# Hedge Fund Risk Transparency

# Hedge Fund Risk Transparency

## UNRAVELLING THE COMPLEX AND CONTROVERSIAL DEBATE

**Leslie Rahl**

*Capital Market Risk Advisors*

Published by Risk Books, a division of the Risk Waters Group.

Haymarket House
28–29 Haymarket
London SW1Y 4RX
Tel: +44 (0)20 7484 9700
Fax: +44 (0)20 7484 9758
E-mail: books@riskwaters.com
Website: www.riskbooks.com

Every effort has been made to secure the permission of individual copyright holders for inclusion.

© Risk Waters Group Ltd 2003

© Incisive Media Investments Limited, Reprinted 2004

ISBN 1 904 339 04 2

British Library Cataloguing in Publication Data
A catalogue record for this book is available from the British Library

Risk Books Managing Editor: Sarah Jenkins
Assistant Editor: Kathryn Roberts

Typeset by Mark Heslington, Scarborough, North Yorkshire

Printed and bound in Great Britain by Antony Rowe Ltd., Chippenham, Wiltshire

# About the Author

**Leslie Rahl** is president of Capital Market Risk Advisors, Inc, a risk management consulting firm serving over 200 institutional clients on six continents. Clients include banks, investment banks, hedge funds, funds of funds and institutional investors. Mrs Rahl was a pioneer of the swaps and derivatives business, and was the originator of the interest rate cap, collar and floor business. Prior to forming Capital Market Risk Advisors, she was president of Leslie Rahl Associates, Inc., a consulting firm specialising in swaps, options and derivative products.

Leslie spent 19 years at Citibank, nine of which were as head of Citibank's Derivatives Group in North America. She launched its caps and collars business in 1983 as an extension of the proprietary options arbitrage portfolio she ran and was a pioneer in the development of the swaps and derivatives business.

Mrs Rahl was named among the Top 50 Women in Finance by *Euromoney* in 1997 and was profiled in both the fifth Anniversary and the tenth Anniversary issues of *Risk* magazine. She was selected among "Who's Who in Derivatives" by *Risk* magazine and was profiled in *Fortune* magazine's column, "On the Rise" and *Institutional Investor*'s "The Next Generation of Financial Leaders".

Leslie was a director of the International Swaps Dealers Association (ISDA) for five years, and she is currently on the Board of Directors of the International Association of Financial Engineers (IAFE) and the Fischer Black Memorial Foundation. She is the Chair of the IAFE's Investor Risk Committee (IRC), the Chair of the Philanthropy Committee of 100 Women in Hedge Funds, a member of the hedge fund committee of the Alternative Investment Management Association (AIMA), a member of the Board of Advisors of The Financial Engineering Programme at the MIT-Sloan School; a senior advisor to the MIT club of NY's partnership with NYC Public Schools and Intel Computer Clubhouses, and is active in all key areas of the industry.

She is the editor of *Risk Budgeting: A New Approach to Investing* published in November 2000 by Risk Books and her articles have appeared in a wide range of publications.

Mrs Rahl received her undergraduate degree in Computer Science from MIT in 1971 and her MBA from the Sloan School at MIT in 1972.

**Kaitlin Rahl** *is currently an analyst and a research assistant and has also undertaken some freelance writing. Ms Rahl is a 2002 Cum Laude graduate of Williams College and a 1998 graduate of Hunter College High School. She is currently deciding between law school, teaching, writing and/or opening an Internet café/bookstore. She resides in Boston, Massachusetts.*

# Acknowledgements

*"The impossible we do right away; the more difficult takes a little longer"*
Mr. Lannon
My 9th grade Math teacher
Friends Seminary 1963

As I said in my first book, "Risk is a journey, not a destination." While I had the good sense to write only portions of my first book and then enlist many friends and colleagues to contribute chapters that I merely organised and edited, for this volume, I allowed my passion and enthusiasm for the subject to overtake my practical instincts and I authored the book in its entirety. Having enormously underestimated the amount of work this endeavour would entail, I am indebted to many people who helped support my folly.

I am incredibly indebted to my stepdaughter Kaitlin, who with a fresh *cum laude* degree in English from Williams willingly took on the challenge of the preliminary editing prior to submission of copy to Risk Books and who, as always, did an outstanding job.

This book would have never been possible if it had not been for the support and assistance of my incredible staff. Lynn Kolk in the editing process and Luis Rodriguez with the intellectual content, put their "blood, sweat and tears" into putting this book together. Thank you! I also want to thank Mary Jane Lupton, Olga Ruiz, Susan Tutundjian, Michael Jensen, Schela Audain and Wendy Fandino for their fantastic administrative support and for stretching their days in order to accommodate their regular jobs as well as assisting me on the book, and my wonderful summer interns, Stephen Rahl and Allison Horwitz, who undertook most of the research for this book. I appreciate the efforts of Adil Abdulali and Anne Laurent in filling in for me on client assignments while I immersed myself in this project, Nandan Pathak for his effort and Adil Abdulali, Jon Lukomnik and Eric Weinstein who contributed immensely to the intellectual content of this book.

I am extremely appreciative of the "perspectives" contributed by Lee Ainslie, Mark Anson, Kelsey Biggers, Richard Bookbinder, William Cook, Jeff Chicoine, Jack Heidt, Pierre F. Jetté, Jean Karoubi, Mike Linn, Bruce Lipnick, Bill McCauley, Sean McGould, Ron Mock, Andrew Pernambuco, Paul Platkin, Pierre-Yves Moix, Michael Rulle, Myron Scholes, Stefan Scholz, Barry Seeman, Mathew Stone, Tom Strauss, John Trammell,

Andrew Weisman, Jay Yoder and Mark Yusko. I am also enormously appreciative of the insight, comments and edits that Leo De Bever of OTTP, Dana Hall of Lighthouse Partners and the 100 Women in Hedge Funds, Paul de Rosa of Peak Partners, and my wonderful husband Andy Rahl, Head of the Bankruptcy and Restructuring Practice of Anderson, Kill & Olick, contributed.

I would also like to thank my wonderful 12-year old son Kevin for putting up with my working at our summer house for most of August on this manuscript and "being around" more than he expected.

# Contents

# Preface

The purpose of this book is to identify, describe and advance the current state of the art as to how and when to measure, manage and disclose hedge fund "risk". Hedge funds are an increasingly popular investment for institutional investors. As institutional investors have begun to embrace hedge funds, their needs – quite different from those of the traditional high net worth hedge fund investors – have triggered a process within some hedge funds of "institutionalisation". An important part of this process has been the increased focus on risk and transparency.

Why do institutional investors want and need transparency?

❏ To know if the manager exhibits style drift.
❏ To meet a prudent man standard.
❏ To understand if the diversification benefits they hope to achieve by investing in alternative assets have been achieved.

But do they really need or want position-level transparency, or is it really risk translucency that they seek?

On the other side of the coin, hedge fund managers have valid apprehensions regarding transparency. The hedge fund manager has efficiency, competitive, and incentive concerns that make increased disclosure policies potentially intrusive and obstructive.

While the road toward increased risk transparency (not necessarily position transparency) for hedge funds is a difficult one and is filled with obstacles, the process is moving forward. This book is an effort to advance this process.

The book is divided into six main sections:

Section I:    Introduction
Section II:   Who invests in hedge funds?
Section III:  Funds of funds
Section IV:   Hedge funds
Section V:    Digging into various hedge fund strategies
Section VI:   Appendices

**Section I** consists of six introductory chapters:

Chapter 1 *What is Risk?* introduces the "galaxy of risks" and offers an historical perspective on the evolution of risk measurement and risk management as well as the language used to describe risk.

Chapter 2 *Types of Risk* introduces the key risks relevant to hedge fund investing:

❑ Market risk.
❑ Credit risk.
❑ Key person risk.
❑ Operational risk.
❑ Reputational risk.
❑ Iceberg risk.
❑ Counterparty risk.
❑ Leverage risk.
❑ Model risk.
❑ Liquidity risk.

❑ Liquidity mismatch risk.
❑ Sensitivity to assumptions risk.
❑ NAV instability risk.
❑ Concentration risk.
❑ Complexity risk.
❑ Borrowing risk.
❑ Short-selling risk.
❑ Derivatives risk.
❑ High watermark risk.
❑ Transparency risk.

Chapter 3 *Risk Transparency/Translucency* introduces the range of risk transparency that currently exists in the hedge fund world from position transparency to risk translucency to opaqueness. This chapter also explores the different perspectives of hedge funds, funds of funds and institutional investors towards transparency and discusses the initiatives under way to bridge the gaps. The chapter also discusses the importance of process transparency and offers useful guidelines on due diligence investigation.

Chapter 4 *Risk Measurement* traces the evolution of risk measurement techniques and then focuses on value-at-risk (VAR), stress testing and risk budgeting.

Chapter 5 *Risk Reporting* explains the difference between "data" and "information" and suggests risk reports that will help both hedge fund managers and their investors "visualise" and track the risk in their portfolios.

Chapter 6 *Hedge Fund Risk Systems* discusses the limitations of commercially available risk management systems for analysing hedge fund risk and compares some of the current commercial offerings.

**Section II** consists of three chapters that focus on hedge fund investing and hedge fund risk from an institutional investor's perspective:

Chapter 7 *An Overview of Institutional Investors* explores hedge fund investing patterns for institutional investors.

Chapter 8 *Plan Sponsors* looks at the unique needs of pension plan sponsors including their fiduciary duties and their heightened awareness of "headline risk". This chapter also includes perspectives on transparency from the following distinguished practitioners:

❑ William Cook, Aegon USA Investment Management, describes Aegon's "deeds-to-action" audit while concluding that transparency is a "pointless push".

❑ Mark Anson, CalPERS, identifies four types of transparency: disclosure, process, position and exposure transparency and the three primary reasons why investors want transparency.

❑ Pierre F. Jetté, CDP Capital, discusses risk budgeting and that his company's risk monitoring is currently based on information calculated by the hedge fund manager.

❑ Paul Platkin, General Motors Pension Plan, explains that less than 40% of managers give position-level transparency and that on the other hand, everyone gives risk exposure transparency. He also explains that unless you have both liquidity and transparency, transparency alone does not help.

❑ Ron Mock, Ontario Teachers Pension Plan, observes that summary risk information may not provide a clear picture of risk or correlation to other funds in the portfolio, and is poor at considering higher moments – an important aspect of risk. Without position reporting, he concludes, it can be hard to get a good estimate of return on risk.

Chapter 9 *Endowments and Foundations* explores the world of hedge fund investing in the world of endowments and foundations. These institutions have been early adopters in the universe of institutional investors as they have the least bureaucratic oversight. There are almost 20 endowments, for example, which invest more than 20% of their assets under management in hedge funds. This chapter also includes perspectives on transparency from the following distinguished practitioners:

❑ Jay Yoder, Smith College, indicates that he relies on his fund of fund managers for additional risk management.

❑ Matthew Stone, The University of Chicago, states that he really does not see much use in full position disclosure for large endowments, other than to satisfy their curiosity and observe that there is always the question of how much of the information that you receive is actionable.

❑ Mark Yusko, The University of North Carolina Chapel Hill, feels that there is no reason why you should need, or even want, full position disclosure and that this ongoing drive for increased transparency is significantly overblown. He also feels that you just have to put your trust in the due diligence you employed when you selected the manager in the first place.

❑ The anonymous Director of Investment Strategies at the endowment of a large university explains that they will not invest unless they get transparency. She feels strongly about getting as much transparency as she can and thinks that there will be segregation in the industry between those who are not transparent and those who are.

**Section III** consists of a single chapter addressing the role of funds of funds and the unique risk issues of fund of fund investing.

Chapter 10 *What is a Fund of Funds?* has its own section in this book because funds of funds play a unique role in the hedge fund/investor interaction. They can fall under the category of investor and, at the same time, they are also a type of fund that investors can select. This dual role provides unique challenges for transparency and risk management. Funds of funds must both:

1. receive sufficient information from the hedge funds in which they invest to perform the portfolio construction, manager selection, diversification, risk management and due diligence responsibilities that they are expected to perform; and
2. provide consolidated information to their ultimate investors.

This chapter also includes the perspectives of the following fund of funds managers:

❏ Bruce Lipnick, Asset Alliance Corporation, explains how his five-person team monitors all their investments, both direct and indirect and also discusses his belief that the benefits of transparency need to be evaluated depending on the strategy used.
❏ Richard Bookbinder, Bookbinder Capital Management, LLC, offers their investors the names of all the managers and feels that greater transparency increases market efficiency and can result in lowering returns.
❏ Jack Heidt, Heidt Capital Fund, asks for total transparency, and finds that about three out of four managers they interview are willing to give that.
❏ John Trammell, Investor Select Advisors, aggregates risk across the transparent and the opaque funds in which they invest by analysing the fund's returns and by evaluating interviews with the managers of such funds. About half their underlying funds offer transparency.
❏ Kelsey Biggers, K2 Advisors, LLC, explains that some strategies will be better suited to risk transparency than others and to be successful, any transparency standard must provide meaningful, actionable information to an investor across multiple managers, while protecting the position-level exposures of the managers. He suggests that one approach may be to transform hedge fund exposures into risk factors before being aggregated by the investor or a third party.
❏ Sean G. McGould, LLC, Lighthouse Partners LLC, demands trans-

parency from all their managers. He feels that transparency allows them to ensure compliance with what the managers have told them they are going to do on a broad level, but cautions that transparency should not be used to fool investors into a false sense of security.

❏ Jean Karoubi, LongChamp Group, indicates that 90% of their managers offer the kinds of transparency he needs. He is not interested in seeing positions but is interested in a detailed risk exposure analysis from each of the funds in which he invests. He rates his managers in terms of approximately 18 factor risk categories (each defined by its benchmark.).

❏ Jeff Chicoine, Mesirow Alternative Strategies Fund, insists on getting transparency but notes that some managers will not give it. All in all, he uses about 14 different statistical measures and gives out as much information as he can because they are insistent on getting transparency from the hedge funds with which they work.

❏ Barry Seeman, AXA, indicates that of the 50 managers they work with, only about four or five do not give them the transparency they want and that the rest give them position-level transparency. He feels that these days, too many people talk about risk management and too few people know what they are talking about.

❏ Tom Strauss, Ramius Capital Group, takes risk reports, coupled with extensive on-site due diligence and plugs them into their own proprietary system for grading managers. He ultimately feels that the greatest risk in this business is the underlying manager risk, not the risk inherent in their position.

❏ Pierre-Yves Moix and Stefan Scholz, RMF Investment Products, indicate that they do not believe it would be wise to ask for full transparency and that the transparency provided to fund of funds investors should entail full transparency of the fund of funds' decision-making process, useful performance reporting, and may be complemented by the reporting of aggregated risk exposures at the portfolio level.

**Section IV** consists of a single chapter, which is an introduction to Hedge Funds. Chapter 11 *An Overview of Hedge Funds* is a comparison of the hedge fund strategies across several factors (ie, performance, coverage by major sources, leverage, risk, etc) that are addressed in Chapters 12 to 20. This chapter also includes perspectives on transparency from the following hedge fund managers:

❏ Lee Ainslie, Maverick Capital, indicates that their investors receive quarterly reports that include a detailed review of the past quarter's performance and of current portfolio positioning. His company holds annual investor meetings at which performance and individual positions are reviewed in depth and investors have the opportunity to explore any other topics with the entire investment team. They also do not provide daily position-level transparency as they believe that such disclosure would be harmful to their investors.

❏ Andrew Pernambuco, Alexandra Investment Management, indicates that they do not use VAR because it does not apply well to convertible arbitrage and that investors can visit their website and are able to query their positions, allocation of P&L, geographic distribution, real leverage, hedge ration and assets under management (AUM).

❏ Michael Rulle, Graham Capital Management, describes how their clients access a GCM website which includes NAV daily, daily VAR, historical VAR, VAR by asset class, and VAR whether long or short. He adds that if their fund investors want transparency beyond what the website offers, they will provide additional information as requested.

❏ Myron Scholes, Oak Hill Capital, believes that it is important to provide the fund's risk exposures to the stakeholders. To this end, creditors and investors receive a VAR report on the aggregate portfolio and a breakdown of exposures geographically and by strategy at each month end. They do not provide position-level transparency on their portfolio because they do not think that this listing gives a good picture of the way they think about the risk of the portfolio and its various strategies.

❏ Bill McCauley, III Offshore, indicates that they include stress testing for the worst-case scenario for each summary position and they have over 1,000 different instruments reduced to 30 different strategies. They aggregate everything and show what would happen if everything moved adversely simultaneously. They provide complete transparency and monthly position reports.

❏ Mike Linn, Omega Partners, offers a tremendous amount of transparency. They will give what you want upon request. They send out a standard report that includes VAR for normal situations, the maximum capital at risk in extreme situations when the correlation goes to one, Sharpe ratios, and other standard measures.

❏ Andrew Weisman, Strativarius Capital Management, offers reports that break down their risk exposure by factors: industry concentrations; geographic concentrations; a breakdown and explanation of the volatility of the portfolio; and their VAR method. They prefer to offer transparency in the form of information rather than offering a book full of positions.

**Section V** contains chapters that discuss in detail the most popular hedge fund strategies and their risk factors.

Chapter 12 *Convertible Arbitrage*
Chapter 13 *Emerging Markets*
Chapter 14 *Long/Short Equity*

Chapter 15 *Event-Driven (including distressed securities and merger arbitrage)*
Chapter 16 *Fixed Income*
Chapter 17 *Global Macro*
Chapter 18 *Managed Futures*
Chapter 19 *Market Neutral*
Chapter 20 *Short Biased*

Each of the preceding chapters are outlined in the following manner:

❏ A description of the strategy.
❏ A list of largest players.
❏ A comparison of coverage of funds within strategy by hedge fund data sources.
❏ An analysis of indices and their components.
❏ An historical performance, by return quartiles, AUM quartiles, source, leverage, Sharpe ratio, etc.
❏ An identification of the key risks of the strategy.
❏ A discussion of the applicability of VAR to the strategy.
❏ A list of key due diligence questions for funds in the strategy.
❏ A brief description of publicly disclosed problems that have affected the strategy.

**Section VI** contains eight appendices.

Appendix 1:  *Hedge Fund Disclosure for Institutional Investors*, findings of the Investor Risk Committee (IRC) on hedge fund risk transparency.

Appendix 2:  *Sound Practices for Hedge Fund Managers*, released by Caxton Corporation, Kingdon Capital Management, LLC, Moore Capital Management, Inc., Soros Fund Management, LLC and Tudor Investment Corporation.

Appendix 3:  *Due Diligence* by Jon Lukomnik of Capital Market Risk Advisors, Inc. (CMRA) from *A Guide to Fund of Hedge Funds Management and Investment* published by the Alternative Investment Management Association Limited (AIMA), October 2002.

Appendix 4:  *Questionnaire for Due Diligence Review of Hedge Fund Managers*, a CMRA-enhanced version of the AIMA due diligence review guidelines for hedge fund managers that is expanded to include a more extensive risk focus.

Appendix 5:  *Risk Standards for Institutional Investment Managers and Institutional Investors*, prepared in 1996 by the Risk Standards Working Group (comprised of eleven plan sponsors) with technical assistance from CMRA.

# SECTION I

# Introduction

# *What is Risk?*

*I'm not afraid of storms, for I'm learning how to sail my ship.*
Louisa May Alcott

## INTRODUCTION

The purpose of this book is to describe and to advance the current state of the art as to how and when to receive, manage and disclose hedge fund "risk". But, what is "risk"?

There is an endless technical debate about the definition of risk. For our purposes, however, risk is the chance of an unwanted outcome. It is a real world concept, not just a mathematical one, and there are many different types of risks that must be managed, as Figure 1 illustrates.

Risk has always existed. One of the best ways to learn about risk is to dissect the publicly disclosed hedge fund losses and problems. Understanding what went wrong can be a powerful tool in preventing future problems. Classic examples from the 1990s include the valuation issues of the Granite and Lipper funds; the impact of haircuts on LTCM, MKP and HRO; and fraud allegations at the Manhattan Fund.[1] The goal is to make new mistakes, not to repeat those that others have already made. Or, as Leo de Bever of Ontario Teachers' Pension Plan observed, "until there is a real blow-up, hedge fund managers in particular will argue that they have a better mousetrap and that risk

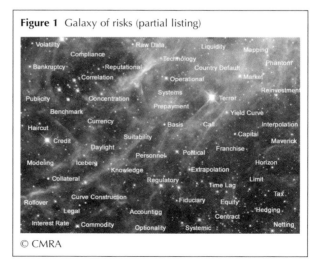

**Figure 1** Galaxy of risks (partial listing)

© CMRA

---

**Table 1** Lessons from the 1990s

❑ AAA is a measure of credit worthiness, not price volatility.
❑ Saving your trading floor tapes can be dangerous.
❑ Assuming that history will always repeat itself is a bad idea.
❑ Purchasing credit protection from a Korean bank on a Korean counterparty is doubling your risk, not mitigating it.
❑ Excessive leverage without deep pockets can kill you.
❑ "Market neutral" does not necessarily mean neutral to the market.
❑ "Kitchen sinks" and other scraps can be dangerous.
❑ Never let your young quants make short-sighted assumptions like "the pound can never leave the snake".
❑ Pegged currencies are no longer low volatility currencies once they de-peg.
❑ Australia is an "emerging market".
❑ Whether the problems in Russia were credit risk or market risk, it does not really matter.
❑ "Default" means different things to different people.

© CMRA

---

measurement is just a bureaucratic way of dealing with something they understand much better than anyone else".[2]

Risk assessment inevitably is dependent on assumptions. But no matter how smart we are or how hard we try, reality is not always consistent with our expectations. Therefore, understanding a portfolio's sensitivity to assumptions is critical. Another essential tool in the risk arsenal is to ask the simple question "what if I'm wrong?".

The ways that people measure and manage risk and the language they use to talk about it are new and have evolved from those used in the 1990s (Table 1 shows some lessons we have learnt from that time). How did people manage risk before measures like value-at-risk (VAR) and tracking error existed? One simplistic method was to limit the investments that could be included in a portfolio. Rules such as "all securities must be AAA and less than three years in maturity" were common. However, as the well-publicised Orange County debacle in 1994 demonstrated, limiting the types of investments does not limit the leverage of a portfolio (Jorion, 2000). Although, 95% of Orange County's portfolio met the three-year final maturity criterion, it contained securities with durations of more than 15 years. Credit ratings are only that – credit ratings. Although they may attempt to rate the ability of the counterparty to pay its obligations, they rate neither its willingness to do so nor the volatility of the price of the security if sold prior to maturity.

Techniques used to control risk used to rely on "guidelines" that were vague and subject to different interpretations (especially after a problem had occurred). Examples include:

❑ Subjective guidelines such as:
  • "Low" interest rate risk;
  • "High" liquidity;
  • "Highly" correlated; and
  • "Hedging is allowed".
❑ Seemingly obvious guidelines that were actually open to interpretation upon further inspection.
  • For example, does "government securities" include:
    – US government securities?
    – Foreign government securities?
    – Age non-structured notes?
    – Barbell strategies such as long the ten-year, short bills, and long bonds?[3]
  • Does "no commodities" include commodity-linked notes?

Despite the experience of working in the financial markets for 30 years, I have yet to figure out how to make money without taking risks. Risk management is not about eliminating risk. It is about ensuring that you both understand what risks you are taking and that the risk/reward equation is in proportion. Risk rules should not extinguish return.

Mathematically, extinguishing risk is equivalent to extinguishing return beyond the risk-free rate of interest.

According to Leo de Bever, "the risks that people confront are often not the ones that matter, but the ones that they can relate to. That's why Boards spend lots of time on real estate and private capital and much less on hedge funds and asset mix risk".

**RISK MANAGEMENT**
The reader should keep in mind the three basic steps of risk measurement and risk management:

1. identifying;
2. measuring; and
3. selecting risks.

The goal of risk management should be to minimise uncompensated, unanticipated and inappropriate risks. To accomplish this goal, a fund needs to understand its risk, understand how its portfolio would behave under adverse conditions, and identify triggers and techniques to be employed if risks exceed risk tolerance. Risk itself is not bad. What is bad is mispriced, mismanaged or unintended risk. As Leo de Bever noted, "my overriding concern is that few people really care about risk as long as it has a return. Our portfolio managers will try to argue their way around me on risk, but in the end risk management is mostly lip service. For example,

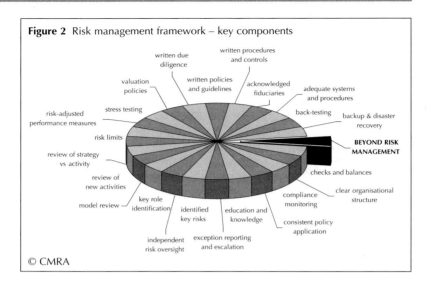

**Figure 2** Risk management framework – key components

© CMRA

hedge funds are deemed to be cash equivalents with better than cash returns. As I look at these issues longer, I realise that our understanding of key risks is very limited. Without falling into the "Chicken Little" sky is falling trap, we make too many assumptions about systemic stability. There is also the assumption that it is easy to identify assets and strategies with above average returns on risk".

Therefore, there are many facets to a robust risk management framework (see Figure 2).

I have learned that only about one-third of the components of a robust risk management framework are quantitative. Mathematics and models are necessary but not sufficient to control risk. Don't get mesmerised by the numbers: while they are important, they are only part of the risk management exercise. There is no substitute for qualitative assessment in investing decisions. The goal of risk management is to provide "risk insight". Often, quantitative reports provide data without providing useful information. This needs to change if risk management is to be effective. It is a waste of time to crunch a lot of risk numbers if one is not able, or not motivated, to use them.

Risk management and risk thinking must be integrated into your ongoing dialogue and decisions. The goal should be to become a "risk aware" organisation. It is only when dialogue and decision making are connected to the risk management process that the full benefit of the effort is realised. To achieve this, however, a common risk language is required.

There are many groups that have an influence on hedge fund risk thinking (see Figure 3).

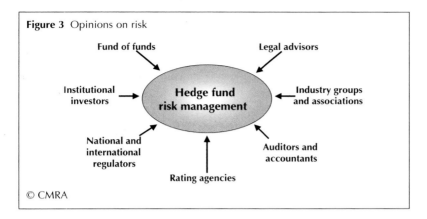

**Figure 3** Opinions on risk

© CMRA

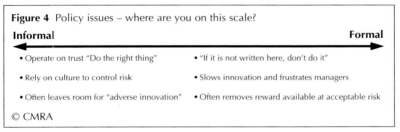

**Figure 4** Policy issues – where are you on this scale?

**Informal**        **Formal**

| | |
|---|---|
| • Operate on trust "Do the right thing" | • "If it is not written here, don't do it" |
| • Rely on culture to control risk | • Slows innovation and frustrates managers |
| • Often leaves room for "adverse innovation" | • Often removes reward available at acceptable risk |

© CMRA

These different groups often have competing, and sometimes seemingly inconsistent, views on the best way for a fund to manage risk.

The way you approach risk management needs to be consistent with your management style. An organisation with a risk management system that is at odds with the corporate culture is working at cross-purposes. Figure 4 illustrates the spectrum of approaches and the associated attitudes.

While most hedge funds are to the left on Figure 5's scale, many investors are further to the right. This dichotomy is one of the underlying cultural differences that creates frustration for both of them. Attempting to impose a formal structure on an informal organisation will not work; the risk management framework needs to relate to the overall management style. I once consulted to a large pension plan where the Chief Executive Officer and the Chief Investment Officer had drastically different opinions, not only about where they wanted to go but also as to where they had been.

No risk management approach can work unless there is organisational buy-

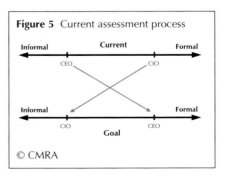

**Figure 5** Current assessment process

© CMRA

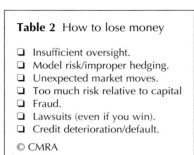

**Table 2** How to lose money

❏ Insufficient oversight.
❏ Model risk/improper hedging.
❏ Unexpected market moves.
❏ Too much risk relative to capital
❏ Fraud.
❏ Lawsuits (even if you win).
❏ Credit deterioration/default.

© CMRA

in and a cultural fit with the organisation. Sometimes cultural changes are required. It is also critical to ensure that account-ability and authority match up. If the person charged with insuring that limits are adhered to does not have the power to deal with limit breeches, the system cannot be effective. The existence of a risk conscious culture is crucial for success.

Risks need to be prioritised, as it is rarely practical or necessary to manage all risk categories with the same intensity of effort. As we will show in the following chapters, some portfolios, for instance, are highly sensitive to volatility levels and the shape of the volatility curve (and, therefore, require robust attention to volatility) while other strategies, such as long/short equity, are largely insensitive to volatility as they generally do not have large options positions. Leveraged portfolios are sensitive to financing arrangements and require significant attention to the risk of haircut changes, while non-leveraged portfolios need not focus on this "star in the galaxy".

Successful and robust risk management does not mean that you will never suffer unexpected and surprising losses (see Table 2). A fund can have an excellent handle on its risk but lose a lot of money because the market zigs when the smart bet, according to available information, was that the market would zag.

Conversely, a poorly risk-managed fund can be "lucky" and make tidy profits despite obliviousness to the perils of its position. Although there should be a correlation between risk and return over time, "time" is often longer than an investor's "time frame". – Beware of the impulse to rely solely on measures that view the world though a rear view mirror and try to avoid the temptation to solve yesterday's problems.

Investors get paid for bearing risk; the fundamental question is whether investors are getting more return when they take more risk.

Risks may be hard to spot and may fly under the radar of simplistic risk systems. Many "unfortunate surprises" have been the result of cross hedging and rollover hedging failures. Understanding these risks is subtle and does not necessarily lend itself to quantification; some risks need to be the focus of sophisticated due diligence. The same is true for instruments that are complex or illiquid. It is important to remember that both risk and return measures see the world through the rear view mirror.

### RISK MANAGEMENT VS RISK MEASUREMENT
Risk management and risk measurement are important but *different* components of a robust risk management process.

Risk *management* is performed by the professionals whose function is to select and manage risk – not necessarily to avoid, prevent or exterminate it. Examples include investment officers, internal and external portfolio managers, traders, hedgers and operational and legal staff. Risk *measurement* is performed by the professionals whose function is to assess and monitor risk. They should ensure that adequate controls and procedures exist in accord with established policies. This function generally resides in independent risk oversight, internal audit, control, compliance, outside consultants and external audit.

### Role of an independent risk manager

Institutional investors, hedge fund managers and funds of funds should consider appointing an independent risk manager. Appendix 5, *Risk Standards for Institutional Investment Managers and Institutional Investors*, contains a further discussion of this and Figure 6 illustrates how such a position might function.

Good risk managers are not "risk police" but rather key members of the investment team. An independent risk manager's responsibilities for a plan sponsor, endowment or foundation generally include:

❏ heading the risk committee, which recommends changes in limits to the finance committee or board;
❏ ensuring that risks are measured in a consistent manner across the firm and aggregating those risks;
❏ recommending changes to risk measurement and reporting that are consistent with industry practice;
❏ recommending appropriate risk controls for new businesses to the finance committee and/or executive committee and/or board;
❏ recommending changes in limits to the finance committee or board;
❏ assisting senior management in setting up a risk-adjusted capital measure;
❏ assisting senior management in assessing risk-adjusted returns;
❏ educating firms at large about complex new products and advances in risk measurement; and
❏ acting as an analytics and data resource for the business group.

An independent risk manager's responsibilities for a hedge fund generally include:

❏ ensuring that risks are measured in a consistent manner across the fund and aggregating those risks;

**Figure 6** Independent risk manager and risk committee

© CMRA

❏ recommending changes to risk measurement and reporting that are consistent with industry practice;
❏ recommending changes in limits to the risk committee;
❏ assisting senior management in assessing risk-adjusted returns;
❏ educating funds at large about complex new products and advances in risk measurement; and
❏ acting as a resource for the fund for analytics and data.

Despite the importance of the risk manager's role, a recent survey of endowments and foundations conducted jointly by *Institutional Investor* and the author's firm, Capital Market Risk Advisors, Inc. (CMRA), found that only 24% of respondents have a risk manager.[4]

## COMPLIANCE AND RISK MANAGEMENT

Compliance and risk management are not synonymous, but rather intersecting universes. Compliance is, however, an important component of risk management. It is crucial that rules are followed and that exceptions are noted and corrected in a timely manner. While there is some overlap between "compliance" and "risk management", each function has a different agenda. "Compliance" focuses primarily on insuring that all rules and regulations are followed; "risk management" focuses on ensuring that risks are understood and that pro-active decisions are made about which risks to take and which to hedge away or avoid.

## CONCLUSION

In general terms, risk is the chance of an unwanted outcome. While one can learn from the history of financial markets and try to avoid them, new risks are found all the time. The goal of risk management is to understand as many risks as possible so that investors can minimise unanticipated and uncompensated risks. Developing a culture of risk management is just as important as quantitative analysis in the quest for managing risk.

1   Zuckerman G., "SEC May Increase Scrutiny of Hedge Funds", May 2002, The Wall Street Journal.
2   Leo de Bever is the senior vice president of Research and Economics at Ontario Teacher's Pension Plan, the largest Canadian pension plan.
3   See the glossary for a definition of Barbell strategies.
4   This report can be found at www.cmra.com.

# Types of Risk

> *You cannot manage outcomes, you can only manage risks.*
> Peter Bernstein, *Against the Gods*

## INTRODUCTION
In this chapter, we will explore the range and diversity of hedge fund risks.

## MARKET RISK
Interest and foreign exchange rate risk, equity and commodity price risk, asset liquidity risk, and the credit risk associated with investments are all frequently included in the market risk category.

Market risk is sometimes measured as the standard deviation of returns (see Figure 1).

However, standard deviation, like any other *single* measure, is insufficient. Some of the other relevant measures of market risk might include:

❏ VAR;
❏ average and net durations;
❏ top 10 positions, winners, losers;
❏ gross long and short exposures;
❏ spread durations;
❏ % exposure especially by sector, gross, net; and
❏ % exposure also by instrument, region.

## CREDIT RISK
Modelling credit risk is significantly more complex than modelling market risk because there are numerous factors driving the value of debt. In addition, return distributions are rarely normally distributed and credit and market

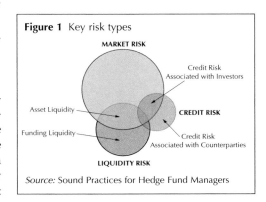

**Figure 1** Key risk types

*Source:* Sound Practices for Hedge Fund Managers

risk can be interrelated. The three main elements of credit risk are exposure, default probability (including market sentiments about possible changes), and loss following default, which is measured by recovery rates.

Two general frameworks for calculating default probabilities have evolved, each with different approaches to modelling the "economics of default". The first method, which is sometimes referred to as "structural modelling", was pioneered by Robert Merton (Merton, 1990). It describes a firm's liabilities as contingent claims issued against the firm's underlying assets. A second class of models, often referred to as "reduced-form" models, attempts to estimate the risk neutral probability of default from prevailing credit spreads quoted in the "market".

Quantitative credit risk modelling has emerged as a major focus of risk management. A new breed of sophisticated quantitative credit models have been built on the extensive mathematical modelling of default and loss probabilities for single obligors, as well as correlations between obligors. Several commercially available approaches have received a great deal of attention, including:

❏ CreditMetrics (JP Morgan);
❏ CreditMonitor (KMV);
❏ RiskCalc (Moody's);
❏ CreditRisk+ (Credit Suisse Financial Products, now Credit Suisse First Boston); and
❏ CreditPortfolioView (McKinsey).

Credit risk can be both specific and generic. For instance, a position in BBB corporate bonds versus treasuries can lose value because the generic BBB credit curve widens versus treasuries. The portfolio can also lose value because the spread of a specific name in the portfolio widens more than the average credit of its rating class and/or because a credit is downgraded. Tracking a portfolio's credit characteristics and understanding its sensitivity to both generic and issue specific credit spreads is an important element of effective risk control (see Figure 2).

The evolution of the credit default swap market has increased hedge funds' ability to hedge credit risk as well as to provide important increased information for the assessment and valuation of credit risk.

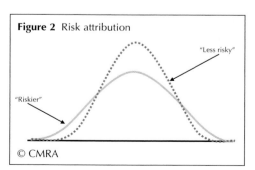

**Figure 2** Risk attribution

"Less risky"

"Riskier"

© CMRA

## KEY PERSON RISK

Dependence upon one or a few key individuals is not uncommon in the world of hedge funds. It is important to remember, though, that the "key person" is not necessarily the boss or the most visible person at the fund. I have seen funds that are dependent on a "kid" in the back office who is the only one who knows how to handle many situations; this kid should be elevated to "key person" status. For example, I remember one instance where "Bob", a twenty-something with a ponytail, was continually referenced in an onsite due diligence meeting as the one who could answer many of the key questions raised, that the key managers in the meeting were unable to answer. The senior people were in the room but "Bob" was not. Needless to say, this was an area of strong caution when evaluating this well-known asset manager.

Key person risk is especially important in smaller, less institutionalised funds. Acknowledging this risk, having a suitable backup plan if something happens to the key person, and advising investors when a key person leaves the firm are part of good risk management.

## OPERATIONAL RISK

Human error, model risk, and exposure to technology risk are present in most hedge fund operations. Methods that are used to measure operational risk include the following quantitative and qualitative elements:

❏ self-assessment;
❏ operational risk indicators: audit scores, staff turnover, trade volume, etc;
❏ compliance monitoring; and
❏ audit oversight.

Operational risk is not new; what is new is that we have coined a name for it. My first introduction to operational risk was in the mid-1970s when two weeks before taking over responsibility for the precious metals business at Citibank, the shelves in the gold vault collapsed. Having a pile of gold bars whose owners could not be easily identified was a risk that the Board of Citicorp could not easily understand. I was summoned to make a presentation at a Board meeting about how we were going to remedy the problem. Despite the much larger risks I personally managed later for the bank, it was the only time I was ever asked to make a presentation to the Board – some risks are more understandable than others.

Once operational risk is measured and quantified, it should be controlled. Operational risk management includes:

❏ separation of functions;
❏ monitoring;
❏ alignment of interests and compensation;
❏ dual entry and reconciliation;
❏ price verification and override control; and
❏ confirmation.

Data entry errors, fraud, system failures and errors in valuation or risk management models are usually included in the operational risk category.

When evaluating operational risk, special attention should be focused on:

❑ services that have been outsourced (remember, delegation does not remove fiduciary responsibilities);
❑ soft dollar arrangements; and
❑ disaster recovery and contingencies.

September 11, 2001 introduced new risks and forced us to focus on risks that we often ignored.

As I wrote in the April 2001 AIMA newsletter in an article called "Survival After the Blaze",

> "Where in your home is your smoke alarm? Chances are good that you know exactly where it is, and chances are also pretty good that when it goes off at 2am, you'll wake up completely confused and have no idea what to do. In today's financial world, this is the way a lot of businesses work as well – we know where the risk management smoke alarms are, but we do not really know what we would do if they were ever to go off".

We have all learned new lessons and remembered old ones:

❑ Back up and recovery and other "mundane" controls are as important as the sexier, quantitative measures.
❑ Stress testing needs to consider the "unthinkable".
❑ Once-in-a-lifetime events seem to occur more and more frequently.
❑ Closed markets, shell-shocked employees functioning at half speed, and offices that permanently disappear must be considered.
❑ Market gaps are an option writer's nightmare.
❑ Primary and back-up sites should not be in the same area – (eg, World Trade Center).
❑ If you chose to liquidate positions held by a manager under duress, would you have access to the list of positions and legal paperwork required?

Documentation basis risk (eg, the differences in unwind procedures between ISDA[1] and GMRA[2] documents) is sometimes also classified as a form of operational risk. In a 1999 survey conducted by CMRA, we found that while 60% of institutions focused on documentation basis risk before the Russian/LTCM crisis, 90% did so after.[3]

During a due diligence review, I asked a major money manager how they complied with the guideline that the asset-backed security (ABS) portfolio they were managing could not have an average duration of greater than five years, they proudly announced that they had a system that "checked that daily". When asked to bring in a copy of the report they used so that we could see it, they disappeared for quite some time and then sheepishly returned and explained that they just realised that the average duration check had been eliminated when they upgraded their system nine months ago!

## REPUTATIONAL RISK

Statements and assumptions that are made in prospectuses and marketing materials but are not clearly defined can be problematic. All written and verbal communications, including monthly letters to investors, are opportunities for "reputational risk" and need to be managed. Even informal communications (eg, emails, recorded telephone conversations and letters) can create "reputational risk".

One investment manager's marketing material clearly stated that their objective was to "maximize risk-adjusted return". However, when asked how they measured "risk" during an assessment they asked me to conduct, they acknowledged that they did not measure or have a standard definition for "risk". This could be disastrous if a client who was losing money decided to blame someone.

Not having written policies and procedures is bad practice; having them and not following them can be disastrous. Litigations are rarely swayed because a party did not have policies and procedures, but can be strongly affected when they existed but were not followed. Therefore, the reader is advised not to agree to guidelines that you cannot implement and track. Meaningful limits need to be both trackable and tracked. Limits such as *average* duration are not meaningful. The guideline is not specific enough to protect the interests of both parties. Be as specific as you can to avoid the possibility of multiple interpretations of guidelines. No matter how well you do your business, expect problems when things go wrong. Preventative measures should be taken not only to prevent misfortunes, but also to protect you from the harsh scrutiny that follows when they do occur.

Another risk is receiving risk information and then doing nothing with it. While institutional investors need information to fulfill their fiduciary responsibilities, having access to information that they do not understand can create liability and/or reduce their ability to maintain that they "didn't know".

Risk branding can be a very effective strategic tool for hedge fund and fund of funds managers and is a significant component of CMRA's business. However, in my experience, risk branding can backfire and create serious reputational risk if you promise things that you don't deliver.

## ICEBERG RISK

One of the important lessons learned from the 1998 Long Term Capital Management (LTCM) crisis was the significance of "iceberg risk". For example, although most dealers at the time knew that LTCM had certain large positions, few understood that what they were seeing was only the tip of the iceberg; other dealers had identical, extremely large exposures. This is iceberg risk! (Further reading on iceberg risk can be found in Weisman and Abernathy, 2000).

## COUNTERPARTY RISK

Counterparty credit risk includes the risks associated with derivative counterparties and margin lenders. It is important to measure and monitor not only current exposure but also the potential future exposure. Suppose, for example, a hedge fund enters into a US$100 million, 10-year interest rate swap with a dealer. The day they enter into the swap, the current exposure (mark-to-market) is minimal. But the risk can increase significantly over 10 years. It is therefore vital to understand the maximum exposure that can be created over time. It is also essential to measure and monitor aggregate counterparty exposures as to maximum potential, expected potential, and current exposure.

A survey CMRA conducted in the aftermath of the Russian/LTCM crisis showed that only 67% of respondents stress tested potential credit exposure to counterparties before the crisis while 85% did so after the crisis.[4] While the respondents to this particular survey were primarily large banks and investment banks, hedge funds might learn a lesson and remember the adage – those who do not learn from history are doomed to repeat it.

## LEVERAGE RISK

Leverage is usually a key ingredient in risk; defining "leverage", however, is a challenge. The most common measure is: gross balance sheet assets to equity (either adjusted for off balance sheet transactions or not). Leverage describes the financing required to achieve a desired (gross) exposure level that is in excess of net asset value (NAV). However, many other variations exist.

❏ Long-only leverage is generally used for arbitrage strategies. It measures leverage as long assets/total capital.
❏ Net leverage can be dangerous. It nets short positions against longs with the idea that the shorts reduce the risk of the longs (which is not always the case).
❏ Gross equity/assets.
❏ Volatility in NAV/equity.
❏ VAR/(cash and borrowing capacity).

❏ Scenario derived VAR/(cash and capacity).
❏ % use of futures, derivatives.

Many strategies achieve leverage through external funding.

Leverage is not necessarily undesirable and, at certain times, can be very helpful in achieving the desired risk/return profile of a strategy. Leverage on a stand-alone basis is not a very useful measure of risk and a high leverage factor does not necessarily imply unacceptably high risk.

Gross and net leverage provide some insight into hedge exposure when comparing similar strategies, but it can be difficult to compare leverage levels across strategies.

In order to evaluate the impact of leverage on risk, it is useful to delever risks and returns by:

❏ Reducing VAR to VAR/US$ AUM for comparative purposes. (Capital under management is preferable when available.)
❏ Specifying the type and amount of leverage.

If you invest in two hedge funds with similar styles but different leverage characteristics, your risk measures need to be appropriately scaled. For example, if you invest US$50 million in each of two equity long/short funds and they each report that they have a monthly average VAR of US$X, then which fund is "riskier"? The answer depends on a number of factors:

1. Which fund is larger?
   A US$50 million investment in a fund with total AUM of US$250 million and a VAR of US$X has twice the risk of a US$50 million investment in a fund with AUM of US$500 million.
2. Which fund is more highly levered?
   A fund with AUM of US$500 million in which you invest US$50 million that is levered two to one is twice as risky as a similar investment that is unlevered through direct borrowing by the manager.
3. Which fund has a higher average beta?
   A US$500 million fund in which you invest US$50 million that is not levered through borrowing but has an average beta of two to one is twice as risky as a similar investment in a fund of the same size and a similar style with a beta of one.
4. Which fund is invested in more liquid stocks?
   A fund with significant investments in stocks governed by Rule 144A or micro caps is going to have higher risk than a fund that invests in liquid large cap stocks if the size and leverage of the investments are similar.

CMRA has developed a risk indicator that attempts to incorporate all of these variables:

$$CMRA\ risk = (invested\ funds\ /\ AUM \times leverage) \times VAR\ average \times beta$$

Once you have selected a measure of "leverage" and clearly communicated it to all constituencies who might need to interpret your delevered risk-adjusted returns, the actual calculation is simple.

Defining a maximum acceptable level of net and gross leverage for each strategy and monitoring these limits closely is an important element of portfolio risk management. If a manager exceeds predefined leverage limits, a red flag should be raised.

The reader is directed to the strategy chapters in Section 4 of this book for a discussion of delevered returns as well as Chapter 11 for a comparison of delevered returns.

## MODEL RISK

Model risk is the risk that the model you use to value your position produces a result that differs from the price at which you can transact, or from the result given by another widely accepted model that is used by competitors and/or market makers. The goal is to be able to mark the position "accurately", not "conservatively" or "aggressively".

Several studies have been conducted on the pricing differences due to the specific model used. In 1992, Leslie Rahl Associates (the predecessor to CMRA) conducted a study on swaption pricing. It found that 43% of the dealers surveyed showed prices on a list of 49 swaption structures where the difference in prices between the maximum and minimum price exceeded 100 basis points (bp)! Price ranges have narrowed since then. Professors Marshall and Siegel concluded in a June 1996 paper that the variance in results between 22 software vendors theoretically using the same approach to valuing instruments was significant.[5] (See Table 1.)

The Bank of England surveyed 40 institutions in 1996 about their option pricing and found that the standard deviation from the mean of option values ranged from 1.9% on European style ¥/Sfr straddles to 52.6% on digital range options on £/DM, as can be seen in Table 2.

---

**Table 1**  Variance in VAR results

| Asset class | Interest rate risk (%) | FX risk (%) | Total VAR (%) |
|---|---|---|---|
| Interest rate swaps | 38 | 31 | 21 |
| FX options | 55 | 24 | 25 |
| Interest rate options | 1 | 51 | 28 |

*Source*: Marshall and Siegel Study, June 1996

---

**Table 2** Summary results for products surveyed (% standard from the mean)

| Products surveyed (plus variations) | Number of responses | Inputs – spot rate | Inputs – implied volatility | Output – value | Output – delta | Output – gamma | Output – vega |
|---|---|---|---|---|---|---|---|
| Digital range option on £/DM | 26 | 0.1 | 4.2 | 52.6 | 19.8 | 39.1 | 29.8 |
| Double barrier (knock-out) option on £/DM | 30 | 0.1 | 4.1 | 48.8 | 18.1 | 33.9 | 31.0 |
| Reverse knock-in (up-and-in) barrier option on £/DM | 33 | 0.1 | 3.2 | 4.6 | 3.2 | 10.7 | 3.8 |
| European-style £/DM straddle | 39 | 0.1 | 2.5 | 2.4 | 3.9 | 3.7 | 0.7 |
| European-style ¥/Sfr straddle | 35 | 0.1 | 8.1 | 1.9 | 4.3 | 12.1 | 13.8 |

*Source*: Bank of England Survey Regarding Option Valuation Models, December 1996

## LIQUIDITY RISK

Liquidity and the lack thereof is probably the risk that has traditionally received the least focus and yet has inflicted the greatest damage. Understanding the liquidity of a portfolio is a critical component of effective risk management.

The scale in Figure 3 shows the prevailing beliefs regarding the duality of liquidity in pricing and transparency in valuation.

Market participants generally view illiquidity in securities markets in one of three ways:

1. As a defect that should be fixed or avoided.
2. As representing an opportunity that should be estimated and priced.
3. As an annoyance that, in most periods, is more profitably ignored than engaged.

Unfortunately, in the case of the all too genuine complexities of hedge fund liquidity, the urge towards radical simplification has often proved an irresistible temptation.

There are multiple facets to liquidity risk in a hedge fund:

❏ Liquidity of the instruments/ strategies vs redemption liquidity/ lock ups.
❏ Potential impact on fund NAV of bid/offer spreads.

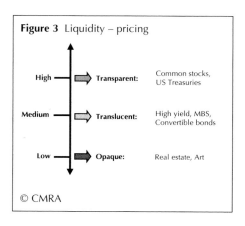

**Figure 3** Liquidity – pricing

High — Transparent: Common stocks, US Treasuries

Medium — Translucent: High yield, MBS, Convertible bonds

Low — Opaque: Real estate, Art

© CMRA

❏ Size of positions vs daily volume traded – number of days to liquidate;
❏ Firmness/stability of NAV.
❏ Borrowing arrangements and sensitivities.
❏ Timing of marks.

### Liquidity of the instruments/strategies vs redemption liquidity/lock ups

Experience has demonstrated that a crisis can dramatically dry up liquidity. While it is a natural human reflex, liquidating the most liquid instruments in a portfolio to meet margin demands can be, and has been in many cases, a death knell. The remaining portfolio is skewed to illiquid instruments and, therefore, even less able to meet the liquidity demands of a fast-moving market than the original portfolio.

A fund that holds large concentrated positions but allows its investors flexible redemption rights has one type of liquidity risk. This type of structural risk can be a red flag for potential investors. If an investor decides to take on this type of liquidity mismatch risk, the investor might ask the following types of questions:

❏ What has been your largest drawdown?
❏ Without exceeding 25% of the daily traded volume in the instruments in your portfolio, how many days would it take to liquidate your portfolio":
  • under "normal circumstances"?
  • under "stressed conditions"?
❏ How wide are the bid/ask spreads in the key positions you hold:
  • under "normal circumstances"?
  • under "stressed conditions"?
❏ How wide did the bid/ask spreads get:
  • during the tech crisis?
  • in the fall of 1998?
❏ Etc.

This type of dialogue is much more meaningful than trying to boil risk down to a single number. Also, this type of dialogue, though time consuming, only has to be done periodically and does not require position-level detail. An investor who conducts the above discussion twice a year and compares notes from one meeting to the next would have a much better handle on liquidity risk than one who received a mathematical answer to such questions.

This mismatch is particularly risky in periods like the fall of 1998 when markets simultaneously experienced high volatility, widening credit spreads, and low liquidity at a time when they experienced high redemptions.

Any mismatch between funding and redemption rules can also cause breakages as Figure 4 indicates.

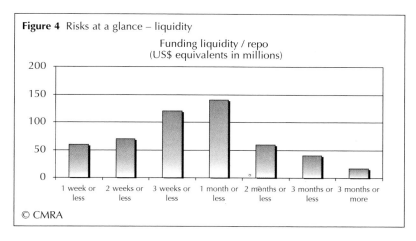

**Figure 4** Risks at a glance – liquidity

Funding liquidity / repo
(US$ equivalents in millions)

© CMRA

Funds of funds, as well as individual hedge funds, typically provide monthly liquidity, while many strategies require longer time periods to be effective.

Some of the ways to measure and monitor liquidity risk and the risk associated with redemption terms include:

❏ worst historical drawdown (cash and capacity);
❏ cash/equity;
❏ VAR/cash and borrowing capacity;
❏ worst historical drawdown (cash and capacity);
❏ asset-liability match (redemption terms);
❏ stress test of NAV stability;
❏ stress test of bid/offer spreads;
❏ stress test of changes to number of days to liquidate; and
❏ stress test of margin haircut sensitivity.

### Potential impact on fund NAV of bid/offer spreads

During periods of market stress, bid/offer spreads tend to widen, further exacerbating the liquidity risk and cost. Additionally, market crises tend to send historical correlation out of the window: all instruments move to a correlation of +1 or –1. While on some level we all know about this correlation truth, it is rarely factored into the risk equation. Strategies such as convergence and basis trades are most vulnerable to this correlation phenomenon. It is critical for such funds' needs to include a measure of this crisis effect and for liquidity to be explicitly addressed in a robust risk management programme.

One of the lessons learned from the Russian/LTCM crisis is that valuing positions at mid-market when positions are large and liquidity is poor can be very misleading.

A fund operating in highly liquid markets with relatively tight bid/offer spreads will be relatively immune to the decision as to whether to mark its positions at the midpoint or take the more conservative approach and mark its long positions to the bid side of the market and its short positions to the offered side of the market.

*Example*

Let us examine the effect of valuing a US$100 million long position of five-year treasury notes at a mid-market level vs a bid level. (A similar argument holds for a short position, with bid price replaced by ask price in the following discussion.) Historical data suggests that the average bid/offer yield spread is 1.05bp for normal periods and 1.83bp for stress periods. Consequently, the difference between the more aggressive (valuing at the mid) and the more conservative (valuing at the bid) approaches in a "normal market" would be:

$$US\$23,699 = (0.000105 \times 4.5 \times 1/2 \times 100 \ million)$$

On the other hand, the same US$100 million position in a stress period renders a difference of:

$$US\$41,282 = (0.000183 \times 4.5 \times 1/2 \times 100 \ million)$$

A portfolio whose manager marked at the mid-market level would not show the extra loss of US$17,583 that it would have shown had it used bid pricing. Clearly, if liquidity is a concern, than bid pricing, though more volatile, would better reflect the value an investor could realise if the position had to be sold.

## Size of positions vs daily volume traded – number of days to liquidate

The number of days to liquidate a portfolio will vary depending both on the liquidity of the instruments held and the relative size of the positions.

In October 1999, CMRA surveyed financial institutions (banks, investment banks, and hedge funds) on the impact of the 1998 crises on their risk management practices. We found that while only 25% of financial institutions made mark-to-market (MTM) adjustments for large/illiquid positions before the crises, 58% did so after.

## Firmness/stability of NAV

All risk management measures assume that you know what today's value of the portfolio is and attempt to measure how much that value can change based on changing circumstances. Some funds, however, are invested in securities with limited liquidity, large bid/offer spreads or other characteristics that make valuation an exercise in estimation.

One of the approaches that I find most helpful for explaining valuation, is by dividing a portfolio into buckets that are then classified by the type of NAV. The NAV type used within every bucket reflects a specific certainty and is color coded. Every bucket then includes the overall portfolio coded as red, blue, purple, etc (see Figure 5).

Due diligence/process transparency questions that can be helpful in understanding valuation practices and the stability of NAV include:

❑ How do you mark your positions to market?
❑ Do you stress test the value of your portfolio against alternative methods for marking the market? What do you conclude?
❑ If you had to (or wanted to) liquidate your portfolio, how long would it take in normal circumstances and in stressed conditions?
❑ What is your data source for volatility?
❑ How do you define a volatility term structure by maturity? By strike?
❑ What is the procedure for marking the portfolios?
❑ Does the manager come up with his/her own marks or are they an average of several broker month-end or day-end quotes? If they are an average, then what is the difference in bond points between the minimum and the maximum? If they are not an average, then what is the manager's method for arriving at its marks?
❑ What type of pricing model do you use?
❑ What sort of trading do you perform with regard to credit derivatives?
❑ How do you deal with correlation assumptions?
❑ How do you hedge FX exposure?
❑ How do you deal with maturity mismatches?
❑ What sort of prepayment model do you use?
❑ How many data sources do you use for MBS?
❑ How do you incorporate off the run issues in your yield curve?
❑ How do you build your volatility curve?
❑ For OTC derivatives, how do you measure counterparty exposure and mark-to-market exposure?

**Mark-to-market vs mark-to-model**

There can be substantial differences between marking to "market" and marking to "model." Pricing models are sensitive to the data inputs and internal differences within the model.

There can also be a substantial difference between theoretical price and market price even when obtained from the same source, as shown in Table 3, using Monis as the example. This table shows that there are differences of as much as six points

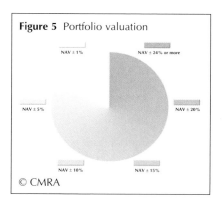

**Figure 5** Portfolio valuation

NAV ± 1%

NAV ± 24% or more

NAV ± 5%

NAV ± 20%

NAV ± 10%

NAV ± 15%

© CMRA

between the theoretical price and the market price as in the case of the AMGN 0% of 2032 convertible bond.

Data reliability can also be a tricky issue when it comes to less liquid instrument derivatives.

Notice that one reason for the difference may be that some of the instruments displayed in Table 4 traded more recently at one source than the other. Another reason can be that a dealer has an axe that is shared with one source and not another.

Differences in volatilities can greatly affect fixed-income instruments with optionality, especially if the option maturity is long-term. Mortgage-backed securities and many of the common fixed-income instruments, such as callable corporate bonds, often have long maturity options embedded in them.

Crisis times can also affect the reliability of data. Typically, when liquidity dries up, or when there is a great deal of uncertainty in the market, bid/ask spreads can grossly widen. In this case, which data input should one use for marking the fund's portfolio? Taking the average is not sufficient because one cannot execute at the average. The wider the bid/ask spread, the further the average is from the execution point.

Securities such as collateralised mortgage obligations (CMOs) can be very illiquid in the secondary market. At month end, managers must poll various broker dealers for prices and the variance in these prices can be huge. In some cases, CMOs are tailor made and only the original dealer, who created the primary market, will be available to create a secondary market. In such cases there will be only one source of price for the security. Figure 6 shows the variance in prices for an inverse floater, Fannie Mae 99-15 SB.

### Borrowing arrangements and sensitivities

Levered funds are sensitive to the haircuts imposed by their lenders. While these do not change frequently, they often change at the most inopportune

---

**Table 3** Theoretical price vs market price

| Convertible bonds | Sample date 1 | Market price (from Monis) | MONIS Absolute theoretical price | % difference |
|---|---|---|---|---|
| AMGN 0% OF 2032 | 28/2/2002 | 71.375 | 77.375 | 7.8 |
| KMG 5.25% OF 2010 | 28/2/2002 | 114.750 | 110.270 | 4.1 |
| AMGN 0% OF 2032 | 28/3/2002 | 70.500 | 72.130 | 2.3 |
| KMG 5.25% OF 2010 | 28/3/2002 | 118.750 | 116.430 | 2.0 |

*Source*: Monis Convertible Bond Pricing Model

---

times. Since the aftermath of the Russian/LTCM crisis, 75% of financial institutions/prime brokers now claim to share their methodologies and the factors that will cause changes in haircuts with their clients as opposed to 42% before the crisis.

## Timing of marks

In a global fund, a question as simple as "when are the positions marked?" can make a difference in volatile markets. As part of CMRA's NAV survey

**Table 4** Interest rate derivatives data comparison of different brokers (as of July 17, 2002)

|  | Garban | Tullets & Tokyo | Difference |
|---|---|---|---|
| **Cap/floor volatilities** | (%) | (%) | (%) |
| 1-year | 41.6 | 42.5 | 0.9 |
| 2-year | 39.8 | 40.4 | 0.6 |
| 5-year | 28.5 | 28.6 | 0.1 |
| 10-year | 22.8 | 22.6 | (0.2) |
| **Swaption volatilities** | (%) | (%) | (%) |
| 1 into 5 | 25.1 | 25.8 | 0.7 |
| 5 into 5 | 18.9 | 19.1 | 0.2 |
| 1 into 10 | 21.9 | 22.3 | 0.4 |
| 10 into 10 | 13.6 | 13.7 | 0.1 |

*Source*: Bloomberg

**Figure 6** Time-series for broker–dealer quotes on an MBS derivative

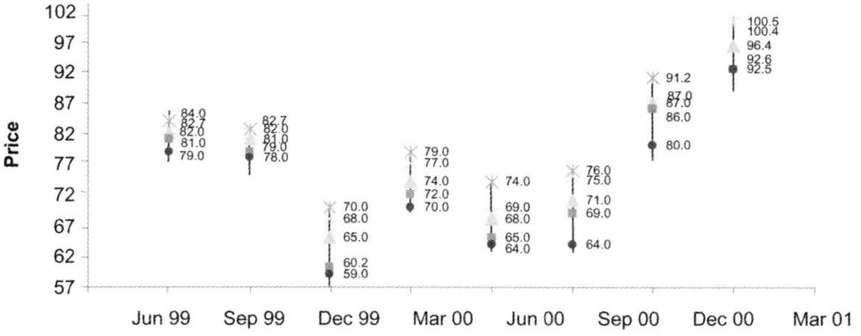

*Note:* Quotes received June 1999 to March 2001 for FNR 99–15 SB and arranged from highest to lowest

© CMRA

in 2001, we found that the methodologies used by funds to mark positions in different time zones vary significantly. The following list indicates some of the methodologies used to mark positions in different time zones.

❏ Adjust all "relevant" prices to NY close.
❏ Adjust cross exchanges trades to same time.
❏ Adjust to futures close in each local market.
❏ 4:00 pm NY Time.
❏ "Fair value pricing" adjustments.
❏ All prices taken at 5:45 Paris time.
❏ Closing prices the day before.
❏ Adjust to futures close in each local market.

## CONCENTRATION RISK

Highly concentrated positions pose their own unique risks. A highly concentrated portfolio lacks the benefits of diversification and can be viewed as having all its eggs in one basket (or just a few). In addition, highly concentrated positions are often large and, therefore, may have less liquidity than moderate sized positions in the same underlying. For example, CMRA valued a control position in a micro cap stock for a client and determined that it might take seven years to liquidate the position. Based on our analysis and with the concurrence of their conditions, the client is now haircutting the value of that investment by 35% to reflect this illiquidity.

## SHORT-SELLING RISK

Shorting securities also has its own unique risks. Short squeezes can and do occur and the cost of borrowing securities can vary significantly over time. Hedge funds with significant short positions are appropriately concerned that transparency might encourage a short squeeze and are, therefore, more reluctant than other funds to be transparent. ABP had just announced at the time of writing that it is to stop lending securities. If other large pension funds were to follow suit, short-selling risk would increase.

## DERIVATIVES RISK

While I was an early pioneer in the over-the-counter (OTC) derivatives business and am very comfortable with all facets of derivatives, I also believe that hedge funds (like any other market participant) that use these instruments require a more robust risk management process than those that limit themselves to less complex investments. A hedge fund using these instruments needs to have the ability to:

❏ reverse-engineer complex products;
❏ quantity report and monitor risks properly;

- ❏ understand mark-to-model issues;
- ❏ independently value the transactions; and
- ❏ measure, monitor and net not only the current counterparty exposure, but also the future potential exposure.

## HIGH WATERMARK RISK

High watermark risk is a phenomenon of poor markets. Hedge fund managers whose performance is down sufficiently that they are well below their "high watermark", and not entitled to incentive fees until the fund returns to the high watermark, are increasingly throwing in the towel and liquidating rather than "working for free".

## TRANSPARENCY RISK

Transparency risk is a two-sided coin. Hedge funds that provide position-level detail to an investor under pressure, against their better judgement as to what is in the best interest of the fund and its investors, are subject to one type of transparency risk. Hedge funds that refuse to provide transparency and/or translucency and insist on remaining opaque, are subject to the risk that institutional investors will steer clear of their funds (which is only a real issue, of course, if they are "open"). Investors in opaque funds, on the other hand, are subject to "transparency risk", as they are not able to judge whether their investment in the opaque funds helps diversify or increases concentration risk in their overall portfolio.

## CONCLUSION – BUT COMPONENTS OF RISK DON'T MOVE IN ISOLATION

While we can isolate the key risks in a hedge fund, the total impact of changing conditions is not simply the sum of the parts. Multiple risk components can and do move at the same time. As Myron Scholes wrote in my first book, *Risk Budgeting – A New Approach to Investing:* "The reputation of financial risk modelling – and options pricing in particular – has been badly damaged by a series of market crises. But critics have misunderstood the changing relationship between credit risk and market liquidity". It is these multifaceted interactions that require VAR and stress testing. See Appendix 2 "Sound Practices" for more detail on types of risk discussed throughout this chapter.

1   ISDA: International Swaps and Derivatives Association.
2   GMRA: Global Master Repurchase Agreement.
3   Available at http://www.cmra.com.
4   Survey available at http://www.cmra.com.
5   See CMRA (1996).

# Risk Transparency/Translucency

*If I am to speak ten minutes, I need a week for preparation; if fifteen minutes,
three days; if half an hour, two days; if an hour, I am ready now.*
Woodrow Wilson

## INTRODUCTION

Risk transparency, which I define as the disclosure of risk attributes, is one
of the key issues facing the hedge fund world today. A May 2001 survey,
*Investments & Pensions – Europe*, found that almost all respondents believed
that lack of transparency was the most important hedge fund issue (see
Figure 1).

The spectrum of choices for hedge fund risk transparency ranges from
completely transparent to opaque, with translucency gaining ground.

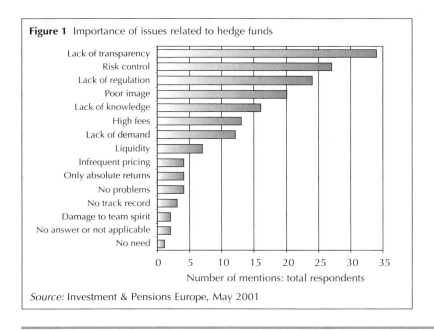

**Figure 1**  Importance of issues related to hedge funds

*Source:* Investment & Pensions Europe, May 2001

## WHAT IS TRANSPARENCY?

Webster's dictionary provides several definitions of "transparency". The first is:

*Having the property of transmitting light through its substance so that bodies situated beyond or behind can be distinctly seen.*

This definition suggests that each position in a portfolio, its "bodies", should be explicitly disclosed, or "distinctly seen". A later definition is:

*Easily understood, manifest, obvious.*

This alternative definition suggests the importance of context and clarity of meaning. The increased "transparency" for which Federal Reserve Chairman Greenspan has been calling is clearly the second version. Investors want to fundamentally *understand* their risks, and not be drowned by a raging flood of data.

## DIFFERENT PERSPECTIVES

Unsurprisingly, hedge fund investors and managers have different perspectives on risk transparency (see Table 1).

## POSITION-LEVEL TRANSPARENCY VS RISK TRANSLUCENCY

The increased focus on hedge fund risk transparency is part of the natural evolution towards "institutionalisation" that is occurring in the hedge fund world. As the investor base for hedge funds expands beyond its traditional core of high net worth individuals to include pension plan sponsors, endowments, and foundations, the needs of investors are

**Table 1** Perspectives on risk transparency

| Institutional investor | Hedge fund |
| --- | --- |
| Adhering to best practice in risk management. | The manager should be given broad discretion and judged on results. |
| Institutional investors need to fully understand the risks in each fund in which they invest. | Many strategies are highly proprietary and hedge fund performance is compromised by disclosure. |
| Institutional quality funds must have infrastructure, stability and a well-defined process that is not dependent on any single individual. | Risk management, compliance and regulatory oversight are a drag on performance. |

changing. Institutional investors are accustomed to having 100% access to the securities used by their traditional managers and to having these positions independently controlled by their custodian. But does an institutional investor really need position-level transparency? While this remains a topic of active debate, the concept of risk *translucency* rather than position-level *transparency* is gaining momentum. With risk tools, position-level transparency allows institutional investors to:

❏ Create their own independent risk analysis of the funds in which they invest.
❏ Aggregate risks and exposures across their hedge funds and fund of funds portfolios.
❏ Aggregate risks and exposures across their entire investment portfolio including both traditional and alternative investments.

But . . .

❏ How many institutional investors actually have the tools and staff to undertake the analysis to interpret the results?
❏ How many institutional investors get position-level transparency for 100% of their investments?

The reality is that while institutional investors say they want and need position-level risk transparency from the hedge funds and funds of funds in which they invest, few are equipped to effectively deal with this type of transparency. A two-inch thick report of positions is of limited value: yes, it is "transparency", but it is not helpful if it is not used or understood.

For position-level data to be of full value it needs to be in machine-readable form and the investor needs both the tools to digest and analyse the details and the skills and experience to interpret the results.

While a two-inch thick printout of positions might give an investor insight into a long/short equity strategy or a distressed debt portfolio, it is unlikely that even a sophisticated investor could gain much insight into a complex fixed-income arbitrage portfolio without the help of analytical tools, which would require machine readable information as a starting point. In addition, no analytical tool, for example, no matter how robust, will pick up the "off-the-balance-sheet" put option embedded in merger arbitrage and other strategies.

## SO WHERE DOES THIS LEAVE US?

While many hedge funds and hedge fund investors have initially equated the need for transparency with a need for full position details, many have rethought what type of transparency they really need and concluded that process transparency and risk profiles/translucency are the real goals.

What is needed is "risk translucency", where a standard set of risk factors can provide investors with a meaningful snapshot of a hedge fund's risk.

Risk translucency is not a list of positions but rather a consistent, aggregatable "risk profile". This is, in fact, the implicit but sometimes unarticulated goal of investors. Accomplishing this goal will require:

❏ A standard industry approach to risk profiling and counting so that results are consistent. There are, for instance, at least eight major approaches to calculating VAR in wide use. A VAR of 11.0 calculated using one method may or may not be lower than a VAR of 12.0 calculated another way. The FX exposure of a foreign bond fund that assumes a three-month forward fully hedges a 10-year exposure is not comparable to the FX exposure of a fund that would view the same exposure as an open US$/FF in three months for nine years and nine months.

❏ An analytical approach to aggregate information. For instance, if you have two convertible arbitrage portfolios, one with a VAR of 5.0 and one with a VAR of 10.0, what is a reasonable approximation of the VAR of the combined portfolios? Does this mean that the VAR is not a "reasonable approximation"? Possibly. So, should we stop worrying about it?

One possible solution is a transparency transformation machine that will take as input, real world funds which refuse to provide transparency information as well as relevant additional information on the fund as time goes by. As output, it will produce a hypothetical transparent fund whose distribution of returns is certain (see Figure 2).

## INVESTOR RISK COMMITTEE

The Investor Risk Committee (IRC), of the International Association of Financial Engineers (IAFE) was launched in January 2000 to provide a forum to discuss the optimum level of disclosure between hedge funds and their investors.[1] Table 2 identifies the members of the IRC's steering committee.

The IRC initiative is widely supported by over 300 institutional investors, hedge funds, funds of funds, and service providers around the world, as well as by AIMA, the global not-for-profit trade association for the hedge fund community. The committee's mission includes education regarding the activities of hedge funds, defining the needs of institutional investors as they increase hedge fund exposure, and providing results that will help investors and managers to benchmark their practices relative to their peers. To date, the IRC has published two reports on hedge fund disclosure for institutional investors and held a series of working sessions in New York, Boston, Chicago, Amsterdam and Stockholm. The IRC continues its work on the next, more detailed phase, which will include suggestions for risk profiles by type of hedge fund strategy and the related needs of institutional investors.

The IRC has concluded that investors have three main objectives in seeking disclosure from managers.

1. *Risk monitoring*: insuring that managers are not taking on risks beyond represented levels in terms of allowable investments, exposures, leverage, etc.
2. *Risk aggregation*: insuring the investors' ability to aggregate risks across their entire investment programme in order to understand portfolio level implications.
3. *Strategy drift monitoring*: insuring the investors' ability to determine whether a manager is adhering to the stated investment strategy or style.

IRC members agree that full position disclosure by managers does not always allow them to achieve their monitoring objectives, and may compromise a hedge fund's ability to execute its investment strategy.

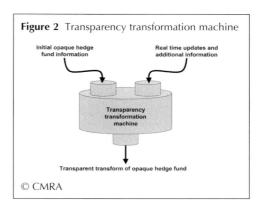

**Figure 2** Transparency transformation machine

Initial opaque hedge fund information

Real time updates and additional information

Transparency transformation machine

Transparent transform of opaque hedge fund

© CMRA

**Table 2** IRC list

**IRC Committee chairs**
Leslie Rahl (Capital Market Risk Advisors) – US
Giovanni Beliossi (First Quadrant) – Europe

**IRC Steering Group members**
Mark Anson (CalPERS)
Tanya Styblo Beder (Caxton Associates)
Thijs Coenen, (ABP Investments)
Phillip DiDio (FRM)
Derek Doupe (Frank Russell Capital)
Leo Lueb (PGGM)
Bill McCauley (III Offshore Advisors)
David K. A. Mordecai (Clinton Group)
Maarten Nederlof (Deutsche Bank)

IRC members also agree that the reporting of summary risk, return, and position information could be sufficient as an alternative to full position disclosure. The Committee has suggested that such summary information should be evaluated on four dimensions:

1. *Content*: describes the quality and sufficiency of coverage of the manager's activities. This dimension covers information about the risk, return, and positions on both an actual and a stress-tested basis.
2. *Granularity*: describes the level of detail. Examples are net asset value (NAV) disclosure, disclosure of risk factors (1, arbitrage pricing theory (APT), 2, VAR, etc), disclosure of tracking error or other risk and return measures at the portfolio level, by region, by asset class, by duration, by significant holdings, etc.

3. *Frequency*: describes how often the disclosure is made. High turnover trading strategies may require more frequent disclosure than private or distressed-debt investment funds where monthly or quarterly disclosure is more appropriate.
4. *Delay*: describes how much of a lag occurs between when the fund is in a certain condition and when that fact is disclosed to investors. A fund might agree to full or summary position disclosure, but only after the positions are no longer held.

Members also agree that detailed reporting is not a substitute for initial and ongoing due diligence reviews, on-site visits, and an appropriate dialogue between investors and managers.

IRC members agree that market, credit, leverage, liquidity, and operational risks are interrelated. Accordingly, exposure to these risks in combination should be included in the dialogue between investors and managers.

The IRC has also developed several alternative ways to classify hedge funds that might be a more useful framework for risk discussions than today's style classifications (see Table 3).

The IRC believes that this alternative nomenclature might eventually replace styles and provide a more useful framework for discussion and comparison.

### Asset class

The asset is the broadest category and defines the market in which the fund operates. The following are the suggested types of asset classes:

❏ interest rates;
❏ equities;
❏ foreign exchange;
❏ commodities; and
❏ multi-class – this is meant to capture "none or some of the above", and specifically includes global macro funds.

### Direction

The direction of the manager's activity in the asset class indicates the net exposure and correlation the manager tends to have with the key risk factor of that asset class. The IRC suggests the following directional classifications:

❏ long;
❏ short;
❏ long/short; and
❏ neutral.

**Table 3** IRC proposed "alternative definitions"

| Strategy | Asset class | Direction | Type | Region | Liquidity | Turnover |
|---|---|---|---|---|---|---|
| Convertible arbitrage | Interest rates Equity FX | L | Convert arbitrage | Any | L/I | L/M |
| Event-driven | Equity Interest rates | L | Merger Credit distressed | Any | L/I | L/M |
| Fixed income | Interest rates FX | L/S/N | Relative value Stat arbitrage Options arbitrage | Any | H/L/I | L/M |
| Long/short equity | Equity | L/S/N | | Any | H/L | L/M/H |
| Emerging markets | Interest rates Equities FX Commodities Multi | L/S/N | Merger Credit distressed Relative value Stat arbitrage Options arbitrage | Emerging markets | L/I | I/M |
| Global macro | Interest rates Equities FX Commodities Multi | L/S | Sector | Any | H/L/I | L/M |
| Managed futures | Interest rates Equities FX Commodities Multi | L/S | | Require Future Markets | H/L | M/H |
| Market neutral | Interest rates Equities FX Commodities | N | | Any | H/L/I | M/H |
| Dedicated short bias | Interest rates Equities FX Commodities | S | Sector | Any | H/L/I | L/M/H |

*Source*: IRC, CMRA

## Type

The type provides more information, particularly in the case of managers who have neutral and/or event driven categories under the previous classification. Greater information is helpful because the risks of these types of activities are not well described by the variation of the asset class index. The following classifications are suggested as a "straw man" to establish the "type" categories for such managers:

*Type (for neutral classification):*
❏ relative value;
❏ convertible arbitrage;

❏ statistical arbitrage;
❏ quantitative/systematic; and
❏ option arbitrage.

*Type (for event classification):*
❏ merger arbitrage;
❏ credit arbitrage; and
❏ distressed securities.

## Region

The region provides information about where the fund is trading. To the degree that this classification places the manager's positions and/or returns in jeopardy, differentiation may be limited to "G-10 countries" and "emerging markets".

## LIQUIDITY

Some funds trade short term and are in instruments that can be traded easily. Others are less liquid either because of their strategies, the types of instruments they hold, or the size of their holdings. The following classifications are suggested as a "straw man" to establish the "strategy" categories for such managers:

❏ *Highly liquid*: most positions can be liquidated in a few days.
❏ *Liquid*: most positions can be liquidated in one to two weeks.
❏ *Illiquid*: positions cannot be easily liquidated, with some taking months.

## TURNOVER

A second approach to classifying liquidity is turnover, which addresses the percentage of portfolio turnover on a monthly or annual basis. The following classifications are suggested as a "straw man" to establish the "turnover" categories for managers.

❏ *Low turnover*: strategies in which the bulk of the positions (>50%) are carried over a month would be considered as low turnover.
❏ *Moderate turnover*: this would include strategies in which the bulk of the positions change during the month, but are carried over from day to day.
❏ *High turnover*: this comprises strategies that involve daily turnover greater than 25%, on at least several days a month.

With this categorisation scheme, a technology fund might be classified as "stocks-long/short-US-highly liquid", while another technology fund might be classified as "stocks-long-US-illiquid". A Japanese distressed debt fund would be "bonds-event-distressed-Japan-illiquid" while a US corporate bond fund would be "bonds-event-credit-US-liquid".

At a June 2002 meeting of the IRC, a quick tally setup was used to allow participants at the meeting to respond anonymously to questions related to hedge fund transparency. The survey found that, at the time, 33% of hedge funds currently provided position-level detail to investors and an additional 17% did not provide position-level data to investors, but would be willing to. 50% of funds indicated that they would not be willing to provide position-level detail but would provide a "risk profile".

But it is a significant challenge for an institutional investor or a fund of funds to combine the risk from the 50% of funds that will provide transparency with the 50% that will not. Opaque hedge funds focused on performance seem solipsistic: they appear to expect to be treated as if they were the entire portfolio rather than one part of it. It seems to me that someone claiming to provide perfect risk profiling on risk/reward information cannot claim that an investor should be satisfied with high returns if there is not attention to correlations with other investments.

Of the hedge funds participating in the survey, those with less than US$500 million in capital were generally willing to provide position-level detail while larger funds were not.

Of the funds that would not provide position-level detail, all were willing to provide concentrations; but only 50% would provide stress test results, 25% would provide sensitivities, and none would provide VAR as part of their "risk profile".

There was wide agreement among the funds represented in the survey that VAR and other risk parameters should be calculated the same way by funds of similar strategies, but there is still an open question as to whether "strategy" should be described by the old or new nomenclature. The IRC survey also found that 80% of the hedge fund participants do think that VAR should be calculated in a uniform way by strategy.

The survey also indicates that of the hedge funds that do not provide VAR to investors, 33% do calculate it internally.

The most recent findings from the IRC came from its long/short equity and convertible arbitrage subcommittees.[2] These committees informally concluded in September 2002 that:

❏ There does not appear to be a suitable, "one size fits all" risk template even for more straightforward strategies such as long/short equity.
❏ Position transparency can be deceiving; it does not capture off-balance sheet risks.
❏ Risk buckets/exposure is preferable to position transparency.

## STUDIES ON TRANSPARENCY

Several studies have been conducted on hedge fund transparency. In a recent survey conducted by CMRA and AIMA, we found that:[3]

❏ 86% of investors indicated that transparency is an issue in selecting hedge funds and funds of funds.
❏ Only 14% of hedge funds indicated that investors request more information than they receive.
❏ Only 7% of funds of funds and 4% of individual hedge funds indicated that they have had potential investors decline to invest based on lack of transparency, but 64% of investors claim they have declined to invest for that reason.
❏ Only 60% of the investors who get full position-level data have their own tools to analyse it; the rest skim the information.
❏ When provided with detailed position information for the funds in which they invest, funds of funds use that information in two ways:
  • 54% review to make sure that the instruments comply with guidelines.
  • 25% input into a risk management system and monitor the risks.
❏ Disclosing detailed position-level information is deemed to compromise the performance of a hedge fund "significantly" or "materially" by only 24% of funds of funds and 36% of hedge funds (see Table 4).
❏ 69% of investors are satisfied with the information they receive from their hedge funds and funds of funds, but 29% of investors have had requests for information turned down by the hedge funds and funds of funds in which they invest.
❏ Most investors regularly receive general fund information from the funds in which they invest.
❏ 66% of funds of funds would find a standard set of "risk factors" very valuable or extremely valuable for portfolio construction and 55% for marketing/client reporting. The key to risk factors is standardisation so that they are aggregatable across an investor's portfolio of funds.

Infovest21 conducted a survey of 104 investors in June and July 2002 and found that:[4]

❏ Liquidity risk and market risk (negative returns) top investor concerns.
❏ Two-thirds of the investors had had a negative surprise regarding a hedge fund manager.
❏ Almost three-quarters say risk transparency is very important to them.
❏ 11% said all their managers provide full transparency, while 15% said none do.
❏ 40% prefer to receive their risk information directly from their manager.

**Table 4** Perceived impact on hedge funds of position-level disclosure

|  | Funds of funds | Hedge funds |
| --- | --- | --- |
| Depends on strategy | 34% | 25% |
| Not at all / minimal impact | 41% | 39% |
| Significant impact / material impact | 24% | 36% |

*Source*: CMRA/AIMA survey

When Infovest21 interviewed hedge fund managers, they found that:

❏ Market risk (negative returns) was managers' top risk.
❏ 86% of managers have risk management systems in place and most of these systems have been developed internally.
❏ Two to five people in the organisation have risk management as their primary responsibility at over half of the hedge funds responding.
❏ 82% provide risk management information on a monthly basis.
❏ Standard deviation, Sharpe ratio, and leverage are the items most often provided to investors. VAR, stress testing, and worst-case analysis were provided least.
❏ Of those managers that do not currently provide risk information to investors, 80% said they would be willing to provide it.
❏ Over 80% would like to provide the information to investors through their own internal system (internally developed or purchased).
❏ Daily reporting and positions were the two items that managers provide to investors least often.

Investors and managers seem to have consistent responses regarding:

❏ *The frequency of information provided.* Over 80% of managers would like to provide the information on a monthly basis. About 70% of investors said their preference was to receive risk information on a monthly basis. While 12% of the investors prefer weekly information, about 9% of the managers provide risk information on a weekly basis.
❏ *The way information is provided.* Over 80% of the managers prefer to provide risk information to investors through their own systems. Only 40% of investors want to receive risk information directly from the manager.

Investors were evenly divided about the types of transparency they desired most.

Deutsche Bank conducted its own alternative investment survey. The results, as indicated in Figure 3 found that 80% of investors wanted hedge

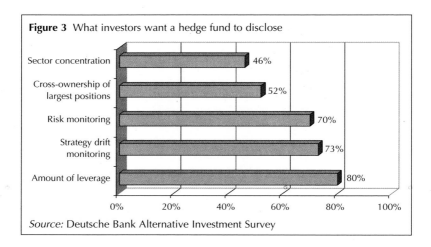

**Figure 3** What investors want a hedge fund to disclose

| | |
|---|---|
| Sector concentration | 46% |
| Cross-ownership of largest positions | 52% |
| Risk monitoring | 70% |
| Strategy drift monitoring | 73% |
| Amount of leverage | 80% |

*Source:* Deutsche Bank Alternative Investment Survey

funds to disclose the amount of leverage they employ, 73% wanted strategy drift monitoring, and 70% wanted risk monitoring.[5]

Table 6 reveals the findings of research undertaken in September 2000 by *Alternative Investment News* that asked hedge fund managers using different investment styles what types of positions they disclose to their investors. The research discovered that the strategies that are most transparent overall are fixed income and merger arbitrage. Accordingly, the least transparent strategies are event-driven and emerging markets.

## PROCESS TRANSPARENCY/DUE DILIGENCE

Process transparency, although less often discussed, is just as important as risk transparency (if not more so). Institutional investors need to be able to satisfy themselves and their ultimate beneficiaries that their investment decisions meet the "prudent man" standard (see Figure 4).

Investors need to be comfortable that:

❑ they have a clear understanding of what the hedge fund manager can and cannot do;
❑ they know that there is a rigorous process within the fund for measuring and evaluating both risk and reward on both an ex-ante and ex-post basis;

**Figure 4** Ongoing risk due diligence

Semi-annual eyeball-to-eyeball due diligence

Risk review and analysis

Quarterly conference calls

Monthly letters, risk profiles, etc

© CMRA

**Table 6** What types of positions do you disclose to investors?

| Investment style | Key long positions (%) | Key short positions (%) |
|---|---|---|
| Distressed | 67 | 17 |
| Merger arbitrage | 54 | 46 |
| Fixed income | 50 | 50 |
| Convertible arbitrage | 43 | 14 |
| Market neutral | 30 | 17 |
| Emerging markets | 25 | 13 |
| Macro | 25 | 25 |
| Event-driven | 9 | 9 |

*Source*: Hennessee Hedge Fund Advisory Group

❏ they understand what the manager's strategy is and what latitude the manager has to stray from that strategy;
❏ the NAV reported is a fair estimate of market value and that they understand the sensitivity of the NAV to valuation methodology;
❏ there are adequate checks and balances in place to avoid fraud, unnecessary operational risk, and conflicts of interest; and ultimately that
❏ the people involved with the fund are honest.

While risk profiles are important, their importance pales in comparison to effective, ongoing due diligence and intelligent manager selection. The eyeball-to-eyeball approach is required and due diligence must be performed by someone not only knowledgeable in the underlying strategy, but also wise to the "ways" of hedge fund managers and skilled at peeling the onion and probing deeply when needed.

While the qualitative futures are paramount, due diligence and manager selection are enhanced by a rigorous, disciplined approach.

Due diligence reviews of both potential and existing managers often treat risk management as a separate, independent activity. Even when a risk management review is included in due diligence, it often includes a look at risk management in isolation, rather than as an integral part of fund management. It is important to identify whether the risk management process in a fund is consistent with the complexity of the strategies used, as well as the management style in which the fund is operating – for example "if it's not written, don't do it" versus "use your judgement".

In addition to standard risk questions, investors should consider the following.

❏ How is Alpha generated?
❏ What are the inherent risks and relevant risk measures?

- What risk mitigation strategies are employed?
- What has performance been based on:
  - realised performance (absolute and, where applicable, benchmark relative)?
  - risk-adjusted performance?
  - *prospective* performance?
  - realised volatility?
  - *prospective* volatility?
- What are the implications of allocation on portfolio construction and when did it last change?
- What are the prospective warning signs of trouble?
- What are the potential blow-up scenarios?

**Some of my best due diligence questions include:**
- When you have a sleepless night, *what* about your fund keeps you awake?
- What have been your best and worst three months and why?
- If you were conducting due diligence on yourself, what would you ask?

**General due diligence questions**
The following are good general risk questions for beginning a dialogue:

- How do you insure the separation of front and back office?
- Who makes the book to market? Who reviews? Who has market authority and override? Who receives report overrides?
- Do you have written policies and procedures? May I please see them?
- How do you manage risk?
- Do you have a designated risk manager?
- Do you include risk limits in your guidelines?
- If someone breaches his or her limits, what happens?
- What are your backup and recovery plans? Have they ever been tested? Where are copies of the plans maintained?
- How do you define leverage? What is the maximum leverage you are allowed? How often are you at or near the maximum? If you were maximum leveraged and your prime broker doubled your haircuts, how much would that cost to fund?
- How much of your borrowing is overnight? Short term? Long term? How has that changed over the past 12 months?
- What is risk? Do you have a risk conscious culture? What defines your culture?
- What is your attitude towards transparency?
- Since you trade in multiple time zones, how do you calculate your NAV?
- How do you evaluate ongoing appropriateness of strategy versus initial premise?

For a more complete discussion of due diligence for funds of funds, the reader is directed to Appendix 4.

Although I strongly believe that many people inappropriately rely on questionnaires and check lists as a substitute for real discussion, a model due diligence guide has been included as Appendix 4 with the hope that it will be used as a discussion guide rather than a check list.

## A BLUEPRINT FOR THE FUTURE

There is a growing industry consensus that standardised strategy-by-strategy risk "profiles" coupled with effective and regular eyeball-to-eyeball due diligence is the most practical and realistic compromise between the needs and constraints of hedge fund managers and their institutional investors. Since I believe that some investors and some funds will still want position-level transparency, many investors and funds of funds will be faced with the challenge of trying to combine position-level details from some managers with "risk profiles" from others. This should provide adequate information for institutional investors to satisfy their fiduciary requirements and their "prudent man" needs, but will fall short for those investors (especially funds of funds) who want to aggregate and mathematically analyse risk and diversification of risks. For example, neither VAR, stress test results, nor convexity are additive. More research will be needed to devise clever ways to correlate funds to portfolios credited for that purpose and to use these correlations to create imperfect but usable aggregations.

I believe that this will also lead to the stratification of the fund of funds market into transparent, translucent, and opaque funds of funds, as well as an unbundling of the manager selection, portfolio construction, due diligence (as illustrated in Figure 4), and risk management duties of fund of funds managers. CMRA has increasingly been asked to perform the function of a fund of funds manager in an unbundled, modular fashion, and we see this unbundling continuing both for our business and for the industry as a whole. Whether performed by a fund of funds manager, a traditional pension consultant, a hedge fund consulting boutique (such as CMRA), or by the investor themself, the components of ongoing risk due diligence are similar.

1   The author is, at the time of writing, the Chair of the Committee.
2   This was under the chairman-ship of Mark Anson, Chief Investment Officer at CalPERS.
3   A guide to Fund of Hedge Funds Management and Investment, October 2002, AIMA, London, UK.
4   Survey Infovest21, June and July 2002.
5   Capital Introduction Group, Deutsche Banc Alex Brown, March 2002.

# Risk Measurement

*Too large a proportion of recent "mathematical" economics are mere concoctions, as imprecise as the initial assumptions they rest on, which allow the author to lose sight of the complexities and interdependencies of the real world in a maze of pretentious and unhelpful symbols.*

*John Maynard Keynes*

## INTRODUCTION

As Figure 1 shows, risk measurement has evolved significantly over time.

I can remember when limits based on 10-year equivalents were state of the art and when viewing all mortgages as having a 12-year average life was a big leap forward. It is sometimes easier to complain about what is wrong with each risk measure (and it is easy to find fault) than to focus on what value we can gain from tracking the measure (however imperfect) over time. Remember, you cannot manage what you cannot measure.

Whatever methods you adopt to measure and monitor the risk in hedge funds, it is important to remember that, while numbers are a vital part of the process, no one should fall into the trap of thinking that numbers mean

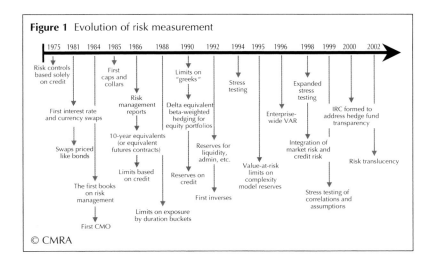

**Figure 1** Evolution of risk measurement

© CMRA

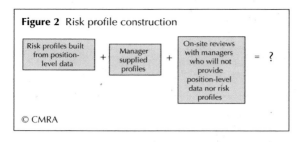

**Figure 2** Risk profile construction

© CMRA

more than they do and that they are the whole story; neglecting context from due diligence and other insights can turn numbers meaningless.

It is also important to remember that most risk and performance measures focus on evaluating the world through a rear view mirror. Before addressing the key tools for risk measurement, it is important to reflect on the fact that institutional investors will continue to receive different levels of information from different funds. Thus, the real world challenge is figuring out how to combine apples and oranges. Figure 2 puts this in a risk management context.

The remainder of this chapter will explore several of the foundations of risk measurement including VAR, stress testing, risk budgeting, and risk-adjusted performance measurement.

It is important to note that the intensity and robustness of risk management needs to be tailored to the complexity of the risk of the strategies.

Simple strategies that use liquid instruments with transparent pricing need less intense risk management oversight than do strategies that are either more complex and use less liquid instruments or that rely upon instruments where pricing is less transparent and marking to model is required (see Figure 3).

## THE HOLY GRAIL – A SINGLE RISK NUMBER

Trying to assess whether someone is overweight based on weight alone is similar to trying to assess a fund's "risk" based on VAR, standard deviation, or stress test results alone. Height and bone size in addition to weight are key factors in assessing the physical fitness of a particular person. Accordingly, a 200-pound man who is 5'7" and small-boned and a 200-pound man who is 6'4" and large-boned are quite different in terms of fitness, even though they weigh the same amount.

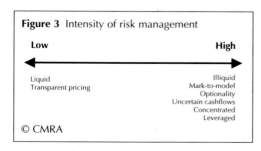

**Figure 3** Intensity of risk management

© CMRA

Why then do we insist on trying to measure risk by a single number? If three factors are required for a simple evaluation of whether someone is fit, why is the need to define "risk" with reference to as many as five or ten measures so hard to accept?

We live in a multi-dimensional world, yet we fight the idea that risk is multi-dimensional. Therefore, just as we refer to a 200-pound man who is 6'4" and large boned as fit, we need to develop a common language to describe risk. Perhaps we might use such terms as "moderate VAR", "high correlation sensitivity", "low directional risk", and "medium validity exposure".

VAR is one, but only one, technique for measuring risk. Figure 4 shows some of the many others.

Each of these measures has merit and no single one of them can describe all facets of risk. It is only when risk is measured in multiple ways that the essence of the risk involved in a given strategy and portfolio can be understood.

But as Leo de Bever of Ontario Teachers Pension Plan pointed out when asked for his comments on this book, "you argue that this has to be a multidimensional measure. I agree. The problem is that it is hard to get people to pay attention to even one risk measure. Risk measurement is a perceived constraint on their ability to earn bonuses".

## VALUE-AT-RISK

VAR is a portfolio measure of risk; it measures the potential loss in a portfolio over a specified time period for a given confidence level. As Philippe Jorion states:[1]

> When implemented at the level of the total plan, VAR allows improved control of portfolio risk and of managers. It cuts through the maze of diversification rules, benchmark portfolios, and investment guidelines. VAR systems allow analysts to make better risk-return tradeoffs. The goal, of course, is not to eliminate risk but rather to get the just reward for risk that managers elect to take.

While it has its limitations, VAR is here to stay as a measure: it has been widely adopted by the regulatory community and bank capital requirements are assessed based on it. It is a useful tool for many hedge fund strategies but not others, in all cases it needs to be supplemental to other measures.

One of VAR's benefits is that it is an intuitive concept and is therefore relatively easy to understand. If a portfolio has a 95% one-month VAR of US$1

**Figure 4** Common risk measures (partial listing)

- Aging
- Alpha
- Bank tracking
- Benchmark equivalents
- Beta
- Bucketed sensitivity
- Concentration
- Convexity
- Correlation
- Country exposure
- Coverage ratios
- Credit rating
- Current risk exposure
- Delta
- Devaluation risk
- Dollar face
- Duration
- DV01
- Effective duration
- Extension risk
- Factor analysis
- Gamma
- Gap analysis
- Likelihood of default
- Loan to valuation ratio
- Mark-to-market
- Mark-to-model
- Option-adjusted spread
- Position reports
- Potential risk exposure
- Prepayment sensitivity
- Relative value
- Rho
- Risk rating
- Scenario analysis
- Sensitivity
- Sharpe/Treynor measures
- Shortfall probability
- Simulation
- Spread analysis
- Standard deviation
- Stress testing
- Theta
- VAR
- Vega

© CMRA

million, this means that the portfolio is not expected to lose more than US$1 million in the month with a 95% level of confidence. Other benefits of VAR are a portfolio measure of risk and a uniform measure of risk across all risk types.

However, VAR is not a worst-case scenario. If I tell you that a given portfolio has a US$1 million one-month VAR at the 95% confidence level, you know nothing about what would happen during the 5% of the time that the portfolio is expected to lose more than US$ 1,000,000. Is the loss likely to be US$1,000,001 or US$10,000,000?

Also, VAR is not a cumulative loss measure. With a VAR of US$1,000,000 month you can lose US$1,000,000 this month and US$1,000,000 next month, and a US$1,000,000 the month after that.

VAR is an important risk measure, but it is not sufficient as the only risk measure used. Risk is multi-faceted and therefore the risk measurement must be multi-faceted, too.

VAR, however, despite its limitations, is a critical component of risk management in the 21st century. While VAR is more meaningful for some hedge fund styles than others, it needs to be supplemented, not ignored.

VAR does not, for instance, effectively measure spread risk or correlation risk. Nor does it effectively capture the additional risks of leverage. It would be a mistake, however, to ignore the value and insight it does provide, just because it is not the "be all and end all".

**Table 1** The three methodologies for calculating VAR – some pros and cons

| Method | Pros | Cons |
| --- | --- | --- |
| **Variance/Covariance** | • Easy to understand<br>• Least computationally intensive<br>• Requires only portfolio level sensitivities | • Cannot capture non-linear risk<br>• Fat tails problem |
| **Monte-Carlo simulation** | • Produces a distribution of profit and loss changes<br>• Allows for multiple periods with rehedging and maturation<br>• Provides greatest level of control over price volatility | • Mathematically intensive (scenario generation)<br>• Parametric – requires distribution and correlation assumptions<br>• Less transparent |
| **Historical simulation** | • Naturally addresses the fat tails problem<br>• Performs well under back testing<br>• Can fully capture non-linear risks | • Relies on history<br>• Computationally-intensive<br>• Data intensive |

## VAR calculation methods

All VARs are not equal. There are three primary methodologies for calculating VAR, as listed below and compared in Table 1, but many additional variations.

1. Variance/Covariance.
2. Historical simulation.
3. Monte Carlo simulation.

There are also many different approaches to data. Some VARs are calculated using one year of data, others using two or five or ten years. Some data sets are carefully scrubbed and cleaned while others are not. Some VARs weigh recent events more than historical ones, while others do not. There is no single VAR of a given portfolio: you can get a very different

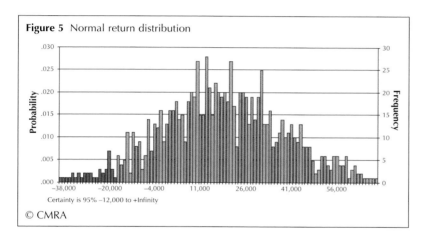

**Figure 5** Normal return distribution

Certainty is 95% –12,000 to +Infinity

© CMRA

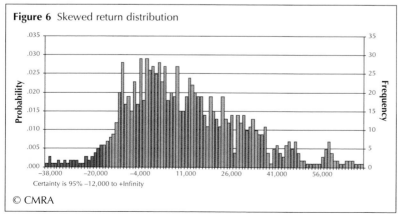

**Figure 6** Skewed return distribution

Certainty is 95% –12,000 to +Infinity

© CMRA

answer depending on the methodology chosen. Therefore, if you invest in two managers with identical investment styles and calculate VAR according to two different methodologies, you could come up with two different numbers. Figures 5 and 6 illustrate that even when you are using the same methodology, such as Monte Carlo simulation in these examples, and data sets, if you make different assumptions about the shape of the underlying distribution, both distributions can have the same 95% VAR of 12, but very different return patterns.

CMRA did a study of the eight most common combinations of the above factors and found that the VAR of three simple portfolios varied by as much as 14 fold, depending on the technique used in the calculation (see Figure 7).

As Figure 8 shows there can be significant differences in VAR when it is calculated using a variance/covariance methodology with equal weightings, as opposed to a historical VAR or a variance/covariance VAR calculated using exponential weighting.

## VAR Choices

There are many choices to be made when implementing a VAR tool in a hedge fund's risk management process:

❏ time horizon;
❏ data: historical or other;
❏ correlation limits;
❏ mathematical engine and quantitative approach;
❏ confidence interval;
❏ stress testing and the role of "outliers"; and
❏ incorporation of qualitative factors.

## Seven cautionary lessons about VAR

Over the years, we have all learned many important lessons:

❏ for instruments with non-linear price function, variance/covariance VAR tends to mis-state risk;
❏ historical VAR and simulation VAR can differ drastically;
❏ mapping can impair VAR calculations;
❏ poor assumptions about diversification can lead to flawed results;
❏ combining square root of T adjusted VARs from different time periods can be misleading;
❏ VARs may be less comparable than they appear; and ultimately
❏ accounting and economic measures may not mix.

There are also many variations to VAR that attempt to incorporate liquidity (see Figure 9), and other factors that an advanced reader might want to consider.

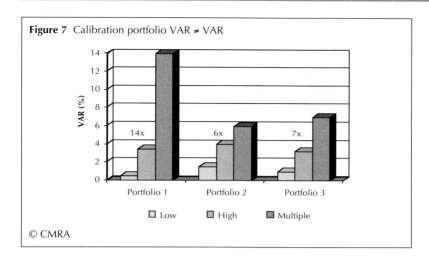

**Figure 7** Calibration portfolio VAR ≠ VAR

Portfolio 1    Portfolio 2    Portfolio 3

☐ Low    ▨ High    ▪ Multiple

© CMRA

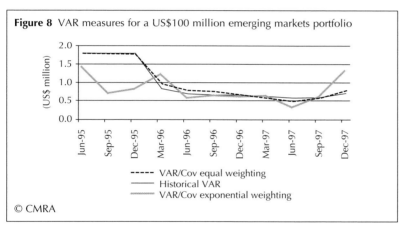

**Figure 8** VAR measures for a US$100 million emerging markets portfolio

- - - - VAR/Cov equal weighting
——— Historical VAR
▬▬▬ VAR/Cov exponential weighting

© CMRA

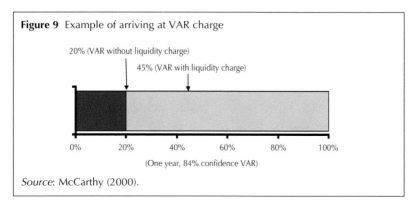

**Figure 9** Example of arriving at VAR charge

20% (VAR without liquidity charge)

45% (VAR with liquidity charge)

0%        20%        40%        60%        80%        100%

(One year, 84% confidence VAR)

*Source*: McCarthy (2000).

Further discussion on the application of VAR across the different hedge fund strategies can be found in the fourth section of the book. The reader is also directed to Appendix 2 "Sound Practices" for a further discussion of VAR and hedge funds.

## STRESS TESTING

Once-in-a-lifetime events seem to occur every few years. There have been 10 Sigma events in at least one major market every year since 1992. In my opinion, too much time is often spent on simplistic market moves and not nearly enough on relationships between markets, volatilities, assumptions embedded in the models, etc. Remember the Federal Financial Institutions Examination Council (FFEIC) test of the 1980s that subjected mortgages to ±50bp or ±100bp type stresses to "rate" the risk of mortgages? How many portfolios were damaged by investments that met the FFEIC test but "exploded" if the yield curve moved in a non-parallel fashion? Figure 10 shows a timeline of when such financial shocks have occurred.

Although none of us can accurately predict what the next "surprise" will be, our approach to risk management must assume that surprises will occur: stress testing needs to consider the "unthinkable". Closed markets, shell-shocked employees functioning at half speed, and offices that disappear permanently must be considered. There was a recurring theme in the questions I was asked by several institutional investors after September 11.

❏ What would I need to prove my rights and get access to my securities if my manager was in the World Trade Center?
❏ If my lawyer was also in the World Trade Center, where would I find the required paperwork?

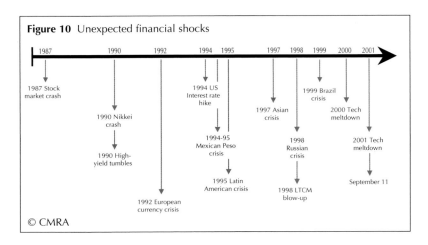

**Figure 10** Unexpected financial shocks

© CMRA

❏ Suppose I wanted to liquidate even a managed account but the records were destroyed, how would I know what positions I owned?

Even well-established correlations have a tendency to vanish during stressed periods. We all know that in a crisis, correlations go to +1 or −1, but this tends to be forgotten when we are between crises. Robust risk management must consider a portfolio's performance under both "stressed" and "normal" conditions. As Figure 11 shows, correlation to the major market indices jumped from almost 0 to 0.9 in one month as a result of the Russian/LTCM crisis.

## Using today's hedge fund strategies

There are many different types of stress tests. For example:

❏ historical events;
❏ scenarios based on "updated" history;
❏ institution-specific scenarios;
❏ extreme standard deviation scenarios;
❏ testing sensitivity assumptions; and
❏ quantitative evaluation of tail events.

Stress testing is an essential tool in the risk arsenal (see Figure 12). Stress tests are needed to evaluate the following:

❏ What variables, given a small move, cause a large move in value or risk estimates.
❏ Which variables important to your portfolio have a high likelihood of change.
❏ What variables or exposures are considered to offset each other. By how much? Are they consistent across investment managers?
❏ How sensitive your NAV is to your assumptions.
❏ How solid your NAV is and how much is model/methodology dependent rather than transparent.

The way you frame your stress test questions can determine the value they add. Perhaps a question such as "what if the Thai Baht devalued but at only half the speed and half the amplitude of the Mexican Peso devaluation?" (as depicted in Figure 13) would have saved a lot of emerging market funds a lot of unexpected pain.

Some of the more subtle stress tests to be considered include:

❏ The impact on your portfolio if the bid/offer spread widens.
❏ The impact of all correlations going to +1 or −1.
❏ The impact if your prime broker increased the haircuts on repos.

❏ Sensitivity to yield curve shape.
❏ Sensitivity to volatility curve level and shape.
❏ Sensitivity to basis risk.
❏ Sensitivity to yield curve creation methodology.
❏ Sensitivity to correlation assumptions.
❏ Sensitivity to model.

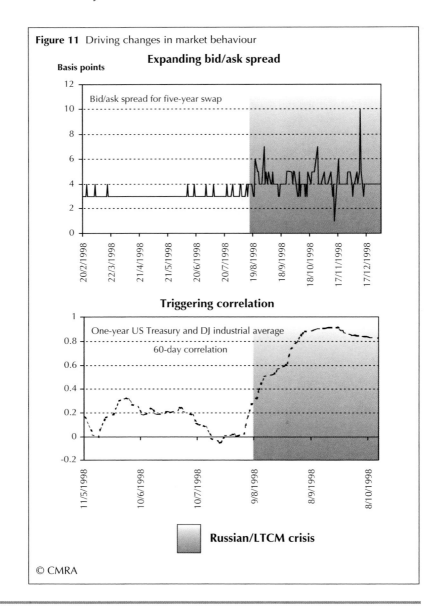

**Figure 11** Driving changes in market behaviour

Selecting potential scenarios that are concerning you can also be an important part of stress testing. This is accomplished by imagining difficult changes in the economic environment over the next 12 months. For instance, we might ask:

❑ What would happen to these strategies if interest rates were to rise?
❑ Which strategies would become more or less correlated?
❑ Which strategies would become more risky?
❑ Which strategies would become less risky?

This stress testing, which runs through a wide range of possible difficult economic environments, allows the fund of funds manager to assemble a portfolio with the potential to earn positive returns in a number of possible economic environments.

Strategies that use instruments with limited price transparency that rely on models to value their portfolios should also stress test against model risk (see Figure 14).

Table 2 shows some of the stressed periods that are frequently used in stress tests. The importance or relevance of the results of stress tests is that they provide the user with usable risk metrics that are fundamental for the decision making process.

**Table 2** Typical stress periods analyses

| Crisis | Scenario | Impact |
| --- | --- | --- |
| **Interest rates 1994** | Unexpected and sharply rising interest rates | • Large drop in S&P 500<br>• Large rise in MSCI World Index<br>• Significant loss in CB arbitrage |
| **Asian crisis 1997** | Balance of payments, exchange rates, and liquidity crisis throughout Asia | • Drop in S&P 500<br>• Large drop in MSCI World<br>• Significant rise in market neutral |
| **Russian/LTCM crisis 1998** | Unexpected collapse of a massive global macro fund, preceded by the Russian crisis | • Large drop in S&P 500<br>• Large drop in MSCI World<br>• Significant loss in sector funds |
| **Tech crash 2000** | NASDAQ plunge, credit crisis | • Large drop in S&P 500<br>• Large drop in MSCI World<br>• Significant loss in sector funds |
| **September 11, 2001** | The "unthinkable" happened | • Equity markets closed for four days<br>• Fed injects largest amount of equity ever |

© CMRA

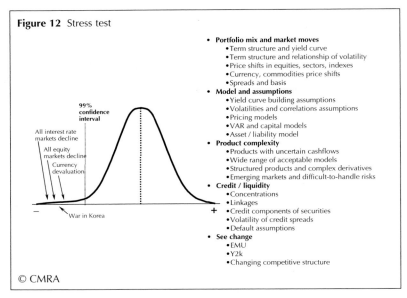

**Figure 12**  Stress test

- **Portfolio mix and market moves**
  - Term structure and yield curve
  - Term structure and relationship of volatility
  - Price shifts in equities, sectors, indexes
  - Currency, commodities price shifts
  - Spreads and basis
- **Model and assumptions**
  - Yield curve building assumptions
  - Volatilities and correlations assumptions
  - Pricing models
  - VAR and capital models
  - Asset / liability model
- **Product complexity**
  - Products with uncertain cashflows
  - Wide range of acceptable models
  - Structured products and complex derivatives
  - Emerging markets and difficult-to-handle risks
- **Credit / liquidity**
  - Concentrations
  - Linkages
  - Credit components of securities
  - Volatility of credit spreads
  - Default assumptions
- **See change**
  - EMU
  - Y2k
  - Changing competitive structure

99% confidence interval

All interest rate markets decline

All equity markets decline

Currency devaluation

War in Korea

© CMRA

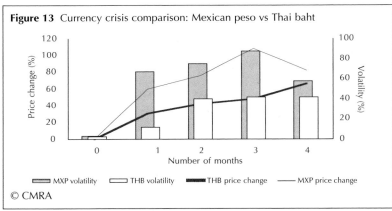

**Figure 13**  Currency crisis comparison: Mexican peso vs Thai baht

Price change (%)

Volatility (%)

Number of months

MXP volatility   THB volatility   THB price change   MXP price change

© CMRA

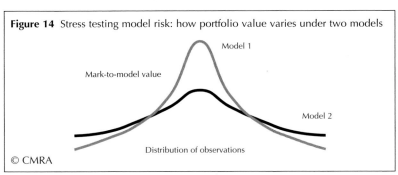

**Figure 14**  Stress testing model risk: how portfolio value varies under two models

Model 1

Mark-to-model value

Model 2

Distribution of observations

© CMRA

**Types of stress tests**
There are three common types of stress tests:

❏ static, single scenario;
❏ static, multiple scenario; and
❏ dynamic simulation.

Their relative strengths and weaknesses are identified below.

*Static, single scenario*
❏ Provides a snapshot of the portfolio.
❏ Reflects only an instantaneous move in interest rates.
❏ Portfolios with optionality can change value significantly with no change in rates.
❏ Does not account for movements in portfolio value due to changes in:
  • shape of the yield curve;
  • basis relationships; and
  • other markets.
❏ Does not permit risk to be viewed on a dynamic basis.
❏ Ability to capture the impact on non-parallel shifts or twists in the yield curve.

*Static, multiple scenario*
❏ Inaccurate for assessing risks in options and non-US-linked positions.
❏ Pre-defined buckets can mask the existence of significant risks within buckets, (ie, a 50bp change reflects no change in the five- to 10-year bucket, but has significant impact on the seven- to nine-year bucket).
❏ Does not permit risk to be viewed on a dynamic basis.

*Dynamic simulation*
❏ Allows testing of multiple shock scenarios on a dynamic basis (ie, over time).
❏ Results are only as good as the underlying assumptions.

An advanced stress test technique is to stress today's portfolio for the worst week experienced during a given crisis. As Figure 15 shows , the extremes experienced in 1998 peaked for Hong Kong 10-year swaps in January, while the Swiss five-year swaps did not peak until the end of December. Even within the US market, the peak occurred at different times (see Figure 16).

**Using alternative definitions of hedge funds**
Once we migrate to the "alternative definition" being discussed by the IRC (see Appendix 1), the following preliminary stress testing framework is

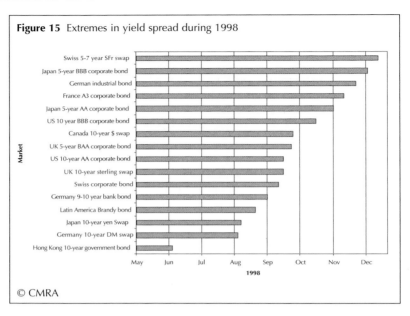

**Figure 15** Extremes in yield spread during 1998

© CMRA

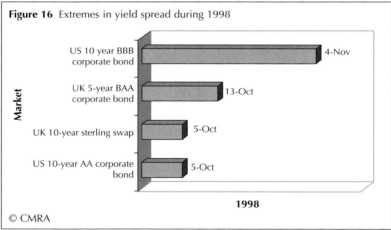

**Figure 16** Extremes in yield spread during 1998

© CMRA

suggested. This framework outlines the key risk factors that, depending on the asset class and direction, provide a valuable tool to stress test their portfolios under different market conditions.

## Asset class

*Interest rates*

- ❏ Term structure and yield curve levels and shapes.
- ❏ Term structure and relationship of volatility.
- ❏ Spreads and basis relationships.
- ❏ Yield curves assumptions.
- ❏ Pricing models.
- ❏ VAR.
- ❏ Products with uncertain cash-flows.
- ❏ Product complexity.
- ❏ Difficult to model risks.
- ❏ Concentrations.
- ❏ Correlations.
- ❏ Credit components of securities.
- ❏ Volatility of credit spreads.
- ❏ Default assumptions.
- ❏ Leverage.
- ❏ Liquidity.
- ❏ Maturity mismatches.
- ❏ Duration.

*Equity*

- ❏ Price shifts in equities, sectors, indices.
- ❏ Products with uncertain cash-flows.
- ❏ Product complexity.
- ❏ Concentrations.
- ❏ Correlations.
- ❏ Leverage.
- ❏ Liquidity.

*FX*

- ❏ Currency, price shifts.
- ❏ Spreads and basis relationships.
- ❏ Pricing models.
- ❏ VAR.
- ❏ Products with uncertain cash-flows.
- ❏ Product complexity.
- ❏ Difficult to model risks.
- ❏ Concentrations.
- ❏ Correlations.
- ❏ Leverage.
- ❏ Liquidity.
- ❏ Maturity mismatches/gap.

*Commodities*

- ❏ Term structure.
- ❏ Commodities prices shifts.
- ❏ Spreads and basis relationships.
- ❏ Pricing models.
- ❏ VAR.
- ❏ Products with uncertain cash-flows.
- ❏ Product complexity.
- ❏ Difficult to model risks.
- ❏ Concentrations.
- ❏ Correlations.
- ❏ Maturity mismatches/gaps.
- ❏ Leverage.
- ❏ Liquidity.

*Multi-Asset Class*

- ❏ Term structure and yield curve levels and shapes.
- ❏ Term structure and relationship of volatility.
- ❏ Price shifts in equities, sectors, indices.
- ❏ Currency, commodities price shifts.

- ❑ Spreads and basis relationships.
- ❑ Yield curves assumptions.
- ❑ Pricing models.
- ❑ VAR.
- ❑ Products with uncertain cash-flows.
- ❑ Product complexity.
- ❑ Difficult to model risks.

- ❑ Concentrations.
- ❑ Correlations.
- ❑ Credit components of securities.
- ❑ Volatility of credit spreads.
- ❑ Default assumptions.
- ❑ Maturity mismatches/gaps.
- ❑ Leverage.
- ❑ Liquidity.

## Direction
*Long*
- ❑ Products with uncertain cash-flows.
- ❑ Product complexity.

- ❑ Difficult to model risks.
- ❑ Securities lending.

*Short*
- ❑ Products with uncertain cash-flows.
- ❑ Product complexity.
- ❑ Difficult to model risks.

- ❑ Margin/haircuts.
- ❑ Leverage.
- ❑ Liquidity.

*Long/short*
- ❑ Spreads and basis relationships.
- ❑ Product complexity.
- ❑ Difficult to model risks.
- ❑ Concentrations.
- ❑ Correlations.

- ❑ Gamma.
- ❑ Margin/haircuts.
- ❑ Leverage.
- ❑ Liquidity.
- ❑ Securities lending.

*Market neutral*
- ❑ Spreads and basis relationships.
- ❑ Products with uncertain cash-flows.
- ❑ Product complexity.
- ❑ Difficult to model risks.
- ❑ Concentrations.

- ❑ Correlations.
- ❑ Gamma.
- ❑ Beta.
- ❑ Leverage.
- ❑ Liquidity.
- ❑ Shorts in sectors, indices.

## Event
- ❑ Pricing models.
- ❑ Product complexity.
- ❑ Difficult to model risks.
- ❑ Concentrations.

- ❑ Correlations.
- ❑ Assumptions.
- ❑ Probability of event's occurrence.

## Region
- ❑ Spreads and basis relationships.

- ❑ Correlations.

## Liquidity

- Bid/offer spread assumptions.
- Concentrations/iceberg risk.
- Difference between current mark-to-market (MTM) and predicted liquidation value.
- Impact of volume increases/decreases.

## Turnover

- Bid/offer spreads.

## Borrowing leverage

- Haircuts.
- Other.

## Complexity

- Pricing models.
- Correlations.

## Options

- Term structure and relationship of volatility.
- Spreads and basis relationships.
- Pricing models.
- Product complexity.
- Difficult to model risks.
- Concentrations.
- Correlations.

## Concentrations

- Sensitivity to time to liquidate.
- Input of elephant effect on NAV.

## Mark-to-market vs mark-to-model

- Spreads and basis relationships.
- Assumptions.
- Pricing models.
- Products with uncertain cash-flows.
- Product complexity.
- Difficult to model risks.
- Concentrations.
- Correlations.

## Market practice

CMRA conducted a survey in the fall of 1999 to understand how market practice had evolved after the Russian/LTCM crisis.[2]

The survey showed that while only 50% of financial institutions stress tested VAR assumptions before the crisis, 80% did so afterwards. Additionally, while only 40% of financial investors stress tested their sensitivity to volatility curve twists before the crisis, 67% did so after.

Each of the hedge fund strategy chapters in Section 4 and Appendix 2, "Sound Practices for Hedge Fund Managers", contain suggestions on relevant stress tests.

## RISK BUDGETING

The goal of risk budgeting is to optimise risk by "spending" each unit of risk efficiently and to avoid holding down any particular element of market risk at the expense of the overall risk profile of the portfolio.

Historically, institutional investors have used asset allocation as the core process by which they determine their investment strategy. The asset allocation process classically starts with the choice of asset classes and follows the direction shown in Figure 17.

Allocating investment dollars is an important tool but it ignores the need to efficiently allocate risk appetite and to reflect the changing dynamics of risk. Asset allocation emphasises return, out-performance, and profit and loss flows. Risk budgeting adds another dimension: it is a function of volatility and correlation as well as a function of dollars. Constant assets in a risk budgeting framework can result in widely fluctuating risk.

Decomposing risk factors across different asset classes and geographies is an important step in risk budgeting.

Risk budgeting is an optimisation exercise; as Figure 18 shows, the objective is not to avoid risk, but to efficiently allocate it as a scarce resource. All else being equal, an investor who maximises risk-adjusted performance will perform better than one who does not.

While risk budgeting and risk-adjusted return management need not necessarily go hand-in-hand, they usually do. Risk budgeting enables a plan sponsor to evaluate the portfolio contribution of various exposures to risk. The first step is to determine current risk exposures. Once a plan sponsor has developed the ability to measure the risk of each of its managers and strategies, using the risk measure as the denominator of the risk-adjusted return equation is a simple and powerful next step. The ultimate accomplishment in the process is to have risk as the basis of "strategic risk management" (see Figure 19).

The effective use of risk

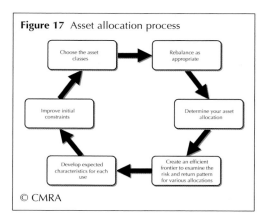

**Figure 17**  Asset allocation process

© CMRA

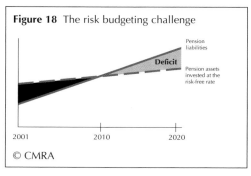

**Figure 18**  The risk budgeting challenge

© CMRA

budgeting requires a sophisticated understanding that not all VAR calculations are the same and that market risk VAR does not cover the galaxy of risks that a portfolio faces. It is important that all portfolios being budgeted using a risk amount adopt a consistent methodology for measuring risk.

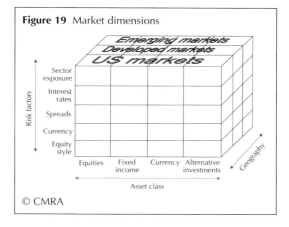

**Figure 19** Market dimensions

© CMRA

While risk budgeting is an innovative and important concept, risk needs to be more broadly defined than VAR and/or traditional risk measures. Stress test results and sensitivities need to be integrated into the denominator of the risk-adjusted reward equation. Stress testing results need to include not only sensitivities to market moves but also the assumptions underlying VAR and mark-to-market NAV.

Risk budgeting alone – or any single approach for that matter – is not the answer. An organisation needs a disciplined approach to risk, one that includes the quantitative aspect but does not rely exclusively on it. I believe strongly that only about one-third of the components of a good risk management approach are quantitative.

## RISK-ADJUSTED PERFORMANCE
While performance measurement is a well-developed science, risk-adjusted performance measurement is still a work in progress. When

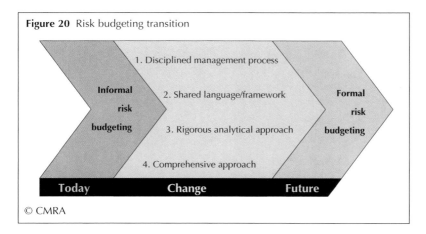

**Figure 20** Risk budgeting transition

Informal risk budgeting

1. Disciplined management process
2. Shared language/framework
3. Rigorous analytical approach
4. Comprehensive approach

Formal risk budgeting

Today    Change    Future

© CMRA

considering candidates for the risk-adjusted performance denominator, a starting point is often market risk. Various techniques are evolving for the measurement of market risk (see Figure 20), but best practice generally includes some combination of VAR, stress test results, and scenario analysis results. One increasingly popular definition of risk is:

*Market risk = highest of (VAR, stress test 1, stress test 2, ... stress test 5, scenario analysis 1, scenario analysis 2, ... scenario analysis 5).*

Stress tests should be chosen based on the nature of the portfolio, but might include:

❑ large market shocks;
❑ changes in correlations;
❑ changes in liquidity;
❑ changes in shape of yield curve;
❑ changes in "sector" definitions;
❑ changes in volatility level; and
❑ changes in shape of volatility curve.

The next challenge is to consider the time horizon over which to measure the risk. One approach might be to match the horizon chosen for return, though longer horizons are generally more useful.

1   Jorion, P., 2001, *Value at Risk: The New Benchmark for Managing Financial Risk*, Second Edition (New York: McGraw-Hill).
2   Capital Market Risk Advisors, 1999, "CMRA Russian/LTCM Survey."

# 5

# *Risk Reporting*

*Things should be made as simple as possible, but not simpler.*
*Albert Einstein*

## DATA ≠ INFORMATION

Meaningful reporting requires the transformation of "data" into "information". Giving someone raw data is often akin to presenting someone looking for a needle with a haystack containing one. We know of many cases in which investors or managers received voluminous, detailed, position-level data and did nothing with it – they could not "see the forest through the trees". Processing information to understand the risk inherent in a portfolio is a complex exercise: simply providing position disclosure does not suffice. Investors require risk information to understand investment risk. Data supplemented with different contexts can mean the difference between "information", "misinformation" and "disinformation".

In order to maximise the value of risk reports they need to be:

❏ understandable;
❏ comparable; and
❏ aggregatable.

The way that risk information is presented can make a huge difference in the value it adds. Creating "risk maps" and "risk dashboards" can be an excellent way to communicate. Peer group comparisons, when possible, are incredibly valuable. Ideally, investors would like to be able to compare, for instance, all convertible arbitrage managers or all fixed income managers to their "peer" universe. However, while this might be enormously useful, it would require access to the sensitivities to different risk factors of all the managers in the peer group. Therefore, comparing a fund to itself over time is a more realistic and achievable goal. While falling short of peer benchmarking, such an evaluation can add significant insight into the style, consistency and performance of a fund.

Analysing risk reports for a fund over time can provide valuable insights. Comparing the ex-ante risk for an individual fund with its target provides both the investor and the investment manager with an assessment of whether the risks taken are consistent with expectations. Significant deviations must be discussed. It can also be useful to analyse a stray portfolio that with 20/20 hindsight would have pushed a manager's guidelines to the limit. For example, one could ask the manager how they expect the fund to behave in particular environments with respect to both performance and volatility. Then, when such an environment is actually encountered, the fund can be checked against the prediction. By trending risk sensitivities, investors can proactively diagnose style drift and avoid surprise shifts in risks/ returns.

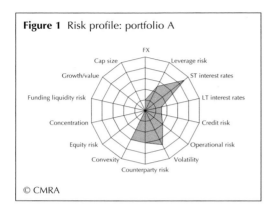

**Figure 1**  Risk profile: portfolio A

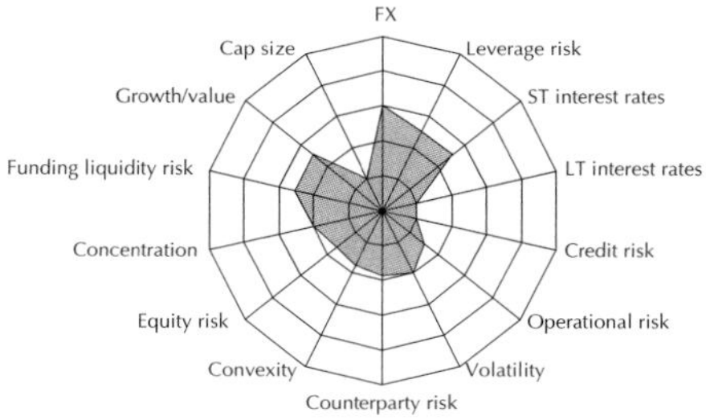

© CMRA

Figures 1, 2 and 3 display the risk profile of three different portfolios across the same set of risk factors. This display is a clear and simple way of understanding what factors drive risks in each one of the portfolios analysed.

Visualising numbers can also add important insight. For example, knowing that a portfolio has a VAR of X is not as informative as seeing the distribution of probabilities (see Figures 4 and 5).

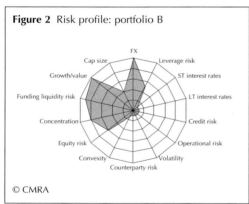

**Figure 2**  Risk profile: portfolio B

© CMRA

Sometimes visualisation tools can provide insight, especially when outliers are involved (see Figure 6).

On the other hand, at times visualisation can create charts that look pretty but are not really informative (see Figure 7).

**Report dimensions**

Risk reporting must be multidimensional in order to effectively reflect the multidimensional nature of risk.

As Figure 8 shows, the dimen-

**Figure 3**  Risk profiles: portfolios A & B combined

© CMRA

**Figure 4** Normal return distribution

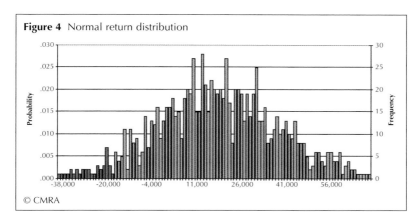

© CMRA

**Figure 5** Skewed return distribution

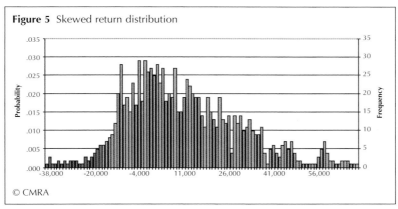

© CMRA

**Figure 6** Quarterly performance

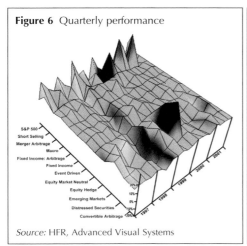

*Source:* HFR, Advanced Visual Systems

**Figure 7** Annualised performance

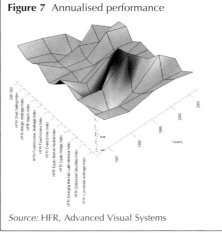

*Source:* HFR, Advanced Visual Systems

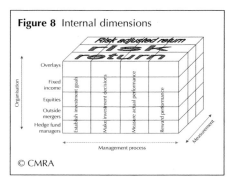

**Figure 8** Internal dimensions

© CMRA

sions across which an institutional investor must be able to aggregate data are potentially daunting.

Individual hedge fund managers have a slightly easier, but still complex, task of meeting the needs of two different audiences for risk reporting – themselves and their investors.

The internal risk reporting needs of hedge fund managers are different from the needs of their investors. Although the push for improved risk transparency is primarily driven by investors, many hedge fund managers are grudgingly finding that risk tools can actually help them better manage their portfolios. Their own risk management needs are not dissimilar to the needs of the bank or investment bank proprietary trading desks of the 1980s from which many hedge fund managers (and I) hail. Nor is the current attitude of many hedge fund managers different from the disdain that many bank and investment bank traders had for risk management tools and techniques when they were first introduced.

Investors' needs, however, are quite different. Investors need risk information from the funds in which they invest for three primary reasons:

1. To assist them in meeting their fiduciary responsibilities and ensuring that the funds in which they invest are appropriately risk managed.
2. To assist them in assessing the overall risks of their portfolio of hedge fund investments as well as their overall portfolio (traditional plus alternative investments).
3. To determine whether or not they are achieving the diversification benefits that they intended from their alternative investments.

The IRC has developed the following preliminary list of topics that a risk profile should address:[1]

❏ option exposure (Greeks);
❏ credit rating;
❏ duration;
❏ sector;
❏ currency;
❏ equity exposure – long, short, net;
❏ derivatives exposure;
❏ capitalisation ranges;
❏ beta;
❏ average position weight;
❏ distribution of returns;

❏ call risk;
❏ counterparties;
❏ top 10 positions; and
❏ geographic concentrations.

Examples of some of the reports that both hedge funds and their investors find useful include:

❏ exposure and VAR's by manager as shown in Figure 9;
❏ each manager's exposure to a reference index as shown in Figure 10;

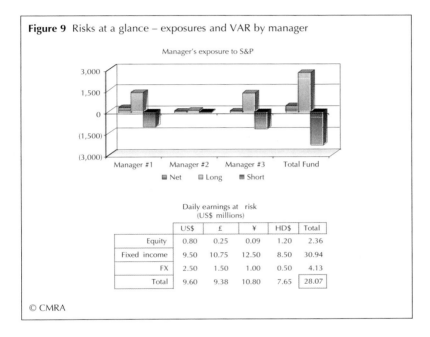

**Figure 9** Risks at a glance – exposures and VAR by manager

Manager's exposure to S&P

Daily earnings at risk
(US$ millions)

|  | US$ | £ | ¥ | HD$ | Total |
|---|---|---|---|---|---|
| Equity | 0.80 | 0.25 | 0.09 | 1.20 | 2.36 |
| Fixed income | 9.50 | 10.75 | 12.50 | 8.50 | 30.94 |
| FX | 2.50 | 1.50 | 1.00 | 0.50 | 4.13 |
| Total | 9.60 | 9.38 | 10.80 | 7.65 | 28.07 |

© CMRA

**Figure 10** Risks at a glance – managers' exposure to S&P

Total diversified VAR: US$16.2 million

Manager #2

Manager #3

Manager #1

*Chart based on non-diversified VAR of US$36.8 million

© CMRA

❏ the net asset allocation exposure of the portfolio as in Figure 11;
❏ funding liquidity analysis as in Figure 12; and finally
❏ sensitivity to yield curve slope as illustrated in Figure 13.

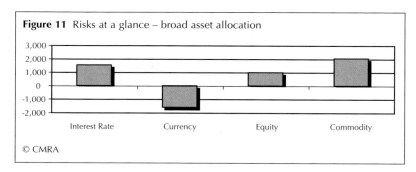

**Figure 11** Risks at a glance – broad asset allocation

© CMRA

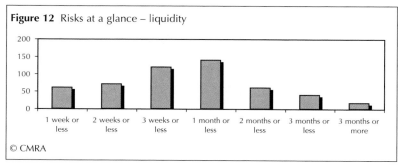

**Figure 12** Risks at a glance – liquidity

© CMRA

**Figure 13** Relationship between changes in the level and the slope of the US Treasury yield curve

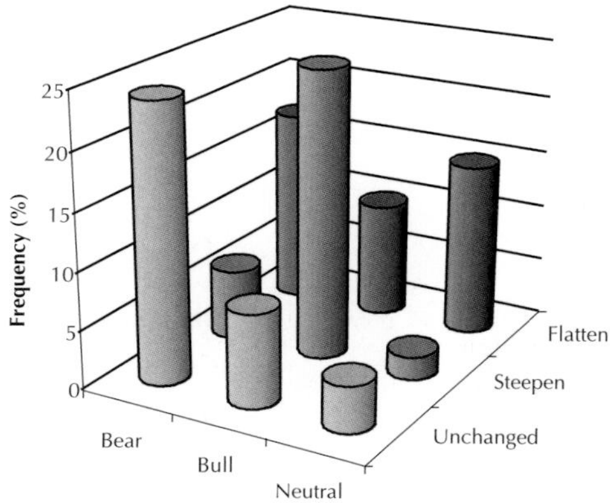

*Source:* Risk Management: Approaches for Fixed Income Markets, Bennett Golub and Leo Tilman

It is important, though, to keep in mind that the best risk reports communicate *comparatively*: risk measures provide perhaps their greatest value when they are looked at over time. Some of the trend reports that are frequently useful include:

❏ VAR trend/style drift analysis as in Figure 14;
❏ mix of credit quality analysis as shown in Figure 15;
❏ prices that are overridden as shown in Figures 16–20;
❏ sensitivity to implied volatility, see Figure 21;
❏ positions with wide bid/offer spreads as in Figure 22;
❏ components of VAR, which are illustrated in Figures 23–30; and finally
❏ components of stress test results, which are shown in Figures 31–40 and Table 1.

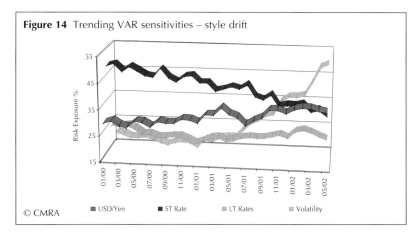

**Figure 14** Trending VAR sensitivities – style drift

© CMRA     ■ USD/Yen     ■ ST Rate     ■ LT Rates     ■ Volatility

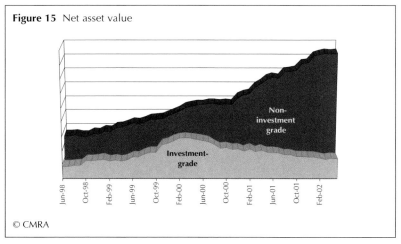

**Figure 15** Net asset value

© CMRA

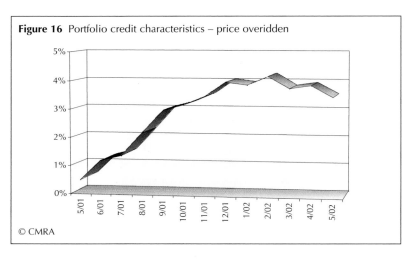

**Figure 16** Portfolio credit characteristics – price overidden

© CMRA

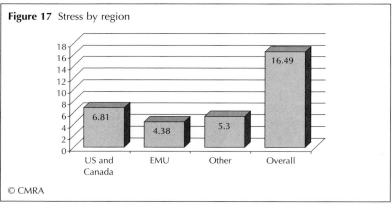

**Figure 17** Stress by region

© CMRA

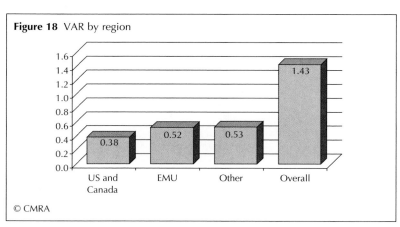

**Figure 18** VAR by region

© CMRA

**Figure 19** Stress by strategy

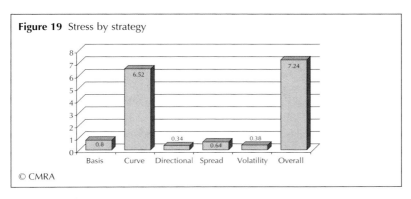

© CMRA

**Figure 20** VAR by strategy

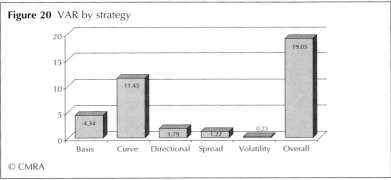

© CMRA

**Figure 21** Factor models reveal changing opportunities for active management

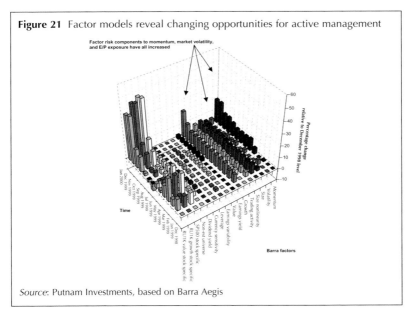

*Source*: Putnam Investments, based on Barra Aegis

**Figure 22** Portfolio interest rate measures – implied volatility +1%

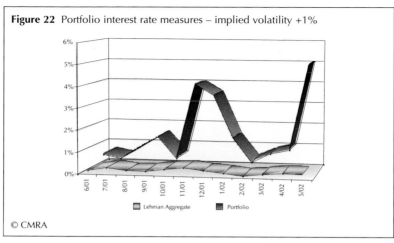

© CMRA

**Figure 23** Portfolio credit characteristics – price overriden with bid/ask spread ≥ 0.5

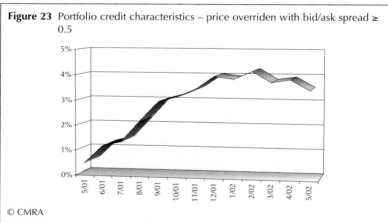

© CMRA

**Figure 24** Term structure VAR

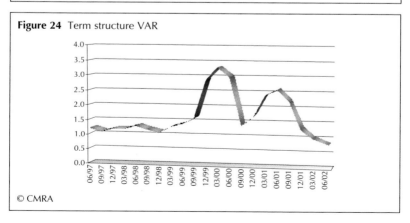

© CMRA

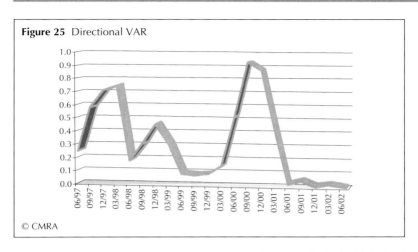

**Figure 25** Directional VAR

© CMRA

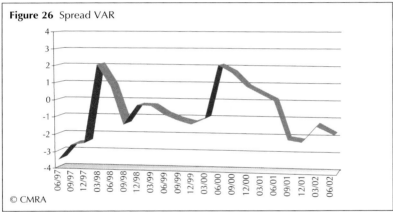

**Figure 26** Spread VAR

© CMRA

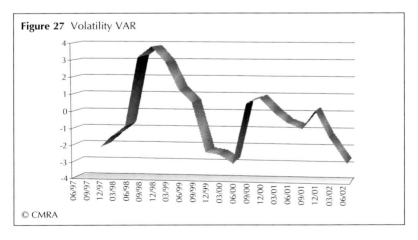

**Figure 27** Volatility VAR

© CMRA

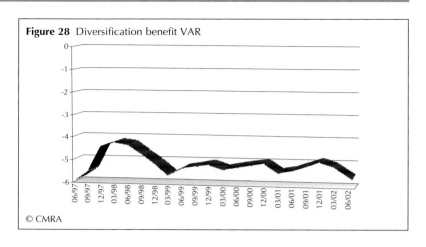

**Figure 28** Diversification benefit VAR

© CMRA

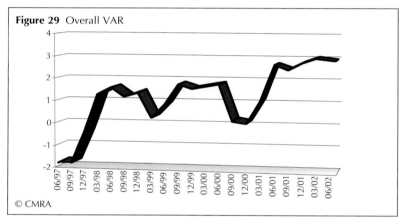

**Figure 29** Overall VAR

© CMRA

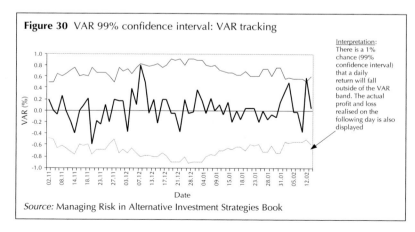

**Figure 30** VAR 99% confidence interval: VAR tracking

Interpretation:
There is a 1%
chance (99%
confidence interval)
that a daily
return will fall
outside of the VAR
band. The actual
profit and loss
realised on the
following day is also
displayed

*Source:* Managing Risk in Alternative Investment Strategies Book

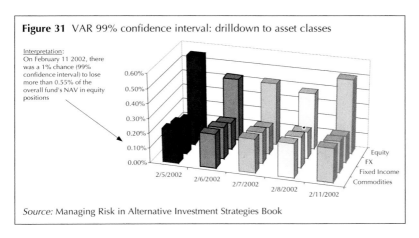

**Figure 31** VAR 99% confidence interval: drilldown to asset classes

Interpretation:
On February 11 2002, there was a 1% chance (99% confidence interval) to lose more than 0.55% of the overall fund's NAV in equity positions

*Source:* Managing Risk in Alternative Investment Strategies Book

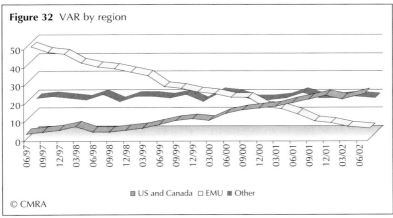

**Figure 32** VAR by region

■ US and Canada □ EMU ■ Other

© CMRA

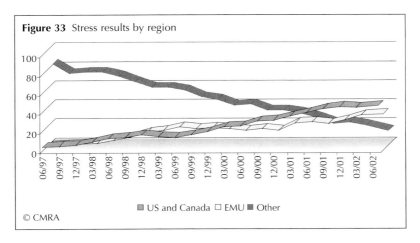

**Figure 33** Stress results by region

■ US and Canada □ EMU ■ Other

© CMRA

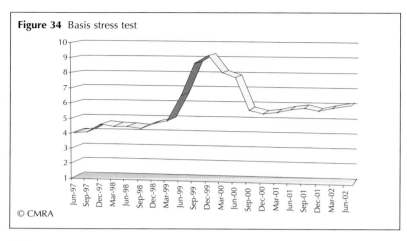

**Figure 34** Basis stress test

© CMRA

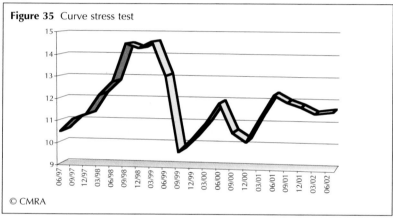

**Figure 35** Curve stress test

© CMRA

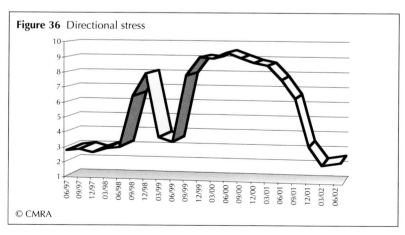

**Figure 36** Directional stress

© CMRA

**Figure 37** Spread stress

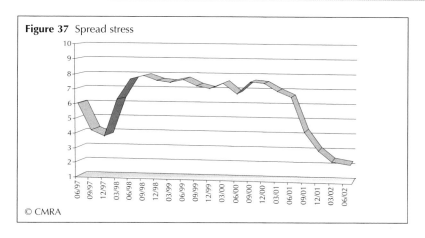

© CMRA

**Figure 38** Volatility stress

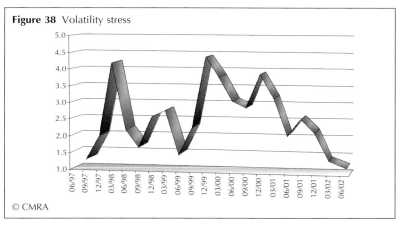

© CMRA

**Figure 39** Diversification benefit stress

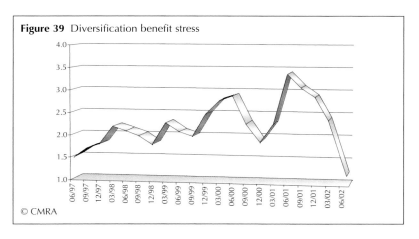

© CMRA

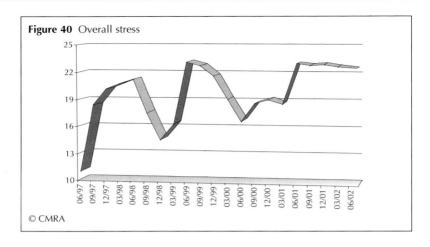

**Figure 40** Overall stress

© CMRA

**Table 1** Stress tests risk report

|  | % | % | % | % |
|---|---|---|---|---|
| Simulated scenario | (10.00) | (5.00) | 5.00 | 10.00 |
| S&P 500 | (1.94) | (0.80) | 1.98 | 5.91 |
| Euro-toxx-50 | (0.98) | (0.39) | 1.01 | 3.04 |
| Nikkei 225 | (0.31) | 0.02 | 0.91 | 2.87 |
|  | 80bp down | 40bp down | 40bp up | 80bp up |
| US government curve | 2.16 | 0.65 | (1.34) | (3.14) |
|  | 30bp down | 15bp down | 15bp up | 30bp up |
| Corporate single A yield spread | 2.01 | 1.01 | (2.02) | (1.04) |
|  | (8.00) | (4.00) | (4.00) | 8.00 |
| €–US$ | 2.38 | 1.19 | (1.04) | (2.01) |
| US$–¥ | (1.62) | (0.34) | 0.56 | 1.98 |
|  | (10.00) | (5.00) | 5.00 | 10.00 |
| GS Commodity Index | 3.13 | 1.11 | (0.71) | (3.01) |
| Historical scenario |  |  |  |  |
| Stock market crash 1987 | (4.91) |  |  |  |
| Bond market crash 1994 | (4.22) |  |  |  |
| Russian default/LTCM crisis 1998 | (5.48) |  |  |  |
| Brasil crisis 1999 | (1.01) |  |  |  |
| September 11, 2001 | (2.79) |  |  |  |

*Source*: Managing Risk in Alternative Investment Strategies: Successful Investing in Hedge Funds and Managed Futures by Lars Jaeger

No matter what level of detailed disclosure a fund selects, meaningful, carefully designed charts can add value for portfolio managers and, when appropriate, investors alike. "A picture is worth a thousand words" is true in risk reporting. The ability to properly visualise risk data is essential to maximise its usefulness. Equally important is the ability to "drill down" as needed: it can be extremely valuable to be able to probe deeper if a trend emerges. The goal is not to have lots of numbers; it is to have risk understanding.

## CONCLUSION

Most risk indicators are "rear view mirror" measures. Many risk reports do not lead to actionable conclusions. Translating risk "data" into meaningful "actionable" information should be the goal of risk reporting.

---

[1] Investor Risk Committee, see http://www.iafe.org.

# 6

# *Hedge Fund Risk Systems*

*I cannot give you the formula for success but, I can give you the*
*formula for failure, which is: "Try to please everybody".*
Herbery Bayard Swope

## INTRODUCTION

Chapter 3 discusses the limitations of position-level reporting and Chapter 4 discusses the pitfalls of risk measures and the need for qualitative due diligence. This chapter discusses the limits of risk management systems. In addition to the foregoing limitations, a major drawback of today's system technology is the lack of integration across the range of functionality that a hedge fund manager needs. As Figure 1 shows, no one system covers the range of functionality from trading a portfolio to portfolio accounting, to portfolio analysis, to performance attribution, to performance measurement, to compliance, and finally to risk management.

This means that most hedge fund and fund of funds managers require

| | Algorithmics | Askari | Barra | BlackRock * | DBRisk | GlobeOp | Measurisk | RiskMetrics | SunGard | Wilshire |
|---|---|---|---|---|---|---|---|---|---|---|
| Trading | ✘ | ■ | ✘ | ■ | ✘ | ■ | ✘ | ✘ | ■ | ✳ |
| Portfolio accounting | ✘ | ■ | ✘ | ■ | ✘ | ■ | ✘ | ✘ | ■ | ■ |
| Portfolio analytics | ■ | ✳ | ■ | ■ | ✘ | ✳ | ✘ | ✳ | ✳ | ■ |
| Market risk management | ■ | ■ | ■ | ■ | ■ | ■ | ■ | ■ | ■ | ■ |
| Credit risk management | ■ | ✘ | ✳ | ⬟ | ✘ | ✳ | ✳ | ■ | ■ | ■ |
| Performance attribution | ✘ | ✳ | ✳ | ■ | ✘ | ✳ | ✳ | ✳ | ■ | ■ |
| Performance measurement | ✘ | ✳ | ✘ | ■ | ✘ | ✘ | ✘ | ✘ | ■ | ■ |

**Figure 1** Range of functionality

* Fixed-income only

✘ No     ■ Yes     ⬟ Limited     ✳ Planned

© CMRA

83

more than one system, which can be a nightmare for integration and consistency.

## COMMERCIALLY AVAILABLE SYSTEMS

While there is a great degree of similarity across commercially available buy-side risk management systems, all systems are not the same; each has its relative strengths and unique capabilities. Therefore, the best solution for a large pension fund primarily focused on large-cap equities will likely not be the best solution for a hedge fund focused on fixed-income arbitrage. Varying management styles also present different requirements: we thus have a clear case of "one size fits nobody".

The long/short equity and convertible arbitrage IRC subcommittees, under the chairmanship of Mark Anson, reviewed three of the commercially available risk templates for these strategies and concluded that, while each template had certain advantages, none was considered sufficient for risk disclosure, as we discuss here:

### System 1
❑ Concentrates on VAR.
❑ Good for measuring market risk: long/short equity, market neutral, statistical arbitrage.
❑ Less viable for convertible arbitrage with credit and volatility spreads.
❑ Does not offer much information on the "Greeks" – delta, gamma, rho, vega and theta risk.

### System 2
❑ Strength is scenario analysis. For example, it can present a scenario for long/short equity and convertible arbitrage when the equity market is down 5% or the credit spreads widen.
❑ Addresses country/currency exposure.
❑ Does not address the Greeks.
❑ Does not address call risk, credit rating exposure, percentage of Regulation D securities.

### System 3
❑ Strength is extensive factor analysis.
❑ Three factors are used to incorporate "twists", shifts and "butterfly" changes in the yield curve.
❑ Not enough information on the Greeks or option exposure, and does not have scenario analysis.

On the other hand, if one views the lack of a uniform technology as a problem, then all investors are facing the same problem. In short, the person with whom you are trading starts with the same problem that you do. An *a priori* across the board handicap in what is often a zero sum game means giving an advantage to those best able to deal with the problem. Therefore, the investor who is best able to make up for the lack of a preferred system by choosing the most appropriate system available and patching its shortcomings may be competitively better off than in the case of everyone having perfect technology. As such, system selection and management can be a source of competitive advantage and profit.

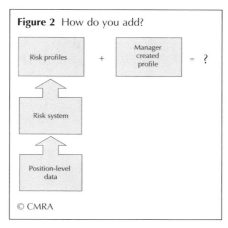

**Figure 2** How do you add?

Another key issue for hedge fund and fund of funds investors is the reality that even if position-level detail is available from some funds, it will not be available from all the funds in which they invest. Therefore, they will need to develop the ability to aggregate bottom-up calculated risk with top-down "risk profiles", which are created from the heuristic findings of due diligence for those funds that are not willing to provide positions (see Figure 2).

Unfortunately, no risk system is a panacea and, in my opinion, too much time is spent agonising over choosing a system. That time would be better spent thinking about what to do with your risk system if you have one.

In addition to the problems of combining bottom-up and top-down analysis (as shown in Figure 3), many users are frustrated by the reporting capabilities from commercially available systems. A preliminary conclusion at a recent IRC subcommittee meeting was that the templates provided by the commercial vendors generally provided either too little or too much information; none offered a comfortable balance.[1] Also, the reports were viewed as having too many numbers and not enough trend information.

Another frustration frequently heard is that users need more education on how to use the tools and translate the information for their Boards.

## VALUE-AT-RISK

There are two levels at which the three basic methods for calculating VAR can be applied. You need to understand the strengths and weaknesses of each approach in order to make an

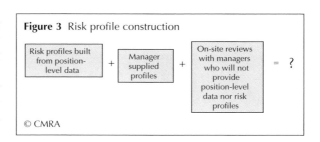

**Figure 3** Risk profile construction

informed decision about the usefulness of VAR. The different methods of calculating VAR have varying abilities to handle optionality (non-linear relations), stress testing, complex fixed income and derivative structures, risk causality, fat tails, non-symmetrical distributions, aggregation of risk from multiple systems, and so on. Furthermore, some of the solutions that these methods produce are difficult to understand and explain (see Figure 4).

In addition to the question of which VAR methodology to use, for equities there is also the question of whether the VAR analysis should be performed at the "security" or "risk factor" level. Even in a data-rich market like the US, equity factor models can explain only 40% of the performance of individual equities. Thus, there is a debate that asks whether the calculation of the risk of equities should be driven by the equity factor model and all other behaviour should be viewed as non-structural specific risk; or whether the risk analysis should be performed at the security level and, subsequently, attributed to the equity risk factors.

While VAR can be an extremely valuable tool, it provides insight only into certain types of risks. There are risks that get missed when we model distributions. Therefore, stress testing is at least equally as important as VAR, but is not handled easily by some systems (see Appendix 6).

## STRESS TESTING

Risk management systems normally perform two types of stress tests. The first is actual crisis "historic scenario", which preserves the embedded historical correlation effects between markets and instruments when the crisis occurred. Examples of such events include the 1987 stock market crisis, the 1994 ERM crisis, the 1998 Russia/LTCM crisis, the 2000–2001 technology meltdown, and the effects of the September 11, 2001 terrorist attacks.[2] While all risk management systems do a good job of calculating

**Figure 4** Suppliers' VAR methodology

| Method | Level | Algorithmics | Askari | Barra | BlackRock | DBRisk | GlobeOp | Measurisk | RiskMetrics | SunGard | Wilshire |
|---|---|---|---|---|---|---|---|---|---|---|---|
| Parametric | Security | ■ | ■ | ■ | ✘ | ✘ | ■ | ✘ | ■ | ■ | ■ |
| Parametric | Risk factor | ■ | ✘ | ■ | ■ | ✘ | ■ | ✘ | ✘ | ✱ | ■ |
| Historic simulation | Security | ■ | ■ | ✱ | ✘ | ✘ | ■ | ✘ | ■ | ■ | ✘ |
| Historic simulation | Risk factor | ■ | ✘ | ■ | ■ | ✘ | ■ | ✘ | ✘ | ✱ | ✘ |
| Monte Carlo simulation | Security | ■ | ■ | ■ | ✘ | ✘ | ■ | ● | ■ | ■ | ✱ |
| Monte Carlo simulation | Risk factor | ■ | ✘ | ■ | ■ | ■ | ■ | ■ | ✘ | ✱ | ✱ |

© CMRA

VAR, their ability to adequately stress test historic scenarios is limited. The limitation is generally not a system functionality problem but rather a data availability problem: most systems do not have adequate data to analyse the impact that a recurrence of one of these historic events could have on a portfolio. Systems that use a variance/covariance matrix as the basis of a parametric or Monte Carlo simulation VAR must prepackage these historic scenarios. Therefore, a user's ability to select a specific scenario depends on whether the supplier has included that event in its system. In particular, correlations across risk factors tend to converge to one (become highly correlated) in times of stress. Therefore, data that replicates this phenomenon is critical. Other relationships that can be captured in complete data are spreads between on-the-run and off-the-run bonds and credit spreads.

Some systems support a wide range of pre-canned stress scenarios, while others more customisation (see Figure 5). See Chapter 4, Risk Measurement, for a more complete discussion of stress testing.

## HOW DIFFICULT IS THE SYSTEM TO IMPLEMENT?
The cost of implementation of a new system can vary dramatically. I am aware of one large money manager spent over US$5 million implementing off-the-shelf packages that required a significant amount of custom integration to combine an equity and fixed-income package. This manager ultimately created a massive data warehouse to consolidate input data and stage output data. On the other extreme, simple hedge funds have implemented ASP solutions within hours and at a minimal cost.

Some suppliers (see Appendix 6) provide significant implementation support and charge on a time and materials basis (either negotiated separately as a fixed cost contract or bundled into the annual price of the system). Other suppliers will refer their client to a third-party integrator.

**Figure 5** Stress test matrix

| | Algorithmics package | Askari package | Askari ASP | Barra package | BlackRock Svc. Bureau | DBRisk ASP | GlobeOp package | Measurisk ASP | RiskMetrics ASP/ package | SunGard package | Wilshire package | Percent yes/average |
|---|---|---|---|---|---|---|---|---|---|---|---|---|
| **Historical scenarios** | | | | | | | | | | | | |
| User can specify a particular time period over which the portfolio should be evaluated? | ■ | ■ | ■ | ● REQ | ■ | ✗ | ● REQ | ✗ | ■ | ■ | ■ | 60% |
| How many prepackaged scenarios does the system supply? | 36 | | | 0 | 20 | 0 | 3 | 21 | 5 | 0 | 0 | 9 |
| **Interactive " what if"** | | | | | | | | | | | | |
| Does the system permit you to evaluate a security that is currently not in the portfolio? | ■ | ■ | ■ | ■ | ■ | ✗ | ✗ | ✳ Mar-02 | ■ | ■ | ■ | 80% |

© CMRA

**Figure 6** Data matrix

| | Algorithmics package | Askari package | Askari ASP | Barra package | BlackRock Svc. Bureau | DBRisk ASP | GlobeOp package | Measurisk ASP | RiskMetrics ASP package | SunGard package | Wilshire package | Percent yes/average |
|---|---|---|---|---|---|---|---|---|---|---|---|---|
| **Risk factors** | | | | | | | | | | | | |
| What is the number of countries covered by factors in the standard set? | | | 45 | 57 | 20 | 46 | 50 | 45/70 | 80 | 50 | 82 | 54 |
| What is the number of factors in the standard set? | | | 445 | 517 | 610 | 610 | 850 | 900 | 830 | 850 | 598 | 690 |
| For an equity security level VAR, can the system provide an analysis of what factors cause the risk in equities? | ✖ | ✖ | ⬟ | ■ | ■ | ■ | ■ | ⬟ | ✖ | ✳ Sep -02 | ✖ | 50% |

© CMRA

## DATA

Data is a huge issue in selecting a system. Some systems provide data and others require the user to provide its own data. Figure 6 specifies some of the data provided.

While some users prefer to use their own data, which has been carefully scrubbed and is consistent with the data used by non-risk systems, many potential users will only consider using a system that provides data (especially if they have no source of their own).

See Appendix 6 for a detailed comparison of buy-side risk management systems.

## CONCLUSION

Since all systems have strengths and weaknesses and none of the systems currently available meet all of the needs of hedge fund managers, funds of funds and/or other investors, prioritising your needs and identifying areas in which you are willing to compromise is probably the best starting point for selecting a system. For example, if multi-asset class is a priority, that will limit your short list to a handful of choices. If complex OTC derivatives are part of the portfolios you need to analyse, the potential universe will be equally small, but not necessarily overlapping with the multi-asset class constraint. If you need historical data as well as daily or monthly updating, this too will eliminate many of the offerings. Rather than tackling a review of many systems, prioritising your needs can reduce the time and energy required to select a system.

1   Http://www.iafe.org.
2   Capital Market Risk Advisors, 2002, "Risk Insights, September 11, 2001," http://www.cmra.com/cgibin/September11.crg.

# SECTION II

# Who Invests in Hedge Funds?

7

# *Institutional Investors*

Broadly speaking, institutional investors are organisations that invest. The category includes pension plan sponsors, endowments, foundations, banks and insurance companies among others. Allocations by institutional investors to hedge funds and other alternative assets have increased dramatically in the late 1990s and early 21st century and that increase is expected to continue. Endowments and foundations in particular have embraced hedge fund investing more aggressively than other institutional investors (see Chapter 9).

High net worth individuals (HNW), however, remain the largest class of hedge fund investors. AIMA estimates that HNW represent 44% of hedge fund investments (see Figure 1).

In a 2001 survey, Barra found that a large majority of hedge fund and fund of funds investments are from the US.[1] Barra also found that the minority of investments in the US are "institutional" (see Table 1).

Some institutional investors have not embraced hedge funds because they are concerned about the risk/return profile or a lack of disclosure or transparency. Others may be prohibited from investing in hedge funds by law or investment policy; others still might fear "headline risk".

## STRATEGIES
Long/short equity remains the most popular hedge fund style among investors according to a Goldman Sachs survey (see Figure 2).[2]

The popularity of long/short equity has recently slipped while the popularity of distressed debt has increased dramatically.

## SOURCING
While most institutional investors do not rely on consultants to source hedge funds, endowments and foundations are more

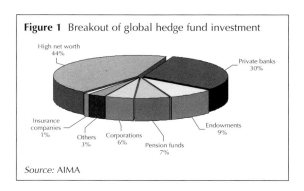

**Figure 1** Breakout of global hedge fund investment

High net worth 44%

Private banks 30%

Insurance companies 1%

Others 3%

Corporations 6%

Pension funds 7%

Endowments 9%

*Source:* AIMA

**Table 1** Estimated global funds of hedge funds market survey, July 2001 (US$ billion)

|  | Corporate pension | Public pensions | Endowments/ foundations | Insurance companies | High net worth | Totals |
|---|---|---|---|---|---|---|
| **United States** | | | | | | |
| Hedge funds | 35 | 28 | 21 | 5 | 261 | 350 |
| Funds of funds | 8 | 5 | 5 | 1 | 50 | 69 |
| Total | 43 | 33 | 26 | 6 | 311 | 417 |
| **Europe** | | | | | | |
| Hedge funds | | | 10 | | 68 | 78 |
| Funds of funds | | | 2 | | 13 | 15 |
| Total | | | 12 | | 81 | 93 |
| **Japan and Asia** | | | | | | |
| Hedge funds | | | | | | 22 |
| Funds of funds | | | | | | 10 |
| Total | | | | | | 32 |
| **Totals** | | | | | | |
| Hedge funds | | | | | 329 | 450 |
| Funds of funds | | | | | 63 | 94 |
| Total | | | | | 392 | 542 |

*Source:* Barra Strategic Consulting Group

likely than pension funds to rely on consultants, as can be seen in Figure 3.

CMRA and other boutique firms who have not traditionally been viewed as "pension consultants" have become active in hedge fund and fund of funds selection, due diligence, and risk management because of the specialised expertise that is required.

Nevertheless, as shown in Figure 4, networking, contacts, and references are still the primary source of hedge fund referrals.

## FEES

The majority of institutional investors believe hedge fund fees, though high, are warranted.[3] A survey published in 2002 by the *Journal of Alternative Investments* reported that 77% of participants believe hedge fund fees are warranted and 80% believe those fees will not come under pressure.

## ALLOCATIONS

Table 2 shows that funds of funds are the most active hedge fund allocators, making allocations 10 or more times a year. Other institutional investors make a new hedge fund investment and/or reallocate AUM much less frequently.

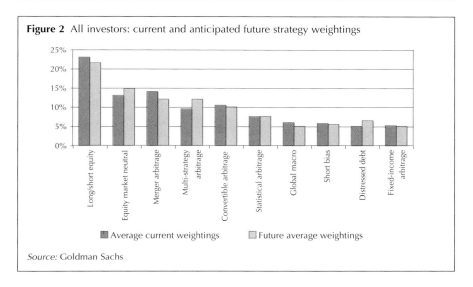

**Figure 2** All investors: current and anticipated future strategy weightings

■ Average current weightings    □ Future average weightings

*Source:* Goldman Sachs

## TRANSPARENCY

As the research behind Figure 5 shows, transparency remains the number one concern of institutional investors.

An informal IRC survey found that 60% of institutional investors get position-level transparency from only 10–25% of their hedge fund managers, while none receive position-level data for 100% of their hedge funds. Only 25% of respondents receive position-level information from 75% or more of their hedge funds.[4] When asked if they were satisfied with the transparency they received, 67% said they were satisfied.

As indicated in Figure 6, which is based on research carried out by Deutsche Bank, when investors were asked what they really wanted to know from a hedge fund

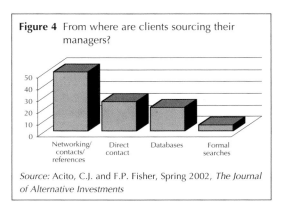

**Figure 3** Percentage of all surveryed participants who use consultants

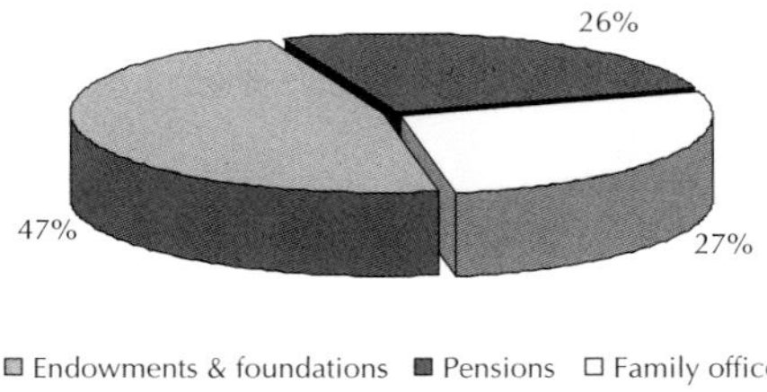

26%

47%

27%

■ Endowments & foundations   ■ Pensions   □ Family office

*Source:* Deutsche Bank Alternative Investment Survey

**Figure 4** From where are clients sourcing their managers?

Networking/ contacts/ references    Direct contact    Databases    Formal searches

*Source:* Acito, C.J. and F.P. Fisher, Spring 2002, *The Journal of Alternative Investments*

**Table 2**  Most frequent number of allocations per year

| | |
|---|---|
| Funds of funds | 10+ |
| Banks | 5 |
| Family offices | 4 |
| Endowments | 2 |

*Source:* Deutsche Bank Alternative Investment Survey

**Figure 5**  Primary investor concerns about investing in hedge funds

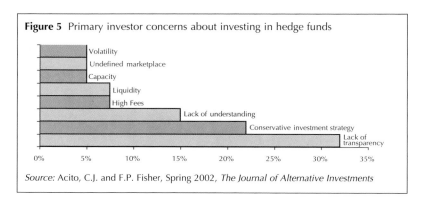

*Source:* Acito, C.J. and F.P. Fisher, Spring 2002, *The Journal of Alternative Investments*

**Table 3**  Risk Standards Working Group

| | | |
|---|---|---|
| **Suzzane Brenner** Rockefeller Foundation | **Michael de Marco** GTE Investment Management | **David Russ** Pacific Telesis Group |
| **Kevin Byrne** The Equitable Companies Inc. | **John Lukomnik** City of New York, Office of Comptroller | **James Seymour** The Common Fund |
| **Christopher Campisano** Xerox Corporation | **Richard Rose** San Diego County Employees' Retirement Association | **Kathy Wassmann** R.R. Donnelley & Sons Company |
| **Mary Cotrill** CalPERS | | **Gregory Williamson** Amoco Corporation |

*Source:* Technical Advisors & Coordinators: Capital Market Risk Advisors, Inc.
*Note:* The Risk Standards, while unanimously endorsed by the RSWG as individuals, do not necessarily represent the views of their respective institutions.

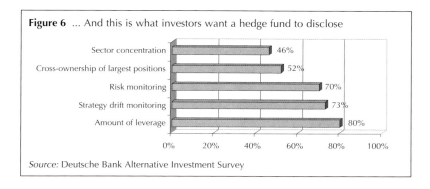

**Figure 6** ... And this is what investors want a hedge fund to disclose

Source: Deutsche Bank Alternative Investment Survey

manager, the majority of respondents said they wanted the amount of leverage employed disclosed and they wanted to understand style drift.[4] See Chapter 3 for an in depth discussion of transparency.

## RISK STANDARDS FOR INSTITUTIONAL INVESTORS AND INVESTMENT MANAGERS

In 1996, CMRA worked with 11 major plan sponsors to develop *Risk Standards for Institutional Investment Managers and Institutional Investors* (see Table 3 and Appendix 5). The mission of the group was:

> *To create a set of risk standards for institutional investment managers and institutional investors.*

The 20 principles the group developed outline an excellent aspirational framework for meeting the risk management needs of institutional investors in their traditional investments. Hedge funds were not specifically addressed in 1996 since so few sponsors were involved in hedge fund investing at the time. While many institutional investors would be delighted if hedge funds could meet these aspirational goals, few do or will and new thinking is needed to adapt these "standards" to an absolute return world.

The Risk Standards Group fully recognised that "talk to action ratio is very high". No institutional investor complies with all of the standards today and implementation approaches must vary by type of institution.

The group worked diligently to tailor the standards to the issues specific to institutional investors including:

❏ longer time horizons, such as holding period or evaluation;
❏ multiple asset classes;
❏ multiple portfolio managers/firms;
❏ distinct fiduciary responsibilities;
❏ heavy reliance on outside data;

❏ historical focus on performance vs risk-adjusted performance; and
❏ increasing dependence on theoretical models.

These standards still form a framework used by many institutional investors and are a good representation of their mindset and issues. While they were not designed to cover hedge fund investing, they do give insight into the risk practices within the institutional investing world that need to be adapted to hedge funds.

The *Risk Standards for Institutional Investment Managers and Institutional Investors* included 20 risk standards focusing on three areas: management standards, measurement standards and oversight standards. These areas cover nine, seven and four standards, respectively.

As Figure 7 shows, the findings included nine management risk standards. The drivers for these management standards included:

❏ Rapid growth in the number of investment managers.
❏ Increased pressure to keep up with "peer" groups.
❏ Quest for differentiation, resulting in aggressive innovation.
❏ Use of exotic asset classes and complex, leveraged, and/or less liquid instruments and markets.
❏ Increased disclosure of unexpected or misunderstood risk, failure of several famous "market neutral" strategies.
❏ Greater number of disagreements related to suitability, fiduciary obligation and risk responsibility.
❏ Realisation that more detailed guidance is required from investors and primary fiduciaries to reduce "revisionist" evaluations of risk and reward.

The findings also included seven measurement risk standards as shown in Figure 8. The drivers for these measurement standards included:

❏ Valuation difficulty became a significant problem during periods of market dislocation (eg, the Fed rate hikes and the Mexican peso devaluation).
❏ The number and complexity of instruments outstripped resources (eg, the "99999999" problem and prices that are constant when markets move).
❏ Only single valuation sources were available for an increasing portion of portfolios.
❏ Widely accepted models produced disparate values for the same instrument/risk, given identical inputs.
❏ "Carbon-dating" became an issue in risk measurement.
❏ Quantitative measures failed to control or identify many loss situations (eg, uni-dimensional measures).
❏ Investors began to focus on risk dollars spent to achieve return.

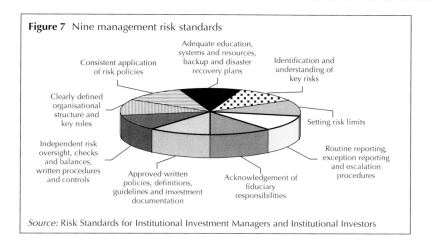

**Figure 7** Nine management risk standards

*Source:* Risk Standards for Institutional Investment Managers and Institutional Investors

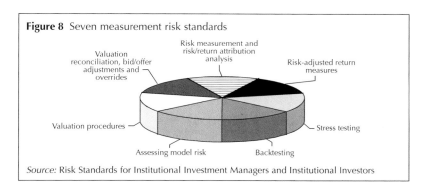

**Figure 8** Seven measurement risk standards

*Source:* Risk Standards for Institutional Investment Managers and Institutional Investors

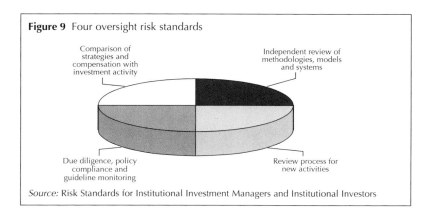

**Figure 9** Four oversight risk standards

*Source:* Risk Standards for Institutional Investment Managers and Institutional Investors

Additionally, as in Figure 9, the findings included four oversight risk standards. The drivers for these oversight standards included:

❏ Guidelines that were out of date facilitated compliance with the letter of the "law" while violating its spirit (eg, "no commodities" yet structured notes were purchased with a commodity-linked return).
❏ Improvements in technology and increased fiduciary awareness led to the ability to ask more questions (eg, by trustees, plan sponsors, supervisors, directors and regulators).
❏ Now-famous surprises led to the need for greater definition of "new" products (eg, power trades, leveraged swaps and structured notes).
❏ Questionnaires and reviews revealed the need for consistency across managers, custodians and others:
  • identical instruments were recorded at different prices;
  • managers and custodians produced conflicting reports due to different models.
❏ The increasing trend to focus on reward and risk at the instrument, manager, and overall portfolio level resulted in a desire to ensure that compensation and fees encourage the type of risk-taking that the primary fiduciary desires.

Understanding the framework of the *Risk Standards* document can give hedge fund managers a better understanding of why institutional investors are asking so many annoying questions. This understanding alone can go a long way towards bridging the gap between institutional investors and hedge fund managers.

When hedge fund managers understand that institutional investors are accustomed to receiving position-level detail on their traditional investors – which can be 25 times the size of their hedge fund investments – they can better appreciate the tension. Also, when hedge fund managers realise that some of the larger institutional investors actually have their own risk management systems, which analyse the risks and concentrations in their traditional investments, it is easier to empathise with (if not satisfy) their desire for position-level data.

## CONCLUSION

Creating a similar framework for hedge fund investing will be a significant step towards increasing the comfort level of institutional investors with hedge fund and fund of funds investing. One approach, proposed by Robert Litterman, Jacques Longerstaey, Jacob Rosengarten and Kurt Winkelmann of Goldman Sachs Investment Management, is outlined in Chapter 7 of my first book, *Risk Budgeting – A New Approach to Investing:*

*In golf it is on the 'fairway'. In baseball it is a 'fair ball'. In football it is 'in bounds'. In portfolio management we also have a name for it. It is the 'green zone'.[5]*

1   Acito. C., and P. Fisher, Spring 2001, "Barra Strategic Consulting Group Survey".
2   1999 Goldman, Sachs & Co. and Frank Russel Company Report on Alternative Investments.
3   Institutional Investor/CMRA Endowment & Foundation Survey, June 2002.
4   Deutsche Bank, Alternative Investment Survey Results, March 2002.
5   Rahl, L., (ed), 2000, *Risk Budgeting: A New Approach to Investing* (London: Risk Books).

# 8

# *Plan Sponsors*

## INTRODUCTION
A plan sponsor refers to the sponsoring entity behind a pension fund. A plan sponsor can be a private business or state or local entity acting on behalf of its employees, a union acting on behalf of its members, or an individual representing his/herself. The plan sponsor acts as a fiduciary for plan participants. This chapter addresses some of the key questions plan sponsors face when investing in hedge funds. The perspectives of several well-known plan sponsors on transparency are also presented throughout this chapter in Panels 1–5.

## BACKGROUND
As a recent survey from the Journal of Alternative Investments found, only 22% of pension funds currently invest in hedge funds.[1] In the UK, the percentage is even lower. But, as Table 1 shows, hedge fund investments by pension plans are up substantially since 1990.

While hedge fund investing by pension funds is increasing, hedge funds do not fit neatly into the traditional pension fund investment methodology. Reasons for the reluctance of plan sponsors to embrace hedge fund investing include:

❏ Adequate data on individual hedge funds is difficult to find (short track records, selection bias, survivorship bias).
❏ Hedge funds invest into strategies rather than assets.
❏ Hedge funds invest *across* traditional asset classes.
❏ Hedge funds use multiple strategies.
❏ Risk, return and correlation with traditional asset classes strongly differ by type of strategy.
❏ Plan sponsors fear "headline risk".
❏ The inability to fit hedge funds into traditional risk/return optimisation frameworks.
❏ Lack of transparency.

**Table 1** Growth of pension fund hedge fund allocation (US$ billion)

| 1990 | 1996 | 2001 |
| --- | --- | --- |
| 2.7 | 5.5 | 9.1 |

*Source*: Hennessee Hedge Fund Survey (January 2000)

## Panel 1

### An interview on transparency with William Cook, Aegon USA Investment Management

Mr Cook is executive vice president of Aegon USA Investment Management, a group with US$83.3 billion of AUM. US$1.25 billion of which is invested across 25 hedge funds.

**What are your strategies?**
All.

**What kind of transparency do you receive from managers?**
One-third of our managers give us full transparency in their offices.

**Are you satisfied with the transparency you receive?**
Yes, or else we wouldn't be there.

**What are your views on transparency?**
It is a pointless push. Business guys have their own reasons: they often want transparency even when it is not actionable.

**What do you do with the information you receive?**
We do what we call a deeds-to-action audit. This is simply to see if the managers are doing what they say they're doing.

**Lots of managers have moved heavily towards cash. Do you consider this a form of strategy drift?**
No, but I would challenge them if they weren't showing the appropriate risk/reward.

**Do you conduct due diligence?**
Yes, both before we invest and afterwards. We have a three-legged process: investment, back office, and a melding of the two.

**Where do you think transparency is headed in the future?**
We will start seeing a divergence between funds that cater to institutional investors – they will offer transparency – and boutique funds that cater to high-net-worth money – they will not have to offer transparency.

## Panel 2

### An interview on transparency with Mark Anson, CalPERS

CalPERS is a public pension fund with US$150 billion of AUM.

**Why do investors want transparency?**
Quite a bit of the recent discussion and research regarding hedge funds centres on whether they are an appropriate investment for institutional investors (Kao, 2002; Asness, Krail and Liew, 2001). The advent of institutions into the hedge fund world inevitably begs the question of whether hedge funds should be "institutionalised." Institutionalisation means three things. First, it means transparency. Second, it means a process. Third, it means relative returns.

There are three primary reasons why investors want transparency. First, investors demand transparency for risk monitoring. This allows the investor to determine whether the hedge fund manager is operating within agreed upon risk levels. For instance, a convertible arbitrage hedge fund manager may agree to limit

The last three reasons are perhaps the biggest for pension funds' slower progress than other categories of institutional investors.

One approach to alleviating the lack of fit with traditional frameworks is to introduce the concept of "transparent frontier" vs "efficient frontier" (see Figure 1).

Just as the "D" word ("derivatives") was a public curse in the 1980s, hedge fund investing is deemed an invitation for bad press in 2002. In addition, plan sponsors are acutely aware of the need to explain their investments to their Boards. They are also sensitive to the scrutiny and second-guessing of their constituents and the press.

A greater awareness and sensitivity to the headline risk that plan sponsors face (especially public plan sponsors whose every move is subject to public and press scrutiny) on the part of hedge fund managers might help them to better understand *why* plan sponsors behave the way they do. When *understanding* the reasons behind a hedge fund manager's request for information from an institutional investor or plan sponsor, the knee-jerk "no" answer often evolves into "I can't give you the position-level detail you are asking for, but I think this risk profile will meet your needs – what do you think?".

### WHICH PLAN SPONSORS ARE INVESTING IN HEDGE FUNDS?
The US$24 billion Pennsylvania State Employees' Retirement System is leading the public pension fund charge into hedge funds with US$2.5 billion, or roughly 10% of its total portfolio, in hedge funds. CalPERS (California Public Employees' Retirement System) has also received significant

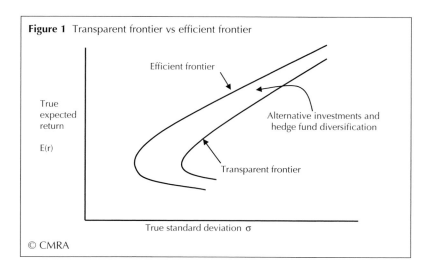

**Figure 1** Transparent frontier vs efficient frontier

Efficient frontier

True expected return

E(r)

Alternative investments and hedge fund diversification

Transparent frontier

True standard deviation σ

© CMRA

leverage to a 1:3 ratio. Or a long/short manager may agree to maintain a net short position of no greater than 25%. Transparency allows the investor to determine whether the hedge fund manager has operated within the established economic parameters of his/her plan.

Investors also desire transparency for risk aggregation. This allows investors to accumulate their risks across their entire hedge fund plan as well as their entire investment portfolio. Only in this manner can an investor determine whether he/she has significant exposure to an industry, economic sector, or sub-sector. Without transparency, an investor may have double or triple bets in a certain industry without realising his/her exposure.

Last, investors require transparency to monitor strategy drift. For instance, as the US economy slowed in 2001, many merger arbitrage deals dried up. As a result, some merger arbitrage managers substituted distressed debt for merger deals. This transformed the risk profile of their hedge funds from one associated with event risk (merger announcements) to one associated with credit risk (distressed debt). Another example is long/short equity managers who suddenly cannot "find good investments" and sit on a significant amount of cash. This manager has transformed from a long/short stock picker to a market timer. The risk in his/her fund is no longer stock specific risk; it is market risk. An investor must ensure that the hedge fund manager stays consistent with his/her chosen investment strategy.

### What does transparency mean?
There are four types of transparency:

1. Disclosure transparency.
2. Process transparency.
3. Position transparency.
4. Exposure transparency.

### What is your prediction as to what best practice will be in 2003? 2005?
I expect exposure transparency, not position transparency, to be the norm. Most investors do not have sufficiently sophisticated risk systems to monitor the individual portfolio positions of hedge fund managers.

## Panel 3

### An interview on transparency with Pierre F. Jetté, of CDP Capital

Mr Jetté is associate vice president of Risk and Return of CDP Capital, a global investment management firm with US$83 billion of AUM.

### How do you look at risk?
We have several objectives for risk management. First, we take a global approach. For any type of client, we must understand the risk of its entire portfolio. We have a proprietary system to measure the risk of multi-asset class portfolios and we take actions to manage the total risk of the fund. Our second objective is to identify the sources of risk across the entire portfolio. We then take actions to manage the concentration of risk. Our third objective is risk monitoring. For each manager, we compare the actual risk level to the risk budget. We also look at style consistency in terms of the sources of risk.

### What systems do you use?
We use a VAR (value-at-risk) approach: the same metric for all asset classes. The methodology we use is a historical simulation (800 days) of all positions. This

press for its planned US$1 billion investment in hedge funds.[2] Public funds as small as the New Haven (Connecticut) Police & Firemen's Pension Fund (US$259 million) have disclosed hedge fund investments, as have large funds like CalSTRS (California State Teachers' Retirement System), State of Wisconsin Investment Board, the Teacher Retirement System of Texas, and the YMCA Retirement Fund.

Public pension funds have committed a combined US$3.5 billion to hedge fund strategies since September 1, 2001, according to published reports (see Tables 2 and 3).

**Table 2**  Table of US pension fund investments in hedge funds

| US pension fund | Total assets (US$ billion) | Size in funds | Strategy |
|---|---|---|---|
| California Public Employee's Retirement System, Sacramento | 159.0 | US$1 billion | N/A |
| City of Montreal Pension Fund | 2.4* | 5% | N/A |
| City of New Orleans Retirement System | 0.4 | US$20 million | Convertible debt |
| Indiana State Teacher's Retirement System, Indianapolis | 6.0 | US$150 million | N/A |
| Louisiana State Employees' Retirement System, Baton Rouge | 6.5 | US$65 million | Merger arbitrage |
| Norfolk County Retirement System, Canton | 0.4 | 3.2% | Market neutral |
| | | 5.1% | Convertible arbitrage |
| North Carolina State Retirement System, Raleigh | 52.0 | 5% | N/A |
| Oklahoma Police Pension & Retirement System, Shawnee | 1.3 | US$25 million/ US$50 million | Multi-strategy |
| | | US$70 million/ US$90 million | Fund of funds |
| Ontario Municipal Employees Retirement System | 35.0* | 5% | N/A |

* C$
*Source*: http://www.HedgeWorld.com

approach captures changing market dynamics and non-linear risk, and it also makes aggregation easy because there is no need for correlation factors.

**What kind of transparency do you receive?**
Hedge funds are the only exception to our process because transparency is not always available. In order to perform our hedge fund risk measurement, we would need full transparency weekly with no time delay. However, this is not acceptable to our hedge fund managers. As an alternative solution, the hedge funds provide their positions to an independent firm, which would compute 800 days of simulation for each hedge fund. This simulation matrix would then be given to us for risk aggregation and measurement

**So how do you measure risk for your hedge funds?**
Right now, in terms of risk monitoring, the hedge fund manager supplies us with VAR, descriptive statistics, and sources of risk. We then compare risk with actual performance. We also perform style monitoring through weekly tracking of the performance of our hedge funds compared to the hedge fund risk indices. Our funds' performances should be consistent with the style index. If it is not, we ask the manager questions.

**Where do you think the industry is headed in terms of transparency?**
The ideal solution is not yet available but alternative solutions are currently being explored. Right now, CDP Capital is using a pragmatic solution. Over the long term I feel that funds that are targeting institutional investors will need to provide transparency.

## Panel 4

### An interview on transparency with Paul Platkin, director of Hedge Fund Investing, General Motors Pension Plan

General Motors Pension Plan has US$70 billion of AUM.

**What percentage of assets do you invest in hedge funds?**
1% of our assets (US$700 million) are allocated to hedge funds. We invest one-quarter of that amount in funds of funds.

**What are your strategies?**
We avoid macro, not because it is a bad strategy but because, as a fiduciary, we cannot invest in a black box. To the extent that a manager will not give position-level transparency, we need both process transparency and risk exposure transparency. The amount of transparency that a macro manager will give does not provide us with enough information to properly monitor investment.

**Of more than 20 managers, how many provide position-level, as opposed to process, transparency?**
Less than 40% of managers give position-level transparency. On the other hand, everyone gives risk exposure transparency. On a monthly basis we get such information as industry tilts, VAR, stress testing, sometimes top-positions, etc.

We maintain a diversified portfolio and, as a result, no more than 5% of our assets are invested with any given manager. Therefore, very specific information is not worth knowing. Also, unless you have liquidity and transparency, transparency alone doesn't help. A friend of mine says that risk reporting is only good for watching your fund blow up in real time. For example, in the short term, there was nothing I could do to divest myself of WorldCom.

**Table 3**  Plan sponsors investing in hedge funds

| | |
|---|---|
| American National Red Cross | Nashville & Davidson County Metro-Emp. Benefit |
| Aon Risk Services | Navy Marine Corps. Relief Society |
| Boeing | New Orleans (LA) Employees' Retirement System |
| California Public Employees' Retirement System | Norfolk (MA) County Employees' Retirement System |
| Citigroup | Oklahoma Firefighters Retirement System |
| City of Winston-Salem (NC) | Oklahoma Police Pension & Retirement System |
| DuPont | Pennsylvania State Employees' Retirement System |
| Eastman Kodak Company | Phillip Morris |
| Episcopal Church | Precision Castparts Corp. |
| Ford Motor | Public Employees' Retirement Fund of Indiana |
| General Electric Co. | Qwest |
| General Motors | San Diego (CA) City Employees' Retirement System |
| Illinois Municipal Retirement Fund | San Diego (CA) County Employees' Retirement System |
| ISPAT Inland | Sisters of the Holy Cross, Inc. |
| Laborers, District Council, Western Pennsylvania | State of Michigan |
| Lehigh Portland Cement Company | Texas Teachers |
| Lighthouse International | The Pentegra Group |
| Massachusetts Bay Transportation Authority | Unisys Corp. |
| Methodist Healthcare | Wayne County (MI) Employees' Retirement System |
| Michelin North America, Inc. | World Bank |

*Source*: Pension & Investments, Nelson's 2002 Surveys of Plan Sponsors and CMRA Analysis

## SIZE OF INVESTMENT

The average investment by a pension fund in a hedge fund is US$16 million (see Table 4), US$6 million less than endowments and foundations.

## TRACK RECORD

Pension funds tend to require longer track records than other investors based on their fear of headline risk coupled with the framework they bring from their traditional investments (see Figure 2).

## TRANSPARENCY

ABP and PGGM,[3] the two largest plan sponsors in Europe,[4] have combined their fund of funds requirements and offered the list of minimum requirements seen in Table 5 for the hedge funds in which they invest as part of the IRC[5] efforts.

While few funds meet all of these requirements, the list provides an excellent discussion document and great insight in the thinking of plan sponsors.

Panels 1–5 follow the issue of transparency into interviews with plan sponsors themselves, giving their views on how transparency affects them and their companies.

**Table 4**  Average size of direct investments (US$ million)

| | |
|---|---|
| Endowments/foundations | 22 |
| Pensions | 16 |
| Funds of funds | 16 |
| Family offices | 8 |
| Banks | 8 |

*Source*: Deutsche Bank Alternative Investment Survey

**What do you do with the transparency that you receive?**
We have a monthly risk reporting cycle: we do a review of risk exposure reporting and make sure that managers are within the boundaries of our expectations. We use this review as the basis for a brief monthly conversation with each of our managers.

**How do you treat funds of funds differently from individual hedge funds in terms of risk reporting?**
It varies. We hold the fund of funds manager accountable for risk monitoring within funds. Funds of funds have the same difficulty that we do with aggregating risk: complicated metrics can't be combined together.

Our focus is different from that of a typical fund of funds. Most funds of funds focus primarily on the investment process and do not focus as much on operations and due diligence. Our approach has a different flavour: we spend time understanding the nature of the business, the operational structure, etc.

I refer to my funds of funds as "off balance sheet head count": we get great insights on the markets from them. A fund of funds has a larger staff to focus on market intelligence. We use them as a risk management tool. I think funds of funds get a bad rap: a good one carries its extra layer of fees. I don't think our plan should be too insular.

**What systems do you use?**
I do most analysis on excel using models that I built myself. We're trying to scrutinise historic returns: historical performance is a good way to understand risk characteristics that will be relevant in the future. We try to understand a manager's investment process; we want a manager with a stable process.

**Where do you think transparency is headed in the future?**
These days most funds of funds are trying to use transparency as a marketing tool; they don't believe it will add any value. Transparency has become the new marketing buzzword. For the future, I hope some of the managers who suffered in June and July 2002 will use that as an opportunity to step up to the plate and provide risk exposure transparency. We're starting to see this now and I'm pleased. I also hope that no more regulatory measures come to pass.

## Panel 5

## Comments on transparency by Ron Mock, Ontario Teachers' Pension Plan (OTPP)

Mr Mock is vice president of Alternative Investments for OTPP, a pension plan with US$68 billion of AUM. He manages OTPP's internal hedge fund with over US$2 billion of AUM.

Early hedge funds attracted capital mostly from high-net-worth individuals. Recent explosive growth in hedge fund assets has in part come from institutions, investing directly or through funds of funds. Individual hedge fund investors did not express much interest in transparency. In contrast, pension plans have a fiduciary obligation to show that funds are invested prudently, and in accordance with the strategies and risk parameters described in portfolio guidelines. OTPP, therefore, strongly supports the hedge fund industry trend to transparency.

Hedge fund managers have historically rejected transparency, arguing that it exposes their proprietary methodologies to reverse engineering, or may hurt returns as market participants become aware of a manager's position. The 1998 failure of Long Term Capital Management (LTCM) and its aftermath stiffened

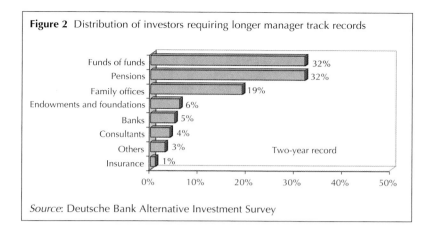

**Figure 2** Distribution of investors requiring longer manager track records

*Source*: Deutsche Bank Alternative Investment Survey

---

**Table 5** Minimum quarter and annual requirements

**Minimum quarter requirements**
❏ Management report covering the issues mentioned above, especially focusing on risk and performances for the total portfolio, per manager and per style.
❏ Review on portfolio allocation as well as proposed changes in the allocation.
❏ Review and outlook on style and sector developments.
❏ Reports on systematic data collection.
❏ Un-audited financial statements (including profit and loss) on the fund of funds portfolio from the investment manager.

**Minimum annual requirements**
❏ Gross and net amount of derivatives in the total portfolio, specified by categories (eg, swaps, futures, etc); number of positions; percent of total long and percent of total short market value.
❏ Confirmation of valuation principles (or changes therein).
❏ Audited financial statements for the underlying hedge fund managers.
❏ Audited financial statements (including profit and loss) on the fund of funds portfolio from the external auditors.

*Source*: ABP/PGGM "requirements" from http://www.iafe.org

---

## CONCLUSION

More institutions are investing in hedge funds or funds of funds or are seriously considering investments, as a way to improve returns. The challenge is that plan sponsors need to educate themselves about hedge funds and modify their traditional investment approach. Many institutions are going through that process now. They need to either get transparency or a investor resolve for position and risk disclosure, as institutional investors and hedge fund managers alike were quite surprised to learn of the leverage employed by LTCM.

Conventional "long only" managers with institutional mandates operate with complete transparency, even though they also use proprietary methodologies. There is no good reason to have different standards for hedge funds. OTPP prefers position uploads to our corporate risk system, preferably on a daily basis. This provides maximum flexibility to calculate various risk measures and to determine return on risk. It will identify excessive leverage, position concentration, and the extent of any changes in short-term portfolio structure that might signify style drift.

As a second best, hedge funds propose to provide not their positions, but aggregate risk characteristics of those positions, eg, a summary value-at-risk (VAR) report, position concentration report, or geographic concentration report. Full transparency may, in these cases, be provided by portfolio position review in the manager's office.

Summary risk information may not provide a clear picture of risk or correlation to other funds in the portfolio, and is poor at considering higher moments an important aspect of risk. For example, VAR is an important metric, but it may be insufficient when hedge fund strategies depart from the underlying assumption of approximate normality of outcomes. Moreover, measured volatility may not be a good risk measure for illiquid securities. Without position reporting, it can be hard to assess such weaknesses, and to get a good estimate of return on risk.

A well-written confidentiality agreement with "no reverse engineering" clauses can go a long way towards providing making hedge fund managers comfortable that their intellectual property rights are protected. Once that issue is resolved, institutional and hedge fund manager interests are ultimately aligned: no prudent institution wants to harm conventional or hedge fund managers' returns, in which they are invested, by violating the confidentiality of manager positions. Transparency will contribute to a better understanding of what hedge fund managers can achieve, increasing the acceptability of hedge funds to pension managers.

Our fund supports the hedge fund industry trend to more complete transparency. It may be a few years before we can claim compliance with our standards of investment management and fiduciary obligations, so we will continue to keep pressing this issue.

"risk profile" and sufficient process transparency to satisfy their needs. This trend indicates that ultimately as they understand hedge fund investments, an increasing number of plan sponsors will be making asset allocations to include hedge funds in their portfolios.

1  Acito, C. J., and F. P. Fisher, 2002, The *Journal of Alternative Investments*, Spring.
2  Http://www.pionline.com, http://www.hedgeworld.com.
3  ABP is the Algemeen Burgerlijk Pensioenfonds. ABP has been the pension fund for government and education authorities in the Netherlands since 1992. PGGM is the Pensioenfonds Voor de Gezondheid en Geestelejk en Maatschappelejk Belangem, the Dutch pension fund for the healthcare and social work sector.
4  Http://www.abp.nl; http://www.pggm.nl.
5  Investor Risk Committee, see http://www.iafe.org.

# 9

# Endowments and Foundations

## INTRODUCTION

Endowments and foundations have embraced hedge fund investing. An endowment is the investing arm of a college or university (Table 1 shows the 10 largest in terms of AUM); a foundation is a non-profit, non-governmental organisation with a principal fund or endowment of its own. These institutions are early adopters within the universe of institutional investors as they have the least bureaucratic oversight.

There are three main types of private foundations: independent, corporate and operating foundations. Independent foundations, the largest category, are grant-making organisations whose funds come from individuals. The Bill and Melinda Gates Foundation was the largest in the US in 2000, with US$21.1 billion of AUM (see Table 2).[1] Corporate foundations are private foundations whose grant funds come from the contributions of a profit-making business, which may or may not remain close to the foundation but is legally a separate entity. Alcoa Foundation was the largest corporate foundation, with US$441 million in assets at the end of 2000.[2] Operating foundations are private foundations that work on whatever projects the establishment charter or governing body decides. These

**Table 1** Top 10 endowments

| Rank | Endowment | AUM (US$ billion) |
|------|-----------|-------------------|
| 1 | Harvard University | 18.8 |
| 2 | Yale University | 10.1 |
| 3 | University of Texas System | 10.0 |
| 4 | Stanford University | 8.6 |
| 5 | Princeton University | 8.4 |
| 6 | Massachusetts Institute of Technology | 6.5 |
| 7 | University of California | 5.6 |
| 8 | Emory University | 5.6 |
| 9 | Columbia University | 4.3 |
| 10 | Washington University | 4.2 |

*Source*: Pension & Investments (December 24, 2001), CMRA Research

**Table 2** Top 10 US foundations by asset size

| Rank | Name | State | Assets (US$ billion) | Do they invest in hedge funds? |
|------|------|-------|----------------------|-------------------------------|
| 1 | Bill & Melinda Gates Foundation | WA | 21.1 | n/c |
| 2 | Lilly Endowment Inc. | IN | 15.6 | No |
| 3 | The Ford Foundation | NY | 14.7 | No |
| 4 | J. Paul Getty Trust | CA | 10.9 | Yes |
| 5 | The David and Lucile Packard Foundation | CA | 9.8 | No |
| 6 | The Robert Wood Johnson Foundation | NJ | 8.8 | Yes |
| 7 | W. K. Kellogg Foundation | MI | 5.7 | Yes |
| 8 | The Andrew W. Mellon Foundation | NY | 4.9 | n/c |
| 9 | The Pew Charitable Trusts | PA | 4.8 | n/c |
| 10 | The Starr Foundation | NY | 4.5 | n/c |

n/c = no comment
*Source*: The Foundation Center, CMRA Research

foundations might conduct research or social welfare projects. If an operating foundation offers any grants, they are generally small compared to the funds used for the foundation's own purposes. The IRS requires all private foundations to pay out 5% of the market value of their assets each year.

According to a recent Institutional Investor/CMRA survey, more than half of endowments and foundations have less than 10% of their total assets invested in hedge funds. However, 57% of those surveyed expect that percentage to rise in the next two years (17% expect it to decline and 26% anticipate that it will remain the same).

Endowments and foundations are less likely to invest in funds of funds than directly in individual hedge funds. 76% of those surveyed have less than 10% of total assets currently invested in funds of funds. Only 42% of those surveyed expect that percentage to rise in the next two years (37% expect it to remain the same and 21% anticipate that it will decline).

According to the 2001 National Association of College and University Business Officers (NACUBO) Endowment Study, 17 schools allocated at least 20% of their endowment assets to hedge funds (see Table 3).[5] 57% of endowments participating in the Institutional Investor/CMRA study indicated that they invest in hedge funds.

On average, independent endowments allocate 8.3% of their assets to alternatives, while public endowments allocate only 4.9% (see Figure 1). One can conclude that independent endowments are early adopters and have less constrictive investment guidelines.

## WHICH ENDOWMENTS AND FOUNDATIONS ARE INVESTING IN HEDGE FUNDS?

In 2001, the University of Virginia's endowment had the largest amount of money, US$656 million, invested in hedge funds, while Yeshiva University had the largest number of hedge fund managers. The five largest endowments (Harvard, Yale, University of Texas, Stamford and Princeton) did not make the top 25 list for endowment investors in hedge funds (see Table 4).

As Table 5 shows, Maverick Capital Funds appears to be the favourite hedge fund among endowments: it has 19 endowments investing US$726 million in total, making it the largest of any fund covered by the NACUBO study. The Commonfund Group has the most endowments, with 46 invested in their fund. (See Chapter 11 for Maverick's "perspective" on transparency).

While hedge fund investing by endowments increased in 2001, other "alternatives" (ie, venture capital and private equity investing) declined, as can be seen in Table 6.

40% of the respondents to a recent Commonfund Institute study reported an overall increase in hedge fund allocations, ranging from 1% to 10% of their endowment portfolio. The study reported no decreases.[6]

When respondents were asked what they hoped to accomplish with the changes they had made or were planning to make regarding their hedge fund allocations, the following comments were made:

❏ "We added hedge funds to provide an asset that doesn't correlate with stocks and bonds, yet has a decent return and low to moderate risk."
❏ "We have increased our commitment to alternative investments in the hopes of higher returns over the long run."
❏ "We invested in hedge funds to cushion heavy equity allocations."

**Table 3** Endowments with greater than 20% allocated to hedge funds

| Institution | % |
| --- | --- |
| SUNY Stony Brook Foundation | 63.1 |
| Reed College | 58.4 |
| Yeshiva University | 51.7 |
| Alfred University | 40.8 |
| Bowdoin College | 40.2 |
| University of Virginia | 38.4 |
| Denison University | 33.5 |
| Brown University | 29.6 |
| College of Wooster | 27.3 |
| Amherst College | 25.9 |
| Oberlin College | 23.2 |
| Hamline University | 22.9 |
| Cranbrook Educational Community | 22.3 |
| Tufts University | 22.1 |
| Mount Holyoke College | 20.7 |
| Cornell University | 20.5 |
| The Catholic University of America | 20.5 |

*Source*: 2001 NACUBO Endowment Study

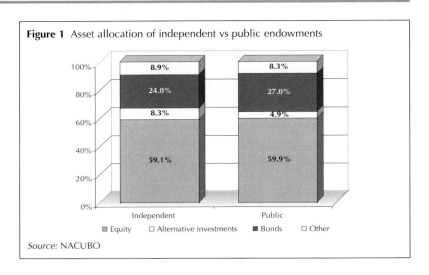

**Figure 1** Asset allocation of independent vs public endowments

*Source:* NACUBO

**Table 4** Top 25 endowments investing in hedge funds

| Institution | Hedge fund investments (US$ million) | Number of hedge fund managers |
|---|---|---|
| University of Virginia | 655.9 | n/a |
| Cornell University | 646.0 | n/a |
| University of Michigan | 484.3 | n/a |
| University of Chicago | 439.5 | 15 |
| Yeshiva University | 429.6 | 29 |
| Brown University | 425.4 | n/a |
| University of Texas System | 383.9 | n/a |
| Emory University | 280.5 | 8 |
| Rice University | 233.5 | n/a |
| Amherst College | 230.8 | n/a |
| University of Minnesota Foundation | 196.2 | n/a |
| Reed College | 187.5 | 10 |
| John Hopkins University | 182.3 | n/a |
| Bowdoin College | 174.1 | n/a |
| UNC at Chapel Hill and Foundations | 161.1 | n/a |
| Denison University | 144.1 | 7 |
| Rider University | 139.4 | 1 |
| Oberlin College | 138.0 | 4 |
| Tufts University | 121.3 | n/a |
| Boston College | 116.5 | n/a |
| Case Western Reserve University | 116.2 | 8 |
| Wellesley College | 110.2 | n/a |
| Middlebury College | 104.1 | 4 |
| University of Southern California | 102.2 | 2 |
| University of Rochester | 189.6 | 6 |

*Source*: 2001 NACUBO Endowment Study

**Table 5** Top 25 hedge funds with endowment investments

| Investment manager | Endowment investments (US$ million) | Number of endowments |
|---|---|---|
| Maverick Capital Funds | 725.6 | 19 |
| Commonfund Group | 573.5 | 46 |
| Pequot Capital Funds | 351.2 | 18 |
| Riverview | 196.2 | 1 |
| Och-Ziff Capital Management Funds | 121.3 | 8 |
| Bank of Ireland | 112.5 | 1 |
| Chilton Funds | 92.7 | 6 |
| Farallon Capital Funds | 91.2 | 4 |
| Blackstone Funds | 80.8 | 8 |
| Bowman Capital Management Funds | 75.9 | 4 |
| Standard Pacific Capital | 74.6 | 5 |
| Everest Capital | 67.4 | 6 |
| Perry Partners Funds | 66.5 | 4 |
| High fields Capital Funds | 58.0 | 3 |
| Ascot Partners | 51.5 | 1 |
| Lone Pine Capital Funds | 50.6 | 3 |
| Satellite Asset Management Funds | 49.6 | 4 |
| Citadel Investment Group | 49.4 | 2 |
| Zweig-DiMenna Funds | 47.1 | 3 |
| Charter Oak Partners LP | 45.1 | 2 |
| Duquesne Capital Management, Inc. | 43.1 | 2 |
| Oak tree Capital Management Funds | 42.8 | 4 |
| Lyster Watson | 40.4 | 1 |
| Moore Capital Management | 39.0 | 3 |
| Kingdon Capital Management Funds | 38.2 | 3 |

*Source*: 2001 NACUBO Endowment Study

**Table 6** Evolution of hedge fund investing (% of AUM)

| | 1999 | 2000 | 2001 |
|---|---|---|---|
| Hedge funds | 2.30 | 2.10 | 2.90 |
| Venture capital | 1.40 | 2.40 | 1.50 |
| Private equity | 0.80 | 1.00 | 0.90 |

*Source*: 2001 NACUBO Endowment Study, Hennessee and CMRA Research

## HEDGE FUND STRATEGIES USED BY ENDOWMENTS AND FOUNDATIONS?

The NACUBO study found that most endowments, independent of size, allocated 40%–50% of their alternative assets to absolute return strategies, hedge funds and distressed securities (see Table 7).

The Institutional Investor/CMRA survey found that funds of funds,

## Panel 1

## Jay Yoder, Director of Investments, Smith College – An endowment with US$860 million of AUM

**What percentage do you invest in hedge funds?**
10%.

**Has this percentage changed over time?**
It's been the same for the last six months, but we only invested in our first hedge fund 13 months ago (July 1, 2001).

**What are your primary strategies?**
We don't have any primary strategies. We have three funds of funds that invest in a wide variety of strategies.

**How do you manage risk?**
Through wide diversification by both manager and strategy. I also rely on our funds of funds managers for additional risk management. I've known two of our three managers for over five years. We also look at performance patterns, correlations, downside protection and volatility measures.

**Do you use a benchmark?**
Yes, a flat 10% benchmark.

**What systems do you use?**
None.

**Where do you think the industry is going in terms of transparency?**
I think the debate will be ongoing. There is no one answer for the industry. Those people who need transparency will find managers who will provide it. Those managers who won't give it will be able to find investors who don't need it.

## Panel 2

## Mathew Stone, Assistant Vice President and Director of Absolute Return Investments, The University of Chicago – The school's endowment is US$3.2 billion.

**What percentage do you invest in hedge funds?**
We invest about 16% in hedge funds; we categorise hedge funds as "absolute return."

**What are your strategies?**
We currently invest in about 20 funds spread across a number of strategies: convertible arbitrage, merger arbitrage, distressed securities, equity restruc-

long/short equity and distressed debt were the most common hedge fund styles chosen by endowments and foundations (see Table 8).

The study also found that long/short equity was the number one strategy chosen by endowments and foundations (see Figure 2).

**Table 7** Average alternative asset class composition as a percentage of total alternative assets

| Investment pool assets | Absolute return | Hedge funds | Distressed securities | Total |
|---|---|---|---|---|
| Greater than US$1.0 billion | 13.1 | 29.0 | 5.7 | 47.8 |
| US$501 million – US$1.0 billion | 8.8 | 31.7 | 7.3 | 47.8 |
| US$100 million – US$500 million | 11.4 | 25.3 | 4.7 | 41.4 |
| Less than US$100 million | 9.3 | 39.4 | 2.2 | 50.9 |
| Public | 9.3 | 28.4 | 3.9 | 41.6 |
| Independent | 11.1 | 32.0 | 4.6 | 47.7 |
| Equally weighted average | 10.6 | 31.0 | 4.4 | 46.0 |
| Dollar-weighted average | 13.9 | 30.2 | 4.5 | 30.2 |

Note: 324 institutions provided alternative asset allocation data. While part of the alternative group of assets, managed futures were not included in this table because the average holdings are too small.

Source: 2001 NACUBO Endowment Study

**Table 8** Most common hedge fund styles by endowments and foundations

| | Number of endowments and foundations |
|---|---|
| Fund of funds | 13 |
| Long/short equity | 12 |
| Distressed debt | 11 |
| Convertible arbitrage | 10 |
| Merger arbitrage | 10 |
| Fixed-income arbitrage | 7 |
| Market neutral | 7 |
| Credit arbitrage | 5 |
| Fixed income | 5 |
| Emerging market | 4 |
| Equity value | 3 |
| Mortgages | 3 |
| Dedicated short bias | 3 |
| Global macro | 3 |
| Managed futures | 1 |

Source: Institutional Investor/CMRA Endowments and Foundations Survey, June 2002

tured, fixed-income arbitrage, mortgage-backed securities, long/short equity in emerging markets and others. We tend to lay off the long/short equity funds. It's been proven that traditional stock picker funds have historically added very little value to large endowments like ours. The theory is that if we're not willing to pay 70 basis points for a traditional stock picker, then we're certainly not willing to pay 170 basis points and a performance fee to another stock picker just because it calls itself a hedge fund. The attitude around here about that is changing, though, because there are some things a market neutral long/short equity fund does that a traditional stock picker doesn't, particularly in a bear market.

**What kinds of transparency do you receive from your hedge funds? Are you satisfied?**
We receive a basic performance/strategy summary that includes a risk report of the standard measures (such as VAR and Sharpe ratios) from just about everyone. We receive full-position disclosure from two of our funds, but we don't really do much with that disclosure. The most I do with that information is really just satisfy my own curiosity. Oftentimes I'll do sample tests to measure against some strategy drift, the fixed-income arbitrage fund that suddenly has half a portfolio of equities, for example, but I really don't see much use in full-position disclosure for large endowments, other than to satisfy our curiosity. I just don't have the time to go through all my funds' portfolios and I don't know any big investor who does. My guess is that the reason why people are interested in full-position disclosure is so that they can plug everything into one of their sophisticated risk systems and have the risk system spit out a bunch of simple, numerical answers. But there are a lot of limitations to risk systems; if a system could figure out everything for me, I'd be out there running a fund for myself. And there is always the question of how much of the information that you receive is actionable. Even if you don't like what a manager is doing, if you feel you're suddenly overexposed in certain areas or if there's some strategy drift, you still have a contract that says you're money is locked up for X number of days, or months, or quarters, or sometimes for years, but the point is that by the time you can get your money out, the underlying conditions will be completely different. So, I see little use in full-position disclosure. Nonetheless, the industry seems to be moving slowly yet inexorably toward increased transparency.

## Panel 3

## Mark Yusko, CIO of The University of North Carolina Chapel Hill – The school's endowment is US$1.1 billion.

### Tell us about your endowment.
We are currently in the process of establishing a private investment management company that will allow us to provide endowment management services for clients other than the university. We will begin offering our programme to the sister schools in the UNC System, such as UNC Asheville, and eventually move on to other clients. We'll offer comprehensive portfolio

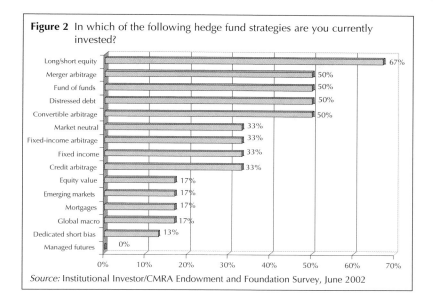

**Figure 2** In which of the following hedge fund strategies are you currently invested?

*Source*: Institutional Investor/CMRA Endowment and Foundation Survey, June 2002

According to a recent Commonfund Institute survey, the greatest increase in allocations among endowments and foundations will be to market neutral, distressed investing and other event-driven strategies. The greatest decreases will be to fixed-income arbitrage, multi-strategy arbitrage and convertible bond arbitrage.

The survey also revealed that long/short equity strategies still comprise the largest chunk of hedge fund assets, representing more than 40% of hedge fund asset investors followed by multi-strategy arbitrage, with an allocation of a little more than 10%. Convertible arbitrage, distressed investing, merger arbitrage and fixed-income arbitrage were next in line, all with allocations of less than 10%.

## FINDING HEDGE FUNDS

Word of mouth serves as the principal means by which institutional investors find hedge funds, next come the prime brokers and direct marketing by managers. After that comes various ways such as conferences, newsletters, consultants and the like.

**Table 9** Average size of direct investment (US$ million)

| | |
|---|---|
| Endowments/foundations | 22 |
| Pensions | 16 |
| Funds of funds | 16 |
| Family offices | 8 |
| Banks | 8 |

*Source*: Deutsche Bank Alternative Investment Survey

management services for endowments and other large investors who do not have the dedicated resources to devote to full-time asset management. Our programme is focused on asset allocation, manager selection and portfolio construction and would focus on directing capital into the right places at the right time; for example, moving out of US equities and into distressed debt right now. Qwest halted trading today on account of a fraud investigation. Qwest has 22 million customers who use its services, so that even taking into account fraud claims, the company has been trading at heavily undervalued prices. There are opportunities out there; you just need to have a strong stomach to make money in the current environment.

**How heavily are you invested in hedge funds?**
We have about 40% of our portfolio with marketable alternative managers. When I first came to UNC there was actually a "ban" against hedge funds, but the definition of a hedge fund was very vague and led to some confusion. When the term was first coined it was hedged funds. Somewhere along the way we lost the "d". Now, any limited partnership with an incentive fee falls under the category of hedge fund. So, with a change in nomenclature to absolute return and opportunistic equity strategies, we now invest in hedge funds.

**What kind of transparency do you receive from your hedge funds?**
I really feel that this ongoing drive for increased transparency is significantly overblown. The transparency we receive in every case is a monthly performance report that includes the market value of the portfolio and a short strategy summary. Sometimes, for certain strategies, such as long/short equity, the report might include the fund's top 10 holdings. But we don't ask for shorts and we don't want individual position disclosure. If a fund offers disclosure we tell them we don't want it and that they shouldn't be offering it to anyone else either. In active management strategies, your competitive advantage is your ability to pick and choose trades. Why would we want our funds giving away their edge?

Even if there weren't competitive concerns about transparency, what am I going to do with a 1-inch thick position report? On page one they might be long tech stock A and on page 86 they might be short tech stock B; sure, it's a pairs trade, but I don't have time to be sifting through hundreds of pages of reports picking out every individual pairs trade. Even if I had all kinds of systems and an entire staff devoted solely to the task of sorting out and aggregating positions across my portfolio, how much of that information is actionable? Am I going to fire a profitable manager if one day he's 14% tech stocks and the next he's 16%?

For a lot of investors it's the lack of regulation and the fear of fraud that inspires their pursuit of increased transparency. I feel that if someone really wants to defraud you, he/she will defraud you. Even with all the position disclosure in the world there isn't much you can do about it. You just have to put your trust in the due diligence you employed when you selected the manager in the first place. The analogy I use is that of your 16-year-old child who just got their license. You have two choices. First, you can get in the passenger seat every time they get behind the wheel, just to make sure that they are being safe and doing everything right. Or second, you can trust that you have a good relationship with them, that they paid attention in driver's

## Properties of hedge funds selected by institutions

*Size of investment*

As can be seen in Table 9, the average investment by endowments and foundations is US$22 million, as compared to US$16 million for plan sponsors. This is probably due to the larger hedge fund allocations in general by endowments and foundations (see Figure 3).

*Track record*

Endowments and foundations do not require manager track records as long as other institutional investors.

*Transparency*

Transparency is a key issue for endowments and foundations in selecting hedge funds and funds of funds according to the Institutional Investor/CMRA survey – 60% of those surveyed considered it to be so. However, it would appear that transparency is less of an issue for large endowments; 41% of endowment and foundation respondents had declined to invest based on a lack of transparency.

The same survey found that only 32% of the respondents had requested more information than hedge funds/funds of funds are willing to provide. For example, some respondents had asked for full position disclosure but received no listing of "short" positions, only that of "long" positions.

Finally, as Figure 4 shows, while most endowments and foundations receive returns information and a monthly management letter, very few receive detailed information such as a list of positions or a breakdown of their strategies by risk factor.

*Risk*

The Institutional Investor/ CMRA survey found that six years after "Risk Standards for Institutional Investors" was published, surprisingly, only

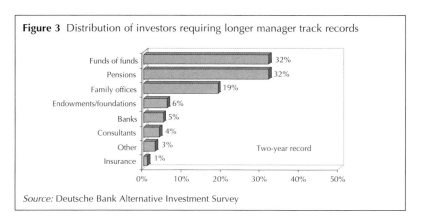

**Figure 3** Distribution of investors requiring longer manager track records

Funds of funds 32%
Pensions 32%
Family offices 19%
Endowments/foundations 6%
Banks 5%
Consultants 4%
Other 3%
Insurance 1%

Two-year record

0%   10%   20%   30%   40%   50%

*Source:* Deutsche Bank Alternative Investment Survey

ed., that you raised them right and that they will drive safely and responsibly. When we invest in a hedge fund we just don't have the time or the resources to sit in the passenger seat all day, every day, going over position reports. Even if we did, the benefit is marginal at best.

One day, you may be going over your reports and find that you don't like your exposure to GM, but by the time you've determined the nature of your overexposure, are you going to drop managers because of it? By the time you've been over the data and analysed it, the entire market could have shifted and suddenly automotive companies look like great bets. Even if you accept the enormous costs of going over everyone's positions, by the time you've crunched all the numbers and put in the analysis, your information is stale and very little of it is actionable.

I've always felt that the key to managing risk with hedge funds is through manager diversification. If you're a big institutional investor, you just can't afford to leave all your assets with a single manager. If you're properly diversified and you've conducted the appropriate due diligence, there's no reason why you should need, or even want, full-position disclosure. Focus on strategy disclosure and determine if the manager is performing well within their specific role within the portfolio. If a manager strays from their stated strategy, loses their edge or begins to do things they do't normally do, such as excessive trading or holding too much cash, then terminate the relationship and move on to another firm. You can actively manage your risk in this area and by having strong relationships with managers; you can save yourself from making a lot of unnecessary trips in that passenger seat.

## Panel 4

## The Director of Investment Strategies at the endowment of a large university

**What percentage of assets do you invest in hedge funds?**
15%

**What are your strategies?**
We don't really have any specific strategies, but I can tell you what we don't invest in. We don't invest in RegD. We stay away from strategies that depend on leverage for their return: I don't like to leverage a nickel to get a dollar. We do like arbitrage strategies and distressed debt. We like to look at our exposures and see what we don't have elsewhere, such as long only or short only.

**How do you feel about transparency?**
I feel strongly about getting as much transparency as I can, possibly because I'm a fiduciary. Also, we have a pension plan which has several billion dollars in assets, so my strong feeling probably comes from the pension plan. We will not invest unless we get transparency.

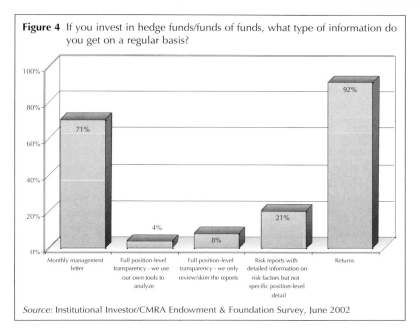

**Figure 4** If you invest in hedge funds/funds of funds, what type of information do you get on a regular basis?

*Source:* Institutional Investor/CMRA Endowment & Foundation Survey, June 2002

44% of endowments and foundations have written risk management policies and procedures (see Appendix 5).[7] Also, only 12% assigned a "risk budget" to their managers.

52% of endowments and foundations with hedge fund/fund of funds investments aggregate and monitor risks across their hedge fund/fund of funds portfolio. However, a higher percentage of endowments than foundations aggregate and monitor risks across the hedge fund/fund of funds in which they invest. One can conclude that investors in funds of funds expect the fund of funds' managers to provide some of the fiduciary oversight that they themselves provide when directly investing in hedge funds.

As Table 10 shows, it would seem that larger endowments have embraced alternatives more enthusiastically than smaller funds.

CMRA's June 2002 survey for *Institutional Investor* found that 61% of endowments and foundations with hedge fund/fund of funds investments were satisfied with the ability of their risk management tools to measure the risks in their portfolios, while 20% were dissatisfied, and 10% were very dissatisfied. 50% of endowments and foundations

**Table 10** Allocation of investments to alternative investments

| Investment pool assets | (%) |
| --- | --- |
| Greater than US$1.0 billion | 26.3 |
| US$501 million – US$1.0 billion | 15.6 |
| US$100 million – US$500 million | 7.4 |
| Less than US$100 million | 3.0 |

*Source:* 2001 NACUBO Endowment Study

**Do you mean position-level?**
That depends on the strategy. Some managers won't talk. I am willing to look at the portfolio in their office or mine because I understand that there's a reluctance to mail or fax it. But I want real-time dialogue with the managers, so I can know what they're buying and why.

**Do you want this transparency because you are concerned about manager dishonesty or style drift?**
Those concerns are really secondary. I just want to know the manager. If I know the manager and have a relationship with him/her, then I may stay with a style drift because I feel comfortable.

**Do you have any systems?**
No.

**Do you believe that hedge funds give up a competitive advantage by offering transparency?**
In some cases they do. But there are two important reasons for transparency: first, it is our money, and they need to trust us; second, their prime brokers and dealers know their positions, and they should worry more about them than about us. Of course there is an obligation to keep information confidential. Also, the effect that transparency has on competitive advantage varies depending on the strategy.

**Where do you think transparency is headed in the future?**
I think there will be segregation in the industry between those who are not transparent and those who are. Right now there are managers that offer transparency to some and not to others. I think this is appropriate, although it would be nice if things could be fair to everyone. There are also other issues that need to be considered. For example, what does one do with the transparency?

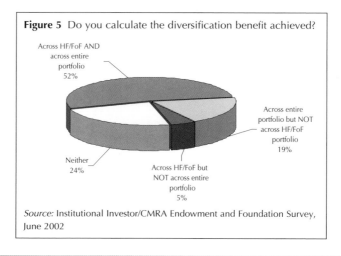

**Figure 5** Do you calculate the diversification benefit achieved?

Across HF/FoF AND across entire portfolio
52%

Across entire portfolio but NOT across HF/FoF portfolio
19%

Neither
24%

Across HF/FoF but NOT across entire portfolio
5%

*Source:* Institutional Investor/CMRA Endowment and Foundation Survey, June 2002

include risk limits in their guidelines. Only 24% of the endowment and foundation participants have a designated risk manager.

Only 52% calculate the diversification benefit across the hedge funds and across the entire portfolio (see Figure 5).

## CONCLUSION

Endowments and foundations are early adopters of hedge fund investing. They have the longest history of investing in hedge funds among institutions. They invest in all styles of hedge funds and are not constrained by any guidelines other than fiduciary responsibility and prudence. The only sure bet is that since endowments and foundations really are investing for the long term, they will continue to be a good fit with hedge funds.

1   Cohen A., 2001, "Time 100: the next Wave/Innovators/Philanthropy/Managing a Foundation – When you have $24 Billion...", *Time Magazine*, November.

2   Tascarella, P., 2001, "Alcoa taps foundation in global giving", *Pittsburg Business Times*, July.

3   Http://www.irs.gov/pub/irs-soi/98eopfin.pdf.

4   Http://www.cmra.com; http://www.aima.org.

5   TIAA-CREF and NACUBO, "2001 NACUBO" Private study.

6   Goldman Sachs Survey.

7   Risk Standards for Institutional Investment Managers and Institutional Investors, Risk Standards Working Group, Copyright (c) 1996 S. Brenner, K. Byrne, C. Campisano, M. Cottrill, M. deMarco, J. Lukomnik, R. Rose, D. Russ, J. Seymour, K. Wassmann, G. Williamson, Capital Market Risk Advisors, Inc.

# SECTION III

# Funds of Funds

# What is a Fund of Funds?

A fund of funds is an investment vehicle that mixes and matches hedge funds and other pooled investment vehicles through funds or managed accounts. A separate section in this book is dedicated to funds of funds because they play a unique role in the hedge fund/investor interaction. This chapter presents the views on transparency of 11 funds of funds' managers that were interviewed for this book.

## INTRODUCTION

Funds of funds are in some ways a category of investor and, at the same time, they are also a type of "fund" that investors can select. This dual role provides unique challenges for transparency and risk management. Funds of funds must do two things:

1. Receive sufficient information from the hedge funds in which they invest to perform the portfolio construction, manager selection, diversification, risk management and due diligence responsibilities that they are expected to perform.
2. Provide consolidated information to their ultimate investors.

Funds of funds must also satisfy institutional investors that both their risk management process and that of the hedge funds in which they invest are robust. This blending of different strategies and asset classes aims to provide a more stable long-term investment return than any of the individual funds. Returns, risk and volatility can be controlled by the mix of underlying strategies and funds. Capital preservation is generally an important consideration. Volatility depends on the mix and ratio of strategies employed. Commonly, a fund of funds will attempt to diversify investment among several different hedge funds based on investment style, track record and the managers' backgrounds. However, there are niche funds of funds that do invest in a single or similar type of strategy.

Funds of hedge funds control one-fifth of the hedge fund market and have been growing at just under 40% yearly since 1997, according to a study by Casey, Quirk & Action.[1]

## Panel 1

### An interview on transparency with Bruce Lipnick, Asset Alliance Corporation

Asset Alliance Corporation is an investment management firm specialising in alternative investment management, specifically hedge funds and hedge fund products, with US$5.3 billion assets. Asset Alliance has a 50% interest in 13 different hedge fund managers.

**What are your strategies?**
We use true hedge funds with no dramatic directional bias, such as JMG Capital and Beacon Hill, with low or no drawdowns. Some of the strategies we use are convertible arbitrage, merger arbitrage, mortgage-backed securities, and long/short equity.

**What kind of transparency do you offer your investors?**
We have a five-person team that monitors all of our investments, both direct and indirect outside allocations. We have our clients sign a simple agreement and then we can give them 100% real-time transparency on our 13 affiliates and on our outside manager allocations. If they prefer to price-off through a third party, that is okay, as we are happy to work closely with outside risk management firms.

Also as a consulting firm, we provide better due diligence and risk measurements than the average traditional consulting firm.

**What systems do you use?**
We use 13 inside managers and 12 outside managers. We're fine with using outside managers as long as they provide complete information. Bennett C. Degen runs our internal monitoring systems. We have to use several different systems along with the appropriate strategy. For example, we use Bear Stearns' system for mortgage-backed securities and another system at Bank America for long/short equities.

**Do you believe transparency hurts strategy?**
It depends on the strategy. Some spread strategies need more secrecy, as you don't want to alert dealers to your positions.

**Where do you think transparency is heading in the future?**
I believe that more institutions and other hedge fund firms will go in the direction that we have gone in.

## Panel 2

### An interview on transparency with Richard Bookbinder of Bookbinder Capital Management, LLC

Bookbinder Capital Management is a fund of funds with US$25 million of AUM in two funds: The Roebling Fund LP (domestic) and Roebling Capital Investment Ltd (international).

**In how many funds do you invest?**
We invest in 14 funds.

Funds of funds perform four major functions:

1. manager selection;
2. portfolio construction and rebalancing;
3. ongoing risk management; and
4. due diligence.

| Table 1 Who invests in funds of funds (%) | |
| --- | --- |
| Family offices | 45 |
| Endowments/foundations | 40 |
| Consultants | 38 |
| Pensions | 30 |

*Source*: Deutsche Bank Alternative Investment Survey

While all are extremely important, they need not be bundled. Increasingly, funds of funds are providing investors with #1, #2, and #3 while permitting them to customise their own portfolios. Some funds of funds are strong in manager selection and portfolio construction but weak in ongoing risk management. It seems inevitable that these functions will increasingly be unbundled.

Some funds of funds have an absolute return target. Their performance objective is either an absolute target or a spread above cash returns. These funds tend to be highly diversified in terms of styles included and number of funds and usually have at least 30 funds and often more than 50 funds in the portfolio. Such funds may emphasise relative value and event-driven styles or cover a wide range of styles. These funds of funds generally have low correlations with the traditional markets.

Another category of funds of funds emphasises individual style, categories, or performance characteristics of hedge funds.

## WHO ARE INVESTORS IN FUNDS OF FUNDS?

Despite a lot of attention being paid to the move by institutions into hedge funds, a recent Goldman Sachs Prime Brokerage Services survey has shown that family offices, private investors, and private banks represent the three largest sources of capital among funds of funds, about 65% of the total. Pension plans, insurance companies, and endowments and foundations represent a little more than 20% of funds of funds' assets.

Similarly, Deutsche Bank's Alternative Investment Survey found that only 40% of endowments and foundations and 30% of plan sponsors invest in funds of funds (see Table 1). The Deutsche Bank Survey also revealed that the largest investors in funds of funds are family offices with 47%, followed by endowments and foundations with 27% and pension plans with 26% (see Figure 1).

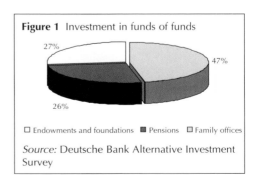

**Figure 1** Investment in funds of funds

27%

47%

26%

□ Endowments and foundations  ■ Pensions  □ Family offices

*Source:* Deutsche Bank Alternative Investment Survey

**Do you plan to change this number?**
Yes, I believe the optimal number of managers is 16 or 17. Redundancy of managers leads to redundancy of investments.

**What are your strategies?**
Absolute return. Opportunistically in a narrow range.

**How do you look at risk?**
We look at historical data. We analyse statistics (Sharpe, Sortino, etc) to see if these have driven the returns. We also look at the due diligence process of on-site manager review as an additional tool to identify and evaluate risk qualitatively.

**What kind of transparency do you receive?**
All of our managers offer transparency, but it varies depending on the strategy. For example, long/short equity will give full transparency that we always review with the manager on a position-by-position basis in the office. Another example is that for non-equities (fixed-income arbitrage or distressed) one should periodically review the long positions with the manager in their office.

**Are you satisfied with the transparency you receive?**
Yes, although satisfied isn't the right word because where we are now is only the first step. I believe there will be an increase in transparency because investors are driving for it. We need to ask why people want transparency. There are two reasons. First, investors need to know for their systems of risk management and due diligence. Second, some investors want to know for the sake of curiosity and gaining some informational insight and competitive ideas into strategies and ideas of hedge fund managers. Our objective for greater transparency is to use risk management to understand the strategy in greater detail.

**What kind of transparency do you offer your investors?**
We give them the names of all the managers that we use along with all of the strategies. We receive transparency on a middle ground level, so we then report to our investors what we believe is time sensitive, such as big gainers or losers, and update in our monthly letters and quarterly reports.

**What systems do you use?**
We do not currently have a formalised system in place, but we are working with our managers to have one within the next 12 months. Our objective is to stress test portfolios and aggregate positions of all strategies.

**How do you think increased transparency would affect the industry in the future?**
I think it could be bad for some strategies, such as distressed. One of the major reasons that investors have historically favoured hedge funds is due to the hedge fund manager's ability to take advantage of market inefficiencies and generate alpha. With greater transparency, it increases market efficiency and can result in lowering returns. On the other hand, investors view greater transparency as lowering the veil of mystery of hedge funds and enabling them to make a more informed investment decision.

## Panel 3

### An interview with Jack Heidt of Heidt Capital Fund

**How big is your fund? What are your primary strategies?**
Heidt Capital Fund is a multi-manager, multi-strategy fund of funds. We work with 14 funds, with a focus on diversification. We currently have about US$40 million

As Figure 2 shows, individual hedge fund investing remains more popular with institutional investors than investing through funds of funds, but 12% of respondents in a Deutsche Bank survey indicated they did both.[2]

## WHAT ARE THE ADVANTAGES AND DISADVANTAGES OF FUNDS OF FUNDS VS INDIVIDUAL HEDGE FUND INVESTMENTS?

Investors and funds of funds prioritise these "advantages" very differently. Table 2 illustrates that while both rank *diversification* as #1, investors rank *risk management* as #2 and funds of funds rank it as #4. Is this because investors believe that funds of funds are providing more "risk management" than they are?

Likewise, investors are much more concerned than funds of funds' managers about their increased exposures to other investors' cashflows when investing in funds of funds and less concerned about the fees as shown in Table 3.

Most funds are built all, or in part, with a bottom-up approach to selecting managers to include in the funds of funds.

Figure 3 shows that funds of funds hold 34% of their hedge fund investments for more than three years.

This could explain why funds of funds and pension funds require longer manager track records than other investors (see Figure 4).

Table 4 tells us that, not surprisingly, funds of funds make more frequent allocations than other investors.

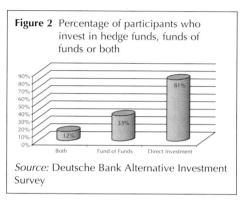

**Figure 2** Percentage of participants who invest in hedge funds, funds of funds or both

*Source:* Deutsche Bank Alternative Investment Survey

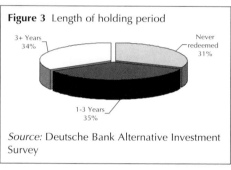

**Figure 3** Length of holding period

*Source:* Deutsche Bank Alternative Investment Survey

**Table 2** Ranking of advantages

| | Rank | |
|---|---|---|
| Advantages | Investors | Fund of funds |
| Diversification | 1 | 1 |
| Risk management | 2 | 4 |
| Capacity/access to funds | 4 | 5 |
| Due diligence | 3 | 3 |
| Manager selection | 5 | 2 |
| Consolidated reporting | 6 | 6 |

*Source*: CMRA/AIMA Survey

135

under management. We focus on market-neutral and event-driven strategies. We also work with net long and net short funds.

**What kind of transparency do you receive from your managers?**
We pretty much ask for total transparency either at our shop or theirs, and we find that about three out of four of the managers we interview are willing to give us that. We want to take their risk measurements, their portfolio, and do a little bit of plugging and see how they are going to add or detract from our portfolio in terms of risks and returns. We are certainly statistically oriented, but we're also interested in doing a lot of qualitative analysis on our managers. Equally important as the transparency issue is due diligence. For me to invest with a manager I have to see that he has good character and a strong record in investing. I also need to see that he has a substantial portion of his own money invested in the fund. When a manager has his kids' college tuition in the fund, he's a lot less likely to take stupid risks and a lot more likely to take an exhaustive, disciplined approach to investing. I also need to see where he's generating his returns; I want to see low beta, volatility, and high alpha, Sharpe ratios, with consistency of returns. Most of the time the funds that match these kinds of criteria are the structured arbitrage type funds, or opportunistic funds, but generally not the macro funds. We find that almost always when a manager has us into his office and goes over his portfolio with us, we can establish an understanding of the fund and whether or not we want to invest in it.

**What kind of transparency do you offer to your investors?**
We work mostly with institutional investors and we find that generally what they want to see is the portfolio broken down into easily digestible categories and numbers. The types of items we look for are VAR calculations, stress testing, written analysis of our strategies, how our funds have done during past stress periods, eg, 1994 and 1998, etc.

**Where do you think the industry is heading?**
I think there will continue to be a trend toward increasing transparency. I think we're going to continue to see more and more funds insisting on things like a five-year lock up in order to protect their capital during bad periods. After 1998 I think everyone realised that this industry is still wide open and really anything can happen.

## Panel 4

### An interview on transparency with John Trammell of Investor Select Advisors

Investor Select Advisors is a fund of funds with US$275 million of assets.

**What are your strategies? How many managers do you invest with?**
We use multiple strategies; and we are now invested in 50 funds.

**How many of your funds offer transparency?**
About half of them do. About 25% of the total number offer daily position transparency, and the number of hedge funds offering transparency is growing rapidly. The sector managers tend to be the most intractable with their transparency.

**How do you aggregate your risk across the transparent and the opaque funds?**
We estimate, based on returns and detailed interviews with managers.

**Table 3** Ranking of disadvantages

| | Rank | |
|---|---|---|
| **Disadvantages** | **Investors** | **Fund of funds** |
| Lack of control/customisation | 2 | 1 |
| Fees | 3 | 1 |
| Exposure to other investors' cashflows | 1 | 3 |
| Decreased transparency | 4 | 2 |

*Source*: CMRA/AIMA Survey

## HOW MANY FUNDS OF FUNDS ARE THERE?

No one knows for sure how many funds of funds there are. Of the publicly available information, the *Directory of Fund of Hedge Funds Investment Vehicles* lists the largest number of funds of funds and covers the largest AUM (see Table 5).[3]

Although no single source contains a comprehensive list of funds of funds with AUM greater than US$1 billion, the list in Table 6 has been compiled based on available sources coupled with CMRA's research.

It is interesting to note, however, that the CMRA/AIMA study found that the sources to which funds of funds report are different from the sources that investors review (see Table 7).[4]

**Table 4** Most frequent number of allocations per year

| | |
|---|---|
| Funds of funds | 10+ |
| Banks | 5 |
| Family offices | 4 |
| Endowment/foundations | 2 |

*Source*: Deutsche Bank Alternative Investment Survey

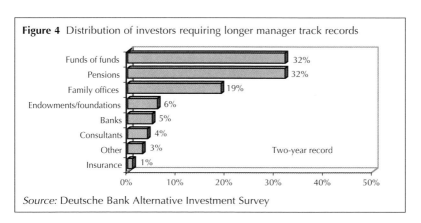

**Figure 4** Distribution of investors requiring longer manager track records

- Funds of funds — 32%
- Pensions — 32%
- Family offices — 19%
- Endowments/foundations — 6%
- Banks — 5%
- Consultants — 4%
- Other — 3%
- Insurance — 1%

Two-year record

*Source:* Deutsche Bank Alternative Investment Survey

**Are you satisfied with the level of overall transparency you receive?**
Yes. We have enough so that we can do appropriate risk analysis. Hedge funds are afraid of what the funds of funds are doing with their transparency, while the institutional investors are afraid of what the funds of funds are not doing with their transparency. For funds of funds, all these questions about risk measurement started simply as a marketing tool. Now, as the measurements have become more sophisticated, they can be useful in better portfolio building.

**What risk tools do you use, both internally for your own use and externally for your investors?**
We use Measurerisk internally. We offer investors monthly VAR, assets by sector and by country, geographic breakdowns of net long and net short, comparison benchmarks, what the various managers are doing, and manager name transparency. We offer the same reports to the funds we invest in, though not many are interested. We can also offer, upon request, for example, our exposure to WorldCom, in a very short period of time.

The fund of funds industry serves as the "de facto" regulator of the hedge fund industry. The funds of funds communicate with each other about such things as problem managers and strategy drift as a control against individual manager risk.

**Are your investors satisfied with the transparency that you provide?**
Yes. There's a tendency for institutional investors to always want more transparency, but we've struck a kind of compromise where everyone seems to be happy. In the end, most institutional investors are more worried about their careers than they are about maximising their returns.

**Where do you think transparency is heading in the future?**
The systems are constantly improving, but that doesn't mean that they are already at a high level. As more people establish the prerequisite structure to synthesise the transparency they receive, more transparency will be offered. In our case, Measurerisk is working for us right now but it is the only system we are ready to handle. As the systems and our infrastructure get more sophisticated, we will probably adopt additional risk management processes.

## Panel 5

### An interview on transparency with Kelsey Biggers of K2 Advisors, LLC

K2 Advisors, LLC is a fund of funds with a broadly diversified portfolio consisting of long/short hedge funds and low volatility hedge funds. The fund has over US$1 billion of AUM.

With regard to risk transparency, we see the industry maturing rapidly and beginning to coalesce around a set of reporting standards. These standards are driven by leading institutional investors in Europe and the US, and industry groups like the Investor Risk Committee.

To be successful, any transparency standard must provide meaningful, actionable information to an investor across multiple managers, while protecting the position-level exposures of the managers. Risk transparency is distinct from position disclosure.

The challenge for our industry is that effective risk analysis always requires holdings-level data. There are a number of ways that holdings can be analysed without being revealed to the market. One approach may be to have analytical software run at all participating managers to transform their exposures into risk

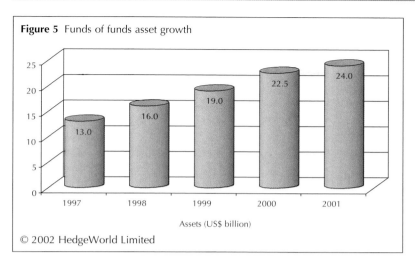

**Figure 5** Funds of funds asset growth

Assets (US$ billion)

© 2002 HedgeWorld Limited

**Table 5** Source of funds of funds information

| Source | Number | AUM (US$ billion) |
|---|---|---|
| Directory of Fund of Hedge Funds Investment Vehicles | 688 | 62.6 |
| Altvest | 315 | 48.4 |
| TASS | 285 | 28.3 |
| HFR | 230 | 31.4 |
| Tuna | 190 | 16.5 |

*Source*: Directory of Fund of Hedge Funds Investment Vehicles, Altvest, TASS, HFR, Tuna

## ASSETS UNDER MANAGEMENT

Overall, as seen in Figure 5, AUM in funds of funds have grown significantly. As Figure 6 illustrates, the number of funds with more than US$50 million almost doubled, from 21 to 40, and the category of funds with more than US$100 million increased 39% between 1994 and 2001.

Funds of funds with AUM greater than US$500 million represent only 3.5% to 7.6% of the funds reporting but account for 38.4% to 57.1% of AUM.

## HOW DO FUNDS OF FUNDS PERFORM?

The general rule that past results are not an indication of future earnings, very much holds true. Funds of funds' performance can vary drastically from one year to another. Furthermore, fund of funds indices vary between data sources. The maximum difference in the various fund of

factors before being aggregated by the investor or a third party. Another approach is to use a third-party service provider to act as a trusted intermediary between the manager and the investor. Still another solution may involve encryption technology to disguise holdings.

We support monthly analysis that is based on direct feeds of holdings data from either fund administrators or prime brokers. The analysis that is most useful to K2 Advisors is an aggregated view across all managers. This analysis will integrate:

❑ frequent performance reporting;
❑ industry, sector and geography exposure reporting;
❑ style-specific leverage measures;
❑ liquidity reporting for concentrated positions;
❑ Value at Risk (VAR) and marginal VAR based on Monte Carlo simulation; and
❑ stress testing.

Resistance to risk transparency will be most acute from underlying managers and embraced most enthusiastically by funds of funds and institutional investors. If the analysis is truly unintrusive and protects the managers' strategies, it will gain widespread acceptance over the next five years. A single industry standard may emerge similar to AIMR performance reporting.

Some strategies will be better suited to risk transparency than others. Long/short equity will be the first strategy to which risk transparency will widely apply. Some strategies may never lend themselves to risk analysis and this should be taken into account when investing in those strategies, particularly when setting exposure limits.

## Panel 6

### An interview with Sean G. McGould of Lighthouse Partners, LLC

Lighthouse Partners is a US$1.3 billion hedge fund of funds manager with experience and expertise in strategies beyond long/short equity, such as short-only, managed futures and other trading-oriented strategies.

Our perspective on hedge fund risk transparency:

1. We demand transparency from all of our managers. Fulfillment of such ranges from the full, position-level transparency of a managed account to more opaque relationships, where we will accept position-level transparency in a manager's office or detailed risk factor reviews at the portfolio level.
2. A core component of our manager research is a manager's thoughtfulness and discipline with respect to risk management. We fundamentally believe that our managers do an excellent job of controlling day-to-day risk. Most use some variation of VAR, which is satisfactory for anticipating normal daily movements. We believe our value added as a fund of funds manager is that we concentrate more on the risk control aspects not adequately captured by VAR. Most observers will agree that correlations are not stable in periods of stress; the unfortunate consequence is that what appear to be independent bets under normal market conditions become similar bets – although the securities traded may be quite different, the common risk factor can be exactly the same under stress. For example, a long / short manager (net long 30%) and a merger arbitrage manager may appear to be completely uncorrelated under normal market conditions. If the equity market sells off dramatically, both managers may start to feel stress because of those market conditions. In the case of the long/short

**Table 6** Funds of funds greater than US$1 billion

| Funds of funds | Assets (US$ billion) |
|---|---|
| RMK | 8.5 |
| Ivy Asset Management | 6.3 |
| Quellos | 6.2 |
| Asset Alliance | 4.5 |
| International Asset Management | 3.7 |
| Haussman Holdings NV | 3.4 |
| Mesirow Alternative Strategies Fund, LP | 3.2 |
| Ramius | 2.8 |
| Brummer & Partners | 2.5 |
| GAM Diversity Inc | 1.9 |
| Xavex Hedge Select Certificates | 1.8 |
| J.P. Morgan Multi-Strategy Fund, Ltd. | 1.8 |
| UBS O'Connor | 1.6 |
| Optima Fund Management | 1.6 |
| Permal Investment Holdings N.V. | 1.5 |
| Pamio | 1.5 |
| Arden | 1.5 |
| Lighthouse Partners | 1.3 |
| Longchamp Group | 1.2 |
| Select Invest | 1.1 |
| Olympia Stars | 1.1 |
| Man-Glenwood Multi-Strategy Fund Ltd. | 1.1 |
| K-2 | 1.1 |
| Mezzacappa Partners, LP | 1.0 |
| Meridian Horizon Fund, LP | 1.0 |
| Leveraged Capital Holdings | 1.0 |
| **Total** | **64.2** |

Source: Altvest, Tuna, TASS, HFR, Directory of Fund of Hedge Funds Investment Vehicles (2001 Edition), CMRA Research

**Table 7** Sources of information used by investors and funds of funds (%)

| | Investors | Funds of funds |
|---|---|---|
| Altvest | 80 | 19 |
| TASS | 38 | 18 |
| Zurich Capital Markets* | 38 | 18 |
| Tuna | 29 | 16 |
| HFR | 50 | 15 |
| CSFB/Tremont | 29 | 10 |
| Hennessee | 60 | 5 |

*Formerly MAR
Source: CMRA/AIMA Research

manager, the net long exposure will hurt them, and in the case of the merger arbitrage manager deal spreads may widen because companies are rethinking their acquisition decisions because of lower valuations. Both losses were caused by the same risk factor – equity price movements – although they may have no overlap in positions.

3. What investors appreciate about our approach is that we see our primary function as identifying the common risk factors among our hedge fund positions, constantly testing those assumptions, and being confident that the portfolio can tolerate them in aggregate under stress.

4. If a fund of funds is properly constructed, there is very little concentrated overlap of underlying securities. It has been our experience over the last 10 years that no single security has cost our portfolio more than a 30bp loss. However, there have been numerous instances over the past decade where common risk factors have cost us more than 1% (the underlying security positions were different but the risk factors were the same). For us, the transparency exercise is looking for compliance with what the managers have told us they are going to do on a broad level (eg, capitalisation, universe of securities, use of leverage). Most relevant to us is a keen understanding of risk exposures and how those exposures will behave in unusual market environments.

5. If we think back to some of the greatest periods of dislocation in the hedge fund industry, it is hard to pinpoint the losses to a single security type. Generally, the losses are caused by a larger risk factor such as equity prices falling or credit spreads widening. These factors cause hedge funds and counterparties to act in a similar manner that propels correlations towards 1.0. A hedge fund investor can know every position in every one of his investments and believe he has very little overlap but can experience significant loss of capital if all the managers are long relatively illiquid instruments and short liquid instruments in a flight-to-quality scenario.

6. We have spent the last five years developing proprietary tools and models that help us identify and quantify individual risk factors that we think are common to hedge funds. These tools are both quantitative and qualitative and are programmed into a continuously expanding database that includes both new data and scenarios.

7. We believe there is too much emphasis placed on being able to see underlying positions for "risk control" purposes and not enough attention being paid to how various investments will interact in a stressful situation. Though an unfortunate analogy, we think of the way we run a fund of funds to be similar to the business of a casino, albeit one with carefully controlled "games". Each of our managers represents a different independent game with a slight edge in favour of our portfolio. Like a casino, we are going to lose money on some of our games some of the time. We do know that over time (if our managers truly have an edge) we will make money as long as we have independent bets (our managers) on the table. In this scenario, we have to spend our time and resources making sure we have independent risk factor bets on the table as opposed to ensuring the dealers at each table are not all holding the same cards.

8. Transparency should not be used to fool investors into a false sense of security. A gratuitous example of this is the loss sustained by investors in Enron, a public company registered under the watchful eye of the SEC and independent accountants. Although everyone had access to their accounts, no one really stopped to ask the question of how they could be so profitable in such a competitive, deregulated industry? No doubt, everyone agrees that more information is better than less, but more raw data should not give investors any additional comfort – particularly in complex hedge fund strategies. Investors should determine what is important, relevant and actionable for their portfolio process and demand that information from all of their managers.

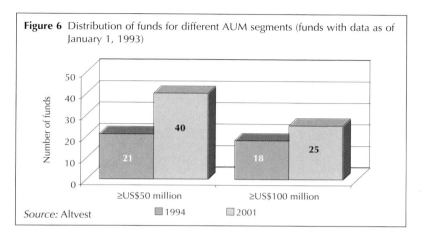

**Figure 6** Distribution of funds for different AUM segments (funds with data as of January 1, 1993)

*Source:* Altvest

funds indices in any of the years from 1997 to 2001 was 26.1% in 1999 between the Altvest Funds of Funds Index and the CSFB/Tremont Index (48.4% vs 22.3%). The difference between these two indices over the five-year period is 10.4% (18.4% vs 8.0%).

## WHICH FUNDS OF FUNDS HAVE THE LARGEST/HIGHEST SHARPE RATIO AND LOWEST CORRELATION?

Tables 8 and 9, kindly provided by HedgeWorld, list the funds of funds with the highest Sharpe ratios and the lowest correlations to the S&P; however, they do not include the full universe of funds, only the funds in The TASS Database. Sharpe ratios should arguably be taken with a grain of salt (as discussed throughout this book) as they are easily "gained" by hedge funds. As Figure 7 shows, the volatility of funds of funds can vary significantly with some unusual funds of funds as high as 70%.

## WHAT HEDGE FUNDS DO FUNDS OF FUNDS ALLOCATE TO MOST FREQUENTLY?

The *Directory of Fund of Hedge Funds Investment Vehicles* reported, as shown in Table 10, that the Tudor GAM Fund had the largest asset allocation (US$348 million) by fund of funds and the Maverick and Kensington Funds were the most favoured by funds of funds.

## WHAT ARE THE MOST POPULAR HEDGE FUND STYLES USED BY FUNDS OF FUNDS?

As Figure 8 indicates, long/short equity hedge funds are the most popular fund of funds investment, but distressed security funds are expected to increase in allocation.

While long/short equity and global macro, on average, are the most popular underlying hedge fund styles, as Table 11 shows, their allocations

## Panel 7

### An interview with Jean Karoubi from LongChamp Group

**How big are you? What are your primary strategies?**
LongChamp began as our family office focused on alternative investments. We have about US$1.2 billion under management and/or some form of advisory service (about US$250 million are discretionary). We invest in all strategies.

**What kind of transparency do you receive from your managers?**
90% of our managers offer the kinds of transparency we need. We'd classify the remaining 10% of our managers as "problem managers" even if some could be among the world's best. Caxton would be our most extreme example, where it's just a complete black box, but they are extraordinarily smart and we still manage to cooperate and obtain some understanding of their risk exposure. We're not really interested in seeing position books or anything like that, but we are interested in a pretty detailed risk exposure analysis from each of our funds. We rate each of our managers in terms of about 18 factor risk categories (each defined by its benchmark), but in the end what we're most interested in seeing from a fund is how well they manage their risk-adjusted returns. We want to see where they're allocating their assets, and we want to do it through an active collaboration with the manager rather than by taking home a position book and trying to figure it out for ourselves. Leverage at the manager level is only one of the key issues for us. By going through an extensive due diligence process with each of our potential managers and then by going through ongoing process with each of our hired managers, we feel that we can protect ourselves from a lot of these risks. Crooks (fortunately there are not that many) will steal from you, but effective due diligence will hopefully protect you from investing with them (we never did). After going through the whole process, if it's clear that the manager is smart, professional and experienced, then we will enjoy becoming his partner. It is then our job to balance all these risks from all those managers and even to overlay protections against tail risks.

**Where do you see the industry going from here?**
One real issue with the hedge fund industry right now, the issue that is going to threaten the industry if it isn't threatening it already, is how over-leveraged a lot of structured products are. From now on I think we're going to see increased regulation and interference from bodies like the SEC. The current investor push we're seeing for increased understanding and aggregation of their investments will only continue to gain momentum. The hedge fund industry is growing at an unprecedented rate, and as a result I think we're going to see increased movement and volatility in the markets as a direct result of hedge fund participation. I see leverage as a real problem, especially as the industry gets bigger. We have hundreds of new funds joining the old ones, many of them getting bigger and bigger, but all of them still borrowing from the same handful of banks. This is a problem. LTCM by itself threatened world financial systems, and although I'd doubt any of the banks today have that much exposure to one fund, I'd say the problem we have today may develop as more dangerous than that of 1998. The first outlier in the market that threatens one of these banks is going to bring the correlation of all these over-leveraged structured products to one, and when the banks are threatened and nobody can get any credit, a mass sell-off is going to hurt even the most responsible funds; fortunately it's not for certain, but if that happens we're going to see a lot money go up in smoke very quickly.

**Table 8** Funds of funds ranked by highest three-year Sharpe ratio

| Rank | Funds of funds | Sharpe ratio | Estimated assets (US$ billion) |
|---|---|---|---|
| 1 | Sumnicht Money Masters Fund II LP | 4.36 | 4 |
| 2 | RMB International Global Spread Capture Fund | 3.84 | 93 |
| 3 | AIG International Relative Value Fund | 3.74 | 206 |
| 4 | Ontario Partners LP | 3.39 | 41 |
| 5 | Coast Diversified Fund Ltd | 3.21 | 159 |
| 6 | GEMS Progressive Fund Ltd (Class T) | 3.00 | 81 |
| 7 | High Sierra Partners I (QP) LP | 2.96 | 89 |
| 8 | California Managed Accounts Fund III LP | 2.93 | 17 |
| 9 | J.P. Morgan Multi-Strategy Fund LP | 2.84 | 133 |
| 10 | Long-Invest USD Fund Ltd | 2.80 | 79 |
| 11 | La Fayette Regular Growth Fund Ltd | 2.79 | 14 |
| 12 | Arden Institutional Advisers LP | 2.66 | 921 |
| 13 | Hermes Neutral Fund | 2.62 | 276 |
| 14 | Raleigh Fund LP | 2.61 | 6 |
| 15 | Arden Advisers LP | 2.55 | 168 |
| 16 | Smart Market Independent Fund LP | 2.50 | 6 |
| 17 | Bodleian Partners LP | 2.48 | 33 |
| 18 | American Masters Opportunity Fund LP | 2.43 | 45 |
| 19 | Upstream Partners LLC | 2.30 | 21 |
| 20 | Sage Capital LP | 2.29 | 137 |

*Source*: TASS

**Table 9** Funds of funds ranked by lowest three-year correlation vs S&P 500

| Rank | Funds of funds | Correlation (%) | Estimated assets (US$ billion) |
|---|---|---|---|
| 1 | Optima Short Fund Ltd | (79) | 4 |
| 2 | Cadogan ContraFund LP | (58) | 4 |
| 3 | Dean Witter Spectrum Select LP | (44) | 241 |
| 4 | Dean Witter Global Perspective Portfolio LP | (40) | 10 |
| 5 | Liberty International Fund | (39) | 8 |
| 6 | Dean Witter Cornerstone Fund 11 LP | (38) | 1 |
| 7 | Goldman Sachs Global Tactical Trading Plc | (37) | 420 |
| 8 | Dean Witter Cornerstone Fund III LP | (33) | 26 |
| 9 | Sperry Persistence Fund Inc | (32) | 46 |
| 10 | FM Global Markets Fund | (27) | 42 |
| 11 | California Managed Accounts Fund III LP | (24) | 17 |
| 12 | Friedberg Global Managers Fund Ltd | (24) | 0 |
| 13 | California Managed Accounts Fund I LP | (23) | 2 |
| 14 | Blue Danube – Diversified Futures Fund (Euro) | (23) | 8 |
| 15 | Futures Portfolio Fund LP | (22) | 7 |
| 16 | High Sierra Partners I (QP) LP | (18) | 89 |
| 17 | Blue Danube – Futures Select (Euro) | (17) | 12 |
| 18 | Securities & Futures Performance Fund Ltd | (15) | 1 |
| 19 | GAM Cross-Market Inc | (15) | 99 |
| 20 | Raleigh Fund LP | (12) | 6 |

*Source*: TASS

## Panel 8

### An interview with Jeff Chicoine of Mesirow Alternative Strategies Fund

**Tell us about your fund**

Mesirow Alternative Strategies Fund is a fund of funds with US$3.2 billion of AUM. We've been in business as hedge fund advisors since 1983 and we started our fund of funds in 1990. Today we are only a fund of funds and our clients are mostly institutional investors. Although these clients are mainly insurance and pension funds, we do have some high net worth investors.

**What strategies do you invest in?**

We invest in low volatility strategies: merger arbitrage, convertible bond arbitrage, distressed securities and long and short-biased hedged equity.

**What kinds of transparency do you receive?**

We need enough information to do our own risk analysis and we also want to be able to determine "manager edge". For example, with merger arbitrage, we want top positions so we can aggregate across the fund. With convertible arbitrage, on the other hand, we want to know sector exposure. We also want to know what kind of leverage the funds we work with employ.

We insist on getting transparency. Unfortunately, some managers won't give it up: it is typically more difficult to get transparency from larger, more established managers.

**Do you calculate VAR?**

Yes, but there are other, better measurements.

**What other calculations do you perform?**

The calculations we perform include market exposure, sector exposure, leverage exposure, stress testing, and weighted active risk. All in all we use about 14 different statistical measures.

**What kinds of transparency do you give your investors?**

We've found that investors increasingly want to perform their own assessments. Most of our investors want sector and currency exposure.

**What strategies are typically more reluctant to give transparency and which give it more freely?**

You can usually get better information from long-biased equity managers. You're not going to get full transparency from short-biased managers.

**Do you think transparency can cause you to surrender your competitive edge?**

We give out as much information as we can because we are insistent on getting transparency from the hedge funds with which we work. We don't believe that giving our investors transparency hurts us because we are a fund of funds. Transparency would probably hurt individual managers more.

**Where do you think the industry is heading in terms of transparency?**

In regards to pension funds, we're seeing transparency becoming increasingly important to them. There is a need for more transparency, whether it comes directly from the hedge fund or is obtained from a third party. I think that the amount of transparency that funds will give in the future will vary by manager and by strategy.

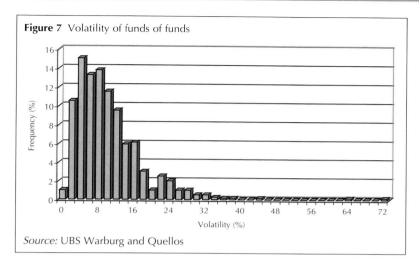

**Figure 7** Volatility of funds of funds

*Source:* UBS Warburg and Quellos

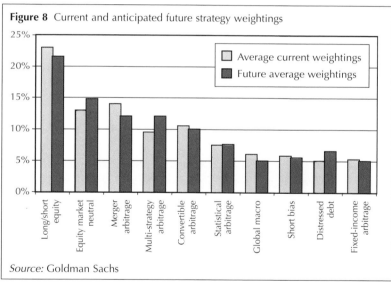

**Figure 8** Current and anticipated future strategy weightings

*Source:* Goldman Sachs

in individual funds of funds vary from a minimum of 3.8% and 3.5%, respectively, to a maximum of 100%.

## LEVERAGE

The reader is asked to note all of the caveats of interpreting leverage data discussed in Chapter 4. Nevertheless, Altvest shows the leverage in funds of funds increasing, as shown in Tables 12 and 13.

In addition, two to four times leverage is often used by high-net-worth

## Panel 9

### An interview with Barry Seeman of the Fund of Funds Unit, AXA

AXA is a French global insurance company with US$300 billion of AUM. US$2 billion (US$1 billion external and US$1 billion internal) allocated to the funds of funds unit.

**Are your strategies diversified?**
Unfortunately, we are fully diversified in terms of strategy. I say unfortunately because, although diversification is the right way to go in the long term, it has been painful in the short term.

**What kind of transparency do you get from your managers?**
Of the 50 managers that we work with, only about four or five don't give us the transparency that we want. The rest give us position-level transparency.

**Have you ever found that what a manager does diverges from what he/she says?**
Since 1997, we've had two or three managers where style drift was an issue.

**What about the managers who don't give you the information you want?**
Those funds represent a much smaller portion of our investments. However, although we've scaled back from uncooperative funds, they are still in our portfolio. On the other hand, we did not invest in LTCM because of their lack of transparency.

**What systems do you use?**
We use a number of in-house systems. One of our VPs put together an Excel-Bloomberg base for looking at risk exposure.

**What do you do with the transparency that you receive?**
These days, too many people talk about risk management and too few people know what they're talking about.

When we receive position-level transparency, we do a few things. We try to gauge style trends; for example, we ask why a sector fund would step outside the sector. In general, we look at issues pertaining to the ways in which they say they will manage the fund: concentration risk issues, position-size, diversification, etc.

We put together a risk assessment. We want to figure out everything that could go wrong with the hedge fund. We want to know how the portfolio is traded: we look for mis-matches between people and pedigree, we look at style. We want to know about the physical infrastructure of the firm: for example, what are their disaster recovery procedures? 95% of our rejection during the due diligence process is over people. These are things we discover during background checks.

We also want to know how much work a manager does before he invests: the due diligence is important. We're very active in talking to our managers.

On the other side of things, what kind of transparency do you give investors?

We give them whatever they need. For a larger institutional investor, we will go down to position-level in the office.

**Are you satisfied with the transparency that you give and get?**
Yes, I'm completely satisfied.

**Where do you think transparency is heading in the future?**
I think the great hedge funds will stay the way they are; from a business-person's standpoint I understand why they won't disclose.

**Table 10** Ranking of most popular underlying hedge funds by number of inclusions

| Fund name | Strategy | Domicile | Assets allocated (US$ million) | No of inclusions | Hedge fund assets (US$ million) | Returns (%) | | |
|---|---|---|---|---|---|---|---|---|
| | | | | | | 1 year | 3 years | Life |
| GAM TFF (Tudor) | Long/short equity | Curacao | 348 | 4 | n/a | 10.7 | 28.0 | 39.0 |
| Crossman Currency Fund | Global Macro | n/a | 288 | 7 | 589 | 65.0 | 17.0 | 61.0 |
| GAM FFT (Trout) | n/a | n/a | 245 | 4 | n/a | n/a | n/a | n/a |
| Medallion Fund | Global Macro | Cayman Islands | 240 | 5 | 1,854 | 66.3 | 19.0 | 32.5 |
| AlphaGen Capella Fund USD | Long/Short Equity | Bermuda | 232 | 4 | 1,058 | n/a | n/a | n/a |
| Moore Global Investments | Global Macro | Cayman Islands | 216 | 7 | n/a | n/a | n/a | n/a |
| Caxton Global Investments Ltd. | CTA/Macro | British Virgin Islands | 212 | 5 | 1,328 | 13.5 | 32.0 | n/a |
| Egerton | Event Driven | British Virgin Islands | 190 | 4 | 612 | 86.0 | 22.0 | 42.6 |
| Eureka Interactive Fund | Long/Short Equity | n/a | 143 | 6 | 390 | 20.9 | n/a | 11.1 |
| Raptor Global Fund Ltd. | Long/Short Equity | n/a | 130 | 5 | 1,894 | 73.0 | 19.0 | 19.8 |
| Maverick Fund Ltd. | Long/Short Equity | Cayman Islands | 125 | 8 | 5,105 | 27.6 | 25.1 | 28.7 |
| Farallon Capital Offshore Investors Inc. | Event Driven | British Virgin Islands | 122 | 5 | n/a | n/a | n/a | n/a |
| Sierra Europe Offshore Fund | Long/Short Equity | Cayman Islands | 118 | 4 | 276 | n/a | n/a | n/a |
| Galleon Technology Fund | Long/Short Equity | Bermuda | 115 | 4 | 1,500 | n/a | 2.0 | 40.4 |
| HBK Ofishore Fund | Convertible Arb | Cayman Islands | 88 | 6 | n/a | n/a | n/a | n/a |
| Kensington Global Strategies Fund | Convertible Arb | Bermuda | 83 | 8 | 1,800 | n/a | n/a | n/a |
| Highbridge Capital Corporation | Convertible Arb | Cayman Islands | 60 | 6 | 3,700 | n/a | n/a | n/a |
| Ivory Capital Ltd. | Long/Short Equity | n/a | 53 | 4 | n/a | 12.0 | 39.0 | 51.0 |
| Kingate Global Fund Ltd. | Equity Market Neutral | British Virgin Islands | 53 | 4 | 1,270 | 40.1 | 12.0 | 78.0 |
| Tudor BVI Global Fund | Global Macro | n/a | 39 | 4 | n/a | n/a | n/a | n/a |
| King Street Capital Ltd. | Event Driven | British Virgin Islands | 36 | 5 | 813 | 44.7 | 13.0 | 18.2 |
| Levco Alternative Fund Ltd. | Event Driven | Cayman Islands | 25 | 4 | 213 | 11.9 | 29.0 | 17.3 |
| Cerberus International Ltd. | Event Driven | Bermuda | 18 | 5 | 1,400 | 12.5 | 29.0 | 47.9 |

*Source:* CMRA research, Directory of Fund of Hedge Funds Investment Vehicles

## Panel 10

### An interview with Tom Strauss of Ramius Capital Group

Ramius Capital Group is a fund of funds with US$2.8 billion of AUM.

**What are your primary strategies?**
Our strategy is an absolute return strategy, focusing on earning 5-10% over the risk-free rate. We invest with about 40 managers, primarily those involved in merger arbitrage, distressed securities, convertible arbitrage, long/short equity, and fixed-income arbitrage. We're most interested in funds that already have a lot of infrastructure in place; it generally goes hand in hand with a very risk-conscious attitude.

**What kind of transparency do you want from your managers and what do you actually receive?**
We're much more interested in getting functional transparency than in just getting maximum transparency. With that in mind, we don't require position-level data. We find that comprehensive risk reports are a lot more useful to us than position data. We don't believe in any magic system that can crunch position data and tell you how to run your portfolio. Instead we take the risk reports, coupled with extensive on-site due diligence and plug them into our own proprietary system for grading managers. Ultimately, we feel that the greatest risk in this business is the underlying manager risk, not the risk inherent in their positions. So, rather than scrutinise every manager's individual position book, we scrutinise every manager: we look at consistency, performance in stress periods, changes in risk/reward over time, etc.

**What kind of transparency do you offer your investors?**
We don't offer manager transparency but we do offer specific portfolio breakdowns by geography, sector concentration, etc.

## Panel 11

### An interview with Pierre-Yves Moix of Stefan Scholz, RMF Investment Products

Stefan Scholz, RMF Investment Products is a fund of funds with US$8.5 billion alternative investments (mostly hedge funds).

Traditionally, hedge fund investments have been perceived as black boxes. However, we think that this view is biased and too simplistic. It is biased because the very same argument could also be made for the proprietary trading desks of the investment banks. Even though these are the largest hedge funds in the world, no investor would dare to ask to have their positions revealed prior to investing in their stocks. This is despite the fact that investment banks lost more money than most hedge funds in the course of the LTCM disaster.

The black box argument is too simplistic since some investors do not understand the nature of hedge fund investing and are not able to differentiate between the various strategies. However, this understanding is required in order to comprehend the level of transparency an investor should ask for and be granted.

Hedge funds are run by specialist managers who use their expertise to exploit arbitrage opportunities, price-value disparities, misunderstood situations, complex to value instruments, temporary price dislocations, etc, and who are willing to take on risks that other market participants cannot handle equally well. Some of these

**Table 11** Funds of fund allocation (%)

| | Average | Minimum (non-zero) | Maximum |
|---|---|---|---|
| Long/short equity | 25.0 | 3.8 | 100.0 |
| Global macro | 20.0 | 3.5 | 100.0 |
| Arbitrage | 19.7 | 6.2 | 64.1 |
| Merger arbitrage | 17.3 | 7.7 | 30.0 |
| Event-driven | 16.5 | 3.5 | 55.0 |
| Distressed | 16.1 | 3.2 | 47.0 |
| Fixed income | 15.6 | 2.8 | 37.0 |
| Capital structure | 13.2 | 13.2 | 13.2 |
| Convertible arbitrage | 11.2 | 4.5 | 21.6 |
| CTA | 8.2 | 6.4 | 9.9 |
| Emerging markets | 7.2 | 5.3 | 9.1 |

*Source*: Directory of Fund of Hedge Funds Investment Vehicles

individuals seeking aggressive returns through funds of funds. Structured products generally offer additional leverage.

## HOW MANY FUNDS DOES IT TAKE TO CONSTRUCT A GOOD FUND OF FUNDS?

The CMRA/AIMA survey indicated that market participants differ significantly on this issue (see Table 14). Not only is there disagreement as to how many funds it takes to make a good fund of funds, but also the

**Table 12** Historical average leverage of funds of funds

| | | | | | 1997–2001 | | |
|---|---|---|---|---|---|---|---|
| 1997 | 1998 | 1999 | 2000 | 2001 | Average | Maximum | Minimum |
| 1.0 | 0.72 | 0.6 | 0.9 | 1.0 | 0.8 | 1.0 | 0.6 |

*Source*: Altvest, CMRA Analysis

**Table 13** Financial leverage of funds of funds in 2002

| Minimum | Average | Maximum | Rank |
|---|---|---|---|
| 1.0 | 1.5 | 3.0 | 10 of 14 |

*Source*: Altvest, CMRA Analysis

opportunities are quick to disappear, thereby requiring secretive investing (eg, arbitrage). Others require certain risk management tools that have to be unknown in order stay effective (eg, stop loss limits). Still others take large macro bets and use investments whose potential profit margins are high.

Taking this into account, it would not be wise to ask for full transparency, ie, full disclosure of all position details, for information-sensitive strategies. A short squeeze or "duplication effect" are just two examples illustrating the (potentially) destructive effect of total transparency. Hence, the demand for complete transparency should be substituted by a call for adequate transparency that fits the underlying strategy. In our opinion, transparency is adequate when it allows one to understand the investments strategy and its associated risks. This in turn admits one to make a prudent investment decision. In general, the level of transparency depends on the liquidity and speed of the strategy.

It is also important to understand that transparency does not necessarily imply economic liquidity, ie, knowing the portfolio positions on say, a daily basis does not necessarily mean that they can also be liquidated within one day. What value does the daily information have in this case? Putting it differently, we are convinced that the detection time and the action time must match.

The impact of liquidity and transparency on the risk control effort of a fund of funds are summarised in the figure below. In this context, risk monitoring is the process of measuring the degree of risk inherent in a given portfolio. As such, it is a passive, backward-looking approach much like an accounting view. Risk management is more than risk monitoring, it employs one set of risk measures to allocate risk optimally among various assets and uses another type of risk measures to monitor exposures and make adjustments. It can only be applied if the fund liquidity allows one to do so. The question mark in the lower right-hand quadrant illustrates the mismatch arising from high transparency and low liquidity: "What do you do with transparency when the liquidity of the underlying assets does not allow you to take the appropriate actions?"

As discussed above, adequate transparency allows one to review all the (risk) factors that are relevant for a prudent investment decision. Hence, we invest only in hedge funds that provide us with at least this level of transparency.

There are also some misconceptions about the transparency that should be provided to fund of funds investors. For some clients, transparency is equivalent to the disclosure of positions or a set of summary statistics concerning the exposures

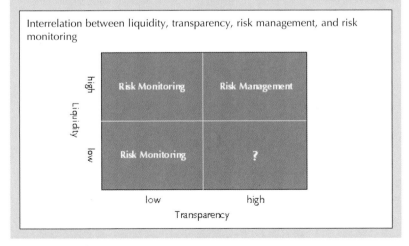

Interrelation between liquidity, transparency, risk management, and risk monitoring

**Table 14** Mix of funds and strategies to create a fund of funds (%)

| Strategies | Funds | | | | | Total |
|---|---|---|---|---|---|---|
| | Under 10 | 10–20 | 20–30 | 30–40 | Over 40 | |
| Under 10 | 13 | 38 | 37 | 13 | 0 | 100 |
| 10–20 | 0 | 0 | 75 | 13 | 13 | 100 |
| Over 20 | 0 | 0 | 100 | 0 | 0 | 100 |
| Combined | 4 | 13 | 70 | 9 | 4 | 100 |

*Source*: CMRA/AIMA Survey

percentage of individual funds of funds allocated to various strategies varies dramatically (see Table 15).

## DUE DILIGENCE

The results from the CMRA/AIMA survey in Table 16 show that hedge funds rate the quality of due diligence they receive from funds of funds as more intense than that of other investors.

Due diligence on existing managers and evaluation of new managers each consume, on average, 30% of a fund of funds manager's time. Some due diligence questions for funds of funds include:

❏ team experience, qualifications;
❏ access to quality hedge fund managers;
❏ thorough, experienced due diligence and risk monitoring;
❏ portfolio construction and rebalancing process;
❏ existing fund diversification across different strategies and different managers;
❏ performance;
❏ investor concentration;
❏ level of disclosure/transparency;
❏ operations and administration;
❏ regulation/compliance; and
❏ growth of AUM.

See Appendix 3 for the reprint of a more complete discussion of due diligence for funds of funds.

## PROBLEMS WITH FUND OF FUNDS SOURCES

The issues for fund of funds indices are similar to the issues for hedge fund indices themselves. See Chapter 11 for a further discussion of indices.

of the single hedge funds underlying their portfolios. As discussed above, this kind of information is not necessarily available for all hedge funds. If it is, as in the case of a fund of managed accounts, the gathering and processing of this information requires appropriate skills and adequate technology. In this context, fund of funds managers have the job of transforming the raw positions and exposure statistics into useful information for the investors.

We think that the transparency provided to fund of funds investors has to be defined more generally. It should entail full transparency of the fund of funds' decision-making process, useful performance reporting, and may be complemented by the reporting of aggregated risk exposures at the portfolio level.

Full transparency of the decision-making process involves the disclosure of the whole investment process, ie, due diligence, style allocation, and portfolio construction methods, as well as the risk management and monitoring process. This transparency allows the investors to feel comfortable with the way hedge funds are selected, monitored and, if necessary, redeemed, as well as with the methods and assumptions underlying the combination of the different styles and managers in a portfolio.

Additionally, full transparency of the decision-making process admits the provision of useful performance reporting. The latter involves much more than allocations and risk-adjusted performance statistics. It discloses the impact of the different investment decisions on the risk/return profile of the portfolio. To this end, risk and return attribution analysis decomposes the contribution of the strategic and tactical asset allocation as well as hedge fund picking on the risk-adjusted performance. The performance comparison of the different investment decisions with pre-defined guidelines and benchmarks gives clients the opportunity to assess the added value of each of them. This analysis has to be done in a portfolio context. Some styles or hedge funds may look unattractive if considered in isolation. The rationale for an allocation towards them may, however, lie in diversification benefits and the avoidance of concentration risk. Performance reporting could be complemented by comments on market developments that may influence the risk/return profile of the portfolio.

Finally, the reporting of aggregated exposures at the portfolio level may be valuable for clients who aim to monitor risk across their entire investment programme. The aggregation of risk exposures requires the definition of a standard set of risk factors that hedge funds may be exposed to. Due to the heterogeneous nature of hedge fund investing, this is not a straightforward task. The Investor Risk Committee of the IAFE has made a first step toward standardisation in their recently published report "Hedge Fund Disclosure for Institutional Investors". The report specifies four dimensions (content, granularity, frequency, delay), which we are beginning to incorporate in our risk monitoring framework. Content and granularity of hedge fund reporting should reveal aggregate exposures to various risk factors such as asset class, sector, currency, region, yield curve, capitalisation, hedge fund strategy, credit quality, liquidity, etc. Additionally, strategy-specific risk factors (Greeks, correlation, etc) should deepen the understanding of the strategies and their associated risks. The appropriate frequency of transparency is a function of asset turnover. Since the information will be disclosed to investors at the portfolio level only, there is no risk to hurt the trading strategy of single managers and therefore no need to delay the disclosure. Hence, the delay should correspond to the normal processing time at the hedge fund level.

Going forward, we are confident that most hedge fund managers will be able and willing to provide the aforementioned information. Large funds of funds are influential hedge fund investors with appropriate expertise and therefore possess a competitive advantage in receiving and processing this information.

## Selection bias

Since hedge funds are not *required* to disclose their performances, only those funds with significantly positive results are likely to report their information. Therefore, the inclusion of top performing hedge funds may overestimate the industry's returns.

No source has a corner on hedge fund manager information. Few managers report their returns data to every source and all fund of funds indices suffer from selection bias.

## Survivorship bias

The survivorship bias occurs because data source vendors only calculate returns for funds that are still in operation and exclude those funds that have gone bankrupt due to poor results or other reasons. Some firms (especially firms that have financial difficulties) stop reporting even when they are still in business.

An interesting pattern that can be seen in Table 17 is that three of the four funds shown and the Altvest Fund of Funds Index exhibit similar performance behaviour between 1998 and 2001 (increasing returns in 1998 and 1999 and decreasing returns thereafter), implying that funds of funds' performances are highly correlated with one another. The table shows, of the 211 funds of funds in Altvest, 153 (or more than 70%) displayed this characteristic. Furthermore, 152 of the 211 funds had correlations greater than 0.5 with Altvest (1998 to 2001 using monthly data). However, only 70 of the 211 funds had correlations greater than 0.7.

Tables 18 and 19 show the methodologies and selection criteria used by Altvest, HFR, Tuna, Zurich and Van Hedge Fund Advisors to build their respective fund of funds indices. As it is shown, these methodologies vary significantly. The data source providers identified build their respective indices with different launch dates. Performance is measured on an equally weighted basis except for Zurich. Monthly rebalancing is the only factor that is common to all funds. Lastly, the

**Table 15** Allocations to various strategies in a good fund of funds (%)

| | Long/short equity | Arbitrage | Global macro | Merger arbitrage | Fixed income | Event-driven | Convertible arbitrage | CTA | Emerging markets | Distressed | Miscellaneous |
|---|---|---|---|---|---|---|---|---|---|---|---|
| Average | 24.6 | 18.0 | 17.6 | 17.3 | 16.6 | 16.4 | 11.8 | 8.2 | 7.2 | 4.1 | 39.3 |
| Minimum | 5.0 | 6.2 | 3.5 | 7.7 | 2.8 | 3.5 | 4.5 | 6.4 | 5.3 | 3.2 | 8.0 |
| Maximum | 100.0 | 34.2 | 100.0 | 30.0 | 37.0 | 55.0 | 21.6 | 9.9 | 9.1 | 5.0 | 69.8 |

*Source:* Alternative Asset Center and CMRA Analysis

number of funds included in the indices varies from 203 for HFR to 295 for Altvest.

## HOW DO FUNDS OF FUNDS PERFORM IN DOWN MARKETS?

When compared to the performance of 16 other strategies, Figure 9 demonstrates that the fund of funds index ranked seventh in the 1994 crisis, fourth in the Russian/LTCM crisis and sixteenth in the dot.com bust.

## TRANSPARENCY

Deutsche Bank found in the results of their survey (recreated in Figure 10) that transparency is the number one issue considered when making investment decisions among funds of funds.

The informal IRC survey in June 2002 found that 60% of funds of funds receive position-level transparency from only 25% of their funds (see Figure 11). This once again makes one wonder how and whether some funds of funds are doing the risk management and due diligence that they claim to be doing.

In the same survey, the IRC ascertained that despite the low level of position-level transparency, 40% of funds of funds are satisfied that they can digest position-level detail.

Figure 12 demonstrates that funds of funds in general are

**Table 16** Rating of quality of due diligence

|  | Rating |
| --- | --- |
| Fund of funds | 1.4 |
| Institutions | 1.7 |
| Consultants | 1.8 |
| High-net-worth individuals | 3.1 |

Note: 1 is highest, 5 is lowest
Source: CMRA/AIMA Survey

**Table 17** Performance (index vs individual funds of funds)

|  | 1998 | 1999 | 2000 | 2001 |
| --- | --- | --- | --- | --- |
| Altvest Fund of Funds Index | 16.9 | 48.4 | 9.6 | 2.3 |
| Best performer 1998: |  |  |  |  |
|     Wahoo Partners, LP (Class C) | 71.4 | 67.8 | 50.2 | 5.8 |
| Best performer 1999: |  |  |  |  |
|     CIBC Oppenheimer Technology Partners, LLC | 40.6 | 100.8 | 2.0 | (1.7) |
| Best performer 2000: |  |  |  |  |
|     High Sierra Partners I (QP), LP | 27.5 | 17.3 | 70.4 | 23.4 |
| Best performer 2001: |  |  |  |  |
|     Triumph Investment Master Fund Ltd. (Class B) | 18.7 | 45.8 | 16.7 | 28.4 |

Source: Altvest

**Table 18** General features and fund of funds index construction

|  | Altvest Fund of Fund Index | HFR Fund of Fund Index | Tuna Fund of Fund Index | The Zurich Fund of Fund Median | Van Hedge Fund of Fund Index |
|---|---|---|---|---|---|
| Launch date | 2000 | 1996 | 1997 | 1994 | N/A |
| Measure of performance | Equally weighted | Equally weighted | Equally weighted | Median weighted | Equally weighted |
| Rebalanced | Monthly | Monthly | Monthly | Monthly | Monthly |
| Included in composite index | No | No | No | No | Yes |
| Number of funds included | 295 | 203 | 388 | 257 | N/A |

*Source*: Directory of Fund of Hedge Funds Investment Vehicles

**Table 19** Selection criteria

|  | Altvest Fund of Fund Index | HFR Fund of Fund Index | Tuna Fund of Fund Index | The Zurich Fund of Fund Median | Van Hedge Fund of Fund Index |
|---|---|---|---|---|---|
| Minimum assets | None | None | None | None | None |
| Minimum track record | None | None | None | None | None |
| Include closed funds | Yes | Yes | Yes | Yes | Yes |
| Require documents | None | Yes | None | Yes | Yes |

*Source*: Directory of Fund of Hedge Funds Investment Vehicles

**Figure 9** Funds of funds performance in downmarkets

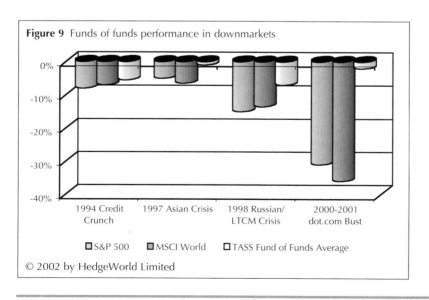

1994 Credit Crunch   1997 Asian Crisis   1998 Russian/ LTCM Crisis   2000-2001 dot.com Bust

☐ S&P 500   ■ MSCI World   ☐ TASS Fund of Funds Average

© 2002 by HedgeWorld Limited

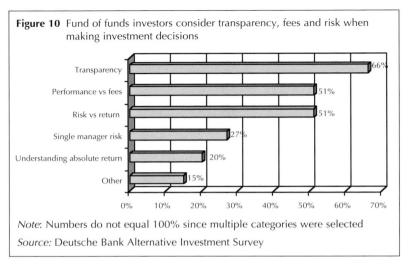

**Figure 10** Fund of funds investors consider transparency, fees and risk when making investment decisions

*Note*: Numbers do not equal 100% since multiple categories were selected

*Source:* Deutsche Bank Alternative Investment Survey

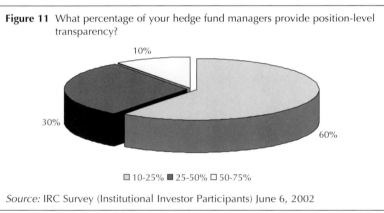

**Figure 11** What percentage of your hedge fund managers provide position-level transparency?

*Source:* IRC Survey (Institutional Investor Participants) June 6, 2002

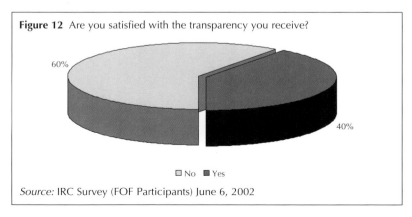

**Figure 12** Are you satisfied with the transparency you receive?

*Source:* IRC Survey (FOF Participants) June 6, 2002

sympathetic with hedge fund managers who are concerned about disclosing position-level detail, with only 36% believing that there is minimal or no impact from such disclosure.

At the IRC meeting, each group (hedge funds, funds of funds and "other") was queried about their attitudes towards hedge fund transparency; 50% of hedge funds, 28% of funds of funds, and 10% of "other" felt that position-level disclosure would have a significant or material impact on a hedge fund's performance (see Table 20).

**Surveys on transparency**

The CMRA/AIMA survey on transparency found that:

❑ Only 7% of funds of funds saw potential investors who declined to invest due to lack of transparency.
❑ 63% of funds of funds would find a standard set of "risk factors" very valuable or extremely valuable for portfolio construction and 56% for marketing/client reporting.
❑ 17% of funds of funds indicated that they have requested "risk profiles" from the hedge funds they invest in and been turned down.

---

**Table 20** Impact of transparency (%)

|                      | Hedge fund | Fund of funds | Other |
|----------------------|------------|---------------|-------|
| Significant impact   | 37         | 14            | 5     |
| Material impact      | 13         | 14            | 5     |
| Minimal impact       | 25         | 14            | 22    |
| Depends on strategies| 25         | 44            | 54    |
| Not at all           | –          | 14            | 14    |

*Source*: IRC Meeting June 6, 2002 (http://www.iafe.org)

---

**Table 21** How do you measure the risks in your fund of funds investments?

| | |
|------|-------------------------------------------------------------------------------|
| 79%  | Rely on detailed conversations with the fund.                                 |
| 66%  | Rely on detailed position information obtained when performing the initial due diligence that you examined. |
| 62%  | Rely on detailed position information periodically obtained that you examine.  |
| 38%  | Rely on correlated historical monthly performance to style benchmarks.        |

*Source*: CMRA/AIMA Survey

When investors were asked "how" they review the risks of the funds in which they invest, 79% answered that they rely on detailed conversations with the fund managers (see Table 21).

**What type of transparency do funds of funds provide to their investors?**
Given that only 10% of funds of funds receive position-level data from at least 50% of their underlying funds, 9% claim to provide position-level transparency to their investors. Perhaps they give only what they get, but this is confusing.

The IRC survey found that 67% of funds of funds provide a "risk profile" to the investors, but most agree that standardising this "risk profile" for consistency across the industry would be helpful.

## FUNDS OF FUNDS RISK MANAGEMENT
The CMRA/AIMA survey found that:

- ❏ 61% of funds of funds include risk limits in their investment guidelines and 79% of funds of funds have written risk management policies and procedures.
- ❏ Only 43% of funds of funds that rely on managers to track their risk vs budget feel that they understand the details of the risk calculations performed by each of their managers and can calibrate and aggregate risk across managers. However, 57% of funds of funds claim to compute VAR for their overall funds of funds; in some cases it is unclear how they do this since some of these same funds reported that they do not receive position-level data.

This makes me wonder: "did we ask the question poorly or is there an inconsistency here?"

## CONCLUSION
While funds of funds are an important player in the hedge fund universe, they are likely to experience a significant shakeout as their functionality is increasingly disaggregated and the level of due diligence and risk management they actually perform comes under increased regulatory scrutiny.

The CMRA/AIMA survey mentioned throughout this chapter found that hedge fund investments made through funds of funds are expected to increase between 2002 and 2004. The survey also found that 93% of funds of funds expect the structured, principal-guaranteed and exchange-traded aspect of the business to stay the same, while 45% of individual hedge funds see future growth in these areas.

1  Casey, Quirk and Action, May 2002, "Fund of hedge funds control 20% of hedge fund market".
2  Alternative Investment Survey Results, March 2002, Deutsche Bank.
3  Directory of Hedge Fund Investment Vehicles, December 2001.
4  Institutional Investor/CMRA, Endowment & Foundation Survey, June 2002.
5  HedgeWorld Limited – Fund of Funds ranked by Lowest standard deviation (3 Year Annualised), Copyright 2002.

# SECTION IV

# Hedge Funds

# An Overview of Hedge Funds

**OUTLINE OF THIS CHAPTER**

This chapter provides perspectives of seven key hedge fund managers as well as an overview of hedge funds including:

❑ What is a hedge fund?
❑ How many hedge funds are there?
❑ Which are the largest hedge funds?
❑ What are the sources for hedge fund data?
❑ How do various hedge fund indices compare?
❑ How much is invested in hedge funds?
❑ Who invests in hedge funds?
❑ Which are the most popular hedge fund strategies?
❑ How have drawdowns affected the various hedge fund styles?
❑ What are the relative performance characteristics of various hedge fund styles?
❑ How do hedge funds correlate with stocks and bonds?
❑ What are the liquidity characteristics of various hedge fund styles?
❑ How do various hedge fund styles perform during stress periods?
❑ How does VAR compare by style?
❑ Where are the risk, return and exposure characteristics of different styles?
❑ What are the correlations between the different hedge fund strategies?
❑ What are the relative Sharpe ratios of each hedge fund style?

The nine chapters in the next section cover the following strategies:

❑ convertible arbitrage;
❑ emerging markets;
❑ equity long/short;
❑ event-driven, including distressed securities and merger arbitrage;
❑ fixed income;
❑ global macro;
❑ managed futures;
❑ market neutral; and
❑ short biased.

## Panel 1

## Perspectives from Lee Ainslie of Maverick Capital

### Maverick Capital's Transparency and Disclosure Philosophy

Maverick Capital's goal is to preserve and grow capital. In order to achieve this goal, the funds are managed as traditional, truly hedged funds, maintaining low net exposure to each region and industry sector in which the funds invest through a balance of long and short equity investments. Maverick manages over US$7 billion and is registered with the SEC as an investment advisor.

We appreciate and respect our investors' desire to have a complete understanding of our investment process and of the risks of our portfolio. As fundamental analysts, we seek exhaustive knowledge of the companies in which we invest, and we expect our investors to seek the same from us. Consequently, we have been committed to thorough, prudent disclosure since our inception.

Investors receive quarterly reports that include a detailed review of the past quarter's performance and of current portfolio positioning. Maverick holds annual investor meetings at which performance and individual positions are reviewed in depth and investors have the opportunity to explore any other topics with the entire investment team. Upon request, investors may receive various reports that show:

❏ long and short performance attribution by region and industry including return on assets, return on equity, dollar profitability and contribution to total performance;
❏ net and gross exposures by region and industry;
❏ long/short ratios by region and industry in absolute and beta-adjusted terms;
❏ number of positions with market capitalisation and liquidity statistics;
❏ detailed trading activity summaries;
❏ current total assets under management and margin availability by fund; and
❏ historical daily performance including volatility and correlation statistics.

All of this information and communication may be supplemented with regular contact with Maverick's investor relations team.

Maverick does not provide daily position-level transparency, as we believe that such disclosure would be harmful to our investors. Such data would allow other market participants to discern current trades, potentially impairing Maverick's ability to obtain optimal prices in these transactions. Furthermore, disclosure of our short portfolio could lead to poor

In each strategy chapter a summary description is followed by a discussion of the following topics:

❏ largest players;
❏ coverage of funds in the strategy by indices and data sources;
❏ an analysis of indices and their components;
❏ historical performance (in terms of returns, AUM leverage, Sharpe ratio, information ratio, etc);
❏ key risks;
❏ applicability of VAR;
❏ due diligence questions; and
❏ major publicly disclosed problems that have affected funds in the strategy.

## WHAT IS A HEDGE FUND?

In general, a hedge fund is a pooled investment vehicle that is privately organised, administered by investment management professionals and not widely available to the public. Many of these funds share a number of characteristics: they hold long *and* short positions, employ leverage to enhance returns, pay a performance or incentive fee to their managers, have high minimum investment requirements, target absolute (rather than relative) returns, and/or may be organised offshore. Hedge fund strategies are relatively unconstrained in terms of short selling, leverage and investment universe. In addition, a hedge fund is not hampered by legal limitations on its investment discretion and can adopt a variety of trading

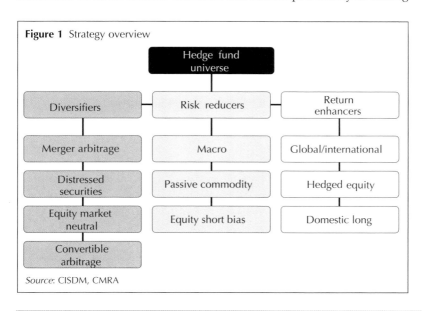

**Figure 1** Strategy overview

*Source*: CISDM, CMRA

relationships with the management teams of the companies in which we hold short positions and could increase the short interest in these positions, which would typically decrease the returns of a successful short. To improve our investors' understanding of our research and strategy, we have always been happy to discuss any position with any of our investors on a periodic basis.

Some investors have argued that such position-level detail could be shared with a handful of trustworthy investors (a classification in which those who make this argument typically believe they belong). In our judgement, we have a duty to treat all investors equally in all regards – including such transparency issues. With over 1,000 investors around the world, we recognise that we must be circumspect in releasing information that could be used in a manner that is detrimental to our ability of achieving our goal of preserving and growing our investors' capital.

We believe that this policy of full transparency and prudent disclosure has served Maverick and our investors well over time. Perhaps more importantly, we are committed to continually improving our investors' understanding and knowledge of our hedged equity strategy.

## Panel 2

### An Interview with Andrew Pernambuco, Principal of Alexandra Investment Management.

Alexandra Investment Management is a convertible arbitrage hedge fund with US$350 million in assets.

**What kind of transparency do you offer your investors?**
We offer our investors more than they seemingly want. Investors can visit our website and are able to query our positions, allocation of profit and loss, geographic distribution, real leverage, hedge ratio, AUM, how we compare to the benchmarks ... basically everything that anyone might want to know. Strangely enough in the four years that we have been offering this kind of transparency, only one person has queried down to the position level. Investors can receive official NAV's from our administrator on a weekly basis if they so desire.

We want investors who understand what we're doing; those that don't might pull their money at an inopportune time – one that's bad for us and for our other investors. Our strategy is a long-term one that has an average duration of three to five years. It is a convergence strategy, which means that there is a certainty that one of three events will happen sometime in the future. These three events are default, maturity and call/put.

strategies. The hedge fund manager will often have his/her own capital (or that of the fund's principals) invested in the hedge fund that he/she manages. Hedge funds are not in themselves an asset class but a type of vehicle that can invest in a variety of asset classes. There are three basic categories of hedge funds (see Figure 1):

1. *Diversifier*: A fund that, among other factors, exploits economic ineffi-ciencies to generate excess returns.
2. *Risk reducer*: A fund that takes positions that reduce the systematic risk of equity portfolios.
3. *Return enhancer*: A fund that exploits informational inefficiency to generate excess returns.

## HOW MANY HEDGE FUNDS ARE THERE?
No one knows for sure how many hedge funds there are, but we do know that the number of hedge funds has increased every year since 1990 (see Figure 2). By the end of 2002, there were approximately 4,500–6,000 hedge funds globally, depending on the source.

## WHICH ARE THE LARGEST HEDGE FUNDS?
The Soros Fund leads the largest hedge funds with US$9.0 billion in AUM. Table 1 shows the 25 largest hedge funds with a total US$113.5 billion in AUM. The available information used to compile this list comes from several major commercial sources and Institutional Investor's The Hedge Fund 100 (referred to henceforth as The Hedge Fund 100) published by Institutional Investor in June 2002. It is interesting to note that 11 of the 25

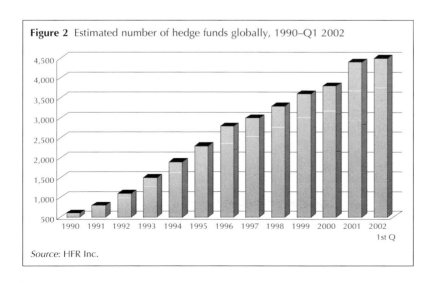

**Figure 2** Estimated number of hedge funds globally, 1990–Q1 2002

*Source*: HFR Inc.

Maturity rarely ever occurs because there's usually a call/put or bankruptcy first. I don't want an investor who doesn't understand that this takes time.

**What kind of risk analysis do you perform?**
We use a number of risk models and software; some proprietary and others from off-the-shelf. We don't use VAR because it does not apply well to convertible arbitrage. It is too static: it does not account for changing volatility over time. We try to identify lumps of risk and adjust our hedges accordingly.

**Are you concerned that transparency diminishes your competitive edge?**
Not at all.

**Do you think transparency can cause other strategies to surrender their competitive edges?**
Yes, probably with distressed debt. However, merger arbitrage and convertible arbitrage can and should be completely transparent.

**Then why do you think some convertible arbitrage funds are not as transparent as yours?**
Older funds probably give less transparency because they are already established. They feel they don't need to; they may possess a sort of hubris.

**Where do you think transparency is headed in the future?**
I think that for the most part investors have already gotten what they want in terms of transparency. I think the big issue is capacity; with individual funds and also for the strategy.

## Panel 3

## An Interview with Michael Rulle, President of Graham Capital Management, a multi-strategy firm.

**Tell us about your company?**
Founded in 1994 by Ken Tropin as a proprietary trading company, Graham Capital Management ("GCM") specialises in 24-hour trading in the global equity, fixed income, foreign exchange and futures markets. GCM manages a wide range of investment strategies, each of which is

**Table 1** The 25 largest hedge funds

| Rank | Fund | Strategy | Assets (US$ billion) |
|------|------|----------|----------------------|
| 1 | Soros Fund | Global macro | 9.0 |
| 2 | Angelo, Gordon & Co. | Multistrategy | 7.0 |
| 3 | Citadel Investment Group | Multistrategy | 5.7 |
| 4 | Renaissance Technologies Corp. | Multistrategy | 5.6 |
| 5 | HBK Investments | Multistrategy | 5.5 |
| 6 | Maverick Fund Ltd. | Equity hedge | 5.1 |
| 7 | Chilton Investment Co. | Multistrategy | 5.0 |
| 8 | Duquesne Capital Mgmt | Multistrategy | 5.0 |
| 9 | ESL Investments | Multistrategy | 5.0 |
| 10 | Highfields Capital Mgmt | Multistrategy | 5.0 |
| 11 | Och-Ziff Capital Mgmt Group | Multistrategy | 5.0 |
| 12 | Kingdon Capital Mgmt | Multistrategy | 4.0 |
| 13 | Lone Pine Capital | Multistrategy | 4.0 |
| 14 | Man Investment Products | Managed futures | 4.0 |
| 15 | Bear Steams Cos. | Multistrategy | 3.9 |
| 16 | Highbridge Capital Corporation | Event-driven | 3.9 |
| 17 | Moore Global Investments | Global macro | 3.8 |
| 18 | Fairfield Greenwich Group's | Market neutral | 3.7 |
| 19 | Andor Capital Mgmt | Multistrategy | 3.6 |
| 20 | GLG Partners | Multistrategy | 3.5 |
| 21 | UBS O'Connor | Multistrategy | 3.5 |
| 22 | Satellite Asset Mgmt | Multistrategy | 3.4 |
| 23 | Baupast Group | Multistrategy | 3.1 |
| 24 | Odey Japan & General Inc. | Equity hedge | 3.1 |
| 25 | Quantum Endowment Fund | Global macro | 3.1 |
| | **Total** | | **113.5** |

Highlighted funds are listed exclusively in The Hedge Fund 100
*Source*: Altvest, CSFB/Tremont, HFR, Tuna, Institutional Investor (June 2002), CMRA Research

largest funds listed, with a total of US$55.8 billion in AUM, were not included in the commercial sources analysed, but were exclusive to The Hedge Fund 100.

## WHAT ARE THE SOURCES OF HEDGE FUND INFORMATION?
Depending on the needs of the investor, there are numerous sources available to provide information about historical performance, AUM, risk/reward, etc. However, while some sources offer more information, others cover a broader range of funds. Of the 298 firms/funds listed in The Hedge Fund 100, 33% (with 45% of the AUM) are not listed in any commercial source. This bias is significant because most of the statistics and published research regarding hedge funds are derived from the commercial sources. However, since many of the largest and most successful funds do not report to the commercial sources, such information is incomplete – covering only the smaller funds. For example, a global

designed to produce attractive risk-adjusted returns and are designed to offer favourable correlation characteristics to traditional and other alternative investments. The firm currently has over 50 employees and almost US$1.8 billion under management.

**What kind of transparency do you offer your investors?**
Our clients access a GCM website which includes NAV daily, daily VAR, historical VAR, VAR by asset class, and VAR whether long/short. The firm uses RiskMetrics as its primary risk management software. Additionally, if an investor has a managed account with us, they also have full transparency for all of their positions. If our fund investors want transparency beyond what the website offers, we will provide additional information as requested.

**Are you concerned that transparency diminishes your competitive edge?**
GCM trades in very liquid markets. We offer our fund investors twice monthly liquidity and our managed account investors daily liquidity. We believe full risk transparency gives greater confidence to investors in our firm, and thus we believe it gives us a competitive edge.

**Where do you think the industry is heading in terms of transparency? Where do you think it should go?**
Investors are demanding greater risk transparency. Third-party systems like RiskMetrics can add value to this process as it provides an industry standard for calculating risk. This is particularly true for multi-strategy or fund of funds investors who seek aggregate risk analysis for their overall portfolios. Additionally, many investors are also requiring managed accounts, which translates into even greater transparency. Finally, investors should demand greater analysis regarding stress test results. Certain strategies may have overall risk understated when relying on traditional VAR analysis alone.

## Panel 4

## An Interview with Myron Scholes, Principal of Oak Hill Capital – a relative-value fund with US$500 million in assets

**What is your perspective on hedge fund risk transparency?**
We believe that it is important to provide the fund's risk exposures to our stakeholders. To this end, creditors and investors receive a VAR report on our aggregate portfolio and a breakdown of exposures geographically

macro index calculated from the global macro funds listed exclusively in The Hedge Fund 100 would exceed all other global macro indices on both an equally weighted and an AUM-weighted basis (see Table 2).

Table 3 shows the distribution of funds by strategy in The Hedge Fund 100 and also shows those exclusive to The Hedge Fund 100. Of this group,

**Table 2** Comparison of 2001 performance of top global macro funds listed in The Hedge Fund 100

| Index | Performance (%) |
|---|---|
| The Hedge Fund 100 exclusively – equally weighted | 17.5 |
| The Hedge Fund 100 exclusively – AUM-weighted | 14.8 |
| Hennessee | 12.4 |
| CSFB/Tremont | 11.5 |
| Tuna | 11.3 |
| HFR | 10.6 |
| Altvest | 7.2 |

*Source*: Institutional Investor (June 2002), Hennesee, CSFB/Tremont, Tuna, HFR, Altvest, CMRA Analysis

**Table 3** Funds in The Hedge Fund 100 categorised by strategy

| | Listed in The Hedge Fund 100 and/or commercial sources | | Listed exclusively in The Hedge Fund 100 | |
|---|---|---|---|---|
| | Number | AUM (US$ billion)* | Number | AUM US$ billion |
| Global macro | 14 | 21.3 | 9 | 29.7 |
| Long/short equity | 95 | 55.5 | 22 | 15.8 |
| Event-driven | 41 | 27.1 | 6 | 4.7 |
| Convertible arbitrage | 17 | 8.3 | 6 | 4.4 |
| Fixed income | 21 | 7.7 | 5 | 3.2 |
| Emerging markets | 10 | 3.7 | 3 | 2.4 |
| Market neutral | 16 | 7.4 | 5 | 1.0 |
| Managed futures | 4 | 4.8 | 0 | 0.0 |
| Short biased | 5 | 1.0 | 0 | 0.0 |
| Multistrategy/other | 75 | 69.8 | 42 | 59.0 |
| **Total** | **298** | **206.7** | **98** | **120.2** |

* The Hedge Fund 100 list has a difference between the firm total and the fund total in AUM. The firm total is US$265.3 billion while the fund total is US$206.7 billion

*Source*: Altvest, Tuna, CSFB/Tremont, HFR, Hennessee, Institutional Investor (June 2002)

and by strategy at each month end. In addition, we deem it important to provide our stakeholders with a stress loss estimate on the entire portfolio and breakdowns by strategy and by region. Stress loss estimates provide investors with loss estimates under extreme circumstances and indicate the percentage of our capital necessary to support each of our strategies given its stress risk.

We provide profit and loss sensitivities to factor exposures to some investors to help them estimate the risk sensitivities of their entire portfolio, which includes our fund as one component. We do not provide position-level transparency on our portfolio because we do not think that this listing gives a good picture of the way we think about the risk of the portfolio and its various strategies. Investors will not be able to ascertain the dynamics of our current strategy set unless we define those dynamics for them. In addition, for competitive reasons, we do not want to disclose the contents of the portfolio. Not only would those who compete with us attempt to reverse engineer our current plans, but also others could attempt to front-run our position adjustments.

Best practice for 2003 and 2005 will be for funds to provide risk attributes and portfolio sensitivities to investors and, more likely, to their advisors, such as fund of funds managers. These advisors will also make regular visits to fund managers to assess expected payoffs and risk attributes. Portfolio optimisation will become more intertwined with risk management.

## Panel 5

## An Interview with Bill McCauley, CEO of III Offshore

III Offshore is a fixed income hedge fund (specifically high-grade fixed income) with four managers and US$2.3 billion assets.

### What kind of transparency do you offer your investors?

We provide complete transparency: our website contains monthly reposition reports. We include stress testing for the worst-case scenario for each summary position and we have over 1,000 different instruments reduced to 30 different strategies. If an investor walks into the office, he can see it all. We give investors as much information as we think they can consume without that information generating more questions than it answers. We have a one-line general explanation on our website in an attempt to avoid the unnecessary questions that result from providing too much unwanted information. This information includes the dollar value of one basis point move in the spread, how that affects each position, and

**Table 4** Summary of hedge funds covered by major commercial sources

| | CSFB/Tremont | | HFR | | Tuna | | The Hedge Fund 100 | | Altvest | | Maximum | |
|---|---|---|---|---|---|---|---|---|---|---|---|---|
| | # of Funds | AUM* | # of Funds | AUM* | # of Funds | AUM* | # of Funds | AUM* | # of Funds | AUM* | # of Funds | AUM* |
| Long/short equity | 269 | 86.7 | 341 | 42.8 | 391 | 29.9 | 81 | 48.9 | 372 | 18.3 | 391 | 86.7 |
| Event-driven | – | – | 169 | 17.0 | 185 | 21.1 | 30 | 26.1 | 91 | 16.8 | 185 | 26.1 |
| Market neutral | 119 | 17.0 | 61 | 7.4 | 155 | 11.9 | 10 | 1.1 | – | – | 155 | 17.0 |
| Fixed income | 70 | 9.3 | 84 | 10.9 | 109 | 14.9 | 18 | 7.3 | 66 | 5.0 | 109 | 14.9 |
| Convertible arbitrage | 25 | 9.5 | 64 | 7.4 | 61 | 8.3 | 25 | 12.5 | 88 | 14.8 | 88 | 14.8 |
| Global macro | 71 | 8.4 | 50 | 12.1 | 46 | 1.0 | 7 | 10.9 | 50 | 5.6 | 71 | 12.1 |
| Emerging markets | 118 | 8.0 | 107 | 4.7 | 32 | 1.0 | 5 | 1.8 | 116 | 8.2 | 118 | 8.2 |
| Managed futures | 164 | 6.5 | 45 | 2.5 | 92 | 3.1 | 3 | 4.7 | 129 | 6.6 | 164 | 6.6 |
| Merger arbitrage | – | – | 59 | 4.5 | 46 | 3.9 | – | – | 35 | 6.3 | 59 | 6.3 |
| Distressed securities | – | – | 37 | 3.2 | 46 | 4.8 | – | – | 22 | 4.2 | 46 | 4.8 |
| Short biased | 16 | 1.0 | 15 | 0.4 | 24 | 1.6 | 5 | 0.6 | 35 | 1.4 | 35 | 1.6 |
| Multistrategy/other | 21 | 10.3 | 27 | 7.3 | 17 | 7.9 | 75 | 69.8 | 17 | 5.4 | 75 | 69.8 |
| **Total** | **852** | **146.4** | **1032** | **112.9** | **1187** | **101.5** | **184** | **113.9** | **1004** | **87.2** | **1421** | **199.1** |

\* AUM = US$ billion

*Source*: Altvest, CSFB/Tremont, HFR, Tuna, Institutional Investor (June 2002)

how it affects the whole portfolio. We also include the per cent of the move, the ten-year swap equivalent of the move, and the worst-case scenario. We also tell investors what can go wrong. We then aggregate everything and show what would happen if everything moved adversely simultaneously. This includes the standard deviation relative to the performance and what percent of the capital is cash. We show on-balance sheet and off-balance sheet leverage.

We only provide this complete information to our investors and our credit officers because we believe that neither can hurt us: our credit officers are behind a Chinese wall and we trust our investors with this information. Our corporate goal is to be the most transparent fund in the industry.

**What systems do you use?**
We have our own proprietary systems.

**Do you think transparency is harmful to your strategy?**
I think it causes us to lose very little competitive edge. However, this is different for other strategies.

**Where do you think transparency is headed in the future?**
Trust is the foundation of capitalism, which is established by transparency.

## Panel 6
## An Interview with Mike Linn of Omega Partners

Omega Partners is a long/short equity fund with US$2 billion in assets. About US$400 million of their capital is institutional.

**What are your primary strategies?**
Omega sprung out of the old Goldman Sachs equity department. We place an emphasis on in-house research and individual stock selection. Our team must first approve every stock we go with. Over the years, we've developed G-10 macro and emerging markets units, focusing on liquid emerging markets and fixed income instruments. For the most part, though, we've historically made our money in the equity markets. Though the non-equity units have performed quite well in certain periods, we've been consistently profitable in stocks. We've never allocated more than 10% to the non-equity units, which is fortunate because in August 1998 our emerging markets unit blew up and dissolved. Then,

long/short equity, global macro and multi-strategy funds comprise a total of 89 funds with US$91.1 billion of AUM. CSFB/Tremont covers the greatest AUM of the commercial sources but not the largest number of funds (see Table 4). Many large hedge funds do not report their data to most of the commercial sources. For example, CMRA has identified 63 multi-strategy funds with a total of US$155 billion in AUM that do not appear in the commercial sources analysed.

To further explore the coverage of the different strategies analysed in the following chapters, CMRA prepared Tables 5 and 6, which list the coverage of each strategy by number of funds and AUM, respectively.

**Table 5** Funds listed in major sources including funds listed exclusively in The Hedge Fund 100

| Strategy | Altvest | CSFB | The Hedge Fund 100 | Tuna | HFR | Maximum | Source |
|---|---|---|---|---|---|---|---|
| Long/short equity | 372 | 269 | 81 | 391 | 341 | 391 | Tuna |
| Event-driven* | 148 | 220 | 30 | 277 | 265 | 277 | Tuna |
| Managed futures | 129 | 164 | 3 | 92 | 45 | 164 | CSFB |
| Market neutral | -- | 119 | 10 | 155 | 61 | 155 | Tuna |
| Fixed income | 66 | 70 | 21 | 109 | 84 | 109 | Tuna |
| Emerging markets | 116 | 118 | 5 | 32 | 107 | 118 | CSFB |
| Convertible arbitrage | 88 | 98 | 25 | 61 | 64 | 98 | CSFB |
| Global macro | 50 | 71 | 7 | 46 | 50 | 71 | CSFB |
| Short biased | 35 | 16 | 5 | 24 | 15 | 35 | Altvest |

*Event-driven includes distressed securities and merger arbitrage

*Source*: Altvest, CSFB/Tremont, Hennessee, HFR, Institutional Investor (June 2002), Tuna, CMRA Analysis

**Table 6** Most comprehensive source for each strategy by AUM

| Strategy | Source | Number | AUM (US$ billion) |
|---|---|---|---|
| Long/short equity | CSFB/Tremont | 269 | 86.7 |
| Event-driven | The Hedge Fund 100 | 30 | 26.0 |
| Managed futures | CSFB/Tremont | 98 | 20.5 |
| Market neutral | CSFB/Tremont | 119 | 17.0 |
| Emerging markets | Tuna | 109 | 14.9 |
| Fixed income | HFR | 50 | 12.1 |
| Convertible arbitrage | Altvest | 116 | 8.2 |
| Global macro | Altvest | 129 | 6.6 |
| Merger arbitrage | Altvest | 35 | 6.3 |
| Distressed securities | Tuna | 46 | 4.8 |
| Short biased | Hennessee | 11 | 3.0 |

*Source*: Altvest, CSFB/Tremont, Hennessee, HFR, Institutional Investor (June 2002), Tuna, CMRA Analysis

in the last few years, a large part of the macro unit has broken off to form its own fund. Now, for the most part we've stuck with our consistently profitable equity strategies. Nowadays, we're primarily long equity – about 70%. We're generally invested pretty evenly in about 70 stocks, so for us a really big equity position would never be more than 5% of the portfolio. We feel that we do a pretty good job of diversifying away a lot of the inherent market risks.

**What kind of transparency do you offer?**
We offer a tremendous amount of transparency. We'll pretty much give you anything you want upon request. We were one of the first funds to offer transparency. In the days before LTCM, transparent funds were few and far between; now you see a lot more transparency out there. But we find that very few people are asking for position-level transparency because there isn't really that much they can do with it. Instead we send out a standard report that includes VAR for normal situations, the maximum capital at risk in extreme situations when the correlation goes to one, Sharpe ratios and a bunch of other standard measures. We get the feeling that there are very few investors out there who actually know how to use transparency, so we're interested in making the report practical, in making the investor feel comfortable. When an investor sees our report it's pretty clear that we put an emphasis on risk management; once they know that, they're very rarely interested in position disclosure.

**Where do you think transparency is headed in the future?**
Since LTCM, and as the industry has become increasingly institution-alised, we've seen the demand for maximum transparency intensify. But I think now we're getting to the point where people have relaxed a little and are starting to show more of an interest in useful transparency, as opposed to maximum transparency.

## Panel 7

## An Interview with Andrew Weisman of Strativarius Capital Management, a startup global macro fund

**What are your strategies?**
We're using some third-party services in order to establish our middle and back offices for us. We feel that this arrangement makes us capable of covering all the bases with our prime broker at a minimum of expense and energy. It also allows us to quickly determine our sector and geographic concentrations.

## HOW DO VARIOUS HEDGE FUND INDICES COMPARE?

There are many differences in the way major hedge fund indices are constructed. Some principal differences are:

❏ *Selection criteria*: Decision rules determine which hedge funds are included in the index. Examples of selection criteria include length of track record, AUM, and restrictions on new investment (see Table 7).

❏ *Style classification*: How each hedge fund is assigned to a style-specific index.

❏ *Weighting*: How much weight a particular fund's return is given in the index varies. Two common weighting approaches are equally weighted and dollar-weighted based on AUM.

❏ *Rebalancing*: How and when assets are reallocated among the funds in a particular index. For example, some funds are rebalanced monthly, while others are rebalanced annually.

❏ *Investability*: Is the index directly or indirectly investable?

It is important to note that the style classifications are self-assigned and are only accurate to a limited extent. Since funds might employ a mixture of styles in their portfolios, classifying them as a single style causes a great deal of information on the fund to be lost. The effects of this problem are highlighted when one sees how divergent the returns/standard deviation profile is for constituent funds within an index.

Table 8 describes in detail how different methodologies are used by

---

**Table 7** Selection criteria for inclusion of funds in indices

| | Zurich Hedge Funds Indices | Zurich Hedge Fund Universe | HFR Hedge Fund Indices | EACM 100 | CSFB/ Tremont Hedge Fund Indices |
|---|---|---|---|---|---|
| **Classification methodology** | Quantitative, independently verifiable | Manager self classification | Manager self classification | Classified by EACM | Classified by Tremont |
| **Minimum assets** | Varies (US$25 million to US$75 million) | None | None | Not | US$10 million |
| **Minimum track record** | US$25 million for at least 2 years | None | None | Not reported | 1 year of US$500 assets |
| **Includes funds closed to new investment** | Yes | Yes | Yes | No | Yes |

*Source:* Zurich, HFR, EACM, CSFB/Tremont

---

**What kind of transparency do you plan to offer your investors?**

In our office we plan to offer pretty much anything they want. We feel that showing an investor that, as a global macro fund, we are long dollars and short yen isn't a serious threat to our performance. We plan to offer reports that break down our risk exposure by factors: industry concentrations, geographic concentrations, a breakdown and explanation of the volatility of the portfolio, and our VAR method, for example. We prefer to offer transparency in the form of processed information rather than offering a book full of positions. For a pension fund manager to take position books from multiple managers and somehow try to aggregate them and come up with a few magic numbers to summarise all the risks in a multibillion-dollar portfolio is a silly exercise; it's a bit like drinking from a fire hose. There's just too much information to process, and even if you have the time and resources, the information is going to be stale by the time you understand it. We prefer to offer our risk information in a more tractable format, broken down by various concentrations and outlining the key risks. Investors can get all this detailed information through our middle and back offices.

some commercial sources in constructing their indices. Most indices are calculated on an equally weighted basis while the CSFB/Tremont style indices use an asset-weighted approach. All of the sources rebalance their indices at fixed time intervals, either monthly or annually, but different indices rebalance at different frequencies.

However, the returns reported by indices using seemingly similar benchmarks could be dramatically different (see Table 9). In 2001, for example, there was a 22.4 difference between Tuna's emerging market index and Altvest's emerging market index (21.7 vs 0.7). Also, for the

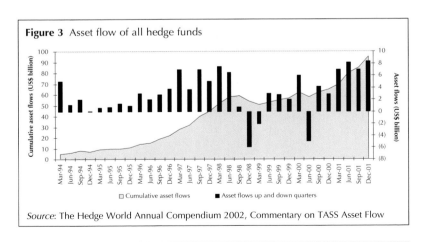

**Figure 3** Asset flow of all hedge funds

*Source*: The Hedge World Annual Compendium 2002, Commentary on TASS Asset Flow

**Table 8** Index construction methods used by suppliers of hedge fund data

| | Overview | Style classification | Weighting | Rebalancing | Gross or net data |
|---|---|---|---|---|---|
| Credit Suisse First Boston/Tremont (CSFB/Tremont) | Index of 339 hedge funds representing US$100 billion in assets. Primary selection criterion is at least US$10 million under management with audited results. If a fund liquidates, its performance remains in the index until the fund becomes inactive to minimise survivorship bias. The index has data going back to 1994. | Nine categories: convertible arbitrage, dedicated short biased, emerging markets, equity market neutral, event-driven, fixed-income arbitrage, global macro, long/short equity and managed futures. | Funds are included on an asset-weighted basis and added or removed on a quarterly basis. | Monthly | All performance figures are net of fees. |
| Evaluation Associates Capital Management Index (EACM100) | Index of 100 funds selected on a discretionary basis. Managers must agree to participate in the index and be willing to accept new assets. They may depart or be replaced at any time. Names of individual managers are not disclosed and EACM disseminates only information on the performance of the index. Launched in 1996 but has data going back to 1990. | Five categories: relative value, event-driven, equity hedge, global asset allocators, and short selling and 13 sub-categories. | Equally weighted by manager. | Annually | All performance figures are net of fees. |
| Hedge Fund Research Index (HFRI) | With more than 1,000 funds, this composite is made up of six daily priced subindices and is one of the largest and most inclusive hedge fund benchmarks. It represents more than US$260 billion of assets and a fund must have at least US$5 million to be included. Launched in 1994, it has information dating back to 1990. | Various sub-indices: convertible bond, equity hedge, event-driven, merger arbitrage, macro, distressed securities, emerging markets, equity market neutral, fixed income, market timing, relative value arbitrage, sector specific, fund of funds, and a weighted composite index. HFR selects only those funds that it views as pure to style. | HFR offers two versions of its aggregate index – equally weighted and AUM-weighted versions. | Monthly | All performance figures are net of fees. |
| Zurich Capital Markets - formerly Managed Account Reports (MAR) | Broad-based index based on a database of 1,500 funds. Its primary criteria for selection are a minimum length track record (at least two years for funds launched prior to January 1998, three years for all funds commencing after that date), a minimum level of assets determined by its particular style of strategy, and a style pure approach to investment. | Four categories: relative value, event-driven, hedged equity, and macro. Each fund is also assigned to one of 10 subgroups, such as merger arbitrage, distressed securities, or convertible hedging. | Equally weighted. | Every three months with a one-month lag. | All performance figures are net of fees. |

*Source:* CSFB/Tremont, Evaluation Associates, Hedge Fund Research Inc. and Managed Account Reports

1997–2001 period, there was an 11.2 difference between Tuna's long/short equity index and Hennessee's long/short equity index (23.0 vs 11.8).

## HOW MUCH IS INVESTED IN HEDGE FUNDS?

The cumulative asset inflow between March 1994 and the end of 2001 was approximately US$87.6 billion (see Figure 3). Over the 1997–2001 period, the overall growth of assets in all hedge fund strategies was 35.1%.

## WHO INVESTS IN HEDGE FUNDS?

As Table 10 indicates, individuals and family offices are currently the largest group of investors in hedge funds but institutional investment is growing. Figure 4 shows how investment in hedge funds grew relative to investment in other alternatives.

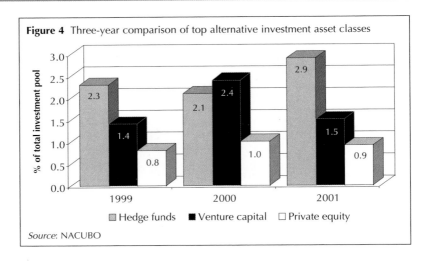

**Figure 4** Three-year comparison of top alternative investment asset classes

*Source*: NACUBO

**Table 9** Maximum differences between returns reported for hedge
fund strategies by different indices

|  | 1997 | 1998 | 1999 | 2000 | 2001 | 1997–2001 |
|---|---|---|---|---|---|---|
| Long/short equity | 13.2 | 18.4 | 15.4 | 14.9 | 8.6 | 11.2 |
| Market neutral | 7.7 | 12.2 | 20.5 | 19.0 | 3.2 | 10.8 |
| Managed futures | 19.8 | 10.4 | 13.3 | 14.4 | 15.5 | 10.7 |
| Emerging markets | 25.5 | 13.9 | 28.0 | 8.3 | 22.4 | 10.6 |
| Global macro | 19.9 | 23.6 | 23.2 | 10.5 | 19.5 | 10.4 |
| Event-driven | 7.6 | 9.9 | 8.2 | 8.6 | 5.2 | 7.3 |
| Short biased | (2.1) | (1.3) | (1.5) | 25.2 | 9.0 | 5.4 |
| Merger arbitrage | 7.0 | 3.7 | 6.2 | 4.7 | 3.7 | 5.0 |
| Distressed securities | 7.0 | 9.5 | 9.0 | 8.0 | 7.7 | 4.4 |
| Convertible arbitrage | 7.2 | 12.2 | 3.6 | 20.3 | 5.0 | 3.4 |

*Source*: Altvest, Tuna, HFR, CSFB/Tremont, Hennessee, EACM, CMRA Research

## WHICH ARE THE MOST POPULAR HEDGE FUND STRATEGIES?

In 2001, US$31.1 billion of net assets flowed into hedge funds with event-driven funds receiving the largest new allocation (see Table 11). The cumulative asset flow in 2001 can be classified into three groups. The first is composed of event-driven, long/short equity and convertible arbitrage; these three strategies received a combined inflow of US$23.3 billion of assets. The second group is composed of market neutral, fixed income and managed futures; these three strategies received an overall inflow of US$6.6 billion. The last group includes the funds in emerging markets, global macro and short biased, which received an inflow of only US$0.7 billion.

As shown in Table 12, since 1994, hedge fund assets have grown from at

**Table 10** Investors in hedge funds (%)

| | Individuals and family offices | Pensions and retirement | Endowments and foundations | Funds of funds | Corporations |
|---|---|---|---|---|---|
| Convertible arbitrage | 47 | 9 | 2 | 18 | 24 |
| Distressed | 42 | 4 | 4 | 32 | 18 |
| Emerging markets | 40 | 12 | 19 | 22 | 8 |
| Europe | 59 | 5 | 2 | 23 | 11 |
| Event-driven | 53 | 6 | 11 | 17 | 14 |
| Financial equities | 61 | 8 | 4 | 20 | 8 |
| Fixed income | 64 | 3 | 7 | 21 | 5 |
| Growth | 32 | 0 | 6 | 47 | 15 |
| Healthcare | 48 | 17 | 7 | 20 | 8 |
| International | 80 | 8 | 3 | 3 | 5 |
| Macro | 69 | 11 | 6 | 12 | 2 |
| Market neutral | 35 | 11 | 11 | 24 | 19 |
| Merger arbitrage | 45 | 8 | 4 | 37 | 6 |
| Multiple arbitrage | 37 | 4 | 7 | 35 | 17 |
| Opportunistic | 58 | 6 | 9 | 15 | 11 |
| Pacific Rim | 31 | 3 | 4 | 56 | 6 |
| Technology | 80 | 6 | 1 | 12 | 1 |
| Value | 58 | 14 | 7 | 10 | 11 |
| 2000 Survey universe total | 53 | 9 | 7 | 20 | 11 |

*Source*: Hennessee Hedge Fund Survey (January 2000)

least US$57.1 billion to US$261.3 billion. While overall hedge fund assets have increased by 24.3% since 1994, the big winners were the long/short equity and event-driven strategies. Other strategies with double-digit growth in assets were convertible arbitrage and market neutral, closely followed by fixed income.

## HOW HAVE DRAWDOWNS AFFECTED THE VARIOUS HEDGE FUND STYLES?

The short biased and emerging market strategies were tied for the maximum drawdown in the 1997–2001 period at −36.6% (see Table 13).

Once again, as Table 14 illustrates, the quality and completeness of the

**Table 11** Net asset flows by strategy in 2001

| Strategy | (US$ billion) |
|---|---|
| Event-driven | 8.3 |
| Long/short equity | 7.9 |
| Convertible arbitrage | 7.1 |
| Equity market neutral | 3.3 |
| Fixed-income arbitrage | 2.1 |
| Managed futures | 1.2 |
| Emerging markets | 0.6 |
| Other | 0.4 |
| Global macro | 0.1 |
| Short biased | – |
| All funds | 31.0 |

*Source*: Hedge World Annual Compendium 2002

**Table 12** Total asset history December 2001 and December 1994 (US$ billion)

| | December 2001 | December 1994 |
|---|---|---|
| Long/short equity | 115.8 | 15.0 |
| Event-driven | 51.2 | 7.2 |
| Global macro | 24.1 | 18.2 |
| Convertible arbitrage | 20.7 | 0.8 |
| Equity market neutral | 17.6 | 1.0 |
| Fixed-income arbitrage | 14.2 | 3.8 |
| Emerging markets | 8.1 | 7.1 |
| Managed futures | 7.7 | 3.6 |
| Other | 1.2 | 0.2 |
| Short biased | 0.7 | 0.2 |
| **All funds** | **261.3** | **57.1** |

*Source*: Hedge World Annual Compendium 2002

data are suspect. Based on what is available in commercial sources, emerging markets demonstrated the widest gap between the lowest reported maximum drawdown of –7.3% and the highest reported maximum drawdown of –36.6%.

## WHAT IS THE LEVERAGE USED BY THE VARIOUS HEDGE FUND STYLES?

Leverage is defined in many ways and the available data are especially limited and inaccurate. (See Chapter 2 for a further discussion of leverage.) Using the best information available, convertible arbitrage showed the highest average leverage of 13.0 in 2002. And, although it had funds with maximum leverage as high as 21.0, global macro's average leverage was only 1.9 (see Table 15). Market neutral appears to be the most levered hedge fund strategy, with more than 50% using a leverage ≥ 2.0 (see Figure 5).

Looking at Altvest's leverage data for the 1997–2001 period given in

**Table 13** Maximum drawdowns by strategy and source, 1997–2001

| Strategy | Source | Maximum drawdown (%) |
|---|---|---|
| Market neutral | Hennessee | (4.6) |
| Merger arbitrage | HFR | (6.2) |
| Managed futures | CSFB | (8.6) |
| Convertible arbitrage | CSFB | (12.0) |
| Event-driven | CSFB | (14.4) |
| Distressed | Hennessee | (15.0) |
| Long/short equity | CSFB | (16.4) |
| Fixed income | HFR | (20.8) |
| Global macro | CSFB | (21.0) |
| Short selling | Altvest/CMRA | (36.6) |
| Emerging markets | HFR | (36.6) |

*Source*: Altvest, CSFB/Tremont, EACM, Hennessee, HFR, Tuna, CMRA Analysis

**Table 14** Difference between maximum drawdowns reported by any source for strategies in 1997–2001

| Style | Drawdown from any source (%) | | |
|---|---|---|---|
| | Lowest | Highest | Difference |
| Emerging markets | (7.3) | (36.6) | 29.3 |
| Global macro | (2.8) | (21.0) | 18.2 |
| Fixed income | (4.1) | (20.8) | 16.8 |
| Long/short equity | (2.9) | (16.4) | 13.6 |
| Short selling | (23.1) | (36.6) | 13.5 |
| Convertible arbitrage | (4.7) | (12.0) | 7.4 |
| Distressed | (9.6) | (15.0) | 5.5 |
| Event-driven | (9.5) | (14.4) | 4.9 |
| Market neutral | (1.2) | (4.6) | 3.4 |
| Managed futures | (5.9) | (8.6) | 2.7 |
| Merger arbitrage | (4.8) | (6.2) | 1.5 |

*Source*: Altvest, CSFB/Tremont, EACM, HFR, Tuna, CMRA Analysis

Table 16, managed futures, convertible arbitrage and global macro have the highest average historical leverage across all the strategies. At the other end of the leverage spectrum, we find short biased/short selling, funds of funds, distressed securities, emerging markets and event-driven. Looking at the most heavily levered funds (first quartile leverage by strategy), as will be shown in the following section, managed futures and convertible

**Table 15** Financial leverage of hedge funds in 2002

| Strategy | Minimum | Average | Maximum |
|---|---|---|---|
| Convertible arbitrage | 1.0 | 3.7 | 13.0 |
| Managed futures | 0.1 | 2.9 | 10.0 |
| Fixed income | 0.0 | 2.1 | 15.0 |
| Global macro | 1.0 | 1.9 | 21.0 |
| Long/short equity | 1.0 | 1.8 | 10.0 |
| Market neutral | 1.0 | 1.7 | 12.0 |
| Merger arbitrage | 0.8 | 1.5 | 2.5 |
| Emerging markets | 1.0 | 1.4 | 3.0 |
| Event-driven | 0.9 | 1.4 | 3.0 |
| Short biased | 1.0 | 1.3 | 2.0 |
| Distressed securities | 1.0 | 1.3 | 2.5 |

*Note*: A leverage of 1 means 100% leverage of that debt=100% of assets

*Source*: Altvest, CMRA Analysis

arbitrage average higher leverage than the other strategies analysed. In addition, long/short equity showed the greatest average difference between first and fourth quartile leverage of any style for which Altvest reported data. Lastly, managed futures and convertible arbitrage had the highest average five-year leverage.

Statistical arbitrage shows the greatest difference between five-year returns on a levered vs delevered basis (see Table 17), while the greatest one-year difference is seen in the returns of fixed income funds (see Table 18).

## WHAT ARE THE RELATIVE PERFORMANCE CHARACTERISTICS OF VARIOUS HEDGE FUND STYLES?

Risk/return measures can provide a very different view of hedge fund performance than return-only measures. They can also vary significantly depending on how risk is defined. Despite its limitations, we have used the Sharpe ratio because it is widely available, but the reader should keep in mind the manipulability of this indicator and its limited definition of "risk". Comparative return, volatility and Sharpe ratio data for 1994–2001 are given in Table 19.

Convertible arbitrage ranked only 10 on a five-year (1997–2001) performance basis, but was first on a risk/return basis due to its relatively low

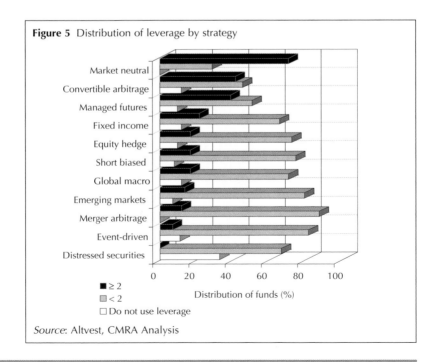

**Figure 5** Distribution of leverage by strategy

Market neutral
Convertible arbitrage
Managed futures
Fixed income
Equity hedge
Short biased
Global macro
Emerging markets
Merger arbitrage
Event-driven
Distressed securities

0   20   40   60   80   100

■ ≥ 2
□ < 2
□ Do not use leverage

Distribution of funds (%)

*Source*: Altvest, CMRA Analysis

**Table 16** Historical financial leverage of hedge funds, 1997–2001

| Strategies | 1997 | 1998 | 1999 | 2000 | 2001 | 1997–2001 Average | Maximum | Minimum |
|---|---|---|---|---|---|---|---|---|
| Managed futures | 2.8 | 3.1 | 2.5 | 2.9 | 2.8 | 2.8 | 3.1 | 2.5 |
| Convertible arbitrage | 2.7 | 3.0 | 2.3 | 2.3 | 2.5 | 2.6 | 3.0 | 2.3 |
| Global macro | 1.9 | 2.2 | 1.7 | 2.1 | 2.2 | 2.0 | 2.2 | 1.7 |
| Merger arbitrage | 1.7 | 2.0 | 1.6 | 2.0 | 1.7 | 1.8 | 2.0 | 1.6 |
| Statistical arbitrage | 1.7 | 1.8 | 1.5 | 1.5 | 1.5 | 1.6 | 1.8 | 1.5 |
| Fixed income | 1.3 | 2.0 | 0.2 | 2.0 | 2.0 | 1.5 | 2.0 | 0.2 |
| Long/short equity | 1.3 | 1.5 | 1.1 | 1.5 | 1.3 | 1.3 | 1.5 | 1.1 |
| Fixed-income arbitrage | 1.3 | 2.2 | 0.9 | 0.9 | 1.0 | 1.3 | 2.2 | 0.9 |
| Sector | 1.3 | 1.6 | 1.0 | 1.0 | 1.0 | 1.2 | 1.6 | 1.0 |
| Distressed securities | 1.1 | 1.4 | 0.9 | 1.4 | 1.0 | 1.2 | 1.4 | 0.9 |
| Event-driven | 1.1 | 1.2 | 1.0 | 1.0 | 1.1 | 1.1 | 1.2 | 1.0 |
| Emerging markets | 1.0 | 1.1 | 0.9 | 1.0 | 1.0 | 1.0 | 1.1 | 0.9 |
| Fund of funds | 0.8 | 1.0 | 0.6 | 1.0 | 0.7 | 0.8 | 1.0 | 0.6 |
| Short biased | 0.3 | 0.6 | 0.1 | 0.3 | 0.1 | 0.3 | 0.6 | 0.1 |
| Maximum | 2.8 | 3.1 | 2.5 | 2.9 | 2.8 | 2.8 | 3.1 | 2.5 |
| Minimum | 0.3 | 0.6 | 0.1 | 0.3 | 0.1 | 0.3 | 0.6 | 0.1 |
| Average | 1.4 | 1.7 | 1.1 | 1.4 | 1.4 | 1.4 | 1.7 | 1.1 |

*Source*: Altvest, CMRA Analysis

**Table 17** Summary of levered and delevered performance of hedge fund strategies, 1997–2001 (%)

| | Maximum return | Minimum return | Average return | Maximum delevered return | Minimum delevered return | Average delevered return | Difference in returns |
|---|---|---|---|---|---|---|---|
| Statistical arbitrage | 29.3 | 1.2 | 16.9 | 18.9 | 0.3 | 7.1 | 9.8 |
| Emerging markets | 37.3 | (4.4) | 16.9 | 18.4 | (1.9) | 8.8 | 8.0 |
| Global macro | 51.9 | 1.2 | 16.8 | 29.5 | 0.6 | 8.9 | 7.9 |
| Merger arbitrage | 35.0 | 1.4 | 14.7 | 18.7 | 0.5 | 7.0 | 7.7 |
| Long/short equity | 38.5 | 1.3 | 14.0 | 19.5 | 0.2 | 6.3 | 7.7 |
| Event-driven | 29.3 | (2.6) | 14.7 | 21.9 | (1.3) | 8.3 | 6.5 |
| Convertible arbitrage | 17.0 | 1.4 | 10.6 | 9.3 | 0.4 | 4.2 | 6.4 |
| Managed futures | 29.3 | (4.5) | 10.5 | 14.9 | (0.8) | 4.2 | 6.3 |
| Fixed income | 17.5 | 4.4 | 9.6 | 10.3 | 0.5 | 4.8 | 4.8 |
| Short selling | 38.9 | (4.6) | 13.7 | 25.5 | (1.0) | 9.3 | 4.4 |

*Source*: Altvest, CMRA Analysis

standard deviation. By the latter measure, short selling appeared to fare the worst. On a five-year return basis, the highest-returning fund in a commercial source was a global macro fund that returned 51.9%. In 2001, the highest-returning fund in a commercial source was a fixed income fund that returned an incredible 174.5%.

Overall, the top 10 funds reporting to commercial sources had an

**Table 18** Summary of levered and delevered performance of hedge fund strategies in 2001 (%)

| | Maximum return | Minimum return | Average return | Maximum delevered return | Minimum delevered return | Average delevered return | Difference in returns |
|---|---|---|---|---|---|---|---|
| Fixed income | 174.5 | (9.6) | 16.6 | 58.2 | (4.8) | 6.1 | 10.5 |
| Convertible arbitrage | 33.5 | (23.2) | 11.7 | 11.7 | (0.9) | 3.2 | 8.5 |
| Managed futures | 99.4 | (67.2) | 6.1 | 49.7 | (18.3) | 1.5 | 4.6 |
| Event-driven | 47.1 | (24.5) | 7.7 | 28.3 | (12.2) | 3.7 | 4.0 |
| Long/short equity | 45.0 | (25.6) | 6.1 | 20.5 | (18.2) | 2.2 | 4.0 |
| Global macro | 139.0 | (64.0) | 5.7 | 69.5 | (48.5) | 2.2 | 3.5 |
| Emerging markets | 49.2 | (41.6) | 5.5 | 25.9 | (17.9) | 2.4 | 3.1 |
| Statistical arbitrage | 17.8 | (12.1) | 4.3 | 8.9 | (3.3) | 1.8 | 2.6 |
| Merger arbitrage | 12.4 | (2.9) | 3.4 | 4.1 | (1.3) | 1.3 | 2.1 |
| Short selling | 15.8 | (44.3) | 0.4 | 10.4 | (20.2) | 0.7 | (0.4) |

*Note*: No data was available for market neutral

*Source*: Altvest, CMRA Analysis

**Table 19** Returns, volatilities and Sharpe ratios of strategies, 1994–2001

| Style | CMRA returns 1994–2001 | Standard deviation 1994–2001 | Sharpe ratio |
|---|---|---|---|
| Long/short equity | 17.7 | 9.7 | 1.2 |
| Equity market neutral | 13.6 | 3.4 | 2.7 |
| Event-driven | 13.0 | 8.2 | 0.9 |
| Merger arbitrage | 12.7 | 3.5 | 2.1 |
| Distressed securities | 12.7 | 6.9 | 1.1 |
| Fixed income | 12.6 | 11.7 | 0.6 |
| Convertible arbitrage | 10.9 | 2.6 | 2.2 |
| Fixed income: high yield | 9.9 | 5.1 | 0.9 |
| Macro | 9.4 | 8.9 | 0.5 |
| Emerging markets | 7.5 | 23.0 | 0.1 |
| Short selling | (1.1) | 18.3 | (0.3) |

*Source*: Altvest, CMRA Analysis

average five-year return of 40.5%, while the bottom 10 had a five-year return of –15.9% (see Table 20).

Using the S&P 500 Index as a reference for calculating information ratios, we can see in Figure 6 that the long/short equity strategy outperformed the other strategies during the boom period. During the bust period, however, the leading strategies were event-driven and convertible arbitrage. We will show that over the 1997–2001 period, the top quartile of long/short equity funds outperformed the top quartiles of the other strategies on both an equally weighted and an AUM-weighted basis.

Table 21 shows the concentration of funds per strategy that account for

60% of AUM. There are three groups, the first of which includes the highly concentrated strategies where less than 10% of the funds comprise 60% of the assets. This group consists of long/short equity and market neutral. The second group includes the strategies where 10%–15% of the funds account for 60% of the assets. It consists of event-driven, global macro, fixed income, managed futures and distressed securities. The third group includes those strategies for which more than 15% of the funds cover 60% of the assets. This group, with the lowest concentration of assets, consists of emerging markets, short biased and convertible arbitrage.

**Table 20**  Best and worst performers: five-year net compound annual returns January 1, 1997–December 31, 2001 (%)

| | |
|---|---|
| Top 10 | 40.5 |
| Top 10% | 30.0 |
| Top 25% | 22.9 |
| Bottom 25% | 1.2 |
| Bottom 10% | (15.9) |
| Bottom 20 | (10.4) |

*Source*: Altest, CSFB/Tremont, HFR, Tuna, CMRA Analysis

As the analyses in the nine strategy chapters that follow will show, the largest funds (the top quartile of funds by AUM) outperformed smaller funds in fixed income, long/short equity, managed futures, market neutral, emerging markets and short biased on both an equally weighted and an AUM-weighted basis. However, the largest funds underperformed smaller funds on both bases in the event-driven, convertible arbitrage,

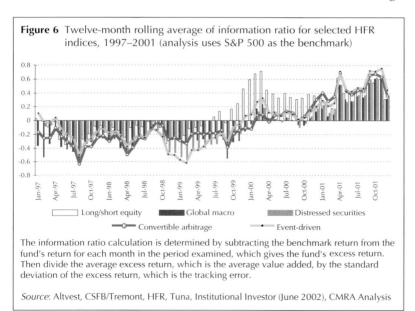

**Figure 6**  Twelve-month rolling average of information ratio for selected HFR indices, 1997–2001 (analysis uses S&P 500 as the benchmark)

Long/short equity   Global macro   Distressed securities
Convertible arbitrage   Event-driven

The information ratio calculation is determined by subtracting the benchmark return from the fund's return for each month in the period examined, which gives the fund's excess return. Then divide the average excess return, which is the average value added, by the standard deviation of the excess return, which is the tracking error.

*Source*: Altvest, CSFB/Tremont, HFR, Tuna, Institutional Investor (June 2002), CMRA Analysis

**Table 21** Distribution of AUM across strategies as of December 2001

| Strategy | Number of funds that represent 60% of AUM | % of total funds that represent 60% of AUM | Total AUM (US$ billion) |
|---|---|---|---|
| Short biased | 5 | 23.8 | 1.9 |
| Convertible arbitrage | 10 | 20.0 | 10.2 |
| Emerging markets | 5 | 17.2 | 2.8 |
| Merger arbitrage | 10 | 16.1 | 4.5 |
| Event-driven | 10 | 14.7 | 11.1 |
| Global macro | 6 | 13.6 | 5.4 |
| Fixed income | 14 | 12.2 | 21.0 |
| Managed futures | 13 | 11.3 | 6.6 |
| Distressed securities | 4 | 11.1 | 3.2 |
| Market neutral | 6 | 6.8 | 8.8 |
| Long/short equity | 34 | 8.9 | 18.3 |

*Source*: Altvest, CSFB/Tremont, HFR, Tuna, CMRA Analysis

merger arbitrage and global macro strategies. Larger distressed funds outperformed smaller funds on an equally weighted basis but underperformed them on an AUM-weighted basis. Again, we urge you to consider the quality of the data before you change your investment strategy!

The index returns reported by different sources can differ dramatically. On a five-year basis, the difference between the highest and lowest returns reported was greatest for short biased funds at 15.4%. As shown in Table 22, short biased funds also showed the largest discrepancies between data sources when the differences between the highest and lowest reported returns are given as a percentage of the average reported return for the strategy. Over the 1997–2001 period, long/short equity demonstrated the highest performance but also the third highest standard deviation.

Even when onshore and offshore funds are intended to track one another, differences in drawdowns and inflows can create different returns. Over the 1994–2000 period, merger arbitrage indices had the highest information ratio and market neutral indices exhibited the greatest discrepancy between onshore and offshore results (see Figure 7). This, of course, again raises a question of data quality.

### HOW DO HEDGE FUNDS CORRELATE WITH STOCKS AND BONDS?

Here again, incomplete and inaccurate data is a serious problem for those trying to analyse hedge fund performance. For example, if we look at only the 65 hedge funds in Altvest with data going back to January 1, 1994, we can conclude that assets in hedge funds have fallen by 1.2%. Whereas, if we look at all the Altvest funds we can conclude that there was a growth of 9.8% (see Table 23).

Analysing the returns of the same 65 Altvest funds we can conclude that their average performance was 8.2%, while the 224 funds with data

**Table 22**  Maximum difference in fund index returns across sources,
1997–2001 (%)

| | 1997 | 1998 | 1999 | 2000 | 2001 | Five-year return difference |
|---|---|---|---|---|---|---|
| Short biased | 12.9 | 36.2 | 39.6 | 25.1 | 22.7 | 15.4 |
| Long/short equity | 13.2 | 18.4 | 15.4 | 10.5 | 8.6 | 11.2 |
| Market neutral | 7.7 | 12.2 | 20.5 | 19.0 | 3.2 | 10.8 |
| Managed futures | 19.8 | 10.4 | 13.3 | 4.3 | 15.5 | 10.7 |
| Emerging markets | 25.5 | 13.9 | 53.8 | 8.3 | 22.4 | 10.6 |
| Global macro | 19.9 | 23.6 | 23.2 | 12.5 | 19.5 | 10.4 |
| Fixed income | 8.2 | 23.1 | 6.3 | 14.8 | 3.1 | 7.8 |
| Event-driven | 7.6 | 9.9 | 8.2 | 8.6 | 5.2 | 7.3 |
| Merger arbitrage | 7.0 | 3.7 | 6.2 | 4.7 | 3.7 | 5.0 |
| Distressed securities | 7.0 | 9.5 | 9.0 | 8.0 | 7.7 | 4.4 |
| Convertible arbitrage | 7.2 | 12.2 | 3.6 | 20.3 | 5.0 | 3.4 |

*Source*: Altvest, Tuna, HFR, CSFB/Tremont, Hennessee, EACM

between 1994 and 1998 turned in a better performance of 11.0%, and the
total Altvest funds returned 10.4% (see Table 24).

Looking at the correlations of the different market indices with the S&P
500 Index given in Table 25, we see that distressed securities and convertible arbitrage both have a low correlation with the index, while event-
driven has a moderately high correlation and equity hedge and merger
arbitrage both have medium correlation with the S&P 500.

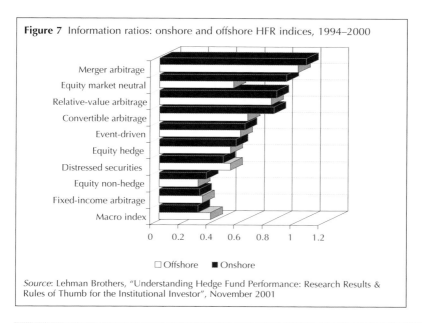

**Figure 7**  Information ratios: onshore and offshore HFR indices, 1994–2000

*Source*: Lehman Brothers, "Understanding Hedge Fund Performance: Research Results &
Rules of Thumb for the Institutional Investor", November 2001

**Table 23** Annualised increases in assets of funds in Altvest, 1994–2001

| Funds with data as of: | Number of funds | Increase (%) |
|---|---|---|
| 01/01/1994 | 65 | (1.2) |
| 31/12/1997 (but not in 01/01/1994) | 224 | 14.2 |
| **Total** | **289** | **9.8** |

*Source*: Altvest, CMRA Analysis

### Correlation with the Lehman Aggregate Composite Bond Index (LCBI)

None of the hedge styles analysed has a strong correlation with the LCBI. Furthermore, correlations change drastically from one year to the next. Note 1998, the year of the Asian crisis and the Russian/LTCM crisis; for many of the strategies, the correlations seem to flip between negative and positive, as shown in Table 26.

### Correlation with the S&P 500 Index

Changes in correlation from one year to the next with the S&P 500 Index do not seem to be as large as the changes in correlation with the LCBI (see Table 27). Global macro and emerging market funds have the highest

**Table 24** Annualised returns of funds in Altvest, 1994–2001

| Funds with data as of: | Number of funds | Return (%) |
|---|---|---|
| 01/01/1994 | 65 | 8.2 |
| 31/12/1997 (but not in 01/01/1994) | 224 | 11.0 |
| **Total** | **289** | **10.4** |

*Source*: Altvest, CMRA Analysis

**Table 25** Correlations between strategy indices and S&P 500 Index

| Strategy | S&P 500 | Lehman Brothers Aggregate Bond Index |
|---|---|---|
| Event-driven | Moderately high | Negative |
| Hedge equity | Mid-level | Negative |
| Merger arbitrage | Mid-level | Negative |
| Distressed securities | Low | Negative |
| Convertible arbitrage | Low | Negative |

*Source*: Zurich Hedge Indices

correlations with the S&P 500. This is partly due to the tendency of global stock markets to follow the US markets. Managed futures is among the least correlated; for this reason, the strategy is commonly preferred by managers to diversify their portfolios.

## WHAT ARE THE LIQUIDITY CHARACTERISTICS OF VARIOUS HEDGE FUND STYLES?

Liquidity is a key risk factor when evaluating hedge funds. As the matrix in Figure 8 shows, different instruments provide the investor with different liquidity properties as well as different correlations to the equity market. As it is discussed in the following strategy chapters, each of the

**Table 26** Rolling correlations with Lehman Aggregate Bond Index, 1997–2001 (%)

| Strategy | 1997 | 1998 | 1999 | 2000 | 2001 | 1997–2001 |
|---|---|---|---|---|---|---|
| Managed futures | 46 | 63 | (30) | 31 | 39 | 46 |
| Emerging markets | 62 | 58 | 18 | 26 | (84) | 35 |
| Event-driven | 57 | (62) | 24 | 30 | 9 | 12 |
| Distressed securities | 40 | (61) | 23 | 17 | 18 | 7 |
| Long/short equity | 60 | (51) | 4 | 45 | (25) | 7 |
| Global macro | 54 | (50) | 6 | 45 | (41) | 3 |
| Merger arbitrage | 23 | (55) | 9 | 8 | 20 | 1 |
| Market neutral | 0 | 0 | 0 | 0 | 0 | 0 |
| Short biased | 0 | 0 | 0 | 0 | 0 | 0 |
| Convertible arbitrage | 0 | 0 | 0 | 0 | 0 | 0 |
| Fixed income | (47) | 48 | (14) | (44) | 30 | (5) |

*Source*: Altvest, CSFB/Tremont, HFR, Tuna, CMRA Analysis

**Table 27** Rolling correlations with S&P 500 Index, 1997–2001 (%)

| Strategy | 1997 | 1998 | 1999 | 2000 | 2001 | 1997–2001 |
|---|---|---|---|---|---|---|
| Global macro | 80 | 88 | 63 | 53 | 76 | 72 |
| Emerging markets | 80 | 87 | 63 | 53 | 76 | 69 |
| Long/short equity | 68 | 84 | 55 | 68 | 72 | 61 |
| Event-driven | 66 | 90 | 57 | 32 | 56 | 60 |
| Merger arbitrage | 46 | 95 | 39 | 10 | 45 | 47 |
| Fixed income | 73 | 35 | 53 | 24 | 65 | 40 |
| Market neutral | 62 | 58 | 18 | 26 | (84) | 35 |
| Distressed securities | 62 | 63 | 50 | 5 | (3) | 35 |
| Convertible arbitrage | 35 | 54 | 43 | 24 | 35 | 35 |
| Managed futures | 64 | (63) | 0 | (3) | (60) | (12) |
| Short biased | (71) | (98) | (71) | (54) | (94) | (78) |

*Source*: Altvest, CSFB/Tremont, HFR, Tuna, CMRA Analysis

different asset classes provides the investor with different diversification opportunities.

## HOW DO VARIOUS HEDGE FUND STYLES PERFORM DURING STRESS PERIODS?

In times of crisis, the composition of an "optimal" portfolio would be quite different from those optimised to perform well in normal times. However, there are some similarities: market neutral and equity hedge funds seem to be the most common haven for crisis-optimal portfolios. Also, the "optimal" allocations vary sharply from one crisis situation to another.

Understanding the behaviour of funds in stressed and non-stressed environments is crucial because, as we know but frequently forget, correlations change dramatically in times of stress and we seem to have a "once-in-a-lifetime" event every few years. Different strategies behave differently under different stress scenarios. Table 28 shows the strategies that performed best and worst in February 1994 when the Federal Reserve surprised the markets by raising interest rates. Although relative-value arbitrage was the best performer during this event, it ranked 14 of 17 during the Russian/LTCM crisis in 1998. Further comparison of strategy performance during stress periods reveals that convertible arbitrage performed poorly during the 1994 and 1998 events, but ranked first during

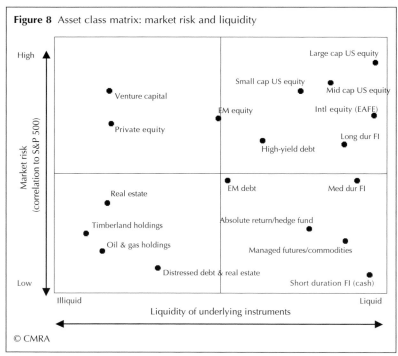

**Figure 8** Asset class matrix: market risk and liquidity

© CMRA

the tech crash of 2000 and the events of September 11, 2001.

On average, market neutral and convertible arbitrage performed the best across the four crises selected. However, convertible arbitrage was one of three strategies with differences greater than seven points between their best and worst performances across these crises.

**Table 28** Best and worst performers in selected crisis periods

| Best | Worst |
|------|-------|
| Relative-value arbitrage | Macro |
| Equity market neutral | Convertible arbitrage |
| High yield | Distressed |

*Source*: CMRA Analysis

Bearing in mind once again the limitations of the Sharpe ratio, the global macro and emerging markets strategies had the lowest average Sharpe ratios during the four crisis periods. The best Sharpe ratio indicators were those of the convertible arbitrage, event-driven and market neutral strategies. The largest differences between maximum and minimum Sharpe ratios across the four periods were exhibited by the relative-value arbitrage, convertible arbitrage and distressed securities strategies (see Table 29).

On a performance basis, only two strategies outperformed the S&P 500 Index during the January 1997–June 2000 boom period: equity hedge and equity non-hedge. In contrast, short biased, which lost 11% in the boom period, recovered significantly during the June 2000– December 2001 bust period with a performance of 22.1% (the highest of all the strategies

**Table 29** Sharpe ratios during periods of stress

| Style | Fed interest rate hike | Russian/ LTCM crisis | Tech crash | September 11 | Average of distressed periods | Maximum– minimum |
|-------|------------------------|----------------------|------------|--------------|-------------------------------|------------------|
| Lehman Aggregate Bond Composite Index | (2.8) | 1.0 | 3.1 | 0.5 | 0.4 | 5.9 |
| Convertible arbitrage | (2.1) | (1.3) | 2.5 | 3.6 | 0.7 | 5.7 |
| Distressed securities | (3.5) | (1.3) | 0.8 | 1.0 | (0.8) | 4.5 |
| Short selling | 3.4 | (0.3) | 1.1 | 0.3 | 1.1 | 3.7 |
| Event-driven | (2.6) | (1.0) | 0.3 | 0.6 | (0.7) | 3.2 |
| Macro | (2.7) | (0.6) | (1.4) | (0.0) | (1.2) | 2.7 |
| Merger arbitrage | (1.1) | (0.4) | 1.1 | (0.5) | (0.2) | 2.2 |
| Equity market neutral | 1.7 | 0.0 | 2.0 | 1.8 | 1.4 | 2.0 |
| S&P 500 Index | (1.6) | 0.0 | (1.7) | (0.4) | (0.9) | 1.7 |
| Emerging markets | (1.0) | (0.4) | (1.5) | 0.1 | (0.7) | 1.6 |
| Long/short equity | (1.3) | (0.1) | (1.3) | 0.2 | (0.6) | 1.5 |
| Fund of funds index | (1.1) | 0.0 | (1.3) | 0.2 | (0.5) | 1.5 |
| Fixed income | 1.5 | 0.5 | 0.7 | 0.2 | 0.7 | 1.3 |

*Source*: Altvest, CSFB/Tremont, HFR, Tuna, Institutional Investor (June 2002), CMRA analysis

analysed). Fixed income and managed futures also staged an outstanding performance during the bust period (see Table 30).

## HOW DOES VAR COMPARE BY STYLE?

Table 31 shows the average VAR and the volatility of VAR for different strategies. Overall, hedge funds have a combined monthly average VAR of 12.8%. According to the analysis, event-driven is the least risky strategy, with an average VAR of 8.5%. Emerging markets is the riskiest strategy, with a VAR of 29.1%. Looking at the evolution of VAR over time, managed futures, dedicated short and global macro saw a reduction in VAR of 6.5%, while emerging markets and fixed-income arbitrage experienced a VAR increase of more than 5%. VAR increased by 3% from 1997 to 2000. Several stress factors could be used to explain the greater sensitivity of the different strategies to VAR over time: the Asian crisis and the high volatility of the equity markets in the boom and bust periods probably hurt the performance of the emerging market and equity-driven strategies.

Figure 9 compares the historical five-year standard deviation with the

**Table 30** Performance comparison between boom and bust periods of the S&P 500 Index, 1997–2001 (%)

|  | Boom January 1997 –June 2000 | Bust June 2000– December 2001 |
|---|---|---|
| Equity hedge | 27.6 | 3.1 |
| Equity non-hedge | 23.3 | 0.5 |
| S&P 500 Index | 22.8 | (13.8) |
| Market timing | 17.1 | 5.0 |
| Event-driven | 17.0 | 9.3 |
| Merger arbitrage | 15.7 | 6.5 |
| Macro | 15.6 | 2.5 |
| Convertible arbitrage | 14.9 | 9.1 |
| Equity market neutral | 14.2 | 12.8 |
| Managed futures | 12.5 | 20.5 |
| Event-driven combined | 12.5 | 8.2 |
| Distressed securities | 12.1 | 8.7 |
| Emerging markets | 11.6 | (6.3) |
| Fixed income (total) | 10.7 | 13.2 |
| Statistical arbitrage | 10.6 | 5.4 |
| Relative-value arbitrage | 10.0 | 11.5 |
| Fixed income: high yield | 6.9 | 1.9 |
| Lehman Aggregate Bond Index | 5.6 | 10.6 |
| Fixed income: mortgage-backed | 5.3 | 19.0 |
| Short selling | (11.0) | 22.1 |

*Source*: Altvest, CSFB/Tremont, HFR, Tuna, CMRA Analysis

standard deviation for the following 18 months. The standard deviation of equity hedge, fixed income and merger arbitrage increased. The disappearance rate, however, was substantially higher for fixed income and merger arbitrage than for the other strategies analysed.

## WHAT ARE THE RISK, RETURN AND EXPOSURE CHARACTERISTICS OF DIFFERENT STYLES?

The risk characteristics of hedge funds vary widely, as shown in Table 32. The risk, return and exposure characteristics of five different hedge fund styles tracked by Zurich are summarised in Table 33. The equity hedge

**Table 31** Components of one-month VAR (99% confidence) for hedge fund strategies

|  | Average VAR | | | | |
|  | 1997 | 1998 | 1999 | 2000 | Average |
|---|---|---|---|---|---|
| Emerging markets | 11.6 | 31.4 | 31.2 | 32.8 | 29.1 |
| Dedicated short | 15.3 | 13.6 | 13.7 | 12.1 | 13.8 |
| Fixed-income arbitrage | 9.8 | 10.5 | 13.3 | 14.9 | 12.0 |
| Long/short equity | 9.2 | 10.2 | 12.5 | 16.8 | 11.9 |
| Managed futures | 12.4 | 10.8 | 11.6 | 10.6 | 11.2 |
| Market neutral | 8.7 | 10.0 | 11.7 | 12.1 | 11.1 |
| All sample | 9.4 | 9.9 | 11.7 | 12.2 | 11.0 |
| Multi-strategy | 9.7 | 10.0 | 11.7 | 11.9 | 10.8 |
| Global macro | 11.9 | 11.0 | 10.2 | 9.8 | 10.6 |
| Convertible arbitrage | 9.3 | 9.6 | 11.3 | 11.0 | 10.5 |
| Event-driven | 8.0 | 8.1 | 8.7 | 9.1 | 8.5 |

*Source*: Assessing market risk for hedge funds and hedge funds portfolios, Francois-Serge Lhabitant, March 2001

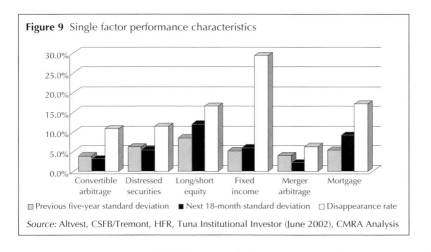

**Figure 9** Single factor performance characteristics

□ Previous five-year standard deviation ■ Next 18-month standard deviation □ Disappearance rate

*Source:* Altvest, CSFB/Tremont, HFR, Tuna Institutional Investor (June 2002), CMRA Analysis

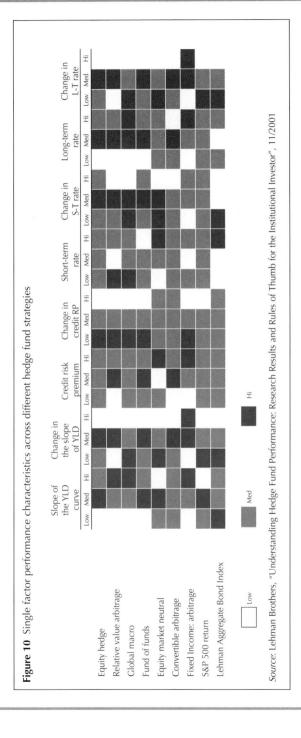

**Figure 10** Single factor performance characteristics across different hedge fund strategies

*Source:* Lehman Brothers, "Understanding Hedge Fund Performance: Research Results and Rules of Thumb for the Institutional Investor", 11/2001

**Figure 10** Continued

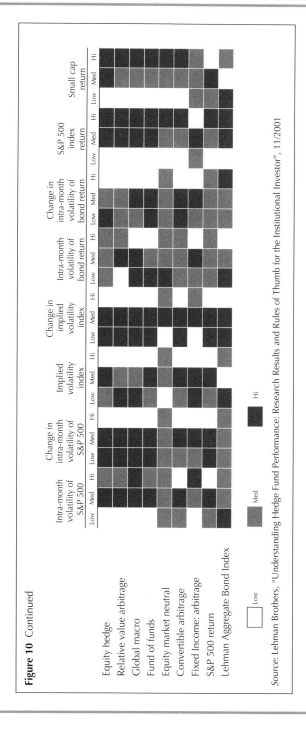

Source: Lehman Brothers, "Understanding Hedge Fund Performance: Research Results and Rules of Thumb for the Institutional Investor", 11/2001

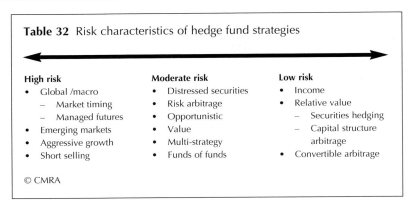

**Table 32** Risk characteristics of hedge fund strategies

| High risk | Moderate risk | Low risk |
|---|---|---|
| • Global /macro | • Distressed securities | • Income |
|   – Market timing | • Risk arbitrage | • Relative value |
|   – Managed futures | • Opportunistic |   – Securities hedging |
| • Emerging markets | • Value |   – Capital structure |
| • Aggressive growth | • Multi-strategy |     arbitrage |
| • Short selling | • Funds of funds | • Convertible arbitrage |

© CMRA

strategy has the highest return of the five styles. It also has the highest volatility and the highest exposure to the equity markets. Convertible arbitrage, on the other hand, does not have as high returns but its volatility is lower and it also has the highest leverage of the strategies analysed.

Lehman Brothers published an interesting study that used the single-factor performance characteristics (see Figure 10) evaluating six hedge fund strategies in light of different market environments. As you can see, the equity hedge strategy is favourably affected when the S&P 500 Index returns are medium or high and when the small-cap returns are medium or high. The slope of the yield curve has a positive influence on the relative-value arbitrage and global macro strategies. Significant changes in the slope of the yield curve are only advantageous to the fixed-income arbitrage strategy. Moderate changes, on the other hand, are more beneficial to most of the strategies analysed, except market neutral and global macro. In addition, high-volatility events in the equity and bond markets do not favour any of the strategies except global macro.

The results can be classified in three groups. The first group consists of those strategies for which the inclusion of the multivariate model significantly improves the overall fit. The second is comprised of those strategies for which the inclusion of the factors only marginally improves the overall fit of the regression models. The third is composed of those strategies for which the inclusion of these factors diminishes the overall fit (see Table 34).

The first group is comprised of 10 strategies that are sensitive to the factors mentioned above. In this group, we find event-driven, fixed income, convertible arbitrage and relative-value arbitrage. The second group includes five strategies that are not as sensitive to the other factors and is composed of the equity-driven strategies (ie, equity hedge, equity non-hedge, market timing and short selling). The third group includes two strategies that show no sensitivity to the factors: statistical arbitrage and market neutral.

**Table 33** Summary of risk, return and exposure of strategies

| | Return to the style | Volatility of return | Downside risk | Exposure | | | | % of return volatility not explained by the style | Sharpe ratio | Leverage |
| | | | | Equity index return | Equity index volatility | Economy wide credit risk | Interest rates | | | |
|---|---|---|---|---|---|---|---|---|---|---|
| Convertible arbitrage | Medium | Low | High | Positive High | Positive Low | Negative Medium | Negative Medium | High | High | High |
| Hedged equity | High | High | Medium | Positive High | Negative Low | Negative Medium | Negative Low | Medium | Medium | Medium |
| Event-driven | Medium | Medium | Medium | Positive Medium | Negative Medium | Negative Low | Negative Low | Low | Medium | Medium |
| Distressed securities | Medium | Medium | Medium | Positive Medium | Negative Low | Negative High | Negative Medium | Medium | Medium | Low |
| Merger arbitrage | Medium | Low | Medium | Positive Medium | Negative Medium | Negative Low | Negative Low | Medium | High | Medium |

*Source*: Zurich Hedge Fund Indices

**Table 34** Sensitivity of strategies to regression factors in Lehman's multivariate model

| Strategy | Change in | | |
|---|---|---|---|
| | Term premia | Credit spread | VIX |
| Emerging markets | 0.04 | 0.00 | (0.10) |
| Sector | 0.03 | (0.08) | (0.22) |
| Distressed securities | 0.02 | (0.12) | (0.42) |
| Event-driven | 0.02 | (0.07) | (0.13) |
| Equity non-hedge | 0.02 | (0.01) | 0.04 |
| Fixed income high yield | 0.02 | (0.10) | (0.31) |
| Equity hedge | 0.01 | (0.07) | (0.22) |
| Relative-value arbitrage | 0.01 | (0.04) | (0.08) |
| Convertible arbitrage | 0.01 | (0.03) | (0.08) |
| Merger arbitrage | 0.01 | (0.08) | (0.26) |
| Fixed income (total) | 0.01 | (0.04) | (0.20) |
| Fixed-income arbitrage | 0.01 | 0.01 | (0.08) |
| Market timing | 0.01 | (0.02) | (0.11) |
| Equity market neutral | 0.00 | (0.01) | (0.11) |
| Macro | (0.00) | (0.08) | (0.23) |
| Statistical arbitrage | (0.01) | 0.15 | 0.21 |
| Short selling | (0.01) | (0.01) | (0.05) |

*Source*: Lehman Brothers Understanding Hedge Fund Performance

Equity non-hedge, emerging markets and global macro ranked at the top in terms of their sensitivity to changes in term premia, credit spread and VIX. On the other hand, the event-driven strategies, as well as convertible arbitrage and relative-value arbitrage, were not as sensitive to the factors in Lehman's multivariate model.

Strategies that exploit differences in the term structure are sensitive to changes in credit spread. Fixed income is consistently ranked eighth and ninth across the 17 strategies analysed. An increasing long-term rate with a more short-term slowing down are signs of an expanding economy, during which credit spreads tend to narrow and the equity market is expected to improve.

Table 35 summarises the major characteristics of the hedge fund strategies analysed using the new IRC-proposed "alternative definitions" (see Appendix 1 for a further discussion of the findings of the IRC on hedge fund risk transparency). For the convertible arbitrage strategy, it describes the direction of the positions taken, which in this case is long. It also describes liquidity as a driving risk factor and turnover is between low and medium. For the event-driven strategy, it describes two of the three types that are covered: merger arbitrage and distressed securities. In the

**Table 35** IRC proposed "alternative definitions"

| Strategy | Asset class | Direction | Type | Region | Liquidity | Turnover |
|---|---|---|---|---|---|---|
| Convertible arbitrage | Interest rates<br>Equity<br>FX | L | Convert arbitrage | Any | L/I | L/M |
| Event-driven | Equity<br>Interest rates | L | Merger<br>Credit distressed | Any | L/I | L/M |
| Fixed income | Interest rates<br>FX | L/S/N | Relative value<br>Stat arbitrage<br>Options arbitrage | Any | H/L/I | L/M |
| Long/short equity | Equity | L/S/N | | Any | H/L | L/M/H |
| Emerging markets | Interest rates<br>Equities<br>FX<br>Commodities<br>Multi | L/S/N | Merger<br>Credit<br>distressed<br>Relative value<br>Stat arbitrage<br>Options arbitrage | Emerging<br>markets | L/I | I/M |
| Global macro | Interest rates<br>Equities<br>FX<br>Commodities<br>Multi | L/S | Sector | Any | H/L/I | L/M |
| Managed futures | Interest rates<br>Equities<br>FX<br>Commodities<br>Multi | L/S | | Require<br>Future<br>Markets | H/L | M/H |
| Market neutral | Interest rates<br>Equities<br>FX<br>Commodities | N | | Any | H/L/I | M/H |
| Dedicated short bias | Interest rates<br>Equities<br>FX<br>Commodities | S | Sector | Any | H/L/I | L/M/H |

*Source*: IRC, CMRA

case of fixed income, the positions can be long, short or neutral. The equity-driven strategies are fundamentally based on liquid stocks and turnover is high. For emerging markets, the assets traded are interest rates, equities, foreign exchange, commodities, etc.

## WHAT ARE THE CORRELATIONS BETWEEN THE DIFFERENT HEDGE FUND STRATEGIES?

Table 36 illustrates the cross-correlations between different hedge fund strategies. All the event-driven strategies (ie, pure event-driven, merger arbitrage and distressed securities) are highly correlated while other correlations are medium to low.

## WHAT ARE THE RELATIVE SHARPE RATIOS OF EACH HEDGE FUND STYLE?

Convertible arbitrage and merger arbitrage funds seem to have the strongest Sharpe ratio values and hedge funds within these investment styles have had the largest increases in AUM. Styles with the largest AUM growth in 1994–2001 were merger arbitrage, relative-value arbitrage, long/short equity, equity non-hedge and convertible arbitrage (see Table 37). The strategy with the least impressive growth over the same period was emerging markets, which experienced a decrease in AUM of 18.4%, mostly due to the performance, volatility and risk/reward characteristics

**Table 36** Summary of cross-correlations of hedge funds by strategy

|  | Convertible arbitrage | Hedged equity | Event-driven | Distressed securities | Merger arbitrage |
|---|---|---|---|---|---|
| **Convertible arbitrage** | 1 | Positive Low | Positive Medium | Positive Medium | Positive Medium |
| **Hedged equity** | Positive Low | 1 | Positive Medium | Positive Medium | Positive Low |
| **Event-driven** | Positive Medium | Positive Medium | 1 | Positive High | Positive High |
| **Distressed securities** | Positive Medium | Positive Medium | Positive High | 1 | Positive Medium |
| **Merger arbitrage** | Positive Medium | Positive Low | Positive High | Positive Medium | 1 |

*Source*: Zurich Hedge Fund Indices

**Table 37** Hedge fund styles with largest AUM growth, 1994–2001

|  | Average annualised growth (%) |
|---|---|
| Merger arbitrage | 35.5 |
| Relative-value arbitrage | 23.4 |
| Equity hedge | 12.0 |
| Equity non-hedge | 11.0 |
| Convertible arbitrage | 10.2 |

*Source*: Altvest, CMRA Analysis

**Table 38** Comparison of rankings by returns and Sharpe ratios, 1994–2001

| Style | Returns | Standard deviation | Sharpe ratio value | Rank based on returns | Rank based on Sharpe ratio | Difference |
|---|---|---|---|---|---|---|
| Convertible arbitrage | 10.9 | 2.6 | 2.2 | 7 | 2 | 5 |
| Merger arbitrage | 12.7 | 3.5 | 2.1 | 5 | 3 | 2 |
| Fixed income: high yield | 9.9 | 5.1 | 0.9 | 8 | 6 | 2 |
| Equity market neutral | 13.6 | 3.4 | 2.7 | 2 | 1 | 1 |
| Macro | 9.4 | 8.9 | 0.5 | 9 | 9 | 0 |
| Emerging markets | 7.5 | 23.0 | 0.1 | 10 | 10 | 0 |
| Short selling | (1.1) | 18.3 | (0.3) | 11 | 11 | 0 |
| Distressed securities | 12.7 | 6.9 | 1.1 | 4 | 5 | (1) |
| Fixed income | 12.6 | 11.7 | 0.6 | 6 | 8 | (2) |
| Equity hedge | 17.7 | 9.7 | 1.2 | 1 | 4 | (3) |
| Event-driven | 13.0 | 8.2 | 0.9 | 3 | 7 | (4) |
| Lehman Aggregate Bond Composite Index | 8.0 | 4.4 | 0.6 | | | |
| S&P 500 Index | 11.9 | 14.5 | 0.4 | | | |
| Fund of Funds Index | 18.8 | 9.0 | 1.4 | | | |

*Source*: Altvest, CMRA Analysis, 183 Funds

described in Chapter 13. Overall, the AUM of hedge funds increased at an annualised rate of 8% between 1994 and 2001; the rise was faster between 1994 and 1998 (approximately 15%) and slowed after 1998.

As shown in Table 38, Sharpe ratios can differ dramatically between time buckets. Emerging market funds, for example, showed a 256% increase in Sharpe ratio for the 1999–2001 period relative to the period 1994–1998, while short biased showed a 182% decline in the ratio within the same time buckets.

Hedge fund performance ranked on the basis of returns gives a very different result to ranking based on Sharpe ratio-adjusted returns. Convertible arbitrage, for example, ranks 10 based on returns between 1994 and 2001 but ranks first on a Sharpe ratio basis. Merger arbitrage, high-yield, long/short equity and statistical arbitrage also demonstrate significant differences in their rankings based on Sharpe ratio. The more volatile strategies – emerging markets and short selling – consistently rank at the bottom in terms of both returns and Sharpe ratio.

# Digging Into Various Hedge Fund Strategies

# 12

# Convertible Arbitrage

## DESCRIPTION OF THE STRATEGY

Ten years ago, convertible arbitrage was a niche strategy that was generally reserved for the proprietary accounts of large banks, brokerage firms and hedge funds. Today, many portfolios use a convertible arbitrage strategy, and it is estimated that convertible arbitrage trades represent more than half of the secondary market trading in convertible securities at the institutional level. Currently there are more than 100 hedge funds that focus on convertible arbitrage. Collectively, they represent over US$15 billion in AUM. The managers of these funds exploit arbitrage opportunities not only in convertible bonds but also in other convertible securities, including convertible preferred, zeros and mandatory convertibles.

Convertibles, or "converts", are a hybrid of equity and debt. Corporations can raise new capital by issuing either equity or debt. At a simple level, issuing equity dilutes earnings per share but has low current financing costs; debt, though not dilutive, may have high financing costs, depending on interest rates and the issuer's credit rating. Converts offer the investor a moderate current income with lower current financing costs. The buyer receives lower current income in exchange for the potential to participate in the equity upside of the company by converting the instrument into an agreed number of the company's common equity shares at an agreed future price. The objective of the strategy is to create a low-volatility asset class that is focused on the preservation of capital while seeking to provide a consistent return above the risk-free rate. The strategy is typically long volatility. As the volatility of the stock price changes, the convertible's value will change due to the commensurate change in the inherent option value (conversion premium).

The "delta" of a convertible bond usually rises with the price of the underlying stock. The portfolio is rebalanced by the sale of shares of the stock when the price of the stock increases, and by the repurchase of those shares when the price of the stock falls. In practice, when the stock price rises, the convertible appreciates more than the "delta" shares of the underlying asset due to "gamma" (the second-order derivative). The reverse happens when the stock falls. As a result, the portfolio generates positive profits regardless of the direction of the move. However, it is essential that the stock prices move!

Like the regular equity and fixed-income markets, convertible instruments have supply- and demand-driven growth rates and size constraints. Changing economic conditions can determine whether corporations will issue new convertible instruments.

Convertible issuance has tripled in size between 1998 and 2001. According to Morgan Stanley, 210 convertible issues totalling US$104.5 billion came to market in 2001, compared with the US$61 billion raised in 2000. This unprecedented growth in 2001 was driven by low interest rates, high levels of volatility in the equity markets and significant cash inflows to asset managers and hedge funds specialising in convertible securities.

Technology, media and telecommunication companies dominated convertible bond issuance in 1998 and 1999. In the first half of 2000, 68% of new issuances came from media/telecom companies, while biotech accounted for 17% (see Figure 1).

As companies within these sectors burned their cash rapidly, their credit quality was lowered, changing the overall risk of these investment vehicles in the market. During the next two years the market became more diverse, with issuance coming from various sectors and higher quality issuers. Investment-grade deals comprised 56.9% of the new convertible issues in 2001 compared to 37.8% in the previous year. Convertible issuance has also been driven by merger activity in the last few years (see Figure 2).

There are several kinds of convertible issues in the market today, including zero-coupon converts, mandatories and structures with contingent convertibility and contingent payment features. Investors have also sought issues with shorter put options that allow them to redeem a convertible early, as well as converts with shorter maturities and higher credit standings. A key characteristic of zero-coupon issuance is that when companies issue zero-coupon convertible bonds they avoid quarterly interest payments but gain tax deductions for the accrued interest.

The growth in convertible issuance has been fuelled by investors who are interested in reducing the volatility of their portfolios with exposure to the volatile equity markets. Empirical studies have shown that convertibles participate in as much as

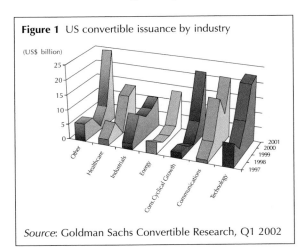

**Figure 1** US convertible issuance by industry

(US$ billion)

*Source*: Goldman Sachs Convertible Research, Q1 2002

70% of the upward movement in equity markets, but only roughly 50% of the downside. This asymmetric Sharpe ratio profile is one of the greatest appeals of convertibles to investors in times of market uncertainty.

In 2000, only about 30% of the secondary market for convertibles in the US was investment-grade, but by 2001 it was up to 65%. The US contrasts with Europe, where 85% of the existing issuance is investment-grade. On a global basis, as of the fourth quarter of 1999, the US represented 31% of the convertible market, with Japan and Europe representing 38% and 24%, respectively (see Figure 3).

Industry experts warn about the liquidity exposure of the US convertible arbitrage market.

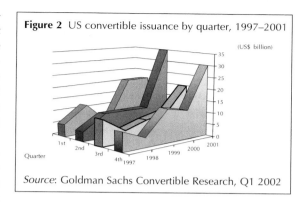

**Figure 2** US convertible issuance by quarter, 1997–2001

*Source*: Goldman Sachs Convertible Research, Q1 2002

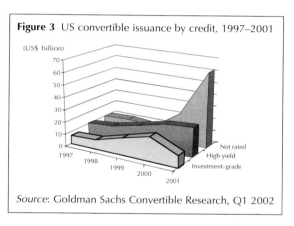

**Figure 3** US convertible issuance by credit, 1997–2001

*Source*: Goldman Sachs Convertible Research, Q1 2002

Convertible arbitrage combines two investments in one strategy to create a position that significantly reduces equity exposure. The first half of the process involves buying a convertible security and the second part involves selling short the underlying common stock. Because the long and short positions are essentially the same security, the correlation between them can be easily determined and a "hedge ratio" can be calculated.

Figure 4 presents a simplified version of the return curve of an arbitrage position. If the stock price decreases, the amount lost on the long convertible position is countered by the amount gained on the short stock position, theoretically creating a stable net position value.

The convertible arbitrage strategy consists of buying a convertible bond which is trading with an implied volatility for the equity that is lower than the anticipated volatility. To insulate the position in the convertible bond from movements in the underlying stock price, the holder then shorts a specified quantity of shares of the underlying; this is commonly known as

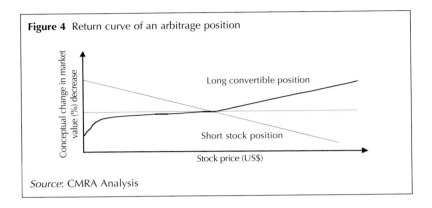

**Figure 4** Return curve of an arbitrage position

*Source*: CMRA Analysis

the "delta" number of shares. Delta is the basic directional risk measure of securities with embedded options, such as convertible bonds.

An important distinction between convertible arbitrage managers is their varied focus on how much the convertible option is in- or out-of-the-money.

Some managers focus on deep-in-the-money convertibles, while others trade mainly out-of-the-money issues (or even "busted convertibles", which are deeply out-of-the-money issues). Depending on how much the option is in- or out-of-the-money, the credit quality of the convertible securities can be an important factor to consider. One concern associated with convertible arbitrage is that if large hedge funds decide to sell as market conditions become less favourable, there could be a wave of selling with no one to buy. A key characteristic of the convertible arbitrage strategy is that the convertible market is not as efficient as the equity market – thus, converts are slightly "undervalued" relative to their common stock price.

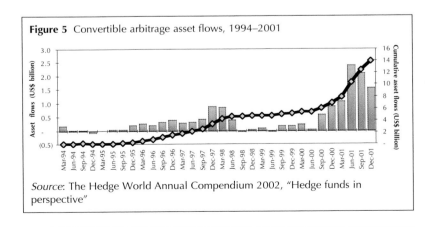

**Figure 5** Convertible arbitrage asset flows, 1994–2001

*Source*: The Hedge World Annual Compendium 2002, "Hedge funds in perspective"

Skilled arbitrageurs search the market for those convertibles that are most "underpriced". Whether the convertible is underpriced by an appropriate discount for illiquidity and complexity or by an arbitrage opportunity is a matter of opinion.

The AUM of convertible bond hedge funds increased from 1994 to 2001 (see Figure 5). The greatest increases occurred in 1996–97 and in 2000–01. It is important to note that the asset flow did not increase substantially in the 1998–2000 period. As of the end of 2001, the cumulative asset flow since March 1994 was US$14 billion. The growth of the assets in the strategy for the 1997–2001 period was 54.6%, the largest growth in assets of the hedge fund strategies.

## EFFECT OF MARKET CONDITIONS

The strategy performs above its historical average when:[1]

❏ the slope of the yield curve is unchanging;
❏ credit risk premium is moderate;
❏ the long-term rate is not high and is unchanging;
❏ the intra-month volatility of the S&P 500 and the implied volatility index are at moderate levels and are not increasing;
❏ the intra-month volatility of bond returns is not increasing; and
❏ the returns on large-cap and small-cap stocks are high.

The strategy underperforms when:

❏ the slope of the yield curve is increasing;
❏ credit risk premium is very low;
❏ the long-term yield is high or is increasing by a large amount;
❏ the intra-month volatility of the S&P 500 and the implied volatility index are high and increasing;
❏ the intra-month volatility of bond returns is increasing; and
❏ the returns on large-cap and small-cap stocks are negative.

## INVESTORS IN THE STRATEGY

Although individuals and family offices form the largest investor group for convertible arbitrage funds, corporations and funds of funds have also begun to make investments. Convertible arbitrage funds have more institutional investments than any of the other strategies (see Table 1).

**Table 1** Investors in the convertible arbitrage strategy

| Investors | (%) |
| --- | --- |
| Individuals and family offices | 47 |
| Corporations | 24 |
| Funds of funds | 18 |
| Pensions and retirement | 9 |
| Endowments and foundations | 2 |

*Source*: Hennessee Hedge Fund Survey (January 2000)

213

**Table 2** Top convertible arbitrage funds with more than US$1 billion in AUM (all sources)

| Rank | Fund | Highest AUM* (US$ billion) |
|------|------|---------------------------|
| 1 | Highbridge Capital Corporation | 3.9 |
| 2 | Kensington Global Strategies Fund | 1.8 |
| 3 | Global Convertible Strategy, Bear Stearns | 1.2 |
| 4 | Deephaven Market Neutral Master Fund LP | 1.3 |
| 5 | CSFB Convertible & Quantitative Strategies Feeder Fund Limited | 1.0 |
| 6 | GEM Convertible Securities Composite | 1.0 |
| 7 | Lydian Overseas Partners LTD (Class A composite) | 1.0 |
| 8 | Stark Investments, LP | 1.0 |
| | **Total** | **12.2** |

*This is the highest AUM for that fund among all the sources

Source: Altvest, Tuna, HFR, Institutional Investor (June 2002), Directory of Fund of Hedge Funds Investment Vehicles, CMRA Analysis.

## WELL-KNOWN PLAYERS

Table 2 includes the convertible arbitrage funds with more than US$1.0 billion in AUM from the major sources.

The Hedge Fund 100 includes one of the top 25 convertible arbitrage funds (with US$1.2 billion in AUM) that is not included in any other source. In addition, of the top 25 funds, 10 funds with US$11.0 billion in AUM (or 58.8% of the total) are among the most popular holdings of funds of funds. Table 3 shows the investments of funds of funds in the convertible arbitrage strategy.

## COVERAGE OF THE STRATEGY IN DIFFERENT SOURCES

There are two groups of indices that can be used to evaluate convertible arbitrage hedge funds. One is based on the performance of the different hedge funds as reported by the major sources. The other includes indices that evaluate the overall convertible bond market. Such indices are HFR's Convertible Bond Index and Goldman Sach's Convertible Bond Index, among others (see Table 4).

## DISTRIBUTION OF FUNDS IN THE STRATEGY

Convertible arbitrage funds are highly concentrated in terms of AUM. Seven convertible arbitrage funds have an overall AUM of US$8.9 billion, representing 60% of the total US$14.8 billion in the strategy (see Figure 6).

**Table 3** Convertible arbitrage investments by fund of funds

| Fund | Holding | % of NAV as of June 30, 2002 |
|------|---------|------------------------------|
| Arden Advisers | Stark | 10.0 |
| Resistant Capital Invest Ltd | Lionhart Global Appreciation Fund | 10.0 |
| Europanel | CSFB CQS | 9.4 |
| Hirst Meta Strategy | Forest Global Convertible Fund | 8.4 |
| Rio Bravo HF | Alexandra Global Investors | 8.3 |
| Attica Global Selector Fund | AIG SoundShore Investors | 7.7 |
| Europanel | Ferox | 7.7 |
| Micado Capital Invest Ltd | Forest Global Convertible Fund | 7.0 |
| Rio Bravo HF | Palladin Overseas Fund | 6.7 |
| Coastal Magnum | Alexandra Global | 6.6 |
| NIBI Target Return Fund | Lydian Overseas Partners | 6.3 |
| Coastal Magnum | West Broadway Global Arb | 6.2 |
| Micado Capital Invest Ltd | Northeast Convertible Arbitrage | 6.0 |
| NIBI Target Return Fund | IG SoundShore Investors | 6.0 |
| KB Lux Spec Opps | Deephaven Market Neutral Fund | 4.6 |
| Absolute Invest AG | Navigator Offshore | 4.5 |
| Europanel | Kallista Fund | 4.5 |
| Leu Prima Global | Forest Folcrum | 4.3 |
| Leu Prima Global | Highbridge Capital | 4.2 |
| Hirst Meta Strategy | Highbridge Capital Corp | 3.0 |

*Source*: Directory of Fund of Hedge Funds Investment Vehicles

**Table 4** Coverage of convertible arbitrage funds by different sources

| Source | Total number of funds | Funds with no AUM data | Total AUM (US$ billion) |
|--------|----------------------|------------------------|--------------------------|
| Altvest | 88 | 14 | 14.8 |
| The Hedge Fund 100 | 25 | N/A | 12.5 |
| CSFB/Tremont | 25 | 0 | 9.5 |
| Tuna | 61 | 3 | 8.3 |
| HFR | 64 | 6 | 7.4 |
| Hennessee | 40 | 0 | 1.4 |

*Source*: Altvest, HFR, Tuna, Hennessee, Hedge Index, CSFB/Tremont, Institutional Investor (June 2002), CMRA Research

### Distribution of funds by quartile of performance

The distribution of convertible arbitrage funds by quartiles of performance and AUM shows several patterns.

The funds in the first quartile of five-year returns account for 45% of the assets in the sample. In addition, in terms of return, the first quartile has

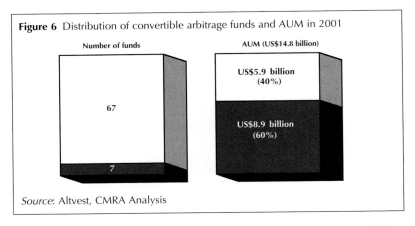

**Figure 6** Distribution of convertible arbitrage funds and AUM in 2001

*Source*: Altvest, CMRA Analysis

the highest volatility by a factor of 3.0, reducing the attractiveness of these funds on a Sharpe ratio basis (see Table 5).

### Distribution of funds by quartile of AUM

The distribution of returns by quartile of AUM of the convertible arbitrage funds shows that the funds in the top quartile have the highest five-year performance of the group (14.49%). The funds in the second and third quartiles have almost the same volatility and their Sharpe ratios are very close (see Table 6).

As the average credit quality has fallen, the best convertible arbitrageurs evaluate these changing macro-driven factors and respond through diversification, hedging away some of the unwanted risks. For example, some arbitrageurs are paying more attention to an issuer's cashflows, debt servicing levels and overall capitalisation, as well as the experience of the management team, transparency, the accuracy of earning reports, etc.

Over the 1994–2001 period, the growth in AUM of convertible arbitrage

**Table 5** Distribution of convertible arbitrage funds by quartiles of five-year performance, 1997–2001

| Return quartiles | Average 1997–2001 equally weighted return (%) | Average 1997–2001 AUM-weighted return (%) | AUM in quartile (US$ billion) | % of total | Average 1997–2001 standard deviation (%) | Sharpe ratio 1997–2001 |
|---|---|---|---|---|---|---|
| 1 | 19.5 | 20.2 | 3.9 | 45 | 13.8 | 1.4 |
| 2 | 14.4 | 14.0 | 1.5 | 17 | 4.5 | 2.3 |
| 3 | 11.1 | 11.6 | 0.8 | 9 | 5.1 | 1.3 |
| 4 | 8.3 | 7.6 | 2.5 | 29 | 4.0 | 1.2 |
| Total | 13.2 | 14.8 | 8.7 | 100 | 6.7 | 1.6 |

*Source*: Altvest, HFR, Tuna, CMRA Analysis based on 37 funds with five-year performance data

**Table 6** Distribution of convertible arbitrage hedge funds by quartiles of AUM, 1997–2001

| AUM quartiles | Average 1997–2001 equally weighted return (%) | Average 1997–2001 AUM-weighted return (%) | AUM in quartile (US$ billion) | % of total | Average 1997–2001 standard deviation (%) | Sharpe ratio 1997–2001 |
|---|---|---|---|---|---|---|
| 1 | 14.5 | 15.6 | 5.9 | 68 | 9.7 | 1.3 |
| 2 | 12.4 | 12.8 | 2.0 | 23 | 5.8 | 1.6 |
| 3 | 12.5 | 13.0 | 0.6 | 7 | 5.5 | 1.4 |
| 4 | 13.3 | 13.8 | 0.2 | 3 | 6.0 | 1.9 |
| **Total** | **13.2** | **14.8** | **8.7** | **100** | **6.7** | **1.6** |

*Source*: Altvest, HFR, Tuna, CMRA Analysis based on 37 funds with five-year performance data

hedge funds had increased at an average annualised rate of 10.2%. These growth levels are exceeded only by merger arbitrage, relative-value arbitrage and equity hedge/non-hedge strategies. In addition, the convertible arbitrage strategy has recorded an average performance of 12.6% between 1997 and 2001.

## PERFORMANCE OF THE STRATEGY
### Returns during boom and bust
Although the S&P 500 outperformed the convertible arbitrage strategy during the boom years of 1997–2000 by an 8% margin (23% compared to 15%), the strategy outperformed the S&P 500 by a margin of 23% (–14% compared to 9%) during the bust period 2000–01. These numbers illustrate the steadiness of the strategy. Although convertible arbitrage is not technically a "market neutral" strategy, it nevertheless performs in both the boom and bust periods of the general market (see Figure 7).

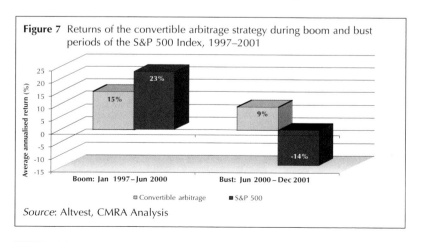

**Figure 7** Returns of the convertible arbitrage strategy during boom and bust periods of the S&P 500 Index, 1997–2001

*Source*: Altvest, CMRA Analysis

217

### Returns from different sources

Altvest covers both the highest number and the largest AUM of the main sources (see Table 7).

The constituents of a particular index can vary substantially in performance. For example, there are 12 convertible arbitrage funds in the Zurich Convertible Arbitrage Index, and the 2001 return for each of these funds ranged from 3.5% to 33.48%, while the 1998–2001 return ranged from 4.41% to 56%. Figure 8 shows the degree of variance of funds in the index.

### Index performance

For the 1997–2001 period, the returns of the Altvest Convertible Arbitrage Index ranked sixth among the 14 hedge fund strategies analysed (see Table 8).

However, comparing the strategy on a Sharpe ratio basis, the convertible arbitrage strategy was consistently at the top of the list (see Table 9).

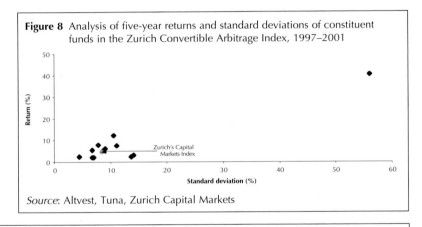

**Figure 8** Analysis of five-year returns and standard deviations of constituent funds in the Zurich Convertible Arbitrage Index, 1997–2001

*Source*: Altvest, Tuna, Zurich Capital Markets

**Table 7** Comparison of convertible arbitrage indices across different sources, 1997–2001

| | 1997 | 1998 | 1999 | 2000 | 2001 | 1997–2001 Return | Sharpe ratio |
|---|---|---|---|---|---|---|---|
| Tuna | 17.0 | 5.9 | 18.0 | 13.3 | 15.5 | 13.9 | 3.8 |
| Altvest | 16.2 | 6.4 | 16.8 | 15.1 | 11.4 | 13.1 | 3.6 |
| CSFB/Tremont | 14.5 | (4.4) | 16.0 | 25.6 | 14.6 | 12.8 | 1.5 |
| HFR | 12.7 | 7.8 | 14.4 | 14.5 | 13.4 | 12.5 | 3.7 |
| Hennessee | 9.8 | 5.9 | 16.2 | 8.6 | 15.1 | 11.1 | 2.8 |
| EACM | 11.7 | 2.6 | 17.0 | 5.3 | 16.4 | 10.5 | 2.1 |
| Maximum difference | 7.2 | 12.2 | 3.6 | 20.3 | 5.0 | 3.4 | 1.7 |
| Average | 14.4 | 3.7 | 16.4 | 14.8 | 14.3 | 12.6 | 2.8 |

*Source*: Tuna, Altvest, CSFB/Tremont, HFR, Hennessee, EACM

Convertible arbitrage tries to eliminate most risks (such as directional risk) by betting on a single risk (such as volatility). When funds hedge their convertible arbitrage portfolios in this way, it generally reduces the overall variance. On a Sharpe ratio basis, convertible arbitrage ranked first during the 1997–2001 period.

Other studies have also shown that, among the strategies with relatively low volatility, convertible arbitrage is a good strategy for investors to diversify into during a downturn. One such study is an analysis by Laurent Favre of UBS and José-Antonio Galeano of Banque Cantonale Vaudoise.[2]

There is a noticeable difference between the CSFB/Tremont Convertible Arbitrage Index and the other indices (see Table 7 and Figure 9). One reason for this variability is the quarterly rebalancing feature of this index: the other indices either are not rebalanced or are rebalanced less frequently. (See Chapter 11 for a discussion of how hedge fund indexes are created.)

### Performance correlations

Convertible arbitrage funds performed poorly during 1994 when the Federal Reserve Bank began to raise interest rates (see Figure 10). During this period the poor performance of high-yield bonds and government bonds, along with the rate increase of 2.25% from February to December, led to a mass dumping of fixed income instruments.

Getting a handle on the ways that fund managers deal with data and NAV issues is important. What is the procedure for marking the portfolios? Does the manager come up with his/her own marks or are they an

**Table 8**  Ranking of the convertible arbitrage strategy against other strategies, 1997–2001

|  | 1997 | 1998 | 1999 | 2000 | 2001 | 1997–2001 | Rank |
|---|---|---|---|---|---|---|---|
| **Return (%)** | 16.2 | 6.4 | 16.8 | 15.1 | 11.4 | 13.1 | 6 of 14 |

*Source*: Altvest, CMRA

**Table 9**  Sharpe ratio of the convertible arbitrage strategy against other strategies, 1997–2001

| 1997 | 1998 | 1999 | 2000 | 2001 | 1997–2001 | Rank |
|---|---|---|---|---|---|---|
| 4.8 | 0.3 | 6.4 | 2.1 | 2.4 | 2.2 | 1 of 14 |

*Source*: Altvest, CMRA

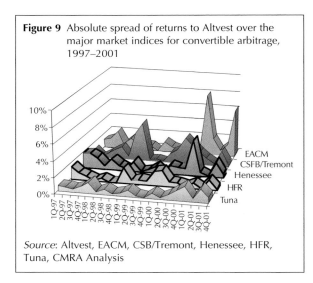

**Figure 9** Absolute spread of returns to Altvest over the major market indices for convertible arbitrage, 1997–2001

*Source*: Altvest, EACM, CSB/Tremont, Henessee, HFR, Tuna, CMRA Analysis

average of several broker month-end or day-end quotes? If they are an average, then what is the difference in bond points between the minimum and the maximum? If they are not an average, what is the manager's method for arriving at his/her marks?

In light of changing market conditions, investors in these kinds of instruments face issues, other than default risk, that are related to the holding time on their positions (holding-period risk). The average duration of the holder's portfolio would also be subject to interest rate risk if the entire yield curve suddenly shifted. Issuing companies also introduce specific risks to a portfolio, such as event risk from acquisition, which might suddenly cause the stock's available supply for short selling to drop. This drop might cause the long convertible bond position's premium to erode.

Arbitrageurs typically seek to hedge some of these market risks and issuer-specific risks through swap deals; they hedge interest rate risk through a mix of different durations and credit securities and derivatives. Asset swaps or credit swaps may also be used to reduce the credit exposure of a portfolio. Some worry that too many assets are concentrated among too

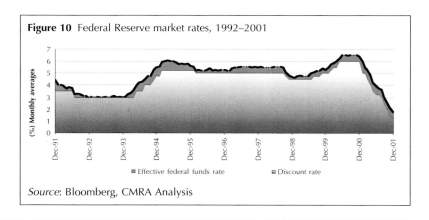

**Figure 10** Federal Reserve market rates, 1992–2001

■ Effective federal funds rate　▨ Discount rate

*Source*: Bloomberg, CMRA Analysis

few hedge fund managers, creating a mismatch between the natural buyers and sellers in the strategy. This creates pockets of illiquidity.

Understanding the valuation process should be a key component of due diligence. Stress testing of a convertible arbitrage fund needs to focus on these assumptions. Whether it should be another factor in the string of risk factors or a multiplicative factor applied to VAR and other risk measures is still a subject of debate by market professionals.

Intuitively, widening credit spreads would hurt the returns of the strategy. Lower default environments, tightening credit spreads and high-volatility environments are generally good for the strategy (see Figure 11).

During the Russian crisis, credit spreads began to shoot up, again resulting in poor performance for many convertible arbitrage funds. However, credit spreads widened so much that many issues were left underpriced in the beginning of 1999, leading to strong recoveries in fund returns that year.

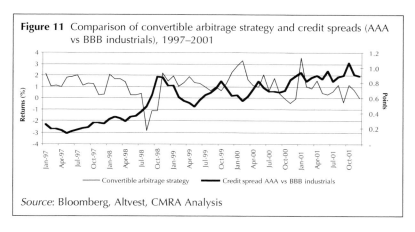

**Figure 11** Comparison of convertible arbitrage strategy and credit spreads (AAA vs BBB industrials), 1997–2001

*Source*: Bloomberg, Altvest, CMRA Analysis

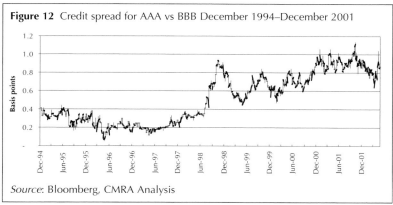

**Figure 12** Credit spread for AAA vs BBB December 1994–December 2001

*Source*: Bloomberg, CMRA Analysis

The Tech crash in 2000 actually helped most convertible arbitrage strategies because volatilities remained high, as did liquidity for the borrowing of stock (to short in order to hedge convertible arbitrage positions).

To conclude, an environment of high volatility, high credit quality and good liquidity seems to be the best environment for convertible arbitrage strategies.

The correlations between the convertible arbitrage index returns and the volatility of the S&P 500 and the Lehman Aggregate Bond Composite Index are 4.3% and –2.4%, respectively. This is counterintuitive given the strategy's dependence on volatility, and is more indicative of the shortfalls of a monthly correlation study when trying to capture a dynamic trading strategy (see Figure 12).

The convertible arbitrage strategy is especially attractive when the yield curve is moderately upward sloping and market volatility is at a moderate level (see Figure 13).

Although the convertible arbitrage index was positively correlated with the S&P 500 from 1996 onwards, the correlation with the Lehman Bond Index kept switching from negative during stressed times to positive during non-stressed times. The convertible arbitrage index shows an increasingly stronger correlation to the HFR Convertible Bond Index, which might be attributable to the strategy itself. While there are many moving parts to convertible arbitrage, its dependence on the convertible securities that are used to drive some of the returns obtained by the strategy itself also drives the correlation (see Table 10).

**Stress period analysis**
When the returns of the index covering different styles during the significant stress periods in the 1990s are annualised, convertible arbitrage seems to have a consistently average performance, ranking anywhere between 6 and 9 out of 14. This is much more stable than, for example, short selling, which performs among the best in some crises and among the worst in others. Table 11 summarises the exposure of the strategy to the different factors outlined above.

We examined the performance of convertible arbitrage funds in different environments during the 1995–2001 period. We looked at the relationship of the excess returns of the strategy to other systematic risk factors critical to the equity markets, including equity volatility (the implied volatility of S&P100 Index options), the market factors measuring the relationship between positive returns for the funds increase when the equity market is performing well, size factors and value factors.

The correlation with the debt-related systematic risk factors is about –50%. Convertible arbitrage funds were most vulnerable (ie, they had large negative excess returns) when systematic risks drastically increased in the debt markets. The correlation between the equity factor and the

**Table 10** Rolling correlations of convertible arbitrage index performance with S&P 500 and Lehman Aggregate Bond Index, 1997–2001 (%)

|                              | 1997 | 1998   | 1999 | 2000   | 2001 |
|------------------------------|------|--------|------|--------|------|
| Lehman Aggregate Bond Index  | 26.2 | (37.7) | 3.2  | (13.4) | 26.3 |
| S&P 500 Index                | 35.1 | 53.5   | 42.9 | 24.2   | 34.5 |
| HFR Convertible Bond Index   | 58.9 | 71.6   | 66.1 | 81.7   | 75.8 |

*Source*: Altvest, HFR, Bloomberg, CMRA Analysis

**Table 11** Summary of risk, return and exposure of convertible arbitrage to different risk factors

|                        |                 | Exposure                  |                                  |                    |                 |          |
|------------------------|-----------------|---------------------------|----------------------------------|--------------------|-----------------|----------|
| Volatility of return   | Downside risk   | Equity index return       | Economy-wide credit risk         | Interest rates     | Sharpe ratio    | Leverage |
| Low                    | High            | Positive low              | Negative medium                  | Negative medium    | High            | High     |

*Source*: Zurich Hedge Fund Indices Spring/Summer 2002

**Figure 13** Comparison of the convertible arbitrage strategy and the volatility of the S&P 500 Index

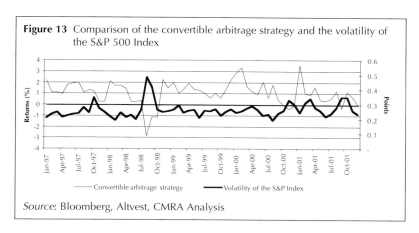

*Source*: Bloomberg, Altvest, CMRA Analysis

performance of convertible arbitrage funds changes only from a small positive to a small negative amount (20% to –24%), indicating that observations from August to October 1998 have a critical impact on the historical risk analysis for the strategy (see Table 12).

Generally, the Sharpe ratio properties of the strategy vary significantly under very different conditions. It seems clear that: (1) high returns came at the expense of high risk; and (2) there are significant differences between Altvest and other benchmarks. For the five-year study period, Altvest shows an average annual return for convertible arbitrage funds of 13.1% per annum. Along with these impressive returns came a relatively low level of risk. With a 3.6% standard deviation, convertible arbitrage investments ranked among the lowest in the hedge fund industry in terms of volatility. The strategy has a Sharpe ratio of 2.1. In contrast, the eight-year CSFB/Tremont Index for convertible arbitrage shows an average annual return of 12.8%, a volatility of 5.2% and a Sharpe ratio of 2.2. The expected volatility for a convertible arbitrage fund is very low. Convertible

**Table 12** Average correlation of convertible arbitrage funds with various risk factors, 1995–2001

| Factor | Overall correlation (%) |
|---|---|
| Equity volatility* | 2 |
| Equity volatility excluding 3Q of 1998 | (31) |
| High yield spread | (39) |
| Treasury volatility** | (44) |
| Swap volatility | (44) |

*The implied volatility of Treasury options
**The implied volatility of the S&P 100 Index options
Source: Financial Analyst Journal – Battle for Alphas, March/April 2002

**Table 13** Returns of convertible arbitrage index during periods of stress (%)

| Russian/LTCM crisis | Tech crash | September 11 |
|---|---|---|
| (6.2) | 10.7 | 8.4 |

Source: Altvest, CMRA Analysis

**Table 14** Sharpe ratio of convertible arbitrage index during periods of stress

| Russian/ LTCM crisis | Tech crash | September 11 | Average of absolute Sharpe ratios | Maximum– minimum |
|---|---|---|---|---|
| (1.1) | 1.3 | 1.2 | 1.2 | 2.4 |

Source: Altvest, CMRA Analysis

arbitrage managers continuously combat the problems of excessive risk, systemic risk, leverage, stale approaches and complacency (see Table 13).

Convertible arbitrage had a Sharpe ratio value of –1.05 during the stress period from August to October 1998. During the equity market downturn and the burst of the technology bubble (ie, the "NASDAQ crash"), convertible arbitrage was able to make a comeback with a 10.7% return. During the stress periods of the technology crash and the events of September 11, 2001, convertible arbitrage ranked in the top half of the strategies (see Table 14).

The convertible bond market as a whole is also prone to liquidity risk. When demand dries up, bid/ask spreads on the bonds can widen significantly. Because convertible bond arbitrage involves the short sale of underlying common stock, the strategy is also subject to stock-borrowing risk. This is the risk that the hedge fund manager will be unable to sustain the short position in the underlying common shares.

In addition, convertible arbitrage hedge funds use varying degrees of leverage, which can magnify both risks and returns. While some conservative convertible arbitrage hedge funds may use only 1.0 times leverage, most are leveraged 4.0 to 7.0 times capital.

Convertible arbitrage hedge fund managers can, and often do, minimise certain risks in their portfolios. For example, short Treasury positions can be used to reduce interest rate exposure and credit swaps can be used to reduce credit risks.

The issuing company always has the option to default on its obligations, so the investor would be essentially short a deep out-of-the-money put on the company's assets. The potential for default brings to bear the kind of financial restructuring skills that distressed securities investors need to master (see Chapter 15).

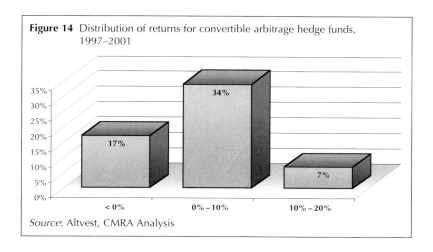

**Figure 14** Distribution of returns for convertible arbitrage hedge funds, 1997–2001

*Source*: Altvest, CMRA Analysis

An attempt to understand the different factors that affect the strategy was developed by Lehman Brothers. They evaluated the strategy in light of three different factors: change in term premia, change in credit spreads and change in VIX. The term premia factor is an indicator of economic expansion or contraction, which is visibly related to any sector strategy. It is no surprise that the strategy is sensitive to the term premia factor (ranked 7 of 17). Managers are expected to group all trades across different sectors in a search for diversification.

With regard to credit spread leverage, volatility and changes in the slope of the yield curve are risk drivers that should be considered. As to leverage itself, as of 2002, convertible arbitrage is among the most levered strategies, with 13 times leverage or higher in some cases. Accordingly, the strategy is clearly affected by credit spreads. In addition, since this strategy exploits differences in the term structure, it should be sensitive to the changes in credit spread, as indicated in Table 15.

As mentioned before, an increase in implied volatility is also related to a decrease in the equity markets. It is interesting to note that the trading strategies in convertible arbitrage benefit from a change in the volatility of the market. Lehman's model did pick up this relationship.

### Range of performance

Most of the convertible arbitrage funds had returns between 0% and 10% for the 1997–2001 period (see Figure 14).

### SHARPE RATIO

Leading academics in the field are increasingly questioning the quality of the Sharpe ratio, especially as it relates to options-based strategies such as convertible arbitrage. According to one, "it is very easy to report artificially higher Sharpe ratios. For example, writing options on very liquid securities".[3] In the case of convertible arbitrage, options can be written as a pretext to hedge the underlying volatility of the instruments in a portfolio.

It is important to realise that even though a high Sharpe ratio is positive,

**Table 15** Sensitivity of the convertible arbitrage strategy to factors from Lehman's multivariate model

| Factor | Coefficient | Rank |
|---|---|---|
| Change in credit spread | 0.000 | 3 of 17 |
| Change in implied volatility | (0.100) | 7 of 17 |
| Change in term premia | 0.011 | 9 of 17 |

*Source*: Lehman Brothers Understanding Hedge Fund Performance

it should also be stable over time. Although convertible arbitrage has a high Sharpe ratio compared to other strategies, it is also the most volatile from one year to another (see Table 16). And, although the Sharpe ratio distribution for convertible arbitrage is skewed to the positive in this particular case, one must be aware of the volatility of Sharpe ratios over time.

### Distribution

While the five-year Sharpe ratio of the funds analysed ranges from 0.15 to 4.45, the 2001 Sharpe ratios ranged from –0.96 to 6.79 (see Figure 15).

As shown in Table 17, the last quartile of convertible arbitrage funds has an average Sharpe ratio of 0.6, 45% of the assets in the sample. The last quartile also has the highest volatility of the sample with an average standard deviation of 12.09%, roughly three times as much as the volatility exhibited by the first two quartiles.

### LEVERAGE

88% of convertible arbitrage funds use leverage (see Chapter 2 for a discussion of leverage). 46% of the funds use a leverage lower than 2.0, and 42% leverage their positions to a level greater than 2.0.

Figure 16 shows that convertible arbitrage funds tend to employ a significant degree of leverage, averaging a ratio of US$3.73 of AUM for

**Table 16** Historical Sharpe ratio of the convertible arbitrage index, 1997–2001

| 1997 | 1998 | 1999 | 2000 | 2001 | 1997–2001 | Volatility of Sharpe ratio |
|------|------|------|------|------|-----------|----------------------------|
| 4.9 | 0.3 | 6.5 | 2.1 | 2.3 | 2.2 | 2.5 |

*Source*: Altvest, CMRA Analysis

**Table 17** Distribution of convertible funds by quartiles of Sharpe ratio, 1997–2001

| Sharpe ratio quartiles | Average 1997–2001 equally weighted return (%) | Average 1997–2001 AUM-weighted return (%) | AUM in quartile (US$ billion) | % of total | Average 1997–2001 standard deviation (%) | Sharpe ratio 1997–2001 |
|------------------------|----------------------------------------------|-------------------------------------------|-------------------------------|------------|------------------------------------------|------------------------|
| 1 | 14.1 | 15.8 | 1.2 | 13.0 | 3.2 | 2.7 |
| 2 | 12.0 | 13.1 | 2.0 | 23.0 | 4.0 | 1.8 |
| 3 | 13.9 | 15.5 | 1.6 | 19.0 | 7.1 | 1.2 |
| 4 | 12.8 | 15.0 | 3.9 | 45.0 | 12.1 | 0.6 |
| Total | 13.2 | 14.8 | 8.7 | 100.0 | 6.7 | 1.6 |

*Source*: Altvest, HFR, Tuna, CMRA Analysis based on 37 funds with five-year performance data

227

each dollar of capital (see Table 18), ranging all the way up to US$13.00 for each dollar of capital. On a historical basis the strategy has maintained an average leverage of 2.7 (see Table 19).

A further analysis of leverage for the strategy for the 1997–2001 period indicates that the first quartile (the group with the lowest leverage) had US$6.7 billion in AUM, while the last quartile had only US$1.6 billion in AUM (see Table 20).

The five-year delevered returns for convertible arbitrage are roughly 6–7 percentage points lower than the reported average returns, as Table 21 shows. While the one-year delevered returns are 9.4 percentage points

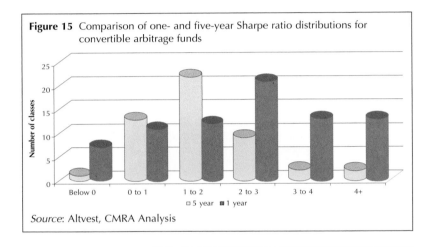

**Figure 15** Comparison of one- and five-year Sharpe ratio distributions for convertible arbitrage funds

□ 5 year  ■ 1 year

*Source*: Altvest, CMRA Analysis

---

**Table 18** Financial leverage of convertible arbitrage funds in 2002

| Minimum | Average | Maximum | Rank |
|---------|---------|---------|------|
| 1.0 | 3.7 | 13.0 | 1 of 14 |

*Source*: Altvest, CMRA Analysis

---

**Table 19** Historical average leverage of convertible arbitrage funds, 1997–2001

| | | | | | 1997–2001 | | |
|------|------|------|------|------|---------|---------|---------|
| 1997 | 1998 | 1999 | 2000 | 2001 | Average | Maximum | Minimum |
| 2.3 | 2.5 | 2.8 | 2.9 | 3.0 | 2.7 | 3.0 | 2.3 |

*Source*: Altvest, CMRA Analysis

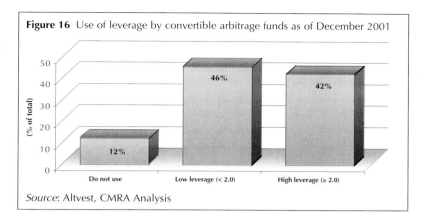

**Figure 16** Use of leverage by convertible arbitrage funds as of December 2001

*Source*: Altvest, CMRA Analysis

lower, the one-year difference is among the highest of all strategies. In general, arbitrage funds tend to take on larger amounts of leverage because they need to enhance the dollar amount of their returns.

## RISK MEASUREMENT

Some of the risks in the convertible arbitrage strategy include short-selling risk, volatility risk, credit risk, liquidity risk and model risk (see Figure 17).

### Short selling risk

The hedging of convertible arbitrage positions requires selling stock short. Sometimes, however, there is an insufficient amount of stock to purchase or no one is willing to sell stocks that can be used by short sellers to cover short positions. This is called a short-squeeze. The risk for convertible arbitrageurs is that during a short-squeeze the fund might be forced to exer-

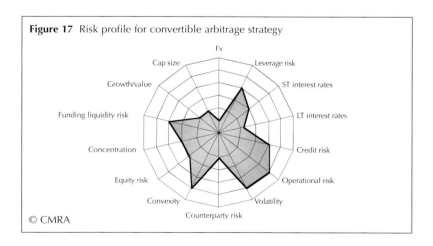

**Figure 17** Risk profile for convertible arbitrage strategy

© CMRA

**Table 20** Distribution of convertible arbitrage funds by quartiles of leverage, 1997–2001

| Leverage quartiles | Minimum leverage in quartile | Maximum leverage in quartile | Average leverage in quartile | Median leverage in quartile | Total AUM in quartile (US$ billion) | % of total AUM |
|---|---|---|---|---|---|---|
| 1 | 0.9 | 1.7 | 1.3 | 1.3 | 6.7 | 53.1 |
| 2 | 1.7 | 3.0 | 2.6 | 2.5 | 1.8 | 14.2 |
| 3 | 3.0 | 4.0 | 3.5 | 3.5 | 2.5 | 19.6 |
| 4 | 4.0 | 35.7 | 7.8 | 5.3 | 1.6 | 13.1 |
| **Total** | **0.9** | **35.7** | **2.7** | **3.0** | **12.6** | **100.0** |

*Source*: Altvest, CMRA Analysis based on 89 funds with five years of leverage data

cise the conversion feature in the bond, thereby losing the option premium and destroying the economics of convertible arbitrage trades.

### Volatility risk

Since convertible arbitrage entails going long the convertible bond, the bond holder is also long the "conversion option" and has a long "vega" position. Vega is the relationship between changes in the price of the bond to changes in the implied volatility of the underlying stock.

### Credit risk

Credit risk is a factor in convertible bond arbitrage. This risk can be reduced at a cost by hedging. Hedging with credit default swaps exposes the fund to the credit risk of the counterparty to the default swap.

### Liquidity risk

Liquidity risk can occur in conjunction with a short-squeeze. Liquidity problems usually occur during crisis situations. The stock market can move adversely, requiring convertible arbitrageurs to dynamically hedge their long option position. However, this can be very difficult when it becomes impossible to short stocks. Precipitously, the arbitrageur can have open directional exposure on its options position. Market moves against the portfolio's directional exposure can reduce profits or even create losses. Often during liquidity crunches, increased haircuts and tighter lending standards may force funds to cover short positions, again damaging the economics of the arbitrage position.

Table 22 shows the leverage of two convertible arbitrage funds with different risk profiles. Clearly, the investor should understand all of the risk factors mentioned here in order to anticipate any "unwanted" surprises.

**Table 21** Summary of levered and delevered performance of convertible arbitrage funds, 1997–2001 (%)

|  | Maximum return | Minimum return | Average return | Maximum delevered return | Minimum delevered return | Average delevered return | Difference in returns levered vs delevered |
|---|---|---|---|---|---|---|---|
| **1997–2001** | 17.0 | 1.4 | 10.6 | 9.3 | 0.4 | 4.2 | 6.4 |
| **2001** | 88.4 | (23.2) | 12.6 | 11.7 | (0.9) | 3.2 | 9.4 |

*Source*: Altvest, CMRA Analysis

## VALUE-AT-RISK
### Overview
The average VAR for the strategy was 10.5 between 1997 and 2000. Convertible arbitrage ranked second of ten strategies analysed (see Table 23).

### Examples
To further understand the implications of convertible bonds for a portfolio, we created seven sample convertible bond portfolios and calculated their VARs. Table 24 describes each portfolio. One of the key characteristics of these portfolios is that we did not apply any hedging techniques (ie, delta hedging, gamma trading, credit hedging, asset swapping, etc).

The results of our calculations suggest that diversification in a convertible bond portfolio helps to reduce VAR. The best example of this is seen in the combination of Portfolios 1 and 2 (Telecom + Technology + Telecom = Portfolio 7). The VARs of Portfolios 1 and 2 are 3.62% and 2.25%, respectively. The resulting VAR of Portfolio 7 is 2.64%, lower than the expected 3.0% of the weighted average of the two VARs combined (see Table 25). Several correlation analyses shown in Tables 26 and 27 give the reader an indication of the market exposure of the portfolios analysed.

## STRESS TESTS
Due to the number of different parameters that affect the price of convertible bonds, the fact that marking-to-model rather than marking-to-market

**Table 22** Convertible arbitrage risk profile

| Manager | Leverage |
|---|---|
| Credit-sensitive manager | 2 to 1 |
| Premium-sensitive manager | 5 to 1 |

*Source*: Hewitt Investment Group

**Table 23** Average VAR calculation for convertible arbitrage, 1997–2000

| 1997 | 1998 | 1999 | 2000 | Average 1997–2000 | Rank |
|------|------|------|------|-------------------|------|
| 9.3  | 9.6  | 11.3 | 11.0 | 10.5              | 2 of 10 |

*Source*: Assessing Market Risk for Hedge Funds and Hedge Funds Portfolios FAME, March 2001 – Research Paper No. 24, Francois-Serge L'habitant

**Table 24** Portfolios included in VAR analysis

| Portfolio | Sectors | Number of bonds in portfolio |
|-----------|---------|------------------------------|
| 1 | Telecom | 7 |
| 2 | Telecom + technology | 12 |
| 3 | Other | 8 |
| 4 | Telecom + other | 15 |
| 5 | Technology | 5 |
| 6 | Telecom + technology + other | 20 |
| 7 | Telecom + technology + telecom | 19 |

*Source*: Bloomberg, CMRA Analysis

**Table 25** Daily VAR calculation with 95% confidence level for mock convertible arbitrage portfolios, 1997–2001

| Portfolios | Sectors | Daily VAR (%) |
|------------|---------|---------------|
| 1 | Telecom | 3.6 |
| 2 | Telecom + technology | 2.3 |
| 3 | Other | 1.4 |
| 4 | Telecom + other | 1.8 |
| 5 | Technology | 3.9 |
| 6 | Telecom + technology + other | 1.8 |
| 7 | Telecom + technology + telecom | 2.6 |

*Source*: Bloomberg, CMRA Analysis

may be necessary in many cases (see the section "Mark-to-market vs mark-to-model" below) and because of the complexity of models that can be used to price the bonds, stress testing is essential. As with all strategies, when one parameter changes the sensitivity of the instrument to another parameter will also change. For example, if the option in a convertible bond is "out-of-the-money," then the sensitivity to volatility (ie, vega) will be very different than when it is "at-the-money". So in a situation where both the volatility and the equity price move by a large amount, adding the results of a report that shocks these separately (when the stock price was at a different level) will not necessarily explain the P&L.

Suggested stress tests for a convertible arbitrage fund include:

❏ term structure and yield curve levels and shapes;
❏ term structure and relationship of volatility;
❏ price shifts in equities, sectors, indices;
❏ spreads and basis relationships;
❏ yield curve assumptions;
❏ pricing models;
❏ VAR;
❏ product complexity;
❏ difficult-to-model risks;
❏ concentrations;
❏ correlations;
❏ credit components of securities;
❏ volatility of credit spreads;
❏ default assumptions;
❏ leverage; and
❏ liquidity.

To demonstrate the need to stress test patterns/groups of changes as well as individual changes, we used the Monis convertible arbitrage system to carry out stress tests on a single convertible bond, Royal Caribbean 0% maturing February 2, 2021 (see Table 28).

In this situation, a test that includes a move in both the stock price and the volatility is far more valuable than one that uses isolated moves. This makes sense intuitively: if the stock price moved by a large amount, the volatility would not stay constant.

Interest rate models and trees (used frequently to price callable or putable bonds – features commonly found in many convertibles) take up computational time. However, there are solutions to this problem. One such solution is the creation of a stress test that mimics historical periods of stress (such as the Russian/LTCM crisis of 1998). A more sophisticated analysis would use principal components, a statistical process of finding movements of market parameters (such as yield curve, stock price, etc) that explain a large part of the variance of those parameters. However, such tools might not be readily available to many hedge funds since highly skilled (and therefore expensive) labour or expensive commercial software is required to calculate such statistics.

The results of stress tests of +100bp interest rate and at 5% increase in volatility vary depending on two factors: the maturity of the bonds and the diversification of the portfolio. In the case of Portfolio 1, 60% of its bonds have maturities of less than 10 years and 40% have a maturity of approxi-

**Table 26** Cross-correlation between selected portfolios (%)

| | Telecom | Technology | Telecom + technology | Other | Telecom + other | Telecom + technology + other | 2*Telecom + technology |
|---|---|---|---|---|---|---|---|
| Telecom | 100 | 44 | 97 | (22) | 10 | 9 | 99 |
| Technology | 44 | 100 | 50 | (3) | 9 | 11 | 48 |
| Telecom + technology | 97 | 50 | 100 | (18) | 14 | 15 | 100 |
| Other | (22) | (3) | (18) | 100 | 95 | 95 | (19) |
| Telecom + other | 10 | 9 | 14 | 95 | 100 | 99 | 13 |
| Telecom + technology + other | 9 | 11 | 15 | 95 | 99 | 100 | 13 |
| 2*Telecom + technology | 99 | 48 | 100 | (19) | 13 | 13 | 100 |

Source: Bloomberg, CMRA Analysis

**Table 27** Correlation between portfolios and major convertible arbitrage indices, 1997–2001 (%)

| Portfolios | Sectors included | Altvest | Tuna | Hennessee | EACM | CSFB/Tremont | HFRI convertible arbitrage index |
|---|---|---|---|---|---|---|---|
| 5 | Technology | 36.5 | 28.9 | 31.3 | 32.4 | 13.7 | 22.2 |
| 6 | Telecom + technology + other | 35.5 | 28.8 | 37.4 | 23.6 | 6.3 | 28.0 |
| 4 | Telecom + Other | 32.0 | 25.4 | 33.1 | 20.8 | 4.3 | 26.0 |
| 2 | Telecom + technology | 27.9 | 24.1 | 26.7 | 23.1 | 4.3 | 17.8 |
| 7 | Telecom + telecom + technology | 23.2 | 20.1 | 21.7 | 20.1 | 2.0 | 14.6 |
| 3 | Other | 20.2 | 12.8 | 21.4 | 3.0 | 5.6 | 23.5 |
| 1 | Telecom | 16.2 | 14.1 | 14.6 | 15.7 | (1.1) | 9.8 |

Source: Altvest, Tuna, Hennessee, EACM, CSFB/Tremont, HFR

**Table 28** Scenario analysis – base case

| | Scenario | Profit and loss impact (US$) |
|---|---|---|
| | Stock price +10% | 136,800 |
| | −10% | (65,800) |
| | Volatility +10% | 193,900 |
| | −10% | (110,700) |

| Stock price | Volatility | Sum of individual impact (US$) | Calculated joint impact (US$) | "Unexplained" profit and loss (US$) |
|---|---|---|---|---|
| +10% | +10% | 330,700 | 434,100 | 103,400 |
| +10% | −10% | 26,100 | (41,800) | (67,900) |
| −10% | +10% | 128,100 | 3,200 | (96,100) |
| −10% | −10% | (176,500) | (147,900) | 28,600 |

Base stock price = US$22.37  Base volatility = 35%  Base bond price = US$38.3147  Face value = US$100 million

*Source*: Monis Convertible Bond Pricing Model, CMRA Analysis

mately 30 years. In Portfolio 2, 80% of its bonds have maturities of 20 years or more. This explains the greater variance in returns for the second portfolio compared to the first for the same 100bp move in interest rates (see Table 29).

## LEVEL OF TRANSPARENCY

A survey published by Alternative Investment News in September 2000 found that convertible arbitrage funds offer the least transparency of all the strategies, but CMRA's experience in dealing with actual managers suggests otherwise (see Table 30).

## DUE DILIGENCE QUESTIONS FOR CONVERTIBLE ARBITRAGE FUNDS

Due diligence questions for a convertible arbitrage hedge fund may include:

❏ What type of pricing model do you use?
❏ How do you mark your positions to market?
❏ Do you stress test the value of your portfolio against alternative methods for marking the market? What do you conclude?
❏ If you had to (or wanted to) liquidate your portfolio, how long would it take in normal times and in stressed times?
❏ What is your data source for volatility?
❏ How do you evaluate your portfolio by maturity? By strike?
❏ Do you use credit derivatives to hedge?

**Table 29** Generic stress testing for sample portfolio analysis, 1997–2001

| Portfolio | Sectors | Daily VAR (%) |
|-----------|---------|---------------|
| 1 | Telecom | (7.3) |
| 2 | Telecom + technology | (6.6) |
| 3 | Other | (16.0) |
| 4 | Telecom + other | (12.6) |
| 5 | Technology | (2.3) |
| 6 | Telecom + technology + other | (17.0) |
| 7 | Telecom + technology + telecom | (6.6) |

*Source*: Bloomberg, CMRA Analysis

Because convertible bonds are dependent on model pricing, it is important to ask about the systems in place to price trades in addition to the portfolio and the calculation of risk parameters. Getting a handle on the ways the fund managers deal with data and NAV issues is important.

❏ What is the procedure for marking the portfolios?
❏ Does the manager come up with his/her own marks or are they an average of several broker month-end or day-end quotes? If they are an average, then what is the difference in bond points between the minimum and the maximum? If they are not an average, what is the manager's method for arriving at its marks?

These last few questions are particularly important if the portfolio is very large because summary reports can disguise danger. For example, running a report that moves volatilities across the board up and down by a certain amount is not enough. Such a report might show that the portfolio is long volatility. Yet when volatilities move up, the portfolio might lose money.

**Table 30** Transparency offered to investors by managers of convertible arbitrage funds (%)

| | Overall level of transparency | | | Positions disclosed to investors | |
|---|---|---|---|---|---|
| Performance | Key positions | View entire portfolio | No transparency | Key long positions | Key short positions |
| 100 | 43 | 0 | 0 | 43 | 14 |

*Source*: Hennessee Hedge Fund Advisory Group

This is because the fund might be net long volatility but might be short a certain sector and long another sector. If volatilities move unevenly, anything is possible. Understanding the volatility "surface" used, the source of the data to create the surface and the methods employed to differentiate the "smile" can be important.

Another focus of due diligence should be on the concentration characteristics of each issue in the portfolio within the market:

❏ Are there a few investors who own entire issues or one-issue ownerships split over a large number of investors?
❏ How much of the fund's portfolio reflects a play on volatility and how much reflects a play on credit?
❏ How can a third party understand whether the "convertible bonds" in which a company is investing really have "convertible" characteristics?

The Association of Convertible Bond Managers (ACBM), a European trade body, takes this last issue seriously. Unlike the US, Europe does not have a regulatory framework for convertible bonds and other equity-linked issues. The ACBM rightly stresses that the adoption of standards will benefit the asset class and, in a way, will make the investment style more transparent.

## DATA AND NAV ISSUES

The dependence of convertible bond funds on mark-to-model pricing as opposed to mark-to-market (see the section "Mark-to-market vs mark-to-model" for further discussion) creates pricing differences among the different broker dealers – especially for illiquid bonds – thereby diminishing the investor's ability to accurately calculate any kind of Sharpe ratio measurement for its portfolios.

The illiquidity and mark-to-model characteristics of the convertibles should be considered as an additional source of risk for which the hedge fund investor should expect additional reward. One approach introduced by Weinsten and Abdulali proposes a two-step process to find the best representative price for a security for which multiple indicative prices are received.[4] The first step is to assign for each indicative price the probability that that price will be the trade price. The assignment of such probabilities represents a preconceived belief and understanding about the market. The second step requires setting a single price that best represents the distribution of the prices received. It is a feature of this framework that the price selected in the second step is closely related to the risk tolerance of the manager investing in these assets. Based on this approach, Weinsten and Abdulali estimate that, with these prices, the benchmark statistics used in portfolio management could be applied to estimate more accurate Sharpe ratio characteristics of these assets.

The convertible bond market is primarily a dealer market and there are few commercial sources that provide market data for convertible bonds. Bloomberg provides some historical data, while Monis offers end-of-day prices for up to 2,300 bonds. Real-time price data must be obtained from dealers. The big dealers for convertibles are Merrill Lynch, CSFB, Goldman Sachs and Morgan Stanley. Smaller dealers like KBC Financial are also a good source for real-time data.

Bloomberg provides end-of-day data for some of the bonds in its database. Even though Bloomberg does not report the exact number of bonds that are available in its database, it does provide terms and conditions information on most outstanding bonds.

As part of the analysis, the prices of eight convertible bonds obtained from three different sources were compared to one another (see Table 31). The prices given by these sources varied by as much as 8.7%.

Typically, bid/ask spreads of convertible bonds for fairly liquid issues are 0.125–0.25 points (price points), whereas they are 0.5–1.0 point for more illiquid issues. Bid/ask spread data from Bloomberg is the closing spread for the day. It is possible for Bloomberg to have slight mismatches in the timings of the bids and asks at the close of the day, resulting in larger spreads (one point, as seen in three of the four quotes in Table 32).

Typically, a round lot in the convertible bond market is US$1 million. From interviews with several funds, we found that convertible arbitrage hedge funds that have US$30–50million of AUM will commonly trade a quarter to half a million principal amount of bonds. On a monthly basis, traded volumes for funds that are about US$500 million of AUM are roughly a quarter to half a billion principal amount, although it varies from fund to fund. Usually, the turnover of such funds occurs two to three times per year.

As an example, let us examine the effect of valuing a US$100 million long position of five-year Treasury notes at a mid-market level vs. a bid level. (A similar argument holds for a short position, with bid replaced by ask in the following discussion.) Historical data suggest that the average bid/offer yield spread is 1.05bp for normal periods and 1.83bp for stress periods.

Consequently, the difference between the more aggressive (valuing at the mid) and the more conservative (valuing at the bid) approaches in a "normal market" would be:

$$US\$23,625 \ (0.000105 \times 4.5 \times 1/2 \times 100 \ million)$$

On the other hand, the same US$100 million position in a stress period renders a difference of

$$US\$41,175 \ (0.000183 \times 4.5 \times 1/2 \times 100 \ million)$$

**Table 31** Price difference between broker dealer quotes

| Convertible bonds | Observation date | Sources | | | Maximum difference between sources | Maximum difference as % of average |
| | | Bloomberg price | MONIS price | Broker dealer price | | |
| --- | --- | --- | --- | --- | --- | --- |
| AES 4.5% of 2005 | 28/03/02 | 63.6 | 67.3 | 61.7 | 5.6 | 8.7 |
| ONIS 5% of 2005 | 19/02/02 | 75.1 | 70.4 | 75.6 | 5.2 | 7.1 |
| ONIS 5% of 2005 | 15/02/02 | 71.6 | 70.3 | 70.3 | 1.3 | 1.9 |
| AES 4.5% of 2005 | 31/12/01 | 87.7 | 88.0 | 87.1 | 1.0 | 1.1 |
| KMG 5.25% of 2010 | 28/03/02 | 119.9 | 118.8 | 118.9 | 1.1 | 0.9 |
| AMGN 0% of 2032 | 28/03/02 | 71.0 | 70.5 | 70.8 | 0.5 | 0.7 |
| KMG 5.25% of 2010 | 28/02/02 | 114.3 | 114.8 | 114.2 | 0.5 | 0.4 |
| AMGN 0% of 2032 | 28/02/02 | 71.3 | 71.4 | 71.2 | 0.2 | 0.2 |

*Source:* Broker Dealer, Bloomberg, Monis, CMRA Analysis

**Table 32** Average bid/ask spreads

| Convertible bonds | Bloomberg | Broker dealer |
|---|---|---|
| ONIS 5% of 2005 | 1 point | Typically 0.125 to 0.25 points |
| KMG 5.25% of 2010 | 1 point | for liquid issues and 0.5 to |
| AMGN 0% of 2032 | 0.25 to 0.50 points | 1 point for illiquid issues |
| AES 4.5% of 2005 | 1 point | |

*Source*: Bloomberg, CMRA Analysis

A portfolio whose manager marked at the mid-market level would not show the extra loss of US$17,550 that it would have shown had it used bid pricing. Clearly, if liquidity is a concern, the bid pricing – though more volatile – would better reflect the value an investor could realise if the position had to be sold.

### MARK-TO-MARKET VS MARK-TO-MODEL

There can be substantial differences between marking to "market" and marking to "model." Convertible bond prices from pricing models are sensitive to the data inputs and internal differences within the model. CMRA looked at how differences in internal features, like tree creation, affected the price and volatility sensitivity of a bond in a particular convertible bond-pricing model. Table 33 shows that the price changes by almost half a point between the 100-node and the 200-node model. The price sensitivity is reduced as the number of nodes used in the model is increased.

Table 34 gives the theoretical prices vs market prices obtained from Monis. The data show that there are differences of as much as six points, as in the case of the AMGN 0% of 2032 convertible bond.

Furthermore, the sensitivity to the volatility of the underlying security depends on the number of nodes. In the case of 100 nodes, the price sometimes falls as volatilities rise. The fluctuations are a lot smoother when 300 nodes are used. Other factors in the model, such as interest rate trees and credit spreads, can also affect prices. Note that volatility and credit spread are largely subjective data inputs. For this reason the theoretical prices that models generate can differ significantly from actual market quotes (see Table 35).

The failure of Lipper & Co.'s prominent convertible arbitrage funds sheds light on the subjectivity that can creep into portfolio valuation. The main reason for their problem was that the portfolio had been mis-marked for a long period of time. Mis-marking can happen, especially when data are not easy to obtain and especially in the case of illiquid securities. There can be several data problems with convertible bonds. First, the volatility that is used to estimate the value of a convertible bond may not be accurate. Unlike exchange-traded options, where volatility is easily and accurately estimated (since these options are liquid), volatility might not be easily verifiable for convertibles. This is because exchange-traded options have a maximum maturity of two years (in the case of LEAPS). Convertibles, on the other hand, can extend all the way to 10 years. Estimating 10-year volatility on the basis of two-year quotes is as much an art as a science.

The typical way to counter such data problems is to poll several brokers of the security. However, the more illiquid the security, the greater the variance of the poll results, which means that the marking of the security might not necessarily be the level at which it would trade. Also, the way these quotes are "averaged" can make a significant difference.

---

**Table 33** Price sensitivity to number of nodes used in valuation

**Spot**

**Base case**

| | |
|---|---|
| Stock price | US$33.37 |
| Volatility | 40% |
| Credit spread | 200bp |
| Bond price | US$43.45 |

*Source*: Monis Convertible Bond Pricing Model

**Theoretical value of Thomson Multimedia 1% 1/1/08**

| # of nodes used in valuation model | Calculated price |
|---|---|
| 100 | 43.45 |
| 200 | 42.98 |
| 300 | 43.07 |
| 500 | 43.06 |

*Source*: Monis Convertible Bond Pricing Model

---

**Table 34** Theoretical price vs market price

| Convertible bonds | Sample date 1 | Market price (from Monis) | MONIS theoretical price | Absolute % difference |
|---|---|---|---|---|
| AMGN 0% of 2032 | 28/02/2002 | 71.375 | 77.375 | 7.8 |
| KMG 5.25% of 2010 | 28/02/2002 | 114.750 | 110.270 | 4.1 |
| AMGN 0% of 2032 | 28/03/2002 | 70.500 | 72.130 | 2.3 |
| KMG 5.25% of 2010 | 28/03/2002 | 118.750 | 116.430 | 2.0 |

*Source*: Monis Convertible Bond Pricing Model

**Table 35** Fluctuations of bond price with changes in volatility (points)

**Spot**

| | |
|---|---|
| Stock price | US$33.37 |
| Volatility | 40% |
| Credit spread | 200bp |
| Bond price | US$43.45 |

*Source*: Monis Convertible Bond Pricing Model

**Fluctuations of bond price with changes in volatility (points)**

| Volatility (%) | 100 nodes | 300 nodes | Difference |
|---|---|---|---|
| 41 | 0.2 | 0.2 | 0.0 |
| 42 | 0.2 | 0.2 | 0.0 |
| 43 | (0.4) | 0.2 | (0.7) |
| 44 | 1.2 | 0.2 | 1.0 |
| 45 | (0.8) | 0.3 | (1.1) |

*Source*: Monis Convertible Bond Pricing Model

Table 36 shows the results of CMRA's survey of eight convertible arbitrage hedge funds on how they obtain data to mark their portfolios and calculate NAVs. As one can see, most funds mark their portfolios using mid prices rather than the more conservative bid (for long) and offered (for short) prices.

Hedge funds typically obtain volatility estimates from the publicly available sources or directly from broker dealers.

In the case of convertible arbitrage hedge funds attempting to neutralise the expense through gamma trading, short-term volatility is needed because the trader must rebalance his/her portfolio a certain number of times each week. To do this, the trader usually tries to obtain the 30- to 45-day at-the-money volatility; Bloomberg is considered a good source. Some hedge fund managers then adjust the volatility based on the "smile" effect, but may just apply the at-the-money volatility to out-of-the-money options. To obtain the volatilities of the option embedded in the convertible bond (to see if it is rich or cheap and therefore whether it is a good investment), traders seek options with maturities similar to the bond option itself. In the case of two-year bonds, LEAPs are commonly used to extrapolate volatility. In the case of 10-year bonds, the trader will sometimes estimate the likelihood of the bond being put or called (if these features exist in the bond) and will try to use the volatility of the stock until the put or call dates. For instance, a 10-year bond with a two-year put might be priced using the two-year volatility for the stock. If nothing else is available, traders will extrapolate long-term volatility from short-term

**Table 36** Marking of long positions

**Marking of long positions**

| Mid | Bid | No answer |
|---|---|---|
| 4 | 2 | 2 |

**Marking of short positions**

| Mid | Offer | No answer |
|---|---|---|
| 5 | 1 | 2 |

**Number of quotes per security**

| 1 only | 1 to 3 | 3+ | No answer |
|---|---|---|---|
| 2 | 4 | 2 | 0 |

**Frequency of quotes**

| Many times a day | Daily | Weekly | Monthly | No answer |
|---|---|---|---|---|
| 1 | 2 | 2 | 3 | 0 |

*Source*: CMRA Analysis

volatility and the extrapolation will be influenced by historical data patterns. Whatever approach is chosen, the value of the portfolio will be sensitive to the assumptions made.

## PUBLICLY DISCLOSED PROBLEMS

Lipper's convertible arbitrage funds attributed its problems to investments in illiquid securities and the events of September 11, 2001. Lipper wrote down as much as 45% of the value of some of its funds. This incident is widely viewed as an isolated one, but we nevertheless believe it is a wake-up call.

Some companies issue convertibles to pay off liabilities caused by earlier issued convertibles (especially those with embedded put options that investors can exercise). Part or all of the payment of the old convertible might be in stock. This can also cause the stock price and the issuer's credit quality to fall. CMRA believes that such incidents have the potential to destabilise some convertible arbitrage portfolios. Table 38 gives more details on the Lipper Funds and the extent of their losses.

**Table 37** Lipper case

| | Lipper Convertibles, LP | Lipper Off-Shore Convertibles | Lipper Convertibles II, LP |
|---|---|---|---|
| **Long positions** 1/1/02 – 26/03/02 | Reduced from over US$1.7 billion to US$200 million | Reduced from US$373 million to US$48 million | Reduced from US$60 million to US$6 million |
| **Short positions** 1/1/02 – 26/03/02 | Reduced from US$1.1 billion to US$160 million | Reduced from US$230 million to US$33 million | Reduced from US$38 million to US$4 million |
| **Net cash** | US$360 million | US$185 million | US$19 million |
| **2002 portfolio sales** | Fraction of 1% of independent third party low bids | Fraction of 1% of independent third-party low bids | Fraction of 1% of independent third party low bids |
| **2001** Decline in book value | 45% | 10% | 17% |
| **1/1/02–26/03/02** Decline in book value | Additional 2% over 2001 | Additional 1% over 2001 | Additional 3% over 2001 |

*Source: Marhedge.com*

1   Lehman Brothers, 2001, "Understanding Hedge Fund Performance: Research Results and Rules of Thumb for the Institutional Investor", November.

2   Favre L., and J. Galeano, 2002, Hedge Fund Managers Question Convertible Arbitrage Study, Financial Products, May 21.

3   Ivo Welch, Professor of finance, Yale University, 2002, Financial Adviser Report, May.

4   Weinsten, E., and A. Abdulali, 2002, "Hedge Fund Transparency: Quantifying Valuation Bias for Illiquid Assets", *Risk Management Magazine*, June.

# 13

# Emerging Markets

## DESCRIPTION OF THE STRATEGY

Emerging market hedge funds typically invest in the debt or equity of emerging (or non-G7) markets. The World Bank defines countries as emerging markets if their per capita GDP is less than US$7,620. Emerging market hedge funds generally focus either on single continents or on the global markets. Although the rewards from investing in emerging markets can be high, so can the risks. These are countries with volatile growth rates, high inflation and are hugely dependent upon how well their governments function. Lack of a business-orientated legal infrastructure and other regulatory restrictions (such as restrictions on short selling) make risk management and hedging difficult.

Investing in emerging market securities offers the opportunity for high rates of return on investment for qualified individuals and institutions that appreciate the potential and risks inherent in dealing in these markets. From 1991 to 1999, emerging market funds focused on political and policy changes in the emerging markets. Many of these funds enjoyed a track record of catching major turning points in emerging market economies, including the Mexican peso devaluation of 1994, the bull markets in Israel and South Africa in the 1990s and the decline of equity markets in Russia and China in 1998.

Emerging market funds grew sharply in 1999, but their success was tied to that of the US equity markets. When the US stock market began to falter at the end of the first quarter of 2000, emerging markets generally suffered as well. Latin American funds experienced the biggest blow. They saw their values fall dramatically after posting strong gains during 1999. On average, the top 25 funds in the group lost 7.9% during 2000.

Emerging market funds try to take advantage of market inefficiencies. These market inefficiencies are continuously explored by fund managers, who look for undervalued assets and purchase them before the market corrects itself. Most emerging markets do not have a market infrastructure comparable to that of the US or the European countries. This makes them very attractive in many ways but at the same time very volatile. Participants in these markets are often faced with political instability, corruption scandals, economic decline and other issues that are very difficult to forecast.

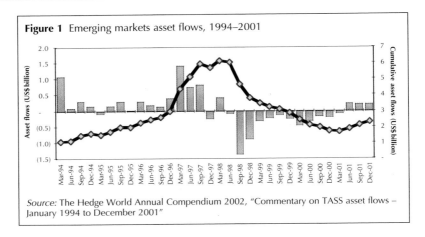

**Figure 1** Emerging markets asset flows, 1994–2001

*Source:* The Hedge World Annual Compendium 2002, "Commentary on TASS asset flows – January 1994 to December 2001"

Funds investing in emerging markets not only research companies in those markets but also look at political and regional issues and maintain close contact with a network of brokers and industry participants in the countries concerned.

The AUM of hedge funds in emerging market funds has had among the lowest growth in the hedge fund universe. Volatility and unsustainable returns have dampened enthusiasm for emerging market funds.

The cumulative flow of assets into emerging market hedge funds has had two cycles (see Figure 1). The first cycle was from 1994 until June 1998, with a continuous flow of assets to a cumulative level of US$1.5 billion. The second cycle was from the second quarter of 1998 to the first quarter of 2001, when there was a continuous outflow of approximately US$2 billion of AUM.

## EFFECT OF MARKET CONDITIONS

In general, the emerging market strategy performs above its historical average when:

❏ The US and European economies are in an expansionary mode.
❏ Credit risk premium is declining.
❏ The US equity markets and the major European markets are rising (the emerging markets often follow these).
❏ Global political stability prevails.

The strategy performs substantially below its historical average when:

❏ The US and European economies are in a recessionary mode.
❏ Credit risk premium is increasing.
❏ High liquidity in emerging markets is not expected.

❏ The US and European equity markets are falling.
❏ Global political instability prevails.

## INVESTORS IN THE STRATEGY

A 2000 survey found that individuals and family offices are the investor groups that invest most in the emerging market strategy funds. This investor group constitutes 40% of the total investor universe for these funds. Funds of funds are the next largest investor group with 22%. The results of the survey are summarised in Table 1.

## WELL-KNOWN PLAYERS

Table 2 lists the top 10 emerging markets funds by AUM. The Hedge Fund 100 covers only three of the top 25 emerging market funds with US$2.4 billion in AUM. This represents 29% of the approximately US$8.3 billion total in the top 25. In addition, of the top 25 funds, four funds with a combined US$0.9 billion in AUM (or 11% of the total) are among the most popular holdings of funds of funds.

## COVERAGE IN DIFFERENT SOURCES

CSFB/Tremont covers the largest number of emerging market funds, but Altvest covers the greatest AUM (see Table 3).

## DISTRIBUTION OF FUNDS IN THE STRATEGY

By December 2001, 8% of the funds comprised an overall AUM of US$2.7 billion, which represented 51% of the US$5.2 billion total AUM of the strategy. The 80 smaller funds that participate in the strategy account for 49% of the assets (see Figure 2).

### Distribution of funds by quartile of performance

Table 4 shows the distribution of funds by quartiles of performance. The highest-returning funds also have the largest AUM and the highest average Sharpe ratio.

### Distribution of funds by quartile of AUM

When dividing the funds by the largest AUM, there does not seem to be a clear correlation between AUM and returns; large AUM does not necessarily mean high returns (see Table 5). Furthermore, the Sharpe ratios are almost the same across quartiles.

**Table 1** Investors in the emerging market strategy

| Investors | (%) |
|---|---|
| Individuals and family offices | 40 |
| Funds of funds | 22 |
| Endowments and foundations | 19 |
| Pensions and retirement | 12 |
| Corporations | 8 |

*Source*: Hennessee Hedge Fund Survey (January 2000)

**Table 2** Top emerging market funds with more than US$1 billion in AUM (all sources)

| Rank | Fund | Highest AUM*<br>(US$ billion) |
|---|---|---|
| 1 | Joho Capital | 2.0 |
| 2 | OCM Emerging Markets | 1.8 |
| 3 | TIFF Absolute Return Pool | 0.8 |
| 4 | Pharo Arbitrage Fund, Ltd. | 0.4 |
| 5 | LCM Global Interest Rate Hedged Fund Aggressive Program | 0.3 |
| 6 | Marathon Master Fund, Ltd. | 0.3 |
| 7 | Sloane Robinson Investment Management | 0.3 |
| 8 | Alexandra Global Investment Fund I, Ltd. | 0.3 |
| 9 | Moore Emerging Markets | 0.2 |
| 10 | Avenue Capital Group | 0.2 |
| | **Total** | **6.6** |

* This is the highest AUM for that fund among all the sources.

*Source*: Altvest, Tuna, HFR, Institutional Investor (June 2002), Directory of Fund of Hedge Funds Investment Vehicles

**Table 3** Coverage of emerging market funds by different sources

| Source | Total number of funds | Funds with no AUM data | Total AUM (US$ billion) |
|---|---|---|---|
| Altvest | 116 | 21 | 8.2 |
| CSFB/Tremont | 118 | 0 | 8.0 |
| HFR | 107 | 4 | 4.7 |
| The Hedge Fund 100 | 5 | 0 | 1.8 |
| Tuna | 32 | 1 | 1.0 |

*Source*: Altvest, HFR, Tuna, CSFB/Tremont, Institutional Investor (June 2002)

In both Tables 4 and 5, the first quartile's AUM is dominated by a single fund, OCM Emerging Markets, which alone has an AUM of US$1.2 billion. The second largest fund in the sample has US$187 million in AUM.

## PERFORMANCE OF THE STRATEGY
### Returns during boom and bust

As shown in Figure 3, emerging market hedge funds underperformed the S&P 500 Index during the boom years of 1997-2000 by an 11% margin (23% for the S&P 500 vs 12%), but during the bust period from 2000–2001 these funds outperformed the S&P 500 by a margin of 8% (–14% for the S&P 500 vs –6%).

**Figure 2** Distribution of emerging market funds and AUM in 2001

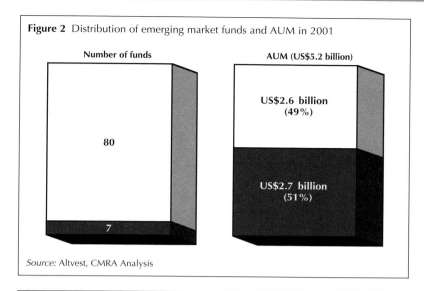

Number of funds

80

7

AUM (US$5.2 billion)

US$2.6 billion
(49%)

US$2.7 billion
(51%)

*Source:* Altvest, CMRA Analysis

**Table 4** Distribution of emerging market funds by quartiles of five-year performance, 1997–2001

| Return quartiles | Average 1997–2001 equally weighted return (%) | Avergae 1997–2001 AUM-weighted return (%) | AUM in quartile (US$ billion) | % of total | Average 1997–2001 standard deviation (%) | Sharpe ratio 1997–2001 |
|---|---|---|---|---|---|---|
| 1 | 28.0 | 25.5 | 1.4 | 51 | 19.3 | 1.3 |
| 2 | 15.3 | 14.8 | 0.6 | 20 | 18.6 | 0.8 |
| 3 | 11.1 | 10.9 | 0.4 | 14 | 8.0 | 0.9 |
| 4 | 3.3 | 2.9 | 0.4 | 15 | 15.3 | 0.2 |
| **Total** | **14.0** | **17.8** | **2.8** | **100** | **15.3** | **0.8** |

*Source*: Altvest, CMRA Analysis based on 29 funds with five-year performance data

**Table 5** Distribution of emerging market funds by quartiles of AUM, 1997–2001

| AUM quartiles | Average 1997–2001 equally weighted return (%) | Avergae 1997–2001 AUM-weighted return (%) | AUM in quartile (US$ billion) | % of total | Average 1997–2001 standard deviation (%) | Sharpe ratio 1997–2001 |
|---|---|---|---|---|---|---|
| 1 | 15.7 | 20.8 | 1.8 | 65 | 16.2 | 0.9 |
| 2 | 8.2 | 8.3 | 0.5 | 18 | 12.6 | 0.7 |
| 3 | 16.0 | 16.1 | 0.3 | 11 | 11.8 | 0.9 |
| 4 | 15.9 | 17.6 | 0.2 | 6 | 20.0 | 0.5 |
| **Total** | **14.0** | **17.8** | **2.8** | **100** | **15.3** | **0.8** |

*Source*: Altvest, CMRA Analysis based on 29 funds with five-year performance data

### Returns from different sources

The difference in returns between the various emerging market hedge fund indices can be significant (see Table 6), with the 1997 performance varying by 25.5 points across the different sources, or 1.2 times the average return of the strategy!

It is important to note that the style indices that many sources use are accurate only to a limited extent. Since funds might employ a mixture of styles in their portfolios, segregating them into a single style causes a great deal of information about the funds to be lost. However, if one attempted to segregate funds into their own individual styles by including their multiple strategies in the style labels, there would be too many permutations and combinations of styles to deal with. The result of this problem can be highlighted when one sees how divergent the returns/standard deviation profile is for the constituent funds of an index. To demonstrate this point an analysis was done on the returns and standard deviations of the constituents of the CSFB/Tremont Emerging Markets Index to show how varied they were. The results are plotted in Figure 4. All the funds in the index were used, except one for which data were unavailable.

### Index performance

For the 1997–2001 period, the compounded returns of emerging market funds ranked among the lowest of the hedge fund strategies analysed (see Table 7).

Emerging market funds have been among the most volatile of funds. Having faced a variety of crises, such as Russia and Asia, their five-year returns have been among the most dismal.

Figure 5 shows the quarterly returns of emerging market fund indices calculated by different commercial sources. There are large differences, for

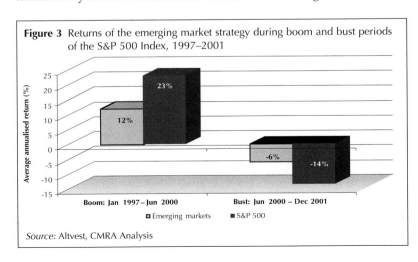

**Figure 3** Returns of the emerging market strategy during boom and bust periods of the S&P 500 Index, 1997–2001

*Source:* Altvest, CMRA Analysis

**Table 6** Comparison of emerging market indices across by different sources, 1997–2001

| | 1997 | 1998 | 1999 | 2000 | 2001 | 1997–2001 Return | Sharpe ratio |
|---|---|---|---|---|---|---|---|
| Tuna | 39.2 | (23.8) | 48.2 | (2.4) | 21.7 | 13.3 | 0.3 |
| Altvest | 13.7 | (27.7) | 72.8 | (5.6) | (0.7) | 5.9 | 0.2 |
| Hennessee | 14.3 | (30.1) | 47.1 | (9.3) | 10.3 | 3.3 | 0.2 |
| HFR | 16.6 | (33.0) | 55.9 | (10.7) | 6.3 | 2.9 | 0.2 |
| CSFB/Tremont | 26.6 | (37.7) | 44.8 | (5.5) | 5.8 | 2.7 | 0.1 |
| Maximum difference | 25.5 | 13.9 | 28.0 | 8.3 | 22.4 | 10.6 | 0.2 |
| Average | 22.1 | (30.5) | 53.8 | (6.7) | 8.7 | 5.6 | 0.2 |

*Source*: Tuna, Altvest, Hennessey, HFR, CSFB/Tremont

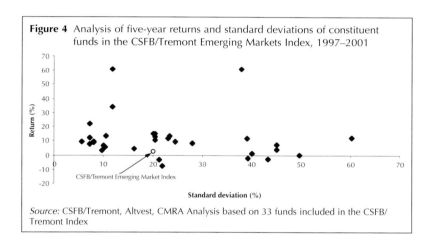

**Figure 4** Analysis of five-year returns and standard deviations of constituent funds in the CSFB/Tremont Emerging Markets Index, 1997–2001

*Source:* CSFB/Tremont, Altvest, CMRA Analysis based on 33 funds included in the CSFB/Tremont Index

instance, between the Altvest and CSFB/Tremont indices. The different index calculation methodologies, along with the different compositions of the funds in the indices, are the main reasons for this difference. See Chapter 11 for a further discussion of index methodologies.

The CSFB/Tremont Index is based on 33 funds, while 20 funds are included in the Altvest source. The two indices have five funds in common. The remaining 28 funds in the CSFB/Tremont Index outperform the remaining 19 funds of the Altvest Index on an equally weighted basis by 10.5 points for the 1998 period. In addition, the CSFB/Tremont Index is AUM-weighted, whereas the Altvest Index (and all the other indices analysed) is equally weighted. This difference in the methodology accounts for the 65% difference between the return of the two indices in 1998.

**Table 7** Ranking of the emerging market strategy against other strategies, 1997–2001

|  | 1997 | 1998 | 1999 | 2000 | 2001 | 1997–2001 | Rank |
|---|---|---|---|---|---|---|---|
| Return (%) Altvest | 13.7 | (27.7) | 72.8 | (5.6) | (0.7) | 5.9 | 12 of 14 |
| Return (%) HFR | 16.6 | (33.0) | 55.9 | (10.7) | 5.8 | 2.9 | 19 of 19 |

*Source*: Altvest, HFR, CMRA Analysis

**Figure 5** Absolute spread of returns to Altvest over the major market indices for emerging markets, 1997–2001

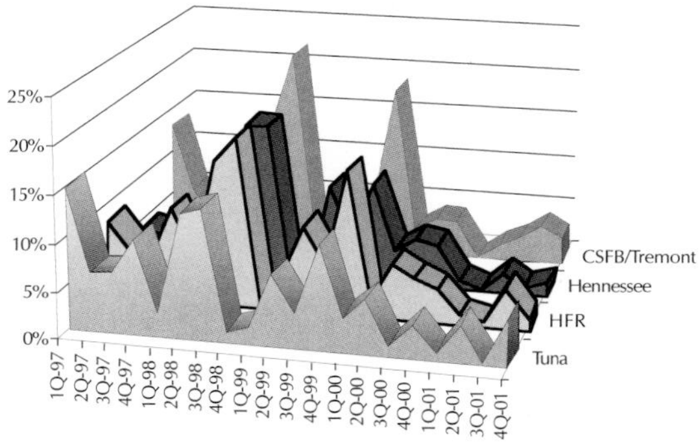

*Source:* Altvest, CFSB/Tremont, Henessee, Tuna, CMRA Analysis

## Performance correlations

The rolling correlations in Table 8 show that emerging market fund returns are highly correlated to the S&P 500 Index. This is because the health of many emerging market economies depends on the US economy. If equity markets fall in the US, emerging markets are likely to follow suit.

## Stress period analysis

As one would expect, the emerging market funds were hit hard during the Russian/LTCM crisis, during which their returns were among the lowest of all the funds (see Table 9).

The emerging market index had a Sharpe ratio of –0.8 during the Russian/LTCM crisis. During the equity market downturn and the burst of the technology bubble, the strategy continued to do poorly with a Sharpe ratio of –1.0 (see Table 10).

Term premia (an indicator of economic expansion) has a great effect on emerging market funds (see Table 11). This strategy involves the purchase of emerging market government debt. Its reliance on US economic health shows how emerging markets in general depend on US economic performance.

### Range of performance
On average, emerging market funds earned between 10% and 20% over the 1997–2001 period (see Figure 6).

## SHARPE RATIO
### Distribution
Bearing in mind the cautions in this book regarding the use of Sharpe ratio analysis for hedge funds, it is interesting to note that the funds with the highest Sharpe ratios are not necessarily those with the highest returns. However, in this strategy they are the ones with the lowest standard deviation (see Table 12).

Due to the volatility of emerging market funds, the Sharpe ratio itself

**Table 8**  Rolling correlations of emerging markets index performance with the S&P 500 and Lehman Aggregate Bond Index, 1997–2001 (%)

|  | 1997 | 1998 | 1999 | 2000 | 2001 |
|---|---|---|---|---|---|
| Lehman Aggregate Bond Index | 54.3 | (49.5) | 5.7 | 44.6 | (41.3) |
| S&P 500 Index | 79.6 | 87.5 | 63.3 | 53.3 | 76.3 |

*Source*: Altvest, CMRA Analysis

**Table 9**  Returns of emerging markets index during periods of stress (%)

| Russian/LTCM crisis | Tech crash | September 11 |
|---|---|---|
| (19.9) | (17.7) | 3.2 |

*Source*: Altvest, CMRA Analysis

**Table 10**  Sharpe ratio of emerging markets index during periods of stress

| Russian/LTCM crisis | Tech crash | September 11 | Average of Absolute Sharpe ratios | Maximum-minimum |
|---|---|---|---|---|
| (0.8) | (1.0) | 0.2 | 0.7 | 1.2 |

*Source*: Altvest, CMRA Analysis

**Table 11** Sensitivity of the emerging market strategy to factors in Lehman's multivariate model

| Factor | Coefficient | Rank |
|---|---|---|
| Change in term premia | 0.038 | 1 of 17 |
| Change in credit spread | (0.120) | 17 of 17 |
| Change in implied volatility | (0.420) | 17 of 17 |

*Source*: Lehman Brothers Understanding Hedge Fund Performance

can vary substantially. Although 18 funds had Sharpe ratios greater than 2.0 in 2001, only one fund had consistently kept up the performance for five years. This observation holds for Sharpe ratios between 1.0 and 2.0 because of the high variance in the ratio. When Sharpe ratios are high, it is not because the volatility of the returns is low but because the returns themselves are very high. However, returns can be sharply negative too, as evidenced by the large number of funds with a one-year Sharpe ratio below 0.0 (see Figure 7).

### LEVERAGE
94% of emerging market hedge funds use leverage (see Chapter 2 for a discussion of leverage). 80% of the funds use a leverage lower than 2.0, and only 14% leverage their positions to a level greater than 2.0 (see Figure 8).

Table 13 shows the minimum, maximum and average leverage of emerging market funds in 2002. Compared to 14 other strategies, emerging market funds are currently among the least leveraged.

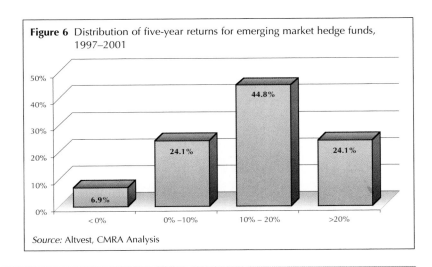

**Figure 6** Distribution of five-year returns for emerging market hedge funds, 1997–2001

*Source:* Altvest, CMRA Analysis

**Table 12** Distribution of emerging market hedge fund quartiles of Sharpe ratio, 1997–2001

| Sharpe ratio quartiles | Average 1997–2001 equally weighted return (%) | Avergae 1997–2001 AUM-weighted return (%) | AUM in quartile (US$ billion) | % of total | Average 1997–2001 standard deviation (%) | Sharpe ratio 1997–2001 |
|---|---|---|---|---|---|---|
| 1 | 17.7 | 21.5 | 1.6 | 58 | 8.2 | 1.6 |
| 2 | 21.3 | 22.1 | 0.3 | 12 | 15.9 | 1.0 |
| 3 | 12.1 | 12.6 | 0.5 | 18 | 12.1 | 0.6 |
| 4 | 6.2 | 3.9 | 0.3 | 12 | 23.8 | 0.1 |
| **Total** | **14.0** | **17.8** | **2.8** | **100** | **15.3** | **0.8** |

Source: Altvest, CMRA Analysis based on 29 funds with five-year performance data

Historically, leverage in emerging market funds has been relatively constant, ranging from 0.9 to 1.1 over the past five years (see Table 14).

Further analysis of leverage for the strategy during the same period (see Table 15) indicates that the first quartile (the group with the lowest leverage) has US$1.7 billion in AUM, while the last quartile has only US$0.9 billion in AUM – indicating that size may indeed matter for this strategy.

Table 16 shows the delevered returns of emerging market funds against their reported returns. The average reported five-year return of emerging market funds is 8.04 percentage points higher than the average five-year delevered return. The difference is smaller in the one-year returns. The five-year returns difference is among the highest of all the other strategies, while the one-year returns difference is in the lower half compared to the

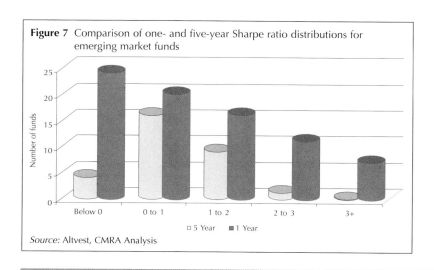

**Figure 7** Comparison of one- and five-year Sharpe ratio distributions for emerging market funds

Source: Altvest, CMRA Analysis

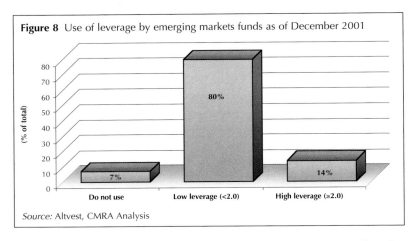

**Figure 8** Use of leverage by emerging markets funds as of December 2001

*Source:* Altvest, CMRA Analysis

other strategies. Leverage has decreased through time, especially after events such as the Russian/LTCM crisis.

## RISK MEASUREMENT

Emerging markets are not easily understood and they experience volatile periods that can only be accounted for by intuitive factors. Stock prices are not directly linked to the performance of the respective issuers – factors such as political uncertainty, economic turmoil, corruption, etc, are the primary drivers of valuation in the space. Accordingly, diversification is a

**Table 13** Financial leverage of emerging market funds in 2002

| Minimum | Average | Maximum | Rank |
|---------|---------|---------|------|
| 1.0 | 1.4 | 3.0 | 11 of 14 |

*Source*: Altvest, CMRA Analysis

**Table 14** Historical average leverage of emerging market funds, 1997–2001

| | | | | | 1997–2001 | | |
|---|---|---|---|---|---|---|---|
| 1997 | 1998 | 1999 | 2000 | 2001 | Average | Maximum | Minimum |
| 1.0 | 1.0 | 0.9 | 1.0 | 1.1 | 1.0 | 1.1 | 0.9 |

*Source*: Altvest, CMRA Analysis

**Table 15** Distribution of emerging markets funds by quartiles of leverage, 1997–2001

| Leverage quartiles | Minimum leverage in quartile | Maximum leverage in quartile | Average leverage in quartile | Median leverage in quartile | Total AUM in quartile (US$ billion) |
|---|---|---|---|---|---|
| 1 | 0.1 | 1.1 | 1.0 | 1.0 | 1.7 |
| 2 | 1.2 | 1.3 | 1.3 | 1.3 | 0.3 |
| 3 | 1.4 | 2.0 | 1.6 | 1.5 | 0.9 |
| 4 | 2.0 | 3.0 | 2.1 | 2.0 | 0.9 |
| **Total** | **0.1** | **3.0** | **1.0** | **1.4** | **3.7** |

*Source*: Altvest, CMRA Analysis

**Table 16** Summary of levered and delevered performance of emerging market funds, 1997–2001 (%)

| | Maximum return | Minimum return | Average return | Maximum delevered return | Minimum delevered return | Average delevered return | Difference in returns levered vs delevered |
|---|---|---|---|---|---|---|---|
| **1997–2001** | 37.3 | (4.4) | 16.9 | 18.4 | (1.9) | 8.8 | 8.0 |
| **2001** | 49.2 | (41.6) | 5.5 | 25.9 | (17.9) | 2.4 | 3.1 |

*Source*: Altvest, CMRA Analysis

fundamental tool for the protection of investments in the emerging markets. Long-term players in these markets experience less volatility as the markets in which they are investing become more developed. Australia, for instance, was surprised to learn in 1997 that it was an emerging market.

Some of the key risk factors that influence emerging market hedge funds shown in Figure 9 include:

### Volatility risk

Emerging markets tend to experience high levels of volatility. Such volatility may lead to substantial risks and returns. While the emerging market strategy index showed a high correlation with the returns of Moody's Equity Fund Emerging Market Index (89%) over the 1997–2001 period, a further comparison of these two indices is also revealing. Figure 10 validates this assessment. The most obvious examples are the August 1998 and September 2001 cases, when the index and the strategy returns shot downwards. The upper plot in Figure 11 compares the returns of the strategy with the volatility of Moody's Equity Fund Index. In 1998, when

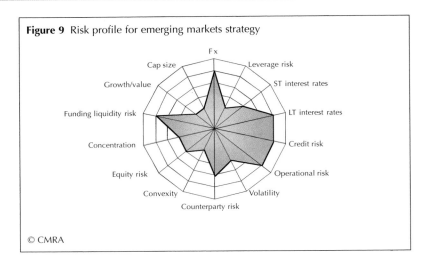

**Figure 9** Risk profile for emerging markets strategy

© CMRA

the volatility of the index jumped to almost 20%, the performance of the strategy dropped.

A comparison between the returns of emerging market hedge funds and the volatility of the Global Emerging Market Sovereign Bond Index reveals another interesting picture.

Over the 1997–2001 period, correlation with this index was a meager 25.1% (lower plot in Figure 11), or nearly none at all. Even though such a low correlation suggests that the returns of the strategy are unrelated to movements of the bond markets, we can see clearly how in October 1998 and September 2001 more volatile markets implied lower returns for the strategy.

### Liquidity risk

There are many factors that can severely stunt liquidity in emerging markets. Short exchange hours can be one such factor. In many countries stock exchanges are open for just a few hours a day and there are no other markets for these stocks. The lack of active repo markets also contributes to liquidity problems. Government restrictions on the convertibility of the local currency to dollars and on shorting of securities further hamper liquidity, as occurred in Asia in 1997. Probably the most important reason for poor liquidity, is poor governance and the lack of depth in legal infra-structure in many of the emerging markets.

### Litigation risk and poor corporate governance risk

Regulatory and legal issues can have a strong impact on emerging market strategies. Ignoring these can result in substantial portfolio losses in any market. In the emerging markets, both issuers and local governments

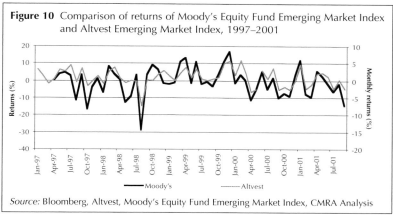

**Figure 10** Comparison of returns of Moody's Equity Fund Emerging Market Index and Altvest Emerging Market Index, 1997–2001

*Source:* Bloomberg, Altvest, Moody's Equity Fund Emerging Market Index, CMRA Analysis

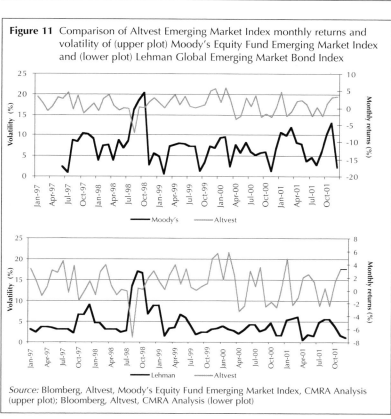

**Figure 11** Comparison of Altvest Emerging Market Index monthly returns and volatility of (upper plot) Moody's Equity Fund Emerging Market Index and (lower plot) Lehman Global Emerging Market Bond Index

*Source:* Blomberg, Altvest, Moody's Equity Fund Emerging Market Index, CMRA Analysis (upper plot); Bloomberg, Altvest, CMRA Analysis (lower plot)

interact in ways that are unfamiliar by US standards; the influence of one on the other is not clearly differentiated, resulting in adverse situations such as monopolies. In such cases investors in the strategy have very little certainty as to the outcome and behaviour of the local players involved.

Litigation in emerging markets often does not proceed in a manner which US observers would consider conducive to stable business operations. The interests of local authorities may get first priority while those of shareholders and investors go ignored. Corporate governance may be extremely poor. Many emerging markets are rife with family-run companies where assets and resources are used for the sole purpose of enriching the family and management.

### Lack of economic information risk

The absence of normal bond markets in many emerging markets has stymied the ability to obtain important economic information and this absence of bond markets also renders unavailable an important benchmark to price non-government debt and gauge risks in these markets.

### VALUE-AT-RISK
### Overview

The emerging market strategy has the lowest VAR out of a sample of 10 strategies analysed in the 1997–2001 period. However, VAR is not necessarily an accurate indicator of risk in emerging markets (see Table 17).

### Example

Take, for example, the 10-year US Treasury and the 20-year Mexican bond. Figure 12 shows their comparative performances. Historical or variance/covariance VAR can often be a lagging indicator of actual risk in returns. On August 14, 1998, the one-month 1% VAR of a 20-year Mexican Sovereign bond was –8.29% (meaning that there was a 1% chance that the one-month loss would exceed –8.29%) while, the actual return between August 14 and September 14, 1998 was –23% because the volatility of the bond suddenly increased from its historical average when Russia defaulted on its debt. This contagion carried over to Latin America, too. Once the history upon which the VAR was calculated incorporated the new volatility, the one-month 1% VAR showed a –25% loss (see Figure 13).

VAR is highly dependent on the assumptions that underlie it. This can be particularly dicey for emerging market securities because they have pockets of extreme volatility not found as often in US securities. These pockets of volatility suggest two possibilities: either the tails of the normal distribution are a lot fatter than these models assume, or the distributions are abnormal. Many risk managers use an alternative way of calculating VAR by assuming that the future price movements of the securities in

**Table 17** Average VAR calculation for emerging market strategy (%)

| 1997 | 1998 | 1999 | 2000 | Average 1997–2000 | Rank |
|------|------|------|------|-------------------|------|
| 11.6 | 31.4 | 31.2 | 32.8 | 29.1 | 10 of 10 |

*Source*: Assessing Market Risk for Hedge Funds and Hedge Funds Portfolios FAME, March 2001 – Research Paper No. 24, Francois-Serge Lhabitant

**Figure 12** Comparative performance of 10-year US Treasury bond and 20-year Mexican bond

*Source:* Bloomberg, CMRA Analysis

question will follow a path similar to the past rather than using the normal distribution assumptions as one solution to the problem. Others use a variety of more sophisticated techniques to capture the non-normal characteristics of the emerging markets.

It can be difficult to get an understanding of the amount that is at stake in extreme market situations. Extreme value (EV) theory tries to address this problem. However, many EV methods have their shortcomings. One such method that aims to quantify this risk involves estimation of the average correlations between the risk factors. However, the data available for emerging market securities during extreme events are too limited to estimate correlations accurately. Simply using average correlations does not capture the asymmetry and non-linearity of the relation between risk factors and correlations. Even EGarch and other techniques that account for asymmetry and non-linearity do not take into account the fact that correlations can change drastically during extreme events. Another method known as "multivariate extreme value theory" involves modelling the tails of multivariate distributions.[1] Since this involves the gathering of simultaneous occurrences of extreme events of all the risk factors, the limited data again pose problems.

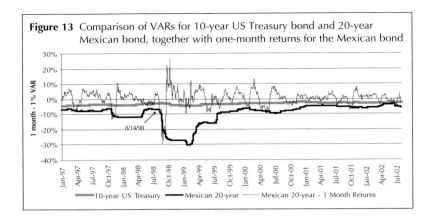

**Figure 13** Comparison of VARs for 10-year US Treasury bond and 20-year Mexican bond, together with one-month returns for the Mexican bond

CMRA believes that a more reliable approach involves the combination of historical simulation and single-factor EV. Historical simulation preserves the correlation structure of risk factors in extreme events, while EV provides a means to project the data out beyond the sample range. The historical data can be used to develop a histogram from which the VAR confidence level that determines the tail event, the EV distribution and the parameters of the EV distribution can be obtained. The VAR can then be calculated for the resulting EV distribution. However, this approach also requires a good stream of data, which can be hard to obtain for many emerging market securities. Furthermore, historical simulations only consider events that have occurred, not events that had a good chance of occurring. This means that if one of these different plausible events occurs in the future, the VAR calculated for the EV distribution will not capture the effect.

### STRESS TESTS

Stress tests are an extremely important component of risk management for an emerging market portfolio. Stress tests for emerging market funds might include:

- ❏ yield curve level and shape;
- ❏ volatility curve level and shape;
- ❏ price shifts in equities, sectors and indices;
- ❏ currency;
- ❏ spread and basis;
- ❏ risks introduced by biases in pricing models (especially for derivatives);
- ❏ correlation;
- ❏ credit risk and default assumptions;

❏ leverage; and
❏ liquidity.

## LEVEL OF TRANSPARENCY

It is unsurprising that emerging market fund managers who participate in more illiquid markets are significantly less willing to provide position-level transparency to their investors than managers of other strategies. One study found that only 25% of the emerging market fund managers surveyed said they would provide full disclosure (see Table 18).

Some emerging market securities can be very illiquid during financial crises. On the other hand, those managers who trade in emerging market sovereigns, which are more liquid than stocks, generally provide investors with more information about their positions.

## DUE DILIGENCE QUESTIONS FOR EMERGING MARKET FUNDS

❏ The diversity of a fund's portfolio is a key issue. Contagion, however, is a fact of life in the emerging market strategy. This was seen during the Russian crisis when investors punished debt from all emerging markets even though it was Russia that defaulted. Currently there is great worry that the Argentinean crisis will carry over to its neighbours. Investors should attempt to find out what hedge funds do in such circumstances.

❏ Investors should attempt to gauge the integrity of the brokers and banks that emerging market funds deal with.

❏ It is a good idea to know what kind of rights a fund would have in a country where it has been the victim of fraudulent activities committed at the expense of the business it has invested in.

❏ Investors should attempt to understand the legal controls that many funds institute. Buying credit protection from a Korean bank on a Korean company can be of questionable value in a crisis. Some funds, such as III Fund, entered into currency forward contracts with well-

**Table 18** Transparency offered to investors by managers of emerging market funds (%)

| | Overall level of transparency | | | Positions disclosed to investors | |
|---|---|---|---|---|---|
| Performance | Key positions | View entire portfolio | No transparency | Key long positions | Key short positions |
| 100 | 25 | 25 | 0 | 25 | 13 |

Source: Hennessee Hedge Fund Advisory Group

known western banks only to find the banks reneging on the contracts during an extreme event. The small print in many of the contracts forgave banks their responsibility in extraordinary scenarios. One well may ask what sense it makes to buy insurance that does not insure.

## DATA AND NAV ISSUES

Due to the volatility and the pockets of poor liquidity in emerging market securities, there can be a big difference between observed prices and executable prices. That means that just because the price of a bond on a quote screen is 90 does not mean you can buy or sell it at that price. Shown in Figure 14 are the bid/ask spreads of a Russian three-year Federal loan bond and an off-the-run five-year (with three years life left) US Treasury note. The average bid/ask spread for the US bond is 1/32, while the average spread for the Russian bond is 19.5 ticks out of 32.

Derivatives in emerging markets are harder to price because their price is dependent on an entire term structure of rates and volatilities. For instance, unlike the US swap curve, which can be built from a series of highly liquid Eurodollar futures contracts with maturities every three months going up to 10 years, emerging market curves can only be constructed with a much smaller number of securities spanning a much sparser maturity spectrum. This means that points between curves need to be interpolated over a greater number of years. For instance, the US Treasury yield curve created by Bloomberg contains 15 bonds of differing maturities, whereas the Russian curve contains only six. In the US case for the first 10 years there is a bond maturity available every year that can be used in the term structure, while the Russian curve has only four bond maturities in the first 10 years, leaving gaps of as much as three years to be interpolated. Hence, the interpolation method alone can cause a huge difference in the marks of many derivatives, rendering NAVs unreliable.

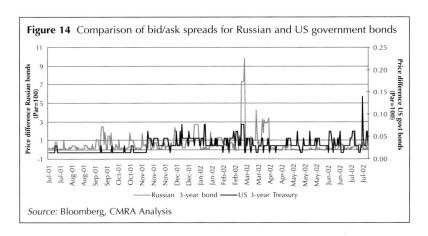

**Figure 14** Comparison of bid/ask spreads for Russian and US government bonds

*Source:* Bloomberg, CMRA Analysis

It is crucial to understand the impact of how variable/unstable the reported NAV is before risk measurement can be put in context as the overall riskiness of the portfolio's potential value can be estimated.

## PUBLICLY DISCLOSED PROBLEMS

In late 1997 the Asia crisis hit Peregrine Investments hard. The collapse of the Hong Kong Stock Market on October 20 resulted in the closure of credit lines to the fund. Peregrine was heavily exposed to Thailand, Indonesia and South Korea, and had ventured into even more unstable places such as Myanmar.[2] Another major reason for Peregrine's collapse was its extremely aggressive investment banking business, through which it helped issue US$2.6 billion of debt for Thai and Indonesian companies between 1996 and 1997. In July and August 1997 investors began to shy away from Asian debt as the economies began to sour. As a result, Peregrine was unable to move the debt off of its books, leaving it with a massive exposure that subsequently led to terrible consequences as the Asian crisis entered full swing.

McGinnis Advisors managed three funds totaling between US$180 million and US$200 million and was heavily invested in Russia just before its default in 1998. Dana McGinnis was quoted as saying "we were not aware that we had this kind of [default] risk because it is unprecedented".[3] However, tail events such as these seem to occur more frequently than the statistics of a normal distribution would imply. This particular tail event caused McGinnis Funds to file for Chapter 11 bankruptcy protection. The other reason for McGinnis' downfall was its failure to read the small print in contracts made between the fund and some banks. Many Russian debt holders had been buying forward foreign currency contracts to protect against a currency devaluation. However, as the rouble fell after the default some banks refused to honour their contracts. Many of these contracts had *force majeure* clauses, which they claimed relieved them of their responsibility to the contract if the Russian government did something "outrageous".

Another publicly disclosed problem included the two hedge funds run by Everest Capital Ltd, which had borrowed approximately 40 cents for each US$1 invested and lost US$1.3 billion of the US$2.7 billion it was managing. Investors included the endowments of Yale and Brown universities. The funds suffered substantial losses in emerging markets, particularly Russian bonds and Latin American stocks.

---

1   Aragones, J.R., C. Blanco and K. Dowd, 2000, "Learning Curve Extreme Value VaR" (2nd article), *Derivatives Week*, March 20.
2   "Peregrine: Hawk turned Prey", *The Economist*, November 22, 1997, www.economist.com.
3   Reed, S., 1998, Emerging Markets, "Pure Carnage", *Business Week*, September 14.

# 14

# Long/Short Equity

## DESCRIPTION OF THE STRATEGY

As the name implies, long/short equity funds hold both long and short positions; however, most do not attempt market neutrality. In the long portfolio the fund is a buyer of stocks; it profits when the stocks in the portfolio rise in price on average and loses when the stock prices fall. In the short portfolio, the fund borrows stocks from another source (usually through securities-lending channels) and then sells the stocks to a third party. The short investor profits when stocks in the short portfolio fall on average and loses when the stocks rise. The goal is that, in the end, the return of the long portfolio is greater than the return of the short portfolio. This is the source of value added. The spread between long and short portfolios is the focus of active management in long/short equity.

Long/short equity strategies have significant flexibility in the use of leverage and short positions. The manager targets returns on the long side as well as on the short side, which ideally results in the doubling of alpha. Depending on the manager, long/short equity strategies have specific exposures to certain industry sectors (sector risk), countries (country risk) and currencies (foreign exchange risk), company sizes (market capitalisation) and styles (value/growth).

This directional strategy involves equity-orientated investing on both the long and short sides of the market. The objective is not to be market-neutral. Managers have the ability to shift from value to growth, from small to medium to large capitalisation stocks, and from a net long position to a net short position. Due to the volatility of the correlation between value and growth, this has been a risky strategy. Managers may use futures and options to hedge. The focus may be by region (eg, US or Europe), or by sector (eg, technology or health care).

The optimal situation is simply for stocks held in long positions to appreciate and stocks held in short positions to depreciate. If the long positions depreciate or the short positions appreciate, the fund typically incurs losses. The worst-case scenario, albeit rare, is for long positions to depreciate and short positions to appreciate simultaneously; this would guarantee a significant loss. Long/short hedge funds usually outperform in bear markets and underperform in strong bull markets.

Long/short equity is both the original and the most popular category of hedge fund. Although the strategy can be traced back to the late 1940s when the A.W. Jones investment partnership bought and shorted stocks in portfolios, it took decades for long/short equity to achieve the popularity it has today. Currently, long/short equity is not among the investment strategies with the highest returns. According to the CSFB/Tremont Hedge Fund Index, the long/short equity average return in 2000 was 2.08%, which is low compared to the index's total return of 4.85%. Long/short equity saw its worst performance ever in 2001 with a return of –3.65%, mainly due to extremely low returns in the first quarter of 4.94%. Also, the events of September 11, 2001 struck long/short equity funds hard, resulting in a performance of –1.57% for that month. Conversely, long/short equity has shown outstanding results in the past: in 1999 it returned 47.23%. However, during the first half of 2002, long/short equity did not greatly improve on its 2001 performance.

One historical concern, which arose when long/short equity investing was first implemented, was that short-selling securities would create tax liabilities for institutional investors who previously had been tax-exempt. The good news came in 1995 when the US Internal Revenue Service removed these concerns in its Ruling 95-8. The ruling made long/short equity a feasible option for tax-exempt investors by exempting from taxation short sales of publicly traded stock through a broker.

Long/short equity hedge funds all invest in equities and all hold both long and short positions. Beyond that, managers' investment strategies vary tremendously. Some managers prefer to maintain a net long bias, while others maintain a net short bias; some use futures or options to hedge market risk; some use leverage, while others do not; some have a style bias (eg, value or growth); some are fundamentally driven and others are technically driven.

One long/short investment strategy is to focus on a particular region. Managers favour this approach because they can become experts in a local market. Although the majority of long/short equity funds concentrate mainly on the United States, in the 1990s there was a significant growth among long/short equity funds in Europe.

Another long/short investment strategy is to focus on a particular sector. The major sector categories are technology, healthcare, financial services, natural resources, biotechnology, consumer goods and energy. Some sector funds trade globally, while others trade regionally. Cambridge (energy), Artis (technology) and Aries (biotech) are three examples of sector funds. Another group of long/short funds has a day-trading orientation. This involves buying and selling stocks at a rapid rate: a stock is rarely held for more than a day or two. Because equity trading changes constantly, funds can go quickly from net long to net short and back again.

There are three primary sources of return in a long/short equity portfolio. The obvious return comes from the spread between the stocks that

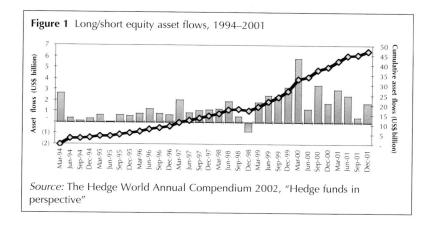

**Figure 1** Long/short equity asset flows, 1994–2001

*Source:* The Hedge World Annual Compendium 2002, "Hedge funds in perspective"

are held long and sold short. This result can be determined by adding the alpha on the long positions and the alpha on the short positions. Typically, the alpha expectations of the strategy are 3.0–6.0%.

The second primary source of return is the interest on the rebate. When a stock is sold short, the proceeds are placed in the lender's custody account and are then invested in short-term securities. The lender receives a small portion of the interest earned, the majority of which is known as the interest rebate. The third primary source of return is the interest on the liquidity buffer. Managers keep some assets liquid in order to maintain the ability to finance unexpected payments, such as those necessary if short stocks appreciate. These liquid assets receive interest, which is the third component of the portfolio return.

Although the 2001 long/short equity return of 8.2% was lower than the five-year historical average performance of 17.4%, the flow of assets to long/short equity (with the exception of December 1998) has maintained its positive trend and has benefited from the boom period. Considering the lackluster performance of the equity markets in 2001, it is unsurprising that, with an average return of 8.2%, the strategy still attracts capital.

As of the end of 2001, the cumulative long/short equity asset flow since March 1994 was approximately US$47 billion (see Figure 1). The growth of the AUM in long/short equity funds for the five-year period 1997–2001 was 38.9%, the third largest growth rate of the hedge fund strategies analysed.

## EFFECT OF MARKET CONDITIONS

Long/short equity performs above its historical average when:[1]

❑ The yield curve is moderately upward sloping and there are no substantial increases or decreases in its slope.

❏ Credit risk premium is declining.
❏ There are no substantial increases or decreases in the short-term rate.
❏ The long-term rate is at a moderate level and is not increasing.
❏ The intra-month volatility of the S&P 500 and the implied volatility index are at moderate levels and are not increasing.
❏ The intra-month volatility of bond returns is declining.
❏ The returns on large cap and small cap stocks are high.

Long/short equity performs substantially below its historical average when:

❏ The yield curve is downward sloping and there are substantial increases in its slope.
❏ Credit risk premium is increasing.
❏ The short-term rate is increasing or decreasing by a substantial amount.
❏ The long-term yield is very low and is increasing.
❏ The intra-month volatility of S&P 500 and the implied volatility index are high or are increasing.
❏ The intra-month volatility of bond returns is increasing.
❏ The returns on large cap and small cap stocks are negative.

## WELL-KNOWN PLAYERS
The long/short equity funds with AUM greater than US$1 billion include those listed in Table 1.

## COVERAGE OF THE STRATEGY IN DIFFERENT SOURCES
Tuna tracks the largest number of funds (391), while CSFB/Tremont covers the greatest AUM. Other major sources and their coverage are listed in Table 2.

## DISTRIBUTION OF FUNDS IN THE STRATEGY
Altvest lists a total of 372 long/short equity funds with US$18.3 billion in assets (see Figure 2); however, 98 of these funds were without AUM data. Of these 372 funds, 34 have US$11.1 billion in AUM, which is 60% of the assets reported. This means that 9% of the funds control 60% of the assets in the strategy.

### Distribution of funds by quartile of performance
First-quartile-performing long/short equity hedge funds returned 33.2% over the five years between 1997 and 2001. The last two quartiles had an average five-year return of 9.2% and, combined, accounted for US$1.7 billion in assets, or 23% of the total AUM. The funds in the first two quartiles have an average five-year standard deviation of 24.6%, which is 1.2

**Table 1** Top long/short equity funds with more than US$1 billion in AUM (all sources)

| Rank | Fund | Highest AUM* (US$ billion) |
|---|---|---|
| 1 | Maverick Fund Ltd. | 5.1 |
| 2 | Chilton Investment Co. US Strategies Fund | 3.5 |
| 3 | Odey Japan & General Inc. (YEN) | 3.1 |
| 4 | Standard Pacific Capital | 2.3 |
| 5 | Andor Technology Perennial Fund | 2.1 |
| 6 | Lone Redwood LP | 2.0 |
| 7 | Omega Partners | 2.0 |
| 8 | Raptor Global Funds | 1.9 |
| 9 | SAC Capital | 1.9 |
| 10 | Raptor Global Fund Ltd. | 1.9 |
| 11 | Galleon Technology Fund | 1.5 |
| 12 | Viking Global Equities LP | 1.5 |
| 13 | Zweig-DiMenna International | 1.5 |
| 14 | Perquot International Fund (Class A) | 1.5 |
| 15 | Lone Cedar Ltd. | 1.4 |
| 16 | Zenit | 1.3 |
| 17 | Eureka Euro Fund | 1.3 |
| 18 | Intrepid Capital Fund (LP, QP, Offshore) | 1.2 |
| 19 | Andor Technology Aggressive Fund | 1.2 |
| 20 | Egerton European Dollar Fund | 1.2 |
| 21 | Viking Global Equities III Ltd. | 1.2 |
| 22 | OCM Emerging Markets | 1.2 |
| 23 | AlphaGen Capella Fund | 1.1 |
| 24 | Orbis Optimal (US$) Fund | 1.1 |
| 25 | Adelphi Europe Fund | 1.1 |
| 26 | AlphaGen Capella Fund US$ | 1.0 |
| | **Total** | **47.6** |

*This is the highest AUM for that fund among all the sources.
Highlighted funds are exclusively in Institutional Investor's The Hedge Fund 100 (June 2002)

*Source*: Altvest, Tuna, HFR, Institutional Investor (June 2002), Directory of Fund of Hedge Funds Investment Vehicles

**Table 2** Coverage of long/short equity funds by different sources

| Source | Total number of funds | Funds with no AUM data | Total AUM (US$ billion) |
|---|---|---|---|
| CSFB/Tremont | 269 | N/A | 86.7 |
| The Hedge Fund 100 | 81 | 2 | 48.9 |
| HFR | 341 | 13 | 42.8 |
| Tuna | 391 | 37 | 29.9 |
| Altvest | 372 | 98 | 18.3 |

*Source*: Altvest, Tuna, CSFB/Tremont, Institutional Investor (June 2002)

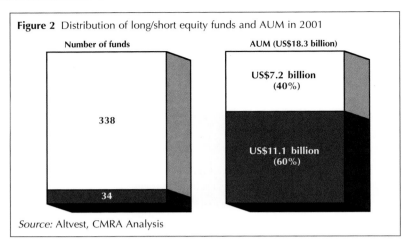

**Figure 2** Distribution of long/short equity funds and AUM in 2001

*Source:* Altvest, CMRA Analysis

points higher than the volatility of the third and fourth quartiles. These findings, presented in Table 3, suggest that size also matters in the long/short strategy.

### Distribution of funds by quartile of AUM

The largest funds showed the best performance on both an equally weighted and an AUM-weighted basis in 1997–2001 (see Table 4). In addition, the five-year returns of the largest funds have the lowest standard deviation (18.7%) of all four quartiles. The best Sharpe ratio results from the combination of the highest returns and the lowest volatility. The second quartile has a five-year return of 11.6%, which is almost 10 points lower than the first quartile's return of 21.5%. The third quartile, with only US$685 million (9% of the total AUM), has the second highest performance. At 20.3%, the resulting beta for this quartile is 3.2, which is the second best of the four quartiles.

**Table 3** Distribution of long/short equity funds by quartiles of five-year performance, 1997–2001

| Return quartiles | Average 1997–2001 equally weighted return (%) | Average 1997–2001 AUM-weighted return (%) | AUM in quartile (US$ billion) | % of total | Average 1997–2001 standard deviation (%) | Sharpe ratio 1997–2001 |
|---|---|---|---|---|---|---|
| 1 | 33.2 | 26.5 | 3.8 | 48 | 32.4 | 1.1 |
| 2 | 17.8 | 18.2 | 2.3 | 29 | 16.9 | 0.8 |
| 3 | 13.3 | 13.0 | 1.0 | 12 | 15.9 | 0.6 |
| 4 | 5.1 | 4.5 | 0.8 | 11 | 25.6 | 0.3 |
| **Total** | **17.2** | **20.1** | **7.8** | **100** | **22.7** | **0.7** |

*Source:* Altvest, CMRA Analysis based on 69 funds with five-year performance data

**Table 4** Distribution of long/short equity funds by quartiles of AUM, 1997–2001

| AUM quartiles | Average 1997–2001 equally weighted return (%) | Average 1997–2001 AUM-weighted return (%) | AUM in quartile (US$ billion) | % of total | Average 1997–2001 standard deviation (%) | Sharpe ratio 1997–2001 |
|---|---|---|---|---|---|---|
| 1 | 21.5 | 22.5 | 5.5 | 70 | 18.7 | 1.1 |
| 2 | 11.6 | 12.5 | 1.4 | 18 | 24.6 | 0.5 |
| 3 | 18.3 | 18.2 | 0.7 | 9 | 21.0 | 0.7 |
| 4 | 17.2 | 16.1 | 0.2 | 3 | 26.4 | 0.6 |
| **Total** | **17.2** | **20.1** | **7.8** | **100** | **22.7** | **0.7** |

*Source:* Altvest, CMRA Analysis based on 69 funds with five-year performance data

## PERFORMANCE OF THE STRATEGY

Regression analyses comparing the growth in AUM in 1999 and 2000 with the strategy's performance in the previous year show conflicting results. As seen in Figure 3, AUM growth in 1999 has a 47% correlation with the performance in 1998. This suggests that positive performance is a factor that drives growth in assets. However, this initial conclusion is contradicted by the results for 2000. As Figure 4 indicates, the correlation between the growth in AUM in 2000 and the average monthly performance in 1999 is only 9%. Both results could be skewed given the different market conditions in 1998 and 1999.

### Returns during boom and bust

The long/short equity strategy outperformed the S&P 500 Index during both the recent boom and bust periods (see Figure 5). This reflects the

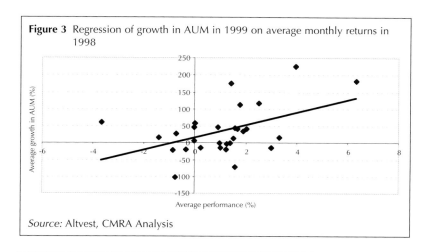

**Figure 3** Regression of growth in AUM in 1999 on average monthly returns in 1998

*Source:* Altvest, CMRA Analysis

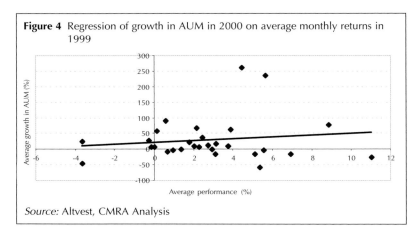

**Figure 4** Regression of growth in AUM in 2000 on average monthly returns in 1999

*Source:* Altvest, CMRA Analysis

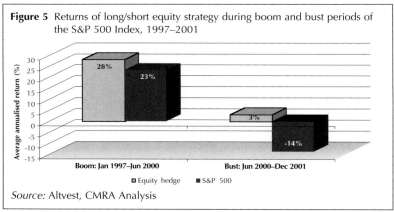

**Figure 5** Returns of long/short equity strategy during boom and bust periods of the S&P 500 Index, 1997–2001

*Source:* Altvest, CMRA Analysis

continuous flow of assets into the strategy during the last decade. The strategy outperformed the S&P 500 by 5% during the boom years of 1997 and 2000, and then outperformed it again by 17% during the bust period 2000–01.

**Returns from different sources**

Summary data for five indices are given in Table 5. The Sharpe ratios for long/short equity are low; they range from 1.11 (according to CSFB/Tremont) to 2.11 (according to Tuna). Also, all indices show a beta close to 1.5, with Tuna reporting one as high as 2.21. This indicates that the volatility of the return of the strategy differs significantly from that of the S&P 500 Index.

The differences between the returns reported by the various long/short equity hedge fund indices can be significant, with the 1998 performance

**Table 5** Comparisons of long/short equity index returns across different sources, 1997–2001

| | 1997 | 1998 | 1999 | 2000 | 2001 | 1997–2001 | |
| | | | | | | Return | Sharpe ratio |
|---|---|---|---|---|---|---|---|
| Tuna | 28.7 | 20.1 | 48.0 | 17.0 | 4.9 | 23.0 | 2.1 |
| Altvest | 24.2 | 14.9 | 45.9 | 16.5 | 1.3 | 19.7 | 1.7 |
| HFR | 23.4 | 16.0 | 44.2 | 9.1 | (1.8) | 17.6 | 1.5 |
| CSFB/Tremont | 21.5 | 17.2 | 47.2 | 2.1 | (3.7) | 15.6 | 1.1 |
| Hennessee | 15.6 | 1.8 | 32.6 | 7.6 | 4.0 | 11.8 | 1.3 |
| Maximum difference | 13.2 | 18.4 | 15.4 | 14.9 | 8.6 | 11.2 | 1.0 |
| Average | 22.7 | 14.0 | 43.6 | 10.5 | 1.0 | 17.5 | 1.6 |

*Source*: Altvest, Tuna, HFR, CSFB/Tremont, Hennessee

varying by 18.37 points across the different sources, or 1.3 times the average return of the strategy of 13.99%. Accordingly, for the year 2000 the maximum difference in returns was 14.92 points, or 1.4 times the average return of 10.47%. The smallest difference of 8.58% was found in 2001.

Long/short equity has performed well over the last five years. Although its performance did not maintain a consistent level, it did hold strong, positive returns – a tendency indicated in all the indices. The Hennesee Long/Short Index underperforms the other indices before 2000, while the CSFB/Tremont Index underperforms the other indices in the 2000–01 period (see Figure 6).

Long/short equity increased slowly in popularity from 1994 through 1997. It had a hard time in 1998, along with most other hedge fund strategies, due to the Russian/LTCM crisis. In contrast, 1999 was an outstanding year for the strategy. Investors continued to show interest in 2000 and 2001, although to a lesser extent than in 1999.

### Index performance

The average performance of the indices covering the strategy indicates that 1999 was a boom year, with an annual performance of 43.58%. 2001 was the worst year, with an average of 0.96%. The Sharpe ratio for the period fluctuates from 1.11 to 2.11, depending on the source. The beta also varies significantly from 1.13 to 2.21. An investor in this strategy must determine the relevance of the different indices available to measure the performance of this asset class. An understanding of the different methodologies used to calculate these indices is fundamental for evaluating the strategy.

As shown in Figure 7, the constituent funds of an index can vary substantially in performance. Of the 150 funds in the CSFB/Tremont Equity Hedge Index, we analysed 65 for which data were available. Of

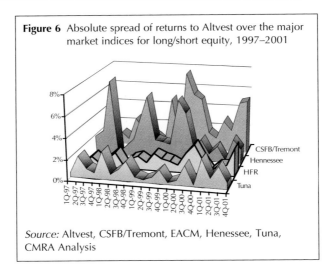

**Figure 6** Absolute spread of returns to Altvest over the major market indices for long/short equity, 1997–2001

*Source:* Altvest, CSFB/Tremont, EACM, Henessee, Tuna, CMRA Analysis

these, the Permal Essex Media & Technology Ltd. Fund had the highest return, with 55.5% over the 1997–2001 period and a standard deviation of 0.4%. Over the same period the Charlemagne Fund LP had the lowest return of 4.9%, with 4.4% standard deviation.

Among the various hedge fund strategies, long/short equity is generally the manager favourite – ranking first in returns and fifth in Sharpe ratio (see Table 6).

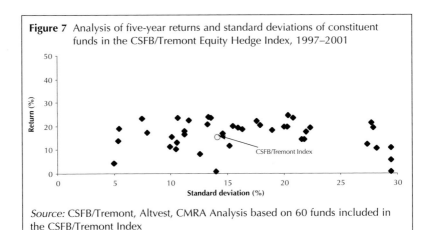

**Figure 7** Analysis of five-year returns and standard deviations of constituent funds in the CSFB/Tremont Equity Hedge Index, 1997–2001

*Source:* CSFB/Tremont, Altvest, CMRA Analysis based on 60 funds included in the CSFB/Tremont Index

**Table 6** Ranking of the long/short equity strategy against other strategies, 1997–2001

|  | 1997 | 1998 | 1999 | 2000 | 2001 | 1997–2001 | Rank |
|---|---|---|---|---|---|---|---|
| Return (%) | 24.2 | 14.9 | 45.9 | 16.5 | 1.3 | 19.7 | 1 of 14 |
| Sharpe ratio | 8.9 | 3.9 | 14.4 | 4.1 | 0.6 | 1.7 | 5 of 14 |

*Source*: Altvest, CMRA Analysis

### Performance correlations

Although liquidity and credit are separate sources of risk exposure for hedge funds in the space, they are nevertheless related because of the problems encountered by hedge funds. There was a 52% correlation between the credit spreads and the returns on the strategy during 2001.

Long/short equity strategies usually have a net long exposure. Long/short equity has substantial exposure to the stock market, and its performance therefore is greatly affected by that of the stock market. It is not surprising that when the equity markets perform well, long/short equity funds generally also perform well. This is shown in Table 7.

A long/short equity strategy, if it is successful, must be volatile. The variance of a position of long only stocks and short positions is the sum of their variances minus 2 times their covariance. But if the covariance is large the arbitrage does not work. Table 8 shows the relationship of the excess returns of the long/short equity strategy to the following risk factors critical to the equity markets: equity volatility, measured as the implied volatility of S&P100 Index options; market factors, measured as the increase of positive returns when the market performs well; size factors; and value factors, measured as returns to high book price companies minus returns to low book price companies. It is evident from the table that long/short hedge funds have strong correlations with all four factors.

**Table 7** Rolling correlations of long/short equity index performance with S&P 500 and Lehman Aggregate Bond Index, 1997–2001 (%)

|  | 1997 | 1998 | 1999 | 2000 | 2001 |
|---|---|---|---|---|---|
| S&P 500 Index | 68.4 | 84.0 | 55.0 | 68.1 | 71.6 |
| Lehman Aggregate Bond Index | 59.7 | (51.7) | 4.4 | 44.6 | (24.8) |

*Source*: Bloomberg, CMRA Analysis

**Table 8** Average correlation of long/short equity funds with various risk factors, 1997–2001

| Factor | Overall correlation (%) |
|---|---|
| Equity volatility* | (39) |
| Market factor | 71 |
| Size factor | 51 |
| Value factor | (75) |

*The implied volatility of the S&P100 Index options (see Figure 8)

Source: Financial Analyst Journal – Battle for Alphas, March/April 2002

## Stress period analysis

On a performance basis, the long/short equity strategy outperformed the S&P 500 Index when the Federal Reserve Bank raised interest rates in 1994, during the Tech crash of 2000 and after the events of September 11, 2001 (see Figure 9). The strategy only outperformed the Lehman Bond Composite Index in 1994.

During the period February–June 1994 when

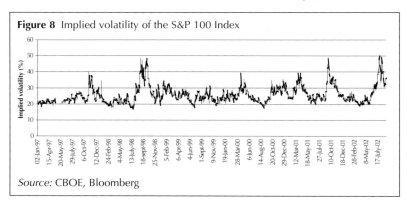

**Figure 8** Implied volatility of the S&P 100 Index

Source: CBOE, Bloomberg

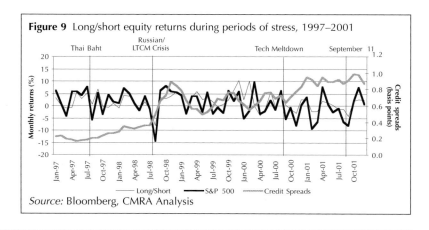

**Figure 9** Long/short equity returns during periods of stress, 1997–2001

Source: Bloomberg, CMRA Analysis

the Fed surprised the markets and raised interest rates, long/short equity provided a performance of 5.8%. Also, during the Russian/LTCM crisis the strategy had a performance 11.2%. During the equity market downturn and the burst of the technology bubble, the strategy was sustainable with a positive return. Index returns and Sharpe ratios for the last three events are shown in Tables 9 and 10, respectively.

The strategy outperformed the S&P 500 in the 1994 crises, the Tech crash and the events of September 11, 2001.

In November 2001, Lehman Brothers evaluated the long/short equity strategy in light of three different factors: change in term premia, change in credit spreads and change in implied volatility. The results are summarised in Table 11.

The long/short strategy is sensitive to the term premia factor (an indicator of economic expansion or contraction). The strategy groups all managers who invest in sectors either through pair trading, cross-trading, etc. Due to the cyclical nature of the economy, one would expect that sectors in an expansionary mode would be investment candidates for managers in the space. With respect to the change in credit spreads – and considering that the strategy is among the most levered with 10 times leverage in some cases, it is surprising that credit spreads did not rank highly in Lehman's regression analysis.

It is interesting to note that even though the trading strategies in equity hedge would benefit from a change in the volatility of the market, the analysis did not pick up this relationship either. In summary, long/short

**Table 9**  Returns of long/short equity index during periods of stress (%)

| Russian/LTCM crisis | Tech crash | September 11 |
|:---:|:---:|:---:|
| 11.2 | 6.9 | 6.2 |

Source: Altvest, CMRA Analysis

**Table 10**  Sharpe ratio of long/short equity index during periods of stress

| Russian/LTCM crisis | Tech crash | September 11 | Average of absolute Sharpe ratios | Maximum-minimum |
|:---:|:---:|:---:|:---:|:---:|
| (0.1) | (1.0) | 0.0 | 0.4 | 1.0 |

Source: Altvest, CMRA Analysis

**Table 11** Sensitivity of the long/short equity strategy to factors in Lehman's multivariate model

| Factor | Coefficient | Rank |
|---|---|---|
| Change in term premia | 0.013 | 7 of 17 |
| Change in implied volatility | (0.130) | 10 of 17 |
| Change in credit spread | (0.070) | 11 of 17 |

*Source*: Lehman Brothers Understanding Hedge Fund Performance

equity is less sensitive to term premia, credit spreads and VIX than other strategies.

### Range of performance
The returns of long/short equity funds vary widely (see Figure 10).

### SHARPE RATIO
### Distribution
As seen in Table 12, the largest quartile by Sharpe ratio includes most of the AUM in the group (53%). There is a clear jump in performance (more than 10 points) between the first quartile and the last quartile. In addition, the last quartile has the smallest AUM. The 1997–2001 Sharpe ratio of the funds analysed ranges from –0.41 to 3.41, and the 2001 Sharpe ratio ranged from –32.8 to 61.8.

Another look at the Sharpe ratio data for the strategy is shown in Figure 11. It shows 77 funds with a negative one-year Sharpe ratio vs eight funds for the five-year Sharpe ratio. The largest category for the five-year Sharpe

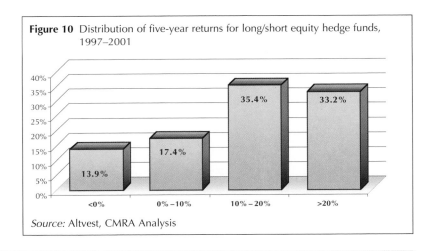

**Figure 10** Distribution of five-year returns for long/short equity hedge funds, 1997–2001

*Source:* Altvest, CMRA Analysis

**Table 12** Distribution of long/short equity funds by quartiles of Sharpe ratio, 1997–2001

| Sharpe ratio quartiles | Average 1997–2001 equally weighted return (%) | Average 1997–2001 AUM-weighted return (%) | AUM in quartile (US$ billion) | % of total | Average 1997–2001 standard deviation (%) | Sharpe ratio 1997–2001 |
|---|---|---|---|---|---|---|
| 1 | 21.0 | 23.9 | 4.2 | 53.0 | 11.9 | 1.5 |
| 2 | 23.5 | 20.2 | 1.4 | 18.0 | 22.8 | 0.8 |
| 3 | 17.1 | 18.3 | 1.0 | 13.0 | 21.5 | 0.5 |
| 4 | 7.6 | 8.8 | 1.2 | 15.0 | 34.1 | 0.1 |
| **Total** | **17.2** | **20.1** | **7.8** | **100.0** | **22.7** | **0.7** |

*Source*: Altvest, CMRA Analysis based on 69 funds with five-year performance data

ratio is in the 0–1 range with 56 funds, whereas the largest category for the one-year ratio is that with ratios greater than three.

### Information ratio

Similar funds that start in different market environments can have completely different results. As shown in Figure 12, in the long/short equity strategy, there is very little difference between the onshore and offshore information ratios.

### LEVERAGE

90% of long/short hedge funds use leverage (see Chapter 2 for a discussion of leverage). 73% of the funds use a leverage lower than two, and only 17% leverage their positions to a level greater than two (see Figure 13).

Many hedge funds in the long/short equity strategy rely on leverage. As

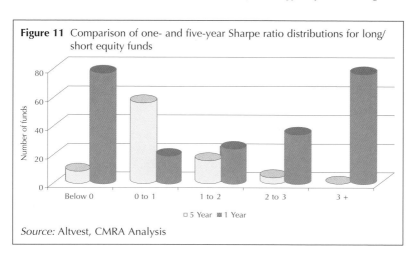

**Figure 11** Comparison of one- and five-year Sharpe ratio distributions for long/short equity funds

*Source:* Altvest, CMRA Analysis

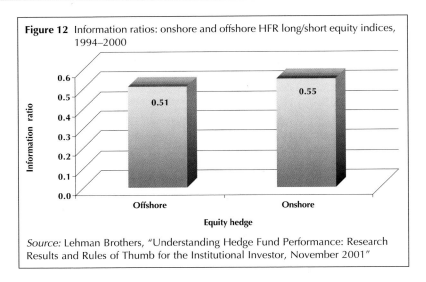

**Figure 12** Information ratios: onshore and offshore HFR long/short equity indices, 1994–2000

*Source:* Lehman Brothers, "Understanding Hedge Fund Performance: Research Results and Rules of Thumb for the Institutional Investor, November 2001"

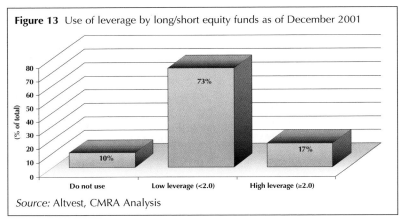

**Figure 13** Use of leverage by long/short equity funds as of December 2001

*Source:* Altvest, CMRA Analysis

is well-known, leverage has a magnifying effect in that it expands small profit opportunities into larger ones and small losses into larger ones. The ranking of the strategy as a user of leverage relative to other strategies in 2002 and historically since 1997 is shown in Tables 13 and 14, respectively.

Funds in the strategy tend to employ a significant degree of leverage, averaging a ratio of US$1.77 AUM for each dollar of capital and ranging all the way up to US$10 of AUM for each dollar of capital. On a historical basis, the strategy has maintained an average leverage ranging from 1.1 to 1.5 in the 1997–2001 period.

When there are adverse changes in the market value of collateral, credit is withdrawn quickly and the subsequent forced liquidations of large

**Table 13** Financial leverage of long/short equity funds in 2002

| Minimum | Average | Maximum | Rank |
|---------|---------|---------|------|
| 1.0 | 1.8 | 10.0 | 5 of 14 |

*Source*: Altvest, CMRA Analysis

**Table 14** Historical average leverage of long/short equity funds, 1997–2001

| 1997 | 1998 | 1999 | 2000 | 2001 | Average | 1997–2001 Maximum | Minimum |
|------|------|------|------|------|---------|-------------------|---------|
| 1.5 | 1.3 | 1.2 | 1.1 | 1.2 | 1.3 | 1.5 | 1.1 |

*Source*: Altvest, CMRA Analysis

positions over short periods of time can lead to widespread financial distress. One example of this was the Russian default in August 1998.

A further analysis of leverage for the strategy during the 1997–2001 period indicates that the first quartile (the group with the lowest leverage) has US$6.8 billion in AUM and the second quartile has US$2.3 billion in AUM. The third and fourth quartiles represent only 17.5% of the assets in the strategy. The results, summarised in Table 15, indicate that most of the funds in the strategy use leverage to improve their return performance.

The nearly eight-point average difference between levered and delevered returns over the 1997–2001 period strongly demonstrates the magnifying factors of leverage (see Table 16).

**Table 15** Distribution of long/short equity funds by quartiles of leverage, 1997–2001

| Leverage quartiles | Minimum leverage in quartile | Maximum leverage in quartile | Average leverage in quartile | Median leverage in quartile | Total AUM in quartile (US$ billion) | % of total AUM |
|--------------------|------------------------------|------------------------------|------------------------------|-----------------------------|-------------------------------------|----------------|
| 1 | 0.3 | 1.0 | 0.8 | 0.9 | 6.8 | 61.8 |
| 2 | 1.0 | 1.2 | 1.1 | 1.1 | 2.3 | 20.8 |
| 3 | 1.2 | 1.8 | 1.5 | 1.5 | 0.8 | 6.9 |
| 4 | 2.0 | 10.0 | 9.3 | 3.6 | 1.2 | 10.6 |
| **Total** | **0.3** | **10.0** | **1.3** | **1.3** | **11.0** | **100.0** |

*Source*: Altvest, CMRA Analysis based on 125 funds with five years of leverage data

**Table 16** Summary of levered and delevered performance of long/short equity funds, 1997–2001 (%)

| | Maximum return | Minimum return | Average return | Maximum delevered return | Minimum delevered return | Average delevered return | Difference in returns levered vs delevered |
|---|---|---|---|---|---|---|---|
| 1997–2001 | 38.5 | 1.3 | 14.0 | 19.5 | 0.2 | 6.3 | 7.6 |
| 2001 | 45.0 | (25.6) | 6.1 | 20.5 | (18.2) | 2.2 | 4.0 |

*Source*: Altvest, CMRA Analysis

## RISK MEASUREMENT

Risk factors that influence the performance of the strategy include volatility, interest rate risk, credit risk, leverage and short-squeeze risk (see Figure 14).

Table 17 summarises the exposure of the long/short equity strategy to the equity index return, economy-wide credit risk, interest rates and leverage.

Some of the risk factors of the strategy are identified below:

### Volatility risk

Volatility in the equity markets may lead to substantial risks and returns. In 2001–02 equity markets were the most volatile, particularly those trading technology stocks, where volatility in July 2002 increased to a record of 50.5%. However, the volatility also extended to fixed-income markets and major currencies. One source of volatility appeared to be the

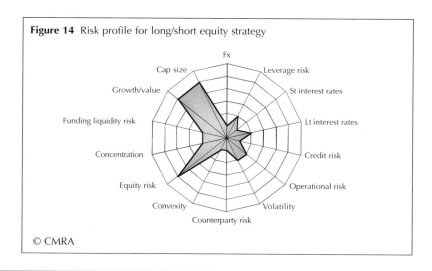

**Figure 14** Risk profile for long/short equity strategy

© CMRA

**Table 17** Summary of risk, return and exposure of long/short equity strategy to different risk factors

| Volatility of return | Downside risk | Exposure | | | Sharpe ratio | Leverage |
|---|---|---|---|---|---|---|
| | | Equity index return | Economy-wide credit risk | Interest rates | | |
| High | Medium | Positive high | Negative medium | Negative low | Medium | Medium |

*Source*: Zurich Hedge Fund Indices Spring/Summer 2002

uncertainty engendered by the economic data released during the period by different companies and the US Government. Not only did the stock markets seem unusually susceptible to such uncertainty, but order flows also appeared to exert an inordinate effect on prices. These conditions set the stage for sharp market declines. Market participants in the US and Europe also seemed to react more forcefully than usual to macroeconomic news.

### Interest rate risk

Interest rate exposure to economic events is a key factor that drives the equity markets. Simply stated, weak equity markets, high unemployment, and a weak economy are more likely to be tied to an aggressive monetary policy that is often viewed as negative by investors in the equity markets.

### Leverage risk

Accounts traded at greater-than-standard leverage will experience greater losses and volatility as well as greater potential for profit.

### Short-squeeze risk

Many hedge fund managers coming from long-only asset management have gone through painful learning experiences in handling the short side.

**Table 18** Average VAR calculation for long/short equity (%)

| 1997 | 1998 | 1999 | 2000 | Average 1997–2000 | Rank |
|---|---|---|---|---|---|
| 9.2 | 10.2 | 12.5 | 16.8 | 11.9 | 7 of 10 |

*Source*: Assessing Market Risk for Hedge Funds and Hedge Funds Portfolios FAME, March 2001 – Research Paper No. 24, Francois-Serge Lhabitant

## VALUE-AT-RISK

### Overview

Interest in the long/short equity strategy increased during the boom days of the equity markets. The growth rate of the AUM in the strategy for the 1997–2001 period was 38.9%. Its performance and volatility characteristics make it an attractive vehicle to enhance the overall risk/reward profile of a traditional portfolio. As Table 18 shows, the long/short equity strategy had the seventh lowest VAR out of a sample of 10 strategies analysed in the period.

### Examples

To further understand the implications of having long/short positions in a portfolio, CMRA created six portfolios, calculated their VARs and performed several stress tests using Riskdata's software. One of the key characteristics of these portfolios is that we did not apply any optionality techniques (eg, delta hedging, gamma trading, credit hedging, asset swapping, etc). Details of the portfolios are given in Table 19.

For each portfolio, CMRA analysed VAR under two different scenarios: a net long and a net short position. The results, presented in Table 20, suggest that diversification in a long/short portfolio helps to reduce VAR. Combining Portfolios 1, 2 and 3 provides the best example of this. The VARs for the net long positions of Portfolios 1 and 2 are 10.5% and 21.4%, respectively. The VARs for Portfolio 4, a diversified portfolio, are 15.1% for the long positions and 16.6% for the shorts. Portfolio 5, the overall diversified portfolio, has a much lower VAR than the expected weighted average of the three VARs combined. Tables 21 and 22 show the cross-correlation of the different portfolios.

**Table 19** Details of example long/short equity portfolios

| Portfolio | Sectors | Number of positions in portfolio |
|---|---|---|
| 1 | Technology | 6 |
| 2 | Telecom | 6 |
| 3 | Other | 8 |
| 4 | Technology + telecom | 12 |
| 5 | Telecom + other | 14 |
| 6 | Telecom + technology + other | 22 |

*Source*: Riskdata, CMRA Analysis

**Table 20** Calculation of daily VAR with 95% confidence level for example portfolios, 1997–2001

| Portfolio | Sectors | Net long (%) | Net short (%) |
|-----------|---------|--------------|---------------|
| 1 | Technology | 10.5 | (24.5) |
| 2 | Telecom | 21.4 | (15.2) |
| 3 | Other | 7.9 | (6.8) |
| 4 | Telecom + other | 15.1 | (16.6) |
| 5 | Telecom + technology + other | 6.8 | (10.1) |

*Source*: Bloomberg, CMRA Analysis, Riskdata provided VAR Calculations

**Table 21** Cross-correlation analysis for net long portfolio (%)

| | Technology | Telecom | Telecoms + + other | Other | Telecoms + technology + other |
|---|-----------|---------|------------------|-------|------------------------------|
| Technology | 100 | | | | |
| Telecom | 23 | 100 | | | |
| Telecom + other | (19) | (49) | 100 | | |
| Other | (13) | (11) | 52 | 100 | |
| Telecoms + technology + other | 61 | 74 | (17) | 36 | 100 |

*Source*: Riskdata, CMRA Analysis

**Table 22** Cross-correlation analysis for net short portfolio (%)

| | Technology | Telecom | Telecoms + + other | Other | Telecoms + technology + other |
|---|-----------|---------|------------------|-------|------------------------------|
| Technology | 100 | | | | |
| Telecom | 37 | 100 | | | |
| Telecom + other | 44 | 89 | 100 | | |
| Other | (4) | (3) | 16 | 100 | |
| Telecoms + technology + other | 80 | 80 | 75 | 21 | 100 |

*Source*: Riskdata, CMRA Analysis

## STRESS TESTS

It is important to note that a basic VAR analysis does not help in under-standing short-squeeze and other risk factors and needs to be combined with stress-testing. Some of the stress tests that should be considered for the long/short equity strategy include:

❏ price shifts in equities, sectors and indices;
❏ spreads and relationships;
❏ concentrations;
❏ correlations;
❏ leverage;
❏ short squeeze; and
❏ liquidity.

The two scenarios considered in Tables 23 and 24 demonstrate the impact on VAR of various changes in securities prices in the selected portfolios. The average impact on the net long positions for a 2% increase in the price of technology stocks is an average 4.1% decrease in the VAR of the net long portfolios and a 1.7% decrease of the VAR of the net short portfolios. On the other hand, the impact of the telecom stocks on VAR varies by portfolio. Telecom has the largest impact on the telecom diversified portfolios, with a 15.3% drop in VAR resulting from a 2% increase in prices. Oil and

**Table 23** Stress-testing on portfolio VAR for net long portfolio (%)

| Long positions | VAR | Technology | | Telecom | | Oil & gas | |
| --- | --- | --- | --- | --- | --- | --- | --- |
| | | +2% | −2% | +2% | −2% | +2% | −2% |
| Technology | 10.5 | (3.3) | (0.1) | 1.6 | 0.9 | (1.9) | (0.4) |
| Telecom | 21.4 | (4.4) | (0.3) | 3.1 | 1.6 | (7.5) | (0.2) |
| Other | 7.9 | (4.1) | (1.8) | (5.1) | (2.3) | (0.2) | 0.0 |
| Telecom + other | 15.1 | (6.4) | (2.3) | (15.3) | (8.8) | (1.5) | (0.8) |
| Telecom + technology + other | 6.8 | (2.2) | (0.4) | 0.5 | 0.1 | (1.0) | 0.1 |

*Source*: Riskdata, CMRA Analysis

**Table 24** Stress-testing on portfolio VAR for net short portfolio (%)

| Short positions | VAR | Technology | | Telecom | | Oil & gas | |
| --- | --- | --- | --- | --- | --- | --- | --- |
| | | +2% | −2% | +2% | −2% | +2% | −2% |
| Technology | (24.5) | (2.2) | (1.1) | (5.0) | (2.6) | (1.4) | (0.4) |
| Telecom | (15.2) | (1.7) | (1.0) | (3.9) | (1.4) | 1.6 | (0.4) |
| Other | (6.8) | (0.3) | (0.2) | (0.4) | (0.1) | (2.4) | (0.3) |
| Telecom + other | (16.6) | (3.9) | (1.0) | (4.5) | (1.8) | 0.3 | (0.3) |
| Telecom + technology + other | (10.1) | (0.4) | (0.4) | (2.5) | (0.6) | (1.8) | (0.3) |

*Source*: Riskdata, CMRA Analysis

gas prices have a smaller impact on the VAR statistics. A 2% increase in the prices of the oil and gas securities causes an average drop in VAR of 2.4% for the net long portfolio and 0.7% for the net short portfolio.

## DUE DILIGENCE QUESTIONS FOR LONG/SHORT EQUITY FUNDS

Some due diligence questions for long/short equity funds include:

- ❏ Does the manager go net long, net short or both?
- ❏ If you had to (or wanted to) liquidate your portfolio, how long will it take under normal circumstances and under stressed conditions?
- ❏ How do you deal with correlation assumptions?
- ❏ How do you hedge foreign exchange exposure?
- ❏ What do you do about maturity mismatches?
- ❏ Do you use the over-the-counter derivatives?
- ❏ How you measure counterparty exposure?
- ❏ How do you mark-to-market?
- ❏ Do you make adjustments for large illiquid positions?
- ❏ Do you mark logs to bid and shorts to offer?
- ❏ Does the manager go net long, short long or both?
- ❏ Does the manager focus on a specific region? If so, which region and why?
- ❏ Does the manager focus on a specific sector? If so, which sector and why?
- ❏ How does the manager handle interest on the rebate?
- ❏ What amount of leverage is used and how does the manager calculate and track it?

## DATA AND NAV ISSUES

Although at first the NAV of a long/short equity fund seems easy to assess, the difficult factor is liquidity. CMRA has seen positions take seven years to liquidate without exceeding 25% of daily volume. When one cannot liquidate an asset for seven years, how is it possible to determine its NAV accurately over the next seven years? Factors that could change the NAV over time include inflation and the volatility of the stock market, as well as the absolute level of the stock market and the relative performance of the individual stocks in the fund compared to its peers.

Another problem with NAV is that it does not take into account the value of asset ownership where a controlling position is involved. Because owning stock represents ownership of a portion of the company, an individual who owns enough stock will have some control over the company's decisions. However, the concept of a control premium, when an investor owns a controlling equity position, dictates that the buyer must pay a control premium. But how much is control worth? Does owning enough stock to obtain control of a company add to NAV or subtract from it due to the cost of the control premium?

## PUBLICLY DISCLOSED PROBLEMS

Examples of publicly disclosed problems in long/short equity funds include the Penta Japan Fund Ltd. Penta was among the largest Japan-focused hedge funds with US$546.7 million of AUM at the end of 1999. It was highly successful in 1999, its first full trading year, with 153.8% returns net of fees. But then 2000 saw a shaky market in Japan, especially in the highly volatile small-cap area, which led to near death for Penta. The fund suffered eight down months, including three when it was down by double digits. Penta lost 47.4% of its value that year. On December 15, 2000, Penta announced to investors that it would temporarily delay withdrawals of some US$120 million in outstanding redemption requests. Penta predicted that allowing liquidation would lead to a mass exodus, leaving the remaining investors with a portfolio consisting of the fund's most illiquid securities. Penta's plan was a success. It lifted the standard 30-day waiting period in February 2001 after the illiquid portion of the fund had shrunk to about 18%, thereby allowing an immediate exit for the investors who had wanted to leave in December. A first-quarter rebound in 2001 brought Penta up more than 8%. It showed a monthly gain of just below 9.3% in March 2001 and outperformed the Nikkei and almost every other global benchmark, including the CSFB/Tremont Hedge Fund Index (which listed 0.3% for the month). As of June 2002, Penta was down 3.3% and at −9.5% year-to-date.

Another example is the Foxhound Fund, which was not as fortunate as Penta. Bulldog Capital Management in Clearwater, Florida, managed Foxhound, which had nearly US$400 million of AUM in February 2000. Like Penta, difficult market conditions caused severe losses for Foxhound. Its assets were reduced to nearly US$40 million in only a few days after harsh markets in March and early April 2000. In its eight-year run, Foxhound had never seen a losing year: in 1999 it was up 332.4%. But the fund ended 2000 down 68.5%. After its severe losses in 2000, Bulldog's management began the process of liquidating Foxhound in March 2001.

---

1   Lehman Brothers. "Understanding Hedge Fund Performance: Research Results and Rules of Thumb for the Institutional Investor." November 2001.

# 15

# *Event-Driven*

## DESCRIPTION OF THE STRATEGY

An event-driven fund, generally speaking, is one that specialises in profiting from a specific "event." The term "event-driven" encompasses several hedge fund strategies but does not describe a single specific approach. For practical purposes, most people break down the event-driven category into three fund groups: pure event-driven, distressed securities and merger arbitrage. Event-driven hedge funds specialise in investment strategies that capture the price movement generated by a significant pending corporate event such as a merger, corporate restructuring, liquidation, financial default or bankruptcy. A fund that calls itself an event-driven fund will probably employ both distressed and merger arbitrage strategies.

### Distressed securities

Distressed security strategies invest in or sell short securities of companies that have been or are expected to be affected by financial difficulties. Financial "distress" can be caused by any number of the following: liquidity problems; excess debt; operational or strategic shortcomings; changes in the competitive marketplace; and legal or regulatory difficulties, among others. Distressed securities managers invest in bank debt, bonds, subordinated debt, trade claims, letters of credit, common stock, preferred stock, warrants and a variety of other hybrid securities. There may also be opportunities to buy specific assets or even entire business units from distressed companies that need to raise cash.

Distressed securities funds benefit from the relative predictability and financial flexibility that US bankruptcy laws and, to a lesser extent, those of a few other countries allow for the restructuring of financially distressed businesses. When a public company with outstanding debt begins to show signs of impending default, the value of both its equity and its debt declines rapidly. Typically, many holders of that company's securities tend to be early sellers of their paper on the market for whatever they can get. This process is enhanced by the fact that many institutional investors – often the largest holders of the now-distressed corporate paper – have internal risk controls or other internal arrangements that do not allow them to hold assets rated below investment-grade. With sellers flooding the market from every direction, a distressed company's securities commonly trade at significant discounts.

It takes a special expertise, not to mention fortitude, to make leveraged bets on the securities of a company about to embark on a financial restructuring process that typically leads to Chapter 11. Unsurprisingly, the buyers who surface in these markets are generally hedge funds. Distressed securities funds can profit from the bankruptcy process in a number of ways. One is through a fundamental-value strategy. Believing that the distressed company is fundamentally sound and will either avoid a bankruptcy filing altogether or file and successfully emerge from the bankruptcy process, a fund will step in and buy up debt at a below-par discount. If the company fares well and the debt rating recovers, the fund can harvest profits equivalent to long equity returns in an up market.

There are two different approaches to implementing a fundamental-value strategy. The first is by acquiring a controlling position in a particular security and being active in the actual restructuring process. The second is to remain passive and to trade in and out. Most distressed hedge funds concentrate primarily on one or the other of these two approaches, but not necessarily to the exclusion of the alternative.

Another strategy a fund might employ is a hedged relative value strategy called "capital structure arbitrage". When a company experiences financial difficulty, there is a tendency for its various financial instruments to become incorrectly priced relative to one another. By buying the cheap instrument (eg, debt) and shorting the overpriced instrument (eg, equity), the fund will profit when the market becomes rational again.

One of the most important skills in distressed investing lies in identifying the true value of a distressed company's assets. In this respect, hedge fund managers who specialise in financial restructuring have a significant competitive advantage over the rest of the general market. Given the high level of uncertainty regarding distressed companies, the markets for their securities tend to be irrational and therefore inefficient. For a truly astute distressed fund manager, there accordingly are significant profit opportunities.

The unique nature of the distressed debt market creates an interesting dichotomy between smaller and larger funds. As there are only a few players willing to buy up distressed debt, the markets tend to be fairly illiquid. This gives an obvious advantage to the small funds, which can be very nimble in a volatile market.

On the other hand, if a fund is big enough to buy up tens or hundreds of millions or, depending on the size of the issuer, even billions of principal amount of debt at a time, it too has an interesting advantage. When a business experiences financial distress, the legal process recognises various constituencies that normally try to engineer a financial settlement. The higher the percentage of the total debt that a participant holds within such a constituency, the greater that participant's ability to influence the outcome. This is known as a "control" position. An important part of the business of control-oriented funds entails working on the financial and legal aspects of the bankruptcy process in order to protect and further their own interests. Hedge funds with a control position can often thereby have a meaningful influence on the outcome of a bankruptcy settlement. The price that trading-oriented funds pay for increased liquidity is to be subjected to the volatility that a bankruptcy judge or the holder of a control position can create in the restructuring process.

### Merger arbitrage

Merger arbitrageurs profit from the spread (called the "arbitrage spread") that results from a merger announcement or takeover. The basic idea is that, when an acquiring company is trading at 60 and the acquired company is trading at 30, by the end of the merger the two stocks should be trading at the same price. A merger arbitrageur will profit by shorting the stock of the acquiring company and going long on the stock of the acquired company. If by the end of the merger the combined stock is trading at 50, the arbitrageur has made 20 points on its long bet and 10 points on its short bet, giving a total of 30 points. In the period leading up to the merger date the spread will get tighter and tighter, so the earlier the arbitrageur gets in, the greater the risk and profit opportunity. The primary risk of this strategy is that, if for some reason the merger does not go through, the stocks will return to their original prices, often causing substantial losses.

CMRA completed a fundamental analysis of the merger arbitrage strategy. The major conclusions of the study were:

❏ the majority of merger arbitrage managers achieve their returns by "drifting" away from the "pure" strategy and taking on significant equity market exposure;
❏ the risk/return performance of the "pure" strategy is attractive (driven by modest returns with low volatility); and
❏ smaller deals (presumably less efficiently valued) generate the highest returns.

The strong performance of the event-driven strategy and its risk characteristics have fuelled growth in AUM. As seen in Figure 1, from 1994 to December 2001 the overall outflow was close to US$25 billion. The largest outflows in assets occurred in the second and third quarters of 1998 (during the Russian/LTCM crisis) and also in June 2000 (during the tech crash). The average growth of assets in the strategy during this period was 35.5%, one of the largest growth rates in assets when compared to the other hedge fund strategies.

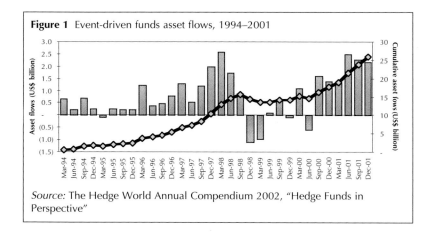

**Figure 1** Event-driven funds asset flows, 1994–2001

*Source:* The Hedge World Annual Compendium 2002, "Hedge Funds in Perspective"

## EFFECT OF MARKET CONDITIONS

Although "events" are theoretically independent of prevailing market conditions, and event-driven funds are often marketed as such, there appears to be little hard evidence to support this. Thus, the strategy performs above its historical average when:

❏ The yield curve is moderately upward sloping and its slope is declining.
❏ Credit risk premium is low.
❏ Short-term rates are not increasing.
❏ Long-term rates are declining.
❏ The implied volatility index is at a low level and is not changing.
❏ The intra-month volatility of the S&P 500 Index is low.

The strategy performs substantially below its historical average when:

❏ Credit risk premium is high.
❏ Short-term rates are increasing by a substantial amount.
❏ The long-term yield is increasing.
❏ The intra-month volatility of the S&P 500 is high.
❏ The returns of large-cap and small-cap stocks are negative.

## INVESTORS IN THE STRATEGY

Financial institutions, individuals, family offices and funds of funds are by far the largest investors in event-driven hedge funds (see Table 1). One disadvantage for distressed securities hedge funds is the lack of liquidity of the underlying positions. Many distressed funds are structured as private equity for this reason.

**Table 1** Investors in the event-driven strategy (%)

| Investors | Event-driven | Distressed securities | Merger arbitrage |
|---|---|---|---|
| Individuals and family offices | 53 | 42 | 45 |
| Funds of funds | 17 | 32 | 37 |
| Corporations | 14 | 18 | 6 |
| Endowments and foundations | 11 | 4 | 6 |
| Pensions and retirement | 6 | 4 | 5 |

*Source*: Hennessee Hedge Fund Survey (January 2000)

## WELL-KNOWN PLAYERS

The top 25 funds by AUM, as consolidated from the major data sources, have a total of US$44.3 billion with 11 funds having an AUM greater than US$1 billion (see Table 2).

The 17 funds exclusively covered by The Hedge Fund 100 represent US$17.4 billion in AUM, which is 80.4% of the consolidated total from all sources – US$21.2 billion. In addition, of the top 25 funds, 13 funds with

**Table 2** Top event-driven funds with more than US$1 billion in AUM (all sources)

| Rank | Fund | Highest AUM* (US$ billion) |
|---|---|---|
| 1 | Och-Ziff Capital Management | 5.0 |
| 2 | Highbridge Capital Corporation | 3.9 |
| 3 | Standard Pacific Capital | 3.1 |
| 4 | Carlson Capital | 3.1 |
| 5 | Perry Partners International, Inc | 2.3 |
| 6 | Farallon Capital Management | 2.0 |
| 7 | Cerberus International, Ltd** | 1.4 |
| 8 | Elliott Associates, LP | 1.0 |
| 9 | Castlerigg International | 1.0 |
| 10 | Appaloosa Investment I | 1.0 |
| 11 | Levco Alternative Fund | 1.0 |
| | **Total** | **24.8** |

*This is the highest AUM for that fund among all the sources
** Distressed securities
Highlighted funds are exclusively in The Hedge Fund 100

*Source*: Altvest, Tuna, HFR, Institutional Investor (June 2002), Directory of Fund of Hedge Funds Investment Vehicles, CMRA Analysis

US$14.3 billion in AUM (or 65.9% of the total) are among the most popular holdings of funds of funds.

## COVERAGE OF THE STRATEGY IN DIFFERENT SOURCES

There are marked differences between the sources that cover event-driven strategies. Tuna covers both the largest number of funds and the highest AUM. A breakdown of coverage by styles and sources is given in Tables 3 and 4.

**Table 3** Coverage of event-driven funds, distressed securities and merger arbitrage by different sources

| Source | Total number of funds | Funds with no AUM data | Total AUM (US$ billion) |
|---|---|---|---|
| **Event-driven** | | | |
| The Hedge Fund 100 | 30 | 0 | 26.0* |
| Tuna | 185 | 8 | 21.1 |
| HFR | 169 | 11 | 17.0 |
| Altvest | 91 | 23 | 16.8 |
| **Distressed securities** | | | |
| Tuna | 46 | 0 | 4.8 |
| Altvest | 22 | 2 | 4.2 |
| HFR | 37 | 1 | 3.1 |
| **Merger arbitrage** | | | |
| Altvest | 35 | 3 | 6.3 |
| HFR | 59 | 5 | 4.5 |
| Tuna | 46 | 4 | 3.9 |
| **Total** | **720** | **57** | **107.7** |

* The Hedge Fund 100 groups all the event-driven strategies into one event-driven strategy.

*Source*: Altvest, HFR, Tuna, Institutional Investor (June 2002)

**Table 4** Summary of event-driven coverage

| Source | Total number of funds | Funds with no AUM data | Total AUM (US$ billion) |
|---|---|---|---|
| Tuna | 277 | 12 | 29.8 |
| Altvest | 148 | 28 | 27.3 |
| The Hedge Fund 100 | 30 | 0 | 26.0 |
| HFR | 265 | 17 | 24.6 |
| **Total** | **720** | **57** | **107.7** |

*Source*: Altvest, Tuna, HFR, Institutional Investor (June 2002).

## DISTRIBUTION OF FUNDS IN THE STRATEGY
Combining the AUM of the three event-driven strategies, 15 funds of 104 surveyed have US$9.7 billion, or 60%, of the AUM that are managed under event-driven strategies (see Figure 2).

### Distribution of funds by quartile of performance
Table 5 shows the different performance ranges of the strategy. The top quartile of event-driven funds represents 38% of the assets and also has the highest return (21.7%). In addition, this quartile has the second highest volatility and its Sharpe ratio (1.1) is the highest of the four quartiles. The third quartile, with an average five-year return of 11.4%, covers 12.0% of the assets. The third quartile also has the lowest standard deviation of the group and a Sharpe ratio of 0.9. The bottom quartile covering the worst performers in the strategy with an average performance of 2.6%, accounts for 32% of the assets.

### Distribution of funds by quartile of AUM
As shown in Table 6, the top quartile by AUM controls 74% of the assets, with an average return of 10.6%. It also has the highest standard deviation (22.8%). The second quartile, with an average performance of 14.1%, has a standard deviation of 11.0%. The last quartile, which represents only 2.0% of the assets, has an average performance of 13.3%. In addition, the smallest funds have the lowest volatility (9.2%) and the highest Sharpe ratio. This analysis, like most analyses of hedge funds, is flawed by the absence of funds managed by a number of major players, including Cerberus International, King Street Capital and Egerton, among others, which collectively control many billions of US dollars of AUM.

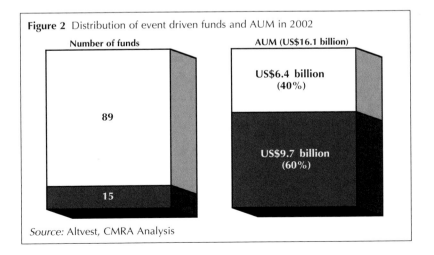

**Figure 2** Distribution of event driven funds and AUM in 2002

Number of funds

89

15

AUM (US$16.1 billion)

US$6.4 billion
(40%)

US$9.7 billion
(60%)

*Source:* Altvest, CMRA Analysis

**Table 5** Distribution of event-driven strategies by quartiles of five-year performance, 1997–2001

| Return quartiles | Average 1997–2001 equally weighted return (%) | Avergae 1997–2001 AUM-weighted return (%) | AUM in quartile (US$ billion) | % of total | Average 1997–2001 standard deviation (%) | Sharpe ratio 1997–2001 |
|---|---|---|---|---|---|---|
| 1 | 21.7 | 22.0 | 3.8 | 38.0 | 17.3 | 1.1 |
| 2 | 14.0 | 14.1 | 1.8 | 18.0 | 10.8 | 1.0 |
| 3 | 11.4 | 11.3 | 1.2 | 12.0 | 8.0 | 0.9 |
| 4 | 2.6 | (1.8) | 3.2 | 32.0 | 19.7 | 0.3 |
| **Total** | **12.6** | **11.7** | **10.0** | **100.0** | **13.8** | **0.8** |

*Source*: Altvest, HFR, Tuna, CMRA Analysis based on 47 funds with five-year performance data

For the 1997–2001 period, the event-driven funds have demonstrated Sharpe ratios as high as 1.55.

## PERFORMANCE OF THE STRATEGY
### Returns during boom and bust
During the great boom and bust period of the equity markets in 1997–2001, event-driven indices performed well against the returns of the S&P 500 Index. During the boom period from January 1997 to June 2000, the event-driven indices underperformed the S&P 500 by 6%, with returns of 17%. However, during the bust period from June 2000 to December 2001, the event-driven strategy outperformed the S&P 500 by a hefty 23%, returning 9%. The distressed securities fund indices also performed well against the returns of the S&P 500. During the boom period the distressed indices underperformed the S&P 500 by 11%, turning in returns of 12%. Lastly, the

**Table 6** Distribution of event-driven hedge funds by quartiles of AUM, 1997–2001

| AUM quartiles | Average 1997–2001 equally weighted return (%) | Avergae 1997–2001 AUM-weighted return (%) | AUM in quartile (US$ billion) | % of total | Average 1997–2001 standard deviation (%) | Sharpe ratio 1997–2001 |
|---|---|---|---|---|---|---|
| 1 | 10.6 | 11.2 | 7.4 | 74 | 22.8 | 0.7 |
| 2 | 14.1 | 13.6 | 1.7 | 17 | 11.0 | 0.9 |
| 3 | 12.7 | 12.8 | 0.7 | 7 | 11.9 | 0.8 |
| 4 | 13.3 | 12.9 | 0.2 | 2 | 9.2 | 1.0 |
| **Total** | **12.6** | **11.7** | **10.0** | **100** | **13.8** | **0.8** |

*Source*: Altvest, HFR, Tuna, CMRA Analysis based on 47 funds with five-year performance data

merger arbitrage indices performed well against the returns of the S&P 500. During the boom period the index underperformed the S&P 500 by 7%, with returns of 16% (see Figure 3). The data strongly suggest that the event-driven strategies live up to their marketing promise of performing well in both favourable and unfavourable market conditions.

According to Zurich Capital Markets, event-driven indices (see Table 7), the merger arbitrage strategy has exhibited an average performance of 10.2% in down markets, 13 points higher than distressed securities and 14.6 points better than event-driven funds. Merger arbitrage also has the lowest volatility by a factor of 2.0 when compared to the event-driven index and of 4.0 when compared to distressed securities funds.

### Returns from different sources
Despite the measured differences in performance for each index and for the three categories of event-driven strategies (see Figure 4), it nevertheless is clear that the event-driven strategies tend to perform well during

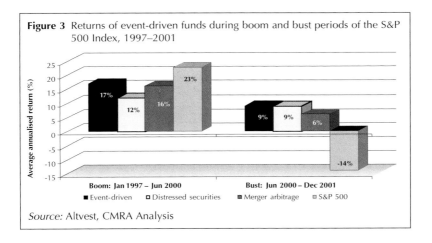

**Figure 3** Returns of event-driven funds during boom and bust periods of the S&P 500 Index, 1997–2001

Boom: Jan 1997 – Jun 2000    Bust: Jun 2000 – Dec 2001
■ Event-driven    □ Distressed securities    ▩ Merger arbitrage    ▤ S&P 500

*Source:* Altvest, CMRA Analysis

**Table 7** Performance of strategy during down markets as indicated by Zurich's Capital Markets' event-driven indices (%)

| Style | Annual return (down markets) | Standard deviation |
|---|---|---|
| Merger arbitrage | 10.2 | 5.3 |
| Distressed securities | (2.8) | 23.8 |
| Event-driven | (4.4) | 10.9 |

*Source:* Zurich Capital Markets

adverse market conditions. Although the event-driven indices certainly did not match the high-flying S&P 500 Index during the late 1990s. Unlike the S&P 500 Index, the event-driven indices continued to enjoy positive returns in the tough market years of 2000 and 2001.

### Event-driven

As seen in Table 8, there was a noticeable difference of 9.94 points in 1998 between the CSFB/Tremont Index and the Altvest Index. The former is based on 77 funds, as opposed to the 74 funds included in the Altvest database. The two indices have 26 funds in common. The remaining 48 funds in the CSFB/Tremont database outperformed the remaining 51 funds of the Altvest Index on an equally weighted basis by 3.5 points. In addition, the CSFB/Tremont Index is AUM-weighted, whereas the Altvest Index (and all other indices analysed) is equally weighted. This difference in methodology accounts for the 35% difference between the returns reported by the two indices in 1998. (See Chapter 11 for a further discussion of index construction.)

The 1998 performance returns of the five event-driven indices varied by 9.94 points across the different sources. For the year 2000, the maximum difference in returns was 8.56 or 1.04 times the average return of 8.24%. In 2001 the different indices converged, with a maximum difference of 5.21%.

1999 was a boom year with an annual performance of 24.73%. 1998 was the least volatile year with an average performance of 0.04%. The Sharpe ratio for the 1997–2001 period fluctuates from 0.16 to 1.08 depending on the source. The beta fluctuates by 1.16, which represents 90% of the average beta for the period.

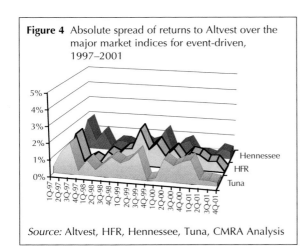

**Figure 4**  Absolute spread of returns to Altvest over the major market indices for event-driven, 1997–2001

*Source:* Altvest, HFR, Hennessee, Tuna, CMRA Analysis

### Distressed securities

There was an evident difference of 9.47 points in 1998 between the Hennessee Index and the Altvest Index. In 2000, the maximum difference in returns was 8.03, or 2.2 times the average return of 3.61%! In 2001 the indices converged more closely, with a maximum difference of 7.74%.

1999 was a boom year with an annual performance of 21.68%. 1998 was the lowest year with an

**Table 8** Comparison of event-driven indices across by different sources, 1997–2001

| | 1997 | 1998 | 1999 | 2000 | 2001 | 1997–2001 Return | 1997–2001 Sharpe ratio |
|---|---|---|---|---|---|---|---|
| Tuna | 27.3 | 0.9 | 30.4 | 3.9 | 11.3 | 14.1 | 0.7 |
| Altvest | 19.6 | 5.1 | 22.3 | 12.4 | 7.2 | 13.1 | 1.1 |
| Hennessee | 22.7 | (2.6) | 24.4 | 10.9 | 12.4 | 13.1 | 0.8 |
| HFR | 21.2 | 1.7 | 24.3 | 6.7 | 10.6 | 12.6 | 1.0 |
| CSFB/Tremont | N/A | (4.9) | 22.3 | 7.3 | 11.5 | 6.8 | 0.2 |
| Maximum difference | 7.6 | 9.9 | 8.2 | 8.6 | 5.2 | 7.3 | 0.9 |
| Average | 22.7 | 0.0 | 24.7 | 8.2 | 10.6 | 12.0 | 0.7 |

Source: Tuna, Altvest, HFR, Hennessee, CSFB/Tremont

average performance of –1.5%. The Sharpe ratio for that period fluctuated from 0.41 to 1.03 depending on the source. Performance during the 1997–2001 period as reported by various indices is summarised in Figure 5 and Table 9.

## Merger arbitrage

There was a 6.15-point difference in 1999 between the HFR Index and the Altvest Index. In 1997 the maximum difference in returns was 7.04, or 50% of the average return of 15.12%. 2000 was a boom year with an annual performance of 17.3%. 2001 was the worst year with an average performance of 2.7%. The Sharpe ratio for the period fluctuated from 0.85 to 2.0 depending on the source. Beta had a maximum fluctuation of 0.93, which represents 75% of the average beta for the period. Details are summarised in Table 10, and the spread of quarterly returns reported by three sources is shown in Figure 6.

## Index performance

The constituents of an index can vary substantially in performance and volatility. There are 77 funds in the CSFB/Tremont Event Driven Index. Of these we analysed 42 constituents for which data are available. The 2001 return for each of these funds ranged from –13.5% to 72.8%; the 1997–2001 return ranged from 6.1% to 18.3%. The degree to which the funds that constitute the CSFB/Tremont Index can vary from the index itself is shown in Figure 7.

Among the 77 funds that make up the CFSB/Tremont event-driven index, 42 funds were analysed. The Palomino Fund Ltd. had the highest return at 18.27% with a standard deviation of 3.9% and the Euro-Partners Arbitrage Fund, Ltd. had the lowest return at 6.1% with a 5.8% standard deviation for the 1997–2001 period.

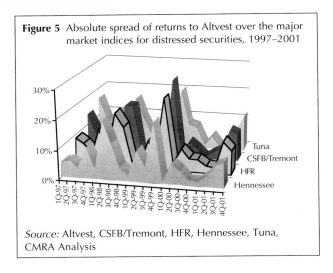

**Figure 5** Absolute spread of returns to Altvest over the major market indices for distressed securities, 1997–2001

*Source:* Altvest, CSFB/Tremont, HFR, Hennessee, Tuna, CMRA Analysis

**Table 9** Comparisons of distressed securities indices across different sources, 1997–2001

| | 1997 | 1998 | 1999 | 2000 | 2001 | 1997–2001 | |
| | | | | | | Return | Sharpe ratio |
|---|---|---|---|---|---|---|---|
| Altvest | 18.3 | 3.0 | 24.8 | 1.6 | 15.5 | 12.3 | 1.0 |
| Tuna | 16.2 | (4.7) | 21.3 | 9.2 | 17.4 | 11.5 | 0.8 |
| EACM | 11.3 | 2.2 | 15.8 | 1.2 | 11.8 | 8.3 | 0.5 |
| Hennessee | 11.3 | (6.5) | 24.8 | 2.4 | 9.6 | 7.8 | 0.4 |
| Maximum difference | 7.0 | 9.5 | 9.0 | 8.0 | 7.7 | 4.4 | 0.6 |
| Average | 14.3 | (1.5) | 21.7 | 3.6 | 13.6 | 10.0 | 0.7 |

*Source:* Altvest, Tuna, EACM, Hennessee

Of the 14 hedge fund strategies defined by Altvest, event-driven, merger arbitrage and distressed securities funds ranked second, sixth and ninth, respectively (see Table 11).

The index performance of the event-driven strategies was consistent with that of the other hedge fund strategies in the stressed period of 1998.

As can also be seen in Table 11, merger arbitrage funds fared better than the rest of the event-driven category in 1998, returning well above the risk-free rate. Although the increased S&P 500 volatility during August and September hurt returns of the primarily equity-based strategy, merger arbitrage funds quickly bounced back at the end of 1998 and performed strongly in 1999. The economic downturn of 2001, along with fewer merger arbitrage deals, is partly the reason for their lacklustre 2001 performance of 4.25%.

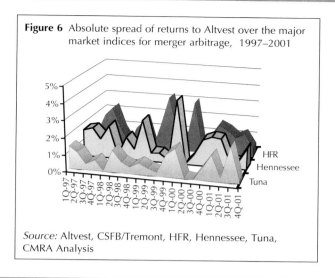

**Figure 6** Absolute spread of returns to Altvest over the major market indices for merger arbitrage, 1997–2001

*Source:* Altvest, CSFB/Tremont, HFR, Hennessee, Tuna, CMRA Analysis

**Table 10** Comparisons of merger arbitrage indices across different sources, 1997–2001

| | 1997 | 1998 | 1999 | 2000 | 2001 | 1997–2001 Return | Sharpe ratio |
|---|---|---|---|---|---|---|---|
| Altvest | 19.1 | 8.9 | 20.4 | 19.6 | 4.0 | 14.2 | 2.0 |
| Hennessee | 14.3 | 7.7 | 16.0 | 17.5 | 3.8 | 11.7 | 1.6 |
| HFR | 16.4 | 7.2 | 14.3 | 18.0 | 2.0 | 11.6 | 1.5 |
| EACM | 12.0 | 5.3 | 14.2 | 14.8 | 0.2 | 9.2 | 0.9 |
| Maximum difference | 7.0 | 3.7 | 6.2 | 4.7 | 3.7 | 5.0 | 1.2 |
| Average | 15.1 | 7.3 | 16.9 | 17.3 | 2.7 | 11.7 | 1.5 |

*Source*: Altvest, Hennessee, Tuna, HFR, EACM

### Performance correlations

The event-driven strategies as a whole (including merger arbitrage and distressed securities) seem to perform above the average when economic conditions are changing. They perform especially well when there is an upward-sloping yield curve with declining long-term yields. These strategies are also an attractive investment when market volatility is at a moderate level.

The data suggest that when the equity market does well, so do event-driven funds (see Table 12). For the 1997–2001 period the correlation between the event-driven indices and the S&P 500 Index was a substantial 60.02%. Distressed securities and merger arbitrage funds had correlations with the S&P 500 of 35.2% and 47.18%, respectively. On the other hand, these funds have little or no correlation with the Lehman Aggregate Bond

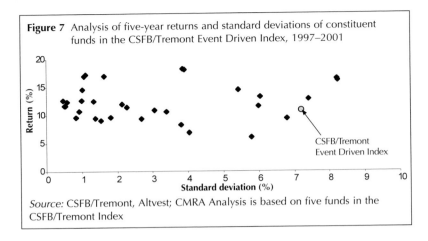

**Figure 7** Analysis of five-year returns and standard deviations of constituent funds in the CSFB/Tremont Event Driven Index, 1997–2001

*Source:* CSFB/Tremont, Altvest; CMRA Analysis is based on five funds in the CSFB/Tremont Index

**Table 11** Ranking of the event-driven strategies against other strategies, 1997–2001

|  | 1997 | 1998 | 1999 | 2000 | 2001 | 1997–2001 | Rank |
|---|---|---|---|---|---|---|---|
| Event-driven | 26.5 | (1.6) | 29.1 | 6.5 | 15.8 | 14.7 | 2 of 14 |
| Merger arbitrage | 18.8 | 7.6 | 18.7 | 15.7 | 4.3 | 12.8 | 6 of 14 |
| Distressed securities | 18.9 | (0.6) | 20.5 | 3.1 | 15.1 | 11.1 | 9 of 14 |

*Source:* Altvest, CMRA Analysis

Composite Index. Thus, event-driven, distressed securities and merger arbitrage indices have demonstrated correlations of only 11.6%, 7.4%, and 1.0%, respectively, with the Lehman index over the period considered.

This suggests that the inclusion of event-driven strategies such as distressed securities and merger arbitrage into a portfolio can be a powerful means of diversification. The correlation properties presented here do not tell the full story about the real benefits of diversification, however. What investors really want is positive correlation in periods when equity and bond portfolios advance and negative correlation in periods when the value of traditional investments declines.

**Stress period analysis**

The Russian default and the subsequent implosion of LTCM's US$125 billion dollar portfolio (approximately US$1.25 trillion in notional value including off-the-books derivative trades) dealt the most crippling blow by far to the event-driven strategies: over the course of only three months, the event-driven and distressed securities indices lost 8.6% and 9.6% of their value, respectively. Interestingly, the merger arbitrage index suffered

**Table 12** Rolling correlations of event-driven indices with S&P 500 and Lehman Aggregate Bond Composite Index, 1997–2001 (%)

| S&P 500 | | | | | | |
|---|---|---|---|---|---|---|
| | 1997 | 1998 | 1999 | 2000 | 2001 | Average |
| Event-driven | 65.8 | 89.5 | 56.6 | 31.8 | 56.4 | 60.0 |
| Distressed securities | 61.9 | 62.5 | 50.0 | 5.0 | (3.3) | 35.2 |
| Merger arbitrage | 46.3 | 95.2 | 39.2 | 10.3 | 44.9 | 47.2 |

| Lehman Aggregate Bond Composite Index | | | | | | |
|---|---|---|---|---|---|---|
| | 1997 | 1998 | 1999 | 2000 | 2001 | Average |
| Event-driven | 56.8 | (61.5) | 24.4 | 29.7 | 8.7 | 11.6 |
| Distressed securities | 40.0 | (60.5) | 23.4 | 16.5 | 17.5 | 7.4 |
| Merger arbitrage | 23.4 | (55.3) | 9.0 | 8.4 | 19.6 | 1.0 |

*Source*: HFR, CMRA Analysis

a relatively small dip of only –0.9%. Due to the flight to quality that resulted from the Russian default, distressed securities funds and event-driven funds suffered major losses as the value of their large holdings of below-investment-grade debt plummeted. Merger arbitrage funds, on the other hand, dealing mostly in corporate equity, were not hurt nearly as much by the jump in the volatility of the S&P 500 as were the event-driven and distressed securities funds.

Compared to the Russian default, the Federal Reserve's interest rate hikes of 1994, the tech crash of 2000-01 and the events of September 11, 2001 had only a minimal effect on the event-driven indices (see Table 13).

Following the Russian/LTCM crisis, distressed securities funds exhibited a Sharpe ratio of event-driven funds –1.3, –0.9 and merger arbitrage funds –0.5 (see Table 14).

An attempt to understand the different factors that affect the strategy was developed by Lehman Brothers, who evaluated the strategy in light of three different factors: change in term premia, change in credit spreads and change in implied volatility.

As mentioned before, the term premia factor can be an indicator of economic expansion or contraction, which is visibly related to any sector strategy. In the case of economic contractions, companies are expected to restructure their operations to respond to deteriorating market conditions. It is no surprise, then, to expect that event-driven strategies are sensitive to term premia.

The different factors that drive change in credit spreads include leverage, volatility and changes in the slope of the yield curve. Event-driven is among the least levered types of strategy.

The results of the Lehman study are summarised in Table 15. On a relative basis, distressed securities and event-driven strategies are more sensitive to changes in term premia than most of the other strategies analysed (this factor ranks them third and fourth, respectively, among the 17 strategies analysed). As mentioned before, an increase in implied volatility is often related to a fall in the equity markets.

It is interesting to note that even though the trading strategies in the event-driven category often benefit from a change in the volatility of the market, the Lehman model did not pick up this relationship. During the boom days of mergers and acquisitions in the 1990s, the Merger Arbitrage Strategy Index showed a negative correlation with the volatility of the S&P 500 Index. In contrast, during the tech meltdown, when volatility in the equity markets started to climb and fewer acquisitions were executed, the index showed a positive correlation. In 2001, when the economy finally slowed down and merger arbitrage activity declined dramatically, the correlation became negative again (see Figure 8).

A simple comparison between the event-driven strategy and the volatility index, plotted in Figure 9, shows that in August 1998 and September 2001 volatility of the Lehman Aggregate Bond Index increased dramatically and merger arbitrage returns declined dramatically.

**Table 13**  Returns of event-driven funds during periods of stress (%)

|  | Russian/LTCM crisis | Tech crash | September 11 |
|---|---|---|---|
| Merger arbitrage | (0.9) | 8.1 | (0.1) |
| Event-driven | (8.6) | 10.1 | 3.8 |
| Distressed securities | (9.6) | 8.3 | 3.4 |

Source: Altvest, CMRA Analysis

**Table 14**  Sharpe ratio of event-driven indices during periods of stress

|  | Russian/ LTCM crisis | Tech crash | September 11 | Average of absolute Sharpe ratios | Maximum-minimum |
|---|---|---|---|---|---|
| Event-driven | (0.9) | 0.6 | 0.7 | 0.8 | 1.7 |
| Distressed securities | (1.3) | 0.5 | 3.1 | 1.6 | 4.4 |
| Merger arbitrage | (0.5) | 1.3 | (0.4) | 0.7 | 1.7 |

Source: Altvest, HFR, Tuna, CSFB/Tremont, Hennessee, CMRA Analysis

**Table 15** Sensitivity of the event-driven strategies to market factors in Lehman's multivariate model

|  | Change in credit spread | Change in term premia | Change in VIX |
|---|---|---|---|
| Distressed securities | (0.08) | 0.021 | (0.22) |
| Event-driven | (0.07) | 0.020 | (0.22) |
| Merger arbitrage | (0.02) | 0.008 | (0.11) |

*Source*: Lehman Brothers "Understanding Hedge Fund Performance"

### Range of performance

The distribution of event-driven funds' returns is concentrated in the 10%–20% range (see Figure 10).

### SHARPE RATIO
### Distribution

Merger arbitrage funds have levered a Sharpe ratio of 3.15 over the 1997–2001 period, ranking merger arbitrage second among the 14 hedge fund strategies defined by Altvest (see Table 16). The ratio has fluctuated significantly, though, ranging from 7.12 in 2000 to a mere 1.22 in 2001. The standard deviation of merger arbitrage's Sharpe ratio fluctuations over the five-year period has been 2.98%. Distressed securities funds and the overall event-driven category follow with rankings of ninth and sixth, respectively, among the 14 hedge fund styles defined by Altvest.

The five-year Sharpe ratio for event-driven funds is highly concentrated (91%) in the 0–1 range. Merger arbitrage also shows a high concentration,

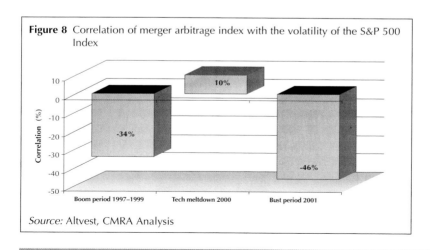

**Figure 8** Correlation of merger arbitrage index with the volatility of the S&P 500 Index

*Source:* Altvest, CMRA Analysis

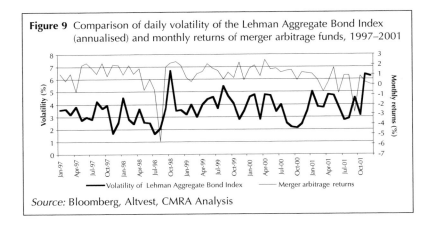

**Figure 9** Comparison of daily volatility of the Lehman Aggregate Bond Index (annualised) and monthly returns of merger arbitrage funds, 1997–2001

*Source:* Bloomberg, Altvest, CMRA Analysis

with 64% of such funds in the 1–2 range. 81% of distressed securities funds had a Sharpe ratio between 0.0 and 2.0 (see Figure 11).

One- and five-year Sharpe ratio distributions for event-driven funds as a whole are compared in Figure 12. Across the different event-driven strategies, 52 (or 30%) of the 176 total funds had a one-year Sharpe ratio from 0.0 to 2.0. For funds with five-year data, there are 93 (or 87%) in the same 0.0 to 2.0 Sharpe ratio category. In addition, 65 funds (or 37%) have a negative one-year Sharpe ratio, as opposed to eight funds (or 7%) for the five-year ratio. Also, 37 funds (or 21%) have a one-year Sharpe ratio greater than 3.0, as opposed to two funds (or 2%) for the five-year indi-cator. These differences could be explained in part by the changing condi-tions in the economy during 2001, which clearly shows an overall Sharpe ratio distribution that is better than the five-year indicator. The one-year

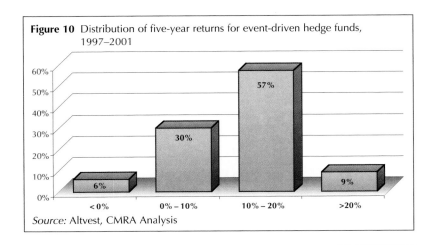

**Figure 10** Distribution of five-year returns for event-driven hedge funds, 1997–2001

*Source:* Altvest, CMRA Analysis

**Table 16** Event-driven fund Sharpe ratios, 1997–2001

|  | 1997 | 1998 | 1999 | 2000 | 2001 | 1997 to 2001 | Standard deviation of Sharpe ratio | Rank |
|---|---|---|---|---|---|---|---|---|
| Merger arbitrage | 6.4 | 1.2 | 6.3 | 7.1 | 1.2 | 3.2 | 3.0 | 2 of 14 |
| Event-driven | 4.4 | (0.1) | 3.9 | 0.7 | 2.5 | 1.6 | 2.0 | 6 of 14 |
| Distressed securities | 3.9 | (0.1) | 4.5 | 0.4 | 3.0 | 1.6 | 2.1 | 9 of 14 |

*Source*: Altvest, CMRA Analysis

Sharpe ratio has 32% of its funds with a value greater than 2.0, as opposed to a mere 1% for the five-year average.

Figure 13 shows a breakdown of the one-year Sharpe ratio for the three categories of the strategy. It is interesting to note how the distributions for merger arbitrage and event-driven funds are similar but differ from the distressed securities funds. 52% merger arbitrage and 43% of event-driven funds had a negative Sharpe ratio in 2001. For distressed securities, the distribution changes because only 9% of these funds had a negative Sharpe ratio in 2001.

An analysis by five-year Sharpe ratio (1997-2001) quartiles of event-driven funds (see Table 17) indicates that the top two quartiles have 37% of the overall AUM in the event-driven category. The first two quartiles also have the lowest standard deviation, with an average of 5.8%. The third and fourth quartiles have an average standard deviation of 15.4%, which is 9.6 points larger than the standard deviation of the first two quartiles.

Analysing the 153 event-driven funds for which there are Sharpe ratio data for 2001, we find that 48.2% of the AUM is accounted for by the first

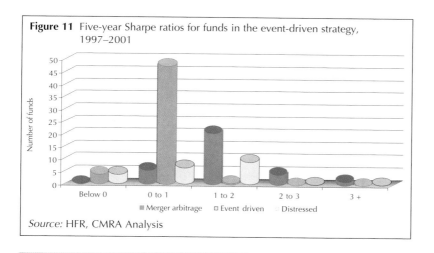

**Figure 11** Five-year Sharpe ratios for funds in the event-driven strategy, 1997–2001

Number of funds

Below 0    0 to 1    1 to 2    2 to 3    3 +

■ Merger arbitrage    ▫ Event driven    Distressed

*Source:* HFR, CMRA Analysis

quartile, which exhibits an average return of 20.6%. The other three quartiles have an average performance of 2.0%, roughly 10 times smaller. The fourth quartile has the smallest AUM, with US$1.9 billion (10.5%) and a negative performance (see Table 18).

In an effort to further understand the three different event-driven strategies, similar analyses were developed for each of the event-driven, merger arbitrage, and distressed securities categories. The results are discussed in the next three sub-sections.

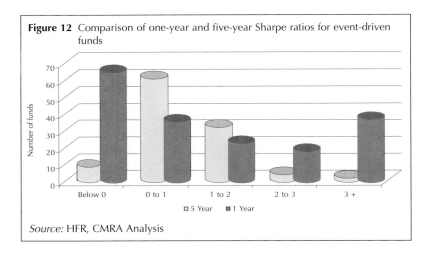

**Figure 12** Comparison of one-year and five-year Sharpe ratios for event-driven funds

*Source:* HFR, CMRA Analysis

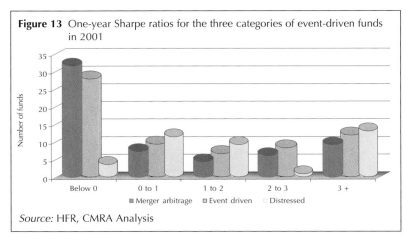

**Figure 13** One-year Sharpe ratios for the three categories of event-driven funds in 2001

*Source:* HFR, CMRA Analysis

**Table 17** Distribution of all categories of event-driven hedge funds by quartiles of Sharpe ratio, 1997–2001

| Sharpe ratio quartiles | Average 1997–2001 equally weighted return (%) | Avergae 1997–2001 AUM-weighted return (%) | AUM in quartile (US$ billion) | % of total | Average 1997–2001 standard deviation (%) | Sharpe ratio 1997–2001 |
|---|---|---|---|---|---|---|
| 1 | 14.4 | 16.5 | 3.1 | 19 | 5.1 | 1.9 |
| 2 | 12.5 | 11.3 | 2.9 | 18 | 6.5 | 1.1 |
| 3 | 14.4 | 17.8 | 4.5 | 28 | 12.4 | 0.8 |
| 4 | 5.3 | 1.8 | 5.6 | 35 | 18.4 | 0.2 |
| **Total** | **11.7** | **10.9** | **16.1** | **100** | **10.6** | **1.0** |

*Source*: Altvest, HFR, Tuna, CMRA Analysis is based on 100 funds with five-year performance data

## Event-driven

Based on a five-year Sharpe ratio, the third quartile has the highest return with 18.1%, but it also has the second largest standard deviation of 18.2% (see Table 19).

Similar results are found for the 2001 Sharpe ratio (see Table 20). As in the case of the five-year analysis, the first quartile has 53.8% of the assets in the strategy as reported by HFR. The average return of the first quartile at 23.7% is the largest of all the quartiles. Table 20 also indicates the significant difference between the returns of the first quartile and those of the second, third and fourth. It is interesting to notice that the fourth quartile does not have the lowest returns of the strategy although it has only 6.7% of the assets, the lowest AUM quartile in the strategy.

**Table 18** Distribution of all categories of event-driven hedge funds by Sharpe ratio for 2001

| Sharpe ratio quartiles | AUM (US$ billion) in quartiles | % of total AUM | Average 2001 return (%) |
|---|---|---|---|
| 1 | 9.1 | 48.2 | 20.6 |
| 2 | 3.9 | 20.9 | 8.2 |
| 3 | 3.4 | 17.9 | 3.2 |
| 4 | 2.0 | 10.5 | (5.5) |
| **Total** | **18.8** | **100.0** | **12.2** |

*Source*: HFR, CMRA Analysis includes 153 event-driven, distressed and merger arbitrage funds

**Table 19** Distribution of event-driven hedge funds by quartiles of Sharpe ratio, 1997–2001

| Sharpe ratio quartiles | Average 1997–2001 equally weighted return (%) | Avergae 1997–2001 AUM-weighted return (%) | AUM in quartile (US$ billion) | % of total | Average 1997–2001 standard deviation (%) | Sharpe ratio 1997–2001 |
|---|---|---|---|---|---|---|
| 1 | 16.3 | 18.5 | 2.2 | 22 | 7.9 | 1.4 |
| 2 | 11.9 | 10.3 | 1.9 | 19 | 6.6 | 1.0 |
| 3 | 18.1 | 21.1 | 3.0 | 30 | 18.2 | 0.7 |
| 4 | 3.4 | (1.7) | 3.0 | 30 | 23.3 | 0.2 |
| Total | 12.6 | 11.7 | 10.0 | 100 | 13.8 | 0.8 |

*Source*: Altvest, CMRA Analysis is based on 47 funds with five-year performance data

## Distressed securities

The results of the five-year Sharpe ratio analysis for distressed securities (see Table 21) indicate that the last quartile has 59.9% of the assets, the highest standard deviation and the lowest performance. The first quartile with the highest return, 13.7%, covers only 3% of the total AUM.

The 2001 Sharpe ratio shows a completely different result (see Table 22). In this case, the second quartile has the largest AUM with US$1.5 billion, or 49.7% of the total, and an average return of 10.0%. The smallest quartile, the fourth, has US$400 million in AUM and the highest average return of 14.3%. The second largest quartile in terms of AUM is the first, with 19.3% of the assets and an average return of 2.9%.

## Merger arbitrage

A comparison of the five-year and one-year Sharpe ratios given in Tables 23 and 24 indicates that for the five-year period the fourth quartile has the largest AUM with 38% of the total. In the case of the one-year Sharpe ratio,

**Table 20** Distribution of event-driven hedge funds by Sharpe ratio for 2001

| Sharpe ratio quartiles | AUM (US$ billion) in quartiles | % of total AUM | Average 2001 return (%) |
|---|---|---|---|
| 1 | 6.0 | 53.8 | 23.7 |
| 2 | 2.6 | 23.5 | 4.9 |
| 3 | 1.8 | 16.1 | 2.0 |
| 4 | 0.7 | 6.7 | 9.7 |
| Total | 11.1 | 100.0 | 14.8 |

*Source*: HFR, CMRA Analysis is based on 68 funds with one-year data

**Table 21** Distribution of distressed securities hedge funds by quartiles of Sharpe ratio, 1997–2001

| Sharpe ratio quartiles | Average 1997–2001 equally weighted return (%) | Avergae 1997–2001 AUM-weighted return (%) | AUM in quartile (US$ billion) | % of total | Average 1997–2001 standard deviation (%) | Sharpe ratio 1997–2001 |
|---|---|---|---|---|---|---|
| 1 | 13.7 | 13.9 | 0.1 | 3 | 4.2 | 2.1 |
| 2 | 11.2 | 12.6 | 0.5 | 17 | 5.5 | 1.0 |
| 3 | 12.8 | 14.6 | 0.6 | 19 | 14.2 | 0.5 |
| 4 | 3.7 | 4.3 | 1.8 | 60 | 16.7 | (0.1) |
| **Total** | **10.1** | **8.0** | **3.0** | **100** | **10.4** | **0.9** |

*Source*: Altvest, CMRA Analysis is based on 47 funds with five-year performance data

**Table 22** Distribution of distressed securities hedge funds by Sharpe ratio for 2001

| Sharpe ratio quartiles | AUM (US$ billion) in quartiles | % of total AUM | Average 2001 return (%) |
|---|---|---|---|
| 1 | 0.6 | 19.3 | 2.9 |
| 2 | 1.6 | 49.7 | 10.0 |
| 3 | 0.6 | 18.6 | 11.7 |
| 4 | 0.4 | 12.5 | 14.3 |
| **Total** | **3.2** | **100.0** | **9.5** |

*Source*: HFR, CMRA Analysis is based on 68 funds with one-year data

the largest quartile in terms of AUM is the second, with US$2.0 billion, or 43.5% of the total.

It is also important to note that the average five-year return of the strategy is 11.4%, as opposed to a modest 7.0% return during 2001. This reduction in return probably reflects the lower number of merger and acquisition deals during 2001. Another important factor in the comparison is the average return of the different quartiles: the average difference is 8.2% higher returns for the funds with five-year data than for the funds with one-year data. The average five-year standard deviations for the first, second, and third quartiles are lower than the fourth quartile's volatility of 8% (see Table 23).

*Information ratio*
As shown in Figure 14, there are significant differences between the information ratios of the three event-driven strategies. The information ratio of merger arbitrage is almost twice that of the event-driven and distressed securities funds. The information ratios for distressed securities are the

**Table 23** Distribution of merger arbitrage hedge funds by quartiles of Sharpe ratio, 1997–2001

| Sharpe ratio quartiles | Average 1997–2001 equally weighted return (%) | Avergae 1997–2001 AUM-weighted return (%) | AUM in quartile (US$ billion) | % of total | Average 1997–2001 standard deviation (%) | Sharpe ratio 1997–2001 |
|---|---|---|---|---|---|---|
| 1 | 13.0 | 13.2 | 0.2 | 8 | 3.4 | 1.4 |
| 2 | 11.8 | 11.3 | 0.8 | 27 | 4.5 | 1.0 |
| 3 | 11.4 | 11.6 | 0.8 | 26 | 5.5 | 0.7 |
| 4 | 9.5 | 9.4 | 1.2 | 38 | 8.0 | 0.2 |
| **Total** | **11.4** | **10.8** | **3.1** | **100** | **5.4** | **0.8** |

Source: Altvest, CMRA Analysis is based on 28 funds with five-year performance data

lowest of the three strategies. This suggests that, although the standard deviation of the strategy is among the lowest, the returns over the long run (9.1% for 1997–2001) have also been generally lower than those for merger arbitrage with 11.0% and event-driven funds with 13.8% for the 1997–2001 period.

## LEVERAGE

Low leverage is a common characteristic of funds in the event-driven strategy (see Figure 15). Most have a leverage ratio of less than 2.0, and only a few use a high leverage. It is notable that 33% of the distressed securities funds do not use leverage at all according to Altvest. (See Chapter 2 for a discussion of leverage.)

Event-driven funds, thus, tend to employ a minimal degree of leverage with an average ratio of US$1.4 AUM for each dollar of capital and a maximum of US$3 AUM for each dollar of capital (see Table 25).

A historical analysis of the three event-driven strategies indicates that

**Table 24** Distribution of merger arbitrage hedge funds by Sharpe ratio for 2001

| Sharpe ratio quartiles | AUM (US$ billion) in quartiles | % of total AUM | Average 2001 return (%) |
|---|---|---|---|
| 1 | 1.2 | 25.5 | 6.9 |
| 2 | 2.0 | 43.5 | 3.7 |
| 3 | 0.5 | 10.5 | 1.6 |
| 4 | 0.9 | 20.5 | (5.2) |
| **Total** | **4.5** | **100.0** | **7.0** |

Source: HFR, Analysis CMRA is based on 62 funds

merger arbitrage is considerably more leveraged than distressed or event-driven investing (see Table 26). Further analysis of leverage in the strategy for the 1997–2001 period indicates that the first quartile (the group with the lowest leverage) of event-driven funds had only US$3.0 billion in AUM, while the last quartile had US$7.3 billion in AUM (see Table 27).

Over five years the leveraged performance of 14.72% for the event-driven category was 6.5 points higher than its delevered returns (see Table 28). Similarly, merger arbitrage showed a 7.7 point difference in its five-year performance.

An analysis for the year 2001 alone shows a smaller difference between delevered and actual performance. In that year the average difference for the event-driven strategy was 4.0. For merger arbitrage funds, which had

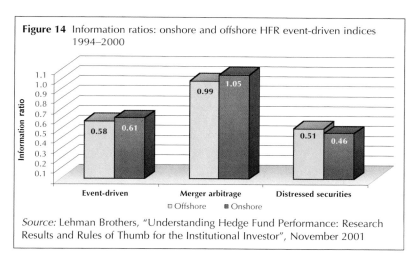

**Figure 14** Information ratios: onshore and offshore HFR event-driven indices 1994–2000

*Source:* Lehman Brothers, "Understanding Hedge Fund Performance: Research Results and Rules of Thumb for the Institutional Investor", November 2001

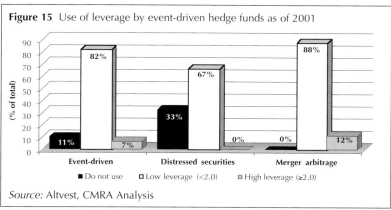

**Figure 15** Use of leverage by event-driven hedge funds as of 2001

*Source:* Altvest, CMRA Analysis

317

a particularly difficult year due to a significant decline in the number of deals, the average difference was 2.1 points, significantly lower than for the five-year period (see Table 29).

## RISK MEASUREMENT

The key risk factors that affect the event-driven strategies are profiled in Figure 16.

Some of the most common risks for an event-driven strategy are deal and regulatory or legal risk. The following subsections identify some of the

---

**Table 25** Financial leverage of event-driven funds in 2002

| Strategy | Minimum | Average | Maximum | Rank |
|---|---|---|---|---|
| Merger arbitrage | 0.8 | 1.5 | 2.5 | 7 of 14 |
| Event-driven | 0.9 | 1.4 | 3.0 | 12 of 14 |
| Distressed | 1.0 | 1.3 | 2.5 | 13 of 14 |

*Source*: Altvest, CMRA Analysis

---

**Table 26** Historical average leverage of hedge funds, 1997–2001

| | | | | | | 1997–2001 | | |
|---|---|---|---|---|---|---|---|---|
| | 1997 | 1998 | 1999 | 2000 | 2001 | Average | Maximum | Minimum |
| Event-driven | 1.0 | 1.1 | 1.2 | 1.2 | 1.2 | 1.1 | 1.2 | 1.0 |
| Distressed securities | 1.4 | 1.0 | 0.9 | 1.0 | 1.2 | 1.1 | 1.4 | 0.9 |
| Merger arbitrage | 2.0 | 1.7 | 1.8 | 1.6 | 1.6 | 1.7 | 2.0 | 1.6 |

*Source*: Altvest, CMRA Analysis

---

**Table 27** Distribution of event-driven funds by quartiles leverage, 1997–2001

| Leverage quartiles | Minimum leverage in quartile | Maximum leverage in quartile | Average leverage in quartile | Median leverage in quartile | Total AUM in quartile (US$ billion) | % of total AUM |
|---|---|---|---|---|---|---|
| 1 | 0.0 | 1.0 | 0.8 | 1.0 | 3.0 | 13.6 |
| 2 | 1.0 | 1.3 | 1.1 | 1.1 | 6.2 | 27.7 |
| 3 | 1.3 | 1.5 | 1.4 | 1.3 | 5.8 | 25.8 |
| 4 | 1.5 | 2.5 | 1.8 | 1.7 | 7.3 | 33.0 |
| **Total** | **0.0** | **2.5** | **1.1** | **1.7** | **22.4** | **100.0** |

* Event-driven funds include distressed securities, event-driven and merger arbitrage funds

*Source*: Altvest, CMRA Analysis based on 167 funds with five years of leverage data

**Table 28** Summary of levered and delevered five-year performance of event-driven funds, 1997–2001 (%)

|  | Maximum return | Minimum return | Average return | Maximum delevered return | Minimum delevered return | Average delevered return | Difference in returns levered vs delevered |
|---|---|---|---|---|---|---|---|
| Event-driven | 29.3 | (2.6) | 14.7 | 21.9 | (1.3) | 8.3 | 6.5 |
| Merger arbitrage | 35.0 | 1.4 | 14.7 | 18.7 | 0.5 | 7.0 | 7.7 |

*Source*: Altvest, CMRA Analysis

**Table 29** Summary of levered and delevered performance of event-driven funds in 2001 (%)

|  | Maximum return | Minimum return | Average return | Maximum delevered return | Minimum delevered return | Average delevered return | Difference in returns levered vs delevered |
|---|---|---|---|---|---|---|---|
| Event-driven | 47.1 | (24.5) | 7.7 | 28.3 | (12.2) | 3.7 | 4.0 |
| Merger arbitrage | 12.4 | (2.9) | 3.4 | 4.1 | (1.3) | 1.3 | 2.1 |

*Source*: Altvest, CMRA Analysis

driving forces behind these risk factors for each category of the strategy. Table 30 summarises the exposure of these categories to some of the factors outlined in Figure 16.

### Event-driven strategy
*Volatility risk*
The securities of corporations facing corporate restructurings, mergers, acquisitions or financial distress are generally highly volatile. Such volatility may lead to substantial risks and returns. In addition, event-driven strategies are exposed to a synthetic short put option. These exposures will not be addressed by even the most robust position-by-position risk tool because they are extrinsic and, therefore, "off-balance-sheet".

While the event-driven indices showed a high correlation with the returns of the S&P 500 Index (56.7%) over the period 1997–2001, a comparison of the event-driven indices with the volatility of the S&P 500 is also instructive. Over this period, the monthly returns of event-driven funds demonstrated a correlation of -49.65% with the volatility of the S&P 500, which means that when volatility goes up, the returns for the strategy go down. A casual glance at Figure 17 reveals this assessment to be accurate. The most obvious examples are the August 1998 and September 2001 cases, when the S&P 500 Index volatility shot up and event-driven returns

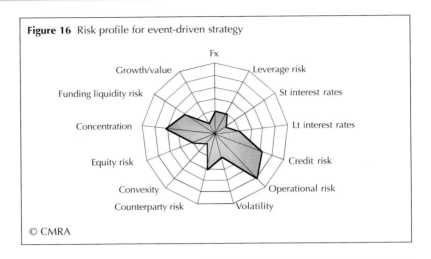

**Figure 16** Risk profile for event-driven strategy

© CMRA

**Table 30** Summary of risk, return and exposure of event-driven strategies to selected risk factors

| | Volatility of return | Downside risk | Exposure | | | | |
| | | | Equity index return | Economy-wide credit risk | Interest rates | Sharpe ratio | Leverage |
| --- | --- | --- | --- | --- | --- | --- | --- |
| Event-driven | Medium | Medium | Positive medium | Negative low | Negative low | Medium | Medium |
| Distressed securities | Medium | Medium | Positive medium | Negative high | Negative medium | Medium | Low |
| Merger arbitrage | Low | Medium | Positive medium | Negative low | Negative low | High | Medium |

*Source*: Zurich Hedge Fund Indices Spring/Summer 2002

plummeted. Some less obvious examples occurred in October 1997 and again in March and April 2001. In these examples we see the volatility reaching over 30% and again the event-driven returns suffer. On the other side of the coin, we see the negative correlation operating again. The event-driven indices generally perform at their best when the volatility of the S&P 500 drops to around 10%, as was the case in February 1998, November and December 1999 and August 2000.

A comparison between the returns of the event-driven strategy and the volatility of the Lehman Aggregate Bond Index reveals another interesting picture (see Figure 18). Over the period 1997–2001 the correlation was a meagre 7.77%, or nearly none at all. Such a low correlation suggests that the returns of the event-driven indices are unrelated to the movements of the bond markets, which in turn indicates that these two instruments would work well together in a portfolio.

## Leverage risk

Event-driven funds with greater than average leverage will experience greater losses and volatility as well as a greater potential for profit.

## Liquidity risk

Most distressed securities and bankruptcy-related transactions can be highly illiquid and difficult to value.

## Legal risk

Regulatory and legal issues can have a strong impact on event-driven strategies. Ignoring these could result in substantial losses in the portfolio in both the US market and markets abroad.

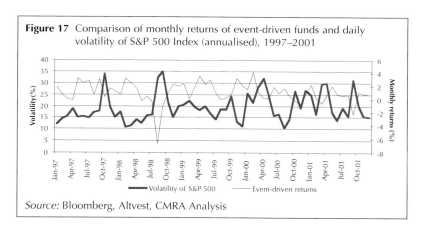

**Figure 17** Comparison of monthly returns of event-driven funds and daily volatility of S&P 500 Index (annualised), 1997–2001

*Source:* Bloomberg, Altvest, CMRA Analysis

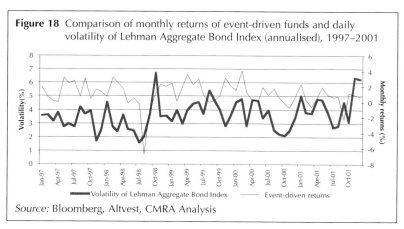

**Figure 18** Comparison of monthly returns of event-driven funds and daily volatility of Lehman Aggregate Bond Index (annualised), 1997–2001

*Source:* Bloomberg, Altvest, CMRA Analysis

### Distressed securities strategy

The risks associated with distressed securities investing are primarily the unique risks associated with each individual case. A sample risk profile is shown in Figure 19. Prevailing trends in the bond markets are far less important than case-specific developments such as, for example, a crucial court ruling. An added diversification bonus to investing in distressed debt funds is that there tends to be a very low correlation between distressed debt and other asset classes.

*Redemption risk*

Investments in distressed securities are relatively illiquid. Extended redemption periods are the norm and most managers seek a long-term commitment of investor capital. Out-of-court restructuring negotiations and bankruptcy proceedings are, by nature, time-consuming and their outcome is uncertain. Distressed securities investments, therefore, have many characteristics that are similar to private equity investments.

*Credit risk*

Any investment in distressed securities involves significant credit risk. The strategy requires correct valuation of the underlying business and its individual securities.

*Liquidity and pricing risk*

Distressed securities have high liquidity risk. Often there is only a very thin market, or even no market at all, for individual securities and positions can be extremely difficult to value.

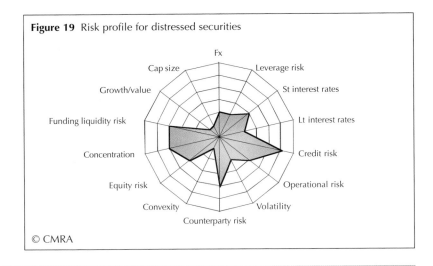

**Figure 19** Risk profile for distressed securities

© CMRA

## Market risk

Especially in situations of falling equity markets and rising interest rates, the performance of distressed securities investments is highly correlated to the broader market. Long-duration debt positions are also exposed to duration and interest rate risk.

## Volatility risk

Distressed securities show a strong negative correlation of –54.42% with the volatility of the S&P 500 Index during the 1997–2001 period. This means that when volatility goes up, returns for the strategy go down, as Figure 20 shows. The most obvious examples were in August 1998 and September 2001, when the S&P volatility shot up and the event-driven returns shot down. Some less obvious examples occurred in October 1997 and July 2001. In these cases the volatility exceeded 30%. As with the event-driven funds, the negative correlation means that distressed security indices generally perform best when the volatility of the S&P 500 drops to around 15%, such as in February 1998, November–December 1999 and July 2001.

A comparison of the returns of the strategy and the volatility of the Lehman Aggregate Bond Index reveals another interesting picture. Over the 1997–2001 period the correlation was a meagre 13.57%. Such a low correlation suggests that the returns of the indices are unrelated to the movements of the bond markets, which in turn indicates that these two instruments would work well together in a portfolio.

## Legal risk

In the financial restructuring process, various stakeholder constituencies typically organise and negotiate with each other to restructure the company and determine who gets what. In this process secured creditors

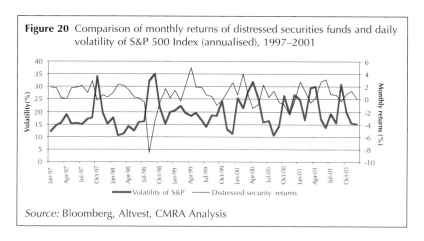

**Figure 20** Comparison of monthly returns of distressed securities funds and daily volatility of S&P 500 Index (annualised), 1997–2001

*Source:* Bloomberg, Altvest, CMRA Analysis

have first priority, unsecured creditors come next and equity comes last. Hybrid securities, such as preferred stock, fall in between one of these three positions. If negotiations break down, the determination of these priorities, as well as a number of other factors, may ultimately be made by a bankruptcy judge, whose decisions generally are not subject to effective review.

*Business and operational risk*

Financially distressed companies generally fall between two extremes on a spectrum. At one extreme, the company is a fundamentally sound, well-managed business with a bad balance sheet; at the other extreme the company's business is fundamentally unsound, unprofitable and incompetently and/or corruptly managed. In the first case, the company should be able to restructure successfully and there will either be a sale or a significant transfer of equity to the creditors. In the second case, the company's business and management require drastic change and the best returns may often be obtained by simply liquidating its assets for their intrinsic value such that the company's business ceases to exist. Obviously, most financially distressed companies fall between these two extremes and the resulting uncertainty of outcome accounts for much of the volatility in the distressed market.

## Merger arbitrage strategy

A risk profile for merger arbitrage funds is shown in Figure 21.

*Volatility risk*

Merger arbitrage funds show a correlation of -28.5% with the volatility of the S&P 500 Index over the 1997-2001 period. This means that when volatility goes up, the returns for the strategy go down.

In order to reflect the changing nature of mergers and acquisitions in the market, we divided the correlation analysis into three periods, as shown earlier in this chapter in Figure 8. Merger arbitrage has a synthetic short put option exposure. As noted above, these exposures will not be picked up by even the most robust position-by-position risk tool because they are extrinsic and therefore "off-balance-sheet".

## VALUE-AT-RISK
### Overview

During the boom period of the late 1990s, the AUM growth of the event-driven strategy for the 1994-2001 period was 35.5%. Its performance and volatility characteristics made it an attractive vehicle to enhance the overall risk profile of a traditional portfolio. The event-driven strategy had the lowest VAR of a sample of 10 strategies analysed for the period 1997-2000, giving it a ranking of one (see Table 31).

VAR measures the likely maximum loss that a portfolio could experience over a finite time horizon at a given confidence level. Typically, the time horizon corresponds to a hypothesis about the holding period, which should reflect the features of the portfolio on which the risk is being measured. The confidence level indicates the frequency of the maximum loss.

The VAR calculations presented in Table 32 are the result of a two-step procedure. The first step estimates systematic risk by calculating risk factors. Each risk factor is derived from a multivariate model that captures the strategy's exposure to a set of market indices. Once the strategy's performance has been deconstructed into several risk factors, the next step is to estimate the overall impact of all factors under the most adverse market conditions. The first step gives the VAR due to market moves, and the second step estimates specific risk. Specific risk is defined as the difference between total risk (observed fund variance) and systematic risk (variance due to the market, ie, hedge fund style). The resulting VAR is the combination of the two risk exposures described above.

## Examples

To further understand the implications of executing the merger arbitrage strategy, three kinds of portfolios of merger arbitrage deals were created. The VAR for each portfolio was then calculated using the Riskdata statistical software. As explained before, in merger arbitrage there are two kinds of outcome. The optimal case would be when the deal in which the manager is investing his/her funds closes, and the investment is therefore fully hedged. As we have seen, in the market this does not always happen.

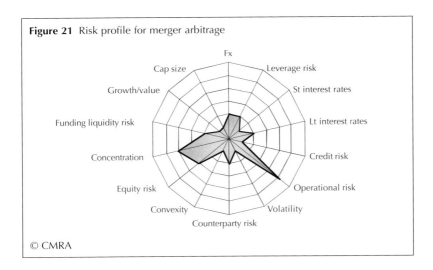

**Figure 21** Risk profile for merger arbitrage

© CMRA

The worst-case scenario is when the deal is not closed or "terminates". The investor is then faced with a short position that is not covered and the downside risk could prove troublesome. The portfolios analysed cover three different events in the space – closed, terminated and pending (not yet closed or terminated).

The total value of the merger arbitrage deals announced in January–August 2002 was US$212 billion (see Table 32). To analyse the relative VAR, we selected three completed, seven pending and four terminated deals for that period. The final value of the completed deals chosen was US$26.5 billion, or 48% of the announced value. The pending deals selected were worth US$73.7 billion, 76% of the announced value, and the terminated deals represented US$58.9 billion.

The first portfolio is comprised of deals that were successfully completed, the second has deals that were pending as of November 2002, and the third includes deals that were terminated (see Table 33). For consistency with the VAR calculation presented in Table 31, we calculated a one-month holding period VAR at the 99% confidence level (see Table 37).

Portfolio 1 includes three stock deals with a combined value of US$26.4

**Table 31** VAR for event-driven funds, 1997–2001 (%)

| 1997 | 1998 | 1999 | 2000 | Average 1997–2000 | Rank |
|------|------|------|------|-------------------|------|
| 8.03 | 8.08 | 8.74 | 9.14 | 8.50 | 1 of 10 |

Source: Assessing Market Risk for Hedge Funds and Hedge Funds Portfolios FAME, March 2001– Research Paper No. 24, Francois-Serge Lhabitant

**Table 32** Stock for stock deals announced, closed and/or terminated between January 1, 2002 and September 1, 2002

| | Announced value | % of total | Number of deals | % of total |
|---|---|---|---|---|
| Completed | 55.1 | 26 | 86 | 57 |
| Pending* | 97.0 | 46 | 48 | 32 |
| Terminated** | 60.0 | 28 | 17 | 11 |
| **Total** | **212.1** | **100** | **151** | **100** |

* Pending deals are reported as of the third quarter of 2002
** Terminated deals includes the GE-Honeywell and Felcor-Merisater deals terminated in the second half of 2001

Source: Bloomberg, CMRA Analysis

billion (see Table 34). All three deals were announced in the first quarter of 2002 and closed in the third quarter of 2002.

Portfolio 2 includes eight deals that have a combined value of US$73.8 billion (see Table 35). All deals were still pending as of the third quarter of 2002.

Portfolio 3 consists of four deals that were announced, did not close and were terminated (see Table 36). The total value of the terminated deals would have been US$58.9 billion.

The application of VAR to event-driven portfolios has several limitations. The non-normality and non-linearity of these corporate events and their limited history, among other things, could skew the results (eg, stable risk measurements could only be achieved under normal market conditions, "tail risk", etc). Nonetheless, the results are very indicative of the risks associated with this investment category. We found that the highest VAR calculation at a 99% confidence level over a one-month holding period was for the terminated deals at 16.9% – 25% higher than the VAR for the completed deals. The VAR results are given in Table 38.

To understand our portfolios better, we calculated VAR on a daily basis for several individual deals, and the results by completion status mirror those of the sample portfolios (see Figure 22). The terminated deals have a higher VAR than the other two types of deals selected.

**Table 33** Details of three portfolios analysed

| Portfolio | Types of deals included | Number of securities in portfolio |
|---|---|---|
| 1 | Completed deals | 6 |
| 2 | Pending deals | 14 |
| 3 | Terminated deals | 8 |

*Source*: Riskdata, CMRA

**Table 34** Transactions included in Portfolio 3 (completed stock deals)

| Buyer | Seller | Deal size (US$ billion) | Terms/ (acquisition target shares) | Announcement date | Completion date |
|---|---|---|---|---|---|
| PHILLIPS PETROLEUM | CONOCO | 25.0 | 0.47 | 18/11/01 | 03/09/02 |
| CIENA CORP | ONI SYSTEMS CORP | .8 | 0.71 | 18/2/02 | 24/06/02 |
| XCEL ENERGY INC | NRG ENERGY INC | .7 | 0.50 | 15/2/02 | 04/06/02 |
| **Total** | | **26.4** | | | |

*Source*: Riskdata, Bloomberg, CMRA Analysis

**Table 35** Transactions included in Portfolio 2 (pending stock deals)

| Buyer | Seller | Deal size (US$ billion) | Terms/ (acquisition target shares) | Announcement date | Expected completion date |
|---|---|---|---|---|---|
| PFIZER INC | PHARMACIA CORP | 64.3 | 1.40 | 15/07/02 | 03/121/02 |
| UNIVISION COMMUNICATIONS INC | HISPANIC BROADCASTING CORP | 3.7 | 0.85 | 12/06/02 | N/A |
| USA NETWORKS INC | HOTEL RESERVATIONS NETWORK | | | 03/06/02 | N/A |
| | TICKETMASTER CORP | 3.6 | 1.77* | 06/06/02 | |
| | EXPEDIA INC | | | 30/06/02 | |
| CARDINAL HEALTH INC | SYNCOR INTERNATIONAL | 1.1 | 0.52 | 14/06/02 | 31/12/02 |
| VEECO INSTRUMENTS INC | FEI COMPANY | 1.0 | 1.36 | 12/07/02 | 31/12/02 |
| SMARTFORCE PLC | SKILLSOFT CORP | .2 | 2.37 | 10/06/02 | 10/09/02 |
| **Total** | | **73.8** | | | |

* Average of terms of three deals

*Source*: Riskdata, Bloomberg, CMRA Analysis

**Table 36** Transactions included in Portfolio 3 (terminated stock deals)

| Buyer | Seller | Deal size (US$ billion) | Terms/ (acquisition target shares) | Announcement date | Termination date |
|---|---|---|---|---|---|
| GENERAL ELECTRIC CO | HONEYWELL INTERNATIONAL INC | 52.7 | 1.06 | 23/10/00 | 02/10/01 |
| TYCO INTERNATIONAL | CR BARD INC | 3.3 | 1.13 | 30/05/01 | 06/02/02 |
| FELCOR LODGING TRUST INC | MERISTAR HOSPITALITY CORP | 2.6 | 0.78 | 10/05/01 | 21/09/01 |
| SMARTFORCE PLC | CENTRA SOFTWARE INC | .2 | 0.43 | 16/01/02 | 02/04/02 |
| **Total** | | **58.9** | | | |

*Source*: Riskdata, Bloomberg, CMRA Analysis

## STRESS TESTS

There are a wide variety of stress tests that should be considered for event-driven strategies. These include:

- ❏ pricing models;
- ❏ products with uncertain cashflows;
- ❏ product complexity;
- ❏ difficult-to-model risks;
- ❏ concentrations;
- ❏ correlations;
- ❏ credit components of securities;
- ❏ assumptions;
- ❏ leverage;
- ❏ liquidity; and
- ❏ underlying assumptions (distributions).

**Table 37** VAR at 99% confidence level for sample portfolios

| Portfolios | VAR (%) |
|---|---|
| Terminated | 16.9 |
| Pending | 15.6 |
| Completed | 13.5 |

*Source*: Riskdata, CMRA

## LEVEL OF TRANSPARENCY

Event-driven and distressed securities managers in more illiquid markets are significantly less willing to increase their transparency for investors. Of the event-driven managers surveyed in 2000, 9% said they would not provide any transparency, while 36% indicated that they provided full disclosure. In contrast, 77% of the merger arbitrage managers surveyed said they would provide total transparency. Results of the survey are summarised in Table 38.

Distressed securities and merger arbitrage managers appear more willing to disclose their key long positions than managers who categorise

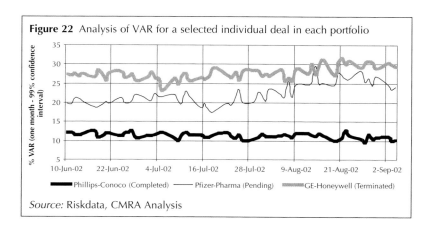

**Figure 22** Analysis of VAR for a selected individual deal in each portfolio

Phillips-Conoco (Completed) — Pfizer-Pharma (Pending) — GE-Honeywell (Terminated)

*Source:* Riskdata, CMRA Analysis

themselves as event-driven, but only merger arbitrage managers appear to be willing to disclose short positions. As noted above, however, position-level transparency fails for these strategies because the synthetic options embedded in them are "off-balance-sheet".

## DUE DILIGENCE QUESTIONS
### Event-driven
❑ What are the competitive advantages of the fund manager relative to other players in the space (ie, information sources, in-depth analytics, etc)?
❑ How would volatility in the stock and/or bond market affect your strategy?
❑ How do you account for the lack of liquidity in your valuations?

### Distressed securities
❑ How do you mark your positions to market?
❑ Do you stress-test the value of your portfolio against alternative methods for marking-to-market? What do you conclude?
❑ How long would it take to liquidate your portfolio?
❑ What is your source for volatility?
❑ Do you use credit derivatives? How?
❑ How do you deal with correlation assumptions?
❑ How do you perform credit and due diligence analysis?
❑ If a controlling investor, what experience and resources do you employ to participate in the financial restructuring process?
❑ What recovery assumptions do you make?

### Merger arbitrage
❑ How do you estimate the likelihood of the success of a deal?
❑ What is your diversification strategy? (By size of deal, type of deal, industry, geography.)

**Table 38** Transparency offered to investors by managers of different types of event-driven funds (%)

| | Overall level of transparency | | | | Positions disclosed to investors | |
|---|---|---|---|---|---|---|
| Strategy | Performance | Key positions | View entire portfolio | No transparency | Key long positions | Key short positions |
| Event-driven | 100 | 36 | 36 | 9 | 9 | 9 |
| Merger arbitrage | 100 | 54 | 77 | 0 | 54 | 46 |
| Distressed securities | 100 | 83 | 67 | 0 | 67 | 17 |

*Source*: Hennessee Hedge Fund Advisory Group

❏ What kind of liquidity considerations do you evaluate when entering into a deal?
❏ How much of your borrowing is overnight? Short term? Long term? How has that changed over the past 12 months?

## DATA AND NAV ISSUES

Due to the volatility and the pockets of poor liquidity found in the distressed securities markets, there can be a big difference between observed prices and executable prices. This means that just because the price of an instrument on a quote screen is 90, it doesn't mean you can buy or sell it at that price.

Derivatives such as CDOs and CLOs that have distressed securities underlying them are harder to price because their price is not regularly quoted. Often the entire issue is owned by a few market participants who do not trade on a regular basis, thereby reducing the amount of data available for such securities. Hedge fund managers have a hard enough time marking their portfolios without introducing a large degree of subjectivity. The recent difficulties of funds in the space, such as Harch International, are prime examples of this situation. Manager intervention alone can cause a huge difference in the marks of many derivatives (ie, CDOs, CLOs, etc), rendering NAVs unreliable. Before risk measurement can be thoroughly understood, it is crucial to understand its impact on the reported NAV. This will allow the investor to better assess the overall riskiness of the portfolio.

## PUBLICLY DISCLOSED PROBLEMS

Publicly disclosed problems within the event-driven strategy have been infrequent. One recent example is Harch International Ltd. Harch was highly successful in 1998, with US$350 million of AUM. As of the end of 2002, the offshore fund had about US$105 million of AUM and the domestic fund US$80 million of AUM. In 2002, Harch suffered from adverse debt market conditions and the fund, which had a quarterly redemption schedule, held back 10% of its redemptions.

# 16

# *Fixed Income*

## DESCRIPTION OF THE STRATEGY

A "fixed income" hedge fund generally involves the trading of any of the following:

- ❑ US government bonds and futures/options related to them;
- ❑ eurodollar futures contracts and options;
- ❑ G7 debt, such as Japanese government bonds;
- ❑ currency futures and options;
- ❑ swaps and repurchase (repo) transactions;
- ❑ municipal bonds;
- ❑ corporate bonds and notes (investment-grade and/or high-yield);
- ❑ structured instruments such as mortgage-backed securities, asset-backed securities and structured notes; or
- ❑ options, caps, collars, floors, forwards and other interest rate and bond-related derivatives.

Fixed-income arbitrage is a generic description for a variety of arbitrage strategies involving different fixed income instruments. The strategy generally seeks to profit by exploiting pricing inefficiencies between related securities and their derivatives. Different types of fixed-income arbitrage trades include yield curve trades (spread positions, including bonds with different maturities), corporate vs Treasury yield spreads, municipal vs Treasury yield spreads, cash vs futures, and on-the-run vs off-the-run bonds. The fixed-income arbitrage universe also includes a variety of strategies involving mortgage-backed securities (MBS), commercial mortgage-backed securities (CMBS), collateralised debt obligations (CDO) and asset-backed securities (ABS). Managers in the strategy vary in terms of how and to what degree they hedge interest rate risks, credit risks, foreign exchange risks and inter-market spread risks. Some managers take "directional bets" with respect to changes in the yield curve or credit spread, while others employ spread trades only.

Fixed income strategies are varied and include those that take directional price risk based on fundamentals or technicals; relative-value movement between instruments of different maturity (sometimes referred to as "yield curve trades"); changes in relative value between different agency and government bonds (spread trades); and sector bets in corporate bonds, emerging markets, high-yield, etc. Strategies that seek to benefit from sources of return other than pure directional movement in prices are generally known as fixed-income arbitrage strategies. However, the term "arbitrage" is rarely used in the academic sense; instead, it describes a directional view of subtle variables such as spread, volatility, prepayment rates or default levels.

In the fixed-income arbitrage world, hedge fund portfolios can be composed of a variety of trading strategies. Most strategies use a relative value philosophy: buy something undervalued or "cheap" and short something overvalued or "rich" with the same risk characteristics. Examples include:

❑ Trades that exploit anomalies in the yield curve and trading off-the-run vs on-the-run bonds.
❑ Relative value trades in credit spreads, such as going long and short corporate bonds or agency bonds with almost identical risk and administrative characteristics but different implied credit spreads in the market.
❑ Relative value trades in option-adjusted spreads, such as going long and short agency bonds or corporate bonds of the same company where there seems to be a discrepancy in the implied prices of the embedded options of the bonds.
❑ Mortgage derivatives, swap and repurchase relationships, and other volatility plays.

Other trading strategies that fixed income funds employ are similar to strategies commonly employed by equity funds, such as long-only, directional spread trading and trend following. Some funds focus on a particular fixed income instrument, such as mortgage-backed securities, while others trade all security types. It is much easier to have short-selling strategies in the fixed income world than for equities, as there are several sectors with deep and liquid repo markets in which one can borrow the shorted security. In addition, interest rate futures contracts (both treasury-based and Libor-based) have huge liquid markets and trade almost 24 hours a day.

Figure 1 shows the flow of assets in or out of fixed income funds. Notice the large outflows after June 1998 following the Russian/LTCM crisis. Further analysis will show that this was one of the major crisis events for fixed income funds. Asset flows to fixed income funds recovered only in the middle of 2001 when it was clear that the technology bubble had burst.

## EFFECT OF MARKET CONDITIONS
In general, fixed income and fixed-income arbitrage funds perform well in the following market conditions:

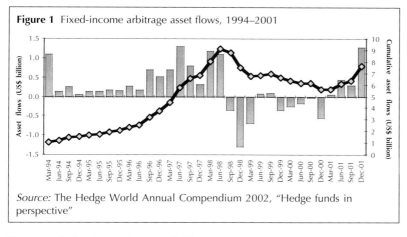

**Figure 1** Fixed-income arbitrage asset flows, 1994–2001

*Source:* The Hedge World Annual Compendium 2002, "Hedge funds in perspective"

❑ upward-sloping and steep yield curves;
❑ low and stable equity and bond volatility; and
❑ decreasing credit risk premiums.

These funds do poorly in the following market conditions:

❑ inverted yield curves;
❑ high and unstable equity and bond volatility; and
❑ increasing credit risk premiums.

### INVESTORS IN THE STRATEGY

Individuals, family offices and funds of funds are by far the largest investors in fixed income hedge funds (see Table 1). One cultural disadvantage for fixed income hedge funds, especially mortgage funds, is that few investors are familiar with fixed income instruments. In contrast, most investors feel that they have a good understanding of equities and, therefore, are comfortable investing in them. Conversely, many do not invest in mortgage funds because they do not adequately understand the strategy.

### WELL-KNOWN PLAYERS

Table 2 includes the largest fixed income funds by AUM covered by the major sources. The table highlights one fund, BlackRock, with US$1.6 billion in AUM that is not covered in the other sources.

Of the top 25 funds, six with a

**Table 1** Investors in the fixed income strategy

| Investors | (%) |
|---|---|
| Individuals and family offices | 64 |
| Funds of funds | 21 |
| Endowments and foundations | 7 |
| Corporations | 5 |
| Pensions and retirement | 3 |

*Source*: Hennessee Hedge Fund Survey (January 2000)

**Table 2** Top fixed income funds with more than US$1 billion in AUM (all sources)

| Rank | Fund | Highest AUM* (US$ billion) |
|------|------|----------------------------|
| 1 | III Fund | 2.3 |
| 2 | Pareto Global Bond Allocation Strategy | 2.0 |
| 3 | SCM Composite | 1.7 |
| 4 | BlackRock | 1.6 |
| 5 | Trinity Fund, Ltd. | 1.3 |
| 6 | Clinton Multistrategy Fund, Ltd. | 1.3 |
| 7 | Vega Asset Management | 1.3 |
| 8 | GAMut | 1.0 |
| | **Total** | **11.2** |

*This is the highest AUM for that fund among all the sources
Highlighted fund is exclusively in The Hedge Fund 100

*Source*: Altvest, Tuna, HFR, Institutional Investor (June 2002), Directory of Fund of Hedge Funds Investment Vehicles, CMRA Analysis

combined US$3.8 billion in AUM are among the most popular holdings of funds of funds. Furthermore, seven funds with a combined total AUM of US$6.1 billion are in The Hedge Fund 100.

## COVERAGE IN DIFFERENT SOURCES
Tuna covers both the largest number and the largest AUM for fixed income hedge funds (see Table 3).

## DISTRIBUTION OF FUNDS IN THE STRATEGY
As Figure 2 shows, 9% of the total 105 funds (from three major commercial sources) managed 51% of the total AUM among fixed income funds.

**Table 3** Coverage of fixed income funds by different sources

| Source | Total number of funds | Funds with no AUM data | Total AUM (US$ billion) |
|--------|----------------------|------------------------|-------------------------|
| Tuna | 109 | 7 | 14.9 |
| HFR | 84 | 6 | 10.9 |
| CSFB/Tremont | 70 | – | 9.3 |
| The Hedge Fund 100 | 21 | 2 | 7.6 |
| Altvest | 66 | 14 | 5.0 |

*Source*: HFR, Tuna, CSFB/Tremont, Institutional Investor (June 2002), Altvest, CMRA Research

## Distribution of funds by quartile of performance

A bird's-eye view of investment in fixed income funds vs the returns shows that funds with larger returns and Sharpe ratios do not necessarily attract the most investors (see Table 4). In fact, the third quartile by performance has the highest AUM.

## Distribution of funds by quartile of AUM

Table 5 shows the distribution of fixed income hedge funds in terms of AUM. The largest two quartiles also have a considerably lower average standard deviation than the others.

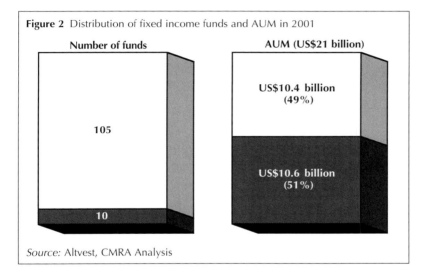

**Figure 2** Distribution of fixed income funds and AUM in 2001

Number of funds

AUM (US$21 billion)

US$10.4 billion (49%)

105

US$10.6 billion (51%)

10

*Source:* Altvest, CMRA Analysis

**Table 4** Distribution of fixed income funds by quartiles of five-year performance, 1997–2001

| Return quartiles | Average 1997–2001 equally weighted return (%) | Avergae 1997–2001 AUM-weighted return (%) | AUM in quartile (US$ billion) | % of total | Average 1997–2001 standard deviation (%) | Sharpe ratio 1997–2001 |
|---|---|---|---|---|---|---|
| 1 | 18.2 | 18.7 | 6.9 | 33 | 15.1 | 1.3 |
| 2 | 9.9 | 8.9 | 4.2 | 20 | 10.9 | 0.9 |
| 3 | 6.4 | 6.3 | 7.7 | 37 | 8.8 | 0.3 |
| 4 | (0.6) | 2.3 | 2.3 | 11 | 15.7 | (0.4) |
| Total | 8.6 | 10.4 | 21.0 | 100 | 12.6 | 0.5 |

*Note:* All funds included in this distribution had at least four years of returns data, with at least nine months of returns data in a year.

*Source:* Altvest, HFR, Tuna, CMRA Analysis based on 115 funds.

## PERFORMANCE OF THE STRATEGY
### Returns during boom and bust
Figure 3 shows the general performance of fixed income funds during boom and bust situations. The funds had consistent returns during the stock market boom and the following bust.

### Returns from different sources
Table 6 shows the returns and Sharpe ratios for the cumulative fixed income strategies. Although the returns vary across the sources, the general trend is consistent. All the indices showed a dip in returns in 1998 during the Russian/LTCM crisis and the ensuing credit crunch (see Table 7).

**Table 5** Distribution of fixed income hedge funds by quartiles of AUM, 1997–2001

| AUM quartiles | Average 1997–2001 equally weighted return (%) | Avergae 1997–2001 AUM-weighted return (%) | AUM in quartile (US$ billion) | % of total | Average 1997–2001 standard deviation (%) | Sharpe ratio 1997–2001 |
|---|---|---|---|---|---|---|
| 1 | 10.3 | 10.8 | 17.0 | 81.0 | 9.1 | 0.8 |
| 2 | 7.8 | 8.7 | 3.2 | 15.0 | 9.0 | 0.7 |
| 3 | 9.9 | 10.5 | 0.8 | 4.0 | 13.5 | 0.5 |
| 4 | 6.2 | 7.0 | 0.1 | 1.0 | 18.9 | 0.1 |
| **Total** | **8.6** | **10.4** | **21.0** | **100.0** | **12.6** | **0.5** |

Note: All funds included in this distribution had at least four years of returns data, with at least nine months of returns data in a year.
Source: Altvest, HFR, Tuna, CMRA Analysis based on 115 funds.

**Figure 3** Returns of fixed income funds during boom and bust periods of the S&P500 Index, 1997–2001

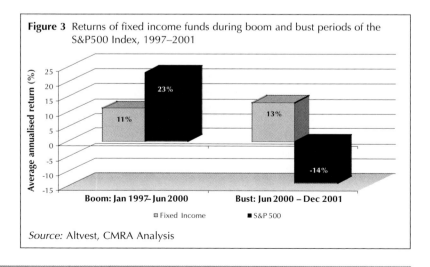

Source: Altvest, CMRA Analysis

**Table 6** Comparison of returns and Sharpe ratios reported by fixed income fund indices, 1997–2001

|  | Return | Sharpe ratio |
|---|---|---|
| Altvest | 11.4 | 0.9 |
| Tuna | 8.8 | 0.5 |
| HFR | 6.6 | 0.4 |
| Hennessee | 3.7 | (0.2) |
| Maximum difference | 7.8 | 1.0 |
| Average | 7.6 | 0.4 |

*Source*: CMRA Analysis, Altvest, HFR, Hennessee, Tuna

Unfortunately, there are no standardised indices and many of the data providers have their own styles or sub-indices. Table 7 also shows the different sub-index returns as calculated by the major commercial sources. All of the fixed income sub-strategies, except the diversified strategy, had low or negative returns during the Russian/LTCM crisis in 1998. Furthermore, all sub-strategies followed a similar trend of high performance in 1997, 1999 and 2001 and poor performance in 1998 and 2001.

It is important to note that the styles and sub-styles that many sources and research papers use are accurate only to a limited extent. Since funds might employ a mixture of styles in their portfolios, segregating them in a single style or sub-style causes a great deal of information on the fund to be lost. For instance, Mortgage Backed Opportunity, LP, which is included in the "fixed-income arbitrage" category by most sources, has a very small arbitrage component. In fact, Mortgage Backed Opportunity is a directional play on the prepayment behaviour of mortgages. If one attempted to segregate funds into their own styles by including their multiple strategies in the style labels, there would be too many permutations and combinations of styles to deal with. The scatter plot in Figure 4 corroborates this point. Notice how divergent the returns and standard deviations are within an index. In this analysis, 17 of the 19 funds that constitute the CSFB/Tremont Fixed-Income Arbitrage Index were included. Data for the two other funds were unavailable.

The annualised increase in assets fell between 1994 and 1998 after increasing briskly before 1994 (see Table 8), while over the same period the annualised performance was relatively consistent. The most likely explanation for the 16.4% drawdown in assets between 1994 and 1998 is the competing equity market, which was enjoying the returns of the boom period.

**Table 7** Behaviour of the fixed income strategies, 1997–2001

|  | 1997 | 1998 | 1999 | 2000 | 2001 | 1997–2001 |
|---|---|---|---|---|---|---|
| **Altvest/ CMRA** | | | | | | |
| Fixed income (diversified)* | 15.4 | 8.9 | 8.3 | 18.2 | 6.8 | 11.4 |
| Fixed income (high-yield) | 15.7 | 2.0 | 3.7 | (0.7) | 7.2 | 5.4 |
| Fixed income (MBS) | 18.5 | (5.7) | 12.5 | (0.0) | 23.8 | 9.3 |
| **HFR** | | | | | | |
| Fixed income (total) | 11.9 | (2.0) | 11.0 | 3.4 | 9.5 | 6.6 |
| Fixed income (high-yield) | 12.5 | (5.3) | 7.4 | (3.0) | 4.6 | 3.0 |
| Fixed income (MBS) | 17.3 | (9.2) | 11.3 | (1.4) | 19.3 | 6.9 |
| Fixed-income arbitrage | 7.0 | (10.3) | 7.4 | 4.8 | 7.6 | 3.1 |
| Fixed income (diversified) | 5.8 | 5.6 | 2.8 | 13.7 | 11.9 | 7.9 |
| **Hennessee** | | | | | | |
| Fixed income (total) | 7.3 | (14.1) | 14.6 | 5.1 | 7.8 | 3.7 |
| **Tuna** | | | | | | |
| Fixed income (total) | 13.8 | 3.8 | 8.6 | 8.2 | 9.9 | 8.8 |
| Fixed-income arbitrage | 14.4 | (5.3) | 18.6 | 6.0 | 9.2 | 8.3 |

\* This includes funds that did not focus on any particular fixed income instruments and generally invest in MBS, Currencies, Futures, Munis etc.

*Source*: Altvest, HFR, Hennessee, Tuna, Bloomberg

**Figure 4** Analysis of five-year returns and standard deviations of constituent funds in the CSFB/Tremont Fixed-Income Arbitrage Index, 1997–2001

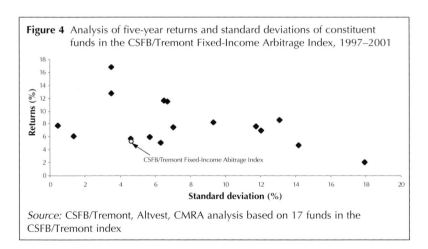

*Source:* CSFB/Tremont, Altvest, CMRA analysis based on 17 funds in the CSFB/Tremont index

Finally, as shown in Figure 5, there are large differences between Altvest's index and the other indices; this is mainly the result of the differences in both the index calculation methodology and the composition of the funds in the indices.

**Table 8** Annualised increase in assets for fixed income funds to 1998

| Inception date | AUM growth (%) | Annualised performance (%) |
| --- | --- | --- |
| Before 1994 | 24.0 | 5.7 |
| Between 1994 and 1998 | (16.4) | 9.8 |
| Before 1998 | 3.8 | 8.5 |

*Source*: Altvest, CMRA Analysis

## Index performance

While the returns of fixed income funds have been generally positive over the five-year period, they have ranked towards the bottom compared to other strategies because, unlike many of the equity funds, they did not share in the long bull market that occurred in the second half of the 1990s. Rankings according to two sources are given in Table 9.

Looking at the Sharpe ratios for the sub-strategies given in Table 10, one can see that focused strategies (such as mortgage-backed securities) seem to have a higher Sharpe ratio than the total or diversified fixed income strategies. However, one can also see that the more focused fixed income strategies have greater variance in their Sharpe ratios than the more general or diversified strategies. Furthermore, all the indices performed poorly in 1998 and had negative Sharpe ratios during that time – this was due to the Russian/LTCM crisis, during which all spread-related fixed income securities performed poorly.

## Performance correlations

Table 11 evaluates the correlation of the performance of the fixed income indices vs several fixed income and equity instruments. Investment opportunities commonly arise just after major market dislocations. The most prominent of these was the Russian/LTCM crisis in 1998. Liquidity dried up and all credit-related fixed income instruments were adversely affected, causing credit spreads to widen across the board. In early 1999 it was possible to find bonds that had become very undervalued. Many of the fixed income fund indices made strong comebacks

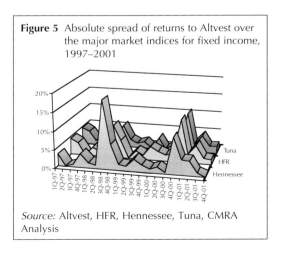

**Figure 5** Absolute spread of returns to Altvest over the major market indices for fixed income, 1997–2001

*Source:* Altvest, HFR, Hennessee, Tuna, CMRA Analysis

**Table 9** Ranking of fixed income strategy returns against other strategies, 1997–2001

| | 1997 | 1998 | 1999 | 2000 | 2001 | 1997–2001 | Rank |
|---|---|---|---|---|---|---|---|
| **Altvest/ CMRA** | | | | | | | |
| Fixed income (diversified)* | 15.4 | 8.9 | 8.3 | 18.2 | 6.8 | 11.4 | 8 of 14 |
| Fixed income (MBS) | 18.5 | (5.7) | 12.5 | (0.0) | 23.8 | 9.3 | 11 of 14 |
| Fixed income (high-yield) | 15.7 | 2.0 | 3.7 | (0.7) | 7.2 | 5.4 | 13 of 14 |
| **HFR** | | | | | | | |
| Fixed income (MBS) | 17.3 | (9.2) | 11.3 | (1.4) | 19.3 | 6.9 | 15 of 19 |
| Fixed income (total) | 11.9 | (2.0) | 11.0 | 3.4 | 9.5 | 6.6 | 16 of 19 |
| Fixed income (high-yield) | 12.5 | (5.3) | 7.4 | (3.0) | 4.6 | 3.0 | 18 of 19 |

* This includes funds that did not focus on any particular fixed income instruments and generally invest in MBS, Currencies, Futures, Munis etc.

*Source*: Altvest, HFR, Hennessee, Tuna, Bloomberg

**Table 10** Sharpe ratios and standard deviations reported by fixed income indices, 1997–2001

| Source | 1997 | 1998 | 1999 | 2000 | 2001 | 1997–2001 | Standard deviation of Sharpe ratio |
|---|---|---|---|---|---|---|---|
| **Altvest/CMRA** | | | | | | | |
| Fixed income (diversified) | 1.2 | 0.8 | 0.4 | 1.3 | 0.5 | 0.9 | 0.4 |
| Fixed income (high-yield) | 2.6 | (0.4) | (0.4) | (1.4) | 0.6 | 0.1 | 1.4 |
| Fixed income (MBS) | 4.4 | (1.3) | 2.6 | (1.4) | 11.1 | 0.8 | 4.7 |
| **HFR** | | | | | | | |
| Fixed income (total) | 2.4 | (1.1) | 1.7 | (0.8) | 1.6 | 0.4 | 1.4 |
| Fixed income (high-yield) | 1.6 | (1.1) | 0.7 | (2.9) | 0.2 | (0.3) | 1.6 |
| Fixed income (MBS) | 7.8 | (1.4) | 2.0 | (1.5) | 5.5 | 0.3 | 3.8 |
| Fixed-income arbitrage | 0.9 | (1.5) | 1.2 | (0.3) | 0.9 | (0.3) | 1.1 |
| Fixed income (diversified) | 0.1 | 0.2 | (0.6) | 1.1 | 1.9 | 0.6 | 0.9 |
| **Hennessee** | | | | | | | |
| Fixed income (total) | 0.3 | (1.6) | 2.6 | (0.3) | 1.3 | (0.2) | 1.4 |
| **Tuna** | | | | | | | |
| Fixed income (total) | 1.8 | (0.3) | 0.9 | 0.5 | 2.1 | 0.9 | 0.9 |
| Fixed-income arbitrage | 6.7 | (0.8) | 4.0 | (0.1) | 2.8 | 0.5 | 2.9 |

*Source*: Altvest, HFR, Hennessee, Tuna, Bloomberg

in 1999 after performing poorly in 1998. During the Russian/LTCM crisis the 10-year Treasury yield rallied and repo rates fell because of a flight to safety, while all credit-related products also fell. Notice the positive correlation between the high-yield index and the 10-year Treasury yield; it

**Table 11** Correlations (%) of fixed income with fixed income and equity instruments, 1997–2001

| 1997–2001 | Total | High-yield | Mortgage backed | Arbitrage | Diversified |
|---|---|---|---|---|---|
| 10-year Treasury yield | 15 | 27 | 9 | 27 | (35) |
| 10-year swap spread | (34) | (27) | (25) | (3) | (15) |
| SPX | 40 | 45 | (8) | (2) | 11 |
| 1-week govt repo | (11) | (8) | (22) | 0 | (22) |
| 3- month govt repo | (4) | 13 | (15) | 11 | (19) |
| 1-week mtg repo | (14) | (11) | (22) | (4) | (24) |
| 3-month mtg repo | (18) | (8) | (15) | (1) | (27) |
| **1997** | | | | | |
| 10-year Treasury yield | (49) | (49) | (11) | 7 | (74) |
| 10-year swap spread | (4) | 7 | 33 | (22) | 19 |
| SPX | 73 | 59 | 22 | 30 | 61 |
| 1-week govt repo | (7) | (24) | (37) | 5 | 16 |
| 3-month govt repo | (72) | (82) | (45) | (18) | (55) |
| 1-week mtg repo | (11) | (27) | (40) | 2 | 12 |
| 3-month mtg repo | (71) | (77) | (40) | (13) | (56) |
| **1998** | | | | | |
| 10-year Treasury yield | 41 | 66 | (14) | 30 | (16) |
| 10-year swap spread | (49) | (76) | (2) | 6 | (46) |
| SPX | 35 | 59 | (16) | (25) | 36 |
| 1-week govt repo | (3) | (16) | (7) | 20 | (18) |
| 3-month govt repo | 56 | 48 | 55 | 72 | 17 |
| 1-week mtg repo | 2 | (10) | (6) | 19 | (12) |
| 3-month Mtg Repo | 49 | 44 | 48 | 66 | 12 |
| **1999** | | | | | |
| 10-year Treasury yield | (14) | 7 | (21) | 11 | (31) |
| 10-year swap spread | (40) | 10 | (70) | 0 | (42) |
| SPX | 53 | 55 | 13 | 24 | 48 |
| 1-week govt repo | (16) | (12) | (18) | 1 | (24) |
| 3-month govt repo | (16) | 21 | (28) | 5 | (27) |
| 1-week mtg repo | (20) | 3 | (19) | 3 | (32) |
| 3-month mtg repo | (20) | 8 | (15) | 17 | (33) |
| **2000** | | | | | |
| 10-year Treasury yield | (45) | 16 | (3) | (1) | (61) |
| 10-year swap spread | (12) | (14) | (48) | 16 | (40) |
| SPX | 24 | 9 | (45) | (15) | 0 |
| 1-week govt repo | (21) | (3) | (49) | 23 | (55) |
| 3-month govt repo | (50) | (15) | (57) | 23 | (70) |
| 1- week mtg repo | (24) | (5) | (55) | 14 | (50) |
| 3-month mtg repo | (45) | (24) | (55) | 33 | (63) |
| **2001** | | | | | |
| 10-year Treasury yield | 36 | 19 | 84 | 57 | 4 |
| 10-year swap spread | (30) | 17 | (28) | (5) | 43 |
| SPX | 65 | 40 | 75 | 72 | (14) |
| 1-week govt repo | (27) | (12) | (13) | (35) | (30) |
| 3-month govt repo | (1) | 43 | (15) | 9 | 10 |
| 1-week mtg repo | (41) | (35) | (15) | (49) | (34) |
| 3-month mtg repo | (52) | (34) | (13) | (46) | (17) |

*Source*: Bloomberg, HFR

would appear that the yield fell due to the flight to quality along with the returns of high-yield and fixed income funds.

### Stress period analysis

Most of the indices performed very poorly during the Russian/LTCM crisis except for fixed income (diversified) calculated using Altvest data (see Table 12). A very large portion of this index contained currency and futures trading funds, some of which had very high returns during the Russian/LTCM crisis. Currencies became very volatile, with the yen/US dollar rate strengthening from 135 to 117 in two days; this caused large windfall gains for currency and futures traders, such as Willowbridge and Legacy Futures, to name two. HFR, on the other hand, defines its diversified fixed income index to be comprised of funds that trade primarily in bonds but do not focus on one particular type of bond (such as MBS or Munis) and employ a variety of trading styles; these were the types of funds that were badly hurt during the Russian/LTCM crisis.

Although most fixed income funds were hurt during the Russian/LTCM crisis, some, especially the MBS and arbitrage funds, did enjoy high, stable returns during the technology bust, a period that lasted more than a year. This is shown by the Sharpe ratios for periods of stress given in Table 13.

There are common market scenarios under which fixed income arbitrage funds can outperform or underperform the market. Because these funds typically need leverage (since they need to short securities), they can borrow only short-term (and roll the borrowing at the end of every period at the then prevailing repo rate) in order to short long maturity or short maturity securities. They can never borrow long-term to do the same. Therefore, an upward-sloping yield curve is essential for obtaining high returns. Table 14 contains a summary of the various risk parameters and their impact on the returns of fixed-income arbitrage funds.

Table 15 shows the excess returns of fixed-income arbitrage funds over Libor in different risk conditions. There is a modest negative correlation of fund returns with high-yield spreads and Treasury and swap volatility (ie, if these decrease, arbitrage funds make greater returns). Equity volatility affects fixed income funds negatively in extreme scenarios (ie, low returns are seen when equity volatilities are either too high or too low). However, the low return in the case of low equity volatility was largely influenced by the Russian/LTCM crisis. If these incidents are excluded, there is a modest negative correlation with equity volatility as well.

The regression results presented in Table 16 show that returns of the fixed-income arbitrage style are dependent on interest rates, credit spreads, interest rate volatility and equity volatility when these four factors are statistically significant. Furthermore, $R^2$ (a measure of the explanatory power of the relation between the factor(s) and the fund

**Table 12** Returns of fixed income indices during periods of stress (%)

| Source | Russian/LTCM crisis | Tech crash | September 11 |
|---|---|---|---|
| **Altvest/ CMRA** | | | |
| Fixed income (diversified) | 6.8 | 14.2 | 4.5 |
| Fixed income (high-yield) | (1.0) | 1.4 | 2.0 |
| Fixed income (MBS) | (7.1) | 20.6 | 8.0 |
| **HFR** | | | |
| Fixed income (total) | (6.6) | 7.7 | 3.5 |
| Fixed income (high-yield) | (9.5) | 1.2 | 1.0 |
| Fixed income (MBS) | (11.6) | 16.8 | 7.0 |
| Fixed-income arbitrage | (13.0) | 5.7 | 3.9 |
| Fixed income (diversified) | 1.1 | 15.9 | 7.7 |
| **Hennessee** | | | |
| Fixed income (total) | (12.8) | 8.0 | 2.8 |
| **Tuna** | | | |
| Fixed income (total) | (0.2) | 8.4 | 3.0 |
| Fixed-income arbitrage | (11.0) | 10.3 | 1.8 |

*Source*: Altvest, CMRA Analysis

**Table 13** Sharpe ratio of fixed income indices during periods of stress

| Source | Russian/ LTCM crisis | Tech crash | September 11 | Average of absolute Sharpe ratios | Maximum- minimum |
|---|---|---|---|---|---|
| **Altvest** | | | | | |
| Fixed income (diversified) | 2.10 | 1.50 | 1.00 | 1.5 | 1.1 |
| Fixed income (high-yield) | (0.10) | 0.20 | 0.50 | 0.3 | 0.6 |
| Fixed income (MBS) | (0.90) | 7.10 | 7.00 | 5.0 | 8.0 |
| **HFR** | | | | | |
| Fixed income (total) | (1.40) | 2.20 | 1.40 | 1.7 | 3.6 |
| Fixed income (high-yield) | (1.10) | 0.30 | 0.20 | 0.5 | 1.4 |
| Fixed income (MBS) | (1.30) | 7.40 | 3.30 | 4.0 | 8.7 |
| Fixed-income arbitrage | (1.70) | 2.10 | 1.00 | 1.6 | 3.8 |
| Fixed income (diversified) | 0.40 | 2.60 | 3.40 | 2.1 | 3.0 |
| **Hennessee** | | | | | |
| Fixed income (total) | (1.20) | 3.40 | 0.90 | 1.8 | 4.6 |
| **Tuna** | | | | | |
| Fixed income (total) | (1.00) | 7.00 | 1.10 | 3.0 | 8.0 |
| Fixed-income arbitrage | (0.10) | 2.90 | 1.30 | 1.4 | 3.0 |
| Fixed income (diversified) | 2.10 | 1.50 | 1.00 | 1.5 | 1.1 |

Source: Altvest, HFR, Tuna, CSFB/Tremont, Hennessee, CMRA Analysis

returns) increases when the other factors are added (note that directional risk is the change in interest rates and credit spreads together), meaning that a combination of factors better explains the returns of the strategy than do individual factors considered separately. Supplementing the above observations, Figures 6 and 7 show that extreme moves in bond markets generally result in lower returns for fixed-income arbitrage funds.

Table 17 contains the results of a single-factor S&P500 regression analysis and a multifactor (S&P500, change in credit spread, change in term premia and change in VIX) regression analysis on fixed income fund indices. As expected, $R^2$ is low when the funds' returns are regressed against the S&P500. There are modest increases in $R^2$ when other factors more relevant to the fixed income strategy are included (such as credit spread and term premia). One reason the increases are modest is the style drift feature of the funds. Each fund within a particular strategy has its

---

**Table 14** Fixed-income arbitrage sensitivity profile

| Risk parameter | Performs well when | Performs poorly when |
|---|---|---|
| Yield curve | upward sloping and steepening | inverted |
| Credit risk premium | high and decreasing | low and increasing |
| Intra month S&P 500 volatility | low and stable | high and increasing |
| Implied volatility index | low and stable | high and increasing |
| Bond return volatility | moderate and stable | high and increasing |
| Large cap stock returns | moderate | high |

*Source*: Lehman Brothers Research

---

**Table 15** Average monthly excess returns of fixed-income arbitrage funds in different risk conditions (with correlations), 1997–2001

| | Rank by change in factor | | | | | | | |
|---|---|---|---|---|---|---|---|---|
| | Down most | | | | | Up most | | Overall |
| Factor | 1 | 2 | 3 | 4 | 5 | 6 | 7 | correlation |
| High-yield spreads | 0.7 | 0.6 | 0.4 | 0.2 | 0.4 | 0.1 | (1.4) | (0.4) |
| Treasury volatility | 0.5 | 0.6 | 0.4 | 0.3 | 0.1 | 0.3 | (1.1) | (0.5) |
| Swap volatility | 0.5 | 0.3 | 0.3 | 0.4 | 0.3 | 0.4 | (1.2) | (0.5) |
| Equity volatility | | | | | | | | |
| Whole period | (0.7) | 0.1 | 0.5 | 0.6 | 0.3 | 0.4 | (0.1) | 0.2 |
| Excluding 9/98 and 10/98 | 0.3 | | | | | | | (0.2) |

*Note*: Returns in percentage points
*Source*: Battle for Alphas, Financial Analysts Journal (March-April 2002)

own position on the market, which might explain why the relationship between fund returns and what the above factors indicate is not strong.

### Range of performance

Figure 8 is the histogram of five-year returns data as seen in Altvest. Although 47% of the funds had single-digit returns, an equal number had double-digit returns.

**Table 16** Hedge fund risk framework: style risk in excess returns of fixed-income arbitrage index vs US high-quality long-only bond fund: statistics, December 1998–December 2002

| Measure | 10-year rate | High-yield spread | Interest rate volatility | Equity volatility | 10-year rate | Directional risk | Four factors |
|---|---|---|---|---|---|---|---|
| **Fixed-income arbitrage index** | | | | | | | |
| Coefficient | 0.2 | (0.2) | (0.2) | 0.1 | 0.1 | 0.3 | 0.6 |
| t-Statistic | 2.4 | (2.3) | (2.3) | 3.8 | | | |
| **Long-only bond fund** | | | | | | | |
| Coefficient | 0.0 | (0.0) | (0.3) | 0.1 | 0.0 | 0.1 | 0.4 |
| t-Statistic | 0.0 | (0.5) | (2.7) | 2.2 | | | |

*Note*: The benchmark for fixed-income arbitrage index is 3m LIBOR, and for the long-only bond fund, it is the Salomon Brothers Broad Investment Grade Index. Active after-fee returns were measured monthly.

*Source*: Battle For Alphas, Financial Analysts Journal (March/April 2002)

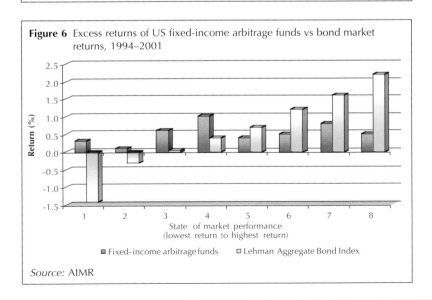

**Figure 6** Excess returns of US fixed-income arbitrage funds vs bond market returns, 1994–2001

*Source:* AIMR

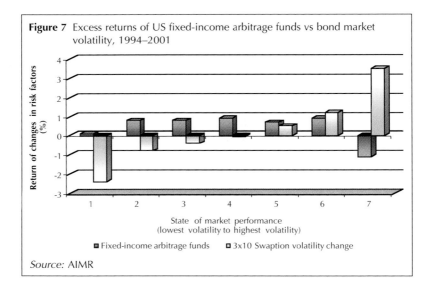

**Figure 7** Excess returns of US fixed-income arbitrage funds vs bond market volatility, 1994–2001

*Source:* AIMR

## SHARPE RATIO
### Distribution

As expected, the Sharpe ratio distributions suggest that fewer funds have higher five-year ratios than one-year ratios. On the whole, the distributions look normal (see Figure 9).

Table 18 shows that there is a clear pattern of increasing returns with increasing Sharpe ratio. This pattern is also retained for AUM. However, notice that the AUMs for the first three quartiles are not very different from one another, so it may not be valid to assert that the highest Sharpe ratios attract the most capital.

### Information ratio

The information ratio for fixed income funds (see Figure 10) has been calculated by taking an average hedge fund index, such as HFR onshore, as a benchmark instead of the Treasury-bill rate as used in the Sharpe ratio

**Table 17** Results of single- and multifactor regressions on selected fixed income indices

|  | S&P 500 | Change in credit spread | Change in term premia | Change in VIX | R-Square (multifactor) | R-Square (single-factor) |
|---|---|---|---|---|---|---|
| Fixed income (total) | 0.1 | (0.0) | 0.007 | (0.1) | 0.3 | 0.2 |
| Fixed-income arbitrage | (0.1) | (0.0) | 0.007 | (0.1) | 0.0 | 0.0 |
| Fixed income: high-yield | 0.1 | (0.1) | 0.018 | (0.3) | 0.4 | 0.2 |

*Source*: Understanding Hedge Fund Performance, Lehman Brothers, November 2001

calculation. The information ratio for fixed income funds is among the lowest of the strategies. This suggests that, though the returns of fixed income funds are among the more stable of the strategies, the returns over the long run have been generally lower than those of other strategies. This may simply reflect the big equity bull market of the 1990s in which equity strategies outperformed the fixed income strategies.

One of the main pitfalls of the Sharpe ratio is not a theoretical one but a problem of data or implementation. The reality of some fixed-income arbitrage is that it relies on the uncertain pricing of illiquid assets. As such, these assets are not easily priced for NAV calculation and often involve manager discretion. The discretion is reflected in a smoothing of returns

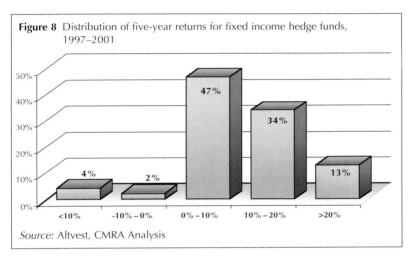

**Figure 8** Distribution of five-year returns for fixed income hedge funds, 1997–2001

*Source:* Altvest, CMRA Analysis

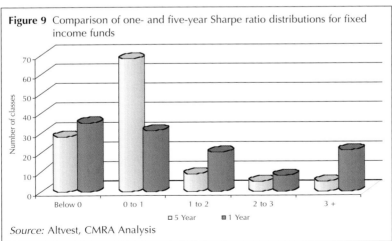

**Figure 9** Comparison of one- and five-year Sharpe ratio distributions for fixed income funds

*Source:* Altvest, CMRA Analysis

**Table 18** Distribution of fixed income funds by quartiles of Sharpe ratio, 1997–2001

| Sharpe ratio quartiles | Average 1997–2001 equally weighted return (%) | Avergae 1997–2001 AUM-weighted return (%) | AUM in quartile (US$ billion) | % of total | Average 1997–2001 standard deviation (%) | Sharpe ratio 1997–2001 |
|---|---|---|---|---|---|---|
| 1 | 15.4 | 16.6 | 7.1 | 34 | 7.5 | 1.8 |
| 2 | 11.5 | 10.1 | 6.2 | 30 | 12.8 | 0.5 |
| 3 | 7.7 | 6.2 | 5.4 | 26 | 14.4 | 0.2 |
| 4 | (0.6) | 2.3 | 2.3 | 11 | 15.7 | (0.4) |
| **Total** | **8.6** | **10.4** | **21.0** | **100** | **12.6** | **0.5** |

*Source*: Altvest, HFR, Tuna, CMRA Analysis based on 115 funds with at least four years of performance data.

that bumps up risk-adjusted returns as measured by the Sharpe ratio. It is extremely unlikely that some of the Sharpe ratios greater than 2.0 would be the same if managers were not masking the true volatility of their positions.[1]

### Leverage

88% of fixed income hedge funds use leverage. 66% of those use a leverage lower than 2.0, and 22% leverage their positions to a level greater than 2.0. Use of leverage as of the end of 2001 is plotted in Figure 11 (see Chapter 2 for a discussion of leverage).

Fixed-income arbitrage is currently among the most levered strategies (see Table 19). On average, the leverage for these funds has been increasing over the years.

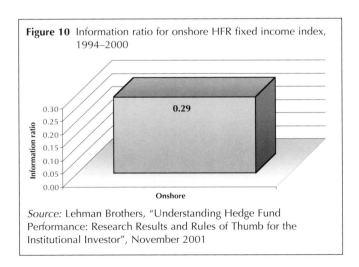

**Figure 10** Information ratio for onshore HFR fixed income index, 1994–2000

*Source:* Lehman Brothers, "Understanding Hedge Fund Performance: Research Results and Rules of Thumb for the Institutional Investor", November 2001

A great deal of leverage is often needed for fixed-income arbitrage trades. For instance, a common trade consists of taking a position in the on-the-run 30-year government bond while simultaneously taking the opposite position in the off-the-run 30-year government bond in order to arbitrage the different yield to maturity of the two bonds. Because the difference in the yield to maturity is too small, LTCM and other hedge funds using similar strategies had to go long and short huge notional amounts of each security to make large dollar profits. A one-basis-point discrepancy in the yield to maturity of the 30-year bond results in an approximate US$1,200 profit per US$1 million notional amount of each long and short position. A US$10 million portfolio would need to go long and short US$416 million of 30-year bonds to make a 5% return (or US$500,000) on this trade.

The leverage distribution of fixed income hedge funds shows an average leverage of 2.4 and a maximum leverage of 12.0.

Fixed income leverage is generally lower than 12.0 (see Table 20). In general, the leverage is lower than that employed by the convertible arbitrage, merger arbitrage and managed futures strategies. On a historical basis, the average financial leverage of the strategy has been growing since 1997 where it was at US$0.9 to US$2.1 in 2002 (see Table 21).

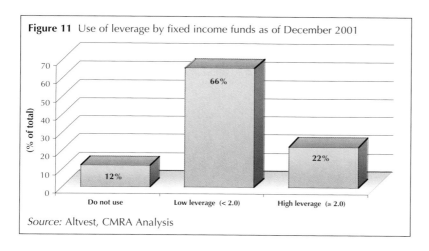

**Figure 11** Use of leverage by fixed income funds as of December 2001

*Source:* Altvest, CMRA Analysis

**Table 19** Financial leverage of fixed income funds in 2002

| Minimum | Average | Maximum | Rank |
|---------|---------|---------|------|
| 0.0 | 2.1 | 15.0 | 3 of 14 |

*Source*: Altvest, CMRA Analysis

351

Although fixed income funds have among the smallest differences between levered and delevered five-year returns (implying that leverage has historically not been very high), in 2001 the difference jumped by almost four percentage points (see Table 22), putting this strategy among the most levered in that year.

**Table 20** Distribution of fixed income funds by quartiles of leverage, 1997–2001

| Leverage quartiles | Minimum leverage in category | Maximum leverage in category | Average leverage in category | Mean leverage in category | Total AUM in category (US$ billion) |
|---|---|---|---|---|---|
| 1 | 0.1 | 1.0 | 0.6 | 0.5 | 0.6 |
| 2 | 1.0 | 1.5 | 1.2 | 1.2 | 0.4 |
| 3 | 1.5 | 3.0 | 2.0 | 2.0 | 0.4 |
| 4 | 3.0 | 12.0 | 5.6 | 4.0 | 1.4 |
| **Total** | **0.1** | **12.0** | **1.3** | **1.6** | **2.9** |

*Source*: Altvest, CMRA Analysis based on 115 funds with at least four years of leverage data

**Table 21** Historical leverage of fixed income hedge funds, 1997–2001

| | | | | | 1997–2001 | | |
|---|---|---|---|---|---|---|---|
| 1997 | 1998 | 1999 | 2000 | 2001 | Average | Maximum | Minimum |
| 0.9 | 1.0 | 1.2 | 1.2 | 2.2 | 1.3 | 2.2 | 0.9 |

*Source*: Altvest, CMRA Analysis

**Table 22** Summary of levered and delevered performance of fixed income funds, 1997–2001 (%)

| | Maximum return | Minimum return | Average return | Maximum delevered return | Minimum delevered return | Average delevered return | Difference in returns levered vs delevered |
|---|---|---|---|---|---|---|---|
| **1997–2001** | 46.3 | 1.3 | 11.8 | 10.3 | 0.8 | 5.2 | 6.6 |
| **2001** | 174.5 | (9.6) | 16.4 | 58.2 | (4.8) | 6.1 | 10.3 |

*Source*: Altvest, CMRA Analysis

**Table 23** Risk factors for fixed income funds and related securities

| Risk category | Basis/risk factors | Fixed income security | Rating | Maturity | Country |
|---|---|---|---|---|---|
| Volatility | Implied Volatility | Caps, Floors, Swaptions, T-Bond Options | | Varies | Varies |
| Mortgages | Mortgage/TSY basis | | | 15,30, others | Mainly US |
| | Mortgage OAS | MBS, IO, PO, CMO | | 15,30, others | Mainly US |
| Credit Spreads | Agency spreads | | | 2, 5, 10 | US |
| | Swap spreads | | | 2, 5, 10, 30 | Varies |
| | Investment grade | Finance, Industrials, | AAA, A, A, BBB | 2, 3, 5, 10, 30 | Varies |
| | | Utilities, Yankees | | | |
| | Corporate spreads | Senior, Subordinate | BB, B, CCC | 10 | US |
| | High-yield spreads | ABS, CMBS, High-yield | AAA to BB and below | | US |
| | CBO/CLO spreads | | | | US |
| | ABS spreads | Auto | | 2 | |
| | | Credit cards | | 2,5,10 | |
| | | Home equity fixed | | 2, 5, 10 | |
| | | Home equity float | | 3 | |
| | | Home equity line of credit | | 3 | |
| | | Manufact. housing | | 2, 5, 10 | |
| | | Student loans | | 2,7 | |
| | | Stranded cost | | 2, 5, 10 | |
| | CMBS | | AAA | 5,7,10 | US |
| | | | AA, A, BBB, BBB-, BB, B | 10 | |

*Source:* Risk Management: Approaches for Fixed Income Markets, Golub, B.W. and L.M. Tilman

## RISK MEASUREMENT

As shown in Table 23, one of the interesting characteristics of fixed income trading is the enormous variety of risks to which funds in the strategy are exposed.

Key risks facing fixed income funds that are difficult to hedge are liquidity, counterparty, convexity and leverage risk. A risk profile for the strategy is presented as Figure 12. Some of these risks are discussed below.

### Convexity risk

This risk is a key issue for funds that trade mortgage-backed securities. Due to prepayments, these bonds can suffer from negative convexity (the bond price does not rise as much as predicted by its duration when yields fall). Notice how option-adjusted duration (OAD) in Table 24 can change for a TAC PO (from 11.4 when interest rates move up 200bp to 4.1 when rates move down 200bp) as compared to a US Treasury (from 10.9 when rates move up 200bp to 14.8 when rates move down 200bp). The TAC PO is experiencing negative convexity.

Convexity is a measure of a bond's change in duration, requiring hedges to be dynamic as opposed to static. Table 25 shows the duration of a 30-year 7.5% Fannie Mae mortgage pass through. Hedging this security would require shorting a four-year Treasury in February. But as the duration increased (because of the change in long-term rates, prepayments and, consequently, convexity) the hedge requirement changed to shorting a seven- to eight-year Treasury by May. Large-scale liquidations by highly levered companies such as Granite Capital MBS Fund caused the market to reach a peak in selling pressure.

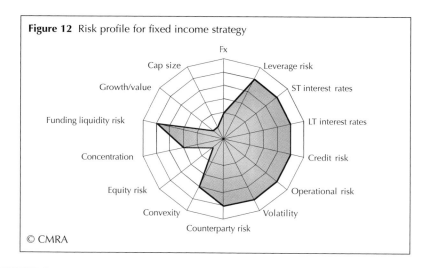

**Figure 12** Risk profile for fixed income strategy

© CMRA

While this risk can be partially hedged by going long options (which have positive convexity or gamma), this can add both a basis risk and a yield curve risk when the options do not exactly match the exposure being hedged. Callable bonds and structured securities with embedded optionality also share this key risk element.

## Credit risk

Credit risk is generally understood to mean the risk of loss due to a credit event such as a delinquency, default or some other such failure of an obligor to meet its repayment obligations. However, as outlined in the discussion of distressed securities funds in Chapter 15, the capital markets price credit risk into a security far earlier than the actual realisation of any credit loss. This repricing of assets due to a change in the perception of the

**Table 24** Duration drifts of selected securities in various interest rate environments

|  | Parallel interest rate shock (basis points) | | | | | | | | | | |
|---|---|---|---|---|---|---|---|---|---|---|---|
|  | +250 | +200 | +150 | +100 | +50 | Base | −50 | −100 | −150 | −200 | −250 |
| US Treasury | | | | | | | | | | | |
| OAV | 69.4 | 73.2 | 77.3 | 81.9 | 86.9 | 92.5 | 98.7 | 105.6 | 113.2 | 121.7 | 131.2 |
| OAD | | 10.9 | 11.3 | 11.8 | 12.2 | 12.7 | 13.2 | 13.7 | 14.3 | 14.8 | |
| OAC | | 2.0 | 2.2 | 2.3 | 2.5 | 2.6 | 2.8 | 2.9 | 3.1 | 3.3 | |
| Duration drift | | 0.9 | 0.9 | 0.9 | 1.0 | 1.0 | 1.0 | 1.0 | 1.1 | 1.1 | |
| Callable corp | | | | | | | | | | | |
| OAV | 78.6 | 81.8 | 85.1 | 88.6 | 92.0 | 95.4 | 98.4 | 100.2 | 100.5 | 100.5 | 100.6 |
| OAD | | 8.0 | 7.9 | 7.8 | 7.4 | 6.7 | 4.9 | 2.1 | 0.3 | 0.1 | |
| OAC | | 0.7 | 0.5 | 0.2 | (0.4) | (1.6) | (4.5) | (6.4) | (0.9) | 0.0 | |
| Duration drift | | 0.0 | (0.2) | (0.4) | (1.0) | (2.0) | (4.8) | (6.4) | (0.9) | 0.0 | |
| Generic MBS | | | | | | | | | | | |
| OAV | 92.5 | 94.6 | 96.7 | 98.8 | 100.8 | 102.6 | 104.2 | 105.3 | 106.1 | 106.8 | 107.6 |
| OAD | | 4.5 | 4.4 | 4.2 | 3.8 | 3.2 | 2.6 | 1.9 | 1.4 | 1.4 | |
| OAC | | 0.1 | (0.1) | (0.4) | (0.8) | (1.1) | (1.4) | (1.3) | (0.3) | 0.1 | |
| Duration drift | | (0.1) | (0.3) | (0.6) | (1.0) | (1.2) | (1.5) | (1.4) | (0.3) | 0.1 | |
| Notional PAC 10 | | | | | | | | | | | |
| OAV | 23.5 | 22.7 | 22.1 | 21.7 | 21.3 | 20.8 | 19.6 | 16.9 | 11.6 | 7.4 | 6.0 |
| OAD | | (6.1) | (4.8) | (3.9) | (4.1) | (8.0) | (19.8) | (47.6) | (82.2) | (75.9) | |
| OAC | | 2.9 | 2.6 | 1.7 | (2.2) | (13.0) | (31.6) | (61.9) | 39.6 | 149.2 | |
| Duration drift | | 2.5 | 2.4 | 1.5 | (2.4) | (13.6) | (35.5) | (84.5) | (27.9) | 91.7 | |
| TAC PO | | | | | | | | | | | |
| OAV | 52.0 | 54.9 | 58.2 | 62.1 | 66.7 | 72.7 | 80.2 | 87.5 | 93.1 | 95.9 | 97.0 |
| OAD | | 11.4 | 12.2 | 13.6 | 15.9 | 18.6 | 18.6 | 14.7 | 9.0 | 4.1 | |
| OAC | | 2.5 | 3.7 | 5.1 | 8.3 | 8.4 | (0.8) | (8.3) | (11.7) | (7.1) | |
| Duration drift | | 1.2 | 2.2 | 3.2 | 5.8 | 4.9 | (4.2) | (10.5) | (12.5) | (7.3) | |

OAC=Option Adjusted Convexity, OAD=Option Adjusted Duration, OAV=Option Adjusted Value

*Source*: Risk Management: Approaches for Fixed Income Markets, Golub, B.W. and L.M. Tilman.

**Table 25** Dealer prepayment forecasts and effective duration for 30-year 7.5% FNMA mortgage-backed security October 1993–May 1994

| Date | Effective duration (years) | Prepayment forecast (%) | 10-year treasury yield (%) | Fed funds (%) |
|---|---|---|---|---|
| 15/10/93 | 3.4 | 21.8 | 5.2 | 3.0 |
| 26/01/94 | 3.5 | 20.8 | 5.7 | 3.0 |
| 09/02/94 | 3.5 | 20.8 | 5.9 | 3.3 |
| 23/03/94 | 4.8 | 11.9 | 6.5 | 3.5 |
| 20/04/94 | 5.3 | 9.5 | 7.0 | 3.8 |
| 17/05/94 | 5.4 | 9.0 | 7.0 | 4.3 |

Source: Bloomberg, Federal Reserve Bank of New York

risks of owning them is called "spread risk" and is the market manifestation of credit risk. Spread refers to the difference between the return of the asset in question and that of a benchmark that captures the prevailing level of interest rates with regard to other non-credit factors such as maturity. After September 11, 2001, the perceived level of future defaults increased substantially as the terrorist shock compounded the loss of investor confidence due to corporate governance scandals such as Enron. Spreads on corporate debt increased accordingly as their prices dropped (see Figure 13).

### Leverage risk

Leverage is a key risk facing many fixed-income arbitrage funds. Leverage can be obtained through repo/reverse repo markets or embedded in optionality. Repos/reverse repos are generally done through the major broker/dealer firms. Ways to reduce this risk include limiting the exposure to any single broker/dealer or counterparty and maintaining a good communication infrastructure so that trades can be executed seamlessly in times of crisis.

### Liquidity risk

Liquidity risk is the possibility that liquidity in the markets might disappear at critical times when funds need to transact. As Nobel laureate Myron Scholes pointed out, a common source of liquidity risk is the risk management systems of hedge funds and large sell-side institutions. These firms and funds commonly trade their portfolios on the basis of "stress-loss limits" (if a portfolio loses a certain amount, all trades have to be liquidated) and "stop-loss limits" (automatic triggers that activate orders to liquidate a security if the price of the security reaches a certain limit).

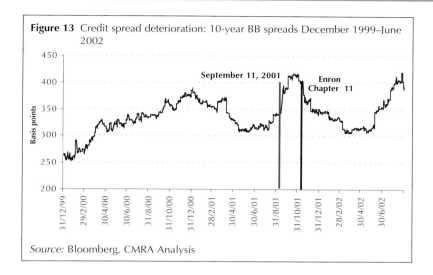

**Figure 13** Credit spread deterioration: 10-year BB spreads December 1999–June 2002

*Source:* Bloomberg, CMRA Analysis

These create a "herd effect" (many funds try to liquidate securities at once) in the market at times of crisis. The market moves so quickly that it is almost impossible to execute trades at these limits. During such times, uncertainty is so great that traders are often unwilling to make a price on securities, causing liquidity crunches.

Another source of liquidity risk is the fact that large sell side institutions are the major providers of liquidity. Most investment banks underwrite many of the complex fixed income securities and derivatives and make markets in these securities. They have to mark their positions to market daily and maintain a high level of transparency because they are often listed companies. Unlike hedge funds, which make money by speculating on securities, sell-side institutions focus on earning revenue from their service business (such as commissions from market-making). If the price of securities on their books threatens their revenue stream, they will sharply reduce liquidity.

Measuring liquidity is not a straightforward business and no widely accepted method exists. A meaningful relationship has been found between liquidity and the spread between on-the-run and off-the-run Treasuries. As liquidity decreases, the yield spread between Treasuries widens significantly. Additionally, there is a strong correlation in the liquidity patterns of similar securities. Note in Table 26 that the correlation between the liquidity premium of the two-year and the 30-year treasury is very low compared to the much higher correlation between the 10-year and 30-year Treasury.

## Spread risk

With the fall in the equity markets, spreads decreased as investors sought investment alternatives to equities. In 1998, several of the fixed income strategy's returns were negatively correlated with changes in swap spreads (their returns fell when swap spreads went up). This was the time of the Russian/LTCM crisis when all credit-related instruments sharply decreased in price. There was also a positive correlation in 1998 between many of the fixed income styles and the 10-year Treasury yield and the three-month government and mortgage repo rates, which implies that the portfolios of many funds contained a high percentage of spread products. 10-year swap spreads for 1997 to mid-2002 are shown in Figure 14.

## Volatility risk

Government bond yield volatilities spike up during periods of crisis and uncertainty. This is clearly seen in the period right after the Russian default in August 1998 and later that same year in September when the LTCM fund had to be restructured (see Table 27). As soon as the spectre of a default of global magnitude was eliminated from the minds of market participants, volatilities receded to lower levels. The difference between short-dated and long-dated volatility has followed an upward trend since the middle of 2000 (Figure 15).

## Yield curve risk

When the Federal Reserve began lowering rates, the curve changed from 59bp on June 30, 2000 to more than 200bp on September 3, 2002 (see Figure 16).

As of October 2002, short-term rates had fallen by almost twice the number of basis points as the long-term rates. Since short-term rates are in the low single digits, short-term volatility has generally increased.

**Table 26** On-the-run US Treasury liquidity premia February 1, 1999–February 1, 2000 (typical fixed income hedges)

| | Liquidity premium (basis points) | | | | Correlations among liquidity premiums | | | |
| | Mean | Std dev | Minimum | Maximum | 2-year | 5-year | 10-year | 30-year |
| --- | --- | --- | --- | --- | --- | --- | --- | --- |
| 2-year | 3 | 2 | 1 | 11 | 1.00 | | | |
| 5-year | 15 | 4 | 5 | 25 | 0.05 | 1.00 | | |
| 10-year | 29 | 6 | 8 | 38 | 0.21 | 0.78 | 1.00 | |
| 30-year | 18 | 4 | 8 | 26 | 0.16 | 0.62 | 0.79 | 1.00 |

*Source*: Risk Management: Approaches for Fixed Income Markets, Golub, B.W. and L.M. Tilman.

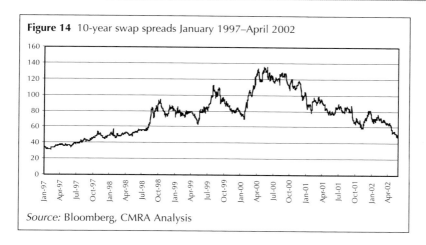

**Figure 14** 10-year swap spreads January 1997–April 2002

*Source:* Bloomberg, CMRA Analysis

**Table 27** US government bond yield volatility during 1998 (January 1, 1998–July 3, 1998 = 100)

|  | January 1– July 3 | July 6– August 14 | August 17– September 22 | September 23– October 15 | October 16– December 31 |
|---|---|---|---|---|---|
| 2-year | 100 | 50 | 161 | 185 | 181 |
| 5-year | 100 | 53 | 149 | 210 | 143 |
| 10-year | 100 | 51 | 132 | 224 | 122 |
| 30-year | 100 | 52 | 154 | 265 | 151 |
| 10-year inflation indexed | 100 | 69 | 94 | 193 | 106 |

*Source*: President's Working Group on Financial Markets

## VALUE-AT-RISK
### Overview

VAR is only a good indicator of the maximum potential loss within a given confidence level if the assumptions used to calculate it are valid. The main assumptions are that probability is normally distributed and that the volatility of assets and their correlation with one another will remain stable. In 1998, these assumptions broke down, rendering VAR numbers meaningless. Many banks and funds bet that spreads between European and emerging market bonds vs US Treasuries would narrow. However, after the Russian default spreads began to widen and the correlations in the markets changed dramatically from those that had been put into the VAR models. VAR is not as effective as stress testing in evaluating the risk in arbitrage type strategies.

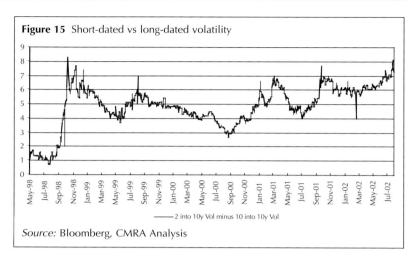

**Figure 15** Short-dated vs long-dated volatility

——— 2 into 10y Vol minus 10 into 10y Vol

*Source:* Bloomberg, CMRA Analysis

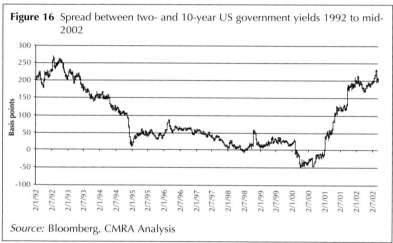

**Figure 16** Spread between two- and 10-year US government yields 1992 to mid-2002

*Source:* Bloomberg, CMRA Analysis

## Examples

To illustrate how a simple portfolio of bonds can have very different levels of risk when viewed from different perspectives, CMRA created a duration-neutral portfolio of two-year, 10-year and 30-year US Treasury notes and bonds. The portfolio's holdings are set out in Table 28.

Even though this portfolio is duration-neutral, a different view is displayed in terms of convexity, risk and average life (see Table 29). Different stress test scenarios give a still different view of the risk (see Table 30). And the VAR analysis shows yet another view of risk (see Table 31).

**Table 28** Composition of example duration-neutral portfolio

| Security | Description | Position | Notional | Duration | Position weighted duration | VAR (95% CI)* (US$) | VAR (99% CI) (US$) |
|---|---|---|---|---|---|---|---|
| 2-year | Treasury: 3.000 02/29/04 | Long | 40,000,000 | 1.5 | 2.7 | (140,778) | (175,774) |
| 10-year | Treasury: 4.875 02/15/12 | Short | (27,502,247) | 7.8 | (9.5) | (177,084) | (221,106) |
| 30-year | Treasury: 5.375 02/15/31 | Long | 10,000,000 | 15.4 | 6.9 | (95,767) | (119,574) |
| | | Net | 22,497,753 | | 0.0 | | |

* 95% chance that loss will be equal to or less than the number in this column

*Source*: CMRA Analysis

When there are sudden crisis situations, the correlation and standard deviation profiles of the securities can change drastically. Consider a portfolio composed of a single corporate bond, hedged by a government bond of similar duration. In this example the corporate bond is AOL Time Warner, 7.75% maturing on June 15, 2005, and the Treasury bond is 6.5% maturing on May 15, 2005.

Figure 17 shows that the hedge would have worked until after July 2002. At that time, bond prices diverged substantially. This is because AOL Time Warner got caught up in the spate of 2002 corporate accounting scandals by coming under market suspicion for its accounting practices. Furthermore, its post-merger performance had been disappointing.

So what would VAR have said? As illustrated in Figure 18, VAR would have shown a loss of 2% to 5% between July 14, 2002, and July 31, 2002, while the actual two-week loss (July 14, 2002 to July 31, 2002) turned out to be between 12% and 13%.

It should be noted that statistics that use historical data, such as VAR, volatility and correlation, generally use the normal distribution; extraordinary events occur in the tails of these distributions. In reality, extraordi-

**Table 29** Example portfolio: risk statistics by time buckets for position-level data

| | Average life | | | |
|---|---|---|---|---|
| | <5 years | 5–10 years | >10 yrs | Total portfolio (US$ million) |
| Positions (US$ million) | 40.0 | (27.5) | 10.0 | 22.5 |
| Position weighted duration | 2.7 | (9.5) | 6.9 | 0.0 |
| Position weighted convexity | 0.1 | (0.9) | 1.5 | 0.7 |

*Source*: CMRA Analysis

**Table 30** Example portfolio: stress-testing scenarios

| Scenario | Profit and loss (US$) |
| --- | --- |
| +200bp parallel shift | 260,257 |
| +100bp parallel shift | 72,758 |
| −100bp parallel shift | 116,121 |
| −200bp parallel shift | 409,031 |
| 0/+50 steepening | (403,228) |
| 50/0 flattening | 434,044 |

Source: CMRA Analysis

nary events occur more often than predicted by a normal distribution: recent examples are the sudden increase in rates in 1994, the Mexican crisis in 1994, the Asian crisis in 1997, the Russian/LTCM crisis in 1998 and the technology crash in 2000–2001 are a few examples. This suggests either that tails are much fatter than most people expect or that distributions are not really normal. For instance, the 5.5-year statistical highlights (ending December 1999) of a particular mortgage fund indicated that its average return was 14.4%, with a standard deviation of 4.1%. It lost money in only five months during the 5.5 years, with a maximum loss of 0.35%. However, in March 2000 this fund lost 5.8%. It then lost 4.5% in May of the same year.

The loss in March was a six-standard deviation event with a probability of one in over a trillion.[2]

**Table 31** Example portfolio: daily VAR for different confidence levels

| Confidence level* (%) | Daily VAR (US$) |
| --- | --- |
| 2 | (139,006) |
| 5 | (111,330) |
| 10 | (86,741) |
| 20 | (56,964) |
| 30 | (35,494) |
| 40 | (17,148) |
| 50 | 0 |
| 60 | 17,148 |
| 70 | 35,494 |
| 80 | 56,964 |
| 90 | 86,741 |
| 95 | 111,330 |
| 98 | 139,006 |

*probability that the gain will be at most what is reported or the loss will exceed what is reported

Source: CMRA Analysis

## STRESS TESTS

Stress testing portfolios comprised of fixed income securities can be very difficult; the prices of such securities depend on multiple factors and stress tests might entail stressing each of the multiple factors together, but there may be too many permutations to make this a realistic exercise. For instance, a parallel shift in the yield curve might give very

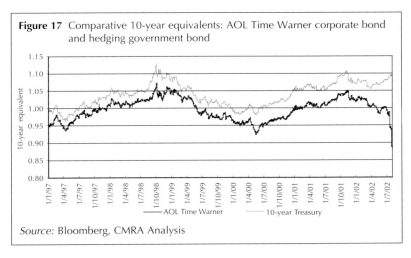

**Figure 17** Comparative 10-year equivalents: AOL Time Warner corporate bond and hedging government bond

*Source:* Bloomberg, CMRA Analysis

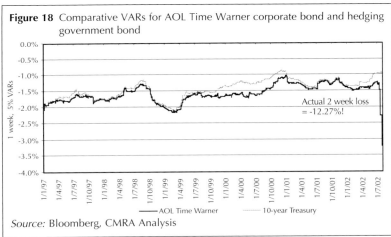

**Figure 18** Comparative VARs for AOL Time Warner corporate bond and hedging government bond

*Source:* Bloomberg, CMRA Analysis

different results from a steepening or a flattening. Consider a portfolio consisting of a long position in US$1 million of 10-year US Treasuries and a short position in US$40 million of two-year US Treasuries. A parallel shift of 300bp will result in a profit or loss of about 2.3%. However, a steepening (where long rates shift up 150bp but short rates shift down 150bp) will result in a loss of 22.4%. For portfolios with instruments containing options, add the effect of the volatility term structure, which can also move (parallel, steepen or flatten) and there are too many combinations of yield curve and volatility curve effects.

In general, stress tests should be done on portfolios in the strategy to see their effect on the following fixed income parameters:

❏ yield curve levels and shapes;
❏ volatility curve levels and shapes;
❏ spreads and basis;
❏ assumptions about the yield and volatility curves;
❏ model quirks and assumptions;
❏ default scenarios;
❏ leverage;
❏ liquidity scenarios; and
❏ correlations.

The nature of some securities might require a special type of stress test. Consider digital options as an example. They are very stable until the underlying security comes close to its strike price. At this point, risk parameters like gamma and vega will change dramatically. If the base case of a stress test is that the option is out-of-the-money, although the stressed case means that the option is in-the-money, the risk parameters will not change much. As long as traders are aware of the existence of such options in their portfolios, there is no problem. However, problems arise if such securities have been "forgotten" in a portfolio containing hundreds of other different securities. The fund's current stress tests might be rendered ineffective.

It is important to note that, during periods of market stress, correlations deviate massively from their historical levels. All instruments move to a correlation of +1 or −1. Many fixed income strategies such as convergence trades and basis trades, are most vulnerable to this correlation phenomenon. It is critical for such funds to include a measure of this crisis effect in their calculations of VAR and other stress tests.

## Transparency level

A CMRA study conducted in 2000 reports the transparency that various fund strategies offered to their investors (see Table 32). Of eight styles of funds, fixed income ranked third in terms of the transparency for key positions and portfolio viewing. Position-level detail without significant tools to interpret it is, however, completely worthless for complex fixed income "strategies".

## DUE DILIGENCE QUESTIONS FOR FIXED-INCOME FUNDS

Below is a useful list of due diligence questions specific to fixed income funds:

❏ What type of pricing model do you use?
❏ How do you mark your positions to market?
❏ Do you stress test the value of your portfolio against alternative methods for marking-to-market? What do you conclude?
❏ If you had to (or wanted to) liquidate your portfolio, how long would it take under normal circumstances and under stressed conditions?

**Table 32** Transparency offered to investors by managers of fixed income funds (%)

| | Overall level of transparency | | | Positions disclosed to investors | |
|---|---|---|---|---|---|
| Performance | Key positions | View entire portfolio | No transparency | Key long positions | Key short positions |
| 100 | 50 | 67 | 0 | 50 | 50 |

*Source*: Hennessee Hedge Fund Advisory Group

❑ What is your data source for volatility?
❑ What sort of trading do you perform with regard to credit derivatives?
❑ How do you deal with correlation assumptions?
❑ How do you hedge foreign exchange exposure?
❑ How do you deal with maturity mismatches?
❑ What sort of prepayment model do you use?
❑ How many data sources do you use for MBS?
❑ How do you incorporate off-the-run issues in your yield curve?
❑ How do you build your volatility curve?
❑ For OTC derivatives, how do you measure counterparty exposure and mark-to-market exposure?

## DATA AND NAV ISSUES

Depending on the type of instrument and its market, the quoted prices on a screen may not be close to executable prices. This is a particularly important issue for NAV calculation and the marking of portfolios. If data are not easily available and their reliability is not good, marking portfolios and calculating NAVs becomes a subjective task.

Some fixed income instruments are traded on exchanges. Generally the quoted price and spread data for these are very reliable and there is a steady stream of recorded history that can be obtained for analysis purposes. Some of the common exchange-traded fixed income instruments include interest rate futures, such as Eurodollar futures, which have very large and liquid markets, and some more exotic ones such as Federal Reserve funds futures, currency futures on all G7 currencies, G7 government bills, note and bond futures, agency futures, and options on all of the foregoing.

Spot currencies and government bonds often trade on the even larger OTC market. This is how all non-exchange traded instruments and derivatives trade. Data reliability for the OTC market depends on the instrument type. The US Treasury market and the spot currency market,

**Table 33** Interest rate derivatives data obtained from different dealers on morning of July 17, 2002

| Cap/floor volatilities | Garban (%) | Tullets & Tokyo (%) | Difference (%) |
|---|---|---|---|
| 1-year | 41.6 | 42.5 | 0.9 |
| 2-year | 39.8 | 40.4 | 0.6 |
| 5-year | 28.5 | 28.6 | 0.1 |
| 10-year | 22.8 | 22.6 | (0.2) |
| **Swaption volatilities** | | | |
| 1 into 5 | 25.1 | 25.8 | 0.7 |
| 5 into 5 | 18.9 | 19.1 | 0.2 |
| 1 into 10 | 21.9 | 22.3 | 0.4 |
| 10 into 10 | 13.6 | 13.7 | 0.1 |

*Source*: Bloomberg

generally put out very reliable data. Many dealers in these instruments actually type in their bids, asks and executed prices directly into terminals provided by companies such as Reuters. Many swap trading desks mark their positions with data provided by GovPx. However, it is important to note that at times of crisis – when liquidity dries up or the market moves too fast – data for these securities as well as for exchange-traded instruments are no longer reliable.

Data reliability can be a tricky issue when it comes to more exotic instruments, such as derivatives. These trade in the OTC market but, unlike Treasuries and spot foreign exchange, which trade every few seconds or minutes, derivatives may trade once a day or even less frequently. Therefore, it is often possible to get day-old data when marks have to be determined. Table 33 contains swaption volatility data from two broker firms. One reason for the difference may be that some of the instruments displayed traded more recently at one source as opposed to the other. Another reason can be that a dealer has an axe that is shown to one source and not another.

Differences in volatilities can greatly affect fixed income instruments with optionality, especially if the option maturity is long-term. Mortgage-backed securities and many of the common fixed income instruments, such as callable corporate bonds, often have long maturity options embedded in them. Table 34 shows how varied dealer quotes can be for different fixed income securities.

Crises can also affect the reliability of data. Typically, when liquidity dries up or when there is a great deal of uncertainty in the market, bid/ask spreads can grossly widen. In these cases, which data input should one use

**Table 34** Mid-market price marks by various dealers for different fixed income security types

| Security type | Description | Coupon | Maturity | Dealer 1 | Dealer 2 | Dealer 3 | Dealer 4 | Maximum-minimum |
|---|---|---|---|---|---|---|---|---|
| US corporate bond | Ameritech Capital | 6.55 | 15/01/28 | 99.1 | 98.9 | 99.2 | 99.5 | 0.5 |
| Generic MBS | FNMA 30 Yr | 8.00 | 01/05/22 | 104.1 | 103.9 | 103.7 | 104.1 | 0.5 |
| ABS | GT_97-1-B1 | 7.23 | 15/03/28 | 100.2 | 100.1 | 100.4 | 100.2 | 0.3 |

(Data obtained 29/07/98)

*Source:* Risk Management: Approaches for Fixed Income Markets, Golub, B.W. and L.M. Tilman.

to mark the fund's portfolio? Taking the average is not sufficient because one cannot execute at the average. The wider the bid/ask spread, the further the average is from the execution point. This issue is illustrated with data for the Russian/LTCM crisis in Figure 19.

Securities such as collateralised mortgage obligations (CMOs) can be very illiquid in the secondary market. At month end managers must poll various broker dealers for prices and the variance in these prices can be huge. In some cases, CMOs are tailor made and only the original dealer who created the primary market will be available to create a secondary market. In such cases there will be only one source of price for the security. Figure 20 shows the variation in prices for an inverse floater, Fannie Mae 99-15 SB.

## PUBLICLY DISCLOSED PROBLEMS

LTCM was a highly leveraged fund forced into a crisis restructuring when its borrowing terms were altered at the same time its highly leveraged positions moved sharply against it. The convergence-type trades that LTCM specialised in performed adversely to an extent that seemed beyond imagination at the time.

Figure 21 shows the spread between the on-the-run and off-the-run treasury yield to maturities. Note the sudden widening during the LTCM crisis; the yield of the on-the-run treasury fell at a higher rate than that of the off-the-run treasury because of the drying up of liquidity and the ensuing short squeeze.

At the time of the LTCM debacle,

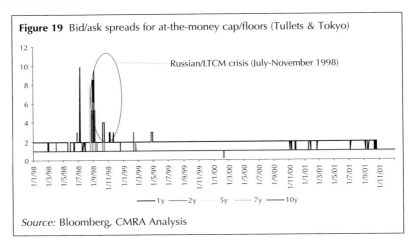

**Figure 19** Bid/ask spreads for at-the-money cap/floors (Tullets & Tokyo)

Russian/LTCM crisis (July–November 1998)

—1y —2y 5y —7y —10y

*Source:* Bloomberg, CMRA Analysis

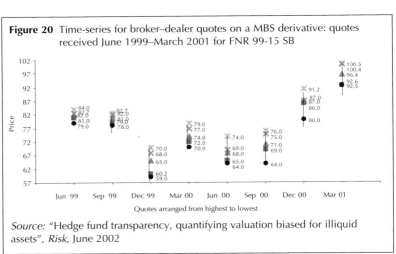

**Figure 20** Time-series for broker–dealer quotes on a MBS derivative: quotes received June 1999–March 2001 for FNR 99-15 SB

Quotes arranged from highest to lowest

*Source:* "Hedge fund transparency, quantifying valuation biased for illiquid assets", *Risk*, June 2002

another fund, Everest Capital Ltd., lost 52% of its value (or US$1.3 billion). Everest had an emerging markets fund that invested in Russian and Latin American bonds that promptly lost 68% of its value when the Russian government defaulted on its debt. The fund's founder, Marko Dimitrijevic, said that "the magnitude of the losses on the Russian debt and the speed at which they occurred were something that I have never encountered since I began working in professional money management 17 years ago."[3] This only highlights the importance of keeping the liquidity and leverage of fixed income products to a manageable level.

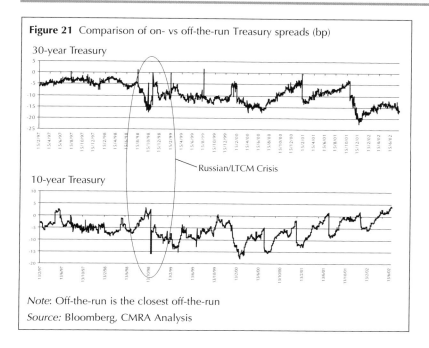

**Figure 21** Comparison of on- vs off-the-run Treasury spreads (bp)

Note: Off-the-run is the closest off-the-run

Source: Bloomberg, CMRA Analysis

1   "Hedge Fund Transparency: Quantifying Valuation Bias for Illiquid Assets", *Risk*, June 2002.
2   Pitfalls of Hedge Funds, Southern Employees Benefit Conference, Michael D. Smith, May 10, 2001, Hewitt Investment Group.
3   The Economy Staggering Losses at Everest Hedge Fund, October 2, 1998, BBC News, UK, news.bbc.co.uk/2/hi/business/184897.stm.

# 17

# *Global Macro*

## DESCRIPTION OF THE STRATEGY

Global macro funds are well known primarily for two reasons: they are among the largest funds in terms of AUM and a number of them are run by managers with celebrity status. Global macro managers seek to generate returns by identifying disparities and placing bets on the relationship between price and underlying value across several markets throughout the world. The classic example of this is the bet that George Soros made against the British pound in 1992. He bet correctly that the British government would allow the pound to break the EMS exchange rate bands dictated at the time. The successful bet is reputed to have made him more than US$2 billion.

In the 1970s and 1980s, managers with roots in the stock market decided to look for opportunities in broader global markets, such as fixed income securities, foreign exchanges and commodities. Because they maintained a private investment structure that allowed them to go long and short (and to use leverage), the term "hedge fund" stuck with them. The strategy they used was described as "global macro". Hedge funds became more fashionable in 1986 after a year of much press about the Tiger Fund and its offshore counterpart, the Jaguar Fund. These funds reaped very high returns on a "global macro play" involving an investment in foreign currency call options. These options were purchased with the macroeconomic expectation that the US dollar would decline against the European currencies and the yen after rising sharply over the preceding four years.

The real downfall of the global macro strategy came in the second half of the 1990s, possibly as a result of the success of Soros and others. Many "copycat" participants squeezed the spreads to unprofitable levels when using moderate leverage. Always volatile, macro trading became increasingly difficult as more players crowded into the arena. According to TASS Research, London, investors took back (or were given back) more than US$20 billion in the three years ending June 30, 2002.

In contrast, in the third quarter of 2002, there was a net inflow of US$543 million into global macro hedge funds, indicating that it may once again become a popular strategy among investors.

Global macro investing (also called "macro" or "opportunistic" investing) is a top-down trading approach that uses global, highly liquid commoditised products such as stocks, indices, bonds and currencies in the equity, fixed income and futures markets. Currently, there are more than 50 hedge funds that focus on global macro, collectively representing more than US$30 billion in AUM. The managers of these funds exploit opportunities, not only in products such as stocks, indices and bonds, but also in other securities, including currencies, fixed income and futures markets.

Macro traders predominantly use three non-distinct approaches: feed-back-based, model-based, and information-based. The feedback-based approach emerged out of managed futures operations. These operations became macro funds due to their increased participation in and focus on financial and currency futures and their cash equivalents. An underlying philosophy is that markets are rational 95% of the time. The non-rational 5% is the key to recognising when a financial "bubble" is starting to grow or burst. In essence, the feedback-based approach is market psychology.

The model-based trader is the first to apply new theories from academic research. The information-based approach uses a bottom-up microeconomic aggregation to look at the macroeconomic picture. Gathering certain information at the micro level (like revenue or balance sheet information) can be done more quickly than it takes to release official macro statistics. The information-based trader usually has a battalion of analysts and a wealth of financial information to support his/her trading decisions.

Macro funds take a macro view of investing. They look at the "big picture", identifying the driving forces that move the different markets around the world. Typically, they forecast important trends and events in economies and nations around the globe. Rather than reviewing the financial statements of individual companies, global macro fund managers create investment ideas from a variety of other sources. Usually they have groups of people placed in different markets who continuously investigate ideas. They are well known for placing both directional (convergence) and non-directional (divergence) trades, which can be made across multiple sectors, markets and instruments as macro conditions dictate.

Figure 1 shows the flow of assets for global macro funds since 1994. There has been an almost continuous decline since 1994. Investor interest in the global macro strategy fluctuated from 1994 to 1997. Then, in 1998, it fell by US$1 billion and in 1999 it fell further by US$7.9 billion. In March 1999, the largest outflow of assets was US$3.2 billion. However, that "record" was surpassed in June 2000 with an outflow of US$5.6 billion.

## EFFECT OF MARKET CONDITIONS

The global macro strategy performs above its historical average when:[1]

❏ The yield curve is upward-sloping and is declining.

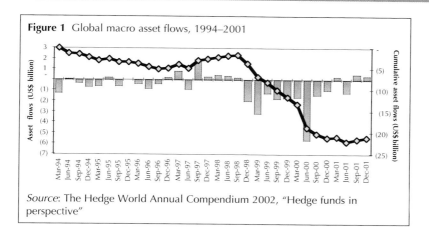

**Figure 1** Global macro asset flows, 1994–2001

*Source*: The Hedge World Annual Compendium 2002, "Hedge funds in perspective"

❑ Credit risk premium is declining.
❑ The short-term interest rate is at a low level and is not increasing.
❑ The long-term rate is at moderate or high levels and is not increasing.
❑ The returns on large-cap and small-cap stocks are high.

The strategy performs substantially below its historical average when:

❑ The yield curve is downward-sloping or there are substantial increases in its slope.
❑ Credit risk premium is increasing.
❑ The short-term interest rate is increasing.
❑ The long-term yield is very low or is increasing by a large amount.
❑ The intra-month volatility of the S&P 500 Index and the implied volatility index are high or are increasing.
❑ The intra-month volatility of bond returns is high or is increasing.
❑ The returns on large-cap and small-cap stocks are negative.

The strategy also appears to be affected when:

❑ The intra-month volatility of the S&P 500 and the implied volatility index are low and not increasing. An analysis comparing the strategy's performance with the volatility of the S&P market gave an overall correlation of 2% for the 1997–2001 period.
❑ The intra-month volatility of bond returns is low to moderate and not changing. The correlation between the strategy and the volatility of Lehman's Bond Investment Grade Index was 1.9% for the 1997–2001 period.

**Table 1** Investors in the global macro strategy

| Investors | (%) |
|---|---|
| Individuals and family offices | 69 |
| Funds of funds | 12 |
| Pensions and retirement | 11 |
| Endowments and foundations | 6 |
| Corporations | 2 |

*Source*: Hennessee Hedge Fund Survey (January 2000)

❑ The correlation between the credit spreads for AAA bonds and BBB rated bonds indicates a −14% for the 1997–2001 period.

## INVESTORS IN THE STRATEGY

Individuals and family offices account for 69% of the investment in global macro funds, which is a higher percentage than for any other fund strategy (see Table 1).

## WELL-KNOWN PLAYERS

The list in Table 2 includes the top global macro funds by AUM covered by the major sources. The Hedge Fund 100 exclusively covers five of the top 25 funds in the strategy, with US$15.5 billion in AUM.

## COVERAGE IN DIFFERENT SOURCES

Table 3 lists the major sources that cover global macro hedge funds. CSFB/Tremont covers the largest number of funds and The Hedge Fund 100 covers the largest AUM.

## DISTRIBUTION OF FUNDS IN THE STRATEGY

Altvest lists a total of 44 funds with US$5.6 billion in assets. As shown in Figure 2, six of these funds have a combined US$3.4 billion in AUM, which

**Table 2** Top global macro funds with more than US$1 billion in AUM

| Rank | Fund | Highest AUM* (US$ billion) |
|---|---|---|
| 1 | Soros Fund | 9.0 |
| 2 | Duquesne Capital Management | 5.0 |
| 3 | Moore Global Investments | 3.8 |
| 4 | Quantum Endowment Fund | 3.1 |
| 5 | Caxton Global Investments | 2.6 |
| 6 | Tudor BVI Global Fund | 2.1 |
| 7 | Essex | 2.0 |
| 8 | Kingate Global Fund, Ltd. – US$ shares | 1.6 |
| 9 | GAMut Investments Inc | 1.1 |
| | **Total** | **30.3** |

*This is the highest AUM for that fund among all the sources.
Highlighted funds are exclusively in The Hedge Fund 100 (June 2002).

*Source*: Altvest, Tuna, HFR, Institutional Investor (June 2002), Directory of Fund of Hedge Funds Investment Vehicles, CMRA Analysis

**Table 3** Coverage of global macro funds by different sources

| Source | Total number of funds | Funds with no AUM data | Total AUM (US$ billion) |
|---|---|---|---|
| The Hedge Fund 100 | 12 | 0 | 23.5 |
| Hennessee | 20 | 4 | 20.5 |
| Altvest | 44 | 14 | 14.8 |
| HFR | 50 | 4 | 12.5 |
| CSFB/Tremont | 71 | 6 | 7.4 |
| Tuna | 46 | 6 | 1.4 |

*Source*: Altvest, HFR, Tuna, Hennessee, Hedge Index, CSFB/Tremont, Institutional Investor (June 2002).

is 62% of the total number of assets. This means that 14% of the funds control over 60% of the assets in the strategy, while the remaining 38 funds have only US$2.1 billion in AUM. It is interesting to note that this is similar to other strategies in the hedge fund space.

### Distribution of funds by quartile of performance

Table 4 shows the performance of 19 global macro hedge funds with five years of performance data (1997–2001). The returns of the first quartile are significantly higher than those of the other three quartiles. In addition, the standard deviation of this quartile is 21.5%. This is significantly higher than the 15.5% and 13.6% standard deviations of the second and third quartiles, respectively. The best performers (first quartile) have only 10% of the assets in the sample. Bear in mind that the publicly available performance data for global macro funds are incomplete as six of the top 10 funds are not listed in any source.

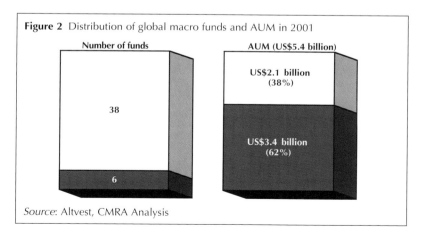

**Figure 2** Distribution of global macro funds and AUM in 2001

Number of funds

38

6

AUM (US$5.4 billion)

US$2.1 billion
(38%)

US$3.4 billion
(62%)

*Source*: Altvest, CMRA Analysis

**Table 4** Distribution of global macro funds by quartiles of five-year performance, 1997–2001

| Return quartiles | Average 1997–2001 equally weighted return (%) | Average 1997–2001 AUM-weighted return (%) | AUM in quartile (US$ billion) | % of total | Average 1997–2001 standard deviation (%) | Sharpe ratio 1997–2001 |
|---|---|---|---|---|---|---|
| 1 | 24.9 | 24.2 | 0.1 | 10 | 21.5 | 0.9 |
| 2 | 12.9 | 12.0 | 0.4 | 28 | 15.5 | 0.7 |
| 3 | 8.4 | 8.5 | 0.6 | 45 | 13.6 | 0.3 |
| 4 | (0.2) | (4.4) | 0.2 | 17 | 26.3 | (0.2) |
| Total | 10.7 | 8.9 | 1.4 | 100 | 19.3 | 0.4 |

*Source*: Altvest, HFR, Tuna, CMRA Analysis based on 18 funds with five-year performance data.

**Table 5** Performance of global macro indices in 2001

| Source | Performance (%) |
|---|---|
| Hennessee | 12.4 |
| CSFB/Tremont | 11.5 |
| Tuna | 11.3 |
| HFR | 10.6 |
| Altvest | 7.2 |
| **Average** | **10.6** |

*Source*: Altvest, HFR, Hennessee, Tuna, CSFB/Tremont, CMRA Analysis

Performance statistics, like other hedge fund statistics, need to be viewed with a skeptical eye. The 2001 performance of the various global macro indices, shown in Table 5, ranged from a high of 12.4% (Hennessee) to a low of 7.2% (Altvest).

The global macro funds included exclusively in The Hedge Fund 100 turned in performances ranging from a high of 31% to a low of 8.2% (see Table 6). A global macro index calculated from the global macro funds listed exclusively in The Hedge Fund 100 would exceed all other global macro indices on both an equally weighted and an AUM-weighted basis (see Table 7).

### Distribution of funds by quartile of AUM

With the distribution of returns of the global macro funds using AUM as a ranking variable, the funds in the second and third quartiles have the highest performance of the group (see Table 8). The largest funds, on the other hand, have the lowest return and the second lowest standard deviation of the sample. Similar to the previous findings, the smallest funds from the third and fourth quartiles have an average volatility of 25.1%, which is almost twice that of the larger funds.

**Table 6**  2001 performance of top 10 global macro funds listed in The Hedge Fund 100

| No. | Fund | AUM (US$ billion) | Performance as of Dec 31, 2001 (%) |
|-----|------|-------------------|-------------------------------------|
| 1 | Moore Global Investments | 3.8 | 10.1 |
| 2 | Caxton Global Investments | 2.6 | 31.0 |
| 3 | Tudor BVI Global Fund | 2.1 | 22.3 |
| 4 | Essex | 2.0 | 31.0 |
| 5 | GAMut Investments | 1.1 | 29.0 |
| 6 | III Fund | 0.8 | 8.5 |
| 7 | III Global | 0.7 | 8.2 |
| 8 | Grossman Global Macro Hedge Fund Ltd. | 0.5 | 24.9 |
| 9 | Aspect Diversified Fund | 0.5 | 15.8 |
| 10 | Tudor Futures | 0.2 | 17.3 |

*Source*: Institutional Investor (June 2002)

**Table 7**  Comparison of 2001 performance of top global macro funds listed in The Hedge Fund 100

| Index | Performance (%) |
|-------|-----------------|
| The Hedge Fund 100 exclusively – equally weighted | 17.5 |
| The Hedge Fund 100 exclusively – AUM-weighted | 14.8 |
| Hennessee | 12.4 |
| CSFB/Tremont | 11.5 |
| Tuna | 11.3 |
| HFR | 10.6 |
| Altvest | 7.2 |

*Source*: Institutional Investor (June 2002), Hennesee, CSFB/Tremont, Tuna, HFR, Altvest, CMRA Analysis

## PERFORMANCE OF THE STRATEGY
### Returns during boom and bust

While the S&P 500 Index outperformed the global macro strategy during the boom years of 1997–2000 by a 7% margin (23% vs 16%), during the bust period the macro strategy outperformed the S&P 500 by a margin of 16% (–14% vs 2%) as shown in Figure 3. These numbers indicate the steadiness of the macro strategy. Though not a "market neutral" strategy in the strictest sense, it is clear that the macro strategy performs in both the boom and bust periods of the general market.

**Table 8** Distribution of global macro hedge funds by quartiles of AUM, 1997–2001

| Return quartiles | Average 1997–2001 equally weighted return (%) | Average 1997–2001 AUM-weighted return (%) | AUM in quartile (US$ billion) | % of total | Average 1997–2001 standard deviation (%) | Sharpe ratio 1997–2001 |
|---|---|---|---|---|---|---|
| 1 | 5.2 | 6.0 | 0.9 | 64 | 13.4 | 0.2 |
| 2 | 14.7 | 14.4 | 0.3 | 24 | 10.8 | 0.9 |
| 3 | 11.4 | 12.1 | 0.1 | 10 | 22.5 | 0.3 |
| 4 | 11.3 | 17.5 | 0.1 | 2 | 27.7 | 0.3 |
| **Total** | **10.7** | **8.9** | **1.4** | **100** | **19.3** | **0.4** |

*Source*: Altvest, HFR, Tuna, CMRA Analysis based on 18 funds with five-year performance data

### Returns from different sources

Tuna's global macro index shows the highest five-year return at 17.0% and Hennessee's shows the lowest at 6.6%. The Sharpe ratios of macro funds are low: they range from 0.9, according to CSFB/Tremont, to 2.9, according to Tuna. Returns and Sharpe ratios are compared in Table 9.

The difference in returns between the various global macro indices can be significant, with the 1998 performance varying by 23.6 points across the different sources, or 3.28 times the average return of the strategy of 7.2%. Similarly, in 1999 the maximum difference in returns was 23.2 points, or 1.6 times the average return of 14.6%. 1998 and 1999 were boom years, whereas 2000 was the worst year, with a performance of 10.5%.

In addition, the Sharpe ratio for the period fluctuates from 0.9 to 2.0 depending on the source. With so many different indicators for the same

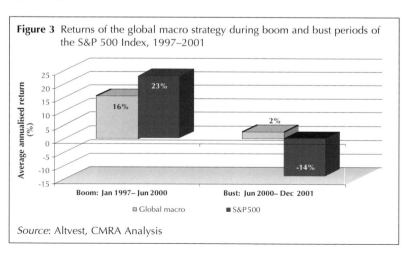

**Figure 3** Returns of the global macro strategy during boom and bust periods of the S&P 500 Index, 1997–2001

*Source*: Altvest, CMRA Analysis

**Table 9** Comparison of global macro indices across different sources, 1997–2001

|  | 1997 | 1998 | 1999 | 2000 | 2001 | 1997–2001 | |
| --- | --- | --- | --- | --- | --- | --- | --- |
|  |  |  |  |  |  | Return | Sharpe ratio |
| Tuna | 26.1 | 20.0 | 12.7 | 12.5 | 14.1 | 17.0 | 2.9 |
| Altvest | 23.6 | 9.4 | 29.0 | 5.6 | 3.3 | 13.7 | 0.9 |
| CSFB/Tremont | 37.1 | (3.6) | 5.8 | 11.7 | 18.4 | 13.1 | 0.9 |
| HFR | 18.8 | 6.2 | 17.6 | 2.0 | 4.9 | 9.7 | 1.3 |
| Hennessee | 17.2 | 4.1 | 7.9 | 5.9 | (1.1) | 6.6 | 1.0 |
| Maximum difference | 19.9 | 23.6 | 23.2 | 10.5 | 19.5 | 10.4 | 2.0 |
| Average | 24.6 | 7.2 | 14.6 | 7.5 | 7.9 | 12.0 | 1.4 |

*Source*: Altvest, Tuna, HFR, CSFB/Tremont, Hennessee, EACM

asset class and such incomplete coverage of the major funds, investors in the global macro strategy should understand the differences between the methods used to calculate the indices (see Chapter 11).

Five of the eight funds in the CSFB/Tremont Global Macro Index were analysed. As Figure 4 shows, the 1997–2001 return ranged from 2.0% to 27.2%. In 2001 the return for each of these funds ranged from 3.5% to 32.5%. Of the five funds analysed, Permal Opportunities Global Fund Ltd., had the highest return, with 21.0% over 1997–2001 and a 2.0% standard deviation. GAMut Investments, Inc. had the lowest return of 10.5% and a 27.2% standard deviation for the same period.

Global macro hedge funds are generally well known in the market place but, compared to other styles, they rank 8 of 14 on a performance basis and 11 of 14 on a Sharpe ratio basis (see Table 10).

**Figure 4** Analysis of five-year returns and standard deviations of constituent funds in the CSFB/Tremont Global Macro Index 1997–2001

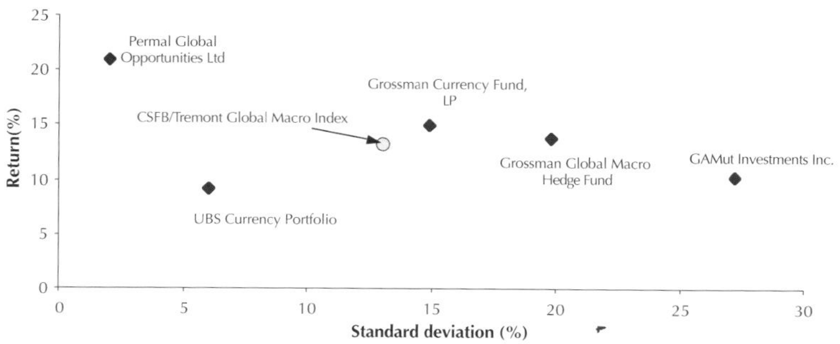

*Source*: CSFB/Tremont, Altvest; CMRA analysis based on five funds in the CSFB/Tremont index

379

### Index performance

As shown in Figure 5, there are significant differences between the returns of the different sources. The maximum difference is 23.6 points for 1998. This could be explained by the methodology and the quality of the information used to create the indices. The comparison across indices shows approximately a 10-point difference in 2000 between CSFB/Tremont and the other indices. CSFB/Tremont is based on nine funds, whereas Altvest includes 50 funds; the two indices have one fund in common. The remaining eight funds in CSFB/Tremont underperformed the remaining funds in Altvest on an equally weighted basis by eight points in 1998. It should be noted that CSFB/Tremont is weighted by AUM, while Altvest (and all the other indices analysed) is equally weighted. This difference in methodology accounts for an additional 10% of the 34% difference between the returns of the indices in 1998. See Chapter 11 for a further discussion of index construction.

### Performance correlations

The global macro strategy has shown some similarities to the equity hedge strategy except that it has also exhibited higher exposure to the bond market as well as systematic trading of forwards, futures and option contracts. For example, the strategy performs very poorly when the slope of the yield curve is increasing and vice versa. Its exposure to the bond market can also be seen from its poor performance when the volatility of bond returns is high. Table 11 shows the correlation of the strategy with the S&P 500 and the Lehman Aggregate Bond Index for the 1997–2001 period.

On a performance basis, the strategy outperformed the S&P 500 Index during the tech crash and the events of September 11, 2001. However, it did not perform as well when compared with the Lehman Bond Composite Index (see Table 12).

Generally, the risk/return properties of the strategy vary significantly, even under slightly different conditions.

For the five-year study period, Altvest showed an average annual return for global macro funds of 13.7% per annum. Along with these impressive

---

**Table 10** Ranking of the global macro strategy against other strategies, 1997–2001

|              | 1997 | 1998 | 1999 | 2000  | 2001  | 1997–2001 | Rank     |
|--------------|------|------|------|-------|-------|-----------|----------|
| Return (%)   | 23.6 | 9.4  | 29.0 | 5.6   | 3.3   | 13.7      | 8 of 14  |
| Sharpe ratio | 1.8  | 0.6  | 2.3  | (0.5) | (0.0) | 0.9       | 11 of 14 |

*Source:* Altvest, CMRA

returns came a relatively high level of risk. With a standard deviation of 9.4%, global macro investments ranked among the highest in the hedge fund industry in terms of volatility. The strategy has a Sharpe ratio of 0.9. In contrast, the eight-year CSFB/Tremont index for global macro showed an average annual return of 13.1%, a volatility of 11.7% and a Sharpe ratio of 0.9. The expected volatility for a macro fund is very high. Macro fund managers continuously combat the problems of excessive risk, systemic

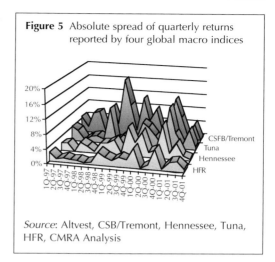

**Figure 5** Absolute spread of quarterly returns reported by four global macro indices

*Source*: Altvest, CSB/Tremont, Hennessee, Tuna, HFR, CMRA Analysis

risk, leverage, stale approaches and complacency. The survival rate of these funds is the lowest among the hedge fund strategies.

**Stress period analysis**

Between February and April 1994, the US and European yield curves shifted upwards by about 150bp after the Federal Reserve unexpectedly raised interest rates. This led to major losses in traditional bond portfolios. Global macro managers suffered most from this unusual interest rate move, with losses of about –10.7%. During this period, global macro ranked 10 of 15 strategies on a risk/reward basis.

The market crisis following the Russian default in August 1998 is also referred to as a "hedge fund crisis". Global macro had a risk/reward (Sharpe ratio) value of 0.1 during the stress period from August to October 1998. During the equity market downturn and the burst of the technology bubble, the global macro strategy returned –1%. Amid the stress periods of the tech crash and the events of September 11, 2001, global macro ranked

**Table 11** Rolling correlations of global macro index performance with S&P 500 and Lehman Aggregate Bond Index, 1997–2001 (%)

|  | 1997 | 1998 | 1999 | 2000 | 2001 |
|---|---|---|---|---|---|
| **Lehman Aggregate Bond Index** | 54.3 | (49.5) | 5.7 | 44.6 | (41.3) |
| **S&P 500 Index** | 79.6 | 87.5 | 63.3 | 53.3 | 76.3 |

*Source*: Altvest, CMRA Analysis

in the bottom third of the strategies. This suggests that, in the 2001–02 period, more funds in the strategy were going net long on the equity market and therefore were more greatly affected by fluctuations in the stock market. Sharpe ratios for these periods are given in Table 13.

In an attempt to understand the different factors that affect the global macro strategy, Lehman Brothers evaluated the strategy in light of three different factors:

1. change in term premia;
2. change in credit spreads; and
3. change in VIX.

The "term premia factor" is an indicator of economic expansion or contraction, which can be applied to any sector strategy. When economies contract, companies are expected to restructure their operations to respond to deteriorating market conditions. Accordingly, it might then be a surprise to find that the strategy is not sensitive to the term premia factor, ranked 15 of 17, as shown in Table 14. The strategy groups all managers who invest in sectors, through pair trading or cross trading, etc. Due to the cyclical nature of the economy, one would expect that sectors in either expansion or contraction mode would be investment candidates for managers in the strategy.

Because the different factors that drive a change in credit spreads are leverage, volatility and changes in the slope of the yield curve, CMRA analysed the exposure of the different strategies to these three factors. As of 2002, global macro was among the most levered strategies, by a factor of 10 or higher in some cases. As a result, the strategy is clearly affected by credit spreads. In addition, the strategies that exploit differences in the

**Table 12** Returns of global macro index during periods of stress (%)

| Russian/LTCM crisis | Tech crash | September 11 |
|---|---|---|
| (2.5) | (1.1) | 25 |

Source: Altvest, CMRA Analysis

**Table 13** Sharpe ratio of global macro indices during periods of stress

| Russian/LTCM crisis | Tech crash | September 11 | Average of absolute Sharpe ratios | Maximum–minimum |
|---|---|---|---|---|
| (0.1) | (0.7) | (0.3) | 0.4 | 1.0 |

Source: Altvest, CMRA Analysis

term structure should be sensitive to changes in credit spread. Global macro is ranked ninth in this regard among the 17 strategies analysed.

An increase in implied volatility is also related to a decrease in the equity markets. It is interesting to note in Table 14 that although many global macro trading strategies would benefit from a change in market volatility, the Lehman model did not pick up this relationship.

### Range of performance

The top 10 performers in Altvest produced very different results over the 1997–2001 period (see Figure 6). The distribution of returns reported indicated that 84.4% of the funds had returns of more than 10%. This is somewhat surprising given the outflow of assets during the same periods, as discussed earlier.

### SHARPE RATIO
### Distribution

The Sharpe ratio is often raised as a major concern for investors in global macro hedge funds. Tables 15 and 16, as well as Figure 7, show the one-year and five-year Sharpe ratios for 2001 and the 1997–2001 period. For 2001, the Sharpe ratio distribution shows that the first quartile had the largest AUM, with US$0.99 billion or 39.3% of the total (see Table 15). This quartile also had a 12.1% average return. The smallest quartile, with 13.8% of the total AUM, had an average return of –10.9%. A comparison of the overall average return of 4.1% for the 46 funds analysed in 2001 with the five-year average return of 10.7% suggests that 2001 was a difficult year for global macro hedge funds.

An analysis of the Sharpe ratio for global macro funds for the period 1997–2001 indicates that the third quartile was the largest, with 40% of the assets for the strategy. The second quartile had a standard deviation of 13.0%, the lowest of the quartiles. The third and fourth quartiles had the lowest returns and the largest standard deviations. It is important to note that of the 18 funds analysed, the funds in the last two quartiles have 57% of the assets.

---

**Table 14** Sensitivity of the global macro strategy to factors from Lehman's multivariate model

| Factor | Coefficient | Rank |
|---|---|---|
| Change in credit spread | 0.040 | 9 of 17 |
| Change in implied volatility | (0.200) | 11 of 17 |
| Change in term premia | 0.003 | 15 of 17 |

*Source*: Lehman Brothers Understanding Hedge Fund Performance

---

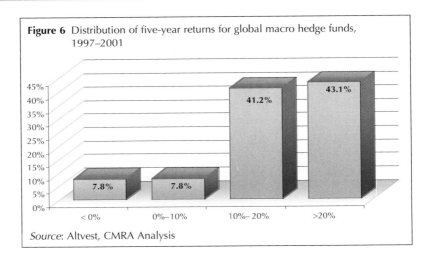

**Figure 6** Distribution of five-year returns for global macro hedge funds, 1997–2001

*Source*: Altvest, CMRA Analysis

As shown in Figure 7, the one-year Sharpe ratios of most of the funds (25 funds, or 55% of the 45 funds analysed) are in the 0.0 to 0.2 range. The figure also shows 12 funds (or 27%) with a negative one-year Sharpe ratio. This contrasts significantly with the five-year data, where the largest number of funds, seven of the 18 analysed (or 37%), had a Sharpe ratio higher than 0.5 and four funds (or 22%) had negative Sharpe ratios.

Most of the funds with negative performances represent from 9.2% to 13.8% of AUM. The smallest funds in the global macro strategy had the lowest Sharpe ratio, the highest volatility and the lowest returns, in contrast to the larger, more established funds. Sharpe ratios can be quite misleading for funds trading in options. Often, funds that short out-of-the-money options can enhance their short-term return. The monthly return can be evened out, resulting in a higher Sharpe ratio. The risks of using

**Table 15** Distribution of global macro hedge funds in 2001 by Sharpe ratio

| Sharpe ratio quartiles | AUM in quartile (US$ billion) | % of total AUM | Average 2001 return (%) |
|---|---|---|---|
| 1 | 1.0 | 39.3 | 12.1 |
| 2 | 0.6 | 24.4 | 3.5 |
| 3 | 0.6 | 22.4 | 0.1 |
| 4 | 0.3 | 13.8 | (10.9) |
| **Total** | **2.5** | **100.0** | **4.1** |

*Source*: Altvest, CMRA Analysis based on 46 funds

**Table 16** Distribution of global macro hedge funds by quartiles of Sharpe ratio, 1997–2001

| Sharpe ratio quartiles | Average 1997–2001 equally weighted return (%) | Average 1997–2001 AUM-weighted return (%) | AUM in quartile (US$ billion) | % of total | Average 1997–2001 standard deviation (%) | Sharpe ratio 1997–2001 |
|---|---|---|---|---|---|---|
| 1 | 20.7 | 15.6 | 0.2 | 17 | 16.0 | 1.0 |
| 2 | 15.9 | 13.9 | 0.4 | 27 | 13.0 | 0.8 |
| 3 | 9.4 | 8.4 | 0.6 | 40 | 20.0 | 0.2 |
| 4 | (0.2) | (4.4) | 0.2 | 17 | 26.3 | (0.2) |
| **Total** | **10.7** | **8.9** | **1.4** | **100** | **19.3** | **0.4** |

*Source*: Altvest, HFR, Tuna, CMRA Analysis based on 18 funds with five-year performance data

optionality to improve overall fund returns can bring additional risks to the portfolio.

### Information ratio
When comparing the returns of onshore and offshore funds in a global macro strategy, investors often look for different performance-related factors. Similar funds that start in different market environments could return completely different results. There is no significant difference between the returns of funds in the strategy that differ merely by their inception. The information ratio for global macro funds is among the lowest of the strategies (see Figure 8). This suggests that the returns over the long run have been generally lower than those of other strategies. Part

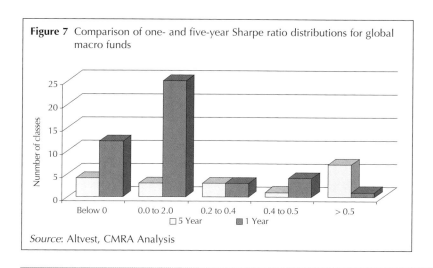

**Figure 7** Comparison of one- and five-year Sharpe ratio distributions for global macro funds

*Source*: Altvest, CMRA Analysis

385

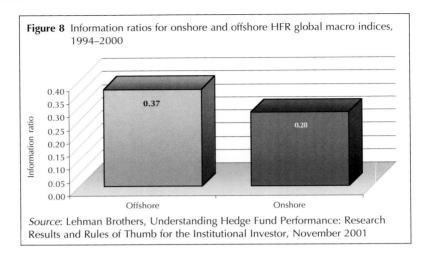

**Figure 8** Information ratios for onshore and offshore HFR global macro indices, 1994–2000

*Source*: Lehman Brothers, Understanding Hedge Fund Performance: Research Results and Rules of Thumb for the Institutional Investor, November 2001

of the reason is that the big equity bull market of the 1990s resulted in equity strategies outperforming global macro strategies.

## LEVERAGE

Many hedge funds rely on leverage. As with most other strategies, if not all, it has a magnifying effect – it expands small profit opportunities into larger ones and small losses into larger losses. Summary leverage data for global macro funds for 2002 are given in Table 17.

Global macro funds tend to employ a significant degree of leverage, averaging a ratio of US$1.92 AUM for each dollar of capital, ranging all the way up to US$21 AUM for each dollar of capital. Actual leverage is probably even greater because it is rare that leverage will be applied to both sides of offsetting bets in the global macro strategy. Historically, the strategy has an average leverage of 1.9, with a high of 2.2 in 1998 and a low of 1.7 in 2001 (see Table 18).

Almost 90% of the global macro hedge funds reporting to Altvest use leverage (see Figure 9). 71% use a leverage lower than 2.0, and another 17% leverage their positions by more than 2.0.

Analysis of global macro leverage for the 1997–2001 period indicates that the first quartile (the group with the lowest leverage) had US$4.3 billion in AUM, while the last quartile had US$8.4 billion in AUM (see Table 19). It appears that, on average, the larger funds have a higher leverage than the smaller funds but, due to the poor quality of the data, this finding might be unreliable.

Because leverage is an important factor that should be considered to better understand the returns of the strategy, CMRA performed an

**Table 17** Financial leverage of global macro funds in 2002

| Minimum | Average | Maximum | Rank |
|---------|---------|---------|------|
| 1.0 | 1.9 | 21.0 | 4 of 14 |

*Source*: Altvest, CMRA Analysis

**Table 18** Historical average leverage of global macro hedge funds, 1997–2001

| | | | | | 1997–2001 | | |
|------|------|------|------|------|---------|---------|---------|
| 1997 | 1998 | 1999 | 2000 | 2001 | Average | Maximum | Minimum |
| 2.1 | 2.2 | 1.7 | 1.8 | 1.7 | 1.9 | 2.2 | 1.7 |

*Source*: Altvest, CMRA Analysis

analysis of 13 funds with available five-year historical leverage data and five-year performance data. The results are presented in Table 20. The nearly eight-point difference between the levered and delevered five-year returns is evidence of the potential magnifying effect of leverage in the strategy.

## RISK MEASUREMENT
Global macro funds are subject to an array of risks including market risk, volatility, leverage, liquidity, foreign debt risk, product complexity and counterparty risk (see Figure 10). The following discussion is intended to promote an understanding of the factors that drive the strategy.

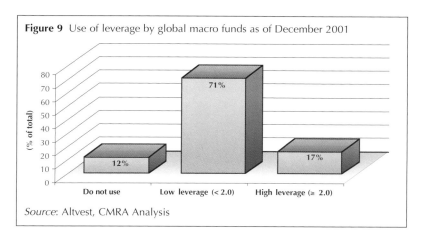

**Figure 9** Use of leverage by global macro funds as of December 2001

*Source*: Altvest, CMRA Analysis

**Table 19** Distribution of global macro funds by quartiles of leverage, 1997–2001

| Leverage quartiles | Minimum leverage in quartile | Maximum leverage in quartile | Average leverage in quartile | Median leverage in quartile | Total AUM in quartile (US$ billion) | % of total AUM |
|---|---|---|---|---|---|---|
| 1 | 0.0 | 1.0 | 0.8 | 0.9 | 4.3 | 18.7 |
| 2 | 1.0 | 1.2 | 1.1 | 1.1 | 6.1 | 26.4 |
| 3 | 1.2 | 2.0 | 1.5 | 1.5 | 4.3 | 18.5 |
| 4 | 0.5 | 16.7 | 6.4 | 2.8 | 8.4 | 36.3 |
| **Total** | **0.0** | **167.0** | **1.9** | **1.3** | **23.1** | **100.0** |

*Source*: Altvest, CMRA Analysis based on 89 funds with five years of leverage data

**Table 20** Summary of levered and delevered performance of global macro funds, 1997–2001 (%)

| | Maximum return | Minimum return | Average return | Maximum delevered return | Minimum delevered return | Average delevered return | Difference in returns levered vs delevered |
|---|---|---|---|---|---|---|---|
| **1997–2001** | 51.9 | 1.2 | 16.8 | 29.5 | 0.6 | 8.9 | 7.9 |
| **2001** | 139.0 | (64.0) | 5.7 | 69.5 | (48.5) | 2.2 | (0.3) |

*Source*: Altvest, CMRA Analysis

## Market risk

Some of the challenges associated with the global macro strategy arise from the lack of an "information edge". For the most part, everybody is informed in real time of global developments and research is easier to come by through modern financial media. This makes it extremely difficult for any one company to get important statistics that would dictate a new market trend. As the average credit quality has fallen, the best global macro managers evaluate these changing macro-driven factors and respond through diversification, hedging away some of the unwanted risks. Market risk often comes in the form of event risk, ie, the risk of macroeconomic and market developments coming out differently than expected by the manager. This includes political developments, sudden currency moves that are often related to regime changes, sudden earnings revisions by key companies, important merger announcements or key firms' management changes.

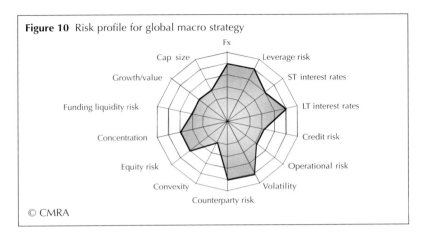

**Figure 10** Risk profile for global macro strategy

© CMRA

### Volatility risk

Investing in markets throughout the world requires investment in highly volatile markets. Such volatility may lead to substantial risks and returns that are generally much larger than in the case of equity or fixed income investments. Currencies, commodity price shifts and products with uncertain cashflows are among the biggest factors of uncertainty that a global macro manager must face. During a crisis, not only can the level of volatility change dramatically, but the smile and shape of the volatility term structure can also change significantly. Figures 11 and 12 illustrate this using currency volatilities during the European exchange rate mechanism (ERM) crisis in 1992.

### Leverage risk

Accounts traded at greater than standard leverage will experience greater losses and volatility as well as a greater potential for profit.

### Liquidity risk

Traded securities may at times be illiquid. Certain exchanges do not permit the trading of particular securities at prices fluctuating beyond certain set limits during a single day's trading. This could prevent the manager from liquidating unfavorable positions promptly and subject clients to substantial losses.

### Foreign debt risk

Unlike the trading of US debt on US exchanges, trading in foreign debt on non-US exchanges is far less neutrally regulated and may be subject to greater risks. For example, some non-US exchanges are "principals' markets" in which no common clearing facility exists and a trader has to rely solely on the broker for performance of the contract.

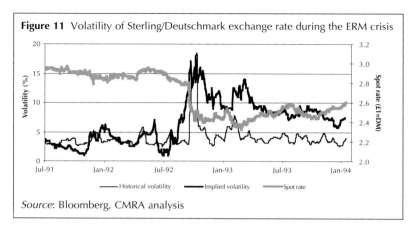

**Figure 11** Volatility of Sterling/Deutschmark exchange rate during the ERM crisis

*Source*: Bloomberg, CMRA analysis

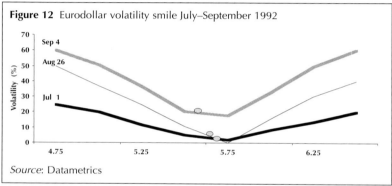

**Figure 12** Eurodollar volatility smile July–September 1992

*Source*: Datametrics

### Product complexity risk

Trading across many different markets, sectors and geographies around the world with many different kinds of products is a very difficult task. Most global macro managers have to rely on incomplete information to make investment decisions on instruments whose associated risks are difficult to model.

### Counterparty risk

OTC markets, including foreign markets, offer less protection against defaults in trading than is available when trading occurs on an exchange. Contracts are not guaranteed by an exchange or clearing house, and a non-settlement or default on the contract by the counterparty could result in the loss of unrealised profits or force the hedge fund manager to cover any commitments to purchase and sell at the current market price.

## VALUE-AT-RISK
### Overview
As Table 21 indicates, the global macro strategy's VAR ranked third among the 10 strategies analysed.

### Examples
To investigate the impact of commodities on a portfolio, CMRA created six sample portfolios and calculated their VARs. Details of the portfolios are given in Table 22. This analysis is helpful for understanding the benefits of having a diversified portfolio of commodities. One key characteristic of these portfolios is that CMRA did not apply any of the hedging techniques that are commonly supported by hedge fund managers in the strategy.

The results, presented in Table 23, suggest that diversification helps to reduce VAR. The best example of this is exhibited by the combination of Portfolios 1 and 3. The resulting VAR is –1.21%, which is lower than the expected average of the two portfolios combined (–2.8%).

CMRA also prepared a cross-correlation table for three managed futures contracts as specified in the sample portfolios. Table 24 shows the cross-correlations between the contracts themselves and between the contracts and the major market indices (eg, the S&P 500 Index and the Lehman Brothers Bond Investment Grade Index). The cross-correlations found across the different portfolios are very low.

**Table 21** Average VAR for global macro strategy (%)

| 1997 | 1998 | 1999 | 2000 | Average 1997–2000 | Rank |
|------|------|------|------|-------------------|------|
| 11.4 | 11.0 | 10.2 | 9.8 | 10.6 | 3 of 10 |

*Source*: Assessing Market Risk for Hedge Funds and Hedge Funds Portfolios FAME, March 2001 – Research Paper No. 24, Francois-Serge Lhabitant

**Table 22** Compositions of diversified global macro portfolios

| Portfolio | Sectors | Number of securities in portfolio |
|-----------|---------|-----------------------------------|
| 1 | Global securities | 7 |
| 2 | Global commodities | 12 |
| 3 | Interest rates | 8 |
| 4 | Securities + commodities | 15 |
| 5 | Securities + interest rates | 5 |
| 6 | Securities + commodities + interest rates | 20 |

*Source*: Bloomberg, CMRA Analysis

**Table 23** Daily VAR with 95% confidence level for diversified global macro portfolios

| Portfolios | Sectors | Daily VAR (%) |
|---|---|---|
| 1 | Global securities | (2.3) |
| 2 | Global commodities | (2.8) |
| 3 | Interest rates | (3.3) |
| 4 | Securities + commodities | (2.8) |
| 5 | Securities + interest rates | (1.2) |
| 6 | Securities + commodities + interest rates | (2.8) |

*Source*: Bloomberg, CMRA Analysis

The components of the different portfolios are not correlated with each other, which would greatly enhance the diversification capabilities of the strategy.

All fund managers go through periods when the performance of their funds is relatively poor. Risk management is principally about ensuring that funds are run in such a way that periods of poor performance do not affect their ability to earn the appropriate level of returns. Risk budgeting is a method of allocating an allowable measure of loss to different aspects of the investment process and then to monitor these measures. As indicated above, VAR measures are typically restricted to a portfolio as a whole, whereas risk budgeting moves down into a single asset class or even a single market.

In a global macro fund, the typical risk budgeting question relates to the weightings that are chosen for each sector traded and how this produces an overall risk for the portfolio. As an example, we will consider the portfolio detailed in Table 25.

Table 25 gives the standard deviation of daily returns for each sector, and if these were just added together the overall portfolio would have a standard deviation of 2.62%. However, the actual standard deviation of daily returns is 1.02%, showing that the range of markets traded offers good diversification benefits.

The highest correlation in the overall sector position defined in Table 25 is that between the equity markets and the interest rates. The question is how large a position should be taken in each market in order to generate the desired sector risk as part of the overall risk portfolio. Figure 13 shows how the volatility increased as the Crude Oil Index began to rise during 1999. It could be argued that this increase in volatility per contract should provide pressure for the types and sizes of contracts being traded in the market. Consequently, we should have expected the number of crude oil contracts traded not to go up during this period. Similar behaviour would have been expected during September 2001, where we can see a sharp jump in volatility, which again should have resulted in a reduction of the crude oil positions. One can then argue that changes in sector volatility and the resulting contribution that each sector makes to the fund's overall result should be observed continuously to match the risk budget in any given period.

**Stress tests**
Due to their potential diversity, global macro funds require a wide-ranging set of stress tests:

❏ Term structure and yield curve levels and shapes.
❏ Term structure and relationship of volatility.
❏ Price shifts in equities, sectors and indices.
❏ Currency and commodity price shifts.
❏ Spreads and basis relationships.
❏ Yield curve assumptions.
❏ Pricing models.
❏ VAR.
❏ Products with uncertain cashflows.
❏ Product complexity.
❏ Difficult-to-model risks.
❏ Concentrations.
❏ Correlations.
❏ Credit components of securities.
❏ Volatility of credit spreads.
❏ Default assumptions.
❏ Leverage.
❏ Liquidity.

**LEVEL OF TRANSPARENCY**
Global macro managers are generally unwilling to reveal their positions, especially their short positions, to anyone – and understandably so. A survey conducted in 2000 found that only 13% of global macro managers indicated that they would provide no transparency. In

**Table 24** Cross-correlations between diversified global macro portfolios (%)

| | Global securities | Global commodities | Interest rate | Securities + commodities | Securities + interest rate | Securities + commodities + interest rate |
|---|---|---|---|---|---|---|
| Global securities | 100 | (2) | (18) | (22) | (36) | (34) |
| Global commodities | (2) | 100 | (9) | (29) | (5) | (4) |
| Interest rate | (18) | (9) | 100 | 13 | 22 | 22 |
| Securities + commodities | (22) | (29) | 13 | 100 | 13 | (6) |
| Securities + interest rate | (36) | (5) | 22 | 13 | 100 | (6) |
| Securities + commodities + interest rate | (34) | (4) | 22 | (6) | (6) | 100 |

*Source*: Bloomberg, CMRA Analysis

**Table 25** Risk budgeting in a diversified global macro portfolio

| Sector | Risk budget | Standard deviation of daily returns (%) |
| --- | --- | --- |
| Equity | 25 | 0.5 |
| Interest rates | 20 | 0.6 |
| Currencies | 15 | 0.4 |
| Agricultural commodities | 18 | 0.6 |
| Metals | 10 | 0.3 |
| Energy | 12 | 0.4 |
| **Total** | **100** | **1.0** |

*Source*: Risk Budgeting for Individual Hedge Funds – A Case Study by Jonathan Riley, RA Asset Management Ltd

contrast, however, 38% of those surveyed said they would provide full disclosure, and 25% would disclose their key positions (see Table 26).

## DUE DILIGENCE QUESTIONS

The factors that drive performance in the strategy must be understood. The investor should seek analytical support in areas such as exposure to long-term interest rates, scenario analysis, the impact of inflationary pressures, trade deficit scenarios, etc. With respect to the overall decision-making process, the fund should be able to demonstrate its ability to replicate and grow its investment model. As outlined in most due diligence questionnaires, one should look for established procedures that drive the investment process. Most importantly, these procedures must be able to recover the process when there is a major market downturn.

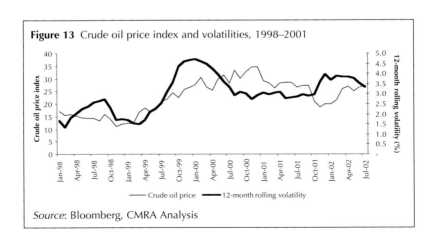

**Figure 13** Crude oil price index and volatilities, 1998–2001

*Source*: Bloomberg, CMRA Analysis

It is important to understand the fund's proprietary techniques to reduce the size of positions in markets where significant gains have been generated in an effort to protect profit from sudden trend reversals. Individual position size should also be analysed, paying close attention to correlation, liquidity and volatility. Risk management reports, like VAR, and their frequency should be evaluated.

The following list summarises some general due diligence questions for the global macro strategy.

❏ What are your unique, competitive advantages?
❏ How do you ensure the separation of front and back office?
❏ Who marks the book to market? Who reviews? Who has market authority and override? Who receives reports regarding overrides?
❏ Do you have written policies and procedures? May I see them?
❏ How do you manage risk?
❏ Do you have a designated risk manager?
❏ Do you include risk limits in your guidelines?
❏ If someone breaches his/her limits, what happens?
❏ What are your backup and recovery plans? Have they ever been tested? Where are copies of the plans kept?
❏ How do you define leverage? What is the maximum leverage you are allowed? How often are you at or near the maximum? If you were at maximum leverage and your prime broker doubled your haircuts, how much would that cost the fund?
❏ How much of your borrowing is overnight? Short term? Long term? How has that changed over the past 12 months?
❏ Do you have a risk conscious culture? What defines your culture?
❏ What is your attitude towards transparency?
❏ Since you trade in multiple time zones, how do you calculate your NAV?

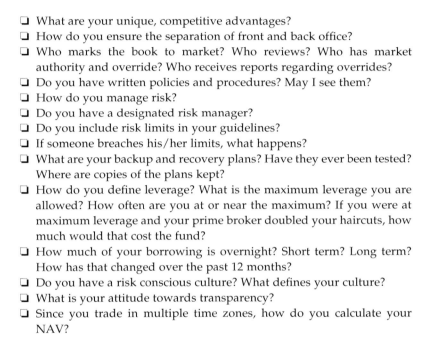

**Table 26** Transparency offered to investors by managers of global macro funds (%)

| | Overall level of transparency | | | Positions disclosed to investors | |
|---|---|---|---|---|---|
| Performance | Key positions | View entire portfolio | No transparency | Key long positions | Key short positions |
| N/A | N/A | 38 | 13 | 25 | 25 |

*Source*: Alternative Investment News, September 2000

## DATA AND NAV ISSUES

Global macro funds often use a number of proprietary computerised mathematical models, coupled with management experience in the securities and futures industries, to administer the implementation of systematic trading programmes in equity, global fixed income, foreign exchange and other financial instruments.

## PUBLICLY DISCLOSED PROBLEMS

### January 1994, Argonaut Capital Partners

The performance of Argonaut Capital Partners, a New York-based macro hedge fund managed by David Gerstenhaber and Barry Bausano (both formerly of Tiger Management), fell 28% between January and July 1994. In addition, Bausano resigned in August 1994 for "personal reasons." Both events resulted in investors withdrawing their money from the fund.[2] Of the initial US$400 million, US$110 million was lost and US$225 million was returned to investors, leaving US$65 million in the fund. The investors were obviously not willing to bear further market risk in addition to the change of manager.

### August 1998, Long Term Capital Management (LTCM)

Technically, LTCM, was an arbitrage operation that made huge macro bets. Its approach was based on the sound theory that assets all over the world are usually under- or overvalued but always ultimately seek their true values. Although the basic idea is valid, LTCM implemented it with such extreme leverage that even small, unpredictable discontinuities had the potential to greatly affect the capital base of the fund. LTCM used extraordinarily sophisticated mathematical computer models to predict and mitigate risks but, in August 1998, an unexpected macro-defying non-linearity occurred that wildly exceeded the parameters of the models: Russia defaulted on its sovereign debt and liquidity around the globe began to dry up rapidly as derivative positions were hastily unwound. LTCM's financial models indicated that the fund should not expect to lose more than US$50 million of capital in a given day, but it was soon losing US$100 million a day. Four days after the Russian default, LCTM's initial US$3 billion capital base lost another US$500 million in a single trading day alone!

### January 2000, Quantum Fund

George Soros' Quantum Fund lost US$600 million, or about 6% of its AUM, with the fall off in technology issues in early 2000.[3] The fund had ended 1999 with a return of 35%, after having been down as much as 19% earlier in the year when a mid-year move into the technology arena was credited for the turnaround. Later, when chief trader Stanley Drucken-miller stepped aside, Quantum was off 22%.

## March 2000, Jaguar Fund

In March 2000, Julian Robertson's Tiger Management LLC liquidated investments in its Jaguar Fund, blaming "irrational markets" for the fund's poor performance. Robertson maintained a policy of value investing, but the fund had suffered a string of losing months since mid-1998, with the combined impact of losses and redemptions greatly reducing the fund's asset base.

## July 2000, Orthagonal Capital Management

In July 2000, MarHedge reported, "With the blush off the global macro rose – Robertson and Soros *q.v.* – London-based Orthogonal Capital Management raised only $10 million by its initial closing on July 3 – far short of the $100 million it had hoped to raise. The new shop, unbashedly global macro, is run by Peter Ahl and Suresh Wadwani, formerly proprietary traders at Barclays Capital and Goldman Sachs. But the company's third principal, Peter Chen, remains confident: Orthogonal has firm indications that more commitments will come in the next two to three months, he said".[4]

## September 2000

Scott Bessent (formerly with Soros Fund Management), after establishing his own firm by raising more than US$1.0 billion for the new fund he was launching, ended plans for a global macro fund because of the administrative difficulties it posed.[5]

Many of the macro funds that have disbanded or scaled back following huge losses – Steinhardt Partners, Odyssey Partners, Soros Fund Management and Tiger Management – were all led by stock pickers. Most of the surviving macro players – Bacon, Jones, Kovner and Trout – originally came from the futures business.[6]

1 Lehman Brothers. "Understanding Hedge Fund Performance: Research Results and Rules of Thumb for the Institutional Investor," November 2001.
2 Zewig, P., 1997, *Business Week*, "The Rich get Richer but the Hedge Fund Players still Trail the S&P", August 25.
3 Mitchell, P., 2000, *Wall Street Journal*, "Soro's Quantum Embraces Technology Feels Squeeze", January 6.
4 Http://www.marhedge.com, Headlines, July 2000.
5 Http://www.marhedge.com, Headlines, September 2000.
6 Atlas, R., 2000, "Macro Macro Man", *Institutional Investor Magazine*, International Edition, July 1.

# 18

# Managed Futures

## DESCRIPTION OF THE STRATEGY

"Managed futures" describes a strategy implemented by professional money managers known as commodity trading advisors (CTAs) who manage client assets on a discretionary basis using global futures and options markets as an investment medium. Investors are attracted to CTAs because they are capable of providing direct exposure to international financial and non-financial asset sectors while offering a means to gain exposure to risk/return patterns that are not accessible in traditional stock and bond portfolios. These managers exploit the low volatility characteristic of the strategy to enhance portfolio returns and participate in a wide variety of new financial products not available in economic environments in which traditional stock and bond investments offer limited opportunities.

Within the group of futures strategies, the industry distinguishes between opportunistic (or active) strategies and passive strategies. Opportunistic futures strategies are characterised by either discretionary trading based on long-term fundamentals and short-term information or proprietary model-based techniques such as trend following, counter-trend trading, spread trading and a variety of others. Passive strategies, in contrast, aim to systematically capture returns available by undertaking professional hedging activities in futures markets. The passive character expresses itself through very low trading frequency and the lack of complex modelling. The significant increase in the contracts available on the futures markets and these markets' increasingly global nature have driven the growth of managed futures. Together, these two factors have expanded the scope of investment opportunities to encompass stock indices, debt instruments, currencies and options as well as conventional commodities.

Managed futures funds seek capital appreciation from movements in the value of futures contracts or other exchange-traded instruments. The strategy generally participates in all major commodities markets – equities, fixed income, currencies, metals, energies and agriculturals – but rarely at the same time. Futures contracts are simply contracts for future delivery of either a financial or physical asset. For example, profits are made by identifying the future supply and demand for orange juice, the trend in the future price of gold, the future movements in the yield curve, or the direction of global stock indices. Managed futures funds rarely move with the general stock market or even with other hedge fund strategies.

Most managed futures managers actively trade worldwide on a 24-hour basis in the equity, fixed income, currency and commodity markets. They use options, futures, forwards and other financial instruments. They also use leverage to amplify the impact of market moves. Most offer their clients systematic and discretionary CTA trading programmes in addition to other proprietary programmes such as long/short equity or global macro. Traditionally, the trading systems utilised by the managers in the strategy rely primarily on technical rather than fundamental information as the basis for their trading decisions. While many use black box computer models to identify trading opportunities, other managers use discretion based on experience. The least adventurous managers use strict trading rules in conjunction with computer models. Their systems are based on the expectation that they can successfully anticipate market events over time using quantitative mathematical models to determine their trading activities rather than attempting to forecast price trends using a subjective analysis of supply and demand.

The managed futures strategy is primarily long term and is designed to participate selectively in profit opportunities that can occur during periods of sustained price trends in a diverse number of US and international markets. The primary objective is to establish positions in markets where price volatility indicates that a potential trend in prices is occurring. The hedge fund manager then mathematically analyses the recent trading characteristics of each market and statistically compares such characteristics to the long-term historical trading pattern of the particular market. These analyses should help the manager benefit from sustained price trends while reducing risk and volatility exposure.

## EFFECT OF MARKET CONDITIONS

The managed futures strategy performs above its historical average when:

❏ The yield curve is moderately upward-sloping and there are no substantial increases or decreases in its slope.
❏ The intra-month volatility of the S&P 500 Index and the implied volatility index are at moderate levels and are not increasing.
❏ Commodity prices are high.

Managed futures perform substantially below historical average when:

❏ The yield curve is downward sloping and there are substantial increases in its slope.
❏ The short-term rate is increasing or decreasing by a substantial amount.

❑ Commodity prices are high.
❑ The intra-month volatility of the S&P 500 Index and the implied volatility index are high or are increasing.
❑ Commodities prices are depressed.

## WELL KNOWN PLAYERS

The largest managed funds in the strategy by AUM covered by the major sources include those listed in Table 1.

The Hedge Fund 100 covers four of the top 25 managed futures funds with US$1.6 billion in AUM, which represents 15.8% of the US$10.1 billion total. In addition, of the top 25 funds, two funds with US$1.3 billion in AUM (or 10.8% of the total) are among the most popular holdings of funds of funds.

## COVERAGE IN DIFFERENT SOURCES

CSFB/Tremont covers the largest number of managed futures funds, but Altvest covers greater AUM (see Table 2).

---

**Table 1** Top managed futures funds with more than US$1 billion in AUM (all sources)

| Rank | Fund | Highest AUM* (US$ billion) |
|------|------|---------------------------|
| 1 | Man Investment Products (London, UK) | 4.0 |
| 2 | Campbell Strategic Allocation Fund | 1.2 |
| 3 | GAMut | 1.1 |
| | **Total** | **6.3** |

*This is the highest AUM for that fund amongst all the sources.

*Source*: Altvest, Tuna, HFR, Institutional Investor (June 2002), Directory of Fund of Hedge Funds Investment Vehicles

---

**Table 2** Coverage of managed futures funds by different sources

| Source | Total number of funds | Funds with no AUM data | Total AUM (US$ billion) |
|--------|-----------------------|------------------------|-------------------------|
| Altvest | 129 | 15 | 6.6 |
| CSFB/Tremont | 164 | N/A | 6.5 |
| The Hedge Fund 100 | 3 | N/A | 4.7 |
| Tuna | 92 | 11 | 3.1 |
| HFR | 45 | 0 | 2.5 |

*Source*: Altvest, HFR, Tuna, CSFB/Tremont, Institutional Investor (June 2002)

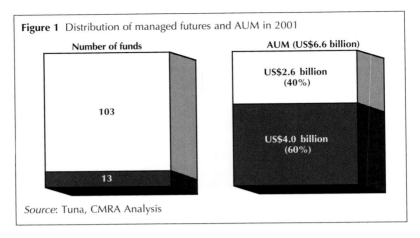

**Figure 1** Distribution of managed futures and AUM in 2001

Number of funds

103

13

AUM (US$6.6 billion)

US$2.6 billion
(40%)

US$4.0 billion
(60%)

*Source*: Tuna, CMRA Analysis

There are no managed futures funds in The Hedge Fund 100 that are not included in the other sources; however, these funds have greater AUM than all the managed futures covered by HFR and Tuna, which consist of funds worth US$3.1 billion and US$2.5 billion, respectively.

## DISTRIBUTION OF FUNDS IN THE STRATEGY

As of December 2001, 13 managed futures funds comprised an overall AUM of US$4.0 billion representing 60% of the US$6.6 billion total in AUM (see Figure 1).

### Distribution of funds by quartile of performance

As shown in Table 3, the first quartile of funds in the strategy had an average five-year returns performance of 20% and US$3.2 billion in assets. The two lowest quartiles had a combined average performance of 3% and only US$0.5 billion in assets, or 12% of the total AUM analysed. The funds

**Table 3** Distribution of managed futures funds by quartiles of five-year performance, 1997–2001

| Return quartiles | Average 1997–2001 equally weighted return (%) | Average 1997–2001 AUM-weighted return (%) | AUM in quartile (US$ billion) | % of total | Average 1997–2001 standard deviation (%) | Sharpe ratio 1997–2001 |
|---|---|---|---|---|---|---|
| 1 | 20.0 | 24.1 | 3.2 | 79 | 24.6 | 0.8 |
| 2 | 11.2 | 11.4 | 0.4 | 10 | 16.2 | 0.4 |
| 3 | 6.9 | 7.8 | 0.3 | 7 | 17.2 | 0.2 |
| 4 | (0.2) | (2.0) | 0.2 | 5 | 10.4 | (0.7) |
| Total | 9.5 | 20.5 | 4.1 | 100 | 22.6 | 0.7 |

*Source*: Altvest, CMRA Analysis based on 60 funds with five-year performance data.

**Table 4** Distribution of managed futures hedge funds by quartiles of AUM, 1997–2001

| AUM quartiles | Average 1997–2001 equally weighted return (%) | Average 1997–2001 AUM-weighted return (%) | AUM in quartile (US$ billion) | % of total | Average 1997–2001 standard deviation (%) | Sharpe ratio 1997–2001 |
|---|---|---|---|---|---|---|
| 1 | 17.0 | 21.7 | 3.6 | 86 | 23.9 | 0.7 |
| 2 | 12.9 | 14.6 | 0.4 | 10 | 15.6 | 0.6 |
| 3 | 7.7 | 9.2 | 0.1 | 3 | 13.1 | 0.3 |
| 4 | 6.2 | 10.5 | 0.0 | 0 | 21.6 | 0.3 |
| Total | 10.9 | 20.5 | 4.1 | 100 | 22.6 | 0.7 |

*Source*: Altvest, CMRA Analysis based on 60 funds with five-year performance data.

in the first quartile, however, had a volatility of 24.6%, which is the highest of all four quartiles.

### Distribution of funds by quartile of AUM

The largest managed futures funds turned in the best performance on both an equally weighted and an AUM-weighted basis (see Table 4). Again, the five-year returns of the largest funds had the highest standard deviation of 23.9%.

The smallest funds (third and fourth quartiles) had the lowest average combined performance and the lowest standard deviation. The AUM of managed futures funds increased at an average annualised rate of 45% between 1994 and 2001. In addition, the strategy recorded an average performance of 16% from 1997 to 2001.

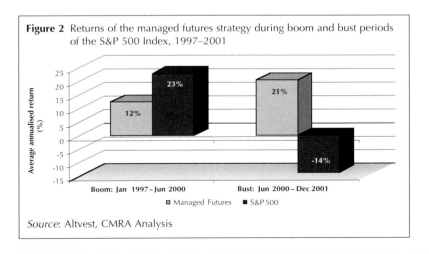

**Figure 2** Returns of the managed futures strategy during boom and bust periods of the S&P 500 Index, 1997–2001

*Source*: Altvest, CMRA Analysis

## PERFORMANCE OF THE STRATEGY
### Returns during boom and bust
As shown in Figure 2, managed futures funds outperformed the S&P 500 Index during both boom and bust periods. This is a strong indicator of the continuous flow of assets into the strategy since the early 1990s.

### Returns from different sources
Differences between the returns reported by the various managed futures indices can be significant, with the 1997 performance varying by 19.8 points across the different sources, or 1.5 times the average return of the strategy of 13.4%. Similarly, in 2001 the maximum difference in returns was 15.5, or 1.8 times the average return of 8.2%. Comparative data for the period are given in Table 5.

### Index performance
The constituents of an index can vary substantially in performance. CMRA analysed 12 of the 31 funds in the CSFB/Tremont Managed Futures Index (see Figure 3). The 2001 return for these funds ranged from –29.0% to 55.0% and the 1997–2001 return ranged from 0.8% to 29.2%. Of the 12 funds analysed, Quadriga AG had the highest five-year return: 29.2% with a standard deviation of 23.3%. The Liberty Global Fund had the lowest five-year return, with 0.8% and a 30.1% standard deviation.

Over the same period, the compounded returns of Altvest's Managed Futures Index ranked 4 of the 14 hedge fund strategies analysed (see Table 6). However, on a risk/reward basis, managed futures ranked 7 of the 14 hedge fund strategies. Studies have shown that the inclusion of managed futures in a traditional portfolio of stocks, bonds and Treasury bills consistently lowers the standard deviation for a given return.[1]

As with other strategies, there is a noticeable difference between the

---

**Table 5** Comparisons of managed futures indices across different sources, 1997–2001

|  | 1997 | 1998 | 1999 | 2000 | 2001 | 1997–2001 | |
| --- | --- | --- | --- | --- | --- | --- | --- |
|  |  |  |  |  |  | Return | Sharpe ratio |
| Altvest | 18.2 | 17.1 | 6.3 | 18.7 | 8.9 | 13.7 | 0.9 |
| Tuna | 22.9 | 21.3 | 8.6 | 8.0 | 6.7 | 13.4 | 1.7 |
| HFR | 9.4 | 10.7 | 4.2 | 13.1 | 6.5 | 8.8 | 2.5 |
| CSFB/Tremont | 3.1 | 20.7 | 4.7 | 4.3 | 1.9 | 4.7 | 0.5 |
| Maximum difference | 19.8 | 10.4 | 13.3 | 14.4 | 15.5 | 10.7 | 2.4 |
| Average | 13.4 | 17.4 | 3.6 | 11.1 | 8.2 | 10.6 | 1.9 |

Source: Altvest, Tuna, HFR, CSFB/Tremont

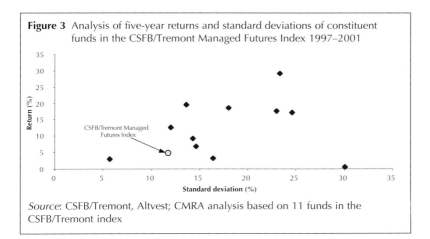

**Figure 3** Analysis of five-year returns and standard deviations of constituent funds in the CSFB/Tremont Managed Futures Index 1997–2001

*Source*: CSFB/Tremont, Altvest; CMRA analysis based on 11 funds in the CSFB/Tremont index

**Table 6** Ranking of the managed futures strategy against other strategies, 1997–2001

|  | 1997 | 1998 | 1999 | 2000 | 2001 | 1997–2001 | Rank |
|---|---|---|---|---|---|---|---|
| **Return** (%) | 18.2 | 17.1 | 6.3 | 18.7 | 17.4 | 18.2 | 4 of 14 |
| **Sharpe ratio** | 4.7 | 4.4 | 0.6 | 4.1 | 5.1 | 1.7 | 7 of 14 |

*Source*: Altvest, CMRA

CSFB/Tremont index and the other indices due to quarterly rebalancing (see Figure 4). For example, in 1997 there was an average 13 point difference. CSFB/Tremont is based on 45 funds; it has 12 funds in common with Altvest. The remaining 33 funds underperformed the remaining funds of Altvest on an equally weighted basis. In addition, CSFB/Tremont is AUM-weighted, whereas Altvest (and all the other indices analysed) is equally weighted. This methodological difference accounts for the 14.4 point difference between the returns of the indices in 2000. See Chapter 11 for a further discussion of index construction.

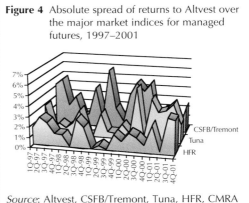

**Figure 4** Absolute spread of returns to Altvest over the major market indices for managed futures, 1997–2001

*Source*: Altvest, CSFB/Tremont, Tuna, HFR, CMRA Analysis

**Table 7** Rolling correlations of managed futures index performance with S&P 500 and Lehman Aggregate Bond Index, 1997–2001 (%)

|  | 1997 | 1998 | 1999 | 2000 | 2001 |
|---|---|---|---|---|---|
| Lehman Aggregate Bond Index* | 46.3 | 62.8 | (29.6) | 31.1 | 38.7 |
| S&P 500 Index | 64.4 | (62.9) | (0.3) | (3.3) | (60.1) |

*This style index for Altvest is the equally weighted average of managed futures funds incepted before 1996, having returns data in Altvest from January 1, 1996 onwards.

*Source*: Altvest, CMRA Analysis

**Table 8** Returns of managed futures index during periods of stress (%)

| Russian/LTCM crisis | Tech crash | September 11 |
|---|---|---|
| 12.7 | 18.3 | 6.0 |

*Source*: Altvest, CMRA Analysis

## Performance correlations

We found a -60% correlation between the S&P 500 Index and returns on the strategy during 2001. Yet, for the same period, the correlation between the Lehman Aggregate Bond Index and the returns of the strategy was 38.7%. This further emphasises the diversification characteristics of the strategy (see Table 7).

## Stress period analysis

When the returns of the managed futures index during significant stress periods in the 1990s are annualised, the strategy seems to have a consistently positive average performance for the events of September 11, 2001 (see Table 8). On the other hand, the results of the Altvest and CSFB/Tremont indices conflict. According to Altvest, the managed futures strategy outperformed all other strategy indices. But, according to CSFB/Tremont, the strategy underperformed 13 of the 16 strategies examined. This inconsistency demonstrates the reliability issues with the various available market indices.

Generally, the risk/return properties of the managed futures strategy vary significantly. Under different conditions, one can observe that:

❏ High returns came at the expense of high risk.
❏ There are significant differences between Altvest and the other benchmarks. For the five-year period, Altvest showed an average annual return for managed futures funds of 13.7% per annum. Along with these impressive returns came a relatively high level of risk, with a 9.6%

**Table 9** Sharpe ratio of managed futures index during periods of stress

| Russian/<br>LTCM crisis | Tech crash | September 11 | Average of absolute<br>Sharpe ratios | Maximum–<br>minimum |
|---|---|---|---|---|
| 1.3 | 1.1 | 0.5 | 1.0 | 0.8 |

*Source*: Altvest, CMRA Analysis

standard deviation. The strategy had a Sharpe ratio of 0.9. By contrast, the eight-year CSFB/Tremont index showed an average annual return of 4.7%, a volatility of 11.7%, and a Sharpe ratio of 0.5.

Managed futures had a Sharpe ratio of 1.3 during the stress period from August to October 1998. During the equity market downturn and the tech crash, the strategy did well with an 18.3% return (see Table 9).

### Range of performance
The distribution of managed futures fund returns reported by Altvest shows that 62% of the funds had a five-year performance between 0% and 10% and only 17% of the funds had a negative performance (see Figure 5).

### SHARPE RATIO
### Distribution
As Table 10 shows, Sharpe ratios for the strategy have not proved stable over time.

As can be seen in Table 11, a clear increase (more than 10 points) in performance occurs between the first quartile and the last two quartiles for

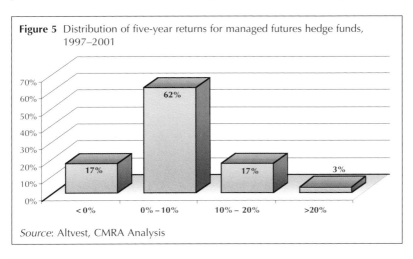

**Figure 5** Distribution of five-year returns for managed futures hedge funds, 1997–2001

*Source*: Altvest, CMRA Analysis

**Table 10** Sharpe ratio of managed futures funds

| 1997 | 1998 | 1999 | 2000 | 2001 | 1997–2001 | Rank |
|------|------|------|------|------|-----------|------|
| 4.6 | 4.4 | 0.6 | 4.1 | 5.1 | 1.7 | 8 of 14 |

*Source*: Altvest, CMRA

funds with at least five years of data. The last quartile has the smallest AUM of the sample (4%) and the first quartile has the largest (32%). The volatility is also significantly larger for the larger funds than for the smaller funds.

Figure 6 shows that the five-year Sharpe ratio of the funds analysed ranged from –0.9 to 2.6, while in 2001, the range was –3.9 to 6.1.

### LEVERAGE

90% of funds in the strategy use leverage. 51% of the funds use a leverage lower than 2.0, and only 39% leverage their positions to a level greater than 2.0. Use of leverage at the end of 2001 and in 2002 is shown in Figure 7 and Table 12, respectively. (See Chapter 2 for a discussion of leverage.)

Managed futures funds employ a significant degree of leverage, averaging a ratio of US$2.94 of AUM for each dollar of capital, ranging all the way up to US$10 of AUM for each dollar of capital. This leverage is probably even larger because it does not reflect the reality that leverage is rarely applied to both sides of offsetting bets in commodities trading.

The historical average leverage for the managed futures strategy has not changed significantly since 1997, as Table 13 shows.

An analysis of leverage for managed futures funds for 1997–2001 indi-

**Table 11** Distribution of managed futures funds by quartiles of Sharpe ratio, 1997–2001

| Sharpe ratio quartiles | Average 1997–2001 equally weighted return (%) | Average 1997–2001 AUM-weighted return (%) | AUM in quartile (US$ billion) | % of total | Average 1997–2001 standard deviation (%) | Sharpe ratio 1997–2001 |
|------|------|------|------|------|------|------|
| 1 | 19.4 | 23.4 | 2.1 | 32 | 40.7 | 0.5 |
| 2 | 15.2 | 13.9 | 1.0 | 16 | 20.7 | 0.4 |
| 3 | 9.0 | 9.1 | 0.6 | 10 | 11.5 | 0.4 |
| 4 | 0.1 | 2.2 | 0.3 | 4 | 10.8 | (0.3) |
| **Total** | **10.9** | **17.3** | **6.3** | **96** | **29.1** | **0.3** |

*Source*: Altvest, HFR, Tuna, CMRA Analysis based on 37 funds with five-year performance data

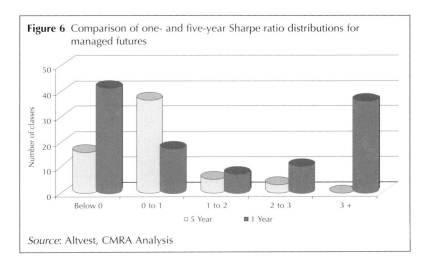

**Figure 6** Comparison of one- and five-year Sharpe ratio distributions for managed futures

□ 5 Year   ■ 1 Year

*Source*: Altvest, CMRA Analysis

---

**Table 12** Financial leverage on managed futures funds in 2002

| Minimum | Average | Maximum | Rank |
|---------|---------|---------|------|
| 0.1 | 2.9 | 10 | 2 of 14 |

*Source*: Altvest, CMRA Analysis

---

cates that the last quartile (the group with the highest leverage) had only US$0.8 billion in AUM while the first quartile (the group with the lowest leverage) had US$1.2 billion in AUM (see Table 14).

During the same five-year period the returns of managed futures funds were 10.5%, which is 6.3 points higher than their delevered returns (see Table 15). The average difference in performance for 2001 between reported returns and delevered returns was –0.3 points.

---

**Table 13** Historical average leverage of managed futures funds, 1997–2001

| | | | | | 1997–2001 | | |
|------|------|------|------|------|---------|---------|---------|
| 1997 | 1998 | 1999 | 2000 | 2001 | Average | Maximum | Minimum |
| 2.9 | 2.8 | 3.1 | 2.8 | 2.5 | 2.8 | 3.1 | 2.5 |

*Source*: Altvest, CMRA Analysis

---

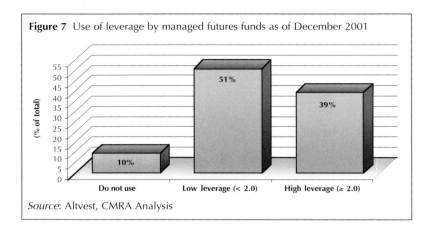

**Figure 7** Use of leverage by managed futures funds as of December 2001

*Source*: Altvest, CMRA Analysis

**Table 14** Distribution of managed futures funds by quartiles of leverage, 1997–2001

| Leverage quartiles | Minimum leverage in quartile | Maximum leverage in quartile | Average leverage in quartile | Median leverage in quartile | Total AUM in quartile (US$ billion) | % of total AUM |
|---|---|---|---|---|---|---|
| 1 | 0.1 | 1.0 | 0.6 | 0.8 | 1.2 | 38.6 |
| 2 | 1.0 | 2.0 | 1.7 | 1.5 | 0.8 | 25.8 |
| 3 | 2.1 | 3.0 | 2.8 | 3.0 | 0.3 | 11.0 |
| 4 | 3.2 | 31.3 | 8.5 | 5.0 | 0.8 | 24.7 |
| **Total** | **0.1** | **31.3** | **2.8** | **2.3** | **3.0** | **100.0** |

Note: Difference in average leverage of 3.4 with 2.82 reported in table before is explained due to a change in the fund information included in the Altvest database when data was obtained.

*Source*: Altvest, CMRA Analysis based on 94 funds with five years of leverage data

## RISK MEASUREMENT

Key risk factors that drive the strategy include volatility, leverage, illiquidity, non-US futures and counterparty risk (see Figure 8).

### Volatility risk

Futures and forward contract prices are highly volatile. This volatility may lead to substantial risks and returns, generally much larger than those from equity or fixed income securities.

### Leverage risk

Accounts traded at greater than standard leverage will experience greater losses and volatility as well as a greater profit potential.

**Table 15** Summary of levered and delevered performance of managed futures funds, 1997–2001 (%)

|  | Maximum return | Minimum return | Average return | Maximum delevered return | Minimum delevered return | Average delevered return | Difference in returns levered vs delevered |
|---|---|---|---|---|---|---|---|
| **1997–2001** | 29.3 | (4.5) | 10.5 | 14.9 | (0.8) | 4.2 | 6.3 |
| **2001** | 15.8 | (44.3) | (0.4) | 10.4 | (20.2) | (0.2) | (0.3) |

*Source*: Altvest, CMRA Analysis

### Illiquidity risk

Futures trading may be illiquid at times. Certain exchanges do not permit trading particular futures at prices that represent a fluctuation in price during a single day's trading beyond certain set limits. This phenomenon could prevent the manager from promptly liquidating unfavourable positions and could subject clients to substantial losses. In addition, the Commodity Futures Trading Commission (CFTC) and various exchanges impose speculative position limits on the number of futures positions a person or group may hold or control in particular futures.

### Non-US futures risk

Unlike trading on US commodity exchanges, trading on non-US commodity exchanges is not regulated by the CFTC and may be subject to greater risks. For example, some non-US exchanges are "principals' markets" in which no common clearing facility exists and a trader may have to rely solely on the broker for performance of the contract.

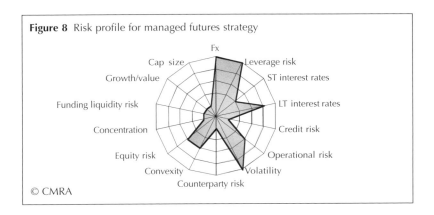

**Figure 8** Risk profile for managed futures strategy

© CMRA

## Counterparty risk

Forward and OTC markets, including foreign currency markets, offer less protection against defaults in trading than is available when trading occurs on an exchange. Forward and OTC contracts are not guaranteed by an exchange or a clearing house, and a non-settlement or default on the contract by the counterparty could result in the loss of unrealised profits or force the hedge fund manager to cover commitments to purchase and sell at the current market price.

## Short risk

Short selling strategies are subject to specific risks because the securities have to be borrowed before they can be sold. The extra steps of borrowing stock, maintaining the corresponding liability and then buying back the shorted stock creates a set of unique risks called "borrowing risks" (or short risks). Certain stocks that a manager would like to short might be unavailable. Short sellers can be subject to squeezes caused by a sudden increase in demand for the stock. A short sale requires collateral and, if the market moves against the short position, additional collateral is required. Thus, insufficient funding is a key liquidity risk for managed futures. The degree of overall borrowing risk is influenced by the manager's relationship with his or her prime broker.

## VALUE-AT-RISK
### Distribution

Since the 1980s, there has been an increasing interest in commodities trading. Its performance and volatility characteristics make it an attractive component of a stock and bond portfolio because it consistently lowers the standard deviation for a given return. The VAR of managed futures funds ranked 5 among the 10 strategies analysed by Francois-Serge Lhabitant (see Table 16).

### Examples

To further understand the implications of having commodities in a managed futures portfolio, CMRA created six sample portfolios and calculated their VARs. One key characteristic of these portfolios is that CMRA

---

**Table 16** Average VAR calculation for managed futures strategy (%)

| 1997 | 1998 | 1999 | 2000 | Average 1997–2000 | Rank |
|------|------|------|------|-------------------|------|
| 12.4 | 10.8 | 11.6 | 10.6 | 11.2 | 5 of 10 |

Source: Assessing Market Risk for Hedge Funds and Hedge Funds Portfolios FAME, March 2001– Research Paper No. 24, Francois-Serge Lhabitant

---

**Table 17** Composition of example diversified managed futures portfolios

| Portfolio | Sectors | Number of bonds in portfolio |
|---|---|---|
| 1 | Energy | 7 |
| 2 | Food | 8 |
| 3 | Interest rate futures | 5 |
| 4 | Energy + food | 15 |
| 5 | Energy + interest rate futures | 12 |
| 6 | Energy + food + interest rate | 20 |

*Source*: Bloomberg, CMRA Analysis

**Table 18** Daily VAR with 95% confidence level for example portfolios calculated for 1997–2001

| Portfolios | Sectors | Daily VAR (%) |
|---|---|---|
| 1 | Energy | 3.3 |
| 2 | Food | 2.8 |
| 3 | Interest rate futures | 3.1 |
| 4 | Energy + Food | 2.8 |
| 5 | Energy + interest rate futures | 1.1 |
| 6 | Energy + food + interest rate | 2.8 |

*Source*: Bloomberg, CMRA Analysis

**Table 19** Cross-correlation for futures contracts and selected market indices (%)

| | Oil | Soy bean | T Bill |
|---|---|---|---|
| Oil | 100 | (1) | 0 |
| Soybean | (1) | 100 | (9) |
| Treasury Bill | 0 | (9) | 100 |
| S&P 500 Index | (10) | 3 | (8) |
| Lehman BIG | (2) | 0 | 47 |

*Source*: Bloomberg, CMRA Analysis

did not apply any of the hedging techniques commonly used by managers in the strategy. Details of the portfolios are shown in Table 17.

The results suggest that diversification in a managed futures portfolio helps to reduce VAR. The best example of this is exhibited in the combination of Portfolios 1 and 3. The resulting VAR is 1.07%, which is lower

**Table 20** Cross-correlation between example managed futures portfolios (%)

| | Energy | Food | Interest rate futures | Energy + food | Energy + interest rate futures | Energy + food + interest rate futures |
|---|---|---|---|---|---|---|
| Energy | 100.0 | 43.7 | 49.7 | 85.9 | 16.6 | 16.1 |
| Food | 43.7 | 100.0 | (9.2) | 87.0 | (2.1) | 15.3 |
| Interest rate futures | 49.7 | (9.2) | 100.0 | 6.5 | 98.7 | 92.2 |
| Energy + food | 85.9 | 87.0 | 6.5 | 100.0 | 10.1 | 12.1 |
| Energy + interest rate futures | 16.6 | (2.1) | 98.7 | 10.1 | 100.0 | 99.9 |
| Energy + food + interest rate futures | 16.1 | 15.3 | 92.2 | 12.1 | 99.9 | 100.0 |

*Source:* Bloomberg, CMRA Analysis

than the expected average of the two portfolios combined, 3.2% (see Table 18).

In addition to the foregoing analysis, CMRA prepared a cross-correlation table of three managed futures portfolios (see Table 20). This table shows the correlations among the contracts themselves.

The results indicate that the components of the different portfolios are not correlated with each other, which would greatly enhance the diversification capabilities of the strategy. In addition, with the exception of the Treasury bill futures, other commodities such as oil and soy bean are not correlated with the S&P 500 or Lehman Bond indices (see Table 19).

## STRESS TESTS

Because portfolios have a propensity to exhibit different risk characteristics when viewed from different perspectives, stress tests can give more accurate insight as to the extent of the portfolio risk than VAR alone. Stress tests for managed futures portfolios include:

❑ Yield curve level and shape.
❑ Volatility curve level and shape.
❑ Price shifts in equities, sectors and indices.
❑ Currency and commodity price shifts.
❑ Spread and basis relationships.
❑ Correlation.
❑ Leverage.

## DUE DILIGENCE QUESTIONS FOR MANAGED FUTURES FUNDS

In general, there are three types of unique questions that should be addressed with managed futures funds. The first has to do with the trading strategy itself, the second with the processes and trading systems in place to manage the risks of the strategy, and the third with the capabilities of the hedge funds to understand risk systematically.

Since most managed futures managers work with several types of trading models across different geographies and different markets, the issue of risk aggregation capabilities should be addressed. The largest hedge funds may trade in approximately 65 markets, including global futures, foreign exchange, fixed income, and stock indices. For example, a report that evaluates futures prices across the different markets is not sufficient because it could show that the portfolio is long in a specific type of sector or market. Yet, when overall market conditions change rapidly, the fund could still lose money if its trader is ignoring which market factors drive risks in the portfolio.

In general, it is important to understand the types of systems and the trade-filtering techniques that are used to mitigate exposure to trendless market conditions. In addition, one should understand the trader's ability to identify and take advantage of significant market trends when they occur. One way to lose in these markets is if the commodity futures, stocks or options fund is not sure in which time frame or trend it is trading, or if it is not matching the target objective price level to the time frame's expected movement. Perhaps the fund wants to capture a move which is expected to take a few days, but, the volatility then increases so that the trend actually ends in a day: if the fund is unaware of this, it will stay in the trade one day too long. The fund will thereby give up all or most of the profit because it expected the trend to last longer. Another common occurrence is the fund that does not use a specific stop-loss order, and a small loss then becomes a large loss.

Some specific questions that should be addressed as part of the due diligence process are:

❏ What type of pricing model do you use?
❏ How do you mark your positions to market (when information is not available)?
❏ Do you stress test the value of your portfolio against alternative methods for marking to market?
❏ If you had to (or wanted to) liquidate your portfolio, how long would it take under normal circumstances and under stressed conditions?
❏ Do you use any kind of optionality to hedge your portfolio?
❏ How do you hedge any foreign exchange or sector exposure?

## DATA AND NAV ISSUES

As opposed to OTC instruments, futures contracts are traded on more than 34 exchanges that provide minute-by-minute pricing information. Table 21 lists some of the best-known exchanges for futures/commodities contracts.

**Table 21** Futures contract exchanges

| No | exchange | Characteristics |
|----|----------|-----------------|
| 1 | Chicago Mercantile Exchange | Quotes and exchange-traded contract information. |
| 2 | The Chicago Board of Trade | World's largest futures and options exchange. |
| 3 | London International Financial Futures Exchange | Major contracts: financial (gilts, short sterling, FTSE index, euribor) commodities (cocoa, coffee, white sugar). |
| 4 | New York Mercantile Exchange | Source for closing prices on metals and petroleum futures and options. |
| 5 | Kansas City Board of Trade | Coverage of the wheat market. Full of useful facts and trivia regarding the wheat trade. |
| 6 | Sydney Futures Exchange | Main contracts: Australian Govt three-year and 10-year bonds, 90-day bills, all ordinaries share price index, equities, greasy wool, wheat. |
| 7 | Minneapolis Grain Exchange | Price coverage and basic contract specifications. |
| 8 | London Metal Exchange | Exchange for non-ferrous base metals. Main contracts: aluminium, copper, nickel, tin, zinc. |
| 9 | Tokyo Grain Exchange | Main contracts: azuki red beans, corn, raw sugar, US soybean, arabica and robusta coffee. |
| 10 | Eurex | Main contracts: euro and Swiss fixed income futures, Eurostoxx, Dax, and SMI index. |
| 11 | Tokyo International Financial Futures Exchange | Main contracts: Euroyen, Euroyen Libor. |
| 12 | Hong Kong Futures Exchange | Main Contracts: Hang Seng Index Futures and Options. |
| 13 | International Petroleum Exchange | Europe's leading energy exchange. Major contracts: Brent crude, gas-oil. |
| 14 | Tokyo Commodity Exchange | Contracts: precious metals (gold, silver, platinum, palladium) others (rubber, cotton yarn, aluminium). |
| 15 | New York Cotton Exchange | Cotton, citrus, sugar, cocoa, FINEX and NYFE. Downloadable quotes, market reports. |
| 16 | MEFF Village | MEFF Renta Fija is the Spanish futures and options exchange. Fixed income, information on contracts, news, publications, training and technology of one of the leading European exchanges. |
| 17 | Korean Futures Exchange | The first dedicated derivatives exchange in Korea. |

(continued)

**Table 21** Futures contract exchanges (continued)

| No | exchange | Characteristics |
|----|----------|-----------------|
| 18 | Singapore Commodity Exchange Limited | Main contracts: rubber and coffee. |
| 19 | European Warrant Exchange | Over 22,000 instruments traded. |
| 20 | Futurecom | The FutureCom Commodity Exchange will announce a commencement date for trading by the end of 2002. Currently scheduling regular mock trading sessions. |
| 21 | New Zealand Futures and Options Exchange | Main Contracts: NZ 90-day bank bill futures, and three- and 10-year bond futures. |
| 22 | Osaka Mercantile Exchange | Contracts: rubber and rubber index futures, cotton yarn, raw silk, aluminium. |
| 23 | Belfox | Belgian futures and options exchange. Main contracts: Bel 20 futures/options, three-month Euribor. |
| 24 | Securities and Futures Authority | UK regulatory body. |
| 25 | Coffee Exchange | Live coffee trading exchange with private trading rooms and auctions. Forums allow interaction with other buyers/sellers. |
| 26 | RedMetor.com | Neutral online exchange for crude oil, electricity, natural gas, and natural gas liquids. Market participants can trade physical, financial and option products. |
| 27 | International French Futures and Options Exchange | Main contracts include long and medium euro national bonds, euribor, CAC40 index, white sugar, rapeseed, and wheat. |
| 28 | Istanbul Gold Exchange | Precious metals market, gold, platinum, silver exchange. |
| 29 | Yokohama Commodity Exchange | Listing both dried cocoon and raw silk futures. |
| 30 | Bombay Commodity Exchange Ltd | Futures trading in castor seeds and castor oil. |
| 31 | Chapel Hill Broadband | Brokers physical and financial deals in all broadband products and services, including channels, dark fiber, collocation facilities and lit fiber. |
| 32 | Australian Macadamia Xchange | Internet exchange registered users can buy and sell macadamia kernel both within Australia and internationally. |
| 33 | Australian Wine Exchange | Offers wine class share IPOs via a prospectus, an investment in wine to be traded on NSX. |
| 34 | Weather Board of Trade | Developer of the NORDIX Weather Index. A standard tradable product to hedge, forecast, speculate, and financially control weather exposure |

*Source*: CMRA Analysis

## PUBLICLY DISCLOSED PROBLEMS

There were several noteworthy negative performers in early 2002. Willow-bridge Associates (Vulcan) saw a steep loss of -29.98% for the month of February. Vulcan's 2001 annual performance was –23.6% and its AUM dropped to US$27.8 million from US$40.2 million in 2000.[2] DUNN Capital Management (WMA) posted a return of –8.07% for February 2002, which brought its past 12-month return to –11.58%. WMA's AUM dropped from US$759.5 milion in 2001 to US$543.1 million in 2002. Its losses were attributed to the trend-following strategies of these two funds.

Most systematic trend followers require two ingredients to perform well: highly volatile markets and modest sustained trends. Throughout the first quarter of 2002, most of the liquid futures markets lacked these ingredients. During this period, intermediate-term trend-following systems were able to generate negative trade signals only to be "stopped out" with losses soon after the positions had been initiated. Long-term trend-following systems were positioned to capture the downward trends that had developed in the Japanese yen, crude oil and soy beans complex. These indications proved to be futile as short-term reversals quickly produced trading losses.

1   The Potential Role of Managed Commodity-Financial Futures Accounts (and/or Funds) in Portfolios of Stocks and Bonds, Prof. John K. Lintner of Harvard University, 1983.
2   CTA Profiles Report, http://www.cta-index.com.

# 19

# *Market Neutral*

## DESCRIPTION OF THE STRATEGY

"Market neutral" is a term that includes many different fund strategies. The key difference between them is the varying degree of risk and neutrality; the common ingredient is the goal that the market should not affect the underlying results of the portfolio. Market neutral funds attempt to hedge against systematic risk by going long and short securities in the same sector, market capitalisation or country.

Various definitions of market neutrality include:

❏ No net cash exposure.
❏ No net beta exposure.
❏ No net duration exposure.
❏ Zero market correlation.
❏ No net sector exposure.

Managers of a market neutral fund sell short instruments that they expect to underperform, buy instruments (often in the same sector) that they expect to outperform, and invest the proceeds in their "cash" portfolio. A market neutral strategy seeks returns in excess of cash. Such strategies are not pure enhanced cash strategies due to the increased risk and increased return possibilities, but are an absolute return investment approach. Another relative value play commonly used by market neutral funds consists of taking long and short positions in different securities of the same issuer. These can be fixed income or emerging market securities. Another popular strategy is ADR (American Depository Receipts) arbitrage, where the fund will go long a security on a foreign exchange and hedge the currency risk when that combination is cheaper than the ADR.

The market neutral strategy has seen increased investment from 1994 to 2001. The only outflow of assets for this strategy was in the third quarter of 1999. A possible explanation for the continuous growth in assets is that even during periods of stress, like the technology crash and the events of September 11, 2001, the strategy continued to produce positive returns of 10.3% and 2.4%, respectively. The growth of the assets in market neutral for the 1997–2001 period has been almost 50%, which is the second largest increase among the hedge fund strategies (see Figure 1).

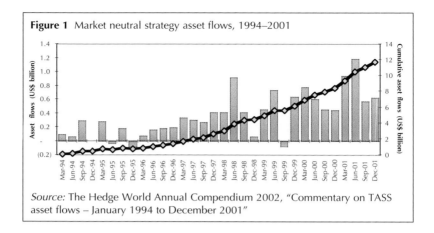

**Figure 1** Market neutral strategy asset flows, 1994–2001

*Source:* The Hedge World Annual Compendium 2002, "Commentary on TASS asset flows – January 1994 to December 2001"

## EFFECT OF MARKET CONDITIONS

Market neutral funds typically perform above their historical average when:[1]

- ❑ The yield curve is moderately upward-sloping and its slope is declining.
- ❑ Credit risk premium is high.
- ❑ The short-term interest rate is at a high level or not increasing.
- ❑ The long-term rate is declining.
- ❑ The implied volatility index is at a moderate level and is not changing.
- ❑ The intra-month volatility of bond returns is low.
- ❑ The returns on large-cap and small-cap stocks are high.

Market neutral funds typically perform below their historical average when:

- ❑ The yield curve is highly upward-sloping or there is a substantial increase in its slope.
- ❑ Credit risk premium is moderate.
- ❑ The short-term interest rate is low and is increasing by a substantial amount.
- ❑ The long-term yield is increasing by a large amount.
- ❑ The intra-month volatility of the S&P 500 Index is high, and the implied volatility index is low or the implied volatility is decreasing.
- ❑ The returns on large-cap and small-cap stocks are negative.

## INVESTORS IN THE STRATEGY

The largest investor group for market neutral funds is individuals and family offices, with 35% of all investments. Funds of funds are second with 24% (see Table 1).

## WELL-KNOWN PLAYERS

The largest market neutral funds by AUM covered by the major sources are listed in Table 2. The Hedge Fund 100 is the only source for two of the top 25 market neutral funds with US$732 million in AUM.

## COVERAGE IN DIFFERENT SOURCES

Table 3 shows the major sources that cover market neutral hedge funds. While Tuna covers the largest number of funds, CSFB/Tremont covers the largest AUM.

## DISTRIBUTION OF FUNDS IN THE STRATEGY

As of December 2001, 10 funds comprised US$7.4 billion of AUM, 62% of the total US$11.9 billion AUM (see Figure 2).

### Distribution of funds by quartile of performance

The results in Table 4 suggest that there is no clear pattern of relationships between either Sharpe ratio and performance or AUM and performance. The highest-performing funds do not have the highest average Sharpe ratio, and though they do have the highest AUM, the third quartile has an equally large AUM, indicating that biggest does not necessarily mean best.

**Table 1** Investors in the market neutral strategy

| Investors | (%) |
| --- | --- |
| Individuals and family offices | 35 |
| Funds of funds | 24 |
| Corporations | 19 |
| Pensions and retirement | 11 |
| Endowments and foundations | 11 |

*Source*: Hennessee Hedge Fund Survey (January 2000)

**Table 2** Top market neutral funds with more than US$1 billion in AUM (all sources)

| Rank | Fund | Highest AUM* (US$ billion) |
| --- | --- | --- |
| 1 | Fairfield Sentry Limited | 3.0 |
| 2 | Davidson Kempner Institutional Partners, L.P. | 1.4 |
| 3 | Clinton Multistrategy Fund, LLC | 1.2 |
| 4 | Deephaven Market-Neutral Fund | 1.2 |
| 5 | Stark Investments, L.P. | 1.0 |
| 6 | Millennium USA, L.P. | 1.0 |
| 7 | GLC Market neutral | 1.0 |
| | **Total** | **9.8** |

*This is the highest AUM for that fund among all the sources.

*Source*: Altvest, Tuna, HFR, Institutional Investor (June 2002), Directory of Fund of Hedge Funds Investment Vehicles

**Table 3** Coverage of market neutral funds by different sources

| Source | Total number of funds | Funds with no AUM data | Total AUM (US$ billion) |
|---|---|---|---|
| CSFB/Tremont | 119 | N/A | 17.0 |
| Tuna | 155 | 17 | 11.9 |
| HFR | 61 | 4 | 7.4 |
| The Hedge Fund 100 | 10 | N/A | 1.1 |

Source: HFR, Tuna, CSFB/Tremont, Institutional Investor (June 2002)

## Distribution of funds by quartile of AUM

Here there is a stronger indication that a fund with greater AUM has higher returns and higher Sharpe ratios. However, as seen in Table 5, that pattern breaks between the second and third quartiles. The sudden drop in AUM from the top quartile to the next is matched by an equally drastic change in the standard deviation. This indicates the possibility that the really successful market neutral hedge funds require managers with special trading skills if they are to maintain high stable returns.

## PERFORMANCE OF THE STRATEGY
### Returns during boom and bust

During the technology crash and the events following September 11, 2001, which, of course, resulted in strong negative returns for the S&P 500 Index, the market neutral strategy showed high positive returns according to the Altvest Index. Figure 3 summarises the boom and bust performance of

**Figure 2** Distribution of market neutral equity funds and AUM in 2001

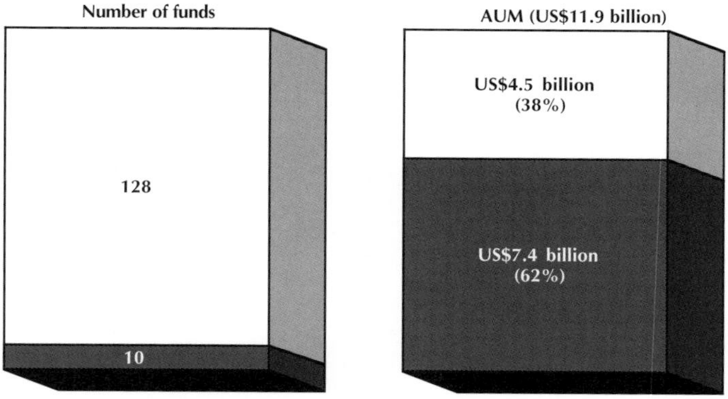

Source: Tuna, CMRA Analysis (analysis does not include 27 funds with no AUM data)

market neutral funds. It implies a relatively low correlation with the S&P 500 Index and stable returns over both good and bad economic conditions.

## Returns from different sources

Differences between the returns reported by the various market neutral hedge fund indices can be significant. The 1999 performance varied by 20.4 points across the different sources, or almost two times the average return of the strategy (see Table 6).

It is important to note that the style indices are only accurate to a limited extent. Since funds might employ a mixture of styles in their portfolios, classifying them under a single style poses problems for analysis because a great deal of specific information about the individual funds is lost. If one did, however, attempt to segregate funds in the strategy by including separate styles, there would be too many permutations and combinations

**Table 4** Distribution of market neutral funds by quartiles of five-year performance, 1997–2001

| Return quartiles | Average 1997–2001 equally weighted return (%) | Avergae 1997–2001 AUM-weighted return (%) | AUM in quartile (US$ billion) | % of total | Average 1997–2001 standard deviation (%) | Sharpe ratio 1997–2001 |
|---|---|---|---|---|---|---|
| 1 | 25.0 | 23.3 | 1.6 | 37 | 14.6 | 1.9 |
| 2 | 13.3 | 13.3 | 1.1 | 25 | 5.3 | 2.6 |
| 3 | 10.3 | 11.0 | 1.6 | 35 | 16.4 | 0.7 |
| 4 | 2.0 | 4.3 | 0.1 | 2 | 12.4 | (0.2) |
| Total | 12.2 | 16.0 | 4.4 | 100 | 12.2 | 1.2 |

*Source*: Altvest, HFR, Tuna, CMRA Analysis based on 25 funds with five-year performance data

**Table 5** Distribution of market neutral funds by quartiles of AUM, 1997–2001

| AUM quartiles | Average 1997–2001 equally weighted return (%) | Average 1997–2001 AUM-weighted return (%) | AUM in quartile (US$ billion) | % of total | Average 1997–2001 standard deviation (%) | Sharpe ratio 1997–2001 |
|---|---|---|---|---|---|---|
| 1 | 15.1 | 15.8 | 3.8 | 87 | 3.9 | 2.5 |
| 2 | 14.3 | 18.8 | 0.5 | 11 | 8.7 | 0.8 |
| 3 | 8.8 | 10.7 | 0.1 | 2 | 9.6 | 1.5 |
| 4 | 10.9 | 7.2 | 0.0 | 0 | 24.4 | 0.2 |
| Total | 12.2 | 16.0 | 4.4 | 100 | 12.2 | 1.2 |

*Source*: Altvest, HFR, Tuna, CMRA Analysis based on 25 funds with five-year performance data

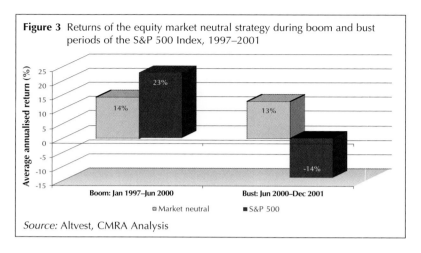

**Figure 3** Returns of the equity market neutral strategy during boom and bust periods of the S&P 500 Index, 1997–2001

*Source:* Altvest, CMRA Analysis

of styles to deal with. The result of this problem is apparent when one sees how divergent the returns/standard deviation profile is for the constituent funds of an index. Note that, for the analysis presented in Figure 4, only 25 of 35 funds constituting the CSFB/Tremont index were chosen because data for the others were not available.

Furthermore, because market neutral indices are based on different funds and calculation methodologies, the performances they report vary from index to index (see Figure 5).

**Index performance**

Comparison of the HFR index for market neutral funds with the indices for the other strategies indicates that the five-year performance is roughly in the middle (see Table 7).

**Table 6** Comparisons of market neutral indices across different sources, 1997–2001

|  | 1997 | 1998 | 1999 | 2000 | 2001 | 1997–2001 | |
|---|---|---|---|---|---|---|---|
|  |  |  |  |  |  | Return | Sharpe ratio |
| CSFB/Tremont | 14.8 | 13.3 | 15.3 | 15.0 | 9.3 | 13.5 | 2.6 |
| HFR | 13.6 | 8.3 | 7.1 | 14.6 | 6.4 | 10.0 | 1.3 |
| Hennessee | 12.3 | 5.1 | (0.8) | 7.1 | 6.1 | 5.9 | 0.3 |
| Tuna | 19.2 | 11.8 | 19.6 | 17.4 | 7.3 | 3.0 | 0.6 |
| Maximum difference | 6.9 | 8.2 | 20.4 | 10.3 | 3.2 | 10.5 | 2.3 |
| Average | 15.0 | 9.6 | 10.3 | 13.5 | 7.3 | 8.1 | 1.2 |

*Source*: CSFB/Tremont, HFR, Hennessee, Tuna,

## Performance correlations

As indicated by Table 8, market neutral funds have weak correlations with all factors; they have negative correlations with equity volatility (–29% during the 1995–2001 period). On the other hand, the strategy shows positive directionality with the equity market factor (ie, the returns of market neutral funds appear to be correlated with the returns of equity markets).

Note in Table 9 that the size factor and the value factor are the differences between the returns and book/price ratios of large and small compa-

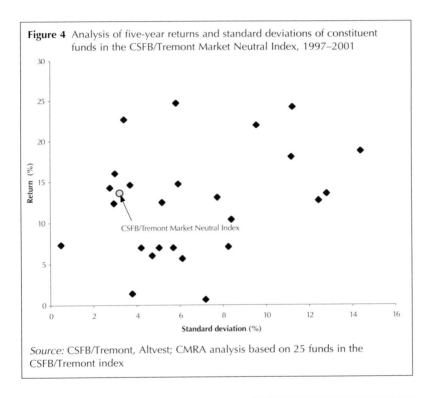

**Figure 4** Analysis of five-year returns and standard deviations of constituent funds in the CSFB/Tremont Market Neutral Index, 1997–2001

*Source:* CSFB/Tremont, Altvest; CMRA analysis based on 25 funds in the CSFB/Tremont index

**Table 7** Ranking of the market neutral strategy against other strategies, 1997–2001

|  | 1997 | 1998 | 1999 | 2000 | 2001 | 1997–2001 | Rank |
|---|---|---|---|---|---|---|---|
| **Return (%)** | 13.6 | 8.3 | 7.1 | 14.6 | 6.4 | 10.0 | 10 of 19 |

*Source:* HFR

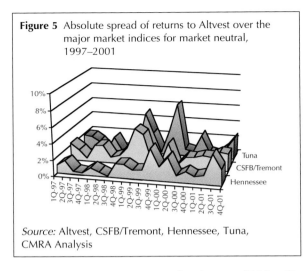

**Figure 5** Absolute spread of returns to Altvest over the major market indices for market neutral, 1997–2001

*Source:* Altvest, CSFB/Tremont, Hennessee, Tuna, CMRA Analysis

nies. In addition, just as before, the strategy has a –9% correlation with the value factor.

However, rolling correlations do not show any clear relationship between market neutral funds and the fixed income or equity markets over longer time spans (see Table 10).

**Stress period analysis**

Looking at the rolling correlations together with the returns of the strategy during periods of stress (Tables 10 and 11), we see a negative correlation with the S&P 500 Index during crises. For instance, while the S&P 500 had positive returns during the Russian crisis, market neutral funds returned –1.7%. Then, when the S&P 500 had negative returns during the technology bust and the events following September 11, 2001, market neutral funds reported positive returns.

Market neutral funds had a Sharpe ratio of –0.9 during the Russian default crisis. During the equity market downturn and the burst of the technology bubble, funds in the strategy made a comeback with a 10.3% return (see Table 11). Sharpe ratios in recent periods of stress are given in Table 12.

Term premia is an indicator of economic expansion. Market neutral strategies are among the least sensitive to changes in this factor (see Table 13). However, changes in implied volatility and credit spread seem to

**Table 8** Correlation of market neutral funds with various risk factors, 1995–2001

| Factor | Overall correlation (%) |
|---|---|
| Equity volatility | (29) |
| Market factor | 50 |
| Size factor | 10 |
| Value factor | (9) |

*Source:* Financial Analyst Journal – Battle for Alphas, March/April 2002

affect the strategy to a greater extent. The high sensitivity to credit spreads is partly the result of the leverage that is employed by some market neutral funds. Many arbitrage funds are also market neutral and must take on leverage to increase their percentage returns. Increases in implied volatility are often related to falling equity markets, resulting in the excess sensitivity to this factor of market neutral funds.

## Range of performance

The returns distribution of market neutral funds for the five years ending in December 2001 (see Figure 6) shows that most market neutral funds, 73%, had five-year returns of between 0% and 20%. A respectable 20% had returns greater than 20%.

**Table 9** Average monthly excess returns of market neutral funds in different risk conditions, 1997–2001

| | Rank by change in factor | | | | | | | Overall correlation |
|---|---|---|---|---|---|---|---|---|
| | Down most | | | | | Up most | | |
| Factor | 1 | 2 | 3 | 4 | 5 | 6 | 7 | |
| Equity volatility | 0.8 | 0.3 | 1.1 | 0.9 | 0.4 | 0.7 | 0.0 | (0.3) |
| Market factor | (0.2) | 0.4 | 0.4 | 0.7 | 0.3 | 1.2 | 1.3 | 0.5 |
| Size factor | 0.2 | 0.5 | 0.8 | 0.5 | 0.8 | 0.8 | 0.6 | 0.1 |
| Value factor | 0.6 | 1.2 | 0.5 | 0.8 | 0.2 | 0.1 | 0.7 | (0.1) |

*Note*: Returns in percentage points

*Source*: Battle for Alphas, Financial Analysts Journal (March-April 2002)

**Table 10** Rolling correlations of market neutral index performance with S&P 500 and Lehman Aggregate Bond Index, 1997–2001 (%)

| | 1997 | 1998 | 1999 | 2000 | 2001 |
|---|---|---|---|---|---|
| **Lehman Aggregate Bond Index** | 78 | (12) | 6 | 43 | 7 |
| **S&P 500 Index** | 62 | 58 | 18 | 26 | (84) |

*Source*: HFR, CMRA Analysis

**Table 11** Returns of market neutral index during periods of stress (%)

| **Russian/LTCM crisis** | **Tech crash** | **September 11** |
|---|---|---|
| (1.7) | 10.3 | 2.4 |

*Source*: HFR, CMRA Analysis

## SHARPE RATIO
### Distribution
When one looks at market neutral funds by quartile of Sharpe ratio (see Table 14), the standard deviation jumps substantially from the top quartile down. Although being in the highest quartile does not necessarily mean the highest return (the second quartile has a better return), the large difference in volatility between the two quartiles perhaps explains the equally large difference in the AUM between the two quartiles.

While many market neutral funds seem to have a recent one-year Sharpe ratio of less than one, the five-year Sharpe ratios distribution is much more uniform (see Figure 7).

### Information ratio
The information ratio for market neutral funds is among the highest of all the strategies. Here, it has been calculated by taking an average hedge fund index as a benchmark instead of the Treasury bill rate as used in the Sharpe ratio calculation. The results, presented in Figure 8, suggest that the returns of market neutral funds over the long run have been generally higher than those of other strategies or that the volatility has been lower.

## LEVERAGE
Figure 9 shows that most market neutral funds, almost 71%, were employing a significant amount of leverage (greater than 2.0) by the end of 2001.

**Table 12** Sharpe ratio of market neutral index during periods of stress

| Russian/LTCM crisis | Tech crash | September 11 | Average of Sharpe ratios | Maximum-minimum |
|---|---|---|---|---|
| (0.9) | 2.7 | 1.1 | 1.6 | 3.6 |

Source: Altvest, CMRA Analysis

**Table 13** Sensitivity of the market neutral strategy to factors in Lehman's multivariate model

| Factor | Coefficient | Rank |
|---|---|---|
| Change in implied volatility | 0.040 | 2 of 17 |
| Change in credit spread | (0.010) | 4 of 17 |
| Change in term premia | 0.002 | 14 of 17 |

Source: Lehman Brothers Understanding Hedge Fund Performance

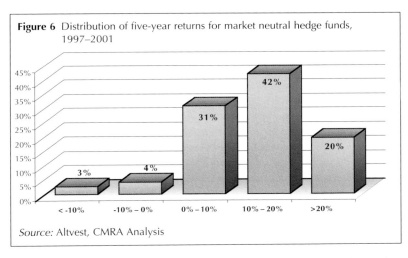

**Figure 6** Distribution of five-year returns for market neutral hedge funds, 1997–2001

*Source:* Altvest, CMRA Analysis

Compared to other hedge fund strategies, market neutral funds employ a median degree of leverage (see Chapter 2 for a discussion of leverage). This is necessary because the shorting of shares or other securities is essential to many market neutral strategies. On a historical basis, market neutral funds exhibit an average leverage of 1.7, with some funds as high as 13.0. Such a big difference emphasises the inconsistencies of data reporting and strategy classification (see Table 15).

## RISK MEASUREMENT

Market neutral funds are exposed to medium levels of funding and operational risk but are sensitive to correlation assumptions and basis risk. The market neutral strategies are typically a combination of fixed income arbitrage strategies and equity hedge strategies. The only way a fund can be

**Table 14** Distribution of market neutral funds by quartiles of Sharpe ratio, 1997–2001

| Sharpe ratio quartiles | Average 1997–2001 equally weighted return (%) | Average 1997–2001 AUM-weighted return (%) | AUM in quartile (US$ billion) | % of total | Average 1997–2001 standard deviation (%) | Sharpe ratio 1997–2001 |
|---|---|---|---|---|---|---|
| 1 | 15.6 | 16.1 | 3.5 | 80 | 3.2 | 3.5 |
| 2 | 19.5 | 18.6 | 0.7 | 15 | 10.3 | 1.5 |
| 3 | 12.7 | 8.4 | 0.2 | 4 | 17.9 | 0.4 |
| 4 | 2.8 | 2.8 | 0.1 | 1 | 16.5 | (0.2) |
| **Total** | **12.2** | **16.0** | **4.4** | **100** | **12.2** | **1.2** |

*Source*: Altvest, HFR, Tuna, CMRA Analysis based on 37 funds with five-year performance data

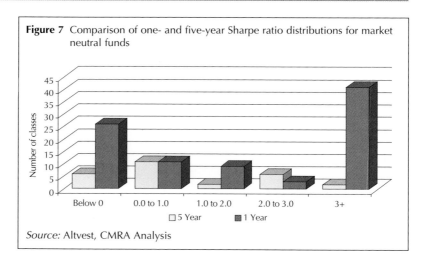

**Figure 7** Comparison of one- and five-year Sharpe ratio distributions for market neutral funds

*Source:* Altvest, CMRA Analysis

market neutral is to take into consideration the non-linear exposures of its holdings. Therefore, many of the risks associated with market neutral strategies are those associated with fixed income and long/short equity. Some of the key risk factors that influence market neutral hedge funds shown in Figure 10 include:

**Market risk**
CMRA believes that it is impossible (especially in the case of fixed income securities) to be truly neutral. If a fund is directionally neutral, it may still

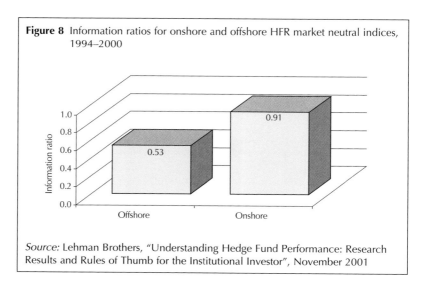

**Figure 8** Information ratios for onshore and offshore HFR market neutral indices, 1994–2000

*Source:* Lehman Brothers, "Understanding Hedge Fund Performance: Research Results and Rules of Thumb for the Institutional Investor", November 2001

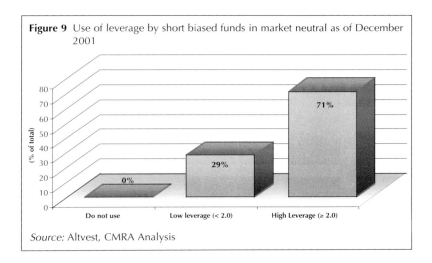

**Figure 9** Use of leverage by short biased funds in market neutral as of December 2001

*Source:* Altvest, CMRA Analysis

be exposed in terms of other risk parameters such as convexity or volatility.

### Beta risk

Just because the beta of a fund is close to zero does not mean that the fund is market neutral. Beta is irrelevant to the strategy because the portfolio could be heavily exposed to other risks, such as volatility or interest rate risk.

### Correlation risk

Often a fund can be directionally neutral by going long a short-term bond and short a duration-weighted amount of a longer-term bond. The fund is neutral to parallel shifts in the term structure, but correlations between the long- and short-term rates mean that these positions could move differently and sometimes even in opposite directions. In such a scenario can one really say that the fund is directionally neutral? Correlations between off-the-run and on-the-run issues are another example of the correlation risks to which many funds in the strategy are exposed.

**Table 15** Financial leverage of market neutral funds in 2002

| Minimum | Average | Maximum | Rank |
|---------|---------|---------|------|
| 1.0 | 1.7 | 13.0 | 5 of 14 |

*Source*: Altvest, CMRA Analysis

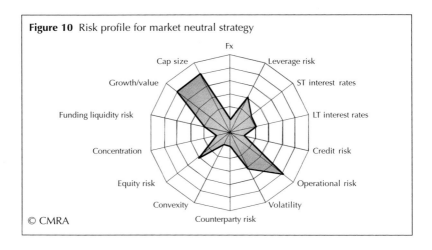

**Figure 10** Risk profile for market neutral strategy

© CMRA

## Leverage and liquidity risk

These are more common with fixed income securities, especially more exotic instruments such as mortgages. However, small-cap stocks and equities of emerging markets can also carry liquidity risk. Since the market neutral strategy involves shorting securities, risks such as short-squeeze can occur in this strategy. To short securities, the fund must maintain some form of leverage and, in adverse market situations, may be at the mercy of the repo desks with which they do business.

## Counterparty and credit risk

Counterparty risk is an unavoidable component of derivative transactions. In addition to the credit risk of the underlying security, there is the solvency risk of the counterparty to the derivative transaction. The counterparty's ability to meet its obligation can be an issue, and assessing the exposure that can build up with a counterparty (current plus potential future exposure) is a key element of effective risk management.

## VALUE-AT-RISK
### Overview

In a recent study the market neutral strategy ranked sixth in terms of VAR for the 1997–2000 period in a sample of 10 strategies (see Table 16). However, as for other arbitrage strategies, VAR is not necessarily an accurate indicator of risk for the market neutral strategy.

In market neutral funds, even if the net exposure of the portfolio remains constant, the VAR can change dramatically. This is caused by the changing correlations and mismatches in the market capitalisations of the long and short positions.

## Examples

To understand this phenomenon further, consider a market neutral portfolio in which an investor goes long the shares of a company and shorts the shares of another company in the same industry sector, such that the dollar value of the long and short positions equal zero. To keep the dollar value of the portfolio neutral, the portfolio manager will have to rebalance the long and short positions. If the correlations of the two stocks change, the VAR can change substantially.

In the example we will consider, a portfolio is constructed by setting up the following long and short positions on May 1, 2002:

❏ Long position: 128 shares of NWRE (Neoware Systems) at US$7.81; long value: US$1,000.
❏ Short position: 41.7 shares of AAPL (Apple Computers) at US$23.98; short value: US$1,000.

Both these stocks are from the computer sector. In this portfolio the long position was kept constant, while the short position was constantly rebalanced so that its dollar value always equalled that of the long position. Therefore, the net market capitalisation in the portfolio was always zero. Observe in Figure 11 how the VAR fluctuated as the correlation of the stocks changed. As the correlation fell, VAR increased. During the period May 5–August 31, 2002, NWRE almost doubled in price while AAPL almost halved in price.

## STRESS TESTS

Because of the propensity for portfolios to exhibit different risk characteristics when viewed from different perspectives, a variety of stress tests should be used. Stress tests can give more accurate insight than VAR into the overall risk in a market neutral portfolio. Tests that should be considered for a market neutral portfolio include:

❏ term structure and yield curve levels and shapes;
❏ term structure and relationship of volatility;

**Table 16** Average VAR (%) for market neutral strategy, 1997–2000

| 1997 | 1998 | 1999 | 2000 | Average 1997–2000 | Rank |
|------|------|------|------|-------------------|------|
| 8.7 | 9.5 | 11.7 | 12.1 | 11.1 | 6 of 10 |

Source: Assessing Market Risk for Hedge Funds and Hedge Funds Portfolios FAME, March 2001 – Research Paper No. 24, Francois-Serge Lhabitant

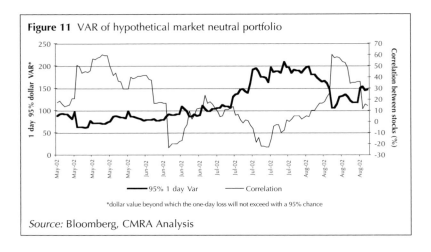

**Figure 11** VAR of hypothetical market neutral portfolio

*Source:* Bloomberg, CMRA Analysis

❏ price shifts in equities, sectors, indices;
❏ currency risk;
❏ spreads and basis relationships;
❏ yield curve assumptions;
❏ pricing models;
❏ VAR;
❏ product complexity;
❏ difficult-to-model risks;
❏ concentrations;
❏ correlations; and
❏ credit components of securities.

## LEVEL OF TRANSPARENCY

A study in 2000 by Hennessee Hedge Fund Advisory Group found that 4% of market neutral managers surveyed indicated that they would provide no transparency (see Table 17). In contrast, 52% said they would provide full disclosure and 43% would disclose their key positions. The study also found that only 30% of market neutral managers surveyed were willing to disclose their key long practices to investors, while even fewer, only 17%, were willing to disclose their short positions.

## DUE DILIGENCE QUESTIONS

Most of the due diligence questions for assessing market neutral funds are similar to those for the underlying asset class. (See Chapters 13, 14 and 16 for discussion on the emerging markets, long/short equity and fixed income strategies).

Due diligence questions generally touch on the traction of pricing models, the foreign exchange exposure of portfolios, funding procedures,

**Table 17** Transparency offered to investors by managers of market neutral funds (%)

| Overall level of transparency | | | | Positions disclosed to investors | |
|---|---|---|---|---|---|
| Performance | Key positions | View entire portfolio | No transparency | Key long positions | Key short positions |
| 100 | 43 | 52 | 4 | 30 | 17 |

*Source*: Hennessee Hedge Fund Advisory Group

the fund's relationship with the repo desks they do business with, correlation and volatility inputs into models, the use of credit derivatives, and the liquidity of the traded instruments.

In addition, market neutral funds must attempt to understand the nature and range of the "neutrality" of the fund's portfolio. No portfolio is entirely neutral; the VAR example given earlier shows how neutrality in one dimension can still mean increasing exposure in the other.

More specific questions could include:

❑ What is the maximum size of market management move that will maintain neutrality? Most market neutral funds are equity funds, many also trade fixed income or other more exotic products.
❑ In such cases, what sort of controls are in place to mark-to-market and /or mark-to-model?
❑ What leverage has been employed and what restrictions might arise with regard to the short positions? (Chapters 16 and 20 on fixed income and short biased funds, respectively, discuss in more detail the operational risks that are inherent in their markets in which funds in the market neutral strategy also trade.)

## DATA AND NAV ISSUES
The data and NAV issues for the strategy are based on the underlying markets for the securities in which investments are made. See the discussions in the long/short equity, fixed-income and emerging market chapters.

## PUBLICLY DISCLOSED PROBLEMS
Askin Capital Management was a victim of illiquidity and mis-marking.[2] Some of the securities that the fund invested in were so complex that there were many differing prices in the dealer community. David Askin, the manager, began using "internal manager marks" to price the portfolio.

Furthermore, the fund bought all its bonds in the repo market and was financed by the repo desks, which resulted in the buyer and the repo desks having a common interest in supporting the securities' prices. Many repo desks lowered their haircut from the usual 15% just to have the fund's business, a practice that created a situation where a sharp fall in prices would hurt both the fund and the repo desks. This, coupled with the funds' internal marking, caused an unsustainable situation whereby the fund was reporting higher than normal marks and the repo desks were attempting to support them. The sudden volatility event that resulted in collapse was the Federal Reserve's interest rate increases in 1994 (for the first time since years of cutting). The fund's repo desks met margin calls by liquidating the fund's portfolio, which caused the fund to lose US$600 million.

1   Lehman Brothers, 2001, "Understanding Hedge Fund Performance: Research Results and Rules of Thumb for the Institutional Investor", November.
2   Clash, J. M., 2001, "No Hedging Here", *Forbes Magazine*, August 6.

# 20

# Short Biased

## DESCRIPTION OF THE STRATEGY

Short selling is the practice of selling securities borrowed from an owner, who is not a seller, with the hope that the price of the securities declines in the market so that they can then be repurchased at a lower price and returned to the lender. Typically, short sales are facilitated by securities-lending operations such as the repo operations of large banks and brokerage firms.

Short biased funds lend cash or other securities pursuant to a repo agreement in exchange for the security they wish to short. If they lend cash, they earn interest that is shared with the broker, subject to the terms of the agreement they have with their brokerage firm. The level of the interest depends on the availability of the securities being lent. If the stock to be shorted is difficult to find or the bond is trading on special terms (government bonds often trade on special at quarter end when corporations need to have them on their balance sheets for accounting purposes), the interest rate that the repo desk will pay the fund is very low. While interest is earned by funds that go short, expenses for these funds include all dividend payments and coupon payments on shorted securities that have to be made by the hedge fund to the repo desk or broker.

Short selling is a specialised skill which is relatively rare among traders. As a result, there are few funds that specialise in short bias and, despite the falling stock market in 2000 and 2001, few short biased funds were launched.

At one time, short selling was a strategy in its own right. However, it became unsustainable during the stock market rally of the 1990s. One prime broker has estimated that the number of short-only managers fell by 75% between 1990 and 2000. Now, many hedge funds follow what is called a short biased strategy in that they will be both long and short, but the net position will be short. Short biased funds typically trade equities, futures and fixed income instruments. They are popular with many funds of funds because they are good investment candidates for mitigating risk through diversification.

## EFFECT OF MARKET CONDITIONS
Generally speaking, the strategy performs above its historical average when there are:

❑ Economic recessions and falling equity markets.
❑ Increase in credit spreads: credit risk premium is increasing.
❑ Higher repo rates.
❑ Low volatility of the S&P 500 Index.

The strategy underperforms its historical average when there are:

❑ Bull markets.
❑ Falling credit spreads.
❑ Lower repo rates.
❑ High volatility of the S&P 500 Index.
❑ Poor liquidity.

## WELL-KNOWN PLAYERS
As shown in Table 1, there are only 10 short biased funds with assets greater than or equal to US$100 million among those covered by the major sources. None of the funds in this list were exclusive to The Hedge Fund 100. Furthermore, the top of the funds of funds holding list contained only two short biased funds, neither of which are listed in Table 1.

**Table 1** Top short biased funds with more than US$100 million in AUM (all sources)

| Rank | Fund | Highest AUM* (US$ billion) |
|------|------|------|
| 1 | Rocker Partners, L.P. | 0.5 |
| 2 | Island Drive Offshore, Ltd. | 0.3 |
| 3 | Compass Holdings, Ltd. | 0.2 |
| 4 | OKUMUS Market Neutral Fund, Ltd. | 0.2 |
| 5 | Bay Resource Partners, L.P. | 0.2 |
| 6 | Prudent Bear Fund, Inc. | 0.2 |
| 7 | Atlas Capital, LP | 0.2 |
| 8 | Arcas International Fund, Ltd. (Covered Interests) | 0.1 |
| 9 | Arcas International Fund, Ltd (Arcas Interests) | 0.1 |
| 10 | Quaestor GlobalNeutral Fund | 0.1 |
| | **Total** | **2.1** |

*This is the highest AUM for that fund among all the sources.

*Source*: Altvest, Tuna, HFR, Institutional Investor (June 2002), Directory of Fund of Hedge Funds Investment Vehicles

## COVERAGE IN DIFFERENT SOURCES

Table 2 shows the major sources of index information for short biased funds. Altvest covers the most funds but Hennessee covers the largest AUM. In contrast to most of the other strategies, no short biased funds are featured exclusively in The Hedge Fund 100.

## DISTRIBUTION OF FUNDS IN THE STRATEGY

12% of the funds (6 of 51) account for almost half of the AUM in the strategy (see Figure 1).

### Distribution of funds by quartiles of performance

The best performing quartile for the 1997–2001 period is also the one with the highest AUM (see Table 3). The same holds true for the Sharpe ratio. Note, however, that the Sharpe ratios are not very different across quartiles.

**Table 2** Coverage of short biased funds by different sources

| Source | Total number of funds | Funds with no AUM data | Total AUM (US$ billion) |
|---|---|---|---|
| Hennessee | 11 | N/A | 3.0 |
| Tuna | 24 | 1 | 1.6 |
| Altvest | 35 | 2 | 1.4 |
| The Hedge Fund 100 | 5 | N/A | 1.1 |
| CSFB/Tremont | 16 | N/A | 1.0 |
| HFR | 15 | 1 | 0.4 |

*Source*: Altvest, HFR, Tuna, Hennessee, CSFB/Tremont, Institutional Investor (June 2002)

**Figure 1** Distribution of short biased funds and AUM in 2001

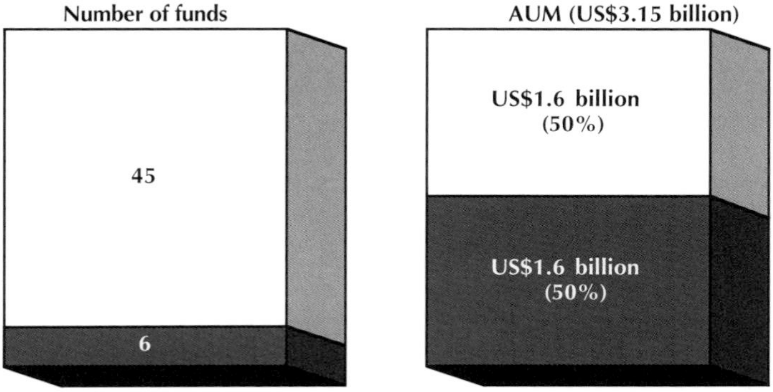

Source: Altvest, CMRA Analysis

**Table 3** Distribution of short biased funds by quartiles of five-year performance, 1997–2001

| Return quartiles | Average 1997–2001 equally weighted return (%) | Avergae 1997–2001 AUM-weighted return (%) | AUM in quartile (US$ billion) | % of total | Average 1997–2001 standard deviation (%) | Sharpe ratio 1997–2001 |
|---|---|---|---|---|---|---|
| 1 | 17.1 | 16.4 | 1.1 | 55 | 21.8 | 0.6 |
| 2 | 8.0 | 8.7 | 0.2 | 10 | 22.9 | 0.3 |
| 3 | 2.1 | 2.2 | 0.4 | 18 | 20.5 | (0.4) |
| 4 | (10.0) | (5.4) | 0.3 | 16 | 45.2 | (0.3) |
| Total | 4.2 | 9.5 | 1.9 | 100 | 27.3 | 0.0 |

*Source*: Altvest, HFR, Tuna, CMRA Analysis based on 21 funds with five-year performance data

### Distribution of funds by quartiles of AUM

Although the quartile with the highest AUM has the highest average return, this pattern does not carry over to the next largest quartile (see Table 4). Note, however, the difference between the total AUMs of the first and second quartiles is similar to that in Table 3. This might indicate that the larger funds are the better performers, which would be consistent with the argument that short selling is a special skill among traders.

### PERFORMANCE OF THE STRATEGY
### Returns during boom and bust

Figure 2 shows, as expected, that the short biased strategy underperformed the S&P500 Index during the boom period and outperformed the index during the bust period.

**Table 4** Distribution of short biased funds by quartiles of AUM, 1997–2001

| AUM quartiles | Average 1997–2001 equally weighted return (%) | Avergae 1997–2001 AUM-weighted return (%) | AUM in quartile (US$ billion) | % of total | Average 1997–2001 standard deviation (%) | Sharpe ratio 1997–2001 |
|---|---|---|---|---|---|---|
| 1 | 11.9 | 12.8 | 1.2 | 63 | 25.4 | 0.3 |
| 2 | 2.9 | 2.5 | 0.5 | 24 | 25.3 | (0.3) |
| 3 | 8.5 | 8.0 | 0.2 | 11 | 19.1 | 0.2 |
| 4 | (7.4) | (3.3) | 0.0 | 2 | 40.9 | (0.3) |
| Total | 4.2 | 9.5 | 1.9 | 100 | 27.3 | 0.0 |

*Source*: Altvest, HFR, Tuna, CMRA Analysis based on 21 funds with five-year performance data

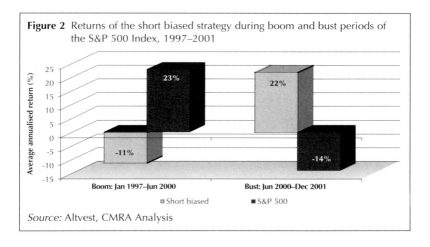

**Figure 2** Returns of the short biased strategy during boom and bust periods of the S&P 500 Index, 1997–2001

*Source:* Altvest, CMRA Analysis

### Returns from different sources

Table 5 shows returns for the cumulative short biased strategies reported by different sources during the 1997–2001 period. As can be seen, there is a great deal of variation in returns across the sources. A major cause of this is that the number of funds that comprise the indices varies dramatically from one index to another. The considerable variation in the mix of funds in each index also has a major impact. For instance, the difference between the returns reported for 1998 by Altvest and HFR (–20.71% and –0.54%, respectively) can be attributed to the mix of funds. 70% of the 10 funds in

**Table 5** Comparisons of short biased indices across different sources, 1997–2001

|  |  |  |  |  |  | 1997–2001 | |
| --- | --- | --- | --- | --- | --- | --- | --- |
|  | 1997 | 1998 | 1999 | 2000 | 2001 | Return | Sharpe ratio |
| Tuna | 10.8 | 12.9 | 15.2 | 9.5 | 17.7 | 13.2 | 0.5 |
| CMRA | 10.3 | (3.3) | (9.3) | 22.2 | 19.1 | 7.1 | 0.1 |
| EACM | (2.1) | (1.3) | (1.5) | 25.2 | 9.0 | 5.4 | 0.0 |
| HFR | 3.9 | (0.5) | (24.4) | 34.6 | 15.7 | 4.0 | (0.0) |
| Hennessee | 7.1 | (23.3) | (9.9) | 30.0 | 12.7 | 1.6 | (0.1) |
| CSFB | 0.4 | (6.0) | (14.2) | 15.8 | (3.6) | (2.0) | (0.3) |
| Altvest | 5.3 | (20.7) | (20.7) | 29.4 | 4.5 | (2.2) | (0.3) |
| Maximum difference | 12.9 | 36.2 | 39.6 | 25.1 | 22.7 | 15.4 | 0.8 |
| Average | 5.1 | (6.0) | (9.3) | 23.8 | 10.7 | 3.9 | (0.0) |

*Note:* CMRA short biased index comprises of funds from Altvest, Tuna and HFR.
*Note:* The Altvest Index was made using funds from Altvest but classifying them as short bias in CMRA.

*Source:* Altvest, Tuna, HFR, CSFB/Tremont, Hennessee, EACM, CMRA Analysis

Altvest had 1998 returns below –20%, whereas only about 33% of the 12 funds in the HFR index had returns below –20%. The two indices had five funds in common. Similarly, the Altvest index had only two funds in common with the Tuna index, which showed a return of 12.91% for 1998. HFR too had a very small number of funds in common with the Tuna index.

A major problem with creating indices for a particular strategy is that the classification of a fund in that strategy might be an approximation as many funds use a mixture of strategies. Furthermore, there is no way of knowing what strategy a fund follows without looking at its portfolio. As a result, the variation of returns of funds within an index can be large.

Figure 3 shows how scattered the returns and standard deviation data can be for the funds that make up an index. Note that the five-year returns vary from –9.62% to 16.4%. The index CMRA chose for analysis was CSFB/Tremont, consisting of eight funds.

The variation in the returns of the short biased strategy is among the highest of all the strategies. As a result, the short biased strategy has one of the lowest Sharpe ratios. One reason for the massive volatility of this strategy was the equity market boom of the 1990s. When the market began its rally in the early 1990s, few thought that it would go on until the end of the decade. Equities, especially internet and technology stocks, reached irrational levels that were not justified by fundamentals. However, many short sellers, especially persistent ones, got burned during this time because the rally continued for several years. This explains the high historical volatility of the strategy's returns. The spread of the various market indices with the Altvest short biased index indicates the significant differences in their composition.

The differences in performance (displayed in Figure 4) change over

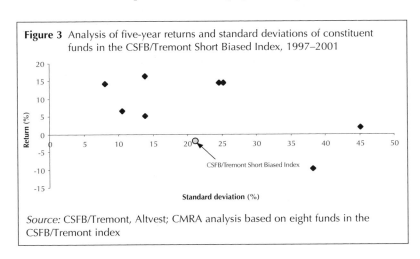

**Figure 3** Analysis of five-year returns and standard deviations of constituent funds in the CSFB/Tremont Short Biased Index, 1997–2001

*Source:* CSFB/Tremont, Altvest; CMRA analysis based on eight funds in the CSFB/Tremont index

time. In some quarters, a 5% difference with the Altvest short biased index was found. This information leads the investor to question the methodologies and validity of information used by the index providers.

### Index performance

As shown in Table 6, the long equity market boom of the 1990s negatively affected the short biased strategy.

### Performance correlations

Correlations of fund performance with various factors are given in Table 7. Correlation with the S&P500 Index is strongly negative. In 1998 the correlation with the swap spread was positive. During the Russian/LTCM crisis, when all markets fell causing short biased funds to perform well, the drying up of liquidity and the ensuing stress resulted in a widening of swap spreads. Also, the correlation with the government bond yield is negative, which shows that during times of stress when investors flock to

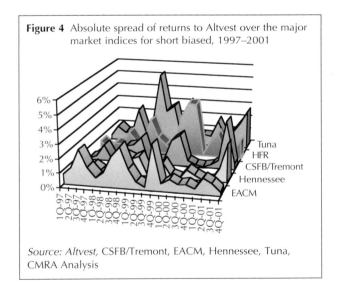

**Figure 4** Absolute spread of returns to Altvest over the major market indices for short biased, 1997–2001

*Source: Altvest*, CSFB/Tremont, EACM, Hennessee, Tuna, CMRA Analysis

**Table 6** Ranking of short biased strategy against other strategies, 1997–2001

|  | 1997 | 1998 | 1999 | 2000 | 2001 | 1997–2001 | Rank |
|---|---|---|---|---|---|---|---|
| Return (%) Altvest | 5.3 | (20.7) | (20.7) | 29.4 | 4.5 | (2.2) | 14 of 14 |
| Return (%) HFR | 3.9 | (0.5) | (24.4) | 34.6 | 15.7 | 4.0 | 17 of 19 |

*Source: Altvest, HFR, CMRA*

**Table 7** Rolling correlations of short biased index performance with S&P500, 1997–2001 (%)

| 1997–2001 | Index Average | Altvest | CSFB/ Tremont | Tuna | HFR | EACM | Hennessee |
|---|---|---|---|---|---|---|---|
| 10-year swap spread | 22 | 29 | 26 | 26 | 13 | 30 | 33 |
| 1-week government repo | 4 | 11 | 14 | 0 | 6 | 8 | 5 |
| 3-month government repo | (2) | (1) | 11 | (4) | 4 | 0 | 0 |
| 10-year treasury yield | (17) | (26) | (13) | (18) | (13) | (16) | (18) |
| S&P 500 Index | (78) | (85) | (80) | (79) | (68) | (85) | (83) |

*Source*: Altvest, HFR, Tuna, CSFB/Tremont, EACM, Hennessee, Bloomberg, CMRA Analysis

the safest securities, such as government bonds, the short biased strategy does well. This same effect can also be observed in 2001.

### Stress period analysis

Short biased strategies do very well in crisis periods because all markets fall during these times. Table 8 lists the returns, as indicated by the various short biased indices, during the Russian/LTCM crisis, the tech crash and the events of September 11, 2001. It is interesting to note, that despite strong returns during the Russian/LTCM crisis, the returns for 1998 were negative in all indices except Tuna. This is because funds in the strategy made money between July and October but lost most or all of their gains by the end of the year. This was probably the result of the short-squeeze caused by the drying up of liquidity, which prevented funds in the strategy from realising their returns during the crisis.

The high Sharpe ratios seen during the tech crash (see Table 9) are primarily due to the windfall gains experienced during steadily falling equity markets. Short biased funds had Sharpe ratios from –0.2 to 0.7

**Table 8** Returns of short biased index during periods of stress (%)

| | Russian/LTCM crisis | Tech crash | September 11 |
|---|---|---|---|
| CMRA | 9.6 | 46.5 | 12.0 |
| Altvest | 0.1 | 39.8 | 7.3 |
| HFR | 7.3 | 68.1 | 7.1 |
| Hennessee | 6.5 | 35.6 | 15.4 |
| Tuna | 13.6 | 31.0 | 11.2 |
| CSFB/Tremont | 9.4 | 43.9 | (4.1) |
| EACM | 14.7 | 38.9 | 8.3 |

*Source*: Altvest, HFR, Tuna, CSFB/Tremont, Hennessee, EACM

(depending on the index) during the Russian/LTCM crisis. During the equity market downturn and the burst of the technology bubble of 2000–01, short biased strategies recovered their performance with an average 43% return across the different indices.

Table 10 gives the results of a single-factor (S&P500 Index) regression and a multifactor (S&P500, change in credit spread, change in term premia, and change in VIX) regression on the short biased index. The $R^2$ value does not change much with the addition of the extra factors, suggesting a strong negative correlation with the S&P500 Index.

### Range of performance

Figure 5 shows distribution of returns reported by Altvest over the 1997–2001 period. The returns of short biased funds are normally distributed, with over half the funds having modest returns between 0% and 10%.

### SHARPE RATIO

### Distribution

In general, the Sharpe ratios for short biased funds are among the lowest of all the strategies. Figure 6 shows that the five-year Sharpe ratio did not exceed 2.0 in any of the funds analysed. Most funds had one- and five-year ratios between 0.0 and 1.0.

**Table 9** Sharpe ratio of short biased index during periods of stress

| Source | Russian/ LTCM crisis | Tech crash | September 11 | Average of absolute Sharpe ratios | Maximum- minimum |
|---|---|---|---|---|---|
| CSFB/Tremont | 0.3 | 2.2 | (0.4) | 1.0 | 2.6 |
| HFR | 0.3 | 2.5 | 0.5 | 1.1 | 2.2 |
| CMRA | 0.4 | 2.2 | 1.0 | 1.2 | 1.8 |
| Altvest | (0.2) | 1.5 | 0.3 | 0.7 | 1.7 |
| Hennessee | 0.2 | 1.6 | 1.0 | 0.9 | 1.4 |
| EACM | 0.6 | 1.6 | 0.4 | 0.9 | 1.2 |
| Tuna | 0.7 | 1.7 | 0.9 | 1.1 | 1.0 |

*Source*: Altvest, HFR, Tuna, CSFB/Tremont, Hennessee, EACM, CMRA Analysis

**Table 10** Single- and multifactor regressions on short biased index

| S&P 500 | Change in credit spread | Change in term premia | Change in VIX | R-Square (multifactor) | R-Square (single-factor) |
|---|---|---|---|---|---|
| (1.1) | 0.2 | (0.007) | 0.2 | 0.5 | 0.4 |

*Source*: Lehman Brothers Research

The quartile distribution of Sharpe ratios shows that, in this strategy, the funds that are generally more stable are also the ones with higher returns (see Table 11).

Sharpe ratios can be quite misleading for funds that short options. Often funds that short out-of-the-money options can enhance their short-term return. The monthly return can be evened out, resulting in a higher Sharpe ratio. However, if the shorting of options is done to manipulate returns and not because the trade has economic merit, there can be serious consequences. It can increase the leverage of the portfolio and, if at some point things go wrong, it can actually end up increasing the volatility of the funds' returns, causing a much lower Sharpe ratio in the long run.

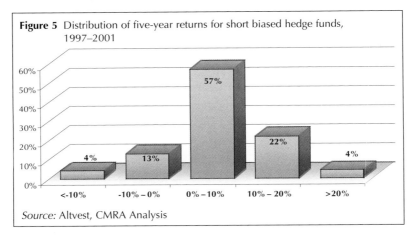

**Figure 5** Distribution of five-year returns for short biased hedge funds, 1997–2001

*Source:* Altvest, CMRA Analysis

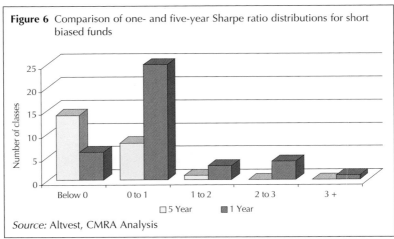

**Figure 6** Comparison of one- and five-year Sharpe ratio distributions for short biased funds

*Source:* Altvest, CMRA Analysis

**Table 11** Distribution of short biased funds by quartiles of Sharpe ratio, 1997–2001

| Sharpe ratio quartiles | Average 1997–2001 equally weighted return (%) | Average 1997–2001 AUM-weighted return (%) | AUM in quartile (US$ billion) | % of total | Average 1997–2001 standard deviation (%) | Sharpe ratio 1997–2001 |
|---|---|---|---|---|---|---|
| 1 | 17.1 | 17.7 | 0.6 | 32 | 18.3 | 0.7 |
| 2 | 8.0 | 12.7 | 0.7 | 34 | 28.3 | 0.2 |
| 3 | 1.2 | 1.6 | 0.4 | 18 | 34.2 | (0.1) |
| 4 | (8.9) | (5.0) | 0.3 | 16 | 26.9 | (0.7) |
| Total | 4.2 | 9.5 | 1.9 | 100 | 27.3 | 0.0 |

*Source*: Altvest, HFR, Tuna, CMRA Analysis based on 21 funds with five-year performance data

## LEVERAGE

92% of short biased hedge funds use leverage (see Chapter 2 for a discussion of leverage). 75% use a leverage lower than 2.0, and only 17% use a leverage greater than 2.0 (see Figure 7).

Many hedge funds rely on the magnifying effect of leverage, but short biased funds have the lowest leverage of all the strategies analysed. (See Table 12 and the five-year leverage data in Table 13.)

The reason short biased funds are among the least levered is partly because there are far fewer securities available for short trading than for long. In order to short stocks, the fund's broker has to look for someone from whom to borrow the stock, and not all investors have margin accounts. For fixed income securities, large portions of an entire issue can be held by a single entity, thereby limiting the number of sources available to short. Table 13 shows the historical leverage for the short biased and the

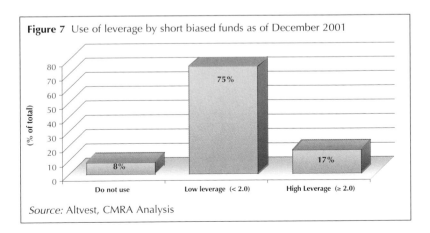

**Figure 7** Use of leverage by short biased funds as of December 2001

*Source:* Altvest, CMRA Analysis

**Table 12** Financial leverage of short biased funds in 2002

| Minimum | Average | Maximum | Rank |
|---------|---------|---------|------|
| 1.0 | 1.1 | 1.5 | 14 of 14 |

Measured as long assets / total capital
*Source*: Altvest, CMRA Analysis

**Table 13** Historical leverage of short biased funds, 1997–2001

|  | 1997 | 1998 | 1999 | 2000 | 2001 | 1997–2001 |
|--|------|------|------|------|------|-----------|
| Short selling | 0.8 | 0.8 | 0.7 | 0.9 | 1.2 | 0.9 |
| Short biased | 0.3 | 0.1 | 0.2 | 0.2 | 0.6 | 0.3 |

*Source*: Altvest, CMRA Analysis

**Table 14** Distribution of short biased funds by quartiles leverage, 1997–2001

| Leverage quartiles | Minimum leverage in quartile | Maximum leverage in quartile | Average leverage in quartile | Median leverage in quartile | Total AUM in quartile (US$ billion) | % of total AUM |
|--------------------|------------------------------|------------------------------|------------------------------|-----------------------------|-------------------------------------|----------------|
| 1 | 0.5 | 0.9 | 0.7 | 0.9 | 0.3 | 52.1 |
| 2 | 1.0 | 1.0 | 1.0 | 1.0 | 0.1 | 16.9 |
| 3 | 1.0 | 1.2 | 1.1 | 1.2 | 0.1 | 20.9 |
| 4 | 1.1 | 5.1 | 3.2 | 3.5 | 0.01 | 10.0 |
| **Total** | **0.5** | **5.1** | **1.5** | **1.1** | **0.6** | **99.8** |

*Source*: Altvest, CMRA Analysis based on 89 funds with five years of leverage data

short selling strategies. In the case of short biased, the 1997–2001 financial leverage of 0.3 is significantly lower than that for short selling of 0.9. As shown in Table 14, the leverage distribution of a sample of short biased hedge funds varies significantly.

The five-year delevered returns are lower than the reported returns by 4.4% on average, whereas the one-year delevered returns are almost the same as the reported returns (see Table 15). This suggests that short biased funds are not highly levered and that part of their portfolio is in cash. There are many limitations to short selling, doing so requires margin cash or collateral deposits which, in many cases, can be equal to a large proportion of the short proceeds.

**Table 15** Summary of levered and delevered performance of short
biased funds in 2001 (%)

|  | Maximum return | Minimum return | Average return | Maximum delevered return | Minimum delevered return | Average delevered return | Difference in returns levered vs delevered |
|---|---|---|---|---|---|---|---|
| 1997–2001 | 38.9 | (4.6) | 13.7 | 25.5 | (1.0) | 9.3 | 4.4 |
| 2001 | 15.8 | (44.3) | 0.4 | 10.4 | (20.2) | 0.7 | (0.4) |

*Source*: Altvest, CMRA Analysis

## RISK MEASUREMENT
Major risks for short biased strategies include leverage, operational and
liquidity risk, volatility, timing, corporate actions and short-squeeze risk
(see Figure 8).

### Leverage risk
Shorting derivatives such as options can greatly increase the leverage of a
fund. Furthermore, a cycle can ensue when one attempts to hedge a short
trade that has gone wrong, especially if the hedge requires the purchase of
the underlying security – as is necessary with shorting calls. In such times,
buying large amounts of the underlying security to hedge the short call
will result in the underlying security increasing in price, with a corresponding increase in loss to the fund.

### Operational and liquidity risk
The short seller has no control over the actions of the securities lender. This
is not a problem in liquid markets, such as the exchange-traded stock
markets. The downside scenario occurs when the securities lender sells its
securities and the broker cannot find another lender to take the original

**Figure 8** Risk profile for short biased strategy

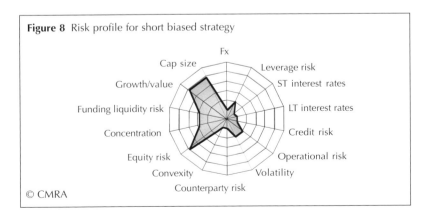

© CMRA

lender's place. In these situations, the short seller can be forced to buy back the securities in order to deliver them to the lender.

### Volatility risk

Volatility risk can complicate the underlying trend of a security and thereby undermine the economics of a short trade. This can happen whenever the price of the security begins to go up sharply after the security is sold short. The fund manager could be correct and the price of the security may decline in the long term. In the interim, however, margin calls can add to the costs of the short seller and lock up capital. Furthermore, a security whose price is very low is never a good candidate for shorting because the volatility risk is skewed to the upside.

### Timing risk

Selling short involves borrowing a security that must be returned to the lender at some point in the future, but the short seller cannot control when the lender will need the security. Therefore, the fund has to be correct about both the direction and the timing of the realisation of the desired return.

### Corporate actions risk

Mergers and takeovers can change the economics of short trades. During the technology boom, many companies used their stocks to pay for the companies they acquired. This resulted in a negative cycle of overvalued stock becoming even more overvalued because of the takeover. The probability of a merger and acquisition of a company must be considered before its stock is sold short. The payment of dividends also hurts short biased strategies because the short seller has to compensate for any dividends that the company might issue. If a dividend announcement is made after a short is initiated, it can add time constraints and costs to the trade, thereby reducing the return.

### Short-squeeze risk

Short-squeezes can render a short trade unprofitable even if the fund trader is correct. This occurs when a short seller attempts to close out the position by buying back the security in the market and no one is willing to sell the security to the trader. In such cases, the position either has to be left open until a more favourable market develops or be closed at a very high cost.

In the case of LTCM, the fund had many sell-side institutions funding it. In return for this funding, LTCM shared trade ideas with these institutions. LTCM put on many short trades along with its investors. When the market went bad, its investors began to liquidate their positions, thereby causing a squeeze that ultimately contributed to LTCM's demise. One example is when LTCM borrowed in yen (when Japanese interest rates were low) and then shorted the yen for the US dollar; the size of its short position amounted to billions of dollars. When the Russian default triggered a global crisis, most institutional investors that shorted the yen began to cover their positions, causing the yen/US dollar exchange rate to move from 135 to 117 in two days. The resulting cost to LTCM was catastrophic.

As is well known, another major issue for short biased funds is the fact that short positions normally have limited gain but no limit to potential losses. For instance, shorting a US$10 stock can only result in a maximum gain of US$10 if the stock price falls to zero. However, if the stock price rises, it can result in an unlimited loss. To mitigate this risk, short biased funds usually trade mid-cap stocks or stocks with a market capitalisation of more than US$1 billion. Diversification also plays a major role in risk control. A prominent short biased fund ensures that a particular stock comprises no more than 2% of its portfolio.

## VALUE-AT-RISK
### Overview/example
In order to see how predictive VAR can be for short biased portfolios, CMRA compared a one-year VAR to the actual one-year performance of three sample portfolios for the strategy. Each portfolio started on July 31, 2001 with a total value of US$10 million, and contained two to three shares (with an equal US dollar amount of each stock within the portfolio). The portfolio composition was as follows:

❑ Portfolio 1: Verizon, Qwest, Sprint.
❑ Portfolio 2: ATT, SBC Communications.
❑ Portfolio 3: Bed Bath & Beyond, Linens n' Things, Inc.

In the preceding year, the correlation between Portfolios 1 and 2 had been high, but neither was correlated with Portfolio 3 (see Table 16).

Since a short biased fund would be net short, a one-year VAR was calculated on long/short combinations of these portfolios, as shown in Table 17.

**Table 16** Correlations (%) between sample portfolios

|  | Portfolio 1 | Portfolio 2 | Portfolio 3 |
|---|---|---|---|
| **Portfolio 1** | 100 | 58 | 23 |
| **Portfolio 2** | 58 | 100 | 15 |
| **Portfolio 3** | 23 | 15 | 100 |

*Source*: Bloomberg Data, CMRA Analysis

**Table 17** Calculation of VAR on long/short combinations of sample portfolios July 31, 2001–July 31, 2002

| | Portfolio value (US$ million) | | Profit and loss (US$ million) | 95% 1-year VAR (US$ million) on 31/07/01 |
|---|---|---|---|---|
| | 31/07/2001 | 31/07/2002 | | |
| Long portfolio 1, Short portfolios 2 and 3 | (10.0) | (11.6) | (1.6) | (10.1) |
| Long portfolio 2, Short portfolios 1 and 3 | (10.0) | (7.5) | 2.5 | (11.2) |
| Long portfolio 3, Short portfolios 1 and 2 | (10.0) | 0.4 | 10.4 | (12.4)* |

*95% chance the profit or loss will never exceed US$12.4 million

*Source*: Bloomberg Data, CMRA Analysis

**Table 18** Correlations (%) between sample portfolios July 31, 2001–July 31, 2002

| | Portfolio 1 | Portfolio 2 | Portfolio 3 |
|---|---|---|---|
| **Portfolio 1** | 100 | 64 | 19 |
| **Portfolio 2** | 64 | 100 | 27 |
| **Portfolio 3** | 19 | 27 | 100 |

*Source*: Bloomberg Data, CMRA Analysis

It was apparent that, while the P&L for the three combinations in Table 17 was within the calculated VAR, the P&L of the third combination was very close to the 95% confidence level VAR (although in a favorable direction). This suggests that it is necessary to estimate the appropriate correlations and volatilities if the VAR numbers for the strategy are to be reliable. The correlation matrix as of July 31, 2002, hardly changed from the previous year (see Table 18).

**STRESS TESTS**
Stress tests that should be considered for this strategy include:

❏ price shifts in equities, sectors, indices, currencies and commodities;
❏ VAR;
❏ products with uncertain cashflows;
❏ product complexity;
❏ difficult-to-model risks;
❏ concentrations;
❏ correlations;
❏ short-squeeze;

❑ liquidity; and
❑ leverage.

## DUE DILIGENCE QUESTIONS

Most of the due diligence questions for assessing short biased funds are similar to those for the underlying asset class. (See Chapters 14, 19 and 20 for discussion on the long/short equity, market neutral and fixed income strategies.)

Due diligence questions generally touch on the understanding of economic and/or corporate conditions drive returns in the strategy, they also measure the fund's relationship with the trading desks they do business with and the liquidity of the traded instruments.

In addition, short biased funds must attempt to understand the composition of the fund's portfolio at all times. No portfolio is exclusively designed to be short biased; the VAR example given earlier shows how the bets in one dimension can still mean increasing exposure in the other. More specific questions for the strategy could include:

❑ What arrangements has the fund made with the broker or repo desk to facilitate short sales?
❑ How liquid are the markets in which the funds participate?
❑ How do the funds operate in a squeeze?

# SECTION VI

# Appendices

# Hedge Fund Disclosure for Institutional Investors

The Investor Risk Committee (IRC) was launched by the IAFE in January, 2000. The IRC consists of individuals from hedge fund investment managers, herein referred to as "managers" and from a variety of institutional investors including pension funds, endowments, foundations, insurance companies, fund of funds and others, herein referred to as "investors".[1]

## INTRODUCTION

Over the past 18 months the IRC has held six working sessions in New York, Boston, and London on the topic "What is the right level of disclosure by hedge funds?". In 2001 the IRC formed 11 smaller working groups to expand the consensus document published by the IRC in October of 2000. The subgroups formed by the IRC cover nine common hedge fund strategies plus a "fund of funds" group to address aggregation issues across strategies. In addition, an "alternate approaches" group was formed as a number of IRC members felt that few hedge funds fit into one of the nine pure strategy types on a consistent basis.

### Highlights from this release

❏ Section I provides expanded detail regarding the 3rd finding from the October 2000 IRC release. The 3rd finding discussed the reporting of summary risk, return and position information as an alternative to full position disclosure and set forth four dimensions: content, granularity, frequency, and delay. This release includes 20 added findings. Where IRC members felt it useful, specific commentary is provided for specific hedge fund strategy types.

❏ Section II provides an alternate framework for classifying hedge funds. This framework eliminates the need to classify a hedge fund by type of strategy. The dimensions of this new framework are asset class, direction, type, region, liquidity and turnover.

The 11 working groups of the IRC are:

1. Convertible arbitrage

2. Event driven
3. Fixed income arbitrage
4. Long/short equity
5. Emerging markets
6. Global macro
7. Managed futures
8. Market neutral
9. Dedicated short bias
10. Fund of funds
11. Alternate approaches

As with the October 12, 2000 document, this is not meant to be the final word. The IRC plans to continue its work and to expand the content of this document in future releases. The goal of the IRC is to provide results that will be useful to investors and managers alike to benchmark their practices relative to their peers.

As in its initial document, the IRC adopts the definition of a hedge fund used in "Sound Practices for Hedge Fund Managers" published in February 2000: "a pooled investment vehicle that is privately organised, administered by a professional investment management firm . . . and not widely available to the public".[2] As such, a wide variety of investment vehicles are included in this definition – small and large (in assets or staff), operating in one market or many, following a single, simple strategy or a combination of complex strategies, operating on-shore or off-shore under varying organisational structures, etc.

*IRC Findings (reprinted from the October 12, 2000 findings)*
1. Investors have three primary objectives in seeking disclosure from managers
   ❏ Risk monitoring: ensuring that managers are not taking on risks beyond represented levels in terms of allowable investments, exposures, leverage, etc.
   ❏ Risk aggregation: ensuring the investors' ability to aggregate risks across their entire investment programme in order to understand portfolio level implications
   ❏ Strategy drift monitoring: ensuring the investors' ability to determine whether a manager is adhering to the stated investment strategy or style
2. IRC members agreed that full position disclosure by managers does not always allow them to achieve their monitoring objectives, and may compromise a hedge fund's ability to executive its investment strategy.

   Despite the fact that many investors receive full position disclosure for many of their investments, the members of the IRC who have participated in the meetings to date were in agreement that full position disclosure by managers is not the solution. Managers expressed significant concerns over the harm that full position disclosure could cause for many common hedge fund strategies (for example macro and risk arbitrage). Investors agreed they did not wish to force disclosure that would be adverse to the manager, and therefore to their investment. In addition, many investors expressed concern over the operational difficulties associated with processing such vast quantities of diverse data.

3. IRC members agreed that the reporting of summary risk, return and position information can be sufficient as an alternative to full position disclosure. Such summary information should be evaluated on four dimensions: content, granularity, frequency, and delay.

❑ Content: describes the quality and sufficiency of coverage of the manager's activities. This dimension covers information about the risk, return and positions on an actual as well as on a stress-tested basis.

❑ Granularity: describes the level of detail. Examples are NAV disclosure, disclosure of risk factors (APT,[3] VAR,[4] etc.), disclosure of tracking error or other risk and return measures at the portfolio level, by region, by asset class, by duration, by significant holdings, etc.

❑ Frequency: describes how often the disclosure is made. High turnover trading strategies may require more frequent disclosure (for example, daily) than private or distressed-debt investment funds where monthly or quarterly disclosure is more appropriate.

❑ Delay: describes how much of a lag occurs between when the fund is in a certain condition and when that fact is disclosed to investors. A fund might agree to full or summary position disclosure, but only after the positions are no longer held.

4. IRC members agreed that usability of any alternative disclosure depends upon sufficient understanding of the definitions, calculation methodologies, assumptions and data employed by the manager. This may be accomplished in a variety of fashions including discussions between investors and managers; by the manager providing for adequate transparency of their process; or via independent verification.

5. IRC members should benchmark their practices relative to their peers. IRC members agreed that a major challenge to peer group performance and risk comparisons as well as aggregation across managers is the use of a variety of calculation methodologies, assumptions and data employed in the market place. IRC members did not, however, feel that "one size fits all", and felt that multiple peer groups may be relevant depending on the nature of the investor as well as the strategies employed by the manager. Investors and managers believe that an industry effort should be made to improve the ability to conduct comparisons across managers as well as multi-manager portfolio analysis.

6. IRC members agreed that detailed reporting is not a substitute for initial and ongoing due diligence reviews, on-site visits and appropriate dialogue between investors and managers.
7. IRC members agreed that market, credit, leverage, liquidity and operational risks are interrelated. Accordingly, exposure to these risks in combination should be included in the dialogue between investors and managers.

## SECTION I

This section provides expanded detail regarding the 3rd finding from the October 2000 IRC release. The 3rd finding discussed the reporting of summary risk, return and position information as an alternative to full position disclosure and set forth four dimensions: content, granularity, frequency, and delay (see above). Overall, IRC members observed that disclosure of information should minimise the possibility that it could adversely impact the fund. This requires limiting the degree of detail that is revealed, closely limiting the recipients and using confidentiality or other protections as necessary. An overarching finding by the IRC for each of the detailed comments that follow is that disclosure should *not* be made if it jeopardises the returns of the fund.

### Dimension #1
*Content*:
Describes the quality and sufficiency of coverage of the manager's activities. This dimension covers information about the risk, return and positions on an actual as well as on a stress-tested basis. Regarding content, the IRC was in agreement that:

❑ VAR can be useful information but should be calculated using an industry-standard definition.
   Currently there is no industry-standard definition for VAR for hedge funds nor is there an industry-standard definition for VAR for many types of firms such as mutual funds, banks or insurance companies. An industry standard definition may be able to be developed for many types of hedge funds and assets classes. However, IRC members noted that while common historical data exist for many asset classes, data do not exist for all asset classes or for many spreads that are traded by hedge funds. Accordingly, for strategies that involve spreads (eg, fixed income arbitrage) and/or specialty assets classes, use of VAR should be discouraged unless it explicitly models the particular "spread" or "specialty asset class" risks in the portfolio. Where use of VAR under an industry standard definition is not possible, simulations of the portfolio under various scenarios are an acceptable substitute.
   The IRC encourages members to cooperate to build the necessary

data required so that all types of assets and spreads may be included in an industry standard definition for VAR. The IRC observes that any development of any industry standard definition – and the necessary data — will take time and must take into account the cost of conversion/implementation to managers. Switching from existing methodologies to an industry standard methodology could result in material and substantial expenditures for many funds.

Pending the development of an industry-standard definition of VAR, managers who use VAR may use methods that are appropriate to their investments. As a consensus on industry standards develops, managers should work to incorporate those standards as soon as practicable if VAR is appropriate for their fund(s). IRC members underscored the value this will have in addressing aggregation issues across managers.

❏ Aggregate measures of a fund's exposure to different types of asset classes can be useful.

Global macro managers and event driven managers – and investors in these types of managers – expressed the concern that disclosure could place the manager's returns in jeopardy. Where possible, profiles of interest to investors include interest rates, equities, commodities and currencies. In addition, volatility and credit, while not considered traditional asset classes, may be of interest to investors for portfolios that involve transactions such as volatility swaps and notes or credit derivatives. Managers may draw from many different types of aggregate measures such as VAR by asset class, marginal VAR by asset class, the absolute value of gross and/or net exposure by asset class, and percentage of overall cash invested per asset class.

❏ Aggregate measures of a fund's exposure to different geographic regions can be useful.

This only should be disclosed if it does not jeopardise the returns of the fund. Global macro managers and event driven managers – and investors in these types of managers – expressed the concern that disclosure could place the manager's returns in jeopardy. Where possible, profiles of interest to investors include US, Euro, other G-7 currencies, and emerging market currencies.

❏ Net asset value (NAV) and stress measures of NAV appropriate to the strategy can be useful.

   ❏ The IRC noted that benchmarks are commonly used to generate the NAV and NAV stress measures for many hedge fund strategy types. The IRC observed that in some cases the use of benchmarks for this type of disclosure might be better replaced by historical simulations. For example, if a market neutral manager in US large cap equities uses the S&P index as a proxy for the long/short positions, this may understate any sector risk that exists in the portfolio. Benchmarks pose a similar issue for arbitrage managers. For such managers, historical simulations designed for the specific risks of the portfolio may be an acceptable substitute. Another useful representation of stress measures is as a percentage impact on capital.

❏ Cash as a per cent of equity can be useful.

Some members of the IRC noted that liquidity as a per cent of equity and/or liquidity expressed relative to VAR may be more appropriate measures for some funds. These measures are an area in which the IRC plans additional work.

❏ Correlation to an appropriate benchmark can be useful.

In addition to correlation with a benchmark, certain investors may also wish to measure the tracking error and information ratio of a portfolio relative to a benchmark. Investors and managers in the IRC unanimously agreed that these are not appropriate for many types of hedge fund managers, particularly those who allocate capital into different types of asset classes and/or strategies during the course of a reporting period.

❏ Delta, gamma and other measures of optionality, as appropriate, can be useful.

❏ Key spread relationships, as appropriate, can be useful.

### Dimension # 2

*Granularity*: describes the level of detail.

Examples are NAV disclosure, disclosure of risk factors (APT, VAR, etc.), disclosure of tracking error or other risk and return measures at the portfolio level, by region, by asset class, by duration, by significant holdings, etc.

❏ Granularity depends on the size of the fund/pool.

For example a small portfolio has little potential market impact so highly granular disclosure could be "costless" and would not jeopardise the manager's positions. For large portfolios, granular disclosure is far from costless and can be ruinous.

Large funds/pools need to limit granularity of reporting sufficiently to protect investors against predatory trading against the manager's positions.

❏ For those funds/pools who will not place the investor's interests at risk through such disclosure, the top 10 single exposures and concentrated sector exposures expressed on a net basis can be useful. Absolute value may be used to protect the directional position of the manager. Some IRC members observed that the availability of information on long equity holdings could be combined with any net holding information to derive short positions and therefore that net position disclosure could be detrimental and should not be made by such funds.

❏ Where it is not possible to disclose the top 10 single exposures, disclo-

sure by asset class and by region can be useful, but should be limited to protect investors against predatory trading against the manager's positions.
❏ To the degree that it is not damaging to the manager's positions – and hence the investor's returns – statistics reported by asset class/ region can be useful if their gross long exposure exceeds 20% of total.

## Dimension # 3
*Frequency*: describes how often the disclosure is made.
High turnover trading strategies may require more frequent disclosure (for example, daily) than private or distressed-debt investment funds where monthly or quarterly disclosure is more appropriate.

❏ Summary statistics can be useful to investors and reported as frequently as monthly. Investor members of the IRC noted that this is consistent with how many of their managers are monitored and that monthly disclosure of risk statistics would be more frequent than what is provided by many mutual funds.
❏ If the strategy is illiquid or exhibits light turnover, then quarterly disclosure may be sufficient. Disclosure can be more frequent (monthly) for portfolios that turn over more frequently.
❏ Performance attribution can be useful to disclose more frequently than risk attribution.
❏ In the monthly disclosure it can be useful to include the previous month's history of daily profit and loss for funds who have investments that are able to be marked to market on a daily basis.

## Dimension #4
*Delay*: describes how much of a lag occurs between when the fund is in a certain condition and when that fact is disclosed to investors. A fund might agree to full or summary position disclosure, but only after the positions are no longer held.

❏ Summary statistics should be disclosed as soon as is practicable following the end of the reporting period (preferably within 10 days) subject to protecting the interests of investors from suffering adverse market impact from that disclosure.
❏ Practically, delay may be viewed as a function of the average holding period in a given strategy.
❏ Disclosure may use generic rather than specific names if the strategy is still active at the time of the disclosure.

## SECTION II[5]

In this section, the IRC provides the following "alternative approach" to hedge fund classifications as a starting point for discussion about disclosure findings. The IRC reiterates that this is an important framework to develop given the lack of "pure" hedge fund types that exist in the market place. The lack of pure hedge funds types – and the fact that many practitioners and academics continue to classify hedge funds by pure types – creates significant noise in many existing hedge fund indices. This calls into question the results of studies that depend upon these classifications. The IRC expects this framework to change substantially as it evolves and is merged with the work in Section I.

The IRC envisions that managers would reclassify themselves as necessary under this framework. For discussion purposes, the IRC classified the activities of traditional and hedge fund managers into the following five types:

### 1. Asset class

The asset class is the broadest category, and defines the market in which the fund operates. The following are the suggested types of asset classes:

❏ Interest rates
❏ Equities
❏ Foreign exchange
❏ Commodities
❏ Multi-class – this is meant to capture "none or some of the above", and specifically includes global macro funds.

### 2. Direction

The direction of the manager's activity in the asset class indicates the net exposure and correlation the manager tends to have with the key risk factor of that asset class. The IRC suggests the following directional classifications:

❏ Long
❏ Short
❏ Long/short
❏ Neutral

The IRC observes that direction may be misleading or impossible to apply to a global macro fund. However, for managers with more consistent investments in one or more asset classes, the following correlation ranges are suggested as a straw man to establish the "direction" categories:

❏ Long            over +0.5
❏ Short           under –0.5

❑ Long/short       between −0.5 and +0.5
❑ Neutral           between −0.2 and +0.2
❑ Event             usually zero, sometimes high (ie, in liquidity or credit crises)

Example: for a large cap US stock fund, the S&P may be an appropriate benchmark against which to calculate correlation for directional evaluation; for a European bond fund it might be the Bund.

The IRC notes that a substantially long-only manager may show low correlation with a benchmark so would be classified as a "neutral". The following net exposure measures are suggested as a straw man to address this:

❑ Long             net exposure over + 60%
❑ Short            net exposure under −20%
❑ Longshort      net exposure between + 20% and + 60%
❑ Neutral           net exposure between −20% and + 20%
❑ Event             net exposure typically between 0% and 20%

To perform the calculation of net exposure take the market value of long exposure minus the market value of short exposure and divide the result by capital.

## 3. Type

The type provides more information, particularly in the case of managers who have "neutral" and/or "event" direction categories under the previous classification. Greater information is helpful because the risk of these types of activities are not well described by the variation of the asset class index. The following classifications are suggested as a straw man to establish the "type" categories for such managers:

*Type (for neutral classification)*
❑ Relative value
❑ Convertible arbitrage
❑ Statistical arbitrage
❑ Quantitative/systematic equity selection
❑ Option arbitrage

*Type (for event classification)*
❑ Merger arbitrage
❑ Credit arbitrage
❑ Distressed debt

## 4. Region

The region provides information regarding where the fund is trading. To the degree this classification places the manager's positions and or returns in jeopardy, differentiation may be limited to "G-10" and "emerging markets." The following classifications are suggested as a straw man to establish the "region" categories for managers:

*G-10*
❏ US and Canada
❏ Euro zone
❏ Other European
❏ Japan
❏ Global

*Emerging markets*
❏ Eastern Europe
❏ Latin America
❏ East Asia
❏ Emerging Market Global

## 5. Liquidity

Some funds trade short-term and are in instruments that can be traded easily. Other funds are less liquid either because of their strategies, the types of instruments they hold, or the size of their holdings. The following classifications are suggested as a straw man to establish the "strategy" categories for such managers:

❏ Highly liquid: most positions can be liquidated in a few days;
❏ Liquid: most positions can be liquidated in one to two weeks;
❏ Illiquid: positions cannot be easily liquidated, with some taking months.

## 6. Turnover

A second approach to classifying liquidity is turnover, which addresses the percentage of portfolio turnover on a monthly or annual basis. The following classifications are suggested as a straw man to establish the "turnover" categories for managers:

❏ Low turnover: strategies that were the bulk of the positions (>50%) were carried over a month would be low turnover.
❏ Moderate turnover: strategies were the bulk of the positions changed during the month, but were carried over from day to day.
❏ High turnover: strategies which involved daily turnover greater than 25%, on at least several days a month.

*Examples of Framework #2 Classification*

With this categorisation scheme, a technology fund might be "stocks-long/short-US-highly liquid" while another technology fund may be classified as "stocks-long-us-illiquid".

A Japanese distressed debt fund would be "bonds-event-distressed-Japan-illiquid" while a US corporate bond fund would be "bonds-event-credit-US-liquid".

## CONCLUSION

IRC members observe that whether using the strategy classification types or the new framework for hedge funds, challenges will still remain to get to peer comparisons and benchmarking. The due diligence process is a critical part of this process. Hence, the IRC reiterates the importance of consensus statement number #6 from its October 2000 document *"IRC Members agreed that detailed reporting is not a substitute for initial and ongoing due diligence reviews, on-site visits and appropriate dialog between Investors and Managers"*.

The IRC's goal is to provide the consensus of a substantial group of managers and investors regarding "What is the right level of disclosure by hedge funds?" The IRC invites all managers, investors and other interested parties to comment and assist this industry group in the evolution of this document. Other interested parties include regulators, industry associations, prime brokers, custodians, consultants and other service providers, among others.

The IRC plans additional forums on related topics, including implementation of these findings, and solicits your input regarding items of interest to you and the IRC's work.[6]

1   See Appendix A for a detailed listing of the IRC's participants to date.
2   This 80-page document may be downloaded from: http://www.mfainfo.org/washington/hedgefunds/HFMSoundPractices.PDF
3   APT refers to the arbitrage pricing theory, but we consider any models that use a linear combination of risk factors that can be combined to explain the risk of a particular holding or portfolio of holdings.
4   VAR refers to Value at Risk, a probabilistic statement about the estimated capital at risk of loss within a given confidence interval over a given period of time.
5   This section is drawn from Richard Bookstaber, "Definitions of Trading Strategies", Working Paper, April, 2001.
6   About the IAFE. The IAFE is a global organisation devoted to defining and fostering the professions of quantitative finance, risk management and financial engineering. Collaboration and networking between academics and practitioners and across different sectors of the practitioner world are major objectives of the IAFE. Over the past 10 years, the Association has pursued its mission of promoting informed exchanges among members to further understanding, share best practices and establish standards on pertinent aspects of finance. The work of the Investor Risk Committee (IRC) on hedge funds is an important part of this mission. Education is a major component of the IAFE's activities. The IAFE sponsors numerous sessions and conferences where new products, strategies, quantitative finance

and technologies are discussed among practitioners and academics and where public policy issues are debated. The IAFE publishes the Journal of Derivatives which represents a merger with the IAFE's former publication the Journal of Financial Engineering. Past issues have carried articles by such luminaries as Nobel Laureates Harry Markowitz and the late Merton Miller. Visit IAFE at *www.iafe.org*.

# Sound Practices for Hedge Fund Managers*

In April 1999, the President's Working Group on Financial Markets (the PWG), comprised of the Secretary of the US Department of the Treasury and the respective chairs of the Board of Governors of the Federal Reserve System, the Securities and Exchange Commission and the Commodity Futures Trading Commission, published its report entitled "Hedge Funds, Leverage and the Lessons of Long-Term Capital Management", (the PWG Report). This report recommended that a number of measures be implemented by financial institutions, regulators and hedge funds to enhance risk management practices.[†] In the section entitled "Enhanced Private Sector Practices for Counterparty Risk Management", it stated:

> A group of hedge funds should draft and publish a set of sound practices for their risk management and internal controls. Such a study should discuss market risk measurement and management, liquidity risk management, identification of concentrations, stress testing, collateral management, valuation of positions and collateral, segregation of duties and internal controls, and the assessment of capital needs from the perspective of hedge funds. In addition, the study should consider how individual hedge funds could assess their performance against the sound practices for investors and counterparties.[1]

## OBJECTIVES OF THIS DOCUMENT
### Respond to the PWG Report
Following the publication of the PWG Report, a group of certain of the largest independent hedge fund managers came together to address the PWG's recommendation to develop and publish sound practices for risk management and internal controls. The views and recommendations set forth in this document reflect the input of this group. The sound practices recommendations that follow are intended to respond to the PWG Report by contributing to a continuing evolution of hedge fund manager practices. Many recommended practices have already been adopted by a number of larger hedge fund managers in recent years, as their growth has resulted in the implementation of more formalised and sophisticated management policies and structures. Other practices were initiated

following the market crisis of August 1998, which created a heightened awareness among all market participants of the need for regular stress testing of market risk models and liquidity analyses. Other recommended practices are aspirational and represent goals that hedge fund managers, depending on their size and objectives, should strive to achieve. Given that the practices recommended were developed by larger hedge fund managers based on their views and business models, many may not be applicable to smaller hedge funds.

### Strengthen hedge fund business practices

As part of this process and as markets continue to evolve, it is anticipated that the recommendations will be further adapted and refined. It is intended that hedge fund managers, by evaluating the recommendations and applying those that suit their particular business model, will strengthen their own businesses while contributing to market soundness by reducing the risk of their own default or failure. In this regard, this document complements the work of the Counterparty Risk Management Policy Group (the CRMPG) in its report of June 1999, which addressed many of these same issues from the perspective of a counterparty credit provider and proposed measures that seek to reduce the risk of defaults that could result in a systemic impact on financial markets.

### One size does not fit all

It is important to recognise in evaluating the recommendations that the hedge fund industry is global and that the strategies, investment approaches and organisational structures of hedge fund managers vary greatly. The variations in organisational structures can be attributed partly to differences in size and partly to the different strategies used by hedge fund managers, which are distinguishable both in terms of their complexity and their product focus. The major strategies include:

❏ macro or global directional investment strategies;
❏ market neutral or arbitrage strategies;
❏ long only, short only or long/short strategies for trading in equities;
❏ event-driven strategies that seek to profit from anticipated events, such as mergers or restructurings;
❏ regional strategies that concentrate on a particular geographic region (such as emerging markets); and
❏ sectoral strategies, which focus on a particular industry and specific asset class strategies (such as currencies).

The complexity of the strategy employed and the breadth of markets covered, combined with the amount of assets under management, will play a large part in determining the operational requirements of a hedge fund manager. For example, the infrastructure needs of a hedge fund manager managing several diversified macrofunds with several billion in net assets will be significantly greater than those of a long-only fund manager that principally trades US equities for a single fund of modest size.

The differences between Long-Term Capital Management (LTCM) and most other hedge fund managers should also be acknowledged. The scale of LTCM's trading activities and the extent of leverage applied by LTCM at the time of its near collapse were unique. LTCM employed particularly high levels of leverage in connection with its arbitrage strategies in order to profit from small discrepancies in the pricing of certain instruments. LTCM sought to leverage such narrow pricing anomalies into attractive returns for its sizeable investor base by borrowing and establishing very large positions to exploit the pricing "spread" it identified. LTCM's massive use of leverage seriously compromised its ability to absorb losses when market conditions moved against it and spreads widened (rather than converging, as predicted). Its situation was further aggravated by its significant investments in illiquid instruments.

The hedge fund managers that developed the recommendations employ primarily global macro trading strategies that involve taking positions in a wide variety of largely liquid markets based on perceived broad economic trends. If a portfolio manager accurately predicts the direction of a market using this strategy, a relatively modest position can generate substantial profits without the use of excessive leverage. Although certain hedge fund managers make use of market neutral or arbitrage/convergence strategies similar to those used by LTCM, the scale of LTCM's trading using these strategies and the levels of leverage assumed by LTCM in connection with such strategies were extraordinary.

### Individualised assessment and application of recommendations

The recommendations are not necessarily the only means of achieving sound practices and they should not be viewed as prescriptive requirements to be rigidly applied by all hedge fund managers. Rather, each hedge fund manager should assess the recommendations based on the size, nature and complexity of its organisation, its strategies and resources, as well as the objectives of the funds it manages, and apply them as appropriate. Certain recommendations may not be relevant or appropriate to every hedge fund manager. In evaluating the relevance of the recommendations and the ability to implement them, hedge fund managers should recognise that, while some recommendations can be implemented easily or unilaterally, others may require substantial planning and significant budgetary commitments, involve internal systems changes and infrastructure development, or negotiation with and co-operation by third parties. It should also be recognised that, while some recommendations have already been widely adopted, many are aspirational in nature or represent emerging practices that generally have not been implemented by hedge fund managers to date. Consequently, the recommendations should not be construed as definitive requirements that could serve as a basis for either auditing hedge fund managers or assessing their financial stability.

## Background on hedge funds

### Hedge fund defined

This document employs the PWG's general definition of a hedge fund ("hedge fund" or "fund"): a pooled investment vehicle that is privately organised, administered by a professional investment management firm (referred to herein as a hedge fund manager), and not widely available to the public. As the PWG Report observed, the term "hedge fund" is used to describe a wide range of investment vehicles, which can vary substantially in terms of size, strategy, business model and organisational structure, among other characteristics. This definition captures most of the types of investment pools that the recommendations seek to address.

### The nature of hedge funds

In assessing the appropriateness of the recommendations for risk management and internal controls, it is important to distinguish the needs of hedge fund managers from those of credit providers, such as banks and other financial institutions that seek to eliminate and minimise the risks of their businesses through hedging, and other risk management methods that seek to reduce risk. Hedge fund managers are in the business of seeking and assuming calculated risks and are retained by the funds they manage to take on such risks in order to achieve the returns sought by their investors. By participating in the market as risk seekers, hedge fund managers play a unique and critical role in financial markets by providing needed liquidity and reducing systemic risk. In this sense hedge funds often act as "risk absorbers" in markets by serving as ready counterparties to those wishing to hedge risk, even when markets are volatile, and, in doing so, reduce pressure on market prices while increasing liquidity. Additionally, hedge fund managers, through their trading based on extensive research, bring price information to the markets, which translates into market price efficiencies. Without the manager's research and commitment of capital, the markets would have potentially wider price spreads, pricing inefficiencies and illiquidity.

Perhaps, most importantly, by standing ready to lose capital, hedge funds act as a buffer for other market participants in absorbing "shocks". The managers that developed the recommendations have each been active investors and market participants for over 10 years in a variety of market environments. Despite having been required to navigate difficult conditions and market crises, these firms have experienced substantial growth in assets and provided investors with attractive returns. Hedge funds also can afford investors valuable portfolio diversification, given that the performance of many hedge fund investments is uncorrelated to that of traditional investments, such as stocks and bonds. Hedge fund managers, like other large investors, are known to market regulators and supervisory authorities. In connection with their trading activities, hedge fund managers currently furnish significant information and reports to regulators (as detailed in the Additional Notes with respect to the United States).

*Relationship of hedge funds and hedge fund managers*

The recommendations assume that a hedge fund is governed by a board of directors, managing member, general partner, trustee or similar individual or entity with the legal authority and responsibility to direct and oversee the activities of the fund (referred to as the fund's "governing authority"). In addition, it is assumed that the assets of each fund are managed by an investment adviser or manager (the "hedge fund manager"), pursuant to an advisory or management agreement with the fund, and that the hedge fund manager is itself governed by a management committee. This committee is a group of executives or other body with the authority and responsibility to direct and oversee the hedge fund manager's trading activities on behalf of the fund ("senior management"). It is recognised, however, that the nature and structure of funds and the relationships with their managers vary substantially. In some cases, a hedge fund may have a formal board of directors, while in other cases the hedge fund manager conducts all material aspects of the hedge fund's management. In addition, the nature and structure of hedge fund managers vary substantially. Certain managers may be primarily governed by a board of directors or supervisory board, while others may be managed by their senior investment personnel. The recommendations also assume the following.

❏ A hedge fund is a separate legal entity managed under contract by the hedge fund manager. A hedge fund has an overall investment objective and may have investment restrictions that cannot be changed without notice to or approval by investors or a governing authority representing investors.

❏ Hedge fund managers may also be, and usually are, investors in the hedge funds they manage and usually are compensated in part based on the performance of the hedge fund. This structure, as well as reputational considerations, create a strong unity of interests between a hedge fund and its manager.

## Risk functions of hedge fund managers

The activities of a hedge fund manager must reflect the fact that the business of a hedge fund is to seek returns by assuming commensurate levels of risk. Hedge fund managers take investment risk, in accordance with their funds' expectations, in order to earn commensurate returns. In this regard, managers must understand the sources of the returns the hedge fund is earning and identify the types and levels of risk associated with these returns. Based on this understanding, hedge fund managers should generally perform the following risk functions.

1. Consistent with its agreement with the hedge fund's governing authority and disclosure made to investors, senior management of the hedge fund manager should determine the appropriate overall level of risk for a particular fund.
2. This overall level of risk should then be allocated (among portfolio managers, strategies, asset classes, etc).
3. Once the risk allocation is determined, portfolio managers should choose the specific risks (consistent with the policies established by senior management) to be assumed, and enter into transactions in order to gain exposure to those risks.
4. The risk actually assumed by a fund must then be analysed and monitored by an independent risk analysis function, or "risk monitoring function". The resulting risk information must be disseminated to senior management and, as appropriate, to portfolio managers.
5. Senior management must ensure that risk levels are acceptable and consistent with established risk policies and parameters.

In summary, senior management are responsible for setting, allocating and controlling risk (Steps 1, 2 and 5); portfolio managers are responsible for putting the plan into action (Step 3); and the "risk monitoring function" is responsible for monitoring and analysing the levels of risk actually assumed by the hedge fund in relation to the risk policies set by senior management, as well as reporting this information to senior management (Step 4).

In the context of hedge fund managers, certain individuals may perform more than one function. For example, a portfolio manager may also be a key member of a hedge fund manager's senior management. Likewise, overlap between senior management and risk monitoring often occurs, eg, it is not uncommon for a senior manager to play an active role in the risk monitoring function. In fact, the smaller the hedge fund manager's organisation, the greater this overlap will likely be. It is critical however, that internal controls ensure the integrity of the risk monitoring function by enforcing its functional independence from the portfolio management (or trading) function.

The management and monitoring of risk is a complex and technical subject and an exhaustive treatment of the topic is beyond the scope of this document. The recommendations seek to address the risk functions of hedge fund managers in a concise manner. The Appendix, "Risk Monitoring Practices for Hedge Fund Managers", seeks to elaborate on the issues related to the recommendations made with respect to risk monitoring.

## ORGANISATION OF THE RECOMMENDATIONS

The recommendations are divided into four major sections. The first addresses the responsibilities of senior management of the hedge fund manager, particularly with respect to establishing risk parameters and monitoring trading activities. The second section proposes sound practices for risk measurement and monitoring to ensure that the risk policies set by senior management are observed. The third section recommends disclosure practices to be observed when dealing with fund investors and boards of directors, counterparties and credit providers, regulatory bodies and the public. The last section proposes sound documentation practices and addresses other legal and compliance issues.

The following key points are fundamental to the recommendations.

*1. Risk allocation and assessment are managed together*
Senior management, in assigning portfolio management and trading responsibilities, should allocate capital and risk based on defined investment objectives and risk parameters, and control the allocations based on information supplied by an independent risk monitoring function. The ultimate monitoring of risk is conducted by senior management and therefore should not be divorced from decisions to allocate risk. This approach may differ from a credit provider's approach to risk management which strives for separation of these functions.

*2. Recognise interplay of different types of risks*
Hedge fund managers must recognise that market, credit and liquidity risks are interrelated, requiring the hedge fund manager to analyse the consequences of the fund's exposure to these risks in combination.

*3. Assess liquidity during stress*
Hedge fund managers should assess how funding liquidity may be compromised during periods of stress and seek to establish reliable sources of financing in order to enhance financial stability in volatile market conditions. In particular, the hedge fund manager should assess how unexpected events may cause losses that may force the liquidation of positions, and the potential "spiral" effects of such a forced liquidation on the value of the portfolios under management and sources of liquidity.

### 4. Use risk-based leverage measures

Recognising that the importance of leverage is the impact it can have on market risk, credit risk and liquidity risk, hedge fund managers should focus on measures of leverage that relate the riskiness of the portfolio to the ability of the fund to absorb that risk – "risk-based leverage". Hedge fund managers should consider tracking the degree to which the fund is able to modify its risk-based leverage, by tracking the relation between the fund's market risk and actions taken. Hedge fund managers also should track traditional, accounting-based measures of leverage, because those traditional measures provide insights into the source of risk-based leverage and how that leverage could be changed.

### 5. Develop informational reports for counterparties

Each hedge fund manager should work with its counterparties to establish periodic reports that will strengthen relationship stability and, in doing so, contribute to market confidence.

### 6. Work with regulators

Hedge fund managers should work with regulators to address their specific market concerns and objectives. As significant participants in a broad array of global markets, hedge funds, like other major financial institutions and other large investors, should be prepared to co-operate with relevant regulators interested in monitoring the markets to reduce systemic risk while preserving the confidentiality of proprietary information.

### 7. Develop consensus on public disclosure

Hedge fund managers should co-ordinate with counterparties and regulators to reach a broad consensus on public disclosure which takes into account the benefits and costs to investors, creditors and the markets.

### 8. Standardise documentation and reflect collateral and default triggers in risk analysis

Each hedge fund manager should seek to standardise its approach to negotiating transaction documentation in order to achieve appropriate levels of consistency with its different counterparties and so that the legal consequences of unexpected losses or market crises (eg, collateral calls, defaults, termination events) are known and may be reflected in stress/scenario testing.

## RECOMMENDATIONS
### Organisational structure and internal controls

Hedge fund managers should clearly define the investment objectives and risk parameters for each fund, and the trading policies and risk limits necessary to achieve these objectives. Managers should adopt an organisational structure that ensures effective monitoring of compliance with investment and valuation policies by allocating defined supervisory responsibilities and maintaining clear reporting lines. Suitably qualified personnel should be retained and adequate systems should be established to produce periodic reporting that permits senior management to monitor trading activities and operations effectively. Internal procedures and periodic independent review processes should seek to ensure the enforcement of policies and identify deviations from those policies. Appropriate controls, reporting and review processes should apply to internal and external managers or traders. Third-party service providers that perform key business functions (such as NAV calculation) also should be subject to appropriate controls and review processes.

### Roles and responsibilities of senior management

Senior management should approve policies and procedures commensurate with the size, nature and complexity of the manager's trading activities and consistent with the directives received from the governing authorities of the hedge funds it manages, and should review and update them when significant market events or changes in strategy occur and otherwise as appropriate.

Policies and procedures should be developed for trading activities, risk analysis, documentation, employee compliance and other key business areas, as appropriate (see specific recommendations under "Risk Monitoring" and under "Legal and Compliance").

Senior management should determine the investment and trading policies to be observed, including targeted risk profiles and parameters, based on the investment objectives of each hedge fund under management.

Senior management should allocate capital and risk based on a fund's performance objectives and targeted risk profile, taking into account the risk analysis produced by the risk monitoring function. Allocations should be re-examined and adjusted periodically (eg, at least once a year and following major market events). Senior management should have an understanding of risk analysis and undertake a rational and reasoned approach to the allocation and distribution of capital and risk among traders, strategies, asset classes and geographical regions.

Senior management should impose appropriate controls over the hedge fund manager's portfolio management and trading activities to ensure that these activities are undertaken on a basis consistent with senior management's allocated investment and trading parameters and with the investment objectives/strategies disclosed to a fund's governing authority and investors. Senior management should analyse and evaluate trading activities by regularly reviewing reports produced by the risk monitoring function. These reports should provide information regarding the risk and performance levels of the investment strategies employed and should identify deviations from trading parameters and risk limits. If the hedge fund manager changes or proposes to change its trading activities on behalf of a fund in a way that is inconsistent with the expectations of the fund's governing authority or differs materially from the disclosure contained in the fund's offering documents, it should inform the governing authority and if appropriate, investors through normal means of investor communication. Amendments should be made as deemed necessary to disclosure/offering documents to ensure that they accurately reflect the nature and risks of the fund's trading activities.

Senior management should formally approve the allocation of capital to all portfolio managers. All portfolio managers, including external portfolio managers, should be subject to controls and review processes commensurate with the amount of assets managed and form of allocation. Where capital is invested with an external portfolio manager in a managed account, applicable trading restrictions/limits, reporting requirements and termination provisions should be clearly defined in written management agreements. The performance of all portfolio managers should be monitored on a periodic basis as appropriate, depending on the form of the allocation – eg, monthly net asset value (NAV) review of a passive investment in a fund versus daily or weekly review of a significant managed account investment.

Senior management should establish formal processes for the approval, monitoring and review of the use of third-party service providers for the performance of key business functions (eg, those related to risk monitoring, valuation, prime brokerage or other administrative functions). While senior management may decide to delegate the selection of actual service providers, they should approve the process by which the selection is made. Key third-party service providers' roles, responsibilities and liability should be clearly defined in written service agreements, and their performance should be periodically reviewed.

### Structure of risk monitoring function

Senior management should establish a risk monitoring function that operates independently of portfolio management functions. The risk monitoring function should be an independent source of information about and analysis of a hedge fund's performance and current risk position, the sources of its risk and resulting exposures to changes in market conditions.

The risk monitoring function should report directly to senior management and be staffed with persons having sufficient experience and knowledge to understand a fund's trading strategies and the nature and risks of its investments. Comprehensive and centralised systems for position and global exposure reporting and risk analysis should function independently of risk selection/portfolio management personnel so that trading activities and operations may be effectively supervised and compliance with trading policies and risk limits can be controlled. The risk monitoring function should produce daily risk reports that present risk measures and appropriate breakdowns by category of risk for review by appropriate members of senior management.

## Valuation

Proper valuation is material both to hedge fund investors and to the risk monitoring process. Hedge fund managers should develop procedures for capturing and verifying prices for the instruments they trade and rely on external pricing sources where available. For net asset value (NAV) purposes, managers generally should value instruments at market value, making adjustments to such values in accordance with generally accepted accounting principles (GAAP) only where market conditions mandate adjustments, recognising that investors will both buy and sell shares of a fund on the basis of NAV. In contrast, hedge fund managers may determine that adjustments to market value are appropriate for risk monitoring purposes in order to enhance the accuracy of risk assessment. Policies for making such adjustments should be approved by senior management. The concepts related to valuation are explored in greater detail in the Appendix.

Hedge fund managers should have pricing policies and procedures for determining a fund's NAV on a periodic basis and for determining its value for risk monitoring purposes on a daily basis. The policies regarding NAV determination should be approved by a hedge fund's governing authority and reviewed by external auditors for compliance with applicable accounting practices. Hedge fund managers should develop procedures and/or systems for capturing pricing data for their positions from independent sources on a daily basis where possible. Procedures for periodically verifying the accuracy of pricing data should also be adopted, and material discrepancies between price sources should be investigated. Where an instrument is not traded actively or where obtaining price information requires significant effort, weekly (or less frequent) pricing may be appropriate depending on the nature and the size of the position.

## Net asset value

Senior management should determine policies for the manner and frequency of computing net asset value based upon applicable GAAP and disclose such policies to investors. Such policies should establish valuation methods that are consistent and fair to both buyers and sellers. Financial assets and liabilities should be valued at "fair value", which is the price at which an item could be exchanged in a current transaction between willing parties, other than in a forced or liquidation sale. Consistent with GAAP, senior management should determine the valuation methods to be used where market prices are not available or are not indicative of fair value (eg, private equity investments may be valued at the lower of cost or market) and disclose such methods to a hedge fund's governing authority.

For an instrument that is actively traded, hedge fund managers should use price quotes available from reliable data vendors. The fair value of a position should be based upon the quoted price for a single trading unit in the most active market. Where price quotes are not available from data vendors, managers should attempt to obtain quotes from independent sources. For thinly traded instruments or those priced using models, hedge fund managers should document the valuation methods used and periodically subject them to independent validation. Dealer quotes and prices generated by models or other estimation methods should be regularly checked against realised prices to gauge their accuracy.

NAV valuations performed by third-party administrators should be regularly reviewed to ensure compliance with valuation policies. Valuations should be periodically validated by independent internal or external review, preferably on a monthly basis, but no less frequently than annually. The accuracy of NAV calculations should be verified by external auditors at least annually to assure compliance with GAAP.

*Risk monitoring valuation*

Senior management should establish policies for determining when risk monitoring valuation methods may differ from NAV for operational or risk analysis reasons. Examples where valuations different from NAV may be appropriate include situations such as those involving unusual position size, legal sale or transfer restrictions, illiquidity, control premiums or unusual hedging or transaction costs.

*Independent review*

A hedge fund manager's internal controls and risk monitoring processes should be subject to periodic independent reviews by either external auditors (at least once annually) or by internal compliance or other independent personnel to ensure that management reporting is complete and accurate and to identify material deviations from internal policies and procedures.

External auditors should report their findings and any recommended actions in writing in the form of a management letter or other appropriate report; the findings of internal reviews should be similarly recorded in writing. Such findings should be relayed to senior management and other recipients to whom they may delegate for appropriate resolution and action. Review of the risk monitoring function should verify compliance with the manager's risk policies and procedures. Review of this function should also address the soundness of internal systems and the qualitative and quantitative methods used (eg, models).

## RISK MONITORING

Current market practice is to focus on three categories of risk that are quantifiable – market risk, credit risk and liquidity risk – and on the less quantifiable operational risk. Market risk relates to losses that could be incurred due to changes in market factors (ie, prices, volatilities and correlations). Credit risk relates to losses that could be incurred due to declines in the creditworthiness of entities in which the fund invests or with which the fund deals as a counterparty. Liquidity risk relates to losses that could be incurred when declines in liquidity in the market reduce the value of the investments or reduce the ability of the fund to fund its investments.

While current market practice is to treat the risks separately, it is crucial for hedge fund managers to recognise and evaluate the overlap that exists between and among market, credit and liquidity risks. This overlap is illustrated in Figure 1 (recognising that the relative sizes of the circles will be different for different strategies):

Consequently, the risk monitoring function should monitor three inter-related variants of market, liquidity and credit risks in combination:

❏ market risk – including asset liquidity and the credit risk associated with investments;
❏ funding liquidity risk; and
❏ counterparty credit risk.

In this framework, the risk sometimes referred to as "sovereign" risk would be included as credit risk, if the potential loss is related to the finan-

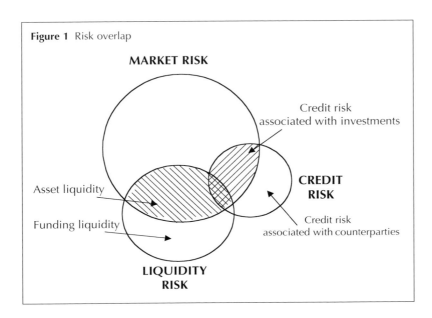

Figure 1 Risk overlap

MARKET RISK

Credit risk associated with investments

Asset liquidity

CREDIT RISK

Funding liquidity

Credit risk associated with counterparties

LIQUIDITY RISK

cial solvency of the sovereign, or as market risk if the potential loss is related to policy decisions made by the sovereign that change the market value of positions (eg, currency controls). The term "event risk" is broader and could incorporate aspects of credit risk and operational risk, as well as some elements of market risk. (For a more detailed discussion of the concepts related to the recommendations in this section, please see the Appendix.)

### Market risk

This encompasses interest rate risk, foreign exchange rate risk, equity price risk and commodity price risk, as well as asset liquidity risk and the credit risk associated with investments.

Hedge fund managers should evaluate market risk, not only for each hedge fund portfolio in aggregate, but also for relevant subcomponents of a portfolio – by strategy, by asset class, by type of instruments used, by geographic region or by industry sector, as appropriate. In addition, the market risk assumed by each individual portfolio manager should be determined. Hedge fund managers should employ a value-at-risk (VAR) model or other consistent framework for measuring the risk of loss for a portfolio (and relevant subcomponents of the portfolio). While the choice of model should be left to each hedge fund manager, the manager should be aware of the structural limitations of the model selected and actively manage these limitations, including the impact of any model breakdown.

A sound market risk-monitoring process should incorporate the confidence level(s) and holding period(s) deemed appropriate depending on the markets traded and the risks assumed. The holding period(s) should reflect the time necessary to liquidate and/or neutralise positions in the portfolio. The role of the risk monitoring function is to identify the factors affecting the risk and return of the fund's investments, both within individual portfolios and across the entire range of activities of the hedge fund manager. Those factors should be incorporated into the risk monitoring process and, where appropriate, be included in the market risk model. Factors commonly incorporated in a market risk model include:

- ❏ level and shape of the interest rate term structure in relevant currencies;
- ❏ foreign exchange rates;
- ❏ equity prices and/or equity indices;
- ❏ commodity prices;
- ❏ credit spreads;
- ❏ non-linearities;
- ❏ volatilities; and
- ❏ correlation.

Hedge fund managers should consider incorporating "asset liquidity" (ie, the change in the value of an asset due to changes in the liquidity of the market in which the asset is traded) as an additional factor. Measures of asset liquidity that may be considered include:

❏ the number of days that would be required to liquidate and/or neutralise the position in question; and
❏ the value that would be lost if the asset in question were to be liquidated and/or neutralised completely within the holding period specified.

Positions managed as a separate account by external portfolio managers on behalf of the fund should be incorporated in the routine risk assessment of the overall portfolio. Passive investments in funds managed by external portfolio managers should be monitored as appropriate.

Hedge fund managers should recognise that market risk measures such as VAR do not give a complete picture of risk in that they assess the risk of "standard" market movements rather than extreme events. Hedge fund managers should actively address these limitations by conducting relevant stress tests and back-testing.

Hedge fund managers should perform "stress tests" to determine how potential changes in market conditions could affect the market risk of the portfolio. Among the potential changes in market conditions that should be considered in stress testing are:

❏ changes in prices;
❏ changes in the shape of term structures; and
❏ changes in correlations between prices.

If the portfolio contains options or instruments with options characteristics, additional changes that should be considered as part of stress testing are:

❏ changes in volatilities; and
❏ changes in non-linearities (also referred to as convexity or gamma).

Hedge fund managers also should consider including the effects of changes in the liquidity of various assets in their stress testing.

For example, hedge fund managers could examine the effects of changing the holding period. A horizon of several days may reveal strings of losses (or gains) that, while individually less than the one-day VAR, in total add up to a significant deviation from the market risk model's predicted distribution. Rather than changing the holding period to reflect the illiquidity of securities or derivatives, the hedge fund manager could gauge the impact of illiquidity by inputting changes for the appropriate market risk factors that are reflective of multiple-day market price movements (as opposed to single-day changes). If specific asset liquidity factors are incorporated in the market risk model (see above), these asset liquidity factors can be "stressed" to examine the impact of (1) changes in the value that could be lost if the position in question were to be liquidated and/or neutralised completely during the standard holding period, or (2) changes in the number of days required to liquidate and/or neutralise the position in question.

Hedge fund managers should incorporate the impact of correlated events into stress testing, where appropriate. They should also consider conducting "scenario analyses" to benchmark the risk of a fund's current portfolio against various scenarios of market behaviour (historical or prospective) that are relevant to the hedge fund manager's trading activities (eg, the October 1987 stock market event, the Asian financial crisis of 1997 or a scenario where concerns about general credit quality lead to dramatic declines in asset values combined with decreases in asset and funding liquidity).

Stress tests/scenario analyses should take into account the impact of legal and contractual relationships.

Hedge fund managers should validate their market risk models through regular back-testing. The distribution of observed changes in the value of the portfolio should be compared to the distribution of changes in value generated by a hedge fund manager's market risk model. If the frequency of changes in the value of the portfolio exceeds the frequency generated by the market risk model (a statistical expectation based on the confidence level of the market risk model), such deviation should be scrutinised to determine its source. If appropriate after investigation, the market risk model should be modified. Potential sources of deviations include:

- a change in the composition of the portfolio between calculation and observation;
- pricing models under/overstated obtainable prices;
- a change in the underlying market, including changes in the volatility, correlation, or liquidity of the factors used in the market risk model; and
- model(s) that did not adequately capture sources of risk.

Even if the frequency of changes in value in excess of that generated by the market risk model is within the expected range, if the observed change in the value of the portfolio differs significantly from the change that would be expected, given the composition of the portfolio and the observed changes in the market factors, hedge fund managers should reconcile the difference.

## Funding liquidity risk

Funding liquidity is critical to a hedge fund manager's ability to continue trading in times of stress. Funding liquidity analysis should take into account the investment strategies employed, the terms governing the rights of investors to redeem their interests and the liquidity of assets (eg, all things being equal, the longer the expected period necessary to liqui-date assets, the greater the potential funding requirements). Adequate funding liquidity gives a hedge fund manager the ability to continue a trading strategy without being forced to liquidate assets when losses arise.

Cash should be actively managed. Hedge fund managers should know where a fund's cash is deployed and the reason for deploying it. Managers should centralise cash management and should evaluate the costs and benefits of leaving excess cash in trading accounts (eg, margin accounts).

Hedge fund managers should employ appropriate liquidity measures in order to gauge, on an ongoing basis, whether a fund is maintaining adequate liquidity. Liquidity should be assessed relative to the size and riskiness of the fund. Possible liquidity measures include:

❑ $Cash^2$/Equity;
❑ $VAR$/(Cash+Borrowing Capacity)[3]; and
❑ Worst historical drawdown/(cash + borrowing capacity).

Hedge fund managers should evaluate the stability of sources of liquidity and plan for funding needs accordingly, including a contingency plan in periods of stress. Hedge fund managers should assess their cash and borrowing capacity under the worst historical drawdown and stressed market conditions (eg, by assuming worst-case haircuts on securities used to collateralise margin borrowings), taking into account potential investor redemptions and contractual arrangements that affect a fund's liquidity (eg, notice periods for reduction of credit lines by counterparties).

Hedge fund managers should periodically forecast their liquidity requirements and potential changes in liquidity measures. Hedge fund managers should perform scenario tests to determine the impact of poten-tial changes in market conditions on a fund's liquidity. Among these scenario tests, hedge fund managers should consider including the poten-tial response to a creditor experiencing a liquidity problem during times of market stress (eg, reluctance to release collateral). Managers should take into account in their liquidity planning redemption "windows" or other rights of investors to redeem their interests. Hedge fund managers should also take into account the relationship between a fund's performance and redemptions and between a fund's performance and the availability of credit lines.

### Counterparty credit risk

Hedge fund managers should establish policies and procedures to manage the fund's exposure to potential defaults by trading counterparties. Hedge fund managers should identify acceptable counterparties, based on a reasonable analysis of creditworthiness, and set appropriate exposure limits. Hedge fund managers should ensure that counterparties' creditworthiness is actively monitored. In addition, credit concentrations relative to exposure limits should be monitored, taking into account settlement risk as well as pre-settlement risk. Procedures should be adopted and enforced to reduce or terminate trading with counterparties whose credit quality falls below an acceptable level or where exposure exceeds set limits. Hedge fund managers should seek to establish appropriate collateral provisions or other forms of credit support in their counterparty agreements and put in place procedures for managing collateral calls between the fund and its counterparties.

### Leverage

Hedge fund managers must recognise that leverage is important, not in and of itself, but because of the impact it can have on market risk, credit risk and liquidity risk – ie, leverage influences the rapidity of changes in the value of the portfolio due to changes in market risk, credit risk, or liquidity risk factors. Consequently, the most relevant measures of leverage are "risk-based" measures that relate the riskiness of a portfolio to the ability of the fund to absorb that risk. Recognising the impact that leverage can have on a portfolio's exposure to market risk, credit risk and liquidity risk, hedge fund managers should assess the degree to which a hedge fund is able to modify its risk-based leverage in periods of stress or increased market risk. Hedge fund managers also should track traditional, accounting-based measures of leverage, which can provide insights into the source of risk-based leverage and how that leverage could be adjusted.

Hedge fund managers should develop and monitor several measures of leverage, recognising that leverage, appropriately defined, can magnify the effect of changes in market, credit or liquidity risk factors on the value of the portfolio and can adversely affect a fund's liquidity.

#### Accounting-based leverage

Hedge fund managers should track traditional accounting-based measures of leverage. Not only are these measures routinely requested by counterparties and credit providers, but they can also contribute to an understanding of leverage measures that incorporate risk. However, hedge fund managers should be aware of the weaknesses of these accounting-based measures, particularly as stand-alone measures of leverage. Accounting-based measures that could be tracked include traditional "balance sheet leverage measures", eg,

"Gross balance sheet assets to equity" = On-balance sheet assets/Equity

and

"Net balance sheet assets to equity" = (On-balance sheet assets

– Matched book assets) / Equity.

Recognising that the preceding measures do not capture off-balance sheet transactions (eg, forward contracts, swaps and other derivatives), hedge fund managers may elect to track other accounting-based measures. While such measures can provide useful information if they are understood fully and interpreted correctly, hedge fund managers must recognise that accounting-based measures of leverage that attempt to include off-balance-sheet transactions are, at best, imprecise measures (eg, accounting-based measures may provide misleading information about offsetting futures positions if they do not have exactly the same expiration date).

*Risk-based leverage*
Hedge fund managers also should track each fund's leverage using "risk-based leverage" measures reflecting the relationship between the riskiness of a fund's portfolio and the capacity of the fund to absorb the impact of that risk. In this sense, some of the liquidity measures noted above can also be viewed as risk-based leverage measures – eg, VAR/(Cash+Borrowing Capacity). Other measures that could perform this function include the following.

❏ The simplest measure of the riskiness of the portfolio is the volatility in the value of the portfolio. This measure could be related to the fund's capital: (Volatility in value of portfolio) /Equity.
❏ VAR has become a widely recognised measure of market risk; so, this measure could be related to the fund's capital: VAR/Equity.
❏ As noted above, market risk measures such as VAR are incomplete measures of market risk because they focus on "standard" market movements rather than extreme events. Consequently, the hedge fund manager should consider assessing the impact of extreme events by comparing a market risk measure derived from analysis of extreme event scenarios (or stress tests) to the fund's capital: (Scenario-derived market risk measure)/Equity.

The hedge fund manager must be aware of limitations of the models used and must guard against placing too much reliance on mathematical measures of leverage alone. (As a case in point, analyses of extreme event scenarios will provide leverage information that is correct *ex-post* only if the "right" scenarios are considered *ex-ante*.) Consequently, it is essential that the hedge fund manager incorporate judgement based on business experience, in conjunction with and in addition to quantitative measures of leverage.

A crucial factor influencing the fund's ability to absorb the impact of extreme market events is the degree to which the fund can modify its risk-based leverage, especially during periods of market stress. During periods of market stress, the manager should understand its ability to reduce risk-based leverage by reducing traditional leverage resulting from either on- or off-balance-sheet transactions or by reducing the level of risk that is being accepted (eg, by changing strategy or the types of assets being held in the portfolio). To track the degree to which the fund is able to modify its risk-based leverage, the hedge fund manager may wish to track variations in the fund's market risk measure (eg, VAR) over time.

### Operational risk

Hedge fund managers should establish procedures to limit the fund's exposure to potential operational risks, including data entry errors, fraud, system failures and errors in valuation or risk measurement models. Hedge fund managers should consider measures to limit or mitigate operational risk, including:

❏ random spot checks of all relevant activities;
❏ effective separation between the risk selection and risk monitoring functions, either by having sufficient staff to avoid overlapping activities or by providing the appropriate level of checks and balances for hedge fund managers that are too small to avoid overlapping staff;
❏ maintenance of a single, centralised position data set (to avoid the errors inherent in maintaining multiple or regionalised data sets); and
❏ establishment of an internal review function.

Hedge fund managers should establish contingency plans for responding to failure of a third-party administrator, credit provider or other party that would affect the market, credit or liquidity risk of a fund. Contingency planning should address responses to a failure of a third party on a fund's ability to meet its obligation, including transfers of activity to back-up clearing systems, credit providers and other service providers and back-up providers.

### DISCLOSURE/TRANSPARENCY

Investors should receive periodic performance and other information about their hedge fund investments. Hedge fund managers should also consider whether investors should receive interim updates on other matters in response to significant events. Hedge fund managers should negotiate with counterparties to determine the extent of financial and risk information that should be provided to them based on the nature of their relationship in order to increase the stability of financing and trading relationships. They should also work with regulators and counterparties to develop a consensus approach to public disclosure. Agreements and other safeguards should be established in order to protect against the unauthorised use of proprietary information furnished to outside parties.

### Reporting to a fund's governing authority and investors

The investment objectives and approach plus the range of permissible investments should be clearly disclosed in a fund's offering documents. Material changes should be disclosed to a fund's governing authority and investors as appropriate.

Hedge fund managers should provide certain base-line standardised performance and other relevant information to all investors, such as:

❏ performance measures, such as quarterly or monthly net asset value calculations and periodic profit and loss;
❏ capital measures, such as total net assets under management and net changes to capital based on new subscriptions less redemptions and the effect of profit and loss;
❏ annual audited financial statements; and
❏ measures that give a view of the fund's risk, such as Sharpe ratios or VAR.

### Reporting to counterparties/credit providers

Hedge fund managers should furnish periodic reports to credit providers and counterparties that extend trading lines or other forms of credit. The extent of disclosure can vary depending on the extent and nature of the relationship with the credit provider. Measures that give a view of the fund's risk and return profile, rather than specific trading positions, should be most useful to credit providers and would not sacrifice the proprietary nature of fund strategies and positions. Possible disclosures include:

❏ performance measures appropriate to the nature of the funds managed, such as periodic changes in NAV; profit and loss volatility; performance attribution by broad product classes (eg, currencies, fixed income, equities and commodities);
❏ capital measures, such as total net assets under management and net changes to capital based on new subscriptions less redemptions and the effect of profit and loss;
❏ market risk measures, such as Sharpe ratios, VAR or scenario-derived market risk measures for each relevant fund; and
❏ liquidity measures, such as cash plus borrowing capacity as a percentage of either equity or VAR.

Appropriate safeguards against a counterparty's unauthorised use of proprietary information should be adopted. Hedge fund managers should provide financial and other confidential information to a counterparty's credit department only, and not to any member of a counterparty's trading desk or department. The counterparty's credit department should confirm, preferably in a written confidentiality agreement or letter, its commitment to restrict the use of, and access to, information furnished by the hedge fund manager to the credit desk. It should also ensure such information is not shared with any trading personnel within the counterparty's organisation or any third-party without the manager's prior written consent.

### Reporting to regulators

Hedge fund managers should work with appropriate governmental authorities to ensure that where large positions have a potential systemic impact, hedge fund managers along with other financial institutions and investors with significant positions comply with applicable large position reporting requirements, while preserving the confidentiality of proprietary information.

The Additional Notes detail existing large trader and large position reporting requirements, as well as other US regulatory filing requirements currently applicable to hedge fund managers depending on either their trading activity or their status as a regulated entity. Similar requirements apply in certain of the other countries where hedge fund managers do business.

### Issues relating to the potential impact of public disclosure on market integrity

Hedge fund managers should co-ordinate with counterparties and regulators to develop a broad consensus approach to public disclosure, evaluating both the benefits and the costs of such disclosure to investors, creditors and the markets.

The dialogue with hedge fund managers, counterparties and regulators should assess the goals to be achieved by public disclosure. To the extent that the purpose of public disclosure is to assist creditors and investors in making informed decisions about the credit they extend or the investments they make, the benefits of the recommendations for improved risk management and internal controls by hedge fund managers and for expanded disclosure to counterparties and investors should be considered. Issues relating to the potential relationship between market integrity and public disclosure should be addressed by broad classes of market participants so that a better understanding of the benefits and costs can be achieved.

Because of the broad recognition (including recognition in the PWG Report) that disclosure of hedge fund's proprietary information on strategies or positions should not be required, any approach to public disclosure should consider what information can be collected, aggregated and disseminated without exposing sensitive strategies or positions.

## LEGAL AND COMPLIANCE

A hedge fund manager's legal/compliance personnel must have the authority and resources to operate independently and effectively. This function should seek to actively manage the legal risks presented by the hedge fund manager's trading, focusing on the documentation governing trading relationships and individual transactions. In particular, hedge fund managers should pursue a consistent and methodical approach to documenting transactions so that the legal consequences of periods of market stress or performance declines may be more clearly anticipated and managed. The legal function should provide the risk monitoring function with useful input in the evaluation of a fund's projected liquidity in stressed environments, including inputs derived from the fund's transaction documentation (eg, terms regarding termination, collateral and margining).

A hedge fund manager's general counsel/senior compliance or legal officer should be recognised as a member of senior management and be granted sufficient authority to manage the legal and compliance affairs of the hedge fund manager independently and effectively.

### Documentation policies

Hedge fund managers should establish transaction execution and documentation management procedures that:

- ❏ ensure timely execution of necessary transaction documents and enforceability of transactions;
- ❏ require that all trading counterparties be pre-approved prior to executing any transactions and verify counterparty authorisations;
- ❏ establish formal documentation requirements for all trading (including confirmation requirements for all off-exchange trades where a master agreement has not been executed with a counterparty);
- ❏ ensure that appropriate security interests are created and perfected when collateral is received as part of a transaction; and
- ❏ where transaction documentation is performed in the operations or similar area, appropriate liaison with the legal/compliance function should be established.

Hedge fund managers should track the status of documentation and the negotiation of key provisions and terms (eg, termination events) using a database or other appropriate mechanism to ensure consistency and standardisation across funds and counterparties to the extent appropriate.

Hedge fund managers should clarify and standardise documentation on a bilateral basis with all counterparties to the extent possible in order to enhance stability during periods of market stress or declining asset levels. In particular, in their counterparty documentation, hedge fund managers generally should evaluate the appropriateness of seeking to:

❏ standardise termination and collateral events as well as events of default, cross-default clauses and the remedies available to a non-defaulting party to achieve consistency in documentation with different counterparties to the extent possible;

❏ minimise the possibility of early termination or collateral calls based upon subjective determinations by avoiding provisions that permit counterparties to terminate or make demands for collateral in their "sole discretion" (eg, avoid "material adverse change" clauses);

❏ include the decline of a counterparty's credit rating as a termination/collateral event;

❏ ensure that provisions addressing NAV declines or other performance-based triggers are structured as collateral or termination events to avoid triggering cross-default provisions under other agreements;

❏ seek grace periods in connection with performance or other termination events so that an orderly liquidation of positions may take place if necessary; and

❏ negotiate commitments from primary credit providers to ensure stability of credit facilities during temporary periods of market stress or declining assets, eg, require that credit providers give written notice within a fixed period prior to termination or reduction of a credit line or other material changes to credit terms.

Hedge fund managers should seek to negotiate bilateral collateral agreements that require each party to furnish collateral, taking into account the relative creditworthiness of the parties. In particular, managers generally should evaluate the appropriateness of seeking to:

❏ ensure satisfactory custodial arrangements are in place and that location and possible uses of collateral are clearly defined;

❏ establish collateral management procedures which permit the hedge fund manager to effectively and regularly value collateral and make calls for collateral from counterparties when permitted;

❏ negotiate thresholds that adjust with the counterparties' credit rating;

❏ ensure that the responsibilities for valuing collateral and determining the amounts of collateral to be delivered or returned are appropriately allocated between the parties to a collateral agreement (eg, by allocating such role to the secured party or the party that is owed collateral); and

❏ negotiate provisions requiring prompt payment of collateral.

Where operational, legal or economic efficiencies would result, hedge fund managers should seek to establish "master/master" or "umbrella" cross-product netting and collateral agreements with counterparties dealing in multiple products using different agreements.

Hedge fund managers should provide input to the risk monitoring function for use in stress/scenario testing as well as liquidity analyses based on legal or contractual relationships, including:

❑ the contractual rights of counterparties to increase margin/collateral requirements, declare events of default or declare termination events in response to a fund's declining assets or other stress scenarios;
❑ the legal or contractual sales restrictions applicable to any investments;
❑ the enforceability of netting provisions in the event of a counterparty's bankruptcy; and
❑ redemption windows for investors.

Hedge fund managers should have appropriate documentation and approval processes for retaining external traders as well as administrators, prime brokers or other third-party service providers.

### Compliance

Hedge fund managers should identify all actual and potential required regulatory filings and clearly allocate responsibility for such filings to appropriate personnel who will supervise and ensure timely compliance with applicable regulations and filing requirements.

Hedge fund managers should require all employees to attest in writing upon hiring and on an annual basis to their acceptance of a "code of conduct" or compliance manual, which should address, where applicable, trading rules and restrictions, confidentiality requirements, procedures to prevent the flow of non-public information from one function to another, compliance with internal policies and procedures and compliance with securities (eg, insider trading) and related laws. The compliance manual/code of conduct should be regularly updated.

### CONCLUSION

In developing these recommendations, the primary goal has been to promote sound risk management and internal controls for the hedge fund industry by identifying practices that would contribute to enhancing the financial stability of large funds managed by hedge fund managers and, in turn, reduce the possibility of their failure due to unexpected market events. While the adoption of the recommendations by hedge fund managers will not reduce market volatility or eliminate the prospect of events leading to unanticipated hedge fund losses, defaults or failures, it is hoped that the adoption of these practices by the largest hedge fund managers, in combination with the implementation by their counterparties of the CRMPG recommendations, will serve to reduce the likelihood of systemic consequences resulting from a hedge fund's default or failure.

The recommendations also seek to emphasise the importance of managerial expertise and discipline to weathering market shocks and crises. While thorough and thoughtful risk measurement and analysis are critical elements of sound hedge fund management, they will not spare the hedge fund manager who refuses to take the steps necessary to preserve appropriate levels of liquidity when faced with stressed market conditions or unexpected losses. For this reason internal controls and policies for addressing stressed market conditions are at least as important as the mechanisms used to anticipate and analyse them.

While most of the recommendations contained in the first two sections may be adopted unilaterally by individual hedge fund managers, the ability to implement them may depend on the availability of qualified personnel and other resources and, consequently, their implementation may not be feasible for smaller hedge fund managers. Furthermore, many of the recommendations relating to disclosure and documentation policies will require negotiation with and acceptance by third parties, and it is hoped that the publication of this document will contribute to generating the industry support and regulatory dialogue that may be necessary to implement these recommended practices.

The recommendations were developed in the belief that the most effective form of oversight is self-evaluation combined with self-discipline. The first line of defence to market stress will always be the managers themselves, and the recommendations are intended to provide a framework of internal policies and controls that will enhance their ability to prudently address unexpected market events or losses.

## APPENDIX

### RISK MONITORING PRACTICES FOR HEDGE FUND MANAGERS

The objective of this Appendix is to elaborate upon the discussion of risk monitoring practices contained in the recommendations. In so doing, this Appendix describes the general array of risk management techniques and methodologies currently available, in addition to addressing the specific techniques and methodologies that should be considered as part of sound risk monitoring practices for hedge fund managers. The latter discussion includes further explanations of valuation, liquidity and leverage from the perspective of hedge fund managers. This appendix begins by providing an overview of the risks faced by a hedge fund manager in the first section.

Valuation procedures are discussed in the following section. While not explicitly part of the risk monitoring function, proper valuation processes are crucial to effective risk monitoring.

The descriptions of the practices for monitoring market risk, funding liquidity risk and leverage form the core of this Appendix and address the following key issues.

❏ Techniques for monitoring market risk that are becoming well-accepted in financial markets – VAR, scenario analyses and stress tests, and back-testing.
❏ The importance of analysing funding liquidity risk. While the measures for monitoring funding liquidity described in this Appendix are used in other industries, hedge fund managers should focus significant attention on funding liquidity given the impact it can have on the viability of a hedge fund.
❏ Leverage in the context of hedge funds. While leverage is not unique to hedge funds, the market risk inherent in a hedge fund, coupled with the constraints imposed by funding liquidity, make the amplifying effect of leverage of particular concern to a hedge fund manager. This Appendix describes a group of static leverage measures, both accounting-based and risk-based leverage measures. Also described in this Appendix are dynamic leverage measures that can provide additional information to the hedge fund manager.

This Appendix concludes with a description of procedures for monitoring counterparty credit risk. Because hedge funds generally deal with counterparties having high credit quality, the credit risk of counterparties may be of less concern to hedge fund managers than the other sources of risk but should nonetheless by appropriately monitored.

## OVERVIEW: THE RISKS FACED BY A HEDGE FUND MANAGER

Effective risk management requires that the hedge fund manager recognise and understand the source of the returns the fund is earning – ie, the risks to which the fund is exposed. Consequently, one of the primary responsibilities of the risk monitoring function is to identify and quantify the sources of risk. While observers often distinguish four broad types of risk – market risk, credit risk, liquidity risk and operational risk[4] – it is important to recognise that these risks are interrelated. Indeed, hedge fund managers should recognise that market risk incorporates elements of credit risk and liquidity risk. Defined most narrowly, market risk focuses on the impact of changes in the prices of (or rates for) securities and derivatives, the volatilities of those prices, and the correlations between pairs of prices on the value of the portfolio. However, the following elements of liquidity risk and credit risk have a similar focus.

❏ Changes in liquidity impact on the value of a security or derivative. This element of liquidity risk is sometimes referred to as asset or "market" liquidity risk.

❏ Changes in the creditworthiness of an entity impact on the value of a security or derivative issued by or indexed to that entity.

Because these three risks all focus explicitly on changes in the value of an asset or the portfolio, hedge fund managers should integrate the monitoring and management of them (ie, view them as a group, rather than individually). Hence, in the section Market risk later in this Appendix, "market risk" will encompass the credit risk associated with assets held in the portfolio and asset (or market) liquidity risk, as well as the more commonly cited market risk factors: interest rate risk, foreign exchange rate risk, equity price risk and commodity price risk.

In addition to having an impact on the value of securities or derivatives held by the hedge fund, changes in funding liquidity can impact on the hedge fund managers' ability to finance its positions. Section 4 (Funding Liquidity Risk), will indicate why this risk is of greater concern to hedge fund managers than to other entities and will describe the techniques that should be used by hedge fund managers to monitor funding liquidity risk.

The hedge fund manager must also consider "leverage". However, leverage is not an independent source of risk; rather, it is a factor that influences the rapidity with which changes in market risk, credit risk or liquidity risk factors change the value of the portfolio. Indeed, it is essential to consider what leverage means – or does not mean – in the context of a hedge fund.

1. A single leverage number may not contain very much information. As will be illustrated in this Appendix, a risk-reducing transaction can increase some leverage measures while decreasing others.
2. The liquidity or price volatility of the position being leveraged is relevant to assessing effective leverage. The leverage employed by a hedge fund that holds one-year Treasury bills with ten-to-one leverage may be of less concern than that employed by a fund levered two-to-one in Russian Ministry of Finance bonds.
3. A hedge fund's capacity to absorb losses – its funding liquidity – is relevant to assessing its effective leverage. Leverage should be measured relative to a fund's capacity to absorb losses. A relatively highly leveraged fund in conventional balance sheet terms may pose a smaller risk than a less levered hedge fund with low cash positions, limited borrowing capacity, or investors that can withdraw their funds on short notice.

In Panel 1, a collection of stylised portfolios and balance sheets are used to illustrate and compare the measures of market risk, funding liquidity risk and leverage.

As noted above, for hedge fund managers, changes in credit quality that

# Panel 1
## Stylised portfolios

In sections 3, 4 and 5, a collection of stylised portfolios and balance sheets are used to illustrate and compare the measures of market risk, funding liquidity risk and leverage that are discussed in the recommendations and this Appendix. As described below, these simple portfolios are composed of various combinations of three hypothetical securities (which are denoted as asset 1, asset 2 and asset 3) and two derivative contracts. Two of the securities are lower risk assets, with annualised volatility of 30% and 25%, respectively. The third asset is a higher risk asset with annual volatility of 60%. The two derivatives are simple futures contracts on the two low risk securities; therefore they have the same volatility as those securities.

Each portfolio is part of a simple balance sheet. It is assumed that US$100 of investor equity funds each strategy. To calculate all of the various risk measures, the stylised balance sheets also indicate a cash position, a futures margin position and a liability account that reflects any financing transactions. The required futures margin is 10% in cash, which is not counted as liquidity. In addition, up to 50% of assets 1, 2, or 3 can be borrowed, and 50% of the proceeds from a short sale are available to finance investments.

For each portfolio various measures of market risk, liquidity and leverage have been calculated. Note that not all the risk measures are relevant for every portfolio.

❏ Portfolios 1 and 2 illustrate positions with identical market risk but different investments to implement the strategy. Portfolio 1 is an unleveraged investment in asset 1 while Portfolio 2 uses the futures contract on asset 1 to implement the same strategy.

❏ Portfolios 3 and 4 are leveraged versions of Portfolios 1 and 2. The use of balance sheet leverage (Portfolio 1) or additional derivatives contracts (Portfolio 2) has the effect of increasing the market risk of both portfolios.

❏ Like Portfolios 3 and 4, Portfolio 5 is more risky than Portfolios 1 and 2; but, instead of employing traditional leverage, the additional risk arises because the manager switches from a lower-risk strategy (invest in asset 1) to a higher-risk investment strategy (invest in asset 3).

❏ Portfolios 6 and 7 use long and short investments to illustrate the effect of a type of hedging by being long in one asset and short in another, that is positively correlated with the first. In Portfolio 6 the strategy is implemented in the cash market, while Portfolio 7 achieves identical market risk using a combination of cash and futures. As discussed later, these portfolios illustrate the complexity that can appear as the portfolio increases in size – although Portfolios 6 and 7 are generally less risky than Portfolios 3 and 4, there are conditions under which they can become significantly more risky.

Portfolios 8 and 9 are used to illustrate the effect of matched book assets-either in the futures market or the cash market-on traditional leverage and liquidity measures. Portfolios 8 and 9 represent the same net positions as Portfolios 1 and 2; but, the positions are established by combining a short position in asset 1 or futures on asset 1 (ie, –20) with long positions in the same asset (ie, 100), rather than only long positions (ie, 80).

**Table 1** Stylised portfolios

| | Unlevered cash vs | | Levered cash vs | | Unlevered high risk | Long/short strategy cash vs futures | | Unlevered strategy with matched book assets | |
|---|---|---|---|---|---|---|---|---|---|
| Portfolio | Cash only | Futures only | Levered cash | Futures | High risk cash | Long/short cash | Long/short mixed | Hedged cash | Hedged futures |
| | *1* | *2* | *3* | *4* | *5* | *6* | *7* | *8* | *9* |
| **Summary balance sheet** | | | | | | | | | |
| Capital | 100 | 100 | 100 | 100 | 100 | 100 | 100 | 100 | 100 |
| Borrowing (outright or repo) | 0 | 0 | 30 | | | | 30 | | |
| Investment | | | | | | | | | |
| Cash market transactions | | | | | | | | | |
| Asset 1 | 80 | | 120 | | | 120 | | 100, –20 | |
| Asset 2 | | | | | | –60 | | | |
| Asset 3 | | | | | 80 | | | | |
| Derivatives market transactions | | | | | | | | | |
| Futures on Asset 1 | | 80 | | 120 | | | 120 | | 100, –20 |
| Futures on Asset 2 | | | | | | | –60 | | |
| Cash | 20 | 92 | 10 | 88 | 20 | 10 | 4 | 10 | 88 |
| Futures margin | 0 | 8 | 0 | 12 | 0 | 0 | 6 | 0 | 12 |

affect the value of the portfolio through a change in the price of securities owned are incorporated into "market risk". However, hedge fund managers are also exposed to counterparty credit risk. Changes in the credit quality of counterparties can impose costs on the hedge fund either in the form of an increase in expected losses due to counterparty failure to perform or by forcing the hedge fund manager to find alternative counterparties.

Operational risks faced by hedge fund managers are much the same as those faced by other financial institutions – data entry errors, fraud, system failures and errors in valuation or risk measurement models. The appropriate techniques and procedures to deal with these risks are, likewise, the same techniques and procedures used by other entities. As noted in the recommendations, these include random spot checks, maintenance of a single, centralised data set, contingency plans for responding to failures in the hedge fund manager's systems or for responding to the failure of a third party service provider.

## VALUATION

As noted in the recommendations, the valuation of positions serves two distinct purposes for the hedge fund manager. In addition to providing the base input to the risk monitoring process, valuation of positions is required for the calculation of NAV, which is the basis for investor subscriptions and redemptions. Hedge fund managers' valuation policies should be objective, fair, and consistent, as outlined below.

❏ Objectivity requires that hedge fund managers either calculate or verify the accuracy of prices independent of the trading/risk selection function. To that end, hedge fund managers should look to reliable price quotes from external sources wherever possible and cost effective to do so.

❏ Fairness recognises that valuation for NAV purposes will determine the prices at which investors subscribe to or redeem from the fund.

❏ Consistency can be achieved through the establishment of recognised procedures or practices. This section will provide more detail on valuation issues than was provided in the recommendations, particularly with respect to valuation for risk monitoring purposes. After restating the principles of NAV valuation, price sources and price validation will be reviewed. Then, the discussion turns to valuation for risk monitoring purposes.

### Net asset valuation

*Fair Value*

As described in the recommendations, for NAV purposes, hedge fund managers generally should value instruments according to generally accepted accounting principles (GAAP) for the appropriate jurisdiction, recognising that investors will both buy and sell shares of a fund on the basis of NAV and that its financial statements must reflect NAV. This generally requires the use of "fair value". For example, under FASB Statement of Financial Accounting Standards 107, the "fair value" of financial assets and liabilities under US GAAP is the amount at which the item could be exchanged in a current transaction between willing parties, other than in a forced or liquidation sale. Calculation of NAV must take into account not only the value of the financial instruments in the portfolio (sometimes referred to as "trading P&L"), but also accruals of interest, dividends and other receivables and fees, expenses and other payables.

*Prices*
Where market prices exist and are indicative of fair value, they should generally be used to compute NAV. For instruments that are actively traded, the fair value should be the product of the number of trading units times the quoted price for a single trading unit in the most active market, even if placing an order to sell (or buy, if short) the holding might affect the price if a market's normal one-day volume might not be sufficient to absorb the quantity held.

For instruments traded in the over-the-counter (OTC) market, hedge fund managers should, to the extent possible, attempt to obtain multiple quotes from dealers active in that market. Where appropriate, the model parameters that the dealer used in determining its valuation should be obtained and analysed. Further considerations on price data are discussed below under "Price Sources".

Senior management should establish the valuation methods to be used for NAV purposes where market prices do not exist or are not indicative of fair value. These methods should be disclosed to a hedge fund's governing authority. For investments in non-traded assets or assets that are extremely illiquid or otherwise difficult to value, hedge fund managers should document the valuation methods used and periodically subject them to independent validation. For example, because there are no objective external price references for private equity investments, hedge fund managers may determine they should be carried at historical cost.5

*Frequency*
Senior management should determine the frequency of computing NAV, which will be needed on each date for which balance sheets are prepared and each interim date on which NAV is disclosed to the governing authority or investors. Some hedge fund managers calculate a daily NAV, while others calculate NAV less frequently.

If initial end-of-day values for portfolio instruments are obtained from the hedge fund manager's trader or other front office staff, such values should be verified with a frequency determined by the materiality of the position. Significant differences between front and back office valuations should be investigated and reconciled. Alternatively, end-of-day valuation may be exclusively the role of back office staff.

Portfolio values used to calculate NAV should also be used for risk monitoring valuation, except as expressly determined otherwise by senior management due to operational or risk analysis reasons as discussed below under "Valuation for Risk Monitoring". However, valuation for risk monitoring purposes will be performed daily even though NAV may be calculated less frequently. Also, the daily expense accruals that must be reflected in NAV are generally not included in the portfolio valuation for risk monitoring purposes, which is instead based on the concept of trading P&L.

*Price sources*
For the following reasons, the appropriate source of price data depends on the position in question.

1. Many of the positions held by hedge funds are securities or derivatives that are listed on organised exchanges or in OTC markets for which reliable price quotes can be obtained from third-party data vendors. For those securities and derivatives, fair value can be based on the "closing" quotation or official closing price of an exchange or prices in the OTC market or other 24-hour markets as they appear on a data vendor screen (observed at the same time on each day).
2. Data vendors may also provide quotations for less actively traded instruments based on a method known as "matrix pricing". Matrix pricing uses market quotes for actively traded securities to approximate the value of a less actively traded security based on comparable characteristics, such as coupon, maturity and risk. Matrix prices can be a useful source of third-party price information, but they should be recognised as modelled prices not transaction prices.
3. Reliable quotes for certain OTC derivative instruments and structured securities may not be available from data vendors, either because the transactions are "one of a kind" or not actively traded. In many cases the only "market" for these securities is with the original counterparty to the transaction. Such instruments can be valued either by obtaining a quote from the originating counterparty or from a pricing model. While a hedge fund manager might be able to obtain quotes from other dealers not party to the original transaction (which would provide a more independent source of pricing information), such an approach may not be practical, for example because it would require disclosure of proprietary position data.

*Price validation*

Hedge fund managers should establish procedures for verifying the accuracy of prices obtained from data vendors, dealers, or other sources. For actively traded instruments, it may be sufficient to establish multiple feeds from data vendors in order to compare and verify their prices. In other cases, the hedge fund manager should establish procedures for verifying the inputs to models and for validating modelled prices. Modelled prices could be validated by comparing them to prices observed in the market or to prices obtained from third parties where possible. As noted in the recommendations, dealer quotes and prices generated by models or other estimation methods also should be regularly checked against realised prices to gauge their accuracy. Hedge fund managers may elect to use external auditors to verify aspects of their pricing and modelling, either as part of an annual audit or an independent review.

Valuation is typically independent of the trading function. However, for certain illiquid or hard to value investments, such as private equity investments, the valuation process may begin with a price obtained from those most familiar with a particular position, ie, the trader or analyst. However, in such situations, the hedge fund manager should take steps to independently (either internally or externally as appropriate) assess the reasonableness of that price.

**Valuation for risk monitoring**

The risk monitoring function typically values positions consistent with the approach taken for the NAV calculation. However, the risk monitoring function is not constrained by the requirements of GAAP. Consequently, in order to examine potential effects on the portfolio of changes in market conditions, the risk monitoring function may use alternative values or may make adjustments to the position values calculated for NAV purposes. Senior management should establish policies for determining when risk management valuation methods may differ from NAV for operational or risk analysis reasons. It would not be appropriate, however, to adjust a long position upward or a short position downward, from its fair value for risk monitoring purposes.

❑ Rather than using mid-market prices, bid prices could be used for long positions and ask prices used for short positions.

❑ Prices may be discounted to reflect the size of a position relative to the market, eg, by using "exit values" rather than fair value. Exit value reflects the likely impact on the market price where the position must be liquidated quickly, such as where the position is significantly larger than historical trading volume during the assumed required exit period.

❑ For an actively traded security held in a large enough quantity and/or involving sufficient indicia of control that a Schedule 13D or similar public disclosure has been made of the position, and therefore where a sale of a portion could not be made anonymously, a downward adjustment from market value may be appropriate.

❏ For instruments subject to legal restrictions on sale or where the market is illiquid or has become disorderly, it may be appropriate to make a downward adjustment from the fair value.

❏ In volatile markets, prices may be discounted if the risk monitoring function does not believe that quoted bids or offers are prices at which a trade could actually be done.

❏ For a less actively traded instrument representing only a small position, and where obtaining price information requires significant effort, weekly (or even less frequent) pricing may be appropriate.

## MARKET RISK

This encompasses the credit risk associated with securities and derivatives in the portfolio and asset liquidity risk, as well as interest rate risk, foreign exchange rate risk, equity price risk, and commodity price risk.

In order that senior management are able to oversee the risks that the hedge fund faces, the risk monitoring function needs to provide them with some useful measure of risk. Measuring the degree to which the portfolio is diversified (eg, the percentages of the portfolio allocated to different asset classes or to different geographical regions) may be useful; however, it is important for the hedge fund manager to recognise and understand the correlations between positions. For complex portfolios, many summary measures of market risk do not reflect such correlations. VAR is a tool which is intended to provide a summary market risk measure which incorporates correlations between positions. VAR measures the maximum change in the value of the portfolio that would be expected at a specified confidence level over a specified holding period. For example, if the 95% confidence level, one-day VAR for a portfolio is US$500,000, one would expect to gain or lose more than US$500,000 in only five of every 100 trading days on average.[6]

Since first being discussed in the Group of 30 Report in 1993,[7] VAR has become a widely-used risk measurement tool among virtually all commercial banks and investment banks.[8] Other market participants are increasingly using the VAR measure as well. A 1998 survey of pension, endowments, and foundations reported that 23% of "large" institutional investors used VAR.[9] Use of VAR by hedge funds is believed to be substantial, if not universal among the larger funds.

*Parameter selection*
In order to calculate a VAR measure, a numbers of parameters must be input; these parameters describe the positions in the portfolio and the

underlying markets. For a given portfolio, the parameters most likely to have a significant impact on the VAR value are the time horizon or holding period (the period of time that would be necessary for the portfolio to be liquidated or neutralised), the confidence level (the probability that the change in the value of the portfolio would exceed the VAR), and the variance-covariance data (which reflects the volatility of the individual market factors and the correlation between pairs of factors). These parameters are explained further below.

❏ The time horizon or holding period used in the VAR calculation is intended to reflect the time period necessary to liquidate (or neutralise) the positions in the portfolio. In practice, if the hedge fund has positions in thinly traded or illiquid instruments, it is difficult to determine the correct liquidation/neutralisation period for the portfolio. Consequently, good practice is to use standard holding periods – eg, one day, three days, five days and 10 days in the base-case VAR calculation and then employ stress tests to determine the degree of holding period risk in the portfolio.

❏ The appropriate confidence level is defined by no mathematical formula; the appropriate confidence level is determined by the business circumstances of the entity. Different types of businesses should and do use different confidence levels. The appropriate confidence level for a specific hedge fund will be a business decision that is determined by the specific circumstances of the fund; and senior management of the hedge fund manager should be actively involved in this determination.

❏ Variance-covariance data are another significant parameter. While the measure of the riskiness of individual market factors (ie, the variances of the market factors) is important, the question of the degree of correlation (ie, covariance) between pairs of market factors is critical, because correlation has such a large impact on the VAR calculation. A number of VAR models use historic correlations. However, since historic correlations are unstable (especially during periods of market stress), the hedge fund manager should employ scenario analyses and stress testing (see below) to ascertain the impact of inaccurate correlation assumptions.

## Beyond a single VAR number
*Scenario analysis, stress testing and back testing*
Hedge fund managers must recognise that a single VAR number is not sufficient to capture all risks faced by the hedge fund and that successful risk management requires the risk monitoring function to analyse both the sensitivity of the VAR to alternative market conditions and the reliability of the VAR calculations.

*Scenario analysis*

By their nature, VAR calculations are based on "typical" market days. Periods of market stress or crisis – the very times of greatest concern – will not be well represented in the data for a typical period; so the resulting VAR number will underestimate the risks of severe markets. To address this limitation, the hedge fund manager should perform scenario analyses regularly, to assess the VAR for the current portfolio in periods of market stress.

In creating scenario analyses, a hedge fund manager should use both historical stress periods – eg, 19 October, 1987, when the equity markets crashed; 4 February, 1994, when the US Federal Reserve changed direction and started increasing US interest rates; 20 December, 1994, when the Mexican peso was devalued – as well as hypothetical periods, designed perhaps to put the most pressure on the current portfolio.

*Stress testing*

Hedge fund managers should stress test the VAR number by changing the parameters of the VAR model. Stress tests permit the hedge fund manager to see what will happen to the VAR number if the actual values of market factors (ie, prices, rates, volatilities, etc) differ from the values used as inputs in the base-case VAR calculation. Of particular concern to hedge fund managers are "breakdowns" in the correlations reflected in current market data. In times of market crisis the correlations between asset prices or rates can change dramatically and unexpectedly, with the result that positions that were thought to be diversifying – or even hedging – end up compounding risk. While it remains difficult to hedge correlation risk, stress tests to evaluate the impact of correlation changes permit the hedge fund manager to help ensure that, when the hedge fund manager selects the assets to be included in the portfolio, the fund is accepting the desired level of correlation risk (and is being compensated for bearing that risk).

Panel 2 contains several illustrative VAR measures for each of the nine stylised portfolios introduced in Panel 1.

*Back testing*

Possibly even more important than analysing the sensitivity of the VAR number is back testing the VAR to see how it performed. By comparing actual changes in the value of the portfolio to the changes generated by the VAR calculation, the hedge fund manager can gain insight into whether the VAR model is accurately measuring a fund's risk.

In back testing, one expects that the portfolio will lose more than the VAR from time to time. For example, a 95% one-day VAR should be exceeded five days in every 100 trading days on average. When the actual changes in the value of the portfolio exceed VAR, the hedge fund manager should determine the source of the discrepancy – ie, whether the VAR measure is flawed or whether this loss is simply one which was expected given the confidence level employed or is attributable to a change in the composition of the portfolio or the market.

## Panel 2

## Illustrative VAR measures for each of the nine stylised portfolios introduced in Panel 1

*Standard VAR*
A 95% one-day VAR is calculated using the historical volatilities for the assets and assuming the correlation between assets is 0.3.

*Stressed VAR 1*
The 95% one-day VAR is re-calculated increasing the volatility of each asset by 50% (ie, to 45% for asset 1, to 37.5% for asset 2 and to 90% for asset 3) and increasing the correlation between all assets to 0.9.

*Stressed VAR 2*
The 95% one-day VAR is recalculated again increasing the volatilities by 50% as above, but decreasing the correlation between assets to zero.

Table 2 provides confirmation of the following general propositions regarding the VAR measures.

❏ Identical positions have the same VAR regardless of whether they are implemented in the cash market (eg, Portfolio 1) or the futures market (eg, Portfolio 2). Identical in this case refers to the fact that the cash and futures positions represent the price risk associated with the same asset and in the same amount. (As discussed below, other risk measures, such as liquidity, are not identical.)

❏ VAR can be increased via traditional balance sheet leverage or the use of additional derivatives contracts. Portfolios 3 and 4 illustrate the effect of leverage on the first two portfolios.

❏ VAR can be increased by choosing higher risk assets, regardless of leverage, as illustrated in Portfolio 5.

❏ A hedge is not always a hedge. The "hedge" established via Portfolios 6 and 7 presumes that Assets 1 and 2 are positively correlated. Under normal conditions (ie, when correlation equals 0.3 in this example) the tendency of asset 1 and asset 2 to move together results in the VAR of Portfolio 6 being similar to the VAR of Portfolio 3 even though the total position size is larger. When the correlation gets more positive (Stressed VAR 1), the hedge is better, and VAR stays relatively unchanged even though overall volatility in the market has increased by 50%. But, when the correlation gets less positive (Stressed VAR 2), the hedge is much less effective and the combined effect of higher volatility and lower correlation results in a significantly larger VAR. As was the case with the earlier portfolios, the use of futures or cash market investments does not change the market risk measure, as evidenced by the identical VAR of Portfolios 6 and 7.

**Table 2** Markets of market risk

| | | Unlevered cash vs | | Levered cash vs | | Unlevered high risk | Long/short strategy Cash vs futures | | Unlevered strategy with matched book assets | |
|---|---|---|---|---|---|---|---|---|---|---|
| Portfolio | | Cash only | Futures only | Levered cash | Futures | High risk cash | Long/short cash | Long/short mixed | Hedged cash | Hedged futures |
| | | **1** | **2** | **3** | **4** | **5** | **6** | **7** | **8** | **9** |
| **Summary balance sheet** | | | | | | | | | | |
| Capital | | 100 | 100 | 100 | 100 | 100 | 100 | 100 | 100 | 100 |
| Borrowing (outright or repo) | | 0 | 0 | 30 | | | | 30 | | |
| Investment | | | | | | | | | | |
| Cash market transactions | | | | | | | | | | |
| Asset 1 | | 80 | | 120 | | | 120 | 120 | 100, –20 | |
| Asset 2 | | | | | | | –60 | –60 | | |
| Asset 3 | | | | | | 80 | | | | |
| Derivatives market transactions | | | | | | | | | | |
| Futures on Asset 1 | | | 80 | | 120 | | | | | 100, –20 |
| Futures on Asset 2 | | | | | | | | | | |
| Cash | | 20 | 92 | 10 | 88 | 20 | 10 | 4 | 10 | 88 |
| Futures margin | | 0 | 8 | 0 | 12 | 0 | 0 | 6 | 0 | 12 |
| **Risk measures** | | | | | | | | | | |
| Standard VAR (Asset Correlation = 0.3) | | 2.50 | 2.50 | 3.76 | 3.76 | 5.01 | 3.61 | 3.61 | 2.50 | 2.50 |
| Stressed VAR 1 (Vol+50%; Asset correlation = .90) | | 3.76 | 3.76 | 5.64 | 5.64 | 7.51 | 3.67 | 3.67 | 3.76 | 3.76 |
| Stressed VAR 2 (Vol+50%; Asset correlation = 0) | | 3.76 | 3.76 | 5.64 | 5.64 | 7.51 | 6.10 | 6.10 | 3.76 | 3.76 |
| Sharpe ratio | | 1.05 | 1.05 | 1.05 | 1.05 | 1.32 | 0.69 | 0.69 | 1.05 | 1.05 |

### Relating earnings and risk

It was noted at the outset that effective risk management requires the hedge fund manager to recognise and understand the risks the fund faces. That, in turn, requires the hedge fund manager to understand the various sources of the fund's earnings, both the size of the earnings and their volatility.

One way that hedge fund managers can accomplish this attribution is by decomposing the daily value changes by market factors. The objective is to determine if the actual changes were what would have been predicted, given the now known changes in the market factors. If the observed change in the value of the portfolio differs significantly from the change that would be expected, given the composition of the portfolio and the observed changes in the market factors, the differences should be reconciled.

Such a source-of-return and source-of-risk attribution process sets the stage for linking performance measurement with risk measurement. The Sharpe ratio is widely used by investors to measure a portfolio's risk-adjusted performance over a specific period.10 The numerator of the Sharpe ratio is a measure of portfolio return during the period; the denominator is a measure of the risk incurred in achieving the return. (For example, over the past decade the Sharpe ratio for the S&P 500 has been approximately 1.2.) Investors prefer high Sharpe ratios to low, since a higher Sharpe ratio indicates that the portfolio earned superior returns relative to the level of risk incurred. There are a number of ways in which return and risk could be calculated. Below is the Sharpe ratio for some arbitrary portfolio – designated as Portfolio j – calculated using the most common conventions for measuring return and risk. The numerator is the return earned on the portfolio $(R_j)$ in excess of the risk-free rate of return $(R_f)$ – ie, the interest rate earned on risk-free securities such as US Treasury securities – over the same period. The denominator – the risk incurred – is measured as the standard deviation of the portfolio's daily return $(\sigma_j)$.

$$(\text{Sharpe Ratio})_j = \frac{R_j - R_f}{\sigma_j}$$

While VAR and the Sharpe ratio contain some similar information, the two measures are different tools, designed for different purposes. VAR is primarily a risk measurement tool. The Sharpe ratio is a summary measure, combining both risk and return information. Moreover, while VAR is a risk measure and the denominator of the Sharpe ratio contains a risk measure, these two risk measures are quite different. The risk measure used in the denominator of the Sharpe ratio is a historical measure; it characterises the actual volatility of the return over some historical period. In contrast, VAR is intended to be a prospective measure of risk.

## FUNDING LIQUIDITY RISK

While other entities face funding liquidity risk, this risk is a more central concern to hedge fund managers than others, because funding liquidity problems can rapidly increase a hedge fund's risk of failure. As is described below, a lack of funding liquidity can contribute to a crisis situation for the hedge fund.

### Liquidity crisis cycle

Hedge fund managers should be concerned about a confluence of risks – ie, market or credit risk events affecting illiquid positions that are leveraged. Such a confluence of events could require the hedge fund to liquidate positions into a market that cascades in price because of a high volume of liquidation orders. Such a situation could be decomposed into the following three stages.

1. A loss that acts as the triggering event.
2. A need to liquidate positions to raise cash, because of this loss. The liquidation may be required either because the fund must post margin with its counterparties or because of redemptions by investors due to the loss.
3. A further drop in the fund's NAV as the market reacts to actions by the fund. Obviously, attempts by the fund to sell in too great a quantity or too quickly for the market liquidity to bear can cause a further drop in prices, precipitating a further decline in the fund's net asset value, and leading in turn to yet a further need to liquidate to satisfy margin calls or redemptions. This downward spiral can be exacerbated if other market participants have information about the fund's positions.

The point of no return comes when the effect of liquidation has a greater impact on the value of the remaining fund position than the amount of cash raised from the liquidation. If this happens, the fund is caught in an accelerating, downward spiral; eventually, it will not be able to satisfy the demands of its creditors or investors. Once the losses move beyond a critical point, it becomes a self-sustaining crisis that feeds off of the need for liquidity, a need imposed by the demands of the fund's creditors and investors. Because of its importance, hedge fund managers should focus significant attention and resources on measuring and managing funding liquidity risk. There exist a range of measures hedge fund managers can use to track funding liquidity risk. Hedge fund managers should monitor the liquidity available in the fund by tracking its cash position (ie, cash and short-term securities issued by high credit-quality entities) and its borrowing capacity (eg, access to borrowings under margin rules or credit lines).

Beyond measures of available liquidity, hedge fund managers should also monitor measures of relative liquidity. Hedge fund managers should relate the measures of liquidity – cash or cash + borrowing capacity – to the need for that liquidity. The following measures are indicators of a fund's potential need for liquidity.

*Equity or NAV*
Generally, a larger fund will require greater levels of liquidity. However, a fund's need for liquidity during periods of market stress is determined not only by the size of the portfolio but also by the characteristics of the assets it holds. Consequently, hedge fund managers need to have measures of potential liquidity needs that reflect the riskiness of the portfolio.

*Worst historical drawdown.*
This indicator provides a measure of risk and of the amount of liquidity the fund has required in the past. This measure is, however, a backward-looking measure of risk and may not be indicative of the fund's current exposure.

*VAR*
As has been argued earlier, VAR is currently the most widely used prospective measure of market risk. Consequently, tracking the ratio of cash (or cash + borrowing capacity) to VAR provides the hedge fund manager with an indication of whether the fund's liquidity relative to its need for liquidity is rising or falling.

**Illustrative liquidity measures**
Panel 3 contains the results of calculating five of the liquidity measures discussed in this section for each of the nine stylised portfolios.

Additional insight about funding liquidity can be gained by looking at the variability in the relative liquidity measure over time. A relative liquidity measure that varies over time is evidence consistent with "effective liquidity" – ie, the assets are liquid and the manager is willing to take advantage of that liquidity.

Beyond simply monitoring liquidity, hedge fund managers should manage liquidity in several dimensions. Foremost is the use of the hedge fund manager's experience and judgement to maintain liquidity levels that are adequate given the risk of loss and/or the likelihood of investor redemptions. Also, hedge fund managers should strengthen lines of communication with their credit providers, providing them with summary measures of the fund's risk and liquidity consistent with the nature of the relationship. Hedge fund managers should actively manage (or monitor) the cash in margin accounts. Similarly, managers should negotiate haircuts and two-way collateral agreements, where appropriate, to further reduce the likelihood of running out of liquidity.

## LEVERAGE

As the recommendations made clear, leverage is not a concept that can be uniquely defined, nor is it an independently useful measure of risk. Never-

---

## Panel 3
## Illustrative liquidity measures

Available liquidity is measured by cash that is not committed as margin, and by cash plus the "borrowing capacity" of the assets. For the three cash market assets, it is assumed that 50% of the value of a long position can be borrowed (ie, assume current Regulation T margin requirements if the three assets were equities). For simplicity, short positions in the assets are assumed to have a 50% margin requirement, in effect, allowing 50% of short trades to be used to fund long positions, or for cash.

Several features of funding liquidity risk measurement are evidenced by the stylised portfolios.

❑ Other things equal, futures (and derivatives in general) require the hedge fund manager to use significantly less cash (at origination) than would an equivalent position established via a cash market transaction. This is evidenced by Portfolios 1 and 2. (However, not reflected in these numbers is the interrelation of market risk, funding liquidity risk and leveraging. While the cash position uses more cash at origination than does the futures position, if the value of the underlying asset were to change dramatically, the resulting margin call on the futures position could have a significant impact on the fund's cash position.)

❑ For the same amount of initial capital, the use of leverage (eg, Portfolios 3 and 4) both consumes borrowing capacity and increases VAR; so, measures of available liquidity and relative measures indicate that liquidity declines.

❑ Use of leverage in the cash market decreases available cash faster than the identical strategy implemented with futures. The increase in traditional balance sheet leverage (ie, use of margin to buy assets) in Portfolio 3 sharply reduces both absolute and relative measures of liquidity since either cash or borrowing capacity is consumed in the process. The identical economic leverage is obtained using futures in Portfolio 4, but the decrease in liquidity is less pronounced. (The caveat about future cash requirements for futures positions that was raised in the first point applies here as well.)

❑ Use of a relative liquidity measure – eg, VAR/(cash +borrowing capacity) – captures the impact of investing in higher risk assets while holding the amount invested constant. Portfolio 5 shows that while absolute liquidity is the same as for Portfolio 1, liquidity relative to VAR has decreased (ie, VAR is a higher percentage of available cash).

❑ Portfolios 6 and 7 illustrate once again that identical market risk portfolios present different funding liquidity risk profiles. Portfolio 7, which uses futures to short asset 2 while borrowing against asset 1 is less liquid than Portfolio 6 which shorts asset 2 in the cash market. The difference is simply that short positions in futures (and derivatives in general) do not generate cash.

---

**Table 3** Measures of liquidity

| | Unlevered cash vs | | Levered cash vs | | Unlevered high risk | Long/short strategy cash vs futures | | Unlevered strategy with matched book assets | |
|---|---|---|---|---|---|---|---|---|---|
| | Cash only | Futures only | Levered cash | Futures | High risk cash | Long/short cash | Long/short mixed | Hedged cash | Hedged futures |
| Portfolio | *1* | *2* | *3* | *4* | *5* | *6* | *7* | *8* | *9* |
| **Summary balance sheet** | | | | | | | | | |
| Capital | 100 | 100 | 100 | 100 | 100 | 100 | 100 | 100 | 100 |
| Borrowing (outright or repo) | 0 | 0 | 30 | | | | 30 | | |
| Investment | | | | | | | | | |
| Cash market transactions | | | | | | | | | |
| Asset 1 | 80 | | 120 | | | 120 | 120 | 100, –20 | |
| Asset 2 | | | | | | –60 | | | |
| Asset 3 | | | | | 80 | | | | |
| Derivatives market transactions | | | | | | | | | |
| Futures on Asset 1 | | 80 | | 120 | | | –60 | | 100, –20 |
| Futures on Asset 2 | | | | | | | | | |
| Cash | 20 | 92 | 10 | 88 | 20 | 10 | 4 | 10 | 88 |
| Futures margin | 0 | 8 | 0 | 12 | 0 | 0 | 6 | 0 | 12 |
| **Standard VAR (asset correlation = 0.3)** | 2.50 | 2.50 | 3.76 | 3.76 | 5.01 | 3.61 | 3.61 | 2.50 | 2.50 |
| **Liquidity measures** | | | | | | | | | |
| Measures of available liquidity | | | | | | | | | |
| Cash | 20 | 92 | 10 | 88 | 20 | 10 | 4 | 10 | 88 |
| Cash + Borrowing capacity | 60 | 92 | 40 | 88 | 60 | 70 | 34 | 60 | 88 |
| Realative measures | | | | | | | | | |
| Cash/Equity | 20% | 92% | 10% | 88% | 20% | 10% | 4% | 10% | 88% |
| (Cash + borrowing capacity)/equity | 60% | 92% | 40% | 88% | 60% | 70% | 34% | 60% | 88% |
| VAR/(Cash + borrowing capacity) | 4.2% | 2.7% | 9.4% | 4.3% | 8.3% | 9.0% | 10.6% | 4.2% | 2.8% |

theless, leverage is important to hedge fund managers because of the impact it can have on the three major quantifiable sources of risk: market risk, credit risk and liquidity risk.

That leverage is not a uniquely defined concept is evidenced by the variety of "leverage" measures used in banking and finance. These measures, that are described in more detail below, may be accounting-based (also referred to as "asset-based") or risk-based. The accounting-based measures attempt to capture the traditional notion of leverage as "investing borrowed funds". Using borrowed money (or its equivalent) enables an investor to increase the assets controlled for a given level of equity capital. Accounting-based measures of leverage relate some measure of asset value to equity. Both returns and risk, relative to equity, are magnified through the use of traditional, accounting-based leverage. The risk-based measures of leverage capture another aspect associated with leverage, namely, the risk of insolvency due to changes in the value of the portfolio. The risk-based measures relate a measure of a fund's market risk to its equity (or liquidity). Although useful in this capacity, as described below, risk-based leverage measures do not convey any information about the role borrowed money plays in the risk of insolvency.

No single measure captures all of the elements that market participants, regulators, or market observers attribute to the concept of leverage. Indeed, examples will be presented in which a risk-reducing transaction increases some leverage measures while decreasing others. This leads to the observation that leverage is not an independently useful concept, but must be evaluated in the context of the quantifiable exposures of market, credit and liquidity.

While continuing to track and use accounting-based measures of leverage, hedge fund managers should focus their attention on measures of leverage that relate the riskiness of the portfolio to the capacity of the fund to absorb that risk – ie, the measures must include elements of market risk (including the credit risk associated with assets in the portfolio) and funding liquidity risk. Hedge fund managers should focus on such measures because traditional accounting-based leverage by itself does not necessarily convey risk of insolvency. To say that one fund is levered two-to-one, while another is unlevered does not necessarily mean that the levered fund is more risky or more likely to encounter liquidity problems. If the levered fund is invested in government securities while the unlevered fund is invested in equities, accounting-based leverage would lead to erroneous conclusions about the riskiness of the two funds. In this sense, accounting-based measures of leverage are arguably deficient since they convey the least information about the nature and risk of the assets in a portfolio.

Risk-based measures (see below) present a measure of market risk (usually VAR) relative to a measure of the resources available to absorb risk (cash or equity). However, in doing so, risk based measures effectively condense several dimensions of risk into a single number. The result of this compression is that some of the detail is lost; the specific effect of leverage is intertwined with dimensions of market, credit and liquidity risk. To illustrate, consider two funds with identical risk-based leverage. One fund employs two-to-one accounting leverage while investing in "low risk" strategies (eg, long/short strategies) using borrowed funds, while the other fund uses no accounting leverage but employs "high risk" strategies (eg, macro-directional) and large cash reserves. One is "high risk" and "high cash" and the other is "low risk" and "low cash/high borrowing", yet each achieves the same risk-based leverage. This comparison high-lights the second reason why leverage measures are not independently useful: more comprehensive measures blend the effect of multiple risk dimensions. To assess the contribution of leverage requires additional information.

**Accounting-based leverage measures**
There exist a number of accounting-based measures of leverage. In addition to the pragmatic recognition that counterparties and credit providers routinely request these measures, a more compelling rationale for calculating these measures is that they can contribute to an understanding of leverage measures that incorporate risk. This is particularly true when accounting and risk-based leverage are tracked over time.

Certain accounting measures can also provide information regarding how much direct or indirect credit in the form of repurchase agreements, short sales, or derivatives are employed by a fund. However, it must be recognised that even these accounting-based measures have serious weaknesses, discussed below, particularly as stand-alone measures of leverage.

The most widely used and generally accepted accounting-based measures of leverage are those that relate items from a fund's balance sheet:

*"Gross balance sheet assets to equity": on-balance-sheet assets/equity*
This straightforward measure is easily calculated from published financial statements; however, it fails to incorporate two important elements of a fund's effective leverage.

1. The risk-reducing effect of on-balance-sheet hedges is not recognised. Adding a hedge to the balance sheet increases assets and thereby increases this leverage measure, even though the transaction may substantially offset the risk of another asset.
2. Derivative instruments, which have historically been carried off-balance-sheet, are not captured11. To the extent derivatives are used to hedge on-balance-sheet assets, this measure will overstate the fund's

effective leverage. By the same token, if a fund's derivatives are used to take outright positions – ie, not as hedges – this measure will understate the fund's effective leverage.

*"Net balance sheet assets to equity": (on-balance-sheet assets – matched book assets)/equity*
While this measure requires more detailed information about the positions in a fund's portfolio, it does provide a partial solution to the shortcomings of the gross-balance-sheet assets to equity measure by including offsets and direct hedges as reflected in "matched book assets". However, two important elements of the fund's effective leverage are still not incorporated.

1. This measure does not reflect portfolio correlation or less direct hedges that fall outside the definition of matched book assets.
2. This measure does not incorporate off-balance-sheet instruments.

Other accounting-based measures have been proposed to capture off-balance-sheet transactions (eg, forward contracts, swaps and other derivatives). Among those measures are the following:

*"Gross accounting leverage": ( on-balance-sheet assets + on-balance-sheet liabilities + gross off-balance-sheet notional)/equity*
Gross accounting leverage incorporates the gross amount of off-balance-sheet derivatives. Such a measure cannot reliably indicate the effective amount of leverage obtained from off-balance sheet transactions because that type of offsetting exposures are not netted. An active derivative user that uses offsetting transactions rather than closeouts to reduce or eliminate positions will accumulate a substantial notional amount of derivatives even though the risk of the position and its effective leverage are quite low.

*"net accounting leverage": ((on-balance-sheet assets – matched book assets) + (on-balance-sheet liabilities – matched book liabilities) + (gross off-balance-sheet notional principal – notional principal of off-balance-sheet transactions used to hedge on-balance-sheet assets or liabilities))/equity*
Net accounting leverage requires still more detail to calculate. Although it reflects matched book assets (liabilities) and off-balance-sheet hedges of balance sheet assets, it still misses off-balance sheet hedges and correlation.

### Risk-based leverage measures

Risk-based leverage measures reflect the relation between the riskiness of a fund's portfolio and the capacity of the fund to absorb the impact of that risk. While not the only measure that could be used, the hedge fund's equity provides a useful measure of "capacity". There are, however, different measures of market risk that could be used as the "riskiness" measure.

*(Volatility in value of portfolio)/equity*

This is a measure of actual performance volatility over a given horizon relative to equity. While useful, it is subject to criticism. Since it is a retrospective measure, it is less useful if the composition of the portfolio changes or if future market conditions are not like historical conditions. Moreover, it does not isolate the effect of financing on the risk of the fund since it includes financed assets.

*VAR/equity*

This measure gives a picture of the fund's capacity to absorb "typical" market movements. The criticism of such a measure is that it does not reflect the risk of the fund's portfolio in extreme markets.

*(Scenario-derived market risk measure)/equity*

To assess the impact of extreme events, the leverage measure could be calculated using a market risk measure derived from analysis of extreme event scenarios (or stress tests). This measure gives senior management information about the hedge fund's ability to absorb extreme market events.

Panel 4 contains the results of calculating all of the accounting-based leverage measures and two of the risk-based leverage measures discussed in this section.

While the preceding leverage measures are the ones most commonly used by hedge fund managers, other measures may be used to analyse leverage. Indeed, because of the interrelation between market risk, funding liquidity risk and leverage, measures of funding liquidity risk described in this section – particularly cash + borrowing capacity relative to VAR – also provide the hedge fund manager with insights about a fund's leverage.

### Dynamic measures of leverage

A crucial factor influencing a fund's ability to absorb the impact of extreme market events is the degree to which a fund can modify its risk-based leverage, especially during periods of market stress.

Treating equity as constant, there are two ways a hedge fund manager could reduce risk-based leverage.

# Panel 4

## Illustrative leverage measures

Table 4 contains the results of calculating all of the accounting-based leverage measures and two of the risk-based leverage measures discussed in this section. Note that "net balance sheet leverage" and "net accounting leverage" are only relevant for Portfolios 8 and 9, because these portfolios are the only ones in which the long and short positions can be netted under accounting rules.

Leverage can be interpreted in several ways: as the use of borrowed money to fund larger asset positions than would otherwise be achievable, and as the use of economic leverage to increase effect of a given change in market prices on the value of fund's equity.

The illustrative portfolios demonstrate several common features of accounting-based and risk-based leverage.

❑ The most common leverage measure, gross balance sheet leverage (or assets/equity) is not indicative of the types of assets employed or the amount of risk assumed. In the illustration, gross balance sheet leverage is the same in Portfolios 1, 2, 4, 5 and 9 even though the risk and investment strategy differ significantly across portfolios. Similarly, while the amount of risk assumed in Portfolio 8 is identical to the risk assumed in Portfolio 1, the levels of gross balance sheet leverage differ.

❑ The purpose of the net balance sheet leverage measure is to adjust for matched book assets. Comparison of net balance sheet leverage with gross balance sheet leverage for Portfolio 8 shows an instance where this occurs.

❑ Gross accounting leverage, which sums assets, liabilities, and futures is not informative about investment strategy (cash versus futures) or the market risk of the portfolio. Note that the riskiest portfolio as measured by VAR – Portfolio 5 – has the lowest accounting leverage. Similarly, Portfolios 1 and 2 are low risk, yet gross accounting leverage varies by 80% between them.

❑ That net accounting leverage adjusts for matched book assets and derivatives that hedge on-balance-sheet positions is seen by comparing gross accounting leverage with net accounting leverage for Portfolios 8 and 9. Note that this measure does not capture the use of a futures position to offset an identical futures position, ie, the matched futures in Portfolio 9. The risk-based leverage measures come closer to capturing the nature of the risks as reflected in the specific strategies. (Note Portfolios 1, 2, 8 and 9.) However, they too miss certain aspects of the risk picture. For example, Portfolios 3 and 4 have the same VAR/Equity, but the cash market strategy employed in Portfolio 3 uses more cash and borrowing capacity, and is therefore riskier from a liquidity standpoint (VAR is 9.4% of liquidity in Portfolio 3 compared to only 4.3% of liquidity in Portfolio 4).

❑ Stress and scenario analysis are essential elements of liquidity and leverage analyses. The long/short strategy employed in Portfolios 6 and 7 is similar in risk-based leverage to Portfolios 3 and 4 until one looks at the stress scenarios. Because of the reliance on correlation, the leverage of Portfolios 6 and 7 is potentially much larger in a period of market stress.

**Table 4** Measures of leverage

| | Unlevered cash vs | | Levered cash vs | | Unlevered high risk | Long/short strategy cash vs futures | | Unlevered strategy with matched book assets | |
|---|---|---|---|---|---|---|---|---|---|
| | Cash only | Futures only | Levered cash | Futures | High risk cash | Long/short cash | Long/short mixed | Hedged cash | Hedged futures |
| Portfolio | 1 | 2 | 3 | 4 | 5 | 6 | 7 | 8 | 9 |
| **Summary balance sheet** | | | | | | | | | |
| Capital | 100 | 100 | 100 | 100 | 100 | 100 | 100 | 100 | 100 |
| Borrowing (outright or repo) | 0 | 0 | 30 | 0 | | | 30 | | |
| Investment | | | | | | | | | |
| Cash market transactions | | | | | | | | 100, –20 | |
| Asset 1 | 80 | | 120 | | | 120 | 120 | | |
| Asset 2 | | | | | | –60 | | | |
| Asset 3 | | | | | 80 | | | | |
| Derivatives market transactions | | | | | | | | | |
| Futures on Asset 1 | | 80 | | 120 | | | | | 100, –20 |
| Futures on Asset 2 | | | | | | | –60 | | |
| Cash | 20 | 92 | 10 | 88 | 20 | 10 | 4 | 10 | 88 |
| Futures margin | 0 | 8 | 0 | 12 | 0 | 0 | 6 | 0 | 12 |
| **Standard VAR (asset correlation = 0.3)** | 2.50 | 2.50 | 3.76 | 3.76 | 5.01 | 3.61 | 3.61 | 2.50 | 2.50 |
| **Leverage measures** | | | | | | | | | |
| Accounting-based measures | | | | | | | | | |
| Gross balance sheet leverage | 1 | 1 | 1.3 | 1 | 1 | 1.6 | 1.3 | 1.2 | 1 |
| Net balance sheet leverage | | | | | | | | 1 | |
| Gross accounting leverage | 1 | 1.8 | 1.6 | 2.2 | 1 | 2.2 | 1 | 1.4 | 2.2 |
| Net accounting leverage | | | | | | | | 1.2 | 1.2 |
| Risk-based measures | | | | | | | | | |
| VAR/Capital | 2.50% | 2.50% | 3.76% | 3.76% | 5.01% | 3.61% | 3.61% | 2.50% | 2.50% |
| Stress 1 VAR/Capital | 3.76% | 3.76% | 5.64% | 5.64% | 7.51% | 3.67% | 3.67% | 3.76% | 3.76% |
| Stress 2 VAR/Capital | 3.76% | 3.76% | 5.64% | 5.64% | 7.51% | 6.10% | 6.10% | 3.76% | 3.76% |

1. If a hedge fund manager wishes to continue an existing investment strategy, risk-based leverage could be reduced by reducing traditional leverage resulting from either on- or off-balance-sheet transactions.
2. A hedge fund manager could reduce risk-based leverage by reducing the level of risk that is being accepted (eg, by changing strategy or the types of assets being held in the portfolio). To track the degree to which the fund is able to modify its risk-based leverage, the hedge fund manager should track variations in the fund's market risk measure (eg, VAR) over time.

The following two measures could be used to track the relationship over time between measures of market risk and actions taken by the hedge fund manager to adjust leverage. Both of these measures consider a short time interval (one or two days – one week); both assume that equity is constant.

*Changes in portfolio market risk*
A decline in a portfolio's market risk measure (eg, VAR) in a period following an increase in that market risk measure in the preceding period, could be evidence of the hedge fund manager's ability to de-lever the portfolio during a period of market stress. (The market risk measure could be VAR or the observed volatility of the value of the portfolio during the relevant period.)

*Relationship between a change in market risk and a subsequent change in cash + borrowing capacity*
All other things equal, if a hedge fund manager is able to reduce the portfolio's accounting-based leverage, the result would be an increase in cash or in borrowing capacity. Therefore, an increase in cash + borrowing capacity in a period following an increase in the market risk measure for the portfolio (eg, VAR) could be evidence of the hedge fund manager's reacting to market stress by reducing leverage.

## COUNTERPARTY CREDIT RISK
Hedge fund managers enter into transactions with a variety of counterparties including banks, securities firms, exchanges and other financial institutions. The risk of loss to the fund as a result of the failure of a counterparty to perform as expected, constitutes counterparty credit risk.

Credit risk is present to some extent in almost any dealing with a third party, including the settlement of securities and derivatives transactions, repurchase agreements, collateral arrangements and margin accounts. It is also present in open derivatives positions where the exposure of one counterparty to another will change over the life of the contract as the contract's value fluctuates. Hedge fund managers should be aware of, and track, concentrations of credit risk with particular counterparties, and where applicable, different regions of the world. The willingness of the manager to enter into a transaction with a specific counterparty should depend on the loss the hedge fund would suffer were the counterparty to default. That, in turn, depends on the magnitude of the fund's exposure to the counterparty and the likelihood of default, ie, the counterparty's credit-worthiness.

An assessment of exposure to a particular counterparty should include analysis of the following elements of exposure.

❑ Current replacement cost. The amount the fund would lose if its counterparty were to become insolvent immediately and the hedge fund manager had to replace the contract in the market.

❑ Potential exposure. A probabilistic assessment of the additional exposure that could result if the counterparty does not default immediately but instead defaults at some date in the future. Potential exposure is particularly applicable to derivatives transactions where exposure is reciprocal and likely to change substantially before the contract expires.

❑ The probability of loss. The likelihood of a default by the counterparty over the relevant time horizon. This is a function of the counterparty's current credit quality, the length of the transaction, and possibly the nature of the transaction itself.

❑ Risk mitigation and documentation. The extent to which collateral, netting provisions or other credit enhancement reduces the magnitude of the exposure to a counterparty. Hedge fund managers can greatly reduce their credit exposure to counterparties by negotiating bilateral netting and collateral provisions in their documentation and establishing document management processes to ensure transactions are documented consistently and in a timely manner.

## ADDITIONAL NOTES

### US REGULATORY FILINGS BY HEDGE FUND MANAGERS

Listed below are regulatory filings (excluding tax-related and state "blue sky" filings) that hedge fund managers may be required to make in the United States depending on either their trading activity or their status as a regulated entity. The filings made to regulators by individual managers will vary depending on the type and volume of trading in which they engage, their business model and the jurisdictions in which they operate. For example, like other market participants and institutional investors, managers are required to make certain filings in the United States if the size of the positions they hold in certain markets reaches "reportable" levels. In addition, some managers are regulated entities in the US or are otherwise subject to a regulatory regime, and, like other similarly situated entities, are required to make certain filings in that capacity. This Appendix lists filings required in the United States where the above circumstances apply to a manager. Hedge fund managers may also be subject to regulatory reporting and filing requirements in the foreign jurisdictions in which they conduct their business.

### Federal reserve – Treasury securities position and foreign exchange transaction reporting

*Large position reporting*

❏ Report of positions in specific Treasury security issues that exceed the large position threshold specified by the US Treasury Department (minimum US$2 billion).

❏ Reports are filed in response to notices issued by the US Department of the Treasury if such a threshold is met.

❏ Reports are filed with the Federal Reserve Bank of New York and are not public.

*Form FC-1*

❏ Report of weekly, consolidated data on the foreign exchange contracts and positions of major market participants.

❏ Reports to be filed throughout the calendar year by each foreign exchange market participant which had more than US$50 billion equivalent in foreign exchange contracts on the last business day of any calendar quarter during the previous year.

❏ The report is filed with the appropriate Federal Reserve Bank acting as agent for the US Department of the Treasury and is confidential.

*Form FC-2*

❏ Report of monthly, consolidated data on the foreign exchange contracts and foreign currency denominated assets and liabilities of major market participants.

❏ Reports to be filed throughout the calendar year by each foreign exchange market participant which had more than US$50 billion equivalent in foreign exchange contracts on the last business day of any calendar quarter during the previous year.

❏ The report is filed with the appropriate Federal Reserve Bank acting as agent for the US Department of the Treasury and is confidential.

*Form FC-3*

❏ Report of quarterly, consolidated data on the foreign exchange contracts and foreign currency denominated assets and liabilities of major market participants.

❏ Reports to be filed throughout the calendar year by each foreign exchange market participant which had more than US$5 billion equiv-

alent in foreign exchange contracts on the last business day of any calendar quarter during the previous year and which does not file Form FC-2.
❏ The report is filed with the appropriate Federal Reserve Bank acting as agent for the US Department of the Treasury and is confidential.

### Treasury auction filings
*Treasury auction*
❏ Treasury security reports filed as necessary. Confirmations must be filed by any customer who is awarded more than US$500 million of US government securities in a Treasury auction. The confirmation must include its reportable net long position, if any.
❏ The confirmation is filed with the Federal Reserve Bank to which the bid was submitted and is not public.

### Treasury international capital forms
*Forms CM, CQ-1 and CQ-2*
❏ Forms filed by US persons who have claims on, or financial liabilities to unaffiliated foreigners, have balances on deposit with foreign banks (in the US or abroad) or otherwise engage in transactions in securities or other financial assets with foreigners. Forms CQ-1 ("financial liabilities to, and claims on, unaffiliated foreigners") and CQ-2 ("commercial liabilities to, and claims on, unaffiliated foreigners") are quarterly reports, which collect data on financial and commercial liabilities to, and claims on, unaffiliated foreigners held by non-banking enterprises in the US, which must be filed when the consolidated total of such liabilities are US$10 million or more during that period. Form CM ("dollar deposit and certificate of deposit claims on banks abroad") is a monthly report whereby non-banking enterprises in the US report their total dollar deposit and certificate of deposit claims on foreign banks, which must be filed when the consolidated total of such claims are US$10 million or more during that period.
❏ The forms are filed with the Federal Reserve Bank of New York are non-public except for aggregate information.

*Form S*
❏ Form filed by any US person who purchases or sells US$2 million or more of long-term marketable domestic and foreign securities in a month in direct transactions with foreign persons.
❏ The form is filed with the Federal Reserve Bank of New York and is non-public except as to aggregate information.

### Securities and Exchange Commission (SEC)
Sale of securities by an issuer exempt from registration under Reg D or 4(6)

*Form D*
❏ Notice of sale filed after securities, such as interests in a private hedge fund, are sold in reliance on a Regulation D private placement exemption or a Section 4(6) exemption from the registration provisions of the 1933 Act. The form is filed with the SEC and relevant states and is publicly available.

## Secondary sale of restricted and control securities under Rule 144

*Form 144*
❏ Form filed as notice of the proposed sale of restricted securities or securities held by an affiliate of the issuer in reliance on Rule 144 when the amount to be sold during any three month period exceeds 500 shares or units or has an aggregate sales price in excess of US$10,000. The form is filed with the SEC and the principal national securities exchange, if any, on which such security is traded and is publicly available.

## Ownership of equity securities publicly traded in the United States

*Schedule 13D*
❏ Disclosure report for any investor, including a hedge fund and its fund manager, who is considered beneficially to own more than 5% of a class of equity securities publicly traded in the US The report identifies the source and amount of the funds used for the acquisition and the purpose of the acquisition.
❏ This reporting requirement is triggered by direct or indirect acquisition of more than 5% of beneficial ownership of a class of equity securities publicly traded in the US Amendments must be filed promptly for material ownership changes. Some investors may instead report on short-form Schedule 13G if they are eligible (see Schedule 13G).
❏ The report is filed with the SEC and is publicly available.

*Schedule 13G*
❏ Short form disclosure report for any passive investor, including a hedge fund and its fund manager, who would otherwise have to file a Schedule 13D but who owns less than 20% of the subject securities (or is in certain US regulated investment businesses) and has not been purchased for the purpose of influencing control.
❏ This reporting requirement is triggered by direct or indirect acquisition of beneficial ownership of more than 5% of a class of equity securities publicly traded in the US Amendments must be filed annually if there are any changes, and either monthly (for US regulated investment businesses) or promptly (for other passive investors) if ownership changes by more than 5% of the class.
❏ The report is filed with the SEC and is publicly available.

*Forms 3, 4 and 5*

❏ Every director, officer or owner of more than 10% of a class of equity securities of a domestic public company must file a statement of ownership. The initial filing is on Form 3 and changes are reported on Form 4. The Annual Statement of beneficial ownership of securities is on Form 5. The statements contain information on the reporting person's relationship to the company and on purchases and sales of the equity securities.

❏ Form 3 reporting is triggered by acquisition of more than 10% of the equity securities of a domestic public company, the reporting person becoming a director or officer, or the equity securities becoming publicly traded, as the case may be. Form 4 reporting is triggered by any open market purchase, sale, or an exercise of options of those reporting under Form 3. Form 5 reporting is required annually for those insiders who have had exempt transactions and have not reported them previously on a Form 4.

❏ The statements are filed with the SEC and are publicly available.

### Registered and unregistered institutional investment managers
*Form 13F*

❏ Quarterly position report for registered and unregistered institutional investment managers (ie, any person, other than a natural person, investing in or buying and selling securities for its own account, and any person exercising investment discretion with respect to the account of any other person) with investment discretion over US$100 million or more in equity securities publicly traded in the United States. Reports contain position information about the equity securities under the discretion of the fund manager, and the type of voting authority exercised by the fund manager.

❏ The reporting requirement is triggered by an institutional investment manager holding equity securities having an aggregate fair market value of at least US$100 million on the last trading day of a calendar year and require a report as of the end of that year and each of the next three quarters.

❏ The reports are filed with the SEC and are publicly available.

### Material associated persons of registered broker-dealers
*Form 17-H*

❏ Material Associated Persons (MAP) reports, filed by registered broker-dealers. Some hedge fund managers are affiliated with registered broker-dealers. MAPs generally include material affiliates and parents and may therefore include an affiliated hedge fund manager or the related hedge fund. Broker-dealers must report (1) organisational chart of the broker-dealer, (2) risk management policies of the broker-dealer,

(3) material legal proceedings, and (4) additional financial information including aggregate positions, borrowing and off-balance sheet risk for each MAP.

❏ The reporting requirement is triggered by status as broker or dealer registered under Section 15 of the Exchange Act.

❏ This report is filed with the SEC quarterly and cumulatively at year-end and is not public.

❏ There are also a variety of filings with the SEC and the securities self-regulatory organisations that must be made by registered broker-dealers and their employees who are associated persons.

## Commodity Futures Trading Commission (CFTC) and National Futures Association (NFA), registered commodity trading advisors (CTAs) and commodity pool operators (CPOs)

*Commodity pool operator and commodity trading advisor registration*

❏ An individual or entity that operates or solicits funds for a commodity pool is generally required to register as a commodity pool operator. As a result, a hedge fund manager may be required to register as a commodity pool operator if the hedge fund trades futures or options on futures and the hedge fund manager operates the fund.

❏ An individual or entity that, for compensation or profit, advises others as to the value of or advisability of buying or selling futures contracts or options on futures must generally register as a commodity trading advisor unless it has provided advice to 15 or fewer persons (including each person in an advised fund or pool) in the past 12 months and does not generally hold itself out to the public as a CTA. Providing advice indirectly includes exercising trading authority over a fund or account. A hedge fund manager, therefore, may also be required to register as a CTA if the related hedge fund trades futures or options on futures.

❏ The documents required for registration as a commodity pool operator or commodity trading advisor are: a completed Form 7-R (which provides CPO or CTA information), a completed Form 8-R (which provides biographical data) and fingerprint card, for each principal (defined to include executive officers, directors and 10% owners), branch office manager and associated person (defined to include persons soliciting fund interests or accounts or supervising persons so engaged), and proof of passage of the Series 3 exam for each associated person and proof of passage of the Series 3 and futures branch office manager exams for each branch office manager.

❏ Applications for registration are filed with and approved by the NFA under authority granted to it by the CFTC and the registration documents are generally public except for fingerprint cards, although confidentiality may be requested for certain information relating to the principals.

*Form 3-R amend. 7-R*
- ❏ Form used to report any changes to information contained in the basic registration Form 7-R.
- ❏ The requirement to file this form is triggered by changes in the information provided in Form 7-R.
- ❏ The form is filed with the NFA and is public, though confidentiality may be requested for certain information relating to the principals.

*Form 8-T associated person termination*
- ❏ Form that must be filed within 20 days of the termination of an associated person, principal or branch manager. The form is filed with the NFA and is generally public.

*Ethics examination for all registered persons*
- ❏ Ethics training is required under CFTC Reg §3.34 for all associated persons and any individual registered as a CPO or CTA. In connection with the annual registration update, each NFA member will receive a report indicating ethics training due or overdue for its associated persons. The member is responsible for providing proof of ethics training to the NFA, and the NFA will confirm this information to the public.

*Annual report*
- ❏ Annual report of a fund that must be filed pursuant to Reg §4.22(c) by that fund's CPO. The annual report must contain certain information, such as actual performance information and fees, and must be distributed to each participant in the fund. The annual report must be filed by a registered CPO with the CFTC within 60 days of the fund's fiscal year-end and is generally publicly available; however, the CFTC is prohibited from disclosing information that would separately disclose the business transactions or market positions of any person or trade secrets or names of any investors.

*CPO/CTA questionnaire*
- ❏ Annual compliance questionnaire concerning its business activities for applicants registered as CPOs or CTAs. The questionnaire is filed with the NFA and is not public.

*NFA self-audits*
- ❏ In order to satisfy their continuing supervisory responsibilities, NFA members must review their operations on an annual basis using a self-examination checklist. The checklist focuses on a member's regulatory responsibilities and solicits information on whether the member's internal procedures are adequate for meeting those responsibilities.

❏ Registered CPOs and CTAs as members of the NFA are required to conduct such self-audit annually.
❏ A written attestation is then signed and dated by the supervisory personnel that they have reviewed the operations in light of the checklist. This attestation is retained by the member and not forwarded to the NFA and as such is not public.

*Claims for exemption*
❏ Filings made pursuant to Reg §4.12(b)(3) (notice of claim for exemption from certain requirements by a CPO that complies with the Securities Act and manages a fund with limited trading in commodity futures and options), Reg §4.7(a)(3) (notice of claim for exemption by a CPO with "qualified eligible participants" as investors), and Reg §4.7(b)(3) (notice of claim for exemption by a CTA advising "qualified eligible clients"). Reg §4.7 provides exemptions for qualifying CPO/CTO applicants from most disclosure and other requirements of CPOs and CTAs.
❏ These statements are filed with the CFTC and NFA and are public.

*Disclosure document*
❏ CPOs and CTAs are generally required to prepare detailed Disclosure documents containing specified information. Such documents are filed with the CFTC and NFA and provided to investors but are not publicly available.
❏ CPOs and CTAs operating under Reg §4.7, however, are exempt from the disclosure document requirement and are required only to provide all material disclosures. In addition, under the exemption provided in Reg §4.8, funds (which would otherwise be treated as commodity pools) with exemptions under Reg §4.12(b) (compliance with the requirements of the Securities Act and certain limits on the trading of commodity futures and options) or which sell interests solely to "accredited investors" and rely on the safe harbour provisions of Rule 506 or 507 of Regulation D under the Securities Act may begin soliciting, accepting and receiving money upon providing the CFTC and the participants with disclosure documents for the fund, which requirement may be satisfied by a private placement memorandum.

*Year-end financial reports for §4.7 funds*
❏ Annual Report requirements for §4.7 funds (ie, funds, which by having only qualified eligible participants, are exempt from the normal disclosure requirements applicable to commodity pools). The form must contain a Statement of Financial Condition, a Statement of Income (Loss), appropriate footnote disclosure and other material information and a legend as to any claim made for exemption.

❏ The annual report is filed with the CFTC, NFA and distributed to each investor, and the report is not public.

## Position reports
*Form 40*
❏ "Statement of Reporting Trader" for persons who own or control reportable positions in futures. A hedge fund and/or hedge fund manager will be required to file a Form 40 if it holds reportable positions. The form must be filed within ten business days following the day that a hedge fund's and/or its managers ' position equals or exceeds specified levels. Such specified levels are set separately for each type of contract. For example, the reportable level for S&P 500 futures is 600 contracts. The Form 40 requires the disclosure of information about ownership and control of futures and option positions held by the reporting trader as well as the trader's use of the markets for hedging. Hedging exemptions from speculative position limits must be reported.
❏ The form is filed with the CFTC and is not publicly available.

*Form 102*
❏ Form filed by clearing members, futures commission merchants (FCMs), and foreign brokers, which identifies persons, including hedge funds, having financial interest in, or trading control of, special accounts in futures and options, informs the CFTC of the type of account that is being reported and gives preliminary information regarding whether positions and transactions are commercial or non-commercial in nature. The form must be filed when the account first becomes "reportable" (ie, when it first contains reportable futures or options positions), and updated when information concerning financial interest in, or control of, the special account changes. In addition, the form is used by exchanges to identify accounts reported through their large trader reporting systems for both futures and options.
❏ The form is filed with the CFTC and is non-public.

## Selected stock and futures exchange reports
Application for exemption from speculative position limits

*Speculative position limit exemption*
❏ Application filed for exemption from speculative position limits. Exchanges generally have speculative position limits for physical commodities and stock index contracts, and the CFTC has speculative position limits for agricultural commodities. Exemptions from such limits are generally available for hedging transactions. Financial

contracts, such as interest rate contracts, do not have such position limits.

❏ For example, under Rule 543 of the Chicago Mercantile Exchange (CME), persons intending to exceed speculative position limits on S&P 500 contracts must either file the required exemption application and receive approval prior to exceeding such limits or receive verbal approval prior to exceeding such limits and, if approved, file the required application promptly thereafter. Generally, an application for any speculative position limit exemption must show that such position is a bona fide hedging, risk management, arbitrage or spread position.

❏ The filing is made with the appropriate exchange in the case of physical commodities and stock index contracts and with the CFTC in the case of agricultural commodities.

## Federal Trade Commission (FTC)
Filings Made Prior to Mergers and Acquisitions

### Hart-Scott-Rodino notice

❏ Notice filed prior to the consummation of certain mergers, acquisitions and joint ventures. After notice is filed there is a waiting period while the FTC and Department of Justice review the competitive effects of the transaction. The notice includes information about the transaction and the participants in the transaction.

❏ The notice and waiting period requirement are generally triggered by the following tests: either the acquiring person or the acquired person must be engaged in US commerce or an activity affecting US commerce, a person with total assets or net sales of US$100 million or more is acquiring voting securities or assets of a person with total assets of US$10 million or more, and as a result of the transaction, the acquiring person will hold 15% or more of the voting securities or assets of the acquired person or an aggregate of US$15 million or more of assets and voting securities of the acquired person. A notice would generally have to be filed for an over US$15 million purchase by a hedge fund with US$100 million in assets if an exemption were not available. Acquisitions of voting securities are exempt from filing if they are made "solely for the purpose of investment" and if, as a result of the acquisition, the securities held do not exceed 10% of the outstanding voting securities of the issuer. Securities are acquired "solely for investment purposes" if the person acquiring the securities has no intention of participating in the formulation, determination, or direction of the basic business decisions of the issuer.

❏ The notice is filed with the FTC and the Department of Justice and is confidential.

\*   This document is reprinted with the permission of the authors. The authors, however, do not endorse any of the other views expressed in this volume.

†   This document has been prepared in response to this recommendation.

1   PWG Report, p37.

2   "Cash" refers to cash plus cash equivalents (short-term, high-quality investments).

3   "Cash + Borrowing Capacity" = cash plus access to borrowings, eg, under margin rules or credit lines.

4   As was noted in the recommendations, "sovereign risk" may be viewed either as "credit risk", if the potential loss is related to the financial solvency of the sovereign, or as "market risk", if the potential loss is related to policy decisions made by the sovereign that change the market value of positions (eg, currency controls). "Legal risk", other than those covered by the preceding discussion of "sovereign risk", would be included as "operational risk".

5   Since illiquid instruments with long holding periods will generally not be included in the daily risk monitoring model, valuing these instruments on a daily basis for Risk Monitoring is not necessary.

6   For a discussion of VAR and VAR calculation techniques, see Philippe Jorion, Value at Risk: The New Benchmark for Controlling Market Risk (McGraw-Hill, 1997).

7   "Derivatives: Practices and Practices", Group of Thirty Global Derivatives Study Group, July 1993.

8   Since 1995, the Basle Committee on Banking Supervision and an IOSCO technical committee have been examining the risk management procedures and disclosures of leading banks and securities firms in the industrialised world. The latest survey, released in December 1999, indicated that virtually all banks and securities firms covered by the survey used VAR techniques to measure market risk.

9   "1998 Survey of Derivative and Risk Management Practices by U.S. Institutional Investors", Risk, August, 1999.

10  The Sharpe ratio is attributed to William F. Sharpe, who described a measure of "return to variability" for use in comparing investment performance.

11  Derivative instruments will be required to be carried on balance sheet under Financial Accounting Standard 133, which was scheduled to become effective in 2000.

# *Due Diligence*

## Jon Lukomnik

CMRA

*Haste makes waste.*
*Measure twice, cut once.*
*Look before you leap.*

## INTRODUCTION[1]

Time and again we are cautioned to examine the rationale for an action before rushing in. With good reason: our ancestors learned that action without a plan risks being wasteful at best, and counterproductive at worst. Yet, when it comes to performing due diligence on a fund of fund (FoF), some potential investors act first, and think later. Indeed, for many, due diligence has become a set of actions to be completed and documented, without thinking as to why they are performing that exact set of actions.

However, gathering a drawer full of documents is not sufficient. Checking references is not sufficient. Running innumerable portfolio simulations is not sufficient. Running criminal investigations on the managers is not sufficient. Speaking with other investors, reviewing the feng shui of the office, checking the phases of the moon, getting the manager so drunk that his tongue loosens, torturing the auditors until they speak – all of these are not sufficient.

While all of the above due diligence techniques may be helpful, or even necessary (well, maybe not torturing the auditors), they are not sufficient when deciding whether or not to invest in a FoF. The reason? Due diligence should mean just what the dictionary says it does: taking the appropriate amount of effort or care. But, until you decide why you are considering investing in that particular FoF, and what that specific FoF manager is supposed to do for you, how are you to know what is relevant? Without that as a benchmark, there is no way to know what is appropriate. Rushing into due diligence before considering the context may often result in a perfunctory, check-the-box approach, in which form is elevated over substance. For due diligence to be successful, it needs to be integrated into the investment management process. That may sound obvious, but arguably many, if not most, investors fail to take that initial step.

(Successful due diligence stems from a careful consideration of the risk implications of the specific investment strategies and instruments employed. Therefore, a potential investor should understand as much as possible about the investment management process, portfolio construction, etc. While some of the trade-offs inherent in the portfolio construction process are addressed below, a full discussion of portfolio construction as well as the risks in each particular underlying hedge fund strategy is clearly beyond the scope of this chapter. Therefore, several other chapters in this book may be of particular interest to investors seeking a deeper knowledge for due diligence purposes.)

### WHY INVEST THROUGH A FUND OF FUND (FOF)?

Let us start at the beginning: why are you investing in a FoF? Only after answering this question can you assess what information is relevant to deciding if a particular FoF is the right one for you.

There are a number of reasons to invest in a FoF, but, in general, they can be divided into top-down portfolio reasons, bottom-up portfolio reasons, and legal/functional reasons as described below.

**Top down reasons:**
are those that relate to the portfolio construction function of the FoF manager. For example:

❑ diversification among a number of underlying hedge funds; or
❑ portfolio construction by the FoF manager to create a desirable risk-return profile unavailable through a single hedge fund.

**Bottom up reasons:**
are those focusing on the underlying managers within the fund. Among these reasons might be:

❑ access to funds which have little or no capacity except through the FoF; or
❑ the FoF manager has the capacity to find great managers before they become common names in the hedge fund community.

**Legal/functional reasons:**
for investing in FoFs include:

❑ Lack of staff resources to select and monitor the multiplicity of hedge fund managers that would be needed to create a diversified hedge fund portfolio, but sufficient skill and resources to select and monitor one or a small number of FoFs.

❏ Comfort with the FoF as a legal intermediary, both for liability and reputational reasons, as well as for ease of reporting.

While much due diligence is common to all manager searches (assessing managerial honesty, ethics, business risk, intelligence, etc), some of the focus should vary depending upon why an investor is seeking a FoF. That is what taking an appropriate level of care means.

Nevertheless, a potential investor is encouraged to read through this entire chapter, rather than jumping to the section of particular interest to him/her, since much of the chapter is relevant to all potential investors.

## DUE DILIGENCE FOR "TOPDOWN" INVESTORS

Diversification and portfolio construction should mean more than the fact that the FoF has many underlying funds. There should be rhyme and reason as to how the underlying funds are selected, weighted, and combined into a FoF. So, the key question for a potential investor is "What is the FoF manager trying to accomplish?". Is it some absolute return objective? Is it some volatility target? Is it a limited loss of principal (draw-down)? Is it a return stream that is not correlated with some other return stream – such as non-correlation with the S&P 500 Index? Or is it some combination of all of the above? And what are the trade-offs in accomplishing that optimal combination because, despite the claims of some, there are always trade-offs.

For example, a high absolute return can be achieved in a number of ways. Perhaps the most common is to allow some directionality (that is, a positive beta to a traditional long-only market benchmark). Since most traditional long-only capital markets trend upwards over time, though perhaps with more volatility than many investors may desire, a common tactic is to use market directionality to boost returns, giving the FoF a "tail wind", so to speak. There is nothing wrong with this. Indeed, the Common Fund, a well-respected multi-manager shop specialising in managing endowments for American educational institutions, targets a beta of 0.3 relative to the S&P 500 Index in one of its major FoFs.[2] The Common Fund believes this is an appropriate level of dampening of the volatility of the S&P, while allowing some benefit from the long-term appreciating quality of the S&P. In other words, the Common Fund has made an explicit, ex-ante decision as to the trade-off it desires between return, volatility and correlation, so as to create what it believes to be an attractive target risk/return/correlation profile for its FoF. Of course, this means that the volatility of the fund may be more than a non-directional fund, and that it may or may not be as good a diversifier for an investor's overall portfolio, which normally will include long-only equities and fixed income, as well as the FoF and other alternative investments. But the trade-off is explicit, and it is up to each potential investor to decide if that risk/return/correlation profile is appropriate or desirable for that particular investor.

Another common method of targeting high absolute returns is to employ leverage, either explicitly at the FoF level, or by combining a number of leveraged underlying funds. Clearly, when this works, it increases returns. But it also increases the drawdown, should something go wrong. Again, there is nothing wrong with this. But an investor should be aware of (and be comfortable with) how the FoF manager is targeting absolute returns, and what trade-off is implied.

Similarly, funds that target non-correlated returns and/or low volatility often make a different trade-off. These funds often combine a number of arbitrage strategies together to make up a large or even dominant portion of the FoF's assets. Individually, each arbitrage fund (such as fixed-income arbitrage, mortgage arbitrage, merger or event arbitrage) may exhibit a desirable low-volatility return pattern. By combining a number of these strategies, the FoF manager can create a FoF that, normally, will have an extremely stabile return pattern.

The key word in the preceding sentence is "normally". To understand why, let us look at how a typical arbitrage works. Traditional treasury arbitrageurs, for example, feature trades where the manager buys an "off-the-run" treasury bond and shorts the "on-the-run" bond; they try to reap an illiquidity premium as the prices converge over time. Other fixed-income arbitrage managers, such as mortgage-backed managers or credit arbitrage managers are also typically long securities common to the underlying asset class and short more liquid instruments, such as treasuries or swaps. These managers often have two sources of return: the illiquidity premium and, sometimes, a basis trade (such as being long credit or prepayment optionality). All these fixed-income arbitrages generally work if the financial markets remain calm. However, what happens during certain stress periods, such as liquidity crunches when there is a flight to quality, is very different. At those times, the liquidity premium expands, leaving all but the most nimble fixed-income arbitrage managers in the unenviable position of watching their short positions become more expensive and their long positions lose value.

Unfortunately, the same market pattern also applies to merger arbitrage, though for different reasons. The risk in merger arbitrage is that the mergers will not happen, so the prices will not converge. Quiescent markets are helpful in consummating mergers, as the value of stock for stock deals does not change materially between deal announcement and closing, allowing merger arbitrage managers to predict time values with a fair amount of certainty. Stressed markets, where there is a flight to quality, often affect stock prices, throwing more volatility into the deal. Moreover, even cash deals are affected in volatile markets, as financing may become more difficult.

In other words, a mathematician might say that the return pattern for many arbitrage patterns is "state dependent", with the variable condition being the liquidity available in the capital markets. Therefore, by "stacking" arbitrage strategies into a single FoF, the FoF manager is dampening volatility in normal markets, but may be increasing the risk of a number of the underlying funds having drawdowns at the same time should markets experience a liquidity crunch (a change of state). This is just what happened to a number of funds in the wake of the Russian crisis and LTCM debacle of 1998. Similarly, many, if not most equity market neutral hedge funds have a systemic bias towards buying stocks that most analysts would classify as "value" stocks, and selling "growth" stocks. In most equity market conditions, that bias is a good trade; in value-trending markets it adds to return, and in trend-less markets it enables the manager to employ his/her stock-picking skill. However, in long-term growth-cycle markets, it can be a killer, as numerous funds discovered during the tech boom of the late 1990s, when FoFs that stacked market neutral equity strategies were hit by significant and ongoing monthly drawdowns.

Once a potential investor understands what the FoF manager is attempting to accomplish in portfolio construction, and what the trade-offs are, two questions naturally follow. The first is:

*"Are you, as the potential investor, comfortable with the targeted risk/return/correlation profile, even assuming it can be accomplished?"*

The answer to this question should be a simple yes or no. Which it is will be a function of the investor's personal utility function or, if an institution, perhaps some set of guidelines or policies. Alternatively, if an asset management company, it might be a business judgement as to the ability to gain clients for such a risk/return/correlation profile product.

If your answer is "yes, you are comfortable", the second question, is an obvious follow-up:

*"Can this FoF manager accomplish the goal?"*

This is where due diligence as it is traditionally practiced really kicks in. The key in performing such traditional due diligence is to "drill down" in each relevant area until you are satisfied. This sounds obvious, but a "tick-the-boxes" approach of going through a set of questions (or the omnipresent due diligence questionnaire) just is not good enough. Think of good due diligence as following a decision tree approach: If it is a line of inquiry that is really important to your decision, you will want to follow all the branches until you reach the leaves. If it is an area where the answer would not affect your decision, one question may be too many.

While everyone starts with an analysis of returns, the reality is that returns are a lagging indicator. A FoF manager cannot manage return directly. He or she must instead manage a process that marshals resources to make good decisions. The returns are a fall-out of the processes and resources and decisions. And that is a problem for a potential investor, because it means that a "perfect" return series is not, in and of itself, an adequate reason to invest. A good, or even a "perfect" return series can mean several things. Hopefully, it means that the FoF manager is skilled (which is why you are considering investing). But he/she could be really lucky – or an outright fraud. The key is to understand why the returns are what they have been. Try to deconstruct the processes and decisions and judge for yourself what the results should have been, then go back and see if the returns confirm or bring into question the manager's skills. You are looking at the past for evidence of what the future's returns are likely to be given a certain set of circumstances. For while most investors believe the disclosure mantra that "past performance does not guarantee future results", good due diligence can tease out indications of future results from an analysis of previous results. Returns alone are never conclusive evidence of skill, but they may provide hints of it, or of its absence.

Perhaps the first question to explore is whether the returns to date have been consistent with the explicit goal of the FoF? If not, then why not? There are innumerable answers to this, including an explicit change of goal. If that is the reason, and you do not ever want to see the goals shift, you might ask why, and what guarantees you have that the goal will not change again. Alternately, you would want to be certain that goal changes are a result of a decision and a process with which you are comfortable.[3] Would the FoF manager do the same thing again, and are you comfortable with his/her answer? Other possible explanations for returns that have deviated from goal are change in investment process or personnel, large cashflows in or out, etc.

Even if the returns are consistent with the explicit goal of the FoF, you should be asking questions. Remember that you cannot buy last year's returns. Your job is to understand how the FoF manufactured last year's returns, so as to judge the replicability of the returns in the future. Try to understand if there was a pattern to the capital markets in which the FoF was invested, and if the strategy is dependent upon that pattern continuing (a variant of the state-dependent question) for the returns to continue? For example, if you saw two funds with annualised returns of 15% and low volatility from 1996–2000, you probably should ask different questions if the first fund specialised in arbitrage strategies and the other is a FoF with a large exposure to long-short equity. For the arbitrage FoF, this author would wish to know how the manager succeeded in weathering 1998 (Russia, LTCM, flight to quality, etc), and whether he/she thought the returns and volatility were dependent on a declining interest rate environment. For the long/short equity FoF, one would wish to ask about the overall net long/short ratios, about market correlations, about how much of the return was due to the world equity markets' phenomenal runs over that time, and about what long-bias sector funds might be included in the FoF. There, you might be concerned about what might happen in a bear market and, particularly, of interest might be the FoF's returns from June 2000 through 2001, when equity markets reversed.

In other words, you are trying to see if the manager has the knowledge and skill necessary to know why the FoF has been successful. You are trying to distinguish between the skillful and the lucky. The two aren't necessarily mutually exclusive. Indeed, the skillful tend to be among the luckiest; remember (the American baseball team) the Brooklyn Dodgers' owner Branch Rickey's dictum: "luck is the residue of design". Translated to the FoF world, luck is sometimes a hallmark of good managers, not a disqualifier, as good managers are able to take advantage of market situations because they understand the underlying strategies and know when and where to employ them. On the other hand, the two don't always go hand-in-hand, and it is your job to find those situations and avoid them.

After you have determined if the manager is skillful, the next job is to discover if he or she has the tools necessary to employ that skill. Let us begin with information, because this is a frequently overlooked component in the analysis. Yet, the question of availability and quality of information permeates almost every aspect of portfolio construction in a FoF, from initial selection of the underlying managers to the ongoing monitoring. Indeed, the state of the art of portfolio construction theory continues to advance rapidly, but the data necessary to implement that new knowledge is often lacking.

Many FoFs use databases to make an initial cut of the funds to be considered for inclusion. However, all of the available databases have their own information issues. No law or regulation requires hedge funds to report, so some of the largest and most successful are not included in the various databases. Few funds actively report to all databases.[4] Survivorship bias is rampant. Closed funds are included in some of the databases but not in others, and they may or may not be investible to the FoF manager. Some databases require a certain minimum track record; others welcome new funds and spinouts. Funds are classified in different ways, so the same fund might be called global macro by one database and multi-strategy by another. These issues play out mathematically as well. Brooks and Kat[5] found that the correlation between the merger arbitrage indices of Tremont/CSFB[6] and that of HFR[7] was only 0.46. Similarly, the correlation matrix comparing the Zurich, Tremont/CSFB and HFR market neutral equity indices shows no correlation higher than 0.31. That is not to say databases have no value. They do. But they are – or should be – starting points for a FoF manager. Beware a FoF manager who is overly reliant on them, who accepts them wholeheartedly at face value, and who does not have his or her own sourcing ability to complement the database.

The quirks in database construction affect how some FoFs model their portfolios as well. A common technique is to take the relatively new style indices and optimise them to give a theoretical allocation: so much to convertible arbitrage, so much to long/short equity, so much to event arbitrage, etc. Again, this is fine as a starting point, but the construction problems of the indices themselves (see above) suggest that optimisations based on these databases will be anything but robust, as the hedge funds themselves will, no doubt, exhibit different return patterns from the style indices, just as no individual stock in and of itself replicates the S&P500 or the FTSE.

Information about the individual funds, therefore, becomes a key component in the portfolio construction process. Again, this sounds obvious. But given the short history of many underlying hedge funds, how accurate will returns-based analyses be when there are only 12 or 24 or 36 data points? Some FoF managers try to deal with those issues by using forward-looking optimisations based around risk factors – and a few go all the way to trying to calculate a value-at-risk (VAR) number. However, given the transparency controversy raging across the hedge fund industry, it is rarely possible for the FoF manager to get the necessary data to do this analysis robustly. You want to discover what level of transparency the FoF manager gets from the underlying hedge funds. And then you want to understand how he or she uses that information to construct the overall FoF portfolio. If the underlying funds all provide position level disclosure, what system does the FoF manager use to analyse and optimise the hundreds, or thousands of positions? How quickly can that analysis be done? And, even if the FoF manager has total position level transparency and a relatively quick analysis, what does that mean in practical terms, since the monthly or quarterly liquidity requirements of the underlying hedge funds make instantaneous rebalancing of the overall portfolio difficult. Does the FoF manager do great analytics that sit on a shelf? Or does he or she take hedges outside the underlying funds – including currency if he or she has any funds denominated in currencies other than that of the overall FoF – but within the FoF structure, effectively acting as a risk manager/overlay manager?

Alternatively, if the underlying funds give risk factor information (such as sectoral exposure or Barra risk factors or credit exposure or duration), how does the FoF manager aggregate those factors? How much confidence does the FoF manager have in the comparability of those factors, since different hedge fund managers can calculate them differently? If, on the other hand, the underlying hedge funds provide even less, how does the FoF manager perform portfolio construction? Of course, once you get the answer to these questions, you might want to examine the periodicity and timeliness of the information the FoF manager receives. The reality is often that the FoF manager uses some managers with full positional transparency, some who give positions on a one-month or longer lagged basis, some who give some risk factors, and some who give "bare bones information". Asking the FoF manager how he or she blends all this varying level of disclosure into a coherent portfolio should give you insight into the level of skill, diligence and creativity of the FoF manager.

Of course, even if your manager has skill and information, resources are necessary to convert those elements into consistent returns. Despite conventional notion, running a FoF is not inexpensive (analysts, analytical systems and normal business costs can be millions of US dollars). Due diligence costs on the underlying managers add up, and high quality FoFs reject many times more hedge fund managers than they accept. FoF managers should have well-trained researchers, and enough of them so that they can give more than a cursory review to hedge funds already allotted to or under consideration. Ask about the background of the researchers. A relatively recent development is the use of contracted due diligence experts. Again, this can be very positive or negative. Be sure to understand who they are and their expertise. Good outside experts can efficiently add perspective and experience, but poor quality due diligence people just "tick the boxes" without the necessary expertise to understand potential problems or, more commonly, how the due diligence efforts on the underlying funds relate to the portfolio construction process. Finally, some FoFs blend inside and outside expertise, using outside experts to either begin the due diligence process or to provide an external viewpoint to either challenge or confirm internal opinions.

Information systems are another key component. How does the FoF manager track data? What risk management tools are available? Are there adequate programmers in-house? What other automated systems does the FoF manager use: accounting, web-based client reporting, etc? What is the technology budget of the FoF and is it anticipated to increase or decrease in the future? Does it appear that the FoF manager understands, anticipates and is willing and able to keep devoting those resources indefinitely into the future?

Finally, if you have invested all this time and effort in selecting a FoF manager, you probably do not want to have to change your selection anytime soon. So spend a little time exploring whether the FoF manager is set up to keep his/her edge over the long term. In addition to the resource availability question mentioned above, you want to see how the FoF manager is positioning for the future. What types of expansion plans are there? Is the FoF manager thinking about selling out or taking a strategic partner or instituting some other form of joint venture? What will the effect be on current investors? Will there be new products launched, and will there be opportunities for you or will they distract the FoF manager from the job you have hired him/her to do? Is there an on-going training programme for staff? Does the FoF manager participate in any of the industry organisations? How else does he/she keep abreast of developments? Is the FoF organisation compensated in a way that encourages good people to stay? Is succession an issue?

### Due diligence for "bottom up" investors

Much of the due diligence carried out by a potential investor seeking a FoF for top down reasons applies equally to an investor seeking a FoF for bottom up reasons. However, other questions – particularly about sourcing of managers – gain increased priority.

Some investors seek a FoF because it can provide capacity to otherwise closed managers or funds. Such investors will want to know how much of the FoF is actually invested in those managers. Is it 20%, 50% or 100%? Can the percentage change over time? How much capacity has the FoF reserved with those managers for future allocations? As important, is the capacity in the specific fund the investor seeks, or is it in a slightly different fund run by the same underlying manager? And, if so, is the risk/return profile of that second fund acceptable? Since the FoF manager charges fees in addition to the underlying manager, does the additional level of fees change the net return to the point where the investor should be concerned, or are the FoF fees a bargain price of entry?

More basically, since a primary reason to invest in such situations is because of capacity constraints, a potential investor should carefully consider the logical implications of that issue. If the underlying hedge fund is closed for capacity reasons, are investments through the FoF company going to get you the risk/return profile you expect, or are new investments in the underlying hedge fund going to dilute returns by stressing capacity? How is the FoF manager tracking that issue? What plans does the FoF manager have for dealing with cash inflows, given the underlying funds' capacity constraints? Will it begin allocating to new managers? Has it reserved capacity with existing managers and, if so, how much? At the FoF level, how much capacity could it take instantaneously? How much over a year? How does that capacity break down by style? What does it think its maximum capacity is? Will it close at that point? (Remember to write down that number and, as AUM approaches the limit, re-ask the question.) If you anticipate making more allocations in the future, can the FoF take it and invest it in the same way as the allocation you are considering today?

Capacity issues affect the FoFs as an organisation as well. Is the staff growing, and how rapidly? Where is it finding analysts? Back office people? How are those new people trained? Are there space limitations? Is the FoF planning any new products, and will they distract the investment staff from your investment? Is the Chief Investment Officer spending too much time marketing, or managing, or is he focused on the portfolio? Ask about distribution of the FoF itself. Are any structured products planned? (Structured products can create hundreds of millions of dollars of inflows.)

Are there any new distribution channels in the works? Any plans to hire/fire/contract direct marketers?

Another type of bottom up FoF is one that specialises in making allocations to newer managers. Even some investors who have fully staffed programmes to invest directly in individual hedge funds choose to use these specialised FoFs, since many of the typical due diligence techniques, such as screening through databases or doing returns-based analyses, are not available. Clearly, finding and vetting new managers requires specialised skills, and, if this is a reason for you considering a FoF, you should be concentrating your due diligence on this area. How does the manager find the underlying funds? Does he/she use prime brokers as sources of information? Lawyers? Accountants? Other service providers? If so, do the hedge funds that use a particular prime broker or lawyer or accountant or other service provider receive disproportionate allocations? Is the FoF effectively a captive marketing organisation for a particular prime broker?

What are the FoF manager's initial screens for new underlying managers? How much of the FoF manager's time is spent scouting new talent, how much in portfolio construction, and how much in other endeavours, such as marketing or client service? Will he or she only invest in new funds that are "spin-outs" from other funds? Does he or she insist that the portfolio team has worked together previously? Will he or she invest in long-only mutual fund managers who leave their shops and set up as hedge fund managers – in traders who have never been portfolio managers?

Among the key concerns when funding new hedge funds is business risk. Running a trading book is a very different skill than dealing with general business issues. Successful hedge funds need to be good traders/investors, but also need to negotiate contracts, rent space, meet payroll, file tax returns, decide which dental option is right for its health care plan, etc. As annoying as such everyday tasks are to every business in the world, they tend to be more annoying to hedge fund managers, who have often left large organisations precisely because they dislike bureaucracies. More than one hedge fund has floundered because its principal had to focus on these general issues, rather than the portfolio. You should understand how the FoF managers view the business risk issues inherent in the underlying funds, and how they try to avoid situations wherein running a business and a portfolio become too much for the underlying hedge fund manager.

So, one valuable skill possessed by some FoF managers is the ability to mitigate business risk. Some do this through their own due diligence efforts on the underlying managers – ie, asking them in detail about their business plans, resources and experiences. Other FoFs specialising in new managers take a different tack. These FoFs (sometimes called incubator funds) provide various business services to the underlying start-up hedge funds. These services can range from general advice, to providing contracted services such as marketing or back office help, to providing facilities such as trading floors, to actually taking an equity stake in the underlying managers either in return for the allocation or in return for cash. There can be more than one business relationship between the underlying hedge fund (or hedge fund management company) and the incubator fund.

These situations make sense, as they mitigate the business risk of the underlying hedge funds and, by allowing the underlying managers to focus on portfolio issues without distraction, can improve performance. However, in such situations it is incumbent on the potential FoF investor to understand the alignment of interests. In the event of an equity interest, is the FoF manager being paid to get the best possible return for the FoF investors, or for itself as an equity investor in the underlying hedge fund management companies? Are there incentives to invest in the underlying fund no matter what the performance? If the FoF manager is providing services such as trading or accounting or marketing, are the fees being charged for those services based on helping the underlying hedge funds, thereby mitigating business risk, or are they a major profit source for the FoF manager? Do they flow back to the FoF investors, or stay with the FoF' management company? Are the agreements in writing? Is there an economic benefit (payment for order flow is a common one) siphoned off from the underlying hedge fund or FoF to a management company or some other affiliated entity? For example, the FoF of one large investment bank required an underlying funds' futures trades be routed through its broker. The result was an 87.5% increase in commission costs – which came right out of investors' returns.

All FoF investors, and particularly bottom up investors, are interested in the sourcing and selection of new managers (whether start-ups or veterans) by the FoF manager. How do new managers get on the radar screen? How many are actually seen and by whom at the FoF? What percentage of managers actually ever gets funded? Will the FoF fund new managers? Spinouts? If a track record is required, how long – and are there exceptions? Will a new underlying manager be "incubated", that is, given a small amount of money for some period of time and watched, before being given a full allocation? How many analysts does the FoF have following how many hedge funds?

Finding new managers is less than half the equation, however. Any good FoF will reject far more hedge fund managers than it allocates to. You want to understand how the FoF manager carries out due diligence. What are the due diligence steps? Who does it? Are managers always visited on site? Is there due diligence on the administrator and prime broker? Are there any criteria that will automatically eliminate a manager from consideration? What are examples of due diligence successes and failures? Has the FoF manager ever picked a manager that later blew up? What did the FoF manager learn from that? Has the due diligence process changed as a result? Has the FoF manager ever avoided a manager that later blew up because of something found in due diligence? Does the FoF manager look at the underlying funds' back offices? It is advisable to ask to see copies of those reports, including hedge funds that were rejected.

### Due diligence for legal/functional reasons

Investors who seek a FoF for legal or functional reasons generally have a top down or bottom up orientation, and their due diligence should include a set of issues similar to those above. However, there is an additional set of issues, as well.

High net worth individuals and family offices may be tax-sensitive. If so, does the FoF manager understand how to maximise after-tax income and is he/she sensitive to reporting requirements in a timely fashion? Does the selection and portfolio construction process consistently seek to maximise after-tax return, or is the tax-efficiency question an add-on?

If the investor is an American pension plan, are they regulated by the Employment and Retirement Income Securities Act (ERISA)? If so, does the portfolio manager run a specialised ERISA account, specialising in underlying managers which understand those regulations? Alternately, will the FoF manager create a managed product or structured product to allow the investor to capture the results of the FoF in a way that satisfies any regulatory needs? In the case of an American tax-free investor, will they be subject to Unrelated Business Income taxes? If an European investor, will they need a FoF accepted by a particular regulator or with a "European passport"? If a bank, what type of capital reserves will be required?

What type of regulatory supervision is there of the FoF manager? When was the last regulatory inspection and what were the findings? Are there any legal actions pending against the FoF or related entities?

More generally, is the investor satisfied with the domicile of the FoF, particularly given the recent increase in sensitivity to money laundering and terrorist financing issues? Is the legal structure of the FoF acceptable?

Leaving the legal/regulatory issues aside, some time should be spent trying to understand the culture of the place. Is there a written procedures manual? Is there a formal risk management function? Is someone tasked with compliance? Is there a Chief Operating Officer? Chief Financial Officer? Is it a two-person shop trying to be nimble, or a 100-person shop trying to be institutional? Are the firm's principals widely quoted in the academic and public press, or do they cultivate privacy? Is the firm a specialist in FoF, or does it run other assets and asset classes?

You might also want to pay attention to the nature of the other investors in the FoF. Some institutions, for example, prefer FoFs that cater to the institutional market only, because they believe that other institutions are less likely to redeem in difficult markets. Others believe institutional investors are more trouble than they're worth, as they move large blocks of cash at a time. Often, having similar investors can give comfort to an investor (as well as to review bodies and regulatory agencies) for a "watch-your-back" reason: fiduciary standards are often based on prudence, which includes an element of what similar-situated entities do. And, having a FoF with experience with your class of investors may mean that the FoF manager understands your reporting requirements.

Of course, some investors want to take the "watch-your-back" rationale even farther. These investors may seek to understand the errors and omissions insurance policies of the FoF. They may also seek principal-guaranteed structures, a topic far beyond the scope of this chapter.

Reporting is a key issue, for a num ber of reasons. Institutional investors often need net asset value's (NAV) quickly for their investment committee meetings, or for their corporate reporting, or for regulatory purposes. For an individual, a single, unified report from a FoF can significantly reduce paperwork and complexity. For a value-added reseller (eg, a private bank selling through to clients, or an insurance company wrapping a FoF into an annuity), reporting is key: can it accommodate your systems? Is it frequent enough for your clients? Ask if there is web-based reporting, and about the security provisions. How many client service people are there? How willing are they to meet your reporting desires? Finally, be aware that slow or improper reporting can often be the tip of the iceberg, signifying some more serious problem lurking below the surface.

Liquidity provisions are also important, though opinions on them vary widely. Some investors like longer lock-up periods (particularly for FoFs which include relatively illiquid assets, such as distressed debt) on the belief that they discourage hot money and better align the capital base of the FoF with the underlying strategies, while many others dislike such provisions. FoF managers occasionally agree to special liquidity privileges (eg, redemption prior to the lock-up period expiration, but for a fee), and may be willing to strike similar agreements with you. Even if you are not interested in such side-letter agreements, you might well want to know if they exist for other investors, and whether or not they advantage or disadvantage you. Also, make sure you understand the real-world effects of redemption policies. If the underlying hedge funds only give partial redemptions, and then "true up" at a later date, either as a result of a final NAV or audited statement, what does that mean for your redemption from the FoF? If there are "side pockets" in some of the underlying funds wherein they can keep the pro rata part of the FoF's money related to a particularly illiquid instrument until that security is monetised (such as cross over funds which include private equity), what does that mean to your investment? Can you ever be given securities instead of cash? Try to discover and understand the liquidity provisions – including all the wrinkles – before investing.

*Check lists*
Thus far, this chapter has avoided a discussion of the standard due diligence check list, and with good reason. Beginning a chapter with a discussion of check list items, rather than with an overview of how due diligence fits into the goal of the investor, is akin to telling a "do-it-yourselfer" to put screw A in flange B without first saying whether you're building a bed or an airplane. Yet, it's a mistake innumerable investors make.

Moreover, check lists tend to become pro forma after a while. Many hedge funds and FoF have had the experience of being given a due diligence check list months, or even years, after an investment has been made. My personal favourite request to fill out such a check list came months after an investment, and was accompanied by the following note: "Sorry to ask you to complete this form. Our internal auditor noticed it wasn't in the file" In other words, the person making the investment thought the check list was worthless, and was just papering the files because a control body said he should. This author remains convinced that the form has never been looked at, to this day.

Nevertheless, check lists are useful for reminding yourself about all the areas for due diligence. You should check references. You should look at the audits. You should understand all the documents. You should understand the returns, assets under management (AUM), changes in personnel, etc. You should check the annual report, ADV or other SEC forms or the Financial Services Authority (FSA) reports or the equivalent regulatory filings (if they exist), monthly commentaries, etc. There is another good reason to use a check list: they can eliminate a particular FoF from consideration quickly. A record of regulatory violations, or a questionable audit, or a less-than stellar reference should warn you away.

If you don't use a check list, you should. Just remember to use it as a tool in the hands of an artist, not a colour-by-numbers template. Numerous good check lists are available from public sources. A good starting point to find one, or to compare yours to, would be the Alternative Investment Management Association, (AIMA).

*Tricks of the trade*
In addition to the above areas, and to the standard check list questions, there are a few "tricks of the trade" worth knowing.

Alignment of interest questions should be asked no matter what your reason for investing (and particularly in the case of FoF's providing services to hedge funds, as discussed above). It is not unheard of for hedge fund management companies to rebate fees to investors, outside of the specific fund structure. This can be a legitimate way of creating distribution, or to allow for volume pricing discounts. And FoFs may use their leverage to gain better fees for their investors. However, rebates can also create certain misalignments of interest. You ought to ask if the FoF manager receives any fee rebates, or, for that matter, any revenues from managers, prime brokers or others. If so, ask to whom those fees accrue: are they put back into the fund, or do they go to the management company? Similarly, has the FoF manager entered into any side letter or other agreements (verbal or written) with any of the underlying managers on any issue whatsoever? Incidentally, there is one alignment of interest question which is commonly asked about underlying hedge funds, but rarely surfaces when discussing FoFs: how much of the principal's net worth is in the FoF, and are there any prohibitions on the principals making hedge fund investments outside of the FoF?

Spend some time looking at the back office of the FoF. Talk to the lower-level professionals there, who may not be as polished in their interactions with potential investors. Are the files as organised as they should be? Have they ever had problems getting out a NAV? What issues have they seen in the last three months?

Internet and private investigator searches are a hot topic at hedge fund conferences. If you feel you need a detective search, by all means, engage one. But remember that the detective has no investment expertise, and certainly cannot make a worthwhile recommendation about investment skill or suitability for your portfolio. And it is likely that most detectives only look at public documentation anyway. Given the proliferation of the Internet, a simple search using a metasearch engine (such as "Google") can give you much of the information for which you would pay a detective. But, please, remember to use those critical facilities you are already using to do due diligence to be appropriately skeptical about Internet sources. Clearly, regulatory violations found at regulatory agencies' websites should figure mightily in your decision process, but casual chat room conversations probably should be discounted.

Do nt be intimidated by a FoF manager who tries to pressure you to invest, either by saying the FoF will close shortly, or by saying you have a short time for due diligence. Be respectful of the manager's time, but remember that the object of the process is to gain an appropriate amount of information to make a decision. If you get comfort from a single question, that is great. But if you don't get comfort from the fourth question, ask the fifth, or the sixth or the seventh, etc. On the other hand, if an area is not of any possible concern to you, don't bother asking a single question. If a manager says he/she cannot give you adequate time to make a decision, politely excuse yourself and move on.

Once you make a decision on whether or not to invest, document it. The level of documentation will vary depending on your situation – investing personal money, fiduciary, proprietary capital of a large organisation, regulatory requirements, etc. One suggestion is to include two items at the time of the investment decision. The first is a common one: why are you investing, what is the manager's edge, why is it a fit, etc. The second item, however, is rarely present. Imagine at the time of the decision what the danger signals would be that would cause you to redeem. If you have picked a manager because of his/her sourcing ability and ability to place money in closed managers, would you redeem if the manager tripled AUM? If you picked a manager for non-correlation, would you redeem if the manager started buying sector funds or long-biased funds? Would you redeem if an underlying fund blew up? What if there was an 85 drawdown in a fund that targets 3% volatility. It seems obvious, but writing down why you would redeem – long in advance of the actual instance – is a wonderful discipline.

Of course, due diligence doesn't stop after an investment. Set up a timetable for formally reviewing the FoF. You may get managerial notes monthly, and you may even speak informally to the manager every month, but establish a schedule for a more formal review, wherein you ascertain whether your reasons for investing initially are still valid and that you are made aware of any changes.

Finally, be aware of the psychology of due diligence. One reason for the perfunctory nature of many due diligences is exactly that – human psychology. By the time a potential investor is doing serious due diligence, chances are there has already been a decision to invest through a FoF. The investor may even have already made a preliminary decision to invest in a specific FoF, based on a database check, recommendation, marketing call or other initial screen(s). At that point, all the inertia is to invest, rather than to decline and then start over with a different FoF. Investing successfully concludes the action the investor desires. Finding something in the due diligence at best delays the action. Nor is the delay linear: given the liquidity requirements of most FoFs, a short delay can create a lag of as much as three months in getting the funds invested. If the investor is working for a fiduciary, it may mean explaining the finding to a committee or some other person. If the finding is really troubling, it may mean restarting the search. While some investors may congratulate themselves on avoiding a disaster, many others will be frustrated in such a situation, feeling, however irrationally, that all the work done up to that point has been a waste and that they have to start over.

## CONCLUSION

In sum, good due diligence experts know why they are investing and what skills/experience/resources/process/culture they seek in a FoF. They are respectful to FoF managers, but not cowed by them. They look at returns, but are not blinded by them. They seek reasons to not invest, rather than to invest, but they understand that not every blemish is disqualifying. They realise that a perfectly good FoF might not be appropriate for their particular need, but also that they may need to compromise. In a phrase, to do due diligence well, you must be skeptical, but not cynical.

1   Successful due diligence stems from a careful consideration of the risk implications of the specific investment strategies and instruments employed. Therefore, a potential investor should understand as much as possible about the investment management process, portfolio construction, etc. While some of the trade-offs inherent in the portfolio construction process are addressed, a full discussion of portfolio construction as well as the risks in each particular underlying hedge fund strategy is clearly beyond the scope of this chapter. Therefore, several other chapters in this book may be of particular interest to investors seeking a deeper knowledge for due diligence purposes.
2   For further reading on Common Fund, see http://www.commonfund.org.
3   While most investors dislike "style drift", some view it as evidence of nimbleness on the part of the manager. A New York-based FoF manager believes that many hedge funds have style drift. The key for him or her is whether the drift is accidental or deliberate. Effectively, they are saying that they don't mind if a state dependent strategy is changed when there is a belief that the underlying state is changing.
4   Liang (2000) found that fewer than 500 funds were included in both the TASS and HFR tables (Liang, B., 2000, "Hedge Funds: The Living and the Dead", Journal of Financial and Quantitative Analysis, September).
5   Brooks, C and H. Kat, 2001, "The Statistical Properties of Hedge Fund Index Returns and Their Implications for Investors" Working Paper, University of Reading.
6   CSFB/Tremont (www.hedgeindex.com).
7   HFR (www.hfr.com).

# Questionnaire for Due Diligence Review of Hedge Fund Managers

## MANAGER INFORMATION

### CONTACT INFORMATION

| |
|---|
| Company name: |
| Address: |
| Telephone: |
| Fax: |
| E-mail: |
| Name of contacts: |
| Title of contacts: |
| Telephone of contacts |
| E-mail of contacts: |

### COMPANY

| |
|---|
| Please give a brief history of the firm: |
| Legal entity: |
| Domicile: |
| Branch offices or other locations, if any: |
| ❏ What functions are performed at these branches and locations? |
| Which regulatory authority is the company registered with? |
| ❏ Type (class): |
| ❏ Date of registration: |
| ❏ Are all the employees registered with the same authority? |
| List any affiliations, directorships and memberships of the company and/or it's principals: |

### COMPLIANCE

| |
|---|
| Who is responsible for compliance in the firm? |
| Please describe any current or potential conflict of interest: |
| Does the firm or advisor have any relationship, which may affect its trading flexibility, eg associated broker/dealer? |
| Please list your accountant and attorney of the company: |
| Is there any material, criminal, civil or administrative proceedings pending or threatened against the firm or any of its principals, or have there ever been any such matters? |
| ❏ If yes, please provide full details: |
| What are the firm's employee own account dealing procedures? |

| |
|---|
| Do any of the firm's principals have other business involvement? |
| ❏ If yes, describe and quantify how much of their professional time is dedicated to each |
| How do you ensure that your marketing materials are consistent and clear? |

## MANAGER ORGANISATION

| |
|---|
| How large is the firm in terms of full time individuals? |
| Describe the firm's ownership structure, name of its owners, their percentage ownership, and their role within the firm |
| Percentage ownership of principals? |
| Short background of principals (education, career background, etc.) |
| |
| ❏ Please, attach information if necessary |
| How many investment professionals (portfolio managers, analysts, etc) in the firm? |
| What are the average years of professional experience in the firm, both years as a professional as well as years in the firm? |
| Please enclose an organisation chart depicting the names of senior managers in charge of the following areas: |
| ❏ Trading: |
| ❏ Reporting, performance analysis: |
| ❏ Research and development: |
| ❏ IT/Programming: |
| ❏ Administration: |
| ❏ Marketing and business development: |
| ❏ Others (please specify): |
| What has been the turnover rate among the firm's personnel? |
| Where do the primary trading, research, and portfolio management activities take place? |
| Where are the accounts maintained? |
| Are outside representatives or consultants used for any activities? If so, give details. |

## MANAGER REFERENCES

| |
|---|
| Please provide at least two references for the firm and for each of the principals involved in the management of the fund |
| ❶ |
| ❏ Name: |
| ❏ Profession: |
| ❏ Company: |
| ❏ Title: |
| ❏ Telephone: |
| ❏ Fax: |
| ❏ E-mail: |
| ❏ Current and past relationship with the firm or its principal: |
| ❷ |
| ❏ Name: |
| ❏ Profession: |
| ❏ Company: |
| ❏ Title: |
| ❏ Telephone: |
| ❏ Fax: |
| ❏ E-mail: |
| ❏ Current and past relationship with the firm or its principal: |

## FUND PROMOTERS

| |
|---|
| What external promoters, if any, have been appointed by the management company for its products? |
| Duration of your professional relationship? |

## FUND INFORMATION

### FUND DETAILS

| |
|---|
| Contact details: |
| ❏ Name: |
| ❏ Address: |
| ❏ Tel: |
| ❏ Fax: |
| ❏ E-mail: |
| ❏ Internet: |
| ❏ Fund structure: |
| ❏ Legal entity: |
| ❏ Domicile: |
| Date of inception: |
| Is the fund listed on any exchanges? |

### FEES

| |
|---|
| Management fee: |
| Administration fee: |
| Incentive fee: |
| Hurdle rate / High water mark: |
| Sales fee: |
| Redemption fee: |
| Any other fees? |
| What costs, if any, are recharged to the fund? |
| Are your fees calculated and charged in terms of equalisation structure by: |
| ❏ Issuing a different series of shares every time shareholders subscribe? |
| ❏ The Equalisation Share method? |
| ❏ The Equalisation and Depreciation Deposit method? |
| ❏ The Equalisation-Adjustment method? |
| ❏ Others (please specify): |
| Do you ever share fees with a third party? |
| Have any investors been granted rebates? Disclose any soft dollar agreement. |

### LIQUIDITY

| |
|---|
| Minimum initial investment: |
| Minimum subsequent investment: |
| Subscription frequency (when): |
| Redemption frequency (when): |
| Redemption notice period: |
| Redemption cash proceeds time period: |
| Do you have any lock-up period or any other liquidity constraints? |
| Do you allow for transfer of shares between nominees? |

## ADMINISTRATOR

| Details: |
| --- |
| ❏ Name: |
| ❏ Address: |
| ❏ Telephone: |
| ❏ Fax: |
| ❏ E-mail: |
| ❏ Name of contact: |
| ❏ Telephone of contact: |
| ❏ E-mail of contact: |
| Duration of your professional relationship? |

## AUDITOR

| Details: |
| --- |
| ❏ Name: |
| ❏ Address: |
| ❏ Telephone: |
| ❏ Fax: |
| ❏ E-mail: |
| Duration of your professional relationship? |

## CUSTODIAN

| Details: |
| --- |
| ❏ Name: |
| ❏ Address: |
| ❏ Telephone: |
| ❏ Fax: |
| ❏ E-mail: |
| Duration of your professional relationship? |

## LEGAL ADVISER

| Details: |
| --- |
| ❏ Name: |
| ❏ Address: |
| ❏ Telephone: |
| ❏ Fax: |
| ❏ E-mail: |
| Duration of your professional relationship? |

## BANKS AND PRIME BROKER

| Please list the banks used by the fund: |
| --- |
| Please list the prime brokers used by the fund, as well as the duration of your professional relationship: |

## DIRECTORS OF FUND

| |
|---|
| Please list the number of directors, their names and the degree of relationship with manager and service providers: |
| Duration of your professional relationship? |

## DATA OVERVIEW

### FUND ASSETS

| |
|---|
| Please list the size of assets by investment vehicle: |
| Please list the size of the fund's net assets: |
| List the total assets under management, and their respective changes over the last year: |
| What percentage of assets is represented by the largest investor? |

### CAPACITY MANAGEMENT

| |
|---|
| What is the maximum capacity of your fund? |
| What is the projected time frame to reach capacity? |
| Will new money be accepted after capacity is reached? |
| How will front / back-office operations be affected in the event of significant increase in assets under management, and what measures will be taken? |

### WITHDRAWALS

| |
|---|
| What were the largest withdrawals in your fund since inception? |
| ❏ Date: |
| ❏ % of equity: |
| ❏ Reasons: |

### MANAGEMENT TEAM'S CO-INVESTMENT

| |
|---|
| What is the total amount invested by the principals/management in the fund and other investment vehicles managed *pari passu* with the fund? |
| Has the management reduced its personal investment? |
| ❏ Date: |
| ❏ Amount: |
| ❏ Reasons: |
| Disclose conditions of subscription / redemptions of team and owners' assets. |

### FUND PERFORMANCE

| |
|---|
| Historical performance since inception: |
| ❏ Monthly NAV's since inception (in table format): |
| ❏ Monthly RoR since inception |
| Please explain any major factors affecting performance and drawdowns (ie, a manager change, a change in strategy, etc): |
| Is the fund performance audited? |

## DRAWDOWNS

| |
|---|
| List the five maximum drawdowns, in percent of equity for each fund, the recovery period, and explain why they have happened: |
| Over the past 12 months, how many daily drawdowns greater than 5% have occurred, and what was the length of recovery? |

## MANAGER TRACK RECORD

| |
|---|
| Number of portfolios / accounts managed by the firm: |
| Number of funds managed / advised by the firm: |
| ❏ Names of these funds: |
| Total assets managed / advised by the firm: |
| Oldest continuously active account: |
| Largest current account: |
| Length of track record: |
| Has the track record been audited: |
| What is your level of portfolio turnover? |
| Average annual commission costs as a percentage of total assets: |
| ❏ Brokerage to equity ratio |
| ❏ Administrator fee to equity ratio |
| ❏ Custodian fee to equity ratio |
| ❏ Auditors' fee to equity ratio |

## STRATEGY

| |
|---|
| Characterise your investment style in terms of: |
| ❏ Strategy: |
| ❏ Hedging: |
| ❏ Market exposure: |
| ❏ Portfolio concentration in terms of amount of instruments and exposure bias (min/max/avg. number of instruments, min/max/avg. long or short bias): |
| ❏ Geographical market focus: |
| List the instrument types you use by percentage: |
| Describe your strategy (in as much detail as possible): |
| What is your trading philosophy? |
| ❏ Do you believe that there are persistent structural inefficiencies in the area you invest in? Please explain: |
| ❏ How do you think these market inefficiencies will change over time? |
| What makes your strategy unique? |
| What makes your strategy different from your peers? |
| Describe your strategy for today's market: |
| What are the strengths / weaknesses of your investment strategy? |
| ❏ Why do you feel you will generate absolute returns? |
| In which markets do you believe your strategy performs best/worst? (Give examples of time periods): |
| ❏ Volatility: |
| ❏ Trends: |
| ❏ Liquidity: |
| ❏ Correlation: |

What is your average holding period for:
- ❏ All investments
- ❏ Profitable investments
- ❏ Losing investments

Does the strategy have a long or short bias?

What investment criteria must new positions meet?

How do you invest new capital into the market?

How do you deal with redemptions?

Have the strategy or trading processes changed over time due to capital flows?

Have you encountered position limit problems? If yes, please explain.

Describe your cash management policy?
- ❏ Do you outsource this function? If so, please give name of provider and method used.

## RISK

### RISK TRANSPARENCY

Are you willing to provide position level detail to Investors on the following basis?
- ❏ Daily
- ❏ Weekly
- ❏ Monthly
- ❏ Other (please specify)

Will you be able to provide this information on the next day or other time frame?

Will this information be in machine-readable format?

If you are not willing to provide any position level detail to investors, will you provide the following risk information?
- ❏ VAR
- ❏ Risk Profile
- ❏ Top 10 positions
- ❏ Stress test results
- ❏ Sensitivities
- ❏ Other (please specify)

### VALUATION TRANSPARENCY

Do you have written valuation policies that I can review?

What percentage of your NAV is based on third party pricing services ?

a) At midpoint

b) At bid for longs

And offer for shorts

Market-to-model vs Market-to-market

c) At estimated mid

d) At estimated bid for longs and offer for shorts

"Overridden"

Do you compare your marks to the marks used by your prime broker for margin purposes?

How significant is the difference?

What is the maximum it has been?

Where on the NAV stability spectrum do you fall (+/- 1bp, +/- 25bp, etc)

Do you communicate to your investor how you make adjustments for liquidity, time zone, etc.?

## LEVERAGE

| |
|---|
| Discuss your leverage exposure policy and its management over different market cycles: |
| What are your portfolio financing constraints/limits? |
| Discuss sensitivity (cost) to LIBOR levels: |
| What has been your maximum leverage? |
| What would be the impact of a doubling of margin requirements at maximum leverage? |
| What is the minimum amount of unencumbered cash or cash equivalents held? |
| How much additional credit can you obtain? |

## HEDGING

| |
|---|
| How is the portfolio hedged? |
| How do you determine size and limits for each position/basket? |
| How often do you re-hedge? |
| Are short positions profit centers? |

## DIVERSIFICATION

| |
|---|
| Discuss the depth of diversification: |
| How do you calculate the correlation between each investment in the portfolio? |
| What are the main sources of marginal risk in your strategy? |
| How has performance been distributed across positions and time? |
| What is your maximum position size vs daily average trading volume? |
| What is the amount of risk reduction due to diversification? |

## RISK MANAGEMENT

| |
|---|
| Do you have a designated risk manager ? |
| ❑ Who are they? |
| ❑ What are their other responsibilities? |
| Please describe the operational risk management policy: |
| How do you measure minimum liquidity of positions? |
| What system/software is used in your middle office? |
| Do you trade options? |
| ❑ What tools do you use to value options? |
| ❑ What tools do you use to calculate the greeks? |
| ❑ What is your typical greek exposure? |
| What is the average holding period for your long positions? |
| What is the average holding period for your short positions? |
| What is your portfolio turnover? |
| What is your maximum sum of worst-case losses of all positions in your portfolio? |
| What is your maximum credit exposure to a counterparty? |
| What is your current currency exposure? |
| How do you manage your currency exposure? |
| How do you measure and monitor counterparty credit risk? |
| What is your best estimate of maximum monetary drawdown the fund could ever suffer (wrong bets together with abnormal market conditions) and what would be the circumstances? |
| How do you assess short recall risk? |
| How many days would it take to liquidate one third of your portfolio? |

How many days would it take to liquidate your entire portfolio?

Do you measure value-at-risk (VAR)?

❏ What is your methodology for VAR?

❏ What has been the maximum VAR?

❏ How well does your methodology back test?

What is the average credit rating of your portfolio?

What stress tests do you perform?

❏ How often are they performed?

❏ How do you use stress test results?

❏ What methodology/data period do you use for your stress testing?

## EXTERNAL CONTROLS

Are any third parties involved in verifying adherence to risk limits, e.g. the fund's administrator?

## LIMITS

Are risk limits included with your guidelines?

What is you leverage limit?

❏ How is it defined?

What is your VAR limit?

Do you use stop losses?

❏ If yes, please explain your approach.

❏ How often are these limits applied?

❏ When were their peaks observed?

Do you have concentration limits?

❏ If so, please describe both the limits and your tracking process.

Do you have counterparty exposure limits?

Do you have portfolio credit limits?

❏ If so, please describe.

Please describe your overall approach to limits and any limits not already addressed.

## INVESTMENT RESEARCH

What outside sources are used?

What proportion of research is generated internally?

Describe the typical flow of an investment idea from inception to a trading position:

Describe your back testing of investment ideas:

Have you published or commissioned any research/academic papers?

## INVESTOR SERVICE / REPORTING

Can your prospectus / offering memorandum be transmitted to us electronically?

Who calculates the NAV?

❏ What is the frequency of calculation?

Do you make any adjustments to the NAV valuation received from your source? If yes, please explain what kind in terms of:
❑ Liquidity
❑ Time zone
❑ Size
❑ Holding period
❑ Other
❑ Percentage of adjustments to total NAV
❑ What instruments subject to adjustments

Can fund performance (NAV, RoR) be transmitted to us electronically on a regular basis, and at what periodicity?

List all reports and correspondence usually sent to clients, and please explain the frequency and the detail the manager reports performance to investors.

Can you provide copies of historical reports?
❑ Please provide examples:

Are investors informed when minor / major changes are made to the trading, money management, or risk control methods?

What databases, publications, or other available sources does the manager regularly report performance figures to?
❑ If none, explain why?

What portfolio data can you provide (electronically) in terms of:
❑ Position:
❑ Concentration:
❑ Exposure:
❑ Performance attributes:
❑ Hedge:

Can all trades be reported on a daily basis to the client?

## ADMINISTRATION

Please indicate any material facts about your fund that are not mentioned in the offering memorandum (domicile, legal issues, political situation, tax etc.)

How do you manage trade data and keep track of open positions?
❑ Please specify the systems in use:

How is performance of each account calculated, and how often?

What type of information is maintained internally on each account?

Is there an electronic feed to brokers and administrators, and how is it used?

Can you link to any third-party risk management systems (like Measurerisk)?

Does your management program automate trade allocations to investor's account?
❑ If not, how are trade allocations to investor accounts executed?

Has this method been audited by a regulatory body?

How are trading errors dealt with?

What contingency plans do you have in terms of:
❑ Computer system fault?
❑ Incapacitated investment decision makers?
❑ Technical failure at Prime Broker's location?
❑ Presence of in-house computer technician?
❑ Back-up systems?

Please attach the most recent disclosure document, information memorandum, and marketing literature.

In the event of amendments to the aforementioned documents, notably the memorandum, please ensure that we will receive those directly from you within reasonable time, as well as copies of proxy's and notification of the Annual General Meeting (the latter only for information purposes).

Please state the name and title of the officer at your firm who has prepared and reviewed this questionnaire.

| | |
|---|---|
| Name: | |
| Date: | |
| Position: | |

# Risk Standards for Institutional Investment Managers and Institutional Investors*

## Risk Standards Working Group+

## FOREWORD

The topic of risk management has commanded ever-greater attention in recent years from the owners of institutional investment funds and those who invest on their behalf. Reports abound of surprises and losses incurred by pension funds, public cash pools, trusts, foundations, endowment funds, institutional investment managers and insurance companies. The fault lay with a variety of causes such as unexpected market moves, failed hedges, insufficient oversight, excessive dependence on theoretical models, too much leverage or credit declines.

Many in the industry realised that guidelines, risk measurement systems and risk management practices required updating. For example, investment guidelines restricting managers to triple-A rated securities had not averted the purchase of highly-leveraged structured notes. Guidelines that restricted average maturity had not prevented the purchase of collateralised mortgage obligations with significant extension risk. The older risk management tools also failed for many in controlling the currency risk from international securities, the high volatility of emerging markets and other alternative asset classes, as well as the illiquidity and lack of transparency of many exotic instruments and private partnerships.

Over the past three years, various financial industry groups published useful guidelines for derivatives. However, no comprehensive document covers the particular problems facing fiduciaries of multi-asset class, multi-manager portfolios. While a few institutions developed their own updated risk standards, it was understandable that their managers, custodians and other providers might resist any single client's demands for costly, complex new systems and procedures – particularly if other clients might soon demand something else. What was needed was a set of widely accepted standards and the clout to give them authority.

To address these issues the Working Group was established in April, 1996 by 11 individuals from the institutional investment community whose mission was:

"To create a set of risk standards for institutional investment managers and institutional investors."

The Working Group consisted of individuals from institutions with varying resources. To properly serve the industry, the proposed Risk Standards had to be general enough so that institutions of *all* sizes could apply them when updating risk measurement and risk management.

The Working Group members reached consensus on all major points and distributed 33 Draft Risk Standards to the Comment Group. Detailed and incisive comments from over 60 respondents provided the basis for a consolidation into the 20 Risk Standards presented herein. All 33 original concepts remain but were regrouped. For example, the Draft Standards on clearly defined organisational structure and key personnel were combined, as were many of the valuation-related Standards. These Risk Standards thus reflect the thoughts and comments of senior managers from roughly 70 entities – institutional investors of all stripes, as well as money managers, broker-dealers, regulators, academics, consultants, custodians and officers of financial exchanges.

The Working Group recognises that few, if any, institutional investors or their internal and external managers have implemented all of these Risk Standards. Much work is required to put them in place. Nonetheless, the Working Group believes these Standards provide a solid foundation for institutional investors, as well as for their internal and external managers, to update and apply risk management policies, practices and procedures in an evolving investment industry.

The Working Group also recognises that implementing these standards will be costly. Technology costs alone for small firms are typically greater than US$100,000 per year; for the largest banks and investment managers such costs can run to US$100 million per year or more. Technology expenses, moreover, are typically only 10–15% of total risk management implementation costs. Scarce valuable time and attention must be expended to implement these standards even in part. There can be no doubt, however, that the deliberate and disciplined approach to understanding, measuring, monitoring and controlling risk suggested by these Risk Standards will help ensure that risks are identified, understood and acceptable.

The Working Group members wish to thank their respective institutions. The Working Group also thanks the Comment Group and all others who participated in preparing this document.

### INTRODUCTION
The Risk Standards that follow provide a guideline, which institutional investors and institutional investment managers may use when planning their own risk measurement and risk management practices. Few, if any,

institutions comply with all of these Standards today. Some of the Standards are in broad use while others are practices only a few institutions have implemented to date.

The manner in which institutional investors and their managers use these Risk Standards depends, in part, on their role. The "Primary Fiduciary" (eg, Boards of Directors, Trustees, Plan Sponsors, Supervisors or their equivalent) of institutional funds can apply these standards to their internal operations and to other subcontractors, mandating compliance from both. The "Manager Fiduciary" (eg, Board of Directors, Trustees, Chief Investment Officer) of internal and external investment managers can use them to update their own risk management and measurement systems, even if not yet required to do so by clients. Implementation of the guidelines also depends on the resources available. For example, small pension plan administrators or other small institutional investors unable to personally verify compliance by subcontractors may need to rely on independent verification by others such as internal or external auditors or consultants.

Implementation should also reflect the risk preferences, resources and capabilities of each organisation. Although this document provides explanations and illustrations to help the reader understand the types of issues each Risk Standard is meant to address, the Working Group deliberately left the specifics of implementation for consideration by each organisation.

These Risk Standards are only one approach to good risk management; other robust frameworks exist. All require knowledgeable, competent, prudent investment management professionals – although a key point of the Standards is that no organisation should rely solely on the knowledge, competence, prudence or honesty of individuals. Even individuals with the best of intentions make mistakes. Sound organisation and high-quality systems are crucial; oversight and checks and balances could have prevented many of the well-known mistakes and investment disasters of recent years.

Risk management must include proper identification, management, measurement and oversight of risk. The Risk Standards are therefore grouped into three categories: *Management*, *Measurement* and *Oversight*. Careful identification and understanding of risks, clear definition and acknowledgment of responsibilities and development and exercise of risk containment procedures with built-in protections against error or abuse are explained in the Risk Standards grouped under *Management*. The next group of Standards focuses on *Measurement* of risk in a timely, consistent manner while warning fiduciaries to be aware of the limitations of quantitative measures. The final set of Standards reviews the careful *Oversight* crucial to any investment program.

Throughout this document, references to "Primary Fiduciary" and "Manager Fiduciary" include their designees; both internal and external investment managers are included in the term "Managers".

### Summary of the 20 Risk Standards[1]

*I. Management[2]*

### Risk Standard 1: Acknowledgment of fiduciary responsibility

Fiduciary responsibilities should be defined in writing and acknowledged in writing by the parties responsible.

### Risk Standard 2: Approved written policies, definitions, guidelines and investment documentation

The Primary and Manager Fiduciaries should approve formal written policies which reflect their overall risk management objectives. The Primary and Manager Fiduciaries also should approve investment guidelines, management agreements and all other contracts that govern investments. Technical terms should be defined. All policies, definitions, guidelines and investment documentation should be reviewed and updated as appropriate and more often if significant market events or changes in strategy occur.

### Risk Standard 3: Independent risk oversight, checks and balances, written procedures and controls

Oversight of compliance with risk policies should be independent of line investment activity and conducted according to up-to-date, written policies and procedures. Front, middle, and back office activities should be separate wherever possible and sufficient checks and balances and appropriate controls should exist. When separation is not possible due to limited staff, alternative checks, balances and controls should be established.

### Risk Standard 4: Clearly defined organisational structure and key roles

Organisational structure and reporting lines should be defined clearly and distributed to all parties. Key personnel and their roles in all front, middle and back office areas should be identified. Changes in key personnel should be communicated immediately to all relevant parties.

### Risk Standard 5: Consistent application of risk policies

The Primary Fiduciary's risk policies should apply both to internal and external managers and should be consistent across similar asset classes and strategies.

### Risk Standard 6: Adequate education, systems and resources, back-up and disaster recovery plans

The Primary and Manager Fiduciaries should ensure that adequate education, systems and resources are available to implement and administer their risk policies. They should also establish and test back-up procedures and disaster recovery plans.

## Risk Standard 7: Identification and understanding of key risks

Risks should be analysed to determine relevancy. This entails understanding strategies and their vulnerabilities, as well as assumptions built into an instrument, system, process, model or strategy. Key risks should be reviewed periodically as well as when significant events occur.

## Risk Standard 8: Setting risk limits

Risk limits should be set for the aggregate portfolio and all individual portfolios. These may include limits on asset classes, individual instruments and specific types of risk.

## Risk Standard 9: Routine reporting, exception reporting and escalation procedures

The Primary and Manager Fiduciaries should specify what positions, risks and other information must be reported and to whom. This policy also should define what constitutes required reporting or an exception to guidelines, to whom the exception should be reported, what action must be taken for different levels of violation and what procedures must be followed for ongoing or increased violations.

*II. Measurement*
## Risk Standard 10: Valuation procedures

All readily priced instruments should be valued daily, less-readily priced instruments at least weekly and non-readily priced instruments as often as feasible and whenever a material event occurs. The pricing mechanism and methodologies must be known, understood, follow written policies and be applied consistently by the Primary and Manager Fiduciaries, Managers, custodian and other subcontractors.

## Risk Standard 11: Valuation reconciliation, bid/offer adjustments and overrides

Material discrepancies in valuations from different sources should be reconciled following established procedures. A procedure for bid/offer adjustments and overrides to valuations should be established in writing and monitored independently.

## Risk Standard 12: Risk measurement and risk/return attribution analysis

The Primary and Manager Fiduciaries should regularly measure relevant risks and quantify the key drivers of risk and return.

## Risk Standard 13: Risk-adjusted return measures

Risk-adjusted returns should be measured at the aggregate and individual portfolio level to gain a true measure of relative performance.

**Risk Standard 14: Stress testing**

Simulation or other stress tests should be performed to ascertain how the aggregate portfolio and individual portfolios would behave under various conditions. These include changes in key risk factors, correlations or other key assumptions and unusual events such as large market moves.

**Risk Standard 15: Back testing**

Risk and return forecasts and models should be back tested at least quarterly and whenever material events occur to assess their reliability.

**Risk Standard 16: Assessing model risk**

Dependence on models and assumptions for valuation, risk measurement and risk management should be evaluated and monitored.

*III. Oversight*

**Risk Standard 17: Due diligence, policy compliance and guideline monitoring**

The Primary and Manager Fiduciaries should perform frequent, independent reviews of all Managers' risk policies and controls. Where policies and controls fall short of the requirements set forth by the Primary or Manager Fiduciaries, plans for future compliance or corrective action should be documented and communicated. Managers should ensure continuing compliance with their clients' risk policies and guidelines.

**Risk Standard 18: Comparison of Manager strategies to compensation and investment activity**

The Primary Fiduciary should require each Manager to submit a statement of strategy and ensure that the Manager's activities and compensation are consistent with that strategy. Key risk and return factors should be documented and reviewed at least annually and updated whenever the strategy changes.

**Risk Standard 19: Independent review of methodologies, models and systems**

All methodologies, models and related systems should be independently reviewed or audited prior to use as well as annually. Significant market moves or changes in market practice should trigger interim reviews.

**Risk Standard 20: Review process for new activities**

The Primary and Manager Fiduciaries should document the review process for permitting the use of new instruments, strategies or asset classes. Policies for initiating new activities should be consistent with the Primary and Manager Fiduciaries' risk and return goals as well as the Manager's strategy and expertise.

*I. Management*

**Risk Standard 1: Acknowledgment of fiduciary responsibility**

*Fiduciary responsibilities should be defined in writing and acknowledged in writing by the parties responsible.*

To avoid misunderstandings, written documents should specify fiduciary assignments made or received. The Primary and Manager Fiduciaries should document the assignment of fiduciary responsibility before the allocation or receipt of assets. Documents should specify and acknowledge in writing the capacity of individuals or organisations to enter into agreements on behalf of the Primary Fiduciary and articulate the nature and limits of each party's status as agent or principal for specific activities. Documents should specify that the Manager Fiduciary has accepted a fiduciary assignment from a Primary Fiduciary and should cover individuals as well as firms.

While the Primary Fiduciary may select a Manager to invest its funds, it *cannot* delegate the responsibilities and liabilities attached to being the Primary Fiduciary. The possibility of lawsuits claiming that a party did not adequately perform its fiduciary responsibilities is a strong motivation to articulate and document fiduciary assignments as well as to monitor compliance carefully.

There are three principal types of accounts with regard to fiduciary responsibility. Each should be defined clearly.

- ❏ *Directed accounts*, for example: "Invest only in S&P 500 stocks and vote with management".
- ❏ *Discretionary accounts*, for example: "Invest in assets of your choice and vote as you wish".
- ❏ *Mixed accounts*, for example: "Invest in common stocks and own 200 names. We will retain voting rights".

For directed accounts, the Primary Fiduciary retains all responsibility for the investment decision, choice of asset class, choice of investment instrument and all associated rights. For discretionary accounts, the Primary Fiduciary delegates broad fiduciary rights. This should be documented to reduce misunderstandings as to the Manager's investment latitude, a common area of dispute when investments go awry. For mixed accounts, the Primary Fiduciary delegates only a portion of its fiduciary duties (the selection of stocks).

Each time the Primary Fiduciary hires a new Manager, or changes the investment guidelines or directives to an existing Manager, both the Primary and Manager Fiduciary should re-define and re-document their fiduciary responsibilities.

### Risk Standard 2: Approved written policies, definitions, guidelines and investment documentation

*The Primary and Manager Fiduciaries should approve formal written policies which reflect their overall risk management objectives. The Primary and Manager Fiduciaries also should approve investment guidelines, management agreements and all other contracts that govern investments. Technical terms should be defined. All policies, definitions, guidelines and investment documentation should be reviewed and updated as appropriate and more often if significant market events or changes in strategy occur.*

Written policies should encompass the investment philosophy and risk appetites of the Primary and Manager Fiduciaries. Typically, these require the creation of more detailed documents and standards for the individual Manager, portfolio or asset class, which include examples specific to the user. For example, a plan sponsor's internal guidelines should provide examples that relate to the management of a pension fund. A Manager's guidelines should provide examples that relate to its specific instruments, portfolio and particular strategy.

Approved written standards applied consistently and appropriately have several advantages over reliance on culture or apprenticeships:

❑ Written standards are less prone to intentional or unintentional omission
❑ Written standards allow those new to an organisation to study the risk management policies of the organisation, rather than to learn by trial and error
❑ Written definitions accompanied by pertinent examples reduce the likelihood of incomplete communications, ambiguities or misinterpretations

Poorly specified guidelines can lead to problems. Guidelines that explicitly allow "hedging," but not "speculation," may or may not permit proxy hedging. An example of a proxy hedge is the use of Swiss francs to hedge the currency risk in a German equity investment. Some may consider this a hedge, based on the assumption that the two currencies will move closely together. Others may consider this speculation because there is no guarantee that the Deutsche Mark and Swiss franc will move together.

Other problems can result from poorly defined permitted investment definitions. A portfolio may satisfy the literal restriction "only government securities are permitted", but violate the intent of the restriction if it contains agency notes whose coupon payment is linked to the return of the stock market. Alternately, two portfolios which meet the guideline requirement that they "maintain an average maturity of five years" may have significant differences in yield curve exposure if one portfolio consists of five-year instruments and the other of a combination of three-month Treasury bills and 30-year bonds.

Common terms that require definition include risk, hedging, speculation, derivative, complex, leverage, benchmark, average maturity, government security and high quality. Descriptors such as material, relevant and significant should also be defined.

In many capital markets, documentation has been developed to limit credit and other exposures. For example, master counterparty agreements for derivatives transactions reduce credit exposure by allowing the netting of payments in the case of default. The current trend to include foreign exchange forwards and options contracts under master swap agreements further reduces counterparty exposure.

The Primary and Manager Fiduciaries should update their policies periodically to reflect changing circumstances, new instruments or other relevant changes. Meaningful changes in an institutional investor's or investment manager's business, strategy, goals, risk appetite, capital requirements, markets or products should trigger formal reviews. Amendments to policies and guidelines should re-affirm what remains and what is changed in the previous document to avoid conflicts between the two versions.

### Risk Standard 3: Independent risk oversight, checks and balances, written procedures and controls

*Oversight of compliance with risk policies should be independent of line investment activity and conducted according to up-to-date, written policies and procedures. Front, middle, and back office activities should be separate wherever possible and sufficient checks and balances and appropriate controls should exist. When separation is not possible due to limited staff, alternative checks, balances and controls should be established.*

Unauthorised trading by individuals can go undetected for months or years if audits or other oversight are insufficient or because other checks and balances are not in place. Traders and portfolio managers who oversee themselves or perform their own portfolio valuations can make mistakes or intentionally understate risk, hide losses or overstate their own performance (and perhaps compensation due). These potential conflicts of interest make it crucial to ensure independent oversight for all major activities and separation of the front office (eg, portfolio management, manager selection, trading, investment research), the middle office (performance and risk measurement, compliance, legal, risk oversight, controllers) and the back office (accounting, administration, operations).

For example, position reports should be monitored by individuals outside the trading group who do not report directly or indirectly to the head of trading. The position reports should verify that investments are as reported by managers, that ownership is properly documented, cash balances reconciled and exceptions reported and acted upon (Risk Standard 9).

Where possible, an independent internal group or individual should perform oversight. Small institutional investors or Managers without a separate risk oversight function should use random audits and develop other internal checks and balances to make the best use of limited resources. The Primary Fiduciary should supervise its Managers closely in these circumstances. Auditors or independent third parties may also be used. Functions checked independently should include such items as:

❏ Oversight of investment activity (Risk Standards 17 and 18)
❏ Limits, monitoring, exception reports and action plans relating to exception reports (Risk Standards 8 and 9)
❏ Valuations and pricing methodologies (Risk Standards 10 and 19)
❏ Stress tests and back tests (Risk Standards 14 and 15)

The Primary and Manager Fiduciaries should verify that Managers conduct independent risk oversight of their employees and activities. Further, the individual or unit of an institutional investor that selects external managers should not be charged solely with overseeing them.

Each organisation should prepare a written plan that contains cost and time estimates of the systems, personnel, training and data necessary for risk oversight (Risk Standard 6).

### Risk Standard 4: Clearly defined organisational structure and key roles

*Organisational structure and reporting lines should be defined clearly and distributed to all parties. Key personnel and their roles in all front, middle and back office areas should be identified. Changes in key personnel should be communicated immediately to all relevant parties.*

To avoid confusion or misunderstandings, the Primary Fiduciary, Managers and subcontractors (such as custodians) should delineate clear responsibility and accountability for all functions, including risk measurement, risk management and oversight. Organisational and functional charts that address both line responsibility and oversight responsibility should be compared to reveal areas where there may be a conflict of interest, inadequate checks and balances, lack of assigned responsibility or unofficial authority (Risk Standards 1 and 3). Functional charts should specify who is authorised to do what – and who is not. For example, a functional chart should specify the individuals authorised to trade and those authorised to clear trades and might explicitly forbid traders to clear trades. An organisational chart should specify the reporting lines for internal audit and other checks and balances to ensure oversight exists for each function and is independent of the area overseen.

Functional charts should be used also to identify all individuals who are vital to the functioning of an organisation. For an institutional investor, the loss of a sole Manager with particular investment or risk management skills might force the sudden, and perhaps unskilled, liquidation of that portfolio. Senior managers are not the only key personnel in an organisation. For example, chaos might follow the abrupt resignation of the only person responsible for maintenance and trouble-shooting of software or systems. Risk policies should include specific provisions for immediate notification of the loss or change in any key personnel. The Fiduciary and its subcontractors should document their succession plans for key personnel and train backups.

### Risk Standard 5: Consistent application of risk policies

*The Primary Fiduciary's risk policies should apply both to internal and external managers and should be consistent across similar asset classes and strategies.*

Because internal managers can pose the same risks as their external peers, culture and proximity are unreliable restraints. Therefore, all Managers should be subject to consistent investment management agreements, written objectives and guidelines (Risk Standard 2). Note that these may vary by asset class or strategy, but policies and performance evaluation should be consistent across the same peer group universe.

Each time the Primary Fiduciary establishes a new portfolio or moves a portfolio, it should provide a copy of its current risk policies to the Manager. A separate document should describe how the risk policies apply to that Manager. If a Manager runs several portfolios for a given client, separate policies should govern each.

### Risk Standard 6: Adequate education, systems and resources, back-up and disaster recovery plans

*The Primary and Manager Fiduciaries should ensure that adequate education, systems and resources are available to implement and administer their risk policies. They should also establish and test back-up procedures and disaster recovery plans.*

Successful implementation of these Risk Standards requires a knowledgeable and responsible fiduciary and well-trained and capable professionals in the front, middle and back office (including adequate systems for position-keeping, processing, settlement, compliance monitoring and reporting). Sufficient funds must be allocated for necessary resources in the systems, personnel and risk oversight areas. All relevant employees (both new and existing) should receive copies of the risk policies and should confirm in writing that they have read and understood them. Employees should receive prompt copies of updates or changes and should sign re-confirmations at least annually.

Back-up and recovery plans are crucial, as physical disasters such as the World Trade Center bombing, the Chicago flood, California earthquakes and hurricanes in the Southeastern US made clear. Financial interruptions such as market trading halts or technological disasters such as systems, communications and power failures or software viruses also have proven the need for back-up and disaster recovery plans.

A disaster plan should include access to duplicate records of investment inventory, legal title to positions, master counterparty agreements, authorities and scheduled cash inflows and payments. It should prepare the organisation to resume operations off-site in a reasonable amount of time if the primary location shuts down and should include access to contingency financing in case of a liquidity crisis.

Back-up and disaster recovery plans are necessary for the Primary and Manager Fiduciaries, custodians and other subcontractors. Each should conduct trial runs to test the adequacy of its plans as well as the plans of those on whom they rely whether these are to be implemented by trained internal staff or outsourced to a specialty firm.

### Risk Standard 7: Identification and understanding of key risks

*Risks should be analysed to determine relevancy. This entails understanding strategies and their vulnerabilities, as well as assumptions built into an instrument, system, process, model or strategy. Key risks should be reviewed periodically as well as when significant events occur.*

Risk comes in many forms including market (eg, price deterioration), credit (default), legal (a contract deemed invalid), operational (systems failure), suitability (sale of inappropriate instruments to a municipal cash pool), asset/liability (mismatch), personnel (loss of a key person), internal liquidity (unexpectedly large demand for cash that forces a fire-sale), market liquidity (wide bid/ask spreads) and dozens of others. The Primary and Manager Fiduciaries should determine which risks are *relevant* to a given portfolio, strategy or instrument by asking such questions as:

❑ What events, even if unlikely, could cause a large change in market value or risk?
❑ How likely are such events to occur?

❏ What risks offset each other? By how much?
❏ How likely is it that these risks will offset each other as expected?
❏ What could go wrong and result in losing more money than is acceptable or increasing risk too much?
❏ What assumptions are built into a model or strategy? Do they make sense?
❏ How reliable are the models on which your risk analysis is based?
❏ How different are the results from other available models?

Identification of relevant risks prevents draining scarce resources on monitoring risks that are not relevant (foreign currency risk in a domestic portfolio) or are extremely improbable (obliteration of a well-established market such as the US equity market). Analyses should distinguish between prohibited risks (currency risk in a domestic bond portfolio), required risks for a strategy or instrument (beta in an equity portfolio), desired risks (credit exposure of a particular name or yield curve risk in a bond portfolio) and those that are subject to established limits (concentration risk).

In order to facilitate the understanding and identification of relevant risks, the Primary and Manager Fiduciaries should clarify what type of risk disclosures it expects from all Managers, subcontractors, counterparties and broker-dealers.

Institutional investors and Managers should re-analyse their risks on a scheduled basis and whenever significant change occurs. Key risks may vary over time due to changes in portfolio composition as well as paradigm changes in markets and economies. For example, the impact of the Mexican peso's collapse on other Latin American markets and even some markets in Asia forced investors to recognise the risk of temporary linkage between falling markets. Parliament's decision that the municipalities of Hammersmith and Fulham were not authorised to enter into certain over-the-counter transactions triggered a review of trade authorisation risk throughout the derivatives markets. Other significant changes in portfolio behaviour, market practice or models should trigger a re-examination of the key risks in a portfolio.

When hiring or reviewing a Manager, investors should consider both the individual Manager's risks as well as how those risks fit within the context of the investor's aggregate portfolio of Managers. Exposures to instruments, strategies and individual Managers should be analysed to ensure they are within limits. A new Manager that trades actively, for example, might increase total trading activity within the aggregate portfolio to a level that the investor or its custodian cannot adequately monitor. On the other hand, a Manager who takes a contrarian, fundamental approach to buying US value stocks may diversify the risk from several managers who trade on momentum.

### Risk Standard 8: Setting risk limits

*Risk limits should be set for the aggregate portfolio and all individual portfolios. These may include limits on asset classes, individual instruments and specific types of risk.*

The Primary and Manager Fiduciaries should establish limits at the instrument, aggregate and individual portfolio level for all relevant risks (Risk Standard 7). Examples of such limits include credit and market risks, net exposure (the combination of long and short positions), tracking error relative to a benchmark (for the individual and the aggregate portfolio), duration risk relative to a benchmark (for a bond portfolio), industry concentration (for an equity or corporate bond portfolio) or the percentage of a portfolio that is "non-readily priced", illiquid or dependent upon theoretical models (Risk Standard 10).

Often, risk limits are expressed in notional terms. For example, "10% of the dollar value of a US bond portfolio may be invested in international bonds". Other limits are expressed through measures of risk such as duration, tracking error or value at risk (VAR) (eg, "10% of the value at risk can be invested in bonds") (Risk Standard 12). Risk limits should be meaningful in the context of the current portfolio and market environment and not solely based on history.

Risk limits, of course, may at times reduce expected returns. The Fiduciary should examine this risk/return tradeoff.

### Risk Standard 9: Routine reporting, exception reporting and escalation procedures

*The Primary and Manager Fiduciaries should specify what positions, risks and other information must be reported and to whom. This policy also should define what constitutes required reporting or an exception to guidelines, to whom the exception should be reported, what action must be taken for different levels of violation and what procedures must be followed for ongoing or increased violations.*

After identifying relevant risks (Risk Standard 7), the Primary and Manager Fiduciaries should specify what positions, risks and other information should be reported, how often and to whom.

An important lesson from the past is that extraordinary performance can lull investors into a false sense of security. Many US bond investors realised the risk implicit in bull market securities after the bond market crashed in 1994; many emerging markets investors awoke to the event risk in some markets after the Mexican peso crashed in late 1994. Similarly, firms and investors questioned the extraordinary performance of rogue traders only after it was too late. It is as important to be as suspicious of unexpected outperformance as of underperformance. Both may indicate mispriced, unintended or misunderstood risks.

Key to effective risk control is an early warning system for problems and violations. It is crucial to rely on established reports and procedures, rather than culture or single individuals to sound the alarm. Both the Primary and Manager Fiduciaries should decide in advance which risk policies, guidelines or limits, if violated, require exception reports, who is responsible for monitoring and reporting exceptions and to whom they must be reported. Exception policies should also include what corrective actions, if any, should take place and within what time-frame, who will monitor the corrective actions and who is authorised to make exceptions to the exception policy.

A typical escalation procedure requires progressively more senior staff to be notified of exceptions which go unaddressed or exceptions which increase.

Oversight of the exception reporting and response process should be performed by individuals independent of those who are directly responsible for monitoring and reporting exceptions. If that is impossible, adequate checks and balances should be established (Risk Standard 3). The Primary and Manager Fiduciaries should ensure that all Managers are subject to consistent reporting, exception reporting and escalation procedure requirements (Risk Standard 5).

*II. Measurement*
## Risk Standard 10: Valuation procedures

---

*All readily priced instruments should be valued daily, less-readily priced instruments at least weekly and non-readily priced instruments as often as feasible and whenever a material event occurs. The pricing mechanism and methodologies must be known, understood, follow written policies and be applied consistently by the Primary and Manager Fiduciaries, Managers, custodian and other subcontractors.*

---

Accurate and frequent valuation is a fundamental aspect of measuring risk and monitoring compliance within the stated strategy and established risk limits. As a practical matter, the frequency of valuation depends on the instrument.

*Readily priced instruments* such as publicly traded securities, exchange-listed futures and options, and many over-the-counter securities and derivatives can be priced daily. These instruments are often tracked and priced by exchanges, data vendors, brokers and dealers. Actual market price information may be obtained either electronically or in published form. Positions or portfolios may be valued or "marked-to-market" on the basis of such quotes.

The Primary and Manager Fiduciaries should each set up procedures for pricing these instruments daily. Often this task is delegated to an external portfolio management service, custodian or pricing service after appropriate procedures, quality controls and checks and balances are established. Pricing may be performed internally, as long as there are appropriate checks and balances and independent verification (Risk Standard 3). The Primary Fiduciary should document and understand the pricing procedures and these should be consistent across all Managers, the custodian and other subcontractors

*Less-readily priced instruments,* such as complex Collateralised Mortgage Obligations (CMO), exotic derivatives, many private placement notes and other custom instruments should be priced as often as possible and at least weekly. Often the values of less-readily priced instruments provided by dealers, custodians and third-party pricing services are based on theoretical models. Because these valuations are not based on market sale prices, these instruments are sometimes said to be "marked-to-model".

For such instruments, the model and pricing mechanism must be made explicit so that they may be verified independently (Risk Standard 19). The Primary and Manager Fiduciaries should document the procedures, including key data assumptions and type of model (such as matrix pricing or option-adjusted spread models). They should also analyse the degree of model risk that exists for such instruments (Risk Standard 16). The Primary Fiduciary should ensure the procedures for similar instruments are consistent across all Managers, the custodian and other subcontractors.

The Primary and Manager Fiduciaries should document the basis of the valuations; for example, firm bid/offers, broker/dealer indications or estimates based on internal models. In all cases, the Primary and Manager Fiduciary should document what methodology will be used, specify the minimum number of brokers or dealers to be polled and establish a policy for selecting a single valuation if there are disparate quotes.

*Non-readily priced assets* such as real estate and private equity stakes are difficult to price frequently. The Primary and Manager Fiduciaries should make explicit what valuation method (such as theoretical model, appraisal, committee estimate or single-dealer quote) should be used to facilitate independent verification (Risk Standard 19).

For such instruments, valuations should be performed as frequently as feasible and whenever a material event occurs. Note that the Primary and Manager Fiduciaries should define "material" (Risk Standard 2). The key drivers of value of a non-readily priced instrument should be determined (Risk Standard 12). Changes in key drivers and key events should trigger a valuation update.

The Primary and Manager Fiduciaries should document the accuracy and reliability of pricing data and ensure that all valuations and risk/return measurements are performed consistently across Managers, the custodian and other subcontractors as well as independently of them

(Risk Standards 3 and 5). The ultimate authority on valuation for each instrument type should be determined by the Primary Fiduciary and stated in writing. Exceptions to any valuation procedures should be known and reported under established policies (Risk Standard 9). The Primary and Manager Fiduciaries should approve explicitly any valuation process that relies upon the Manager who holds the asset. Investors should also take care that multiple valuations do not ultimately depend on a single pricing source.

The Primary and Manager Fiduciaries should allocate the necessary resources to value non-readily priced instruments. To the degree this increases the cost of holding certain investments, the increased cost should be considered when measuring performance.

For all instrument types, the Primary and Manager Fiduciaries should determine whether the pricing agent has incentives to inflate or deflate valuations. Finally, valuations should be reported and all trades recorded and documented on a timely basis (generally daily).

### Risk Standard 11: Valuation reconciliation, bid/offer adjustments and overrides

*Material discrepancies in valuations from different sources should be reconciled following established procedures. A procedure for bid/offer adjustments and overrides to valuations should be established in writing and monitored independently.*

Differences in valuations between different Managers or between Managers and custodians or other subcontractors should be reconciled under established procedures at least monthly, or more frequently if material differences occur. If consistent valuation procedures are applied by the Managers, custodian and other subcontractors, any price differences can usually be explained by error, bid/offer spread adjustments or valuation overrides.

For all instruments, the Primary and Manager Fiduciaries should approve and document the mechanism for any bid/offer adjustments. For example, complex engineered securities tailored to meet the needs of a specific Manager may contain a substantial bid/offer spread that reflects illiquidity, operational burdens on the dealer, the cost of innovation and a dealer mark-up. The bid/offer adjustment may be proposed by the Manager in order to amortise the bid/offer spread over the life of the asset. Bid/offer adjustments may be required for simple instruments as well. Large positions in readily priced stocks or bonds may be valued by custodians and others based on closing prices for small round lots and thus reflect an inadequate bid/offer spread. The degree to which the bid/offer spread is (or is not) included in initial and ongoing valuations should be established under a written policy and monitored.

Overrides are adjustments made by a Manager to valuations provided by independent parties under established valuation procedures (Risk Standard 10). Typically, overrides occur during periods of market dislocation when a Manager believes the independent valuation is incorrect. Although their belief at times may be well-founded, all overrides should be reported and investigated if the differences in valuation are material.

The Primary and Manager Fiduciaries should establish written policies and procedures that set forth the circumstances, notification and approval process for all overrides. These policies and procedures should be communicated to all relevant parties such as the Primary and Manager Fiduciaries, relevant oversight staff and custodians. In addition, the number and magnitude of overrides should be tracked and reviewed by the Primary Fiduciary on an ongoing basis to confirm that all material adjustments have been investigated and that practices are consistent with the override policy.

### Risk Standard 12: Risk measurement and risk/return attribution analysis

*The Primary and Manager Fiduciaries should regularly measure relevant risks and quantify the key drivers of risk and return.*

The Primary and Manager Fiduciaries should measure the total risk in the overall portfolio, individual portfolio and each instrument. Then, they should perform attribution analyses to determine the various risks and returns posed by each instrument or portfolio.

Value at risk (VAR) is one widely used method for creating a common unit of measurement for risk. It is the maximum dollar (or other currency) amount that a position or portfolio is expected to lose within a specified period of time given a specified probability. There are a number of approaches to computing VAR. The results are quite sensitive to the assumptions made and model used, and both should be understood (Risk Standard 16). One common VAR method for which data is widely available is a parametric approach using historical volatility and correlations between assets.

Other risk measures commonly used include duration, beta, standard deviation, semi-variance, tracking error and drawdown size. It is important to verify that the risk measure chosen captures the relevant risks (Risk Standard 7).

Institutional investors and institutional investment managers also should perform both risk and return attribution analyses of all portfolios along all relevant dimensions. A *return attribution analysis* looks at historical performance of a portfolio to determine the key drivers of returns. A *risk attribution analysis* looks at the key sources of risk and the volatility of returns in the current or anticipated portfolio to determine the key drivers of risk. For example, a risk attribution analysis of a US bond portfolio might quantify duration, yield curve, convexity and sector risk in absolute terms or relative to a benchmark. A risk attribution analysis of a US equity portfolio might use a risk factor model to quantify the various sources of absolute and benchmark-relative risk.

The Primary and Manager Fiduciaries also can use risk attribution analysis to monitor whether a Manager is adhering to its stated strategy (Risk Standard 18) and to measure aggregate factor risks from multiple Managers or portfolios. Individual portfolio managers can use risk attribution analysis to make sure they are not taking more of a given risk than their limits allow and to ensure broad diversification of risk.

## Risk Standard 13: Risk-adjusted return measures

*Risk-adjusted returns should be measured at the aggregate and individual portfolio level to gain a true measure of relative performance.*

Investors should compare all Managers on a risk-adjusted basis. By taking into account both the risk and return sides of the equation, risk-adjusted return measures enable investors to evaluate better the relative performance of two managers. Risk-adjusted measures also highlight instances in which a manager's outperformance is due to incurring misunderstood, mispriced, unintended or undisclosed risks.

Consider, for example, two portfolios that each returned 200 basis points (bp) over the same bond index for a given year. The first portfolio manager invested in US Treasury securities; the second purchased distressed debt in emerging markets. A risk-adjusted measure applied to the 200 bp of outperformance of each one would adjust for the differing market volatility, credit risk and foreign exchange risk between the two portfolios and show that the first portfolio may be more desirable on a risk-adjusted return basis.

Risk-adjusted return measures also permit a more meaningful comparison of a Manager's performance relative to its benchmark. If a Manager exceeds the benchmark return by 20%, but takes 30% more risk, his performance is less impressive than if he achieved the same excess return with risk equal to or less than the benchmark.

Common measures of risk-adjusted returns include the information ratio, Sharpe Ratio, Treynor Measure and Sortino Ratio. It is important to verify that the risk-adjusted measure chosen captures the relevant risks (Risk Standard 7).

## Risk Standard 14: Stress testing

*Simulation or other stress tests should be performed to ascertain how the aggregate portfolio and individual portfolios would behave under various conditions. These include changes in key risk factors, correlations or other key assumptions and unusual events such as large market moves.*

All investors, internal managers and external managers should test the likely impact of various market conditions or other events on the value of an instrument, portfolio or strategy by performing stress tests. These are typically simulations, which may be performed on a scenario, historical, simulation or random sampling basis (Monte Carlo analysis).

Strategies that pose little risk under normal market conditions may fall apart when the abnormal occurs. Alternately, strategies that hold up under large market moves (stock market crashes, huge interest rate swings) may fall apart under more subtle changes. Investors and managers should test both the impacts of large market moves and of combinations of small market moves to identify those that are likely to affect the portfolio. For example, a relative value trade that involves selling the 10-year Treasury and buying the five-year is much more sensitive to the spread between 10-year and five-year rates than to equal increases or decreases in both rates (parallel shifts of the yield curve). Other relevant stress tests include how risk and return change under the use of different assumptions or models (Risk Standard 16). Emphasis should be placed on stress testing the key risk factors identified in Risk Standard 7. Events that would breach risk limits, strategy goals, liability targets or asset allocation ranges should be monitored and acted upon.

Stress tests should be performed at least quarterly and whenever material events occur at the aggregate fund and manager portfolio level, incorporating asset/liability issues as relevant. "Material events" include significant changes in the market as well as in the strategy or composition of a Manager's portfolio or a change in Managers. The Primary Fiduciary should ensure that a consistent, well-defined process is used by all Managers as well as at the portfolio level. Assumptions embedded in the stress testing process should also be stress tested. The stress testing process should also be back tested to see whether the process would have forecasted accurately past outperformance, past underperformance and performance under past market shocks (Risk Standard 15).

Note that the same stress test on a portfolio with stable composition may reveal little impact at one time and great impact at another without any change in market conditions. This is most often true of options-based and mortgage portfolios, whose risk characteristics change over time.

Finally, stress tests should take into account all types of leverage and related cash flows, including such items as:

❏ Loans (reverse repurchase agreements)
❏ Instruments that control leveraged market positions (options)
❏ Instruments with internal leverage (structured notes with embedded leverage or high-Beta stocks)
❏ Initial and variation margin requirements (exchange-traded or over-the-counter futures, forwards or options)

## Risk Standard 15: Back testing

*Risk and return forecasts and models should be back tested at least quarterly and whenever material events occur to assess their reliability.*

Institutional investors and Managers should back test all models and forecasts of expected risk, return and correlations for instruments, asset classes and strategies. Back tests involve evaluating how a strategy, instrument or model actually performed for a given period versus what was predicted by a risk or return forecast. Comparing back testing results to actual experience also helps to evaluate the robustness of an estimate for a strategy, instrument or model. This provides a useful framework for assessing the strategy's, instrument's or model's value as an investment or risk management tool.

Typical questions a back test helps to answer include:

❏ How would the strategy, instrument, risk forecast or model have performed under certain past stressful market conditions (such as the Mexican peso devaluation, the stock market crash, the European currency crisis, the Federal Reserve rate hikes during 1994 or the 1973 oil shock)?
❏ Was past performance or risk due to the presence of a sustained bull or bear market condition or other market condition (steep yield curve, strong technology sector, large cap performance)?
❏ What economic conditions provide the best environment for the strategy, instrument or model?
❏ When has the strategy, instrument or model not performed well?

Back tests should also be performed in the overall portfolio or fund context. This may help the investor to assess the risk of multiple strategies failing under similar market or economic conditions.

## Risk Standard 16: Assessing model risk

*Dependence on models and assumptions for valuation, risk measurement and risk management should be evaluated and monitored.*

Virtually all market participants are exposed to mark-to-model risk. The degree of exposure depends upon the type and concentration of less-readily priced and non-readily priced instruments (Risk Standard 10) in individual and aggregate portfolios and on the type of valuation, risk and strategy models used. The Primary and Manager Fiduciaries should evaluate and monitor both the extent to which their management of risk and return changes under different models and assumptions that are widely used in the market place, as well as the degree to which the percentage of assets changes from readily priced to other valuation categories (see Risk Standard 10) from period to period. Dependence on assumptions within models should be stress tested (see Risk Standard 14). Important dimensions of model risk to analyse include:

❑ Data integrity (eg, curve construction, differing sources of data, representativeness and statistical significance of samples, time of day data is extracted, data availability and errors)
❑ Definition and certainty of future cash flows (formula-driven cash flows or flows that depend on an option)
❑ Formula, algorithm or other mathematical engine (Black-Scholes versus Hull and White for options valuation)
❑ Liquidity assumptions (length of time to liquidate and bid/ask spreads)
❑ Model parameter selection (selection of spreads, discount rates, scenario and stress test parameters, probability intervals, time horizon, correlation assumptions)

*III. Oversight*
**Risk Standard 17: Due diligence, policy compliance and guideline monitoring**

---

*The Primary and Manager Fiduciaries should perform frequent, independent reviews of all Managers' risk policies and controls. Where policies and controls fall short of the requirements set forth by the Primary or Manager Fiduciaries, plans for future compliance or corrective action should be documented and communicated. Managers should ensure continuing compliance with their clients' risk policies and guidelines.*

---

Before committing new or additional funds, the Primary Fiduciary should establish an ongoing due diligence process for reviewing a prospective investment strategy or Manager, including risk management, risk measurement and risk oversight capabilities and compliance with these Risk Standards. The process should be documented to avoid incomplete, inadequate or inconsistent reviews (Risk Standards 2 and 5). The due diligence process may be carried out through a combination of meetings, telephone interviews and written questionnaires.

The Primary and Manager Fiduciaries should independently verify compliance with risk policies and other requirements at least annually at both the aggregate and individual portfolio level and whenever a material change or exception occurs (Risk Standard 9). The Primary and Manager Fiduciaries should require Managers to provide notification of any material change and affirm in writing at least annually that they are in compliance with these requirements and other investment guidelines. Guideline compliance monitoring should be an ongoing and possibly daily task, its frequency depending on the nature of the guidelines and limits.

One form of compliance review is a risk audit by an independent third party. If this is not practicable or affordable, the Primary and Manager Fiduciaries should internally verify compliance with guidelines and regulations, ensuring that staff members performing this task are independent of those whose compliance they review (Risk Standard 3).

### Risk Standard 18: Comparison of Manager strategies to compensation and investment activity

---

*The Primary Fiduciary should require each Manager to submit a statement of strategy and ensure that the Manager's activities and compensation are consistent with that strategy. Key risk and return factors should be documented and reviewed at least annually and updated whenever the strategy changes.*

---

Typically, the Primary Fiduciary selects a Manager based on the Manager's perceived skill and value of the strategy. The Primary Fiduciary should understand each Manager's strategy and rationale for trades. If, in the case of a discretionary "black box" strategy, the Primary Fiduciary decides to go ahead without a full understanding of the strategy and trade rationale (Risk Standards 7 and 12), it should recognise and document it is doing so. In all cases, the Primary Fiduciary should require each Manager to draw up a strategy statement that explains the strategy's key risk and return features.

For example, an international equity manager should explain the degree to which the strategy seeks risk and return from country, stock and currency selection (Risk Standards 7, 12 and 13). A provider of portfolio insurance or of a currency overlay strategy should explain the risk and return expected from dynamic hedges or options and the degree to which it needs stable, continuous or highly liquid markets to succeed. A contrarian value manager or asset allocater should explain the risk that positions may do nothing, or even lose value, for some time before gaining value.

The Primary and Manager Fiduciaries should perform risk and return attribution analysis to verify that activity is consistent with the stated strategy and to reveal any style drift. Marked deviation from the performance of similar strategies executed by other Managers should be reported and investigated (Risk Standard 9). The Primary and Manager Fiduciaries also should review the strategy statement to ensure consistency with its objectives and its overall risk and return goals in context of its asset allocation and Manager concentration.

Finally, the Primary and Manager Fiduciaries should understand how each Manager's compensation structure aligns (or does not align) with the Fiduciary's interests and whether the compensation encourages or discourages the Manager to stick to the stated strategy.

The Primary and Manager Fiduciaries should require Managers to verify periodically that strategy statements are accurate and to update them whenever a material change occurs. This should be accompanied by random or other reviews of investment activity and portfolio holdings to verify compliance with the stated strategy. The Primary and Manager Fiduciaries should require Managers to record and report all transactions on a timely basis (Risk Standard 9) and should obtain an independently verified current statement of positions at a frequency appropriate to the strategy (Risk Standard 3). If position information is not available, as may be the case for certain commingled funds and hedge funds, the investor should request verifiable risk information.

### Risk Standard 19: Independent review of methodologies, models and systems

---

*All methodologies, models and related systems should be independently reviewed or audited prior to use as well as annually. Significant market moves or changes in market practice should trigger interim reviews.*

---

The Primary and Manager Fiduciaries should appoint an independent third party to review the soundness of valuation methodologies, models and related systems. If this is not possible, an internal group should perform such assessments, with appropriate checks and balances. Reviews should follow established procedures and be documented to reflect their scope and completion.

Reviews of methodologies, models and related systems should be specific to the instrument, asset class or individual Manager's style. Examples of items to address include:

- ❏ How appropriate are the models chosen to value the instrument?
- ❏ How do the valuations compare with those calculated by others?
- ❏ How appropriate are the assumptions and data to the model of choice?
- ❏ How thorough is the effort to independently verify the choice of model and assumptions?
- ❏ How sensitive is the portfolio to the timing of data capture and the

valuation calculation? How does this affect risk and return measurement and related reporting?

❏ Does the methodology provide a consistently high or low picture of an instrument's or portfolio's risk and return characteristics?

❏ How would the risk and return picture change under alternative assumptions (including stress scenarios), models and methodologies?

## Risk Standard 20: Review process for new activities

*The Primary and Manager Fiduciaries should document the review process for permitting the use of new instruments, strategies or asset classes. Policies for initiating new activities should be consistent with the Primary and Manager Fiduciaries' risk and return goals as well as the Manager's strategy and expertise.*

Typically, no new instrument, asset class or strategy should be permitted without review. Alternatively, the Primary and Manager Fiduciaries should set pre-established limits as to the degree of new activity allowed and specify interim reporting required prior to formal review. The review process should set forth the risk and return dimensions on which the new activity will be evaluated and require the manager to submit all relevant information. The Primary and Manager Fiduciaries should consider additional items such as Manager skill and whether additional valuation, back office/settlement, counterparty oversight, execution, authorities/resolutions and reporting capabilities are needed to engage in the new activity.

One advantage of the review process for new activities is that it sets a time frame for responding to new ideas. This manages expectations, ensures consistent review across opportunities and limits the likelihood of too little scrutiny during busy periods and too much during slow periods.

To avoid excessive reliance on a Manager and unexpected or unintended levels of risk, the Primary and Manager Fiduciaries should weigh carefully the risks of an excessively broad or permissive policy such as, "If an investment is not banned, you may make it". To avoid missing opportunities and reducing returns, however, the Primary and Manager Fiduciaries should be careful not to be too prohibitive. An excessively narrow or restrictive policy might state, "If the specific investment is not listed here, you may not make it". To avoid missing special opportunities and to enable managers to make reasoned judgments, some Primary and Manager Fiduciaries allow a small amount of "new" activity (or a maximum amount of "new" activity) outside of the official review process. That activity, however, should become part of the official review process within a stated period of time.

**The Working Group***

Suzanne Brenner
*Associate Director of Investments*
The Rockefeller Foundation

Kevin Byrne
*Vice President & Treasurer*
The Equitable Companies Inc.

Christopher J. Campisano, CFA
*Manager, Trust Investments*
Xerox Corporation

Mary Cottrill, CFA
*Principal Investment Officer*
CalPERS

Michael deMarco
*Director, Risk Management*
GTE Investment Management
Corporation

Jon Lukomnik
*Deputy Comptroller for Pensions*
City of New York
Office of the Comptroller

Richard Rose
*Chief Investment Officer*
San Diego County Employees'
Retirement Association

David Russ
*Director, Investment Management*
Pacific Telesis Group

James D. Seymour
*Vice President*
The Common Fund

Kathy Wassmann
*Manager, Trust Investments*
R.R. Donnelley & Sons Company

Gregory T. Williamson
*Investment Manager*
Amoco Corporation

**The Comment Group***

Jeffery V. Bailey
*Director, Employee Benefit
Investments*
Dayton Hudson Corporation

J. Carter Beese, Jr.
*Vice Chairman*
Alex Brown International

Afsaneh Mashayekhi Beschloss
*Director, Pension Department*
The World Bank Group

Alan D. Biller
*President*
Alan D. Biller & Associates, Inc.

Robert E. Butler
*Regulatory Compliance Consulting
Group*
Price Waterhouse LLP

Charles T. Connell
*Vice President*
Chase Manhattan Bank

Roger G. Clarke
*Chairman*
Analytic TSA Global Asset
Management

Raymond P. Dalio
*Chairman*
Bridgewater Associates, Inc.

William L. Dawson
*Senior Vice President, Chief Risk &*
*Compliance Officer*
Mellon Trust

Patrick de Saint-Aignan
*Managing Director*
Morgan Stanley & Co., Inc.

Ron S. Dembo
*President & CEO*
Algorithmics, Inc.

Gordon E. Dickinson
*Senior Vice President*
Callan Associates, Inc.

Nancy C. Everett, CFA
*Deputy Chief Investment Officer*
Virginia Retirement System

Stephen C. Fan
*President*
Fan Asset Management

Don Fehrs
*Director of Fixed Income,*
Risk Management and Special
Situations
Investment Office
University of Notre Dame

William C. Fletcher, CFA
*President*
Independence Investment
Associates, Inc.

Chris H. Fuller
*Vice President*
Alliance Capital Management
Corporation

Betsy Glaeser
*Director, Capital Markets Group*
Deloitte & Touche

Frederick L.A. Grauer
*Chairman*
BZW Barclays Global Investors

Orim Graves
*Vice President*
Segal Advisors

Jeffrey E. Gundlach
*Group Managing Director*
Trust Company of the West

Robert W. Harless
*Manager, Structured Products*
Lotsoff Capital Management

W. Van Harlow III
*Director, Investment Research &*
*Analysis*
Fidelity Investments

Gary B. Helms
*Vice President for Investments*
The University of Chicago

Robert W. Kopprasch
*Managing Director*
Smith Barney Capital Management

Ian D. Lanoff
*Principal*
Groom and Nordberg

Ronald Layard-Liesching
*Partner & Director of Research*
Pareto Partners

Robert B. Litterman
*Partner*
Goldman, Sachs & Co.

Andrew W. Lo
*Harris & Harris Group Professor*
MIT Sloan School of Management

Charles M. Lucas
*Director, Market Risk Management*
American International Group, Inc.

Desmond Mac Intyre
*Director, Risk Management*
General Motors Investment
Management Corporation

Katherine Busboom Magrath, CFA
*Partner & Chief Investment Officer*
ValueQuest, Ltd.

Howard L. Margolin
*Partner*
Arthur Andersen

Harry S. Marmer
*Principal*
William M. Mercer Limited

James F. Muzzy
*Managing Director*
Pacific Investment Management
Company

Julie O'Donnell
*Director, Private Transactions*
Ameritech

Virginia R. Parker
*President*
Parker Global Strategies

Thomas K. Phillips
*Managing Director*
Rogers, Casey & Associates, Inc.

Richard A. Pike
*President*
RP Consulting Group, Inc.

William H.S. Preece, Jr.
*Director, Retirement Funds*
Abbott Laboratories

Bluford H. Putnam
*Managing Director, Chief Strategist*
Bankers Trust Company

Richard H. Redding
*Vice President, Index Products
Marketing*
Chicago Mercantile Exchange

Craig Scholl
*Asset Allocation Manager*
Hewlett-Packard Company

Charles A. Service
*Vice President, Capital Management
and Trust Investments*
Unisys Corporation

Frederick Settelmeyer
*Senior Vice President*
Mellon Trust

William Sharpe
*STANCO 25 Professor of Finance*
Stanford University

Elisa K. Spain
*Senior Vice President*
The Northern Trust Company

Casey J. Sylla
*Chief Investment Officer*
Allstate Insurance Company

Thomas Szczesny
*Senior Vice President*
The Bank of New York

Martin E. Titus, Jr.
*Principal*
KPMG Peat Marwick LLP

Francis H. Trainer, Jr.
*Senior Vice President*
Sanford C. Bernstein & Co., Inc.

R.L. (Jay) Vivian, CFA
*Director of Risk Management*
IBM Retirement Funds

Ashbel C. Williams, Jr.
*President*
Schroder Wertheim Investment
Services, Inc.

Arnold S. Wood
President
Martingale Asset Management

1 *Note*: Throughout this document, references to the "Primary Fiduciary" and/or "Manager Fiduciary" include their designees. References to the "Manager" include both the internal and the external investment manager.

2 Throughout this document, references to the "Primary Fiduciary" and/or "Manager Fiduciary" include their designees. References to the "Manager" include both the internal and the external investment manager.

# Appendix 6

# *Buy-Side Risk System Comparison Matrix*

## Capital Market Risk Advisors

The conventions used in the comparison matrix are as follows:

**Matrix answers**

■ Yes    ● No    ◆ Partial    ✚ Planned

**Matrix comments**

REQ      On request
SUB      If separately subscribed to data
Aug-02   Date for planned addition
[1]      All other comments in footnotes

Blank boxes indicate no response from the system provider

# VAR

| | Most common approach — VAR – H=Historic M=Monte Carlo P=Parametric | What is the level at which VAR is typically calculated (factor or security)? | Parametric (Variance/Covariance) — Can the system calculate a parametric VAR at the equity security level? | Can the system calculate a parametric VAR at the equity factor level? | Historical using factor model — Can the system calculate a historical simulation VAR at the equity security level? | Can the system calculate a historical simulation VAR at the equity factor level? |
|---|---|---|---|---|---|---|
| Per cent Yes/Average | | | 60% | 60% | 60% | 60% |
| Wilshire package | P | F | ● | ■ | ● | ● |
| SunGard package | HMP | SF | ■ | ✚ Jan-02 | ■ | ✚ Jan-02 |
| RiskMetrics ASP/package | HM | S | ■ | ● | ■ | ● |
| Measurisk ASP | M | F | ● | ● | ● | ● |
| GlobeOp package | HMP | SF | ■ | ■ | ■ | ■ |
| DBRisk ASP | M | F | ● | ● | ● | ✚ [2] |
| BlackRock Svc. bureau | P | F | ● | ■ | ● | ■ |
| Barra package | P | F | ■ | ■ | ✚ Aug-02 | ■ [1] |
| Askari ASP | H | S | ■ | ● | ■ | ● |
| Askari package | H | S | ■ | ● | ■ | ● |
| Algorithmics package | HM | S | ■ | ■ | ■ | ■ |

## VAR

| Question | Algorithmics package | Askari package | Askari ASP | Barra package | BlackRock Svc. bureau | DBRisk ASP | GlobeOp package | Measurisk ASP | RiskMetrics ASP/package | SunGard package | Wilshire package | Per cent Yes/Average |
|---|---|---|---|---|---|---|---|---|---|---|---|---|
| **Monte Carlo** | | | | | | | | | | | | |
| Can the system calculate a Monte Carlo VAR at the equity security level? | ■ | ■ | ■ | ■ | ● | ● | ■ | ● | ■ | ■ | ● | 60% |
| Can the system calculate a Monte Carlo VAR at the equity factor level? | ■ | ● | ● | ■[3] | ■ | ■[4] | ■ | ■[5] | ● | + Jan-02 | + Jun-02 | 80% |
| **Risk factor causality** | | | | | | | | | | | | |
| For an equity security level VAR, can the system provide an analysis of what factors cause the risk in equities? | ● | ◆[6] | ◆[7] | ■ | + Jun-02 | ■[8] | ■ | ◆[9] | + Dec-02 | + Sep-02 | ● | 60% |
| For an equity security level VAR, can the system provide an analysis of what sector factors cause the risk? | ● | ◆[10] | ◆[11] | ■ | + Jun-02 | ■ | ■ | ■ | + Dec-02 | + Sep-02 | ■ | 80% |
| For an equity security level VAR, can the system provide an analysis of what style factors cause the risk? | ● | ● | ● | ■ | + Jun-02 | ■ | + Mar-02 | ● | + Dec-02 | + Sep-02 | ■[12] | 70% |
| For an equity security level VAR, can the system provide an analysis of specific risk? | ● | ■ | ■ | ■ | + Jun-02 | ■ | ■ | ■ | ■ | + Sep-02 | ■ | 90% |
| Can the system support the analysis of what factors cause the risk in fixed income? | ■ | ■ | ■ | ■ | ■ | ■ | ■ | ■ | ■ | ■ | ■ | 100% |
| Can the system support key rate analysis? | ■ | ■ | ■ | ◆ | ■ | ■ | ■ | ■ | ■ | ■ | ■ | 90% |

## VAR

| | Can the system support tilt/kink/parallel shift analysis? | Can the system support analysis of credit spreads? | Can the system support analysis of volatility? | Can the system measure risk both in absolute and relative to a benchmark? | Can the system aggregate common risks across entire portfolio (eg, FX exposure inherent in holding non-US securities, other exchange-sensitive instruments, and direct FX positions)? | Select — Can the user select the historical period? | Can the user select the holding period? | Can the system select the confidence interval? | Is the data used for equities performance data (adjusted for dividends and corporate actions) and not prices? |
|---|---|---|---|---|---|---|---|---|---|
| **Per cent Yes/Average** | 70% | 90% | 90% | 100% | 100% | 70% | 100% | 90% | 90% |
| Wilshire package | ■ | ■ | ■ | ■ | ■ | ■ | ■ | ● | ■ |
| SunGard package | ■ | ■ | ■ | ■ | ■ | ■ | ■ | ■ | ■ |
| RiskMetrics ASP/package | + Dec-02 | ■ | ■ | ■ | ■ | ■ | ■ | ■ | ● |
| Measurisk ASP | ● | ■ | + Jan-02 | ■ | ■ | ◆ REQ | ■ | ■ | ■ |
| GlobeOp package | ■ | ■ | + Jan-02 | ■ | ■ | ■ | ■ | ■ | ■ |
| DBRisk ASP | ● | + Jun-02 | + Dec-02 | ■ | ■ | ◆ REQ | ■ | ■ | + Dec-02 |
| BlackRock Svc. bureau | ■ | ■ | ■ | ■ | ■ | ■ | ■ | ■ | + Jun-02 |
| Barra package | ■ | ◆ | ● | ■ | ■ | ◆ REQ | ■ | ■ | + Aug-02 |
| Askari ASP | ● | ■ | + Dec-01 | ■ | ■ | ■ | ■ | ■ | ■ |
| Askari package | ● | ■ | + Dec-01 | ■ | ■ | ■ | ■ | ■ | ■ |
| Algorithmics package | ■ | ■ | ■ | ■ | ■ | ■ | ■ | ■ | ■ |

# VAR

### Distribution

| Package | Can the system calculate VAR based on the actual distribution? | Can the system calculate VAR based on the assumption of normality? | Can the system calculate the expected shortfall? | Can the system provide the full distribution of returns? | Can the system support the calculation of the counterparty credit risk? | Can the system calculate the current net exposure? | Can the system net exposures based on the appropriate rules? | *Sensitivity* Can the system calculate the impact on VAR of eliminating a position? | Can the system calculate the impact on VAR of eliminating a risk factor? |
|---|---|---|---|---|---|---|---|---|---|
| Per cent Yes/Average | 100% | 90% | 40% | 100% | 60% | 60% | 60% | 100% | 80% |
| Wilshire package | + Jun-02 | + Jun-02 | ● | + Jun-02 | ● | ● | ● | ■ | + Jun-02 |
| SunGard package | ■ | ■ | ■ | ■ | ■ | ■ | ■ | ■ | ■ |
| RiskMetrics ASP/package | ■ | ■ | ■ | ■ | ■[14] | ■ | ■ | ■[21] | ◆[26] |
| Measurisk ASP | ■ | ■ | ● | ■ | ● | ● | ● | ■[20] | ■[25] |
| GlobeOp package | ■ | ■ | ■ | ■ | ■ | ■ | ■ | ■[19] | ■ |
| DBRisk ASP | ■ | ● | ● | ■[13] | ● | ● | ● | + Dec-02 | ■[24] |
| BlackRock Svc. bureau | ■ | ■ | ● | ■ | ● | ● | ● | ■ | ■ |
| Barra package | ■ | ■ | ● | ■ | + Jun-02 | + Jun-02 | + Jun-02 | ■[18] | ■ |
| Askari ASP | ■ | ■ | ● | ■ | ■ | ■ | ■ | ■[17] | ◆[23] |
| Askari package | ■ | ■ | ● | ■ | ■ | ■ | ■ | ■[16] | ◆[22] |
| Algorithmics package | ■ | ■ | ■ | ■ | ■ | ■ | ■ | ■[15] | ■ |

## VAR

| Package | Can the system calculate the impact on VAR of eliminating a subportfolio? (100%) | Can the system calculate the impact on VAR of a small change in the holdings of a position? (90%) | Can the system calculate VAR intra-day based on changes in holdings? (40%) | Can the system calculate an earnings at risk and a cash flow at risk? (60%) | Can the system market-to-market valuation of the derivative exposures? (80%) | Can the system mark-to-market valuation non-derivative exposures? (80%) | Can the system support clients analysis of hedge? (50%) | Can the system maintain the relationship between the asset and the related hedge? (30%) | Can the system support the 8125 rule? (20%) |
|---|---|---|---|---|---|---|---|---|---|
| Wilshire package | ■ | ■ | ● | ● | ■ | ■ | ■ | ● | ● |
| SunGard package | ■ | ■ | ■ | ◆ [33] | ■ | ■ | ● | ■ | ● |
| RiskMetrics ASP/package | ■ | ■ [32] | ■ | + Dec-02 | ■ | ■ | ■ | ● | ● |
| Measurisk ASP | ■ | + Mar-02 | ● | ■ | ■ | ■ | ■ | ■ [34] | ■ |
| GlobeOp package | ■ | ■ [31] | ● | + REQ | ■ | ■ | ● | ● | ● |
| DBRisk ASP | ■ | ● | ● | ● | ■ | ■ | ● | ● | ● |
| BlackRock Svc. bureau | ■ | ■ | + Feb-02 | + Jun-02 | ■ | ■ | ■ | ■ | ■ |
| Barra package | ■ | ■ [30] | ● | ● | ● | ● | ● | ● | ● |
| Askari ASP | ■ | ■ [29] | ● | + Dec-01 | ● | ● | ● | ● | ● |
| Askari package | ■ | ■ [28] | ● | + Dec-01 | | | | | |
| Algorithmics package | ■ | ■ [27] | ■ | ■ | ■ | ■ | ■ | ● | ● |

FASB 133 (section divider between the fourth and fifth questions)

| VAR | Can the system support retrospective testing of the test? | Pension | Can the system model future liabilities as cash flows? | Can the system calculate surplus at risk? | Can the system calculate the time to liquidate an equity holding based on average market turnover and a percent of market turnover an investor is willing to capture? |
|---|---|---|---|---|---|
| Per cent Yes/Average | 20% | | 100% | 40% | 30% |
| Wilshire package | ● | | ■ | ● | ● |
| SunGard package | ● | | ■ | ◆ | ● |
| RiskMetrics ASP/package | ● | | ■ | ■ | ● |
| Measurisk ASP | ■ | | ■ | ■ | ■ |
| GlobeOp package | ● | | ■ | ● | ■ |
| DBRisk ASP | ● | | ■ | ■ | ✛ |
| BlackRock Svc. bureau | ■ | | ■ | ● | ● |
| Barra package | ● | | ■ | ● | ● |
| Askari ASP | ● | | ■ | ■ | ● |
| Askari package | ● | | ■ | ■ | ● |
| Algorithmics package | ● | | ■ | ● | ● |

## Models

| Model | API for proprietary models? | Import proprietary yield curves? | Develop their own curves? | Interest rate sensitivity? | Spread sensitivity? | Volatility based on historical volatility? | Volatility based on implied volatility? | Embedded options incl. callable bonds? | Convertible bonds? |
|---|---|---|---|---|---|---|---|---|---|
| **Per cent Yes/Average** | 50% | 80% | 60% | 100% | 100% | 80% | 80% | 100% | 100% |
| Wilshire package | ● | ■ | ■ | ■ | ■ | ■ | ■ | ■ | ■ |
| SunGard package | ■ | ■ | ■ | ■ | ■ | ■ | ■ | ■ | ■ |
| RiskMetrics ASP/package | ● | ■ | ◆ REQ | ■ | ■ | ■ | ■ | ■ | ■ |
| Measurisk ASP | ● | ■ REQ | ■ | ■ | ■ | ● | + Mar-02 | ■ | ■ |
| GlobeOp package | ■ | + REQ | ◆ REQ | ■ | ■ | + Dec-01 | + Dec-01 | ■ | ■ |
| DBRisk ASP | ● | ● | ● | ■ | + | + Dec-02 | + Dec-02 | ■ | ■ |
| BlackRock Svc. bureau | ● | ● | ● | ■ | ■ | ■ | ■ | + Dec-02 | ■ |
| Barra package | + Aug-02 | ■ | ■ | ■ | ■ | ● | ● | ■ | ■ |
| Askari ASP | ■ | ■ | ■ | ■ | ■ | ■ | ◆ 36 | ■ 38 | ■ |
| Askari package | ■ | ■ | ■ | ■ | ■ | ■ | ◆ 35 | ■ 37 | ■ |
| Algorithmics package | ■ | ■ | ■ | ■ | ■ | ■ | ■ | ■ | ■ |

Column group headings: "Bonds" (interest rate sensitivity, spread sensitivity) and "Volatility" (historical volatility, implied volatility, embedded options, convertible bonds).

## Models

| Question | Wilshire package | SunGard package | RiskMetrics ASP/package | Measurisk ASP | GlobeOp package | DBRisk ASP | BlackRock Svc. bureau | Barra package | Askari ASP | Askari package | Algorithmics package | Per cent Yes/Average |
|---|---|---|---|---|---|---|---|---|---|---|---|---|
| **MBS (pricing engine)** | | | | | | | | | | | | |
| Can the system use Derivative Solutions for its MBS pricing engine? | ● | ■ | ■ | ● | ● | ■ | ■ | ● | ● | ● | ● | 40% |
| Can the system use Davidson for its MBS pricing engine? | ● | ● | ● | ■ | ● | ● | ● | ● | ● | ● | ■ | 20% |
| Can the system use Chasen for its MBS pricing engine? | ● | ● | ● | ● | ● | ● | ● | ● | ■ | ■ | ● | 10% |
| Can the system use a proprietary MBS pricing engine? | ■ | ● | ● | ● | ✚ Jun-02 | ● | ■ | ■ | ● | ● | ● | 40% |
| **ABS (pricing engine)** | | | | | | | | | | | | |
| Can the system use Derivative Solutions for its ABS pricing engine? | ● | ■ | ● | ● | ● | ■ | ■ | ● | ● | ● | ● | 30% |
| Can the system use Davidson for its ABS pricing engine? | ● | ● | ● | ■ | ● | ● | ● | ● | ● | ● | ■ | 20% |
| Can the system use a proprietary ABS pricing engine? | ■ | ● | ● | ● | ✚ Jun-02 | ● | ● | ■ | ● | ● | ● | 30% |
| **Prepayment model** | | | | | | | | | | | | |
| Can the system use Davidson for its prepayment model? | ✚ Feb-02 | ■ | ● | ■ | ● | ● | ■ | ● | ● | ● | ■ | 50% |
| Can the system use Espiel for its prepayment model? | ● | ■ | ● | ● | ● | ● | ■ | ● | ● | ● | ● | 20% |

## Models

| | Can the system use Derivative Solutions for its prepayment model? | Can the system use Bond Market Association data for its prepayment model? | Can the system use a proprietary prepayment model? | Can the system model risks of default? | Can the system model risks of upgrades/downgrades? | Can the system model collateralised loan obligations and collateralised bond obligations? | Can the system model futures and forwards? | Swaps | Can the system model plain vanilla swaps? | Can the system model amortising swaps? | Can the system model index amortising swaps? | Can the system model asset or total return swaps? |
|---|---|---|---|---|---|---|---|---|---|---|---|---|
| Per cent Yes/Average | 30% | 10% | 40% | 30% | 40% | 20% | 100% | | 100% | 80% | 70% | 90% |
| Wilshire package | ● | ● | ■ | ● | ● | ● | ■ | | ■ | ■ | ■ | ■ |
| SunGard package | ■ | ● | ● | ■ | ■ | ● | ■ | | ■ | ■ | ■ | ■ |
| RiskMetrics ASP/package | ■ | ● | ● | ● | ● | ● | ■ | | ■ | ■ | + Dec-02 | ■ |
| Measurisk ASP | ● | ● | ● | ● | ● | ● | ■ | | ■ | ■ | ◆ REQ | ■ |
| GlobeOp package | ● | ● | + Jun-02 | ● | ● | ◆40 | ■ | | ■ | ■ | + REQ | ■ |
| DBRisk ASP | ■ | ● | ● | ● | ● | ● | ■ | | ■ | ● | ● | ■ |
| BlackRock Svc. bureau | ● | ● | ■ + Jun-02 | ■ | ■ | ■ | ■ | | ■ | ■ | ■ | ■ |
| Barra package | ● | ● | ■ | ● | ■ | +Aug-02 | ■ | | ■ | ◆41 | ■ | +Aug-02 |
| Askari ASP | ● | ■ | ● | ● | ● | ● | ■ | | ■ | ■ | ● | ● |
| Askari package | ● | ● | ● | ● | ● | ● | ■ | | ■ | ■ | ● | ● |
| Algorithmics package | ● | ● | ● | ■39 | ■ | ● | ■ | | ■ | ■ | ■ | ■ |

## Models

| | Basis swaps? | Credit default swaps? | Constant maturity swaps and constant maturity treasury? | Equity index swaps? | Volatility swaps? | Options | Options on cash bonds (European and American)? | Caps and floors? | Credit default options? | Currency options (European and American)? | Equity options (European and American)? |
|---|---|---|---|---|---|---|---|---|---|---|---|
| **Per cent Yes/Average** | 100% | 70% | 90% | 100% | 50% | | 100% | 100% | 60% | 100% | 100% |
| **Wilshire package** | ■ | ■ | ■ | ■ | ■ | | ■ | ■ | ■ | ■ | ■ |
| **SunGard package** | ■ | ■ | ■ | ■ | ● | | ■ | ■ | ■ | ■ | ■ |
| **RiskMetrics ASP/package** | ■ | ● | ■ | ■ | + Dec-02 | | ■ | ■ | ● | ■ | ■ |
| **Measurisk ASP** | ■ | ● | ■ | ■ | ● | | ■ | ■ | ● | ■ | ■ |
| **GlobeOp package** | ■ | + Jun-02 | ■ | ■ | + REQ | | ■ | ■ | + Jun-02 | ■ | ■ |
| **DBRisk ASP** | ■ | ● | ● | ■ | ● | | ■ | ■ | ● | ■ | ■ |
| **BlackRock Svc. bureau** | ■ | + Dec-02 | ■ | ■ | ■ | | ■ | ■ | + Dec-02 | ■ | ■ |
| **Barra package** | ■ | ■ | + Aug-02 | ■ | | | ■ | ■ | ■ | ■ | ■ |
| **Askari ASP** | ■ | + | ■ | ■ | ● | | ■ | ■ | ● | ■ | ■ |
| **Askari package** | ■ | + | ■ | ■ | ● | | ● | ■ | ● | ■ | ■ |
| **Algorithmics package** | ■ | ■ | ■ | ■ | ● | | ■ | ■ | ■ | ■ | ■ |

Can the system model basis swaps?
Can the system model credit default swaps?
Can the system model constant maturity swaps and constant maturity treasury?
Can the system model equity index swaps?
Can the system model volatility swaps?
Options
Can the system model options on cash bonds (European and American)?
Can the system model caps and floors?
Can the system model credit default options?
Can the system model currency options (European and American)?
Can the system model equity options (European and American)?

## Models

| Product | Can the system model equity index options (European and American)? | Can the system model options on futures (European and American)? | Can the system model swaptions (European and American)? | Barrier (knock-in/out) | Can the system model barrier or knock-in/out on an interest rate? | Can the system model barrier or knock-in/out on an index? | Can the system model binary options? | Can the system model quanto options? | Can the system model repos and reverse repos? | Alternative investments | Can the system model distressed debt? | Can the system model convertible arbitrage? |
|---|---|---|---|---|---|---|---|---|---|---|---|---|
| Per cent Yes/Average | 100% | 100% | 100% | | 90% | 80% | 80% | 60% | 90% | | 20% | 80% |
| Wilshire package | ■ | ■ | ■ | | ■ | ■ | ● | ● | ■ | | ■ | ● |
| SunGard package | ■ | ■ | ■ | | ■ | ● | ■ | ■ | ■ | | ● | ■ |
| RiskMetrics ASP/package | ■ | ■ | ■ | | ■ | ■ | +REQ | +REQ | ■ | | ● | ■ |
| Measurisk ASP | ■ | ■ | ■ | | ■ | ■ | ■ | +REQ | ■ | | +Mar-02 | ■ |
| GlobeOp package | ■ | ■ | ■ | | ■ | ■ | ■ | +REQ | ■ | | ◆[44] | ■ |
| DBRisk ASP | ■ | ■ | ■ | | ◆[42] | ◆[43] | ● | ■ | ■ | | ● | ■ |
| BlackRock Svc. bureau | ■ | ■ | ■ | | ■ | ■ | ● | ■ | ● | | ● | ● |
| Barra package | ■ | ■ | ■ | | ■ | + | ■ | ● | ● | | ● | ■ |
| Askari ASP | ■ | ■ | ■ | | ■ | ■ | ■ | ● | ■ | | ● | ■ |
| Askari package | ■ | ■ | ■ | | ■ | ■ | ■ | ● | ■ | | ● | ■ |
| Algorithmics package | ■ | ■ | ■ | | ■ | ■ | ■ | ■ | ■ | | ● | ■ |

## Models

| Question | Algorithmics package | Askari package | Askari ASP | Barra package | BlackRock Svc. bureau | DBRisk ASP | GlobeOp package | Measurisk ASP | RiskMetrics ASP/package | SunGard package | Wilshire package | Per cent Yes/Average |
|---|---|---|---|---|---|---|---|---|---|---|---|---|
| Can the system model event driven strategies including merger arbitrage? | ● | ● | ● | ■ | ● | ● | ✚ Mar-02 | ■ | ✚ Dec-02 | ● | ● | 40% |
| Can the system model real estate? | ● | ● | ● | ● | ● | ● | ● | ◆ 45 | ● | ● | ● | 00% |
| Proxy |  |  |  |  |  |  |  |  |  |  |  |  |
| Can the system proxy with an equity? | ■ | ■ | ■ | ■ | ✚ Jun-02 | ■ | ✚ Mar-02 | ■ | ■ | ■ | ■ | 100% |
| Can the system proxy with an index? | ■ | ■ | ■ | ■ | ✚ Jun-02 | ■ | ✚ Mar-02 | ■ | ■ | ■ | ■ | 100% |
| Can the system proxy with a risk factor? | ● | ● | ● | ■ | ✚ Jun-02 | ■ | ✚ Mar-02 | ■ | ✚ Dec-02 | ■ | ■ | 80% |
| Can the system beta adjust the proxy? | ■ | ■ | ■ | ■ | ✚ Jun-02 | ● | ■ | ■ | ■ | ■ | ■ | 90% |
| Can the system proxy using a combination of multiple equities or indices? | ■ | ■ | ■ | ● | ✚ Jun-02 | ■ | ✚ Mar-02 | ■ | ✚ Dec-02 | ■ | ■ | 90% |
| Can the system perform multiple regressions to determine proxy coefficients? | ● | ■ | ■ | ● | ✚ Jun-02 | ● | ✚ Mar-02 | ● | ● | ● | ● | 30% |

## Data

| | Does the system provide historical data? | What is the length of longest history that the system provides? | What is the length of history adjusted for the Euro? | What is the periodicity (monthly, weekly, daily) of the longest history? | What is the length of the period for which you have daily data? | What is the length of the historical period that your users typically use to calculate VAR (historical, VAR/covariance matrix)? | What is the length of the period generally used to calculate the profit and loss in the calculation of VAR? | History – user definition — Does the system provide the user control of the historical period? |
|---|---|---|---|---|---|---|---|---|
| Per cent Yes/Average | 90% | | | | | | | 40% |
| Wilshire package | ■ | 1977 | 1987 | Monthly | 1995 | 1981 | Unlimited | ■ |
| SunGard package | ■ | 1970 | 1970 | Daily | 1970 | Flexible | 1 Day | ● |
| RiskMetrics ASP/package | ■ | 1997 | 1997 | Daily | 1997 | Flexible | 1 Day | ■ |
| Measurisk ASP | ■ | 1980 | 1980 | Daily | 1980 | 2 Years | 1 Month | ◆ REQ |
| GlobeOp package | ■ | 1970 | 1970 | Daily | 1970 | 2 Years | 10 Days | ◆ REQ |
| DBRisk ASP | ■ | 1992 | 1996 | Weekly | 1998 | 3 Years | Varies | ◆ REQ |
| BlackRock Svc. bureau | ■ | 10 years | 2 years | Daily | 2-3 years | 252 days | 1 year | ◆ REQ |
| Barra package | ■ | 27 years | No problem | Monthly | 1994/1999 | Varies | 10 days | ◆ 46 |
| Askari ASP | ■ | 1995 | 1995 | Daily | 1995 | Flexible | Flexible | ■ |
| Askari package | ● | | | | | | | ■ |
| Algorithmics package | ● | | | | | | | ■ |

## Data

| | Per cent Yes/Average | Wilshire package | SunGard package | RiskMetrics ASP/package | Measurisk ASP | GlobeOp package | DBRisk ASP | BlackRock Svc. bureau | Barra package | Askari ASP | Askari package | Algorithmics package |
|---|---|---|---|---|---|---|---|---|---|---|---|---|
| **Weighting** | | | | | | | | | | | | |
| Can the system equal weight history? | 60% | ■ | ● | ■ | ◆ REQ | ◆ REQ | ■ | ■ | ● | ■ | ■ | ■ |
| Can the system exponentially weight history? | 80% | ■ | ● | ■ | ■ | ◆ REQ | ■ | ■ | ■ | ■ | ■ | ■ |
| Can the system support custom weighting of history for parametric or Monte Carlo VAR? | 30% | ■ | ● | ◆ | ◆ REQ | ◆ REQ | ■ | ● | ● | ◆ | ◆ | ■ |
| **Scrubbing** | | | | | | | | | | | | |
| Does the supplier scrub equity data? | 80% | ■ | ● | ■ | ■ | ■ | ■[47] | ■ | ■ | ■ | ● | ● |
| Does the supplier scrub fixed income data? | 80% | ■ | ● | ■ | ■ | ■ | ■[48] | ■ | ■ | ■ | ● | ● |
| **Market closed** | | | | | | | | | | | | |
| When data is not available because the market is closed does the supplier roll the last available data forward? | 70% | ■ | ● | ■ | ■ | ■ | ● | ■ | ■ | ■ | ● | ● |
| When data is not available because the market is closed does the supplier interpolate the missing days after the market reopens? | 30% | ● | ● | ■ | ■[49] | ● | ● | ● | ● | ■ | ● | ● |

## Data

| | User override of data — Can the user override history and retain the adjustment? | If the user overrides historical equity data and a corporate action (eg, split) requires the restatement of history, does the system produce the appropriate calculation? | Can the user override static data (eg, pe) and retain the override? | Download terms and conditions | Does the system interface to Bloomberg to retrieve terms and conditions? | Does the system interface to IDC to retrieve terms and conditions? | Sources | Does the system use Bloomberg data? | Does the system use Barra data? | Does the system use Datastream data? |
|---|---|---|---|---|---|---|---|---|---|---|
| Per cent Yes/Average | 20% | 10% | 40% | | 70% | 30% | | 50% | 30% | 30% |
| Wilshire package | ● | ● | ● | | ■ | ■ | | ■ | ● | ● |
| SunGard package | ● | ■ | ● | | ■ | ■ | | ■ | ● | ● |
| RiskMetrics ASP/package | ■ | ● | ■ | | ✚ Jan-02 | ● | | ● | ● | ● |
| Measurisk ASP | ● | ● | ● | | ■ | ● | | ■ | ● | ■ |
| GlobeOp package | ● | ● | ● | | ■ | ● | | ■ | ● | ● |
| DBRisk ASP | ● | ● | ● | | ■ | ● | | ■ | ■ | ■ |
| BlackRock Svc. bureau | ● | ● | ■ | | ● | ● | | ● | ■ | ● |
| Barra package | ● | ● | ■ | | ■ | ● | | ● | ■ | ● |
| Askari ASP | ● | ● | ● | | ● | ■ | | ● | ● | ■ |
| Askari package | ■ | ● | ■ | | ● | ● | | ● | ● | ● |
| Algorithmics package | ■ | ● | ■ | | ● | ● | | ● | ● | ● |

| Data | Does the system use EJV data? | Does the system use IDC data? | Does the system use MSCI data? | Does the system use Reuters data? | Does the system use Intex data? | Does the system use Chasen data? | Does the system use Trepp data? | Does the system use Muller data? | Does the system use DataMetrics data? | Does the system use Extel data? | Risk factors | What is the number of countries covered by factors in the standard set? | What is the number of factors in the standard set? |
|---|---|---|---|---|---|---|---|---|---|---|---|---|---|
| Per cent Yes/Average | 10% | 40% | 40% | 10% | 80% | 30% | 10% | 40% | 30% | 30% | | 54 | 690 |
| Wilshire package | ● | ■ | ■ | ● | ✚ Mar-02 | ■ | ● | ■ | ● | ■ | | 82 | 598 |
| SunGard package | ● | ■ | ● | ● | ■ | ■ | ● | ● | ■ | ● | | 50 | 850 |
| RiskMetrics ASP/package | ● | ● | ● | ● | ● | ● | ● | ● | ■ | ● | | 80 | 830 |
| Measurisk ASP | ● | ● | ■ | ● | ■ | ● | ● | ● | ● | ■ | | 45/70 | 900 |
| GlobeOp package | ● | ● | ● | ● | ✚ Jun-02 | ● | ● | ● | ● | ● | | 50 | 850 |
| DBRisk ASP | ● | ● | ■⁵⁰ | ● | ■ | ● | ● | ● | ● | ● | | 46 | 610 |
| BlackRock Svc. bureau | ■ | ■ | ● | ■ | ■ | ● | ■ | ■ | ● | ● | | 20 | 610 |
| Barra package | ● | ● | ■ | ● | ■ | ● | ● | ● | ● | ■ | | 57 | 517 |
| Askari ASP | ● | ■ | ● | ● | ● | ■ | ● | ■ | ✚ | ● | | 45 | 445 |
| Askari package | ● | ● | ● | ● | | ● | ● | ● | ● | ● | | | |
| Algorithmics package | ● | ● | ● | ● | ■ | ● | ● | ● | ● | ● | | | |

| Data | Algorithmics package | Askari package | Askari ASP | Barra package | BlackRock Svc. bureau | DBRisk ASP | GlobeOp package | Measurisk ASP | RiskMetrics ASP/package | SunGard package | Wilshire package | Per cent Yes/Average |
|---|---|---|---|---|---|---|---|---|---|---|---|---|
| What is the number of fixed income factors in the standard set (spreads and volatility factors counted separately)? | | | 400 | 200 | 300 | 400 | 400 | 450 | 750 | 400 | 198 | 389 |
| What is the number of foreign exchange factors in the standard set? | | | 45 | 57 | 50 | 60 | 50 | 50 | 80 | 50 | 120 | 62 |
| What is the number of equity factors in the standard set (volatilities counted separately)? | | | 0 | 260 | 260 | 150 | 400 | 400 | 0 | 400 | 280 | 239 |
| What is the number of sector factors for the US model? | | | 0 | 54 | 54 | 54 | 10 | 9 | 0 | 10 | 39 | 26 |
| What is the number of style factors for the US model? | | | 0 | 13 | 13 | 13 | 0 | 0 | 0 | 0 | 3 | 5 |
| For an equity security level VAR, can the system provide an analysis of what factors cause the risk in equities? | ● | ● | ◆51 | ■ | ■ | ■52 | ■ | ◆53 | ● | + Sep-02 | ● | 50% |
| For equities, can the system provide an analysis of what sector factors contribute to the risk? | ● | ● | ◆54 | ■ | ■ | ■ | ■ | ■ | ● | + Sep-02 | ■ | 70% |
| For equities, can the system provide an analysis of what style factors contribute to the risk? | ● | ● | + | ■ | ■ | ■ | + Mar-02 | ● | ● | + Sep-02 | ■55 | 70% |

# Data

## Specific

| Package | For equities, can the system provide a stock specific risk assuming that the residual risk of the equity is independent of all other equities? | For equities, can the system provide a stock specific risk recognising the actual correlation between the residuals and that of all other equities? | For equities, does the system recognise the relationship between ADRs and the underlying stock? | For equities, does the system recognise the relationship between multiclass shares of the same company? | For equities, does the system recognise the relationship between shares traded in multiple countries? | What is the number of countries for which equity data is provided? | What is the number of equities covered? |
|---|---|---|---|---|---|---|---|
| Per cent Yes/Average | 70% | 10% | 30% | 10% | 10% | 46 | 41111 |
| Wilshire package | ■ | ● | ● | ● | ● | 82 | 55000 |
| SunGard package | + Sep-02 | + Sep-02 | + Sep-02 | + Sep-02 | + Sep-02 | 45 | 45000 |
| RiskMetrics ASP/package | ● | ● | ● | ● | ● | 45 | 45000 |
| Measurisk ASP | ■ | ● | ● | ● | ● | 45 | 45000 |
| GlobeOp package | ■ | ● | ● | ● | ● | 50 | 45000 |
| DBRisk ASP | ■ | ● | ● | ● | ● | 46 | 45000 |
| BlackRock Svc. bureau | ■ | ● | ■ | ● | ● | + Jun-02 | + Jun-02 |
| Barra package | ■ | ● | ■ | ● | ● | 57 | 45000 |
| Askari ASP | ● | ■ | ■ | ■ | ■ | 45 | 45000 |
| Askari package | ● | ● | ● | ● | ● | 0 | 0 |
| Algorithmics package | ● | ● | ● | ● | ● | 0 | 0 |

## Equity coverage

The last two columns above ("What is the number of countries for which equity data is provided?" and "What is the number of equities covered?") belong to the Equity coverage section.

## Data

### Equity fundamental data

| | Does the system provide the market capitalisation of equities? | Does the system provide the price-to-earnings, price-to-book, and dividend yield of equities? | Does the system provide performance data (price appreciation plus dividends plus value of any corporate actions)? | Does the system provide the debt-to-equity of companies? | Does the system provide the MSCI index level data? | Does the system provide the Russell indices? | Does the system provide the MSCI constituency? | Does the system provide the Russell index constituency? |
|---|---|---|---|---|---|---|---|---|
| Per cent Yes/Average | 70% | 60% | 50% | 50% | 100% | 100% | 20% | 20% |
| Wilshire package | ■ | ■ | ■ | ■ | ■ | ■ | ◆ SUB | ◆ SUB |
| SunGard package | ■ | ■ | ● | ● | ■ | ■ | ◆ SUB | ◆ SUB |
| RiskMetrics ASP/package | ● | ● | ● | ● | ■ | ■ | ◆ SUB | ◆ SUB |
| Measurisk ASP | ■ | ● | ● | ● | ■ | ■ | ■[56] | ■[57] |
| GlobeOp package | ■ | ■ | ■ | ■ | ■ | ■ | ◆ SUB | ◆ SUB |
| DBRisk ASP | ● | ● | ● | ● | ■ | ■ | ● | ● |
| BlackRock Svc. bureau | + Jun-02 | + Jun-02 | + Jun-02 | + Jun-02 | + Jun-02 | + Jun-02 | + Jun-02 | + Jun-02 |
| Barra package | ■ | ■ | ■ | ■ | ■ | ■ | ◆ SUB | ◆ SUB |
| Askari ASP | ■ | ■ | ■ | ■ | ■ | ■ | ◆ SUB | ◆ SUB |
| Askari package | ● | ● | ● | ● | ■ | ■ | ◆ SUB | ◆ SUB |
| Algorithmics package | ● | ● | ● | ● | ■ | ■ | ◆ SUB | ◆ SUB |

*Equity indices — Indices*

*Constituency*

## Data — Government curve

| Government curve | Per cent Yes/Average | Wilshire package | SunGard package | RiskMetrics ASP/package | Measurisk ASP | GlobeOp package | DBRisk ASP | BlackRock Svc. bureau | Barra package | Askari ASP | Askari package | Algorithmics package |
|---|---|---|---|---|---|---|---|---|---|---|---|---|
| What is the number of countries for which government curves are provided? | 26 | 26 | 31 | 31 | 25 | 45 | 28 | 23 | 24 | 27 | 0 | 0 |
| What is the number of other countries for which government curves are provided? | 2 | 0 | 0 | 0 | 0 | 0 | 0 | 0 | 14 | 2 | 0 | 0 |
| Does the system provide a government curve for Argentina? | 20% | ● | ● | ● | ● | ■[59] | ■[58] | ● | ● | ● | ● | ● |
| Does the system provide a government curve for Australia? | 90% | ■ | ■ | ■ | ■ | ■ | ■ | ■ | ■ | ■ | ● | ● |
| Does the system provide a government curve for Austria? | 90% | ■ | ■ | ■ | ■ | ■ | ■ | ■ | ■ | ■ | ● | ● |
| Does the system provide a government curve for Belgium? | 90% | ■ | ■ | ■ | ■ | ■ | ■ | ■ | ■ | ■ | ● | ● |
| Does the system provide a government curve for Brazil? | 20% | ● | ● | ● | ● | ■ | ■[60] | ● | ● | ● | ● | ● |
| Does the system provide a government curve for Canada? | 90% | ■ | ■ | ■ | ■ | ■ | ■ | ■ | ■ | ■ | ● | ● |

| Data | Per cent Yes/Average | Does the system provide a government curve for Chile? | Does the system provide a government curve for China? | Does the system provide a government curve for Columbia? | Does the system provide a government curve for Czech Rep? | Does the system provide a government curve for Denmark? | Does the system provide a government curve for Euro? | Does the system provide a government curve for Finland? | Does the system provide a government curve for France? | Does the system provide a government curve for Germany? |
|---|---|---|---|---|---|---|---|---|---|---|
| | | 10% | 10% | 10% | 30% | 90% | 90% | 90% | 90% | 90% |
| Wilshire package | | ● | ● | ● | ● | ■ | ■ | ■ | ■ | ■ |
| SunGard package | | ● | ● | ● | ■ | ■ | ■ | ■ | ■ | ■ |
| RiskMetrics ASP/package | | ● | ● | ● | ■ | ■ | ■ | ■ | ■ | ■ |
| Measurisk ASP | | ● | ● | ● | ● | ■ | ■ | ■ | ■ | ■ |
| GlobeOp package | | ■[61] | ■[62] | ■[63] | ■ | ■ | ■ | ■ | ■ | ■ |
| DBRisk ASP | | ● | ● | ● | ● | ■ | ■ | ■ | ■ | ■ |
| BlackRock Svc. bureau | | ● | ● | ● | ■ | ■ | ■ | ■ | ■ | ■ |
| Barra package | | ● | ● | ● | ● | ■ | ■ | ■ | ■ | ■ |
| Askari ASP | | ● | ● | ● | ● | ■ | ■ | ■ | ■ | ■ |
| Askari package | | ● | ● | ● | ● | ● | ● | ● | ● | ● |
| Algorithmics package | | ● | ● | ● | ● | ● | ● | ● | ● | ● |

| Data | Does the system provide a government curve for Greece? | Does the system provide a government curve for Hong Kong? | Does the system provide a government curve for Hungary? | Does the system provide a government curve for India? | Does the system provide a government curve for Indonesia? | Does the system provide a government curve for Ireland? | Does the system provide a government curve for Israel? | Does the system provide a government curve for Italy? | Does the system provide a government curve for Japan? |
|---|---|---|---|---|---|---|---|---|---|
| Per cent Yes/Average | 80% | 60% | 40% | 40% | 30% | 90% | 10% | 90% | 90% |
| Wilshire package | ■ | ■ | ● | ● | ● | ■ | ● | ■ | ■ |
| SunGard package | ■ | ■ | ■ | ■ | ■ | ■ | ● | ■ | ■ |
| RiskMetrics ASP/package | ■ | ■ | ■ | ■ | ■ | ■ | ● | ■ | ■ |
| Measurisk ASP | ● | ■ | ● | ● | ● | ■ | ■ | ■ | ■ |
| GlobeOp package | ■ | ■ | ■ | ■ | ■ | ■ | ● | ■ | ■ |
| DBRisk ASP | ■ | ● | ● | ● | ● | ■ | ● | ■ | ■ |
| BlackRock Svc. bureau | ■ | ■ | ● | ● | ● | ■ | ● | ■ | ■ |
| Barra package | ■ | ● | ● | ● | ● | ■ | ● | ■ | ■ |
| Askari ASP | ■ | ● | ■ | ■ | ● | ■ | ● | ■ | ■ |
| Askari package | ● | ● | ● | ● | ● | ● | ● | ● | ● |
| Algorithmics package | ● | ● | ● | ● | ● | ● | ● | ● | ● |

| Data | Does the system provide a government curve for Malaysia? | Does the system provide a government curve for Mexico? | Does the system provide a government curve for Netherlands? | Does the system provide a government curve for New Zealand? | Does the system provide a government curve for Norway? | Does the system provide a government curve for Peru? | Does the system provide a government curve for Philippines? | Does the system provide a government curve for Poland? | Does the system provide a government curve for Portugal? |
|---|---|---|---|---|---|---|---|---|---|
| Per cent Yes/Average | 20% | 30% | 90% | 90% | 90% | 10% | 30% | 50% | 80% |
| Wilshire package | ● | ● | ■ | ■ | ■ | ● | ● | ■ | ■ |
| SunGard package | ● | ● | ■ | ■ | ■ | ● | ● | ■ | ■ |
| RiskMetrics ASP/package | ● | ● | ■ | ■ | ■ | ● | ● | ■ | ■ |
| Measurisk ASP | ● | ■ | ■ | ■ | ■ | ● | ■ | ● | ● |
| GlobeOp package | ■ | ■ | ■ | ■ | ■ | ■[64] | ■ | ■ | ■ |
| DBRisk ASP | ● | ■ | ■ | ■ | ■ | ● | ● | ● | ■ |
| BlackRock Svc. bureau | ● | ● | ■ | ■ | ■ | ● | ● | ● | ■ |
| Barra package | ● | ● | ■ | ■ | ■ | ● | ● | ■ | ■ |
| Askari ASP | ■ | ● | ■ | ■ | ■ | ● | ■ | ● | ■ |
| Askari package | ● | ● | ● | ● | ● | ● | ● | ● | ● |
| Algorithmics package | ● | ● | ● | ● | ● | ● | ● | ● | ● |

| | Russia | Singapore | Slovakia | South Africa | South Korea | Spain | Sweden | Switzerland | Taiwan |
|---|---|---|---|---|---|---|---|---|---|
| Per cent Yes/Average | 10% | 70% | 10% | 60% | 20% | 80% | 90% | 90% | 10% |
| Wilshire package | ● | ■ | ● | ■ | ● | ■ | ■ | ■ | ● |
| SunGard package | ● | ■ | ● | ■ | ● | ■ | ■ | ■ | ● |
| RiskMetrics ASP/package | ● | ■ | ● | ■ | ● | ■ | ■ | ■ | ● |
| Measurisk ASP | ● | ● | ● | ● | ● | ■ | ■ | ■ | ● |
| GlobeOp package | ■[65] | ■ | ■[66] | ■ | ■ | ■ | ■ | ■ | ■ |
| DBRisk ASP | ● | ■ | ● | ■ | ■ | ■ | ■ | ■ | ● |
| BlackRock Svc. bureau | ● | ■ | ● | ● | ● | ● | ■ | ■ | ● |
| Barra package | ● | ● | ● | ■ | ● | ■ | ■ | ■ | ● |
| Askari ASP | ● | ■ | ● | ● | ● | ■ | ■ | ■ | ● |
| Askari package | ● | ● | ● | ● | ● | ● | ● | ● | ● |
| Algorithmics package | ● | ● | ● | ● | ● | ● | ● | ● | ● |
| **Data** | Does the system provide a government curve for Russia? | Does the system provide a government curve for Singapore? | Does the system provide a government curve for Slovakia? | Does the system provide a government curve for South Africa? | Does the system provide a government curve for South Korea? | Does the system provide a government curve for Spain? | Does the system provide a government curve for Sweden? | Does the system provide a government curve for Switzerland? | Does the system provide a government curve for Taiwan? |

| Data | Does the system provide a government curve for Thailand? | Does the system provide a government curve for Turkey? | Does the system provide a government curve for UK? | Does the system provide a government curve for US? | Does the system provide a government curve for Venezuela? | Swap curve | What is the number of countries for which swap spreads are provided? | Does the system provide a swap curve for Argentina? | Does the system provide a swap curve for Australia? |
|---|---|---|---|---|---|---|---|---|---|
| Per cent Yes/Average | 30% | 20% | 90% | 90% | 00% | | 27 | 10% | 90% |
| Wilshire package | ● | ● | ■ | ■ | ● | | 26 | ● | ■[67] |
| SunGard package | ■ | ● | ■ | ■ | ● | | 24 | ● | ■ |
| RiskMetrics ASP/package | ■ | ● | ■ | ■ | ● | | 24 | ● | ■ |
| Measurisk ASP | ● | ■ | ■ | ■ | ● | | 43 | ■ | ■ |
| GlobeOp package | ■ | ■ | ■ | ■ | ● | | 41 | ● | ■ |
| DBRisk ASP | ● | ● | ■ | ■ | ● | | 10 | ● | ■ |
| BlackRock Svc. bureau | ● | ● | ■ | ■ | ● | | 24 | ● | ■ |
| Barra package | ● | ● | ■ | ■ | ● | | 26 | ● | ■ |
| Askari ASP | ● | ● | ■ | ■ | ● | | 28 | ● | ■ |
| Askari package | ● | ● | ● | ● | ● | | 0 | ● | ● |
| Algorithmics package | ● | ● | ● | ● | ● | | 0 | ● | ● |

| Data | Does the system provide a swap curve for Austria? | Does the system provide a swap curve for Belgium? | Does the system provide a swap curve for Brazil? | Does the system provide a swap curve for Canada? | Does the system provide a swap curve for Chile? | Does the system provide a swap curve for China? | Does the system provide a swap curve for Columbia? | Does the system provide a swap curve for Czech Rep? | Does the system provide a swap curve for Denmark? |
|---|---|---|---|---|---|---|---|---|---|
| Algorithmics package | ● | ● | ● | ● | ● | ● | ● | ● | ● |
| Askari package | ● | ● | ● | ● | ● | ● | ● | ● | ● |
| Askari ASP | ■ | ■ | ● | ■ | ● | ● | ● | ■ | ■ |
| Barra package | ■ | ■ | ● | ■ | ● | ● | ● | ■ | ■ |
| BlackRock Svc. bureau | ■ | ■ | ● | ■ | ● | ● | ● | ● | ■ |
| DBRisk ASP | ● | ● | ● | ■ | ● | ● | ● | ● | ● |
| GlobeOp package | ■ | ■ | ■[70] | ■ | ● | ■[72] | ● | ■ | ■ |
| Measurisk ASP | ■ | ■ | ■ | ■ | ■ | ■ | ● | ■ | ■ |
| RiskMetrics ASP/package | ● | ● | ■ | ■ | ● | ● | ● | ■ | ■ |
| SunGard package | ● | ● | ■ | ■ | ● | ● | ● | ■ | ■ |
| Wilshire package | ■[68] | ■[69] | ● | ■[71] | ● | ● | ● | ● | ■[73] |
| Per cent Yes/Average | 60% | 60% | 40% | 90% | 10% | 20% | 00% | 60% | 80% |

| Data | Does the system provide a swap curve for Euro? | Does the system provide a swap curve for Finland? | Does the system provide a swap curve for France? | Does the system provide a swap curve for Germany? | Does the system provide a swap curve for Greece? | Does the system provide a swap curve for Hong Kong? | Does the system provide a swap curve for Hungary? | Does the system provide a swap curve for India? | Does the system provide a swap curve for Indonesia? |
|---|---|---|---|---|---|---|---|---|---|
| Per cent Yes/Average | 70% | 60% | 70% | 70% | 60% | 80% | 40% | 40% | 50% |
| Wilshire package | ■[74] | ■[75] | ■[76] | ■[77] | ■[78] | ■[79] | ● | ● | ● |
| SunGard package | ■ | ● | ● | ● | ● | ■ | ■ | ■ | ■ |
| RiskMetrics ASP/package | ■ | ● | ● | ● | ● | ■ | ■ | ■ | ■ |
| Measurisk ASP | ● | ■ | ■ | ■ | ■ | ■ | ■ | ■ | ■ |
| GlobeOp package | ■ | ■ | ■ | ■ | ■ | ■ | ■ | ■ | ■ |
| DBRisk ASP | ● | ● | ■ | ■ | ● | ● | ● | ● | ● |
| BlackRock Svc. bureau | ■ | ■ | ■ | ■ | ■ | ■ | ● | ● | ● |
| Barra package | ■ | ■ | ■ | ■ | ■ | ■ | ● | ● | ● |
| Askari ASP | ■ | ■ | ■ | ■ | ■ | ■ | ● | ● | ■ |
| Askari package | ● | ● | ● | ● | ● | ● | ● | ● | ● |
| Algorithmics package | ● | ● | ● | ● | ● | ● | ● | ● | ● |

| Data | Does the system provide a swap curve for Ireland? | Does the system provide a swap curve for Israel? | Does the system provide a swap curve for Italy? | Does the system provide a swap curve for Japan? | Does the system provide a swap curve for Malaysia? | Does the system provide a swap curve for Mexico? | Does the system provide a swap curve for Netherlands? | Does the system provide a swap curve for New Zealand? | Does the system provide a swap curve for Norway? |
|---|---|---|---|---|---|---|---|---|---|
| Per cent Yes/Average | 60% | 10% | 70% | 90% | 40% | 20% | 60% | 80% | 80% |
| Wilshire package | ■[80] | ● | ■[81] | ■[82] | ● | ● | ■[83] | ■[84] | ■[85] |
| SunGard package | ● | ● | ● | ■ | ■ | ● | ● | ■ | ■ |
| RiskMetrics ASP/package | ● | ● | ● | ■ | ■ | ● | ● | ■ | ■ |
| Measurisk ASP | ■ | ■ | ■ | ■ | ■ | ■ | ■ | ■ | ■ |
| GlobeOp package | ■ | ● | ■ | ■ | ■ | ■ | ■ | ■ | ■ |
| DBRisk ASP | ● | ● | ■ | ■ | ● | ● | ● | ● | ● |
| BlackRock Svc. bureau | ■ | ● | ■ | ■ | ● | ● | ■ | ■ | ■ |
| Barra package | ■ | ● | ■ | ■ | ● | ● | ■ | ■ | ■ |
| Askari ASP | ■ | ● | ■ | ■ | ● | ● | ■ | ■ | ■ |
| Askari package | ● | ● | ● | ● | ● | ● | ● | ● | ● |
| Algorithmics package | ● | ● | ● | ● | ● | ● | ● | ● | ● |

| Data | Does the system provide a swap curve for Peru? | Does the system provide a swap curve for Philippines? | Does the system provide a swap curve for Poland? | Does the system provide a swap curve for Portugal? | Does the system provide a swap curve for Russia? | Does the system provide a swap curve for Singapore? | Does the system provide a swap curve for Slovakia? | Does the system provide a swap curve for South Africa? | Does the system provide a swap curve for South Korea? |
|---|---|---|---|---|---|---|---|---|---|
| Per cent Yes/Average | 00% | 40% | 60% | 60% | 20% | 70% | 00% | 70% | 20% |
| Wilshire package | ● | ● | ■[87] | ■[88] | ● | ■[90] | ● | ■[91] | ● |
| SunGard package | ● | ■ | ■ | ● | ● | ■ | ● | ■ | ● |
| RiskMetrics ASP/package | ● | ■ | ■ | ● | ● | ■ | ● | ■ | ● |
| Measurisk ASP | ● | ■ | ■ | ● | ■ | ■ | ● | ■ | ■ |
| GlobeOp package | ● | ■[86] | ■ | ■ | ■[89] | ■ | ● | ■ | ■ |
| DBRisk ASP | ● | ● | ● | ● | ● | ● | ● | ● | ● |
| BlackRock Svc. bureau | ● | ● | ● | ■ | ● | ■ | ● | ● | ● |
| Barra package | ● | ● | ■ | ■ | ● | ● | ● | ■ | ● |
| Askari ASP | ● | ● | ● | ■ | ● | ■ | ● | ■ | ● |
| Askari package | ● | ● | ● | ● | ● | ● | ● | ● | ● |
| Algorithmics package | ● | ● | ● | ● | ● | ● | ● | ● | ● |

| Data | Spain | Sweden | Switzerland | Taiwan | Thailand | Turkey | UK | US | this country |
|---|---|---|---|---|---|---|---|---|---|
| Per cent Yes/Average | 70% | 80% | 90% | 40% | 50% | 20% | 90% | 90% | 20% |
| Wilshire package | ■[92] | ■[93] | ■[94] | ● | ● | ● | ■[98] | ■[99] | ● |
| SunGard package | ● | ■ | ■ | ■ | ■ | ● | ■ | ■ | ● |
| RiskMetrics ASP/package | ● | ■ | ■ | ■ | ■ | ● | ■ | ■ | ● |
| Measurisk ASP | ■ | ■ | ■ | ■ | ■ | ■ | ■ | ■ | ■ |
| GlobeOp package | ■ | ■ | ■ | ■[95] | ■[96] | ■[97] | ■ | ■ | ■[100] |
| DBRisk ASP | ■ | ● | ■ | ● | ● | ● | ■ | ■ | ● |
| BlackRock Svc. bureau | ■ | ■ | ■ | ● | ● | ● | ■ | ■ | ● |
| Barra package | ■ | ■ | ■ | ● | ● | ● | ■ | ■ | ● |
| Askari ASP | ■ | ■ | ■ | ● | ■ | ● | ■ | ■ | ● |
| Askari package | ● | ● | ● | ● | ● | ● | ● | ● | ● |
| Algorithmics package | ● | ● | ● | ● | ● | ● | ● | ● | ● |

Column questions: Does the system provide a swap curve for Spain? / for Sweden? / for Switzerland? / for Taiwan? / for Thailand? / for Turkey? / for UK? / for US? / for this country?

## Data

| Corporate Spreads | Algorithmics package | Askari package | Askari ASP | Barra package | BlackRock Svc. bureau | DBRisk ASP | GlobeOp package | Measurisk ASP | RiskMetrics ASP/package | SunGard package | Wilshire package | Per cent Yes/Average |
|---|---|---|---|---|---|---|---|---|---|---|---|---|
| What is the number of countries for which corporate curves are provided? | 0 | 0 | 3 | 1 | 1 | 0 | 3 | 1 | 2 | 2 | 20 | 3 |
| What is the total number of corporate curves provided? | 0 | 0 | 12 | 55 | 68 | 0 | 33 | 35 | 26 | 26 | 179 | 43 |
| What is the number of corporate curves provided for Argentina? | | | | | | | | | | | | |
| What is the number of corporate curves provided for Australia? | | | | | | | | | | | 8 | 8 |
| What is the number of corporate curves provided for Austria? | | | | | | | | | | | 8 | 8 |
| What is the number of corporate curves provided for Belgium? | | | | | | | | | | | 8 | 8 |
| What is the number of corporate curves provided for Brazil? | | | | | | | | | | | | |
| What is the number of corporate curves provided for Canada? | | | 3 | | | | | | | | 8 | 6 |
| What is the number of corporate curves provided for Chile? | | | | | | | | | | | | |

| Data | Algorithmics package | Askari package | Askari ASP | Barra package | BlackRock Svc. bureau | DBRisk ASP | GlobeOp package | Measurisk ASP | RiskMetrics ASP/package | SunGard package | Wilshire package | Per cent Yes/Average |
|---|---|---|---|---|---|---|---|---|---|---|---|---|
| What is the number of corporate curves provided for China? | | | | | | | | | | | | |
| What is the number of corporate curves provided for Columbia? | | | | | | | | | | | | |
| What is the number of corporate curves provided for Czech Rep? | | | | | | | | | | | | |
| What is the number of corporate curves provided for Denmark? | | | | | | | | | | | | |
| What is the number of corporate curves provided for Euro? | | | 4 | | | | 4 | | 10 | 10 | 8 | 7 |
| What is the number of corporate curves provided for Finland? | | | | | | | | | | | 8 | 8 |
| What is the number of corporate curves provided for France? | | | | | | | | | | | 8 | 8 |
| What is the number of corporate curves provided for Germany? | | | | | | | | | | | 8 | 8 |
| What is the number of corporate curves provided for Greece? | | | | | | | | | | | 8 | 8 |

| Data | Hong Kong | Hungary | India | Indonesia | Ireland | Israel | Italy | Japan | Malaysia |
|---|---|---|---|---|---|---|---|---|---|
| Per cent Yes/Average | 8 | | | | | 8 | 8 | 6 | |
| Wilshire package | 8 | | | | | 8 | 8 | 8 | |
| SunGard package | | | | | | | | | |
| RiskMetrics ASP/package | | | | | | | | | |
| Measurisk ASP | | | | | | | | | |
| GlobeOp package | | | | | | | | 4 | |
| DBRisk ASP | | | | | | | | | |
| BlackRock Svc. bureau | | | | | | | | | |
| Barra package | | | | | | | | | |
| Askari ASP | | | | | | | | | |
| Askari package | | | | | | | | | |
| Algorithmics package | | | | | | | | | |

Column questions: *What is the number of corporate curves provided for Hong Kong? / Hungary? / India? / Indonesia? / Ireland? / Israel? / Italy? / Japan? / Malaysia?*

| Data | Algorithmics package | Askari package | Askari ASP | Barra package | BlackRock Svc. bureau | DBRisk ASP | GlobeOp package | Measurisk ASP | RiskMetrics ASP/package | SunGard package | Wilshire package | Per cent Yes/Average |
|---|---|---|---|---|---|---|---|---|---|---|---|---|
| What is the number of corporate curves provided for Mexico? | | | | | | | | | | | | |
| What is the number of corporate curves provided for Netherlands? | | | | | | | | | | | 8 | 8 |
| What is the number of corporate curves provided for New Zealand? | | | | | | | | | | | | |
| What is the number of corporate curves provided for Norway? | | | | | | | | | | | | |
| What is the number of corporate curves provided for Peru? | | | | | | | | | | | | |
| What is the number of corporate curves provided for Philippines? | | | | | | | | | | | | |
| What is the number of corporate curves provided for Poland? | | | | | | | | | | | | |
| What is the number of corporate curves provided for Portugal? | | | | | | | | | | | 8 | 8 |
| What is the number of corporate curves provided for Russia? | | | | | | | | | | | | |

| Data | What is the number of corporate curves provided for Singapore? | What is the number of corporate curves provided for Slovakia? | What is the number of corporate curves provided for South Africa? | What is the number of corporate curves provided for South Korea? | What is the number of corporate curves provided for Spain? | What is the number of corporate curves provided for Sweden? | What is the number of corporate curves provided for Switzerland? | What is the number of corporate curves provided for Taiwan? | What is the number of corporate curves provided for Thailand? |
|---|---|---|---|---|---|---|---|---|---|
| Per cent Yes/Average | | | | | 8 | 8 | 8 | | |
| Wilshire package | | | | | 8 | 8 | 8 | | |
| SunGard package | | | | | | | | | |
| RiskMetrics ASP/package | | | | | | | | | |
| Measurisk ASP | | | | | | | | | |
| GlobeOp package | | | | | | | | | |
| DBRisk ASP | | | | | | | | | |
| BlackRock Svc. bureau | | | | | | | | | |
| Barra package | | | | | | | | | |
| Askari ASP | | | | | | | | | |
| Askari package | | | | | | | | | |
| Algorithmics package | | | | | | | | | |

| Data | Algorithmics package | Askari package | Askari ASP | Barra package | BlackRock Svc. bureau | DBRisk ASP | GlobeOp package | Measurisk ASP | RiskMetrics ASP/package | SunGard package | Wilshire package | Per cent Yes/Average |
|---|---|---|---|---|---|---|---|---|---|---|---|---|
| What is the number of corporate curves provided for Turkey? | | | | | | | | | | | | |
| What is the number of corporate curves provided for UK? | | | | | | | | | | | 8 | 8 |
| What is the number of corporate curves provided for US? | | | 5 | 55 | 68 | | 25 | 35 | 16 | 16 | 27 | 31 |
| Number of corporate curves provided for this country? | | | | | | | | | | | | |
| Muni/provincial/local | 0 | 0 | | | | 0 | | | | | | |
| What is the number of countries for which provincial curves are provided? | 0 | 0 | 1 | 1 | 1 | 0 | 1 | 1 | 1 | 1 | 1 | 1 |
| What is the number of provincial/ local curves provided for Argentina? | | | 1 | 4 | 11 | 0 | 4 | 20 | 5 | 5 | 11 | 6 |
| What is the number of provincial/ local curves provided for Australia? | | | | | | | | | | | | |
| What is the number of provincial/ local curves provided for Austria? | | | | | | | | | | | | |

| Data | What is the number of provincial/ local curves provided for Belgium? | What is the number of provincial/ local curves provided for Brazil? | What is the number of provincial/ local curves provided for Canada? | What is the number of provincial/ local curves provided for Chile? | What is the number of provincial/ local curves provided for China? | What is the number of provincial/ local curves provided for Columbia? | What is the number of provincial/ local curves provided for Czech Rep? | What is the number of provincial/ local curves provided for Denmark? | What is the number of provincial/ local curves provided for Finland? |
|---|---|---|---|---|---|---|---|---|---|
| Algorithmics package | | | | | | | | | |
| Askari package | | | | | | | | | |
| Askari ASP | | | | | | | | | |
| Barra package | | | | | | | | | |
| BlackRock Svc. bureau | | | | | | | | | |
| DBRisk ASP | | | | | | | | | |
| GlobeOp package | | | | | | | | | |
| Measurisk ASP | | | | | | | | | |
| RiskMetrics ASP/package | | | | | | | | | |
| SunGard package | | | | | | | | | |
| Wilshire package | | | | | | | | | |
| Per cent Yes/Average | | | | | | | | | |

| Data | Algorithmics package | Askari package | Askari ASP | Barra package | BlackRock Svc. bureau | DBRisk ASP | GlobeOp package | Measurisk ASP | RiskMetrics ASP/package | SunGard package | Wilshire package | Per cent Yes/Average |
|------|---|---|---|---|---|---|---|---|---|---|---|---|
| What is the number of provincial/ local curves provided for France? | | | | | | | | | | | | |
| What is the number of provincial/ local curves provided for Germany? | | | | | | | | | | | | |
| What is the number of provincial/ local curves provided for Greece? | | | | | | | | | | | | |
| What is the number of provincial/ local curves provided for Hong Kong? | | | | | | | | | | | | |
| What is the number of provincial/ local curves provided for Hungary? | | | | | | | | | | | | |
| What is the number of provincial/ local curves provided for India? | | | | | | | | | | | | |
| What is the number of provincial/ local curves provided for Indonesia? | | | | | | | | | | | | |
| What is the number of provincial/ local curves provided for Ireland? | | | | | | | | | | | | |
| What is the number of provincial/ local curves provided for Israel? | | | | | | | | | | | | |

| | What is the number of provincial/ local curves provided for Italy? | What is the number of provincial/ local curves provided for Japan? | What is the number of provincial/ local curves provided for Malaysia? | What is the number of provincial/ local curves provided for Mexico? | What is the number of provincial/ local curves provided for Netherlands? | What is the number of provincial/ local curves provided for New Zealand? | What is the number of provincial/ local curves provided for Norway? | What is the number of provincial/ local curves provided for Peru? | What is the number of provincial/ local curves provided for Philippines? |
|---|---|---|---|---|---|---|---|---|---|
| Per cent Yes/Average | | | | | | | | | |
| Wilshire package | | | | | | | | | |
| SunGard package | | | | | | | | | |
| RiskMetrics ASP/package | | | | | | | | | |
| Measurisk ASP | | | | | | | | | |
| GlobeOp package | | | | | | | | | |
| DBRisk ASP | | | | | | | | | |
| BlackRock Svc. bureau | | | | | | | | | |
| Barra package | | | | | | | | | |
| Askari ASP | | | | | | | | | |
| Askari package | | | | | | | | | |
| Algorithmics package | | | | | | | | | |
| **Data** | | | | | | | | | |

| Data | What is the number of provincial/local curves provided for Poland? | What is the number of provincial/local curves provided for Portugal? | What is the number of provincial/local curves provided for Russia? | What is the number of provincial/local curves provided for Singapore? | What is the number of provincial/local curves provided for Slovakia? | What is the number of provincial/local curves provided for South Africa? | What is the number of provincial/local curves provided for South Korea? | What is the number of provincial/local curves provided for Spain? | What is the number of provincial/local curves provided for Sweden? |
|---|---|---|---|---|---|---|---|---|---|
| Per cent Yes/Average | | | | | | | | | |
| Wilshire package | | | | | | | | | |
| SunGard package | | | | | | | | | |
| RiskMetrics ASP/package | | | | | | | | | |
| Measurisk ASP | | | | | | | | | |
| GlobeOp package | | | | | | | | | |
| DBRisk ASP | | | | | | | | | |
| BlackRock Svc. bureau | | | | | | | | | |
| Barra package | | | | | | | | | |
| Askari ASP | | | | | | | | | |
| Askari package | | | | | | | | | |
| Algorithmics package | | | | | | | | | |

| Data | Per cent Yes/Average | Wilshire package | SunGard package | RiskMetrics ASP/package | Measurisk ASP | GlobeOp package | DBRisk ASP | BlackRock Svc. bureau | Barra package | Askari ASP | Askari package | Algorithmics package |
|---|---|---|---|---|---|---|---|---|---|---|---|---|
| What is the number of provincial/local curves provided for Switzerland? | | | | | | | | | | | | |
| What is the number of provincial/local curves provided for Taiwan? | | | | | | | | | | | | |
| What is the number of provincial/local curves provided for Thailand? | | | | | | | | | | | | |
| What is the number of provincial/local curves provided for Turkey? | | | | | | | | | | | | |
| What is the number of provincial/local curves provided for UK? | | | | | | | | | | | | |
| What is the number of provincial/local curves provided for US? | 8 | 11 | 5 | 5 | 20 | 4 | | 11 | 4 | 1 | | |
| What is the number of provincial/local curves provided for Venezuela? | | | | | | | | | | | | |
| MBS (cash flow generator) | | | | | | | | | | | | |
| Does the system use Intex for MBS cash flows? | 80% | ● | ■ | ✛ Aug-02 | ■ | ✛ Jun-02 | ■[101] | ■ | ■ | ● | ● | ■ |
| Does the system use Chasen for MBS cash flows? | 30% | ■ | ■ | ● | ● | ● | ● | ● | ● | ■ | ● | ● |

## Data

| Question | Algorithmics package | Askari package | Askari ASP | Barra package | BlackRock Svc. bureau | DBRisk ASP | GlobeOp package | Measurisk ASP | RiskMetrics ASP/package | SunGard package | Wilshire package | Per cent Yes/Average |
|---|---|---|---|---|---|---|---|---|---|---|---|---|
| Does the system use Trepp for MBS cash flows? | ● | ● | ● | ● | ■ | ● | ● | ● | ● | ● | ● | 10% |
| **ABS (cash flow generator)** | | | | | | | | | | | | |
| Does the system use Intex for ABS cash flows? | ■ | ● | ● | ■ | ■ | ■ [102] | + Jun-02 | ■ | ● | ■ | + Mar-02 | 80% |
| Does the system use Davidson for ABS cash flows? | ■ | ● | ● | ● | ● | ● | ● | ■ | ● | ■ | ● | 30% |
| **Bond indices** | | | | | | | | | | | | |
| What is the number of bond indices provided? | 1 | 1 | 1 | 0 | 2 | 1 | 1 | 1 | 2 | 1 | 3 | 1 |
| Does the system provide CSFB bond indices? | ◆ SUB | ◆ SUB | ◆ SUB | ◆ SUB | ● | ◆ SUB | ◆ SUB | ◆ SUB | ◆ SUB | ◆ SUB | ◆ SUB | 00% |
| Does the system provide JP Morgan bond indices? | ◆ SUB | ◆ SUB | ◆ SUB | ◆ SUB | ◆ | ◆ SUB | ◆ SUB | ◆ SUB | ■ | ◆ SUB | ■ [103] | 20% |
| Does the system provide Lehman bond indices? | ◆ SUB | ◆ SUB | ◆ SUB | ◆ SUB | ◆ | ◆ SUB | ◆ SUB | ◆ SUB | ◆ SUB | ◆ SUB | ◆ SUB | 00% |
| Does the system provide Lipper bond indices? | ◆ SUB | ■ | ■ | ● | ● | ◆ SUB | ◆ SUB | ◆ SUB | ◆ SUB | ◆ SUB | ◆ SUB | 00% |
| Does the system provide Merrill Lynch bond indices? | ■ | ◆ SUB | ◆ SUB | ◆ | ■ | ■ | ■ | ■ | ■ | ■ | ■ | 90% |
| Does the system provide Morgan Stanley bond indices? | ◆ SUB | ◆ SUB | ◆ SUB | ● | ● | ◆ SUB | ◆ SUB | ◆ SUB | ◆ SUB | ◆ SUB | ◆ SUB | 00% |
| Does the system provide Salomon bond indices? | ◆ SUB | ◆ SUB | ◆ SUB | ◆ SUB | ■ | ◆ SUB | ◆ SUB | ◆ SUB | ◆ SUB | ◆ SUB | ■ SUB | 20% |

## Data

| Question | Algorithmics package | Askari package | Askari ASP | Barra package | BlackRock Svc. bureau | DBRisk ASP | GlobeOp package | Measurisk ASP | RiskMetrics ASP/package | SunGard package | Wilshire package | Per cent Yes/Average |
|---|---|---|---|---|---|---|---|---|---|---|---|---|
| What is the number of bond indices for which constituents are provided? | 1 | 1 | 1 | 1 | 2 | 1 | 1 | 1 | 2 | 1 | 3 | 1 |
| Does the system provide CSFB bond index constituents? | ◆SUB | ◆SUB | ◆SUB | ◆SUB | ● | ◆SUB | ◆SUB | ◆SUB | ◆SUB | ◆SUB | ◆SUB | 00% |
| Does the system provide JP Morgan bond index constituents? | ◆SUB | ◆SUB | ◆SUB | ◆SUB | ◆ | ◆SUB | ◆SUB | ◆SUB | ■ | ◆SUB | ■SUB | 20% |
| Does the system provide Lehman bond index constituents? | ◆SUB | ◆SUB | ◆SUB | ◆SUB | ◆ | ◆SUB | ◆SUB | ◆SUB | ◆SUB | ◆SUB | ◆SUB | 00% |
| Does the system provide Lipper bond index constituents? | ◆SUB | ◆SUB | ◆SUB | ◆SUB | ● | ◆SUB | ◆SUB | ◆SUB | ◆SUB | ◆SUB | ◆SUB | 00% |
| Does the system provide Merrill Lynch bond index constituents? | ■ | ■ | ■ | ■ | ■ | ■ | ■ | ■ | ■ | ■ | ■ | 100% |
| Does the system provide Morgan Stanley bond index constituents? | ◆SUB | ◆SUB | ◆SUB | ◆SUB | ● | ◆SUB | ◆SUB | ◆SUB | ◆SUB | ◆SUB | ◆SUB | 00% |
| Does the system provide Salomon bond index constituents? | ◆SUB | ◆SUB | ◆SUB | ◆SUB | ■ | ◆SUB | ◆SUB | ◆SUB | ◆SUB | ◆SUB | ■SUB | 20% |
| Does the system provide data in FX? | ● | ● | ■ | ■ | ■ | ■ | ■ | ■ | ■ | ■ | ■ | 90% |
| Does the system provide data on commodities? | ● | ● | ■ | ● | ● | ■ | ■ | ■ | ■ | ● | ● | 50% |

## Data

| Question | Per cent Yes/Average | Wilshire package | SunGard package | RiskMetrics ASP/package | Measurisk ASP | GlobeOp package | DBRisk ASP | BlackRock Svc. bureau | Barra package | Askari ASP | Askari package | Algorithmics package |
|---|---|---|---|---|---|---|---|---|---|---|---|---|
| Does the system provide data on direct investments in real estate (not REITs)? | 00% | ● | ● | ● | ◆[104] | ● | ● | ● | ● | ● | ● | ● |
| **Volatilities** | | | | | | | | | | | | |
| Does the system provide historical volatility data? | 70% | ■ | ■ | ■ | ● | ■ | ✚ Dec-02 | ■ | ● | ■ | ● | ● |
| Does the system provide market implied volatility data? | 80% | ■ | ■ | ■ | ✚ Mar-02 | ✚ Dec-01 | ✚ Dec-02 | ■ | ● | ✚ Dec-01 | ● | ● |
| If so, does the system provide a smile? | 60% | ● | ■ | ■ | ✚ Mar-02 | ✚ Dec-01 | ● | ■ | ● | ✚ Dec-01 | ● | ● |
| If so, does the system provide volatility over maturities? | 60% | ● | ■ | ■ | ✚ Mar-02 | ✚ Dec-01 | ● | ■ | ● | ✚ Dec-01 | ● | ● |

## Stress test

| Historical scenarios | User can specify a particular time period over which the portfolio should be evaluated? | How many prepackaged scenarios does the system supply? | Does the system provide a prepackaged scenario of the '1987 stock' crisis? | Does the system provide a prepackaged scenario of the '1990 Nikkei' crisis? | Does the system provide a prepackaged scenario of the '1990 high yield' crisis? | Does the system provide a prepackaged scenario of the 'Gulf War' crisis? | Does the system provide a prepackaged scenario of the '1992 currency' crisis? | Does the system provide a prepackaged scenario of the '1993 mortgage' crisis? |
|---|---|---|---|---|---|---|---|---|
| Per cent Yes/Average | 60% | 9 | 30% | 20% | 20% | 30% | 20% | 30% |
| Wilshire package | ■ | 0 | ● | ● | ● | ● | ● | ● |
| SunGard package | ■ | 0 | ● | ● | ● | ● | ● | ● |
| RiskMetrics ASP/package | ■ | 5 | ■ | ✚ | ✚ Dec-02 | ■105 | ✚ | ✚ Dec-02 |
| Measurisk ASP | ● | 21 | ■ | ● | ● | ■ | ● | ■ |
| GlobeOp package | ◆ REQ | 3 | ● | ● | ● | ● | ● | ● |
| DBRisk ASP | ● | 0 | ● | ● | ● | ● | ● | ● |
| BlackRock Svc. bureau | ■ | 20 | ■ | ■ | ■ | ■ | ■ | ■ |
| Barra package | ◆ REQ | 0 | ● | ● | ● | ● | ● | ● |
| Askari ASP | ■ | | ● | ● | ● | ● | ● | ● |
| Askari package | ■ | | ● | ● | ● | ● | ● | ● |
| Algorithmics package | ■ | 36 | ● | ● | ● | ● | ● | ● |

## Stress test

| | Does the system provide a prepackaged scenario of the '1994 rate hike' crisis? | Does the system provide a prepackaged scenario of the '1994 Mexico' crisis? | Does the system provide a prepackaged scenario of the '1995 Latin America' crisis? | Does the system provide a prepackaged scenario of the '1997 Asian' crisis? | Does the system provide a prepackaged scenario of the 'Fall 1998' crisis? | Does the system provide a prepackaged scenario of the '2000 technology' crisis? | Does the system provide a prepackaged scenario of the '2001 technology' crisis? | Shock scenarios | Does the system provide the ability to shock a security independent of other holdings? |
|---|---|---|---|---|---|---|---|---|---|
| Per cent Yes/Average | 40% | 30% | 20% | 30% | 40% | 30% | 30% | | 60% |
| Wilshire package | ● | ● | ● | ● | ● | ● | ● | | ■ |
| SunGard package | ● | ● | ● | ● | ● | ● | ● | | ■ |
| RiskMetrics ASP/package | + Dec-02 | ■[106] | + | ■[107] | ■ | ■ | ■ | | ■ |
| Measurisk ASP | ■ | ■ | ● | ■ | ■ | ■ | ■ | | ● |
| GlobeOp package | ● | ● | ● | ● | ● | ● | ● | | ● |
| DBRisk ASP | ● | ● | ● | ● | ● | ● | ● | | ● |
| BlackRock Svc. bureau | ■ | ■ | ■ | ■ | ■ | ■ | ■ | | ■ |
| Barra package | ● | ● | ● | ● | ● | ● | ● | | ● |
| Askari ASP | ■ | ● | ● | ● | ● | ● | ● | | ■ |
| Askari package | ● | ● | ● | ● | ● | ● | ● | | ■ |
| Algorithmics package | ● | ● | ● | ● | ■ | ● | ● | | ■ |

## Stress test

| | Does the system provide the ability to shock a factor independently of other securities/factors? | Does the system provide the ability to shock a security or risk factor and have other securities/risk factors move based on historical correlations? | Provide Greeks | Does the system provide the Greeks on a security level? | Does the system provide the Greeks for a portfolio or subportfolio? | Interactive "what if" | Does the system permit you to evaluate a security that is currently not in the portfolio? |
|---|---|---|---|---|---|---|---|
| Per cent Yes/Average | 100% | 90% | | 100% | 90% | | 80% |
| Wilshire package | ■ | ■ | | ■ | ● | | ■ |
| SunGard package | ■ | ■ | | ■ | ■ | | ■ |
| RiskMetrics ASP/package | ■ | ■ | | ■ | ■ | | ■ |
| Measurisk ASP | + Apr-02 | + Apr-02 | | ■ | ■ | | + Mar-02 |
| GlobeOp package | ■ | ■ | | ■ | ■ | | ● |
| DBRisk ASP | ■ | ■ | | ■ | ■ | | ● |
| BlackRock Svc. bureau | ■ | ■ | | ■ | ■ | | ■ |
| Barra package | + Dec-02 | + Dec-02 | | + Aug-02 | + Aug-02 | | ■ |
| Askari ASP | ■ | ● | | ■ | ■ | | ■ |
| Askari package | ■ | ● | | ■ | ■ | | ■ |
| Algorithmics package | ■ | ■ | | ■ | ■ | | ■ |

# Related applications

## Portfolio construction

| Question | Per cent Yes/Average | Wilshire package | SunGard package | RiskMetrics ASP/package | Measurisk ASP | GlobeOp package | DBRisk ASP | BlackRock Svc. bureau | Barra package | Askari ASP | Askari package | Algorithmics package |
|---|---|---|---|---|---|---|---|---|---|---|---|---|
| Can the system provide a portfolio optimiser? | 70% | ■ | ✚ Dec-02 | ✚ Dec-02 | ● | ✚ Jun-02 | ● | ◆[108] | ■ | ✚ | ✚ | ■ |
| Can the system provide a quadratic optimiser? | 70% | ■ | ✚ Dec-02 | ✚ Dec-02 | ● | ✚ Jun-02 | ● | ● | ■ | ✚ | ✚ | ■ |
| Can the system provide a stochastic optimiser? | 10% | ● | ● | ● | ● | ● | ● | ● | ● | ● | ● | ■ |
| Can the system support fixed income portfolio optimisation? | 80% | ■ | ✚ Dec-02 | ✚ Dec-02 | ● | ✚ Jun-02 | ● | ■ | ■ | ✚ | ✚ | ■ |
| Can the system support equity portfolio optimisation? | 80% | ■ | ✚ Dec-02 | ✚ Dec-02 | ● | ✚ Jun-02 | ● | ✚[109] | ■ | ✚ | ✚ | ■ |
| Can the system support equity portfolio optimisation by sector? | 80% | ■ | ✚ Dec-02 | ✚ Dec-02 | ● | ✚ Jun-02 | ● | ✚[110] | ■ | ✚ | ✚ | ■ |
| Can the system support equity portfolio optimisation by style? | 50% | ■ | ✚ Dec-02 | ● | ● | ✚ Jun-02 | ● | ✚[111] | ■ | ● | ● | ● |
| Can the system support the identification of a best hedge? | 90% | ■ | ✚ Dec-02 | ✚ Dec-02 | ✚ May-02 | ■ | ● | ✚[112] | ■ | ✚ | ✚ | ■ |
| Can the system generate portfolio recommendations? | 90% | ■ | ■ | ✚ Dec-02 | ✚ May-02 | ■ | ● | ■ | ■ | ✚ | ✚ | ■ |
| Can the system perform performance attribution? | 70% | ■ | ✚ Dec-02 | ✚ Dec-02 | ✚ May-02 | ✚ Jan-02 | ● | ◆[113] | ✚ | ✚ | ● | ● |
| Can the system perform performance attribution for fixed income portfolios? | 80% | ■ | ✚ Dec-02 | ✚ Dec-02 | ✚ May-02 | ✚ Jan-02 | ● | ■ | ✚ | ✚ | ● | ● |

## Related applications

| System | Can the system perform portfolio attribution for equity portfolios? | Can the system perform portfolio attribution for equity portfolios by sector? | Can the system perform portfolio attribution for equity portfolios by style? | Can the system provide AIMR compliant performance measurement? | Can the system provide credit risk management capabilities? | Can the system provide a basic trading system? | Can the system perform portfolio accounting? | Can the system provide operational risk management analysis capabilities? |
|---|---|---|---|---|---|---|---|---|
| Per cent Yes/Average | 80% | 80% | 70% | 30% | 60% | 40% | 30% | 20% |
| Wilshire package | ■ | ■ | ■ | ■ | ■ | + [117] | ■ | ● |
| SunGard package | + Dec-02 | + Dec-02 | + Dec-02 | ◆ [114] | ■ | ■ | ◆ [118] | ■ |
| RiskMetrics ASP/package | + Dec-02 | + Dec-02 | + Dec-02 | ● | ◆ [115] | ● | ● | ● |
| Measurisk ASP | + May-02 | + May-02 | + May-02 | ● | + Apr-02 | ● | ● | ● |
| GlobeOp package | + Jan-02 | + Jan-02 | ● | ● | + Jun-02 | ■ | ■ | ● |
| DBRisk ASP | ● | ● | ● | ● | ● | ● | ● | ● |
| BlackRock Svc. bureau | + Jun-02 | + Jun-02 | + Jun-02 | ■ | ◆ | ■ | ● | ● |
| Barra package | + | + | + | ● | + Aug-02 | ● | ● | ● |
| Askari ASP | + | + | + | + | ● | ◆ [116] | ■ | ● |
| Askari package | ● | ● | ● | ● | ● | ◆ | ● | ● |
| Algorithmics package | ● | ● | ● | ● | ■ | ● | ● | ■ |

## Infrastructure

| | Portfolio | Does the system permit unlimited number of levels in portfolio hierarchy? | Does the system support a fund of fund logic or handles commingled funds? | Does the system permit one to structure multiple hierarchies in parallel? | Does the front end application permit the user to scroll up and down the portfolio hierarchy? | Does the front end application permit the use to blast down to the lowest level of the hierarchy? | User defined fields | Does the system support an unlimited number of user defined fields? | Can the front end system access the user defined fields as if it were a standard field? | Can the report writer access the user defined fields as if they were standard fields? |
|---|---|---|---|---|---|---|---|---|---|---|
| Per cent Yes/Average | | 90% | 70% | 100% | 90% | 80% | | 50% | 80% | 80% |
| Wilshire package | | ■ | ● | ■ | ✛ Jul-02 | ■ | | ■ | ■ | ■ |
| SunGard package | | ■ | ■ | ■ | ● | ● | | ■ | ■ | ■ |
| RiskMetrics ASP/package | | ■ | ● | ■ | ■ | ■ | | ■ | ■ | ■ |
| Measurisk ASP | | ■ | ■ | ■ | ■ | ■ | | ◆ REQ | ■ | ■ |
| GlobeOp package | | ■ | ■ | ■ | ■ | ■ | | ◆ REQ | ■ | ■ |
| DBRisk ASP | | ● | ■ | ■ | ■ | ◆[119] | | ● | ● | ● |
| BlackRock Svc. bureau | | ■ | ■ | ■ | ■ | ■ | | ● | ■ | ■ |
| Barra package | | ■ | ■ | ■ | ■ | ■ | | ■ | ■ | ■ |
| Askari ASP | | ■ | ■ | ■ | ■ | ■ | | ● | ● | ● |
| Askari package | | ■ | ■ | ■ | ■ | ■ | | ● | ● | ● |
| Algorithmics package | | ■ | ● | ■ | ■ | ■ | | ■ | ■ | ■ |

## Infrastructure

| Question | Per cent Yes/Average | Wilshire package | SunGard package | RiskMetrics ASP/package | Measurisk ASP | GlobeOp package | DBRisk ASP | BlackRock Svc. bureau | Barra package | Askari ASP | Askari package | Algorithmics package |
|---|---|---|---|---|---|---|---|---|---|---|---|---|
| Does the system permit the user to create securities and input time series data (for alternative investments such as hedge funds and real estate)? | 70% | ■ | ■ |  | ■ | ◆ REQ | ■ | ● | ■ | ■ | ■ | ■ |
| Query/select/calculate |  |  |  |  |  |  |  |  |  |  |  |  |
| Does the system permit the user to query/select/calculate based on a single field (eg, all holdings in which 'sector' = 'technology')? | 80% | ■ | ■ | ■ | ■ | ◆ REQ | ● | ■ | ■ | ■ | ■ | ■ |
| Does the system permit the user to query/select/calculate based on logical conditions (eg, pe < 10)? | 60% | ■ | ■ | ● | ■ | ◆ REQ | ● | ● | ■ | ■ | ■ | ■ |
| Does the system permit the user to query/select/calculate based on multiple logical tests can be combined with 'and' or 'or'? | 60% | ■ | ■ | ● | ✚ Mar-02 | ◆ REQ | ● | ● | ■ | ■ | ■ | ■ |
| Can the results of the screening be stored in a user defined field (eg, if pe<15 then set field to "value")? | 30% | ■ | ■ | ● | ■ | ◆ REQ | ● | ● | ● | ● | ● | ● |
| When performed |  |  |  |  |  |  |  |  |  |  |  |  |
| Can the query/select/calculation logic be applied on loading? | 60% | ● | ■ | ■ | ■ | ◆ REQ | ● | ■ | ● | ■ | ■ | ■ |

## Infrastructure

| Question | Per cent Yes/Average | Wilshire package | SunGard package | RiskMetrics ASP/package | Measurisk ASP | GlobeOp package | DBRisk ASP | BlackRock Svc. bureau | Barra package | Askari ASP | Askari package | Algorithmics package |
|---|---|---|---|---|---|---|---|---|---|---|---|---|
| Can the query/select/calculation logic be retained and reused (not updated if the data that went into selecting the positions has changed)? | 60% | ● | ■ | | ■ | ◆ REQ | ● | ■ | ■ | ■ | ■ | ■ |
| Can the query/select/calculation logic be dynamically performed based on the current status of all the data? | 50% | ■ | ■ | ● | ◆ REQ | ◆ REQ | ● | | ● | ■ | ■ | ■ |
| **Benchmarks** | | | | | | | | | | | | |
| **Weighting** | | | | | | | | | | | | |
| Can the system apply the standard weighting of the benchmark (most benchmarks are cap weighted)? | 100% | ■ | ■ | ■ | ■ | ■ | ■ | ■ | ■ | ■ | ■ | ■ |
| Can the system equal weight the constituents in calculating a benchmark? | 70% | ■ | ■ | ■ | ◆ REQ | ◆ REQ | ◆ REQ | ■ | ■ | ■ | ■ | ✚ Jun-02 |
| Can the system cap weight the constituents in calculating a benchmark? | 70% | ■ | ■ | ■ | ◆ REQ | ◆ REQ | ◆ REQ | ■ | ■ | ■ | ■ | ✚ Jun-02 |
| Can the system custom weight the constituents when calculating a benchmark? | 70% | ■ | ■ | ■ | ◆ REQ | ◆ REQ | ◆ REQ | ■ | ■ | ■ | ■ | ■ |
| Does the system permit the user to create a benchmark by providing weights to be applied to other benchmarks? | 70% | ■ | ■ | ■ | ◆ REQ | ◆ REQ | ◆ REQ | ■ | ■ | ■ | ■ | ■ |

## Infrastructure

| Package | Limits | Does the system permit limits to be established by the user? | Does the system provide an internal limit except tracking capability? | Does the system feed exception messages into an email system? | Front end | Does the system provide full front including a comprehensive inquiry/update/calculate capability to the user? | Does the front end support a flexible user defined output table? | Does the front end permit the user to drag and drop the results into Excel? | Does the front end display the results in graphical form? | Is the front end intranet/internet based? |
|---|---|---|---|---|---|---|---|---|---|---|
| Per cent Yes/Average | | 80% | 90% | 70% | | 90% | 90% | 80% | 90% | 100% |
| Wilshire package | | ■ | ■ | ● | | ■ | ■ | ■ | ■ | ■ |
| SunGard package | | ■ | ■ | ■ | | ■ | ■ | ■ | ■ | ■ |
| RiskMetrics ASP/package | | ■ | ■ | ■ | | ■ | ■ | ■ | ■ | ■ |
| Measurisk ASP | | ◆[121] | ■ | + Apr-02 | | ■ | ■ | ■ | ■ | ■ |
| GlobeOp package | | ■ | ■ | + REQ | | ◆[122] | ■ | ■ | ■ | ■ |
| DBRisk ASP | | ◆[120] | ● | ● | | ■ | + Sep-02 | ● | ■ | ■ |
| BlackRock Svc. bureau | | ■ | ■ | ● | | ■ | ● | ■ | ● | ■ |
| Barra package | | ■ | ■ | ■ | | ■ | ■ | ■ | ■ | ■ |
| Askari ASP | | + Jun-02 | + Jun-02 | + Jun-02 | | ■ | ■ | ■ | ■ | ■ |
| Askari package | | + Jun-02 | + Jun-02 | + Jun-02 | | ■ | ■ | ■ | ■ | ■ |
| Algorithmics package | | ■ | ■ | ■ | | ■ | ■ | ● | ■ | ■ |

# Infrastructure

| Report writer | Per cent Yes/Average | Wilshire package | SunGard package | RiskMetrics ASP/package | Measurisk ASP | GlobeOp package | DBRisk ASP | BlackRock Svc. bureau | Barra package | Askari ASP | Askari package | Algorithmics package |
|---|---|---|---|---|---|---|---|---|---|---|---|---|
| Does the system permit you to print the output table/screen? | 100% | ■ | ■ | ■ | ■ | ■ | ■ | ■ | ■ | ■ | ■ | ■ |
| Does the system support automated report generation of standard reports? | 70% | ■ | ■ | ■ | ■ | ■ | ● | ■ | ● | ● | ● | ■ |
| Does the system include a basic report writer? | 70% | ■ | ◆[123] | ■ | ■ | ■ | ■ | ■ | ■ | ● | ● | ● |
| Does the report writer include enhanced formatting (eg, italics, fonts, shading)? | 40% | ● | ◆[124] | ■ | ■ | ■ | ● | ■ | ● | ● | ● | ● |
| Does the report writer permit page breaks and page makeup logic? | 50% | ■ | ◆[125] | ● | ■ | ■ | ■ | ■ | ● | ● | ● | ● |
| Does the report writer support calculations? | 40% | ■ | ◆[126] | ● | ■ | ■ | ● | ■ | ● | ● | ● | ● |
| Does the report writer recognise the portfolio hierarchy and permit the user to automatically work its way down the hierarchy? | 60% | ■ | ■ | ● | ■ | ■ | ■ | ■ | ● | ● | ● | ● |
| Can the system report the information for the nth worst day? | 50% | ■ | ■ | ■ | ● | ■ | ● | ● | ● | ■ | ■ | ● |
| Does the report writer permit reporting over time? | 60% | ● | ■ | ■ | ■ | ■ | ■ | ■ | ● | ● | ● | ● |

| Infrastructure | Does the report writer permit VAR to be run for different historical time periods and shown on the same report? | Interface | Does the system permit you to access all the data through OLE-DB? | Does the system import external data? | Does the system generate /csv files to be uploaded to other systems? | Data distribution systems | Does the system provide an automated interface to Bloomberg? | Does the system provide an automated interface to Fame? | Does the system provide an automated interface to Factset? | Does the system provide an automated interface to Datastream? | Does the system provide an automated interface to IDC? |
|---|---|---|---|---|---|---|---|---|---|---|---|
| Per cent Yes/Average | 50% | | 20% | 90% | 100% | | 30% | 30% | 30% | 30% | 30% |
| Wilshire package | ● | | ● | ■ | ■ | | ■ | ■ | ■ | ■ | ■ |
| SunGard package | ● | | ■ | ■ | ■ | | ■ | ■ | ■ | ■ | ■ |
| RiskMetrics ASP/package | ■ | | ● | ■ | ■ | | ● | ■ | ● | ● | ● |
| Measurisk ASP | ■ | | ● | ■ | ■ | | ● | ● | ● | ● | ● |
| GlobeOp package | ■ | | ● | ■ | ■ | | ● | ● | ● | ● | ● |
| DBRisk ASP | ■ | | ● | ● | ■ | | ● | ● | ■ | ● | ● |
| BlackRock Svc. bureau | ■ | | ● | ■ | ■ | | ● | ● | ● | ● | ● |
| Barra package | ● | | ● | ■ | ■ | | ■ | ● | ● | ● | ● |
| Askari ASP | ● | | ■ | ■ | ■ | | ● | ● | ● | ■[128] | ■[130] |
| Askari package | ● | | ■ | ■ | ■ | | ● | ● | ● | ■[127] | ■[129] |
| Algorithmics package | ● | | ● | ■ | ■ | | ● | ● | ● | ● | ● |

## Infrastructure

| Question | Per cent Yes/Average | Wilshire package | SunGard package | RiskMetrics ASP/package | Measurisk ASP | GlobeOp package | DBRisk ASP | BlackRock Svc. bureau | Barra package | Askari ASP | Askari package | Algorithmics package |
|---|---|---|---|---|---|---|---|---|---|---|---|---|
| **Data retention** | | | | | | | | | | | | |
| Does the system retain the daily market data? | 100% | ■ | ■ | ■ | ■ | ■ | ■ | ■ | ■ | ■ | ■ | ■ |
| Does the system retain the daily holdings data? | 100% | ■ | ■ | ■ | ■ | ■ | ■ | ■ | ■ | ■ | ■ | ■ |
| Does the system retain the results in a data format? | 100% | ■ | ■ | ■ | ■ | ■ | ■ | ■ | ■ | ■ | ■ | ■ |
| Does the system retain the results in a report format? | 80% | ■ | ■ | ■ | ■ | ■ | ● | ■ | ■ | ■ | ■ | ● |
| **Security** | | | | | | | | | | | | |
| **By user** | | | | | | | | | | | | |
| Does the system provide security by function be controlled for each user? | 90% | ■ | ■ | ■ | ■ | ■ | ● | ■ | ■ | ■ | ■ | + Mar-02 |
| Does the system provide security by portfolio be controlled by user? | 80% | ● | ■ | ■ | ■ | ■ | ■ | ■ | ■ | ● | ● | + Mar-02 |
| **Control access to custom** | | | | | | | | | | | | |
| Does the system restrict access to custom curves? | 30% | | | ■ | ■ | ■ | ● | ● | | ● | | |
| Does the system restrict access to custom indices/benchmarks? | 50% | | | ■ | ■ | ■ | ● | ■ | | ■ | | |

## Infrastructure

| | Restrict access to custom factors? | Control access to user defined fields? | Encrypt communication over the internet? | ASP provides multi-site disaster recovery? | For ASPs, supplier satisfy all compliance requirements of a broker-dealer? | For ASPs, can supplier turn around the processing by the next morning? | Operating system | Run with NT 4 Server operating system? | Run with Novell Netware 4.1 operating system? | Run with HP Unix operating system? |
|---|---|---|---|---|---|---|---|---|---|---|
| Per cent Yes/Average | 20% | 30% | 60% | 50% | 50% | 90% | | 90% | 17% | 17% |
| Wilshire package | | | | | | ■ | | ■ | ■ | ● |
| SunGard package | | | | | | ■ | | ■ | ● | ◆[131] |
| RiskMetrics ASP/package | ■ | ■ | ■ | ■ | ■ | ■ | | ■ | ● | ● |
| Measurisk ASP | ● | ■ | ■ | ■ | ■ | ✚ Jun-02 | | | | |
| GlobeOp package | ■ | ■ | ■ | ● | ■ | ■ | | | | |
| DBRisk ASP | ● | ● | ■ | ■ | ● | ● | | | | |
| BlackRock Svc. bureau | ● | ● | ■ | ■ | ■ | ■ | | ● | ● | ● |
| Barra package | | | | | | ■ | | ■ | ● | ● |
| Askari ASP | ● | ● | ■ | ■ | ■ | ■ | | ■ | ● | ● |
| Askari package | | | | | | ■ | | | | |
| Algorithmics package | | | | | | ■ | | ■ | ● | ■ |

## Infrastructure

| | Unix Solaris OS | Windows 2000 OS | *Database* Oracle database | Microsoft SQL database | Sybase database | *Architecture* Client server | Desktop application | ASP application |
|---|---|---|---|---|---|---|---|---|
| Per cent Yes/Average | 50% | 100% | 67% | 67% | 50% | 60% | 50% | 70% |
| Wilshire package | ● | ■ | ● | ● | ● | ■ | ■ | ● |
| SunGard package | ◆132 | ■ | ■ | ■ | ■ | ■ | ■ | ● |
| RiskMetrics ASP/package | + Sep-01 | ■ | + Dec-02 | ■ | ● | ■ | ■ | ■ |
| Measurisk ASP | | | | | | ● | ● | ■ |
| GlobeOp package | | | | | | ● | ● | ■ |
| DBRisk ASP | | | | | | ● | ● | ■ |
| BlackRock Svc. bureau | ■ | ■ | ● | ● | ■ | ■ | ■ | ■ |
| Barra package | ● | ■ | ■ | ■ | ● | ■ | ■ | + Dec-02 |
| Askari ASP | ● | ■ | ● | ■ | ● | ● | ● | ■ |
| Askari package | | | | | | ■ | ■ | ● |
| Algorithmics package | ■ | ■ | ■ | ● | ■ | ■ | ● | ● |

Column questions:
- Does the application run with the Unix Solaris operating system?
- Does the application run with the Windows 2000 operating system?
- *Database* — Does the application run with an Oracle database?
- Does the application run with a Microsoft SQL database?
- Does the application run with a Sybase database?
- *Architecture* — Is the system available as a client server application?
- Is the system available as a desktop application?
- Is the system available as an ASP application?

## Business profile

| | Algorithmics package | Askari package | Askari ASP | Barra package | BlackRock Svc. bureau | DBRisk ASP | GlobeOp package | Measurisk ASP | RiskMetrics ASP/package | SunGard package | Wilshire package | Per cent Yes/Average |
|---|---|---|---|---|---|---|---|---|---|---|---|---|
| Year entered business | 1989 | 1997 | 1997 | 1975 | 1994 | 1995 | 2000 | 1999 | 1994 | 1994 | 1972 | 1991 |
| **Staff** | | | | | | | | | | | | |
| What is the total number of staff dedicated to market risk management systems? | 550 | 76 | 76 | 450 | 200 | 24 | 110 | 46 | 145 | 200 | 178 | 198 |
| What is the number of development staff dedicated to market risk management systems? | 200 | 23 | 23 | 80 | 60 | | | 13 | 48 | | 55 | 68 |
| What is the number of financial engineering staff dedicated to market risk management systems? | 150 | 5 | 5 | 60 | 18 | 12 | 5 | 7 | 7 | | 18 | 31 |
| What is the number of data management staff dedicated to market risk management systems? | 10 | 10 | 10 | 60 | 30 | 8 | | 5 | 18 | | 37 | 24 |
| What is the number of client services staff dedicated to market risk management systems? | 100 | 11 | 11 | 150 | 70 | | | 15 | 26 | | 52 | 54 |
| What is the number of other staff dedicated to market risk management systems? | 90 | 27 | 27 | 100 | 22 | 4 | | 6 | 46 | | 16 | 39 |
| **Licensees** | | | | | | | | | | | | |
| What is the total number of users? | 155 | 8 | 5 | 1500 | 32 | 20 | 24 | 24 | 375 | 120 | 482 | 301 |

## Business profile

| Business profile | Algorithmics package | Askari package | Askari ASP | Barra package | BlackRock Svc. bureau | DBRisk ASP | GlobeOp package | Measurisk ASP | RiskMetrics ASP/package | SunGard package | Wilshire package | Per cent Yes/Average |
|---|---|---|---|---|---|---|---|---|---|---|---|---|
| What is the number of sell-side users? | 140 | 2 | 2 | 150 | 3 | 1 | | 0 | 160 | 105 | 10 | 63 |
| What is the number of buy-side users? | 15 | 6 | 3 | 1350 | 29 | 19 | | 24 | 122 | 15 | 472 | 228 |
| What is the number of plan sponsor users? | 0 | 0 | 2 | 150 | 13 | 6 | | 8 | 8 | 0 | 30 | 24 |
| What is the number of corporate users? | 2 | 1 | 0 | 75 | 0 | 2 | | 3 | 47 | 0 | 28 | 17 |
| What is the number of money manager users? | 9 | 2 | 0 | 1200 | 2 | 2 | | 2 | 21 | 10 | 365 | 179 |
| What is the number of hedge fund or fund of fund users? | 0 | 2 | 0 | 30 | 0 | 7 | | 6 | 22 | 4 | 6 | 8 |
| What is the number of insurance users? | 2 | 0 | 0 | 30 | 3 | 0 | | 3 | 9 | 1 | 28 | 8 |
| What is the number of prime broker users? | 2 | 0 | 1 | 20 | 0 | 1 | | 0 | 10 | 0 | 0 | 4 |
| What is the number of other buy-side users? | 0 | 1 | 0 | 0 | 11 | 1 | | 2 | 5 | 0 | 15 | 4 |
| Can the supplier provide an operational risk assessment? | ● | ● | ● | ● | ● | ● | ● | ■ | ● | ● | ● | 10% |
| Implementation support | | | | | | | | | | | | |
| As part of implementation support, does the supplier provide support in installing the software? | ■ | ■ | | ■ | | | | | ■ | ■ | ■ | 60% |

| Business profile | As part of implementation support, does the supplier provide support in extracting the required data? | As part of implementation support, does the supplier provide support in building the database? | As part of implementation support, does the supplier provide support in processing and loading the data? | As part of implementation support, does the supplier provide support in developing custom reports? | As part of implementation support, does the supplier provide support at your site? | As part of implementation support, does the supplier provide the full support or recommends third-party? | On-going support | As part of on-going support, does the supplier provide unlimited phone support? | As part of on-going support, does the supplier permit you to visit their offices? |
|---|---|---|---|---|---|---|---|---|---|
| Per cent Yes/Average | 70% | 100% | 100% | 80% | 90% | 100% | | 100% | 100% |
| Wilshire package | ■ | ■ | ■ | ■ | ■ | ■ | | ■ | ■ |
| SunGard package | ■ | ■ | ■ | ■ | ■ | ■ | | ■ | ■ |
| RiskMetrics ASP/package | ■ | ■ | ■ | ■ | ■ | ■ | | ■ | ■ |
| Measurisk ASP | ● | ■ | ■ | ■ | ■ | ■ | | ■ | ■ |
| GlobeOp package | ■ | ■ | ■ | ■ | ■ | ■ | | ■ | ■ |
| DBRisk ASP | ● | ■ | ■ | ● | ■ | ■ | | ■ | ■ |
| BlackRock Svc. bureau | ■ | ■ | ■ | ■ | ■ | ■ | | ■ | ■ |
| Barra package | ■ | ■ | ■ | ■ | ■ | ■ | | ■ | ■ |
| Askari ASP | ● | ■ | ■ | ● | ● | ■ | | ■ | ■ |
| Askari package | ● | ■ | ● | ● | ■ | ■ | | ■ | ■ |
| Algorithmics package | ■ | ■ | ■ | ■ | ■ | ■ | | ■ | ■ |

## Business profile

| | As part of on-going support, does the supplier provide standardised training courses? | How many standardised training courses does the supplier typically offer per year? | As part of on-going support, does the supplier provide support at your site? | Does the supplier permit an ASP user to migrate to an in-house application? |
|---|---|---|---|---|
| Per cent Yes/Average | 50% | 10 | 100% | 50% |
| Wilshire package | ■ | 5 | ■ | ■ |
| SunGard package | ■ | 12 | ■ | ■ |
| RiskMetrics ASP/package | ■ | 12 | ■ | ■ |
| Measurisk ASP | ● | 0 | ■ | ● |
| GlobeOp package | ● | 0 | ■ | ● |
| DBRisk ASP | ● | 0 | ■ | ● |
| BlackRock Svc. bureau | ● | 0 | ■ | ● |
| Barra package | ■ | 0 | ■ | ✚ Dec-02 |
| Askari ASP | ● | 0 | ■ | ■ |
| Askari package | ● | 0 | ■ | ■ |
| Algorithmics package | ■ | 75 | ■ | ● |

653

1  Developed but not yet implemented.
2  This is planned for 2002 and will be accelerated at client request.
3  Developed but not yet implemented.
4  This has been released for equities.
5  Measurisk performs a multiple regression of the performance of each stock and the nine sectoral indices provided for each country and uses the result as the coefficients for the 9 sectoral risk factors.
6  Provides correlation with user defined sector benchmarks but does not include any style benchmarks and does not provide attribution.
7  Provides correlation with user defined sector benchmarks but does not include any style benchmarks and does not provide attribution.
8  Attribute risk to equity risk factor but does not present details.
9  Measurisk performs a multiple regression of the performance of each stock and the nine sectoral indices provided for each country and uses the result as the coefficients for the nine sectoral risk factors.
10  Askari does not supply equity sectors.
11  Askari does not supply equity sectors.
12  Cap, growth/value, momentum.
13  Graphic presentation.
14  Aggregate by counterparty with flexible netting agreements.  Current and future (simulation based) potential exposure.
15  Marginal.
16  Incremental.
17  Incremental.
18  Marginal.
19  Marginal.
20  Marginal.
21  Marginal.
22  Can eliminate fixed income and currency factors but not equity factors.
23  Can eliminate fixed income and currency factors but not equity factors.
24  Incremental VAR, sensitivity to 1% change, and What If calculator.
25  Marginal.
26  Can eliminate fixed income and currency factors but not equity factors.
27  Marginal 1%.
28  Marginal VAR.
29  Marginal VAR.
30  Marginal.
31  Incremental.
32  Incremental.
33  Client has customise to do this.
34  Interfaced to FXPress.
35  Equities target Sept-01.
36  Equities target Sept-01.
37  Kalotay model.
38  Kalotay model.
39  Uses more than transition matrix to generate scenario for credit migrations (PCRE).
40  Implemented for hedge fund underlying.
41  Equity only.
42  Because of interpolation of P&L might be slightly off.
43  Because of interpolation of P&L might be slightly off.
44  Limited to Bloomberg fair market curves.
45  Proxy.

**46** No for parametric and Monte Carlo; yes for historical.

**47** From Barra or via beta mapping to index.

**48** Via Intex and Bloomberg.

**49** Roll forward until market reopens and then interpolate for interim days.

**50** Via BARRA.

**51** Provides correlation with user defined sector benchmarks but does not include any style benchmarks and does not provide attribution.

**52** Attribute risk to equity risk factor but does not present details.

**53** Measurisk performs a multiple regression of the performance of each stock and the nine sectoral indices provided for each country and uses the result as the coefficients for the nine sectoral risk factors.

**54** Askari does not supply equity sectors.

**55** Cap, growth/value, momentum.

**56** Supplier uses constituents, but can't redistribute without separate contract.

**57** Supplier uses constituents, but can't redistribute without separate contract.

**58** USD curve.

**59** Brady or Intl curve.

**60** USD curve.

**61** Brady or Intl curve.

**62** Brady or Intl curve.

**63** Brady or Intl curve.

**64** Brady or Intl curve.

**65** Brady or Intl curve.

**66** Brady or Intl curve.

**67** Dec-02.

**68** Dec-02.

**69** Dec-02.

**70** Curve implied from NDF or FWD FX.

**71** Dec-02.

**72** Curve implied from NDF or FWD FX.

**73** Dec-02.

**74** Dec-02.

**75** Dec-02.

**76** Dec-02.

**77** Dec-02.

**78** Dec-02.

**79** Dec-02.

**80** Dec-02.

**81** Dec-02.

**82** Dec-02.

**83** Dec-02.

**84** Dec-02.

**85** Dec-02.

**86** Curve implied from NDF or FWD FX.

**87** Dec-02.

**88** Dec-02.

**89** Curve implied from NDF or FWD FX.

**90** Dec-02.

**91** Dec-02.

**92** Dec-02.

**93** Dec-02.

**94** Dec-02.

95  Curve implied from NDF or FWD FX.

96  Curve implied from NDF or FWD FX.

97  Curve implied from NDF or FWD FX.

98  Dec-02.

99  Dec-02.

100  Curve implied from NDF or FWD FX.

101  Derivative solutions.

102  Derivative solutions.

103  If user subscribes to data.

104  Index level proxy.

105  Dec-02.

106  Dec-02.

107  Dec-02.

108  Fixed income.

109  To be determined.

110  To be determined.

111  To be determined.

112  To be determined.

113  Fixed income.

114  Not integrated.

115  Not fully integrated.

116  Plan to integrate with Bloomberg and potentially other trading systems.

117  Two beta accounts.  Plan to fully introduce in Oct-02.  Target is small accounts.

118  Not integrated.

119  Supported for equities.

120  Limits can be established on VAR/TE, or the change in VAR/TE.

121  Account level only.

122  Strong and flexible presentation of analysis, less of a turnkey package.

123  Works with ODBC report writers plus optional web reporting module.

124  Works with ODBC report writers plus optional web reporting module.

125  Works with ODBC report writers plus optional web reporting module.

126  Works with ODBC report writers plus optional web reporting module.

127  Batch download.

128  Batch download.

129  Interactive link.

130  Interactive link.

131  Can run UNIX as database.

132  Can run UNIX as database.

# Appendix 7

# *Glossary*

**Acquisition (see Mergers and acquisitions)** A type of financial transaction or strategy that seeks to profit from a price differential perceived with respect to related or correlated instruments in different markets and typically involves the simultaneous purchase of an instrument in one market and the sale of the same or related instrument in another market.[1]

**AIMA** The Alternative Investment Management Association, a global, not-for-profit trade association for hedge funds, managed futures and managed currencies.[2]

**Alpha** A static measure that reflects the value of the investment relative to the index at any given time. It is the expected rate of return for the hedge fund manager when the rate of return is zero for the specified benchmark.

**Arbitrage** The simultaneous buying and selling of a security at two different prices in two different markets, resulting in profits without risk. Perfectly efficient markets present no arbitrage opportunities but seldom exist.

**At-the-money** An option is at-the-money if the strike price of the option is equal to the market price of the underlying security. For example, if stock A is trading at 60, then the A 60 option is "at-the-money".

**AUM** Assets under management.

**Average life** The average number of years that each dollar of unpaid principal remains outstanding. Average life is computed as the weighted average time to the receipt of all future cashflows, using as the weights the (US) dollar amounts of the principal paydowns.

**Bankruptcy** Insolvency proceedings under Chapter 11 of the US Bankruptcy Code. Such proceedings normally result in either the transfer of ownership of the ongoing enterprise from stockholders to creditors or the sale of the assets of the ongoing enterprise and the distribution of the sale proceeds to the creditors. A third possibility, known as Chapter 7, is that the assets of the enterprise may be auctioned or sold separately, whereupon the enterprise ceases to exist as such.

**Basis point (bp)** In the bond market, the smallest measure used for quoting yields. Each percentage point of yield in bonds equals 100 basis points. Basis points are also used for interest rates. An interest rate of 5% is 50bp greater than an interest rate of 4.5%.

**Basis trading** The purchase or sale of a futures contract and the offsetting purchase or sale of an instrument that is deliverable into the contract. Synthetic option positions can be created through basis trading.

**Benchmark** The performance of a predetermined set of securities, used for comparison purposes. Such sets may be based on published indexes or may be customised to suit an investment strategy.

**Beta** Used to measure the risk or volatility of the hedge fund manager relative to a specified benchmark; it represents the change in return for every 1% change in the index. If the beta is more than 1, the investment typically gains or loses more than the index. Beta measures the slope of the curve that depicts the investment's performance.

**Bid/offer spread** Dealers quote two-way prices, the lower of which is known as the bid price (the price at which the holder can sell shares) and the higher is the offer price (the price at which the holder can buy shares). The bid/offer spread is determined by a number of factors: the underlying price of the equity, the sector liquidity, volatility, takeovers, corporate actions, etc.

**Bond–futures arbitrage** A hedge fund strategy that involves a portfolio manager buying a particular bond and selling the futures contract on the bond.

**Boom period of S&P500** The period from January 1997 to June 2000 – a period of high performance in the equity markets reflecting in a high S&P.

**Bust period of S&P500** The period beginning June 2000 to December 2001 – a period of low performance in the equity markets.

**Call option** An option contract that gives its holder the right (but not the obligation) to purchase a specified number or share of the underlying stock at the given strike price, on or before the expiration date of the contract.

**Callable bond** A bond that can be "called" by the issuer before the bond matures. The power to call a bond gives the issuer a way to respond to falling interest rates. Callable bonds often pay higher rates than non-callable bonds to compensate for the uncertainty.

**Capital under management** The pre-leverage amount of investor capital.

**Cap** A term used in interest rate derivative parlance to represent an instrument that has a payoff if interest rates go above a preset level. The level is known as the cap strike and need not be a constant. For example, a 4% strike, five-year maturity, three-month Libor cap would pay a quarterly rate, calculated as the difference (Libor − 4%) whenever this difference was positive. The difference would be multiplied by the notional amount of the cap to calculate the payment, and the calculations would be made quarterly for five years.

**Chapter 11** The chapter in the US Bankruptcy Code that contains the provisions for court-supervised reorganisation of debtor companies. See *Bankruptcy.*

**Collateralised mortgage obligation (CMO)** A security backed by a pool of pass-through mortgages, structured so that there are several classes of bondholders with varying maturities and risk profiles, called tranches. The principal payments from the underlying pool of pass-through securities are used to retire the bonds on a priority basis as specified in the prospectus.

**Commodity** Food, metal, or another physical substance that investors buy or sell.

**Compliance** A management function that monitors the rules and regulations governing the business of a company and the response to any violations.

**Concentration** Arises when a significant percentage of a hedge fund's portfolio is exposed to the same or similar *market factors* or other risk factors, increasing the risk of losses caused by adverse market or economic events affecting such risk factors. Hedge fund managers may have concentrations with respect to asset classes, industry sectors, regions, or other relevant areas.

**Confidence level** The degree of assurance that a specified failure rate is not exceeded. VAR is often expressed as the amount that a portfolio could lose over a 1-, 10- or 30-day time horizon at a 95% or 99% level of comfort.

**Control premium** The price difference between the market price per share of an individual security and the price per share of a block of such securities that carries the power to control a corporation.

**Convertible arbitrage** A hedge fund strategy that involves a portfolio manager buying convertible securities and selling the underlying equities, believing the convertibles to be underpriced.

**Convergence** The movement of the price of a futures contract toward the price of the underlying cash *commodity*. At the start, the contract price is higher because of time value. But as the contract nears expiration, and time value decreases, the futures price and the cash price converge. Also applies to spread trades such as emu convergence.

**Convergence strategies** A hedge fund strategy that involves a portfolio manager believing that a market factor (eg, equity volatility) is too high or too low and will revert to more normal levels. The manager buys the underpriced asset and sells the corresponding overpriced asset.

**Convexity** See *gamma*.

**Corporate restructuring** Generally speaking, any restructuring of the liability and stockholders equity components of a financial balance sheet, normally undertaken because the issuer does not generate enough cash-flow to service its debt and other liabilities. Restructuring may include deferral of principal or interest payments on debt, equitisation of debt or other liabilities, and, in bankruptcy, modification or termination of burdensome contractual commitments. Restructuring is normally done with reference to the outcome that would ensue in a Chapter 11 bankruptcy proceeding even where no such proceeding occurs.

**Correlation** A standardised measure of the relative movement between two variables, such as the prices of two different securities. The level of correlation between two variables is measured on a scale of -1 to +1. If two variables move up or down together, they are positively correlated. If they tend to move in opposite directions, they are negatively correlated.

**Counterparty** A third party that enters into transactions with a hedge fund, usually a bank or broker/dealer.

**Counterparty risk** The risk that the other party to an agreement will default and the amount that could be at risk. See Chapter 2 for a discussion of counterparty risk.

**Credit risk** The risk that an issuer of debt securities or a borrower may default on his obligations, or that the creditworthiness of the borrower will decline, affecting the value of their securities. See Chapter 2 for a further discussion of credit risk.

**Cross-correlation** A measure of how closely aligned the timing of movements in activity are for two series of return over their up and down cycles. The cross-correlation statistic for two time series can range from −1 to 1. In general, the closer the cross-correlation is to value of 1 the more in *phase* and *synchronised* the return cycles will be. A value of −1 would indicate that the two series move perfectly in a *counter-cyclical* direction. A value near zero indicates that there is no statistical relationship between the series.

**Day trading** "Day trading" means that a trader tries to make money buying and selling stocks *during the day* taking advantage of the daily price movement. Day trading is a very short-term trade: it can take an hour, minutes, or just a few seconds. A day trader will try to make anything from 1/16, 1/8, to 1/4 of a point on a 1,000 stock purchase.

**Delta** The Greek letter most commonly used for *duration*, is the change in price of a security with respect to a risk factor. In the context of bonds and interest rates, the duration of a bond is defined as a per cent change in price for a one per cent yield of the bond. Usually the present value of a basis point (bp) is calculated and multiplied by 100 to arrive at the duration. In the context of options on securities, the delta of an option is the extent by which the price of the option changes with respect to the underlying security. Delta is usually not a constant and is dependent on the price of the underlying. In market parlance, if the context is not clear, one talks about "interest rate delta" or "option delta" to distinguish between the uses.

**Derivative** A financial instrument, such as an option, or future, whose value is derived in part from the value and characteristics of another security, the *underlying* order.

**Directional trades** Trades that are designed to benefit from a directional move in the market. Examples include long a stock or short a bond.

**Distressed securities** A security of a company undergoing or expected to undergo *bankruptcy* or restructuring in an effort to avoid insolvency. A hedge fund strategy that involves a portfolio manager purchasing the securities of companies that are restructuring, being reorganised, or have filed for bankruptcy protection in the belief that they are undervalued.

**Divergence** When two or more averages or indices fail to show confirming trends. For example, when the Dow goes down on the same day that Nasdaq goes up.

**Diversification** An investment strategy that involves buying a variety of investment instruments that are not highly correlated to each other in order to reduce the risk of a portfolio.

**Due diligence** The process of reviewing and assessing a fund's performance, management team, processes, etc.

**Duration** A measure of price sensitivity to a change in a market variable. The common usage in fixed income, as in "duration of a bond" is the per cent change in price for a basis point (bp) change in yield to maturity.

**Endowment fund** An investment fund established for the support of an institution such as a college, private school, museum, hospital and foundations.

**Equity** In the context of investing, a synonym for stocks or shares of companies. When used in connection with accounting, equity refers to the amount by which the assets of an entity exceed its liabilities.

**Event driven** An investment strategy that seeks to profit from anticipated events, such as mergers or restructurings.

**Event risk** The risk that the value of a security or other instrument will change due to an unexpected takeover or corporate restructuring or an unanticipated change or event in the market environment (eg, a natural disaster or industrial accident) or in the regulatory environment.

**Execution costs** The difference between the execution price of a security and the price that would have existed in the absence of a trade.

**Factor exposure** The sensitivity of the value of a security to an isolated market risk or factor. In fixed income, for example, credit risk and interest rate risk are both factors. One could break down interest rate risk into other sub-factors, such as two-year and ten-year interest rate risk. In equities, exposure to technology (sector risk), large vs small cap exposure, and growth vs value are all factors.

**Fair value** Generally refers to the price at which a single unit of an instrument would trade between disinterested parties in an arm's length transaction. Fair value does not generally take into account control premiums or discounts for large or illiquid positions.

**Family office** A company set up to manage a small number of wealthy families' money. At a minimum, a family office has an administrative staff to manage the various brokerage accounts, private investments, memberships in organisations and boards, and charitable contributions that comprise a portfolio.

**Fat tails** A term used in statistics to describe a higher probability of the occurrence of extreme events than that prescribed by a normal distribution. The term comes from the visual representation of a distorted bell curve. The higher probabilities associated with events far from the mean cause the area under the curve far from the mean to be substantial, rather than asymptomatically disappearing.

**Floor** A term used in interest rate derivative parlance to represent an instrument that has a payoff if interest rates go below a preset level. The level is known as the floor strike and need not be a constant. For example, a standard 4% strike, five-year maturity, three-month Libor floor would pay a quarterly rate calculated as the difference (4% - Libor), whenever the difference was positive. The difference would be multiplied by the notional amount of the cap to calculate the payment, and the calculation would be made quarterly for five years.

**Forward contract** A cash market transaction in which delivery of the underlying is deferred until after the contract has been made. Although the delivery is made in the future, the price is determined at the initial trade date.

**Foundation** An entity that exists to support a charitable institution, and which is funded by an endowment or donations.

**Fund of funds** A hedge fund strategy that aims to enhance returns while reducing risk by allocating capital among different hedge funds.

**Fundamental analysis** Security analysis that seeks to detect misvalued securities through an analysis of the firm's business prospects. Research analysis often focuses on earnings, dividend prospects, expectations for future interest rates, and risk evaluation of the firm.

**Future** A term used to designate all contracts covering the sale of financial instruments or physical commodities for future delivery on an exchange.

**Gamma** In the context of options, gamma (the Greek letter most commonly used for *convexity*) is the rate of change of *delta*, with respect to the change in price of the underlying. In the context of fixed-income securities, gamma is the rate of change of delta with respect to a change in the relevant interest rate. For a fixed-income security, if one approximates the price/yield relationship or curve with a polynomial, the delta is the first order coefficient and gamma is the second order coefficient. In other words, if delta is the slope of the tangent line at a point on the price/yield curve, gamma is the error of the tangent approximation.

**Global macro** A hedge fund strategy that involves establishing market positions to take advantage of perceived broad economic trends and changes anticipated by the hedge fund manager.

**Greeks** The generic name for option specific risk factors such as *delta*, *gamma*, *vega*, *rho*, and *theta*.

**Haircut** The margin or difference between the actual market value of a security and the value assessed by the lending side of a transaction.

**Hedge fund** Generally a pooled investment vehicle that is privately organised and administered by investment management professionals and not widely available to the public. Many hedge funds share a number of characteristics: they hold long and short positions, employ leverage to enhance returns, pay a performance or incentive fee to their hedge fund managers, have high minimum investment requirements, target absolute (rather than relative) returns and/or may be organised offshore. In addition, hedge funds are generally not constrained by legal limitations on their investment discretion and can adopt a variety of trading strategies. The hedge fund manager will often have his/her own capital (or that of his/her principals) invested in the hedge fund he/she manages.

**Hedge fund strategies** The strategies are *global macro, fund of funds, market neutral* (this includes *long/short equity, stock-futures arbitrage, bond-futures arbitrage, convertible arbitrage,* and *convergence strategies*), *long only, short only, event driven* (this includes *risk arbitrage* and *distressed securities*), and specialised strategies.

**High water mark** This is a pre-determined return level (determined based on historical performance). Returns below this level cannot be charged an incentive fee by the manager. In an environment where returns are poor, this can encourage managers to liquidate rather than "to work for free".

**HNW** High net worth individuals.

**Hurdle rate** A term used in the calculation of incentive compensation for hedge funds. A hurdle rate is typically a return percentage that a hedge fund has to achieve, under which the manager does not get an incentive compensation. The federal funds rate is often used as a hurdle rate, the rationale being that until the risk-free rate is achieved, the manager should not get paid.

**IAFE** International Association of Financial Engineers. This organisation was formed in 1992 and currently has about 2,000 members worldwide. The organisation aims to define and foster the field of quantitative finance.

**Index** Statistical composite that measures changes in the economy or in financial markets, often expressed in percentage changes from a base year or from the previous month. Hedge fund indices measure the ups and downs of hedge funds reflecting market prices and weighing of the companies on the index.

**Information ratio** The ratio of expected return to risk, as measured by *standard deviation*.

**Institutional investors** Organisations that invest, including insurance companies, depository institutions, pension funds, investment companies, mutual funds and endowment funds.

**Institutionalisation** The gradual domination of financial markets by institutional investors, as opposed to individual investors.

**Investment style** Style can be a combination of the type of instruments the fund trades, such as fixed income or stocks, and the type of positions the fund puts on, such as arbitrage or trend following.

**Investor risk committee (IRC)** A group of hedge fund managers, fund of fund managers, and institutional investors working on the issue of hedge fund risk transparency. See *www.iafe.org*.

**Kitchen sinks** Mortgage-backed securities composed of the scraps and pieces of other mortgage-backed securities.

**Large cap** Companies with large market capitalisations. Although a large cap stock is currently defined as a company that has a value of US$10 billion or more, this definition has changed over time with the stock market. A decade ago, a large cap stock was a company worth US$1 billion or more.

**Leverage** Financial leverage is the degree to which an investor or business is using borrowed money, measured by the debt/equity ratio. Many hedge funds rely on leverage. It has the effect of a magnifying glass: it expands small profit opportunities into larger ones but also expands small losses into larger losses. There are several definitions of leverage. Long-only leverage is commonly used by convertible arbitrage funds; this gauge measures leverage as long assets / total capital. Gross leverage is simply (total longs + shorts) / total capital. Net leverage nets short positions against longs with the idea that the shorts reduce the risk of the longs (which is not always the case).

**Liquidation** Any transaction that offsets or closes out a long or short position. Liquidation can also refer to the dissolution of a fund.

**Liquidity** A market is liquid when it has a high level of trading activity, allowing buying and selling with minimum price disturbance.

**Long only** A hedge fund strategy that involves a portfolio manager seeking to purchase undervalued stocks or stocks likely to appreciate.

**Long position** An owner of 1,000 shares of stock is said to be "long the stock". An options position where a person has executed one or more option trades where the net result is that they are an "owner" or holder of options (ie, the number of contracts bought exceeds the number of contracts sold).

**Long/short equity** A hedge fund strategy that involves a portfolio manager being long one portfolio of equities and short another. If the returns of the two portfolios are positively correlated, the riskiness of the entire portfolio will be reduced.

**Long-term rate** This refers to interest rates that are 10 years or more in maturity. There are many long-term rates, such as the ten-year swap rate and the ten-year treasury rate.

**Margin** A certain amount of assets that must be deposited in a margin account in order to secure a portion of a party's obligations under a contract. For example, to buy or sell an exchange-traded futures contract, a party must post a specified amount that is determined by the exchange, referred to as an "initial margin". In addition, a party will be required to post a "variation margin" if the futures contracts change in value. Margin is also required in connection with the purchase and sale of securities where the full purchase price is not up front or the securities sold are not owned by the seller.

**Margin call** A demand for additional funds because of adverse price movement. Margin calls can also be triggered by increased haircuts.

**Market factors** Refers collectively to interest rates, foreign exchange rates, equity prices, commodity prices, and indices constructed from these rates and prices, as well as their *volatility* and *correlation*.

**Market neutral** A hedge fund strategy that involves establishing market positions to take advantage of perceived mispricings of related or correlated assets. "Perceived mispricings" are situations in which the portfolio manager believes that a market factor is out of equilibrium and will revert over time. Mathematically-calculated "arbitrages" can exist between the cash market and derivatives markets, where the price in one market is different from the price implied by the other.

**Mark to model** The value derived for a security or transaction that is based on a model rather than actual observed prices.

**Mean–variance analysis** This portfolio analysis concept was developed during Markowitz's time. The idea behind it is that variance is a measure of risk. Mean–variance analysis entails minimising risk (variance) for a particular expected return (mean), or maximising expected return for a particular level of risk.

**Merger and acquisition (M&A)** An acquisition in which all assets and liabilities are absorbed by the buyer.

**Merger arbitrage** A trading strategy that seeks to benefit from stock price movements driven by one company merging with or buying another company. A typical transaction involves shorting the stock of the buyer and purchasing the stock of the company being bought. The difference between the stock prices narrows as the transaction moves towards completion.

**Model** A program or process that is designed to create a depiction of reality through graphs, pictures, or mathematical representations.

**Model risk** The risk that the model chosen and inputs used to value securities and transactions differ from the valuation that other widely used models would produce and are different from observed market prices.

**Net asset value (NAV)** A term used to represent the *equity* in a fund. NAV is the sum of all the values of the assets in a fund minus all the liabilities, including debt and accrued costs (eg, accounting and legal costs).

**Non-directional trades** Trades and strategies that depend on changes in correlations in factors such as volatilities, correlations, basis, or yield curves, rather than absolute up or down moves in the market.

**Off the run** A term used in the debt markets to distinguish between the most recent issuance of a particular note or bond (usually of a single maturity) and previous issuances of similar securities. For example, the US government regularly auctions 10-year maturity notes. The most recently issued note is usually the most liquid and is known as the on the run 10-year note. All previously issued 10-year notes are referred to as the off the run 10-year notes, and currently have maturities less than their original 10 years.

**On the run** The most recently issued (and therefore typically the most liquid) government bond in a particular maturity range.

**Operational risk** The risk of loss due to system breakdowns, employee fraud or misconduct, errors in models or natural or man-made catastrophes, among other risks. It may also include the risk of loss due to the incomplete or incorrect documentation of trades. Operational risk may be defined by what it does not include: market risk, credit risk and liquidity risk.

**Optionality (non-linear relations)** Any presence of an option-like payoff in a security or portfolio.

**Performance attribution analysis** The decomposition of a money manager's performance results to explain the reasons why those results were achieved.

**Plan sponsors** The entities that establish pension plans, including private business entities acting for their employees; state and local entities operating on behalf of their employees; unions acting on behalf of their members; and individuals representing themselves.

**Portfolio construction** The process by which instruments are managed as a whole: the portfolio. Every new instrument adds risk to the portfolio and portfolio managers take on positions based on the types of risk to which they wish to be exposed. Furthermore, other instruments hedge away risks that need to be avoided or minimised.

**Portfolio manager** A person who invests and manages an amount of capital allocated to it by a hedge fund manager on behalf of a hedge fund. Portfolio managers may be either employees of the hedge fund manager or external managers who are actively managed by the hedge fund manager or with whom the hedge fund manager makes a passive investment.

**Portfolio optimisation** The traditional portfolio optimisation problem attempts to simultaneously minimise the risk and maximise the returns. To this end, historical quantitative analysis and forecasting are carried out in order to optimise the risk/return relationship.

**Position-level transparency** Disclosure of all actual positions in a portfolio.

**Prepayment risk** The possibility that the bond principal will be prepaid in part or in whole before the stated maturity date. Examples of bonds with prepayment risk are bonds callable by the issue and mortgage-backed securities. In the case of callable bonds, the prepayment risk is easier to model since the prepayment incentive depends on a single economic factor: whether the issuer can prepay the bond and reissue it at a lower interest rate. However, the prepayment risk is much harder to model in the case of mortgage bonds. Homeowners' prepayment incentive depends on several factors: personal, economic and geographic. Prepayments can greatly influence a bond's performance; they can cause bonds to exhibit negative convexity, capping the price of the bond as interest rates fall, thereby capping returns. Furthermore, securities such as interest only bonds (which do not prepay principal but whose cashflows depend to a great extent of the level of prepayments) can lose a great deal of value as prepayments increase.

**Process transparency** A high level of process transparency is the opposite of a "black box", in which no details of the investment algorithm and internal controls are provided.

**Prudent man standard** A term used to govern business relationships when no precise rules exist. It is used to prescribe rules of behaviour between parties such as brokers and their clients, or management and shareholders.

**Put option** The right to sell (or put) a fixed amount at a fixed price within a given time frame.

**Putable bonds** Bonds with an embedded put option.

**Quartile** Statistic that divides the observations of a numeric sample into four intervals, each containing 25% of the data. The lower, middle and upper quartiles are computed by ordering the data from smallest to largest and then finding the values below which fall 25%, 50% and 75% of the data.

**Rebalancing** Realigning the proportions of assets in a portfolio or the hedge of an option.

**Rebate** Negotiated return of a portion of the interest earned by the lender of stock to a short seller.

**Repo** An agreement in which one party sells a security to another party and agrees to repurchase it on a specified date for a specified price.

**Rho** The dollar change in a given option's price that results from a 1% change in interest rates.

**Risk adjusted ratio** A term used to describe various measurements that seek to normalise returns for the differences in risk associated with achieving these returns. The most common measure is the *Sharpe ratio*, which takes the absolute return, subtracts the risk-free return, and then divides by the volatility of the returns.

**Risk arbitrage** A hedge fund strategy that involves a portfolio manager buying the stock of a company that he/she believes will be acquired and selling the stock of the company that he/she believes will be the acquirer.

**Risk attribution** The deconstruction of a hedge fund's risk profile to explain the source of the risks.

**Risk budgeting** The process by which risk is allocated and the return on risk is maximised.

**Risk measurement** The process by which a risk manager attempts to monitor the risk of a portfolio or entity. This entails ensuring that adequate controls and procedures exist and are applied in a disciplined fashion that comply with the laws. This function is usually carried out by auditors, financial controllers and compliance departments.

**Risk mitigation** A term that describes neutralising measured risk exposure by some offsetting position or by reducing the positions that are causing the exposure.

**Risk profile** This is the high level risk landscape of a fund. It is the output of a good risk management tool, not the input.

**Risk/reward ratio** See *Sharpe ratio*.

**S&P500** A widely followed benchmark of stock market performance, the S&P500 includes 400 industrial firms, 40 financial stocks, 40 utilities and 20 transportation stocks.

**Scenario analysis** This is the process by which portfolio risks are measured by subjecting the portfolio to "what-if" market situations based on historical events. Another variation is stress testing, which often entails moving stocks, interest rates, volatilities and other risk parameters on a statistical or historical basis and monitoring the performance of the portfolio from such moves.

**Sector** A group of securities that are similar with respect to maturity, type, rating, industry and/or coupon.

**Sharpe ratio** A key risk/reward ratio used to compare the rate of reward with the risk of gaining that reward. The formula is the annualised geometric rate of return minus rate of return on a risk-free investment divided by the annualised arithmetic standard deviation, developed by Professor William R. Sharpe of Stanford University.

**Short only** A hedge fund strategy that involves a portfolio manager selling stocks that he/she believes will decline in value.

**Short position** Occurs when stocks are sold that are not yet owned. Securities must be borrowed, before the sale, to make "good delivery" to the buyer.

**Short-term rate** This term refers to interest rates that are two years or fewer in maturity. These rates can determine the cost of liquidity and other borrowing rates, such as repurchase agreements.

**Small cap** These are usually companies with small market capitalisations. While a small cap stock is currently understood as one with a value of US$300 million–US$2 billion, this definition has changed over time with the stock market.

**Spread** The excess of the price or yield on a particular security or instrument relative to a benchmark. For example, the "spread over Treasury" is the difference between the yield for a certain fixed income instrument and the yield for a comparable US Treasury security.

**Standard deviation** Technically, a statistical measure of the dispersion of a set of numbers around a central point. Standard deviation measures the *volatility*, or uncertainty, of investment returns and is therefore commonly used to measure the risk of a portfolio. The higher the standard deviation of a portfolio, the higher the uncertainty of the portfolio's return.

**Stock–futures arbitrage** A hedge fund strategy that involves a portfolio manager buying a basket of stocks and selling the corresponding stock index futures or vice versa.

**Strategy drift** When the stated strategy of a fund diverges from the actual strategy. An example would be a diversified equity long only fund ending up with a 50% fixed income allocation.

**Stress test** A general term for the practice of subjecting a *model* (eg, a VAR model) to inputs that are adjusted to represent extreme or unusual changes in *market factors*. The sources of stress may be actual historical changes in *market factors* or hypothetical changes.

**Swap** A swap is an agreement between two parties to exchange cashflows in the future. The most general swap is the interest rate swap, where one party pays a fixed rate in exchange for a floating interest rate. A hybrid of this is the currency swap, where one payment is made in one currency while the other is made in a different currency. There are all sorts of complex swaps in the market today, many having embedded options. Credit default swaps and volatility swaps are gaining popularity.

**Swaption** An option on a swap. The buyer of a swaption has the right to enter into a swap agreement by some specified date in the future. The writer of the swaption becomes the counterparty to the swap if the buyer exercises.

**Term structure of interest rates** Relationship between interest rates on bonds of different maturities usually depicted in the form of a graph often called a *yield curve*.

**Theta** Also called time decay, the ratio of the change in an option price to the decrease in time to expiration.

**Tracking error** In an indexing strategy, the *standard deviation* of the difference between the performance of the *benchmark* and the replicating portfolio.

**Translucency** A risk profile without the underlying positions.

**Transparency** This term is often equated with position level data.

**Underlying** The interest rate, currency, equity or community instrument that the parties agree to exchange in a derivative contract.

**Value-at-risk (VAR) model** VAR is a statistical method of estimating the quantifiable chance (usually a given confidence level) of a particular quantifiable loss within a particular time frame. There are many ways VAR is calculated: these include the variance/covariance method, which models the statistics using historical data; and Monte Carlo simulations, which estimate future values of the portfolio based on pre-determined parameters. More sophisticated methods of calculating VAR, such as extreme value theory (EVT), or GARCH, focus on tail events to fine-tune loss estimates.

**Vega** The sensitivity of an option's price to a change in volatility.

**Volatility** Volatility is a statistic that measures the amount an instrument or rate will deviate from its historical average path or trend. Usually volatility is measured by the *standard deviation* of a random variable. In option parlance, it is important to note the difference between historical and implied volatility. Historical volatility is the *standard deviation* of a random variable; implied volatility is the volatility that is extrapolated from the options price: it is a measure of what option buyers are perceiving future volatility of the underlying security to be.

**Volatility of return** Measures the relative level of volatility for funds in a particular style.

**Volatility surface** This term is used in the fixed income world, where the *yield curve* is made up of several random variables (rates of different maturities), each with a volatility of its own. Furthermore, each of these yields have forwards (commonly used to price forward starting swaps or constant maturity swaps) that also have their own volatilities (commonly obtainable from caps, floors and swaptions). A 10-year rate can have forward rates at the one-year point, two-year point and so on, each having their own volatility. For each point on the term structure, out-of-the-money, at-the-money and in-the-money options have their own "smile". These can be pooled together to form a matrix, or a "surface", that describes the volatility for the term structure (both spot and forward) as a whole.

**Yield curve** At any point in time, a yield curve is the graphical representation of the various yields at which different maturities of similar bonds trade. An example of a yield curve is that of the US Treasuries of different maturities. Another yield curve is the "swap curve" that is derived from Libor futures contracts. Discount factors calculated from these two curves are commonly used to value fixed income financial instruments.

**Yield curve risk** Yield curve risk is the possibility that the curve will move, resulting in changes in the values of fixed income instruments. There are many dimensions of yield curve risk facing investors in fixed income instruments. Two common ways to measure yield curve risk are "key rate duration" and principal component decomposition". Key rate duration is calculated as the sensitivity, measured as a per cent price change (duration) to a small (usually one basis point) shock in each point on the yield curve. Principal component decomposition is a mathematical construct that seeks to decompose any yield curve movement into basic factors. The standard solution has three factors that can be used to construct any yield curve movement to a high degree of accuracy. These factors are a parallel shift, a steepening where long maturity yields increase and short maturity yields decrease, and a butterfly-type movement that consists of short maturity and long maturity yields decreasing and middle maturity yields increasing.

**Yield curve shape** The shape of the *yield curve* is determined by the relative level of the different maturity interest rates. Often the economic conditions in a country have a strong influence on the shape of the *yield curve*. For example, in economic downturns, the *yield curve* can become negatively shaped (meaning that short-term rates are higher than long-term rates) due to the sudden need for funds for the corporate sector.

**Worst case analysis** This is a form of scenario analysis, where the portfolio is subjected to sharp or "worst case" market moves to determine performance and uncover risks. While the scenarios that can be used are subjective to the risk monitors, sophisticated statistical methods, such as principal components, are commonly used.

1   President's Working Group on Financial Markets 2000, p. III-1.
2   URL:http://www.aima.org/.

# Appendix 8

# *Bibliography*

**Abdulali, A., and E. Weinstein,** 2002, "Hedge Fund Transparency: Quantifying Valuation Bias for Illiquid Assets", *Risk,* June, pp. S25–S28.

**Acar, E.,** 2001, *Added Value in Financial Institutions* (New Jersey: Financial Times Prentice-Hall).

**Acar, E., and P. Lequeux,** 1999, "Currency Overlay: Active Versus Passive Management", *AIMA Newsletter,* June, pp. 36–8.

**Acar, E., and H. Pederson**, 2001, "Which Currency Benchmarks for an Active International Investor?", *AIMA Newsletter,* April, pp. 17–19.

**Acar, E., and S. Satchell**, 1998, *Advanced Trading Rules* (Oxford: Butterworth-Heinemann).

**Ackermann, C.,** 1998, "The Impact of Regulatory Restrictions on Fund Performance: A Comparative Study of Hedge Funds and Mutual Funds", *FMA Presentation,* October.

**Ackermann, C., R. McEnally and D. Ravenscraft**, 1999, "The Performance of Hedge Funds: Risk, Return and Incentives", *The Journal of Finance,* IV(3), June.

**Advanced Visual Systems Inc.,** Data Visualisation Provider, (http://www.dvs.com).

**Agarwal, R., and D. Schirm,** 1995, *Global Portfolio Diversification: Risk Management, Market Microstructure, and Implementation Issues* (London: Academic Press).

**AIMA**, 2002, "Guide to Sound Practices for European Hedge Fund Managers", (http://www.aima.org/SoundPracticesEurope.pdf).

**AIMR**, 1998, "Alternative Investing", (Charlottesville, VA: AIMR Publication).

**AIMR,** 1999, *Standards of Practice Handbook: 1999*, Eighth Edition (Georgia: Professional Book Distributors).

**Alexander, C., I. Giblin and W. Weddington**, 2001, "Cointegration and Asset Allocation: A New Active Hedge Fund Strategy", (http://www.ismacentre.rdg.ac.uk).

**Allenbridge Group PLC**, 2000, "Primer on Hedge Funds of Funds Benchmark Criteria: Investor Protection in Unregulated Investment Schemes", November.

**Altvest Hedge Funds Database,** (http://www.investorforce.com).

**Andersen**, 2002, "Investing in Hedge Funds, A Survey on the Risk Approach Adopted by the Swiss Marketplace", (http://www.andersen.com/switzerland).

**Anson, M.,** 1999, "Maximizing Utility with Commodity Futures Diversification", *The Journal of Portfolio Management,* 25(4), pp. 86–94, Summer.

**Anson, M.**, 1998, "Spot Returns, Roll Yield, and Diversification with Commodity Futures", *The Journal of Alternative Investments,* Winter, pp. 1–17.

**Anson, M.**, 2002, "Funds of Funds vs Individual Hedge Funds", in: Capital Market Risk Advisors (ed) and AIMA Research, *A Guide to Fund of Hedge Funds Management and Investment*, October, pp. 10–15.

**Asness, C., R. Krail, J. Liew and AQR Capital Management, LLC**, 2000, "Do Hedge Funds Hedge?", December, (http://manager.hedgeworld.com/research/download/ssrn_id252810_code001208510.pdf).

**Bacon, L. M.**, 2000, "Can Institutions Afford to Ignore Hedge Funds?", Keynote speech at the 2000 Hedge Fund Symposium, April, London.

**Bain, W. G.**, 1996, *Investment Performance Measurement* (Cambridge: Woodhead Publishing Limited).

**Barham, S.**, 2001, *Starting a Hedge Fund – a US Perspective* (Bermuda: ISI Publications Limited).

**Barham, S., and I. Hallsworth**, 2002, *Starting a Hedge Fund – a European Perspective* (Bermuda: ISI Publications).

**Barra Strategic Consulting Group**, 2001, "Fund of Hedge Funds – Rethinking Resource Requirements" (http://www.cqallc.com/whitepapers/index.asp).

**Beder, T. S.**, 1995, "Guidelines for a Brave New Pension World", *Derivatives Strategy*, November, pp. 58–62.

**Beder, T. S.**, 1994, "Learning from Fund Losses in Derivatives", *Treasury & Risk Management* November/December, pp. 52–3.

**Beeman, D.**, 2002, "Portfolio Construction", in: Capital Market Risk Advisors (ed) and AIMA Research, *A Guide to Fund of Hedge Funds Management and Investment*, October pp. 38–43.

**Bekier, M.**, 1996, "Marketing Hedge Funds - A Key Strategic Variable in Defining Possible Roles of an Emerging Investment Force" (Berne: Peter Lang AG, European Academic Publishers).

**Bernstein, J.**, 1992, *Strategic Futures Trading: Contemporary Trading Systems to Maximize Profits* (Chicago: Dearnborn Trade Publishing).

**Bernstein, P. L.**, 1996, *Against the Gods: The Remarkable Story of Risk* (New York: John Wiley & Sons).

**Bernstein, P. L.**, 1992, *Capital Ideas - The Improbable Origins of Modern Wall Street* (New York: The Free Press).

**Bogle, J. C.**, 1991, "Investing in the 1990s: Remembering of Things Past and Things Yet to Come", *The Journal of Portfolio Management*, Spring, pp. 5–14.

**Bogle, J. C.**, 1998, "The Implication of Style Analysis for Mutual Fund Performance Evaluation", *The Journal of Portfolio Management*, Summer, pp. 34–42.

**Boucher, M.**, 1999, *The Hedge Fund Edge: Maximum Profit/Minimum Risk Global Trend Trading Strategies* (New York: John Wiley & Sons).

**Bousbib, G.**, 2000, "The Infrastructure Challenge: Empowering the Stakeholder through the Successful Deployment of Technology and Data", in: *Risk Budgeting: A New Approach to Investing*, L. Rahl (ed), (London: Risk Books) pp. 249–80.

**Boyle, P. P., and F. Boyle**, 2001, *Derivatives: The Tools that Changed Finance* (London: Risk Books).

**Brittain, B., and Lyster Watson & Company**, 2001, "Hedge Funds and the Institutional Investor", *Journal of International Financial Management & Accounting*, Summer, 12(2).

**Brorsen, B. W.**, 2002, "Performance Persistence for Managed Futures", *Institutional Investor Journal*, Spring, 4(4), pp. 57–61.

**Brown, S. J., W. N. Goetzmann and R. G. Ibbotson**, 1997, "Offshore Hedge Funds: Survival and Performance, 1989–1995", *National Bureau of Economic Research Working Paper Series*.

**Brown, S. J., W. N. Goetzmann, R. G. Ibbotson and S. A Ross**, 1992 , "Survivorship Bias in Performance Studies", *Review of Financial Studies*, 5(4), pp. 553–80.

**Brown, S. J., W. N. Goetzmann and J. Park**, 1997, "Conditions for Survival: Changing Risk and the Performance of Hedge Fund Managers and CTAs", Working Paper, Yale/SOM, November (http://papers.ssrn.com/sol3/papers.cfm?abstract_id=58477).

**Brown, S. J., W. N. Goetzmann and J. Park**, 2000, "Hedge Funds and the Asian Currency Crisis", *The Journal of Portfolio Management*, 26(4), pp. 95–101.

**Burghardt, G., and S. Kirshner**, 1997, *Treasury Options for Institutional Investors*, Chicago Board of Trade, Market Data Corporation, (Chicago Board of Trade).

**Burghardt, G., T. Belton, M. Lane and R. McVey**, 1991, *Eurodollar Futures and Options: Controlling Money Market Risk* (Chicago: Probus Publishing Co.).

**Burghardt, G., T. Belton, M. Lane and J. Papa**, 1993, *The Treasury Bond Basis* (Chicago: Probus Publishing).

**Butler, D.**, 2001, "Equalisation – Is it Worth the Heartache? (Part II)", *AIMA* Newsletter, pp. 7–12.

**Capital Market Risk Advisors,** 1996a, "Bank of England Survey Regarding Option Valuation Models".

**Capital Market Risk Advisors,** 1996b, "Marshall and Siegel Study – Value at Risk: Implementing a Risk Measurement Standard".

**Capital Market Risk Advisors,** 2000, "Transparent to Opaque and Everything In Between", *AIMA Newsletter*, January/February, (http://www.cmra.com/cgibin/benign.cgi).

**Capital Market Risk Advisors,** 2002a, "How to Select a Buy-Side Risk Management System Comparison Matrix" (http://www.cmra.com/cgi-bin/Systems.cgi).

**Capital Market Risk Advisors,** 2002b, "Haircuts: Going to the Collateral Barber", (http://www.cmra.com/cgibin/haircuts.cgi).

**Capital Market Risk Advisors,** 2002c, "Merger Arbitrage Fund, Do They Deliver What They Promise?" (http://www.cmra.com/cgi-bin/MergerArb.cgi).

**Capital Market Risk Advisors,** 2002d, "Hedge Fund Survey Overview", (http://www.cmra.com/cgi-bin/HF.cgi).

**Capital Market Risk Advisors,** 2002e, "NAV/Fair Value Practices Survey Overview", (http://www.cmra.com/cgi-bin/nav.cgi).

**Capital Market Risk Advisors,** 2002f, "Risk Budgeting: The Next Step of the Risk Management Journey", in: L. Rahl (ed), *Risk Budgeting: A New Approach to Investing*, (London: Risk Books) pp. 3–25, (http://www.cmra.com/cgi-bin/budgeting.cgi).

**Capital Market Risk Advisors,** 2002g, "Risk Insights, Lessons Learned" (http://www.cmra.com/cgibin/Lessons.cgi).

**Capital Market Risk Advisors,** 2002h, "Risk Insights, September 11, 2001" (http://www.cmra.com/cgibin/September11.cgi).

**Capital Market Risk Advisors,** 2002i, "Risk Standard for Institutional Investment Managers and Institutional Investors", (http://www.cmra.com/cgi-bin/InstInv.cgi).

**Capital Market Risk Advisors,** 2002j, "Risk Standards Overview", (http://www.cmra.com/cgi-bin/Standards.cgi).

**Capital Market Risk Advisors,** 2002k, "Survival After the Blaze", (http://www.cmra.com/cgi-bin/survival.cgi).

**Capital Market Risk Advisors,** 2002l, "Overview and Highlights of Survey", in: *A Guide to Fund of Hedge Funds Management and Investment*, Capital Market Risk Advisors (ed) and AIMA Research, October, pp. 4–9.

**Capital Market Risk Advisors** (ed) and **AIMA**, 2002, *A Guide to Fund of Hedge Funds Management and Investment*, October (AIMA Research).

**Caslin, J.,** 2001, "Hedge Funds", presented to the Society of Actuaries in Ireland, October 9.

**Cass, D.,** 2000, "French Connection", *Risk,* April, p. 100.

**Chance, D. M., and R. R. Trippi,** 1995, *Advances in Futures and Options Research*, pp. 251–65 (New York: JAI Press).

**Chande, T.,** 1999, "Controlling Risk and Managing Investor Expectations by Modeling the Dynamics of Losses in Hedge Funds and Alternative Strategies", *Derivatives Quarterly,* 5(3), Spring, pp 52–8.

**Chandler, B.,** 1998, *Investing with the Hedge Fund Giants – Profits Whether Markets Rise or Fall* (London: Financial Times Pitman Publishing).

**Chandler, B.,** 1994, *Managed Futures: An Investor's Guide* (New York: John Wiley & Sons).

**Chopra, N., J. Lakonishok and J. Ritter,** 1992, "Measuring Abnormal Performance", *Journal of Financial Economics*, pp. 235–68.

**Chung, S. Y.,** 2000, "The Risks and Rewards of Investing in Commodity-Based Indices", *The Journal of Alternative Investments,* 3(1), Summer, pp. 21–31.

**Coleman, T. S.,** 2000, "Compensating Fund Managers for Risk-Adjusted Performance", *AIMA Newsletter.*

**Coleman, T. S.,** 2002, "Funds of Funds and Fees", in: *A Guide to Fund of Hedge Funds Management and Investment*, Capital Market Risk Advisors (ed) and AIMA Research, October, pp. 62–3.

**Connors, L. A., and B. E., Hayward,** 1995, *Investment Secrets: Hedge Fund Manager,* (New York: McGraw-Hill Trade).

**Cottier, P.,** 1997, *Hedge Funds and Managed Futures: Performance, Risks, Strategies and Use in Investment Portfolios* (Bern: Verlag Paul Haupt).

**Cowles, A.,** July 1933, "Can Stock Market Forecasters Forecast?", Econometrica, 1, pp. 309–24.

**Crapple, G.,** 1999, "Are All Alternative Assets Hedge Funds?", *The Journal of Alternative Investments,* 1(4), pp. 79–84.

**Crerend, W. J.,** 1998, *Fundamentals of Hedge Fund Investing – A Professional Investor's Guide* (New York: McGraw-Hill).

**Cullen, I.,** 1999a, "Managed Futures Funds in Europe", *AIMA Special Report.*

**Cullen, I.,** 1999b, "Marketing Hedge Funds", *AIMA Special Report.*

**Cullen, I., and H. Parry,** 2000, *Hedge Funds: Law and Regulation*, Special Report (London: Sweet & Maxwell).

**Culp, C. L., R., Mensink and A. M. P. Neves,** 2000, "Value-at-Risk for Asset Managers", in: *Risk Budgeting: A New Approach to Investing,* L. Rahl (ed), (London: Risk Books) pp. 83–102.

**Daniel, K., M. Grinblatt, S. Titmanand and R. Wermers,** 1997, "Measuring Mutual Fund Performance with Characteristic-Based Benchmarks", *The Journal of Finance*, 52(3), pp. 1035–58.

**De Bever, L., W. Kozun and B. Zvan,** 2000, "Risk Budgeting in a Pension Fund", in: *Risk Budgeting: A New Approach to Investing*, L. Rahl (ed), (London: Risk Books) pp. 283–97.

**De Marco, M., and T. E. Petzel,** 2000, "Risk Budgeting with Conditional Risk Tolerance", in: *Risk Budgeting: A New Approach to Investing*, L. Rahl (ed), (London: Risk Books) pp. 299–329.

**DeRosa, D.,** 1996, *Managing Foreign Exchange Risk* (Ontario: Irwin Professional Publishing).

**Deutsche Bank,** 2000, "The Capital Guide to Alternative Investments", UK, ISI Publications.

**Diz, F.,** 1999, "CTA Survivor and Nonsurvivor: An Analysis of Relative Performance", *The Journal of Alternative Investments*, 2(1), Summer, pp. 57–71.

**Dunbar, N.,** 2000, *Inventing Money: The Story of Long-Term Capital Management and the Legends Behind It* (New York: John Wiley & Sons).

**Dunlevy, J.,** 1999, "An Overview of Basic Mortgage (MBS) Structures", Beacon Hill Asset Management, March.

**Edwards, F. R.,** 1999, "Do Hedge Funds Have a Future?", *The Journal of Alternative Investments*, 2(2), Fall, pp. 63–8.

**Edwards, F. R.,** 1999, "Hedge Funds and the Collapse of Long Term Capital Management", *Journal of Economic Perspectives*, 13(2), Spring, pp. 189–210.

**Edwards, F. R., and J. Liew,** 1999, "Hedge Funds versus Managed Futures as Asset Classes", *The Journal of Derivatives*, 6(4), Summer, pp 45–64.

**Edwards, F. R., and J. Park,** 1995, "Do Managed Futures Make Good Investments", *The Journal of Futures Markets*, Graduate School of Business, Columbia University, Papers No. 95–32.

**Eichengreen, B.,** 1998, "Hedge Funds and Financial Market Dynamics", Occasional Paper, International Monetary Fund.

**Eichengreen, B., and D. Mathieson,** 1999, "Hedge Funds: What Do We Really Know?", IMF, *Economic Issues*, 19.

**Elton, E., and M. Gruber,** 1991, *Modern Portfolio Theory and Investment Analysis* (New York: John Wiley & Sons).

**Elton, E., M. Gruber and C. Blake,** 1996, "The Persistence of Risk-Adjusted Mutual Fund Performance", *Journal of Business*, 69(2), pp. 133–57.

**Epstein, C. B.,** 1992, *Managed Futures in the Institutional Portfolio* (New York: John Wiley & Sons).

**Fama, E. F.,** 1970, "Efficient Capital Markets: A Review of Theory and Empirical Work", *The Journal of Finance*, 25, pp. 383–417.

**Fama, E. F.,** 1998, "Market Efficiency, Long-Term Returns, and Behavioral Finance", *Journal of Financial Economics*, 49(3), pp. 283–306.

**Farrell, J. L.,** 1997, *Portfolio Management Theory & Application* (New York: McGraw-Hill).

**Favre, L., J. A. Galeano,** June 2000, "Portfolio Allocation with Hedge Funds: Case Study of a Swiss Institutional Investor".

**Fortune,** 1966, "Personal Investing – Those Fantastic 'Hedge Funds'" April, pp. 15–20.

**Fothergill, M., and C. Coke,** 2000, "Deutsche Bank Report on Funds of Hedge Funds", November.

**Fox-Andrews, M., and N. Meaden,** 1992, *Futures Fund Management* (New Jersey: Prentice Hall Trade).

**Fox-Andrews, M., and N. Meaden,** 1995, *Derivatives Markets and Investment Management* (New Jersey: Prentice Hall/Woodhead-Faulkner).

**Froot, K.,** 1995, "Hedging Portfolios with Real Assets," *The Journal of Portfolio Management,* Summer, pp.60–77.

**Fung, W., and D. A. Hsieh,** 1997, "Empirical Characteristics of Dynamic Trading Strategies: The Case of Hedge Funds", *The Review of Financial Studies,* 10(2), pp. 275–302.

**Fung, W., and D. A. Hsieh,** 1999, "A Primer on Hedge Funds", Working Paper, Fuqua School of Business, Duke University.

**Fung, W., and D. A. Hsieh,** 2000, "Measuring The Market Impact of Hedge Funds", Working Paper, *Journal of Empirical Finance,* 7 (2001), pp. 1–36.

**Fung, W., and D. A. Hsieh,** 1998, "Pricing Trend Following Trading Strategies: Theory and Empirical Evidence," Final Report to The Foundation For Managed Derivatives Research, September.

**Gitlin, A. W. and C. C. Peters,** 1993, *Strategic Currency Investing* (Chicago: Probus Professional Publications).

**Goetzmann, W. N., J. Ingersoll and S. A. Ross,** 1998, "High Water Marks", Yale School of Management Working Paper, January.

**Goldman, Sachs & Co. and Financial Risk Management Ltd.,** 1998, "Hedge Funds Demystified – Their Potential Risk in Institutional Portfolios", July.

**Goldman Sachs & Co. and Financial Risk Management Ltd.,** 2000, "Hedge Funds Revisited", Pension & Endowment Forum.

**Greer, R.,** 1994, "Methods for Institutional Investment in Commodity Futures", *The Journal of Derivatives,* Winter, pp. 28–36.

**Grinblatt, M., and S. Titman,** 1989, "Mutual Fund Performance: An Analysis of Quarterly Portfolio Holdings", *Journal of Business,* 62, pp. 393–416.

**Grinhold, R., and R. Kahn,** 2000, "The Efficiency Gains of Long-Short Investing," *Financial Analysts Journal,* November/December, pp. 40–53.

**Grossman, S.,** 1976, "On the Efficiency of Competitive Stock Markets Where Traders have Diverse Information", *The Journal of Finance,* 31, pp. 573–85.

**Hale, T.,** 2001, "Old Principles – New Focus", Albion Strategic Consulting.

**Hammer, D.,** 1991, *Dynamic Asset Allocation: Strategies for the Stock, Bond, and Money Markets* (New York: John Wiley & Sons).

**Haugen, R. A., and Jorion, P.,** 1996, "The January Effect: Still There after All These Years", *Financial Analyst Journal,* 52 (1), pp. 27–31.

**HedgeWorld,** 2001, *Annual Compendium 2001: The Definitive Hedge Fund Reference Guide.*

**Hedgeworld,** 2002, *Annual Compendium 2002: The Definitive Hedge Fund Reference Guide.*

**HedgeWorld** Reports Library, (http://www.hedgeworld.com/research).

**Hedge Fund Research,** 2000, "Market Neutral and Hedged Strategies", August.

**Heim, R. G., and H. S. Meyers,** 2001, "An Overview of U.S. Hedge Fund Regulation", *AIMA Newsletter,* September.

**Hills, R.,** 1996, *Hedge Funds: An Introduction to Skill-Based Investment Strategies,* (London: Rushmere Wynne Limited).

**Hirsch, A. B.,** 2000, "Risk Obsession: Does it Lead to Risk Aversion?", in: *Risk Budgeting: A New Approach to Investing*, L. Rahl (ed), pp. 159–73.

**Hopkins, S.,** 2000, "On Phenomenal Growth Track", Investment & Pensions Europe, June, (http://www.ipeonline.com/article.asp?article=10574).

**Horwitz, R., and L. Rodriguez,** 2001, "Merger Arbitrage Funds, Do They Deliver What They Promise?", (http://www.cmra.com/cgi-bin/MergerArb.cgi).

**Howell, M.,** 2000, "Tactical Style Selection", *AIMA Newsletter*, September.

**Ikenberry, D. L., R. L.Shockley and K. L. Womack,** 1998, "Why Active Fund Managers Often Underperform the S&P 500: The Impact of Size and Skewness", *Journal of Private Portfolio Management*, 1(1), pp. 13–26.

**IMF** (Prepared by the FSF HLI Working Group), Background Note on the Hedge Fund Industry.

**Ineichen, A. M.,** 2000, "In Search of Alpha – Investing in Hedge Funds", (UBS Warburg), October.

**Ineichen, A. M.,** 2001, "The Search for Alpha Continues – Do 'Fund of Hedge Funds' Managers Add Value?", UBS Warburg, September.

**Ineichen, A. M.,** 2001, "The Myth of Hedge Funds: Are Hedge Funds Ahead of the Storm?", October.

**INDOCAM/Watson Wyatt**, 2000a, "Alternative Investment Review Relating To The Continental European Marketplace", November.

**INDOCAM/Watson Wyatt**, 2000b, "Alternative Investment Review Relating To The United Kingdom Marketplace", March.

**INDOCAM/Watson Wyatt**, 2000c, "Alternative Investment Review Relating To The United States Marketplace", March.

**Institutional Investor,** 2002, "The Hedge Fund 100", *Institutional Investor*, June, pp. 43–52.

**Irwin, S., C. Zulauf and B. Ward,** 1994, "The Predictability of Managed Futures Returns", *The Journal of Derivatives*, Winter, pp. 20–7.

**ISI Publications,** 2001a, *The Capital Guide to Alternative Investments*, Second Edition, (Bermuda: ISI Publications Limited).

**ISI Publications,** 2000b, *A Global Guide to Marketing Funds*, First Edition, (Bermuda: ISI Publications Limited).

**ISI Publications,** 2001c, *The Capital Guide to Offshore Funds*, Fifth Edition, (Bermuda: ISI Publications Limited).

**Jacobs, B. I.,** 1998, "Controlled Risk Strategies in Alternative Investing", ICFA Continuing Education, *AIMR*, August, 5, pp. 70–81.

**Jacobs, B. I., and K. N. Levy,** 1999, "Alpha Transport with Derivatives", *The Journal of Portfolio Management*, 25(5), pp. 55–60, Special Issue.

**Jaeger, L.,** 2002a, *Managing Risk in Alternative Investment Strategies: Investing in Hedge Funds and Managed Futures* (New York: Financial Times Prentice Hall).

**Jaeger, L.,** 2002b, "The Significance of Liquidity and Transparency for Multi-manager Hedge Fund Portfolios", in: *A Guide to Fund of Hedge Funds Management and Investment*, Capital Market Risk Advisors (ed) and AIMA Research, October, pp. 44–7.

**Jaffer, S.,** 1998, *Alternative Investment Strategies* (London: Euromoney Publications).

**Jensen, G., R. Johnson and J. Mercer,** 2000, "Efficient Use of Commodity Futures in Diversified Portfolios", *Journal of Futures Market,* 20(5), pp. 489–506.

**Jorion, P.,** 2000, "Risk Management Lessons from Long-Term Capital Management" January IFCI Risk Institute, Geneva, Switzerland.

**Jorion, P.,** 2001, *Value at Risk: The New Benchmark for Managing Financial Risk,* Second Edition (New York: McGraw-Hill).

**Kahn, R. N.,** 1998, "Bond Managers Need to Take More Risk", *The Journal of Portfolio Management,* Spring, pp. 70–6.

**Karavas, V. N.,** 2000, "Alternative Investments in the Institutional Portfolio", *The Journal of Alternative Investments,* 3(3), pp. 11–26.

**Kat, H.,** 2001, "Hedge Fund Mania – Some Words of Caution", Working Paper, ISMA Centre, (http://www.ismacentre.rdg.ac.uk).

**Kat, H., and G. Amin,** 2001a, "Hedge Fund Performance 1990–2000", Working Paper, ISMA Centre (http://www.ismacentre.rdg.ac.uk).

**Kat, H., and G. Amin,** 2001b, "Hedge Fund Performance 1990–2000: Do the Money Machines Really Add Value?", Working Paper, ISMA Center, (http://www.ismacentre.rdg.ac.uk).

**Kat, H., and G. Amin,,** 2001c, "Welcome to the Dark Side: Hedge Fund Attrition and Survivorship Bias Over the Period 1994–2001", Working Paper, ISMA Centre, December.

**Kaufman, P. J.,** 1987, *The New Commodity Trading Systems and Methods* (New York: John Wiley & Sons).

**Keating, C., and W. F. Shadwick,** 2002, "A Universal Performance Measure", Finance Development Centre, London, January.

**Klein, R. A., and J. Lederman,** 1994, *Global Asset Allocation: Techniques for Optimizing Portfolio Management* (New York: John Wiley & Sons).

**Klein, R. A., and J. Lederman,** 1995a, *Hedge Funds: Investment and Portfolio Strategies for the Institutional Investor* (New York: McGraw-Hill Trade).

**Klein, R. A., and J. Lederman,** 1995b, *Market Neutral: Long/Short Strategies for Every Market Environment* (New York: McGraw-Hill Trade).

**Klein, R. A., and J. Lederman,** 1996, *Derivatives Risk and Responsibility: The Complete Guide to Effective Derivatives Management and Decision-Making* (New York: McGraw-Hill Professional Publishing).

**Kline, D.,** 2000, *Fundamentals of the Futures Market* (New York: McGraw-Hill Trade).

**Klopfentstein, G. and J. Stein,** 1993, *Trading Currency Cross Rates* (New York: John Wiley & Sons).

**Kuhn, T. S.,** 1962, *The Structure of Scientific Revolutions* (University of Chicago Press).

**Kutzen, T.,** 1999a, "The Perfect Hedge Fund (part I)", *AIMA Newsletter,* June.

**Kutzen, T.,** 1999b, "The Perfect Hedge Fund (part II)", *AIMA Newsletter,* September.

**Lake, R.,** 1996, *Evaluating and Implementing Hedge Fund Strategies: The Experience of Managers and Investors* (London: Euromoney Publications).

**Lavinio, S.,** 1999, *The Hedge Fund Handbook – A Definitive Guide for Analyzing and Evaluating Alternative Investments* (New York: McGraw-Hill Trade).

**Lederman, J., and M. Pettis,** 1998, *The New Dynamics of Emerging Market Investment: Managing Sub-Investment-Grade Sovereign Risk* (London: Euromoney Publications).

**Leibowitz, M. L., L. N. Bader and S. Kogelman,** 1995, *Return Targets and Shortfall Risk: Studies in Strategic Asset Allocation* (New York: McGraw-Hill Trade).

**Lequeux, P.,** 2000, *Alternative Investments: Managed Currencies* (London: Euromoney Publications).

**Lequeux, P.,** 1999, *Financial Markets Tick by Tick* (New York: John Wiley & Sons).

**Leslie Rahl Associates,** 1992, "Mark to Market Issues of Less Liquid OTC Products".

**Liang, B.,** 1999, "On the Performance of Hedge Funds", *Financial Analysts Journal*, July/August, 55(4), pp. 72–85

**Liang, B.,** 2000, "Hedge Funds: The Living and the Dead", *Journal of Financial and Quantitative Analysis*, September, pp 309–26.

**Liang, B.,** 2001, "Hedge Fund Performance: 1990–1999", *Financial Analysts Journal*, January/February, pp. 11–18.

**Litterman, R., J. Longerstaey, J. Rosengarten and K. Winkelmann,** 2000, "Risk Budgeting for Active Investment Managers", in: *Risk Budgeting: A New Approach to Investing*, L. Rahl (ed), (London: Risk Books) pp. 131–58.

**Lo, A. W., and C. A. MacKinlay,** 2002, *A Non-random Walk Down Wall Street* (New Jersey: Princeton University Press).

**Lofthouse, S.,** 1995, *Reading in Investments* (New York: John Wiley & Sons).

**Lukomnik, J.,** 1999a, "Culture Clash: Why Institutions Don't Allocate to Hedge Funds", *AIMA Newsletter*, September/October.

**Lukomnik, J.,** 1999b, "Not All Alpha is Created Equal", *FOW Supplement*, October, pp. 10–12.

**Lukomnik, J.,** 2002, "Due Diligence", in: *A Guide to Fund of Hedge Funds Management and Investment*, Capital Market Risk Advisors (ed) and AIMA Research, October, pp. 55–61.

**Malkiel, B. G.,** 1995, "Returns from Investing in Equity Mutual Funds, 1971 to 1991", *The Journal of Finance*, 50(2), pp. 549–72.

**Mansi, C., and A. Macdonald,** 2002, "Selecting, Benchmarking and Monitoring Funds of Hedge Funds", in: *A Guide to Fund of Hedge Funds Management and Investment*, Capital Market Risk Advisors (ed) and AIMA Research, October, pp. 34–7.

**Markowitz, H. M.,** 1959, *Portfolio Selection: Efficient Diversification of Investments* (New York: John Wiley & Sons).

**Martin, G.,** 2000, "Making Sense of Hedge Fund Returns: What Matters and What Doesn't?", *Derivatives Strategy*, Center for International Securities and Derivatives Markets, University of Massachusetts.

**McCafferty, T. A.,** 1994, *Winning with Managed Futures: How to Select a Top Performing Commodity Trading Advisor* (Chicago: Probus Professional Publishing).

**McCarthy, M.,** 2000, "Risk Budgeting for Pension Funds and Investment Managers Using VAR", in: *Risk Budgeting: A New Approach to Investing*, L. Rahl (ed), (London: Risk Books) pp. 103–30.

**McCarthy, D., T. Schneeweis, and R. Spurgin,** 1997, "Informational Content in Historical Performance", *Journal of Futures Market*, May, pp.44-7.

**McMillan, L. G.,** 1980, *Options as a Strategic Investment* (New York Institute of Finance).

**Meyers, H. S., and R. G. Heim,** 2001, "An Overview of U.S. Hedge Fund Regulation", *AIMA Newsletter*, September.

**Miller, M. H.,** 1997, *Merton Miller on Derivatives* (New York: John Wiley & Sons).

**Miller, M., and M. Scholes,** 1972, "Rate of Return in Relation to Risk: A Re-examination of Some Recent Findings", in: *Studies in the Theory of Capital Markets*, M. Jensen (ed) (Praeger Publishers, New York) pp. 47–78.

**Moix, P., and C. Schmidhuber,** 2001, "Fat Tail Risk: The Case for Hedge Funds (part I)", *AIMA Newsletter*, September.

**Moriyama, E.,** 2001, "Asset Management Revolution: How to Protect Your Yen Asset Through Risk Diversification and Alternative Investment Strategy Vehicle", (Japan: Daini-Kaientai).

**Morgan Stanley DW,** Quantitative Strategies Team, 2000, "Why Hedge Funds Make Sense" November, (http://www.morganstanley.com/institutional/primebrokerage/hedgefunds_make_sense.pdf).

**Mulinacci, A.,** 2001, "Regulation: Italian Hedge Funds – A Look at Internal Regulations", September, KPMG.

**Naik, N. R., and V. Agarwal,** 1999a, "Multi-Period Performance Persistence Analysis of Hedge Funds", London Business School, December.

**Naik, N. R., and V. Agarwal,** 1999b, "On Taking The 'Alternative' Route: Risks, Rewards, Style and Performance Persistence of Hedge Funds", London Business School, December.

**Naik, N. R., and V. Agarwal,** 2000, "Performance Evaluation of Hedge Funds with Option-Based and Buy-and-Hold Strategies", *Journal of Financial and Quantitative Analysis*, September, pp.1–52.

**National Association of Pension Funds**, 2001, "Hedge Funds Made Simple: What a Trustee Needs to Know", National Association of Pension Funds.

**Nederlof, M.,** 1995a, "Risk Management Programs (AIMR)", ICFA Continuing Education, October.

**Nederlof, M.,** 1995b, "Structures in the City", DFM, April, pp. 17f.

**Nederlof, M.,** 1995c, "Warning Signs", DFM, July/August pp. 17–19.

**Nederlof, M.,** 1996, "Delegating in the Dark: A Threat to Realizing Maximum Alpha", in: *Alpha, The Positive Side of Risk*, Investors Press, 2, pp. 64–77.

**Nesbitt, S. L.,** 2002, "2002 Wilshire Report on State Retirement Systems: Funding Levels and Asset Allocation", Wilshire Associates, Inc.

**Nicholas, J. G.,** 1999, *Investing in Hedge Funds: Strategies for the New Marketplace* (New Jersey: Bloomberg Press).

**Nicholas, J. G.,** 2000a, "Market Neutral and Hedged Strategies", in: *Risk Budgeting: A New Approach to Investing*, L. Rahl (ed.) (London: Risk Books), pp. 175–247.

**Nicholas, J. G.,** 2000b, *Market Neutral Investing: Long/Short Hedge Fund Strategies* (New Jersey: Bloomberg Press).

**Owen, J. P.,** 2000, *The Prudent Investor's Guide to Hedge Funds: Profiting from Uncertainty and Volatility* (New York: John Wiley & Sons).

**Park, J. M., and J. C. Straum,** 1998, "Performance Persistence in the Alternative Investment Industry", Working Paper, Paradigm Capital Management Inc.

**Perold, A. F.,** 1999, "Long-Term Capital Management, L.P. (A)", Harvard Business School Publication, November.

**Peters, C., and B. Warwick,** 1996, *The Handbook of Managed Futures and Hedge Funds – Performance, Evaluation and Analysis* (New York: McGraw-Hill Trade).

**President's Working Group on Financial Markets**, 1999, "Hedge funds, Leverage, and the Lessons of Long-Term Capital Management", April, (http://www.aima.org).

**President's Working Group on Financial Markets**, 2000, "Sound Practices for Hedge Fund Managers", February, (http://www.aima.org).

**Purcell, D., and P. Crowley,** 1999, "The Reality of Hedge Funds", *The Journal of Investing*, 8(3), pp. 26–44.

**Raffkind, E. D., and F. Lacy,** 1998, "Frequently Asked Questions Concerning Investment Limited Partnerships (Hedge Funds) (http://articles.corporate.findlaw.com/library/firms/ag/pdf/agp000039.pdf).

**Rahl, L.,** 2000, *Risk Budgeting: A New Approach to Investing* (London: Risk Books).

**Rahl, L.,** 2001, "Survival After the Blaze", *AIMA Newsletter*, April.

**Rahl, L.,** 2002a, "Performance Measurement & Attribution", *Investment/Financial Services Review*, February.

**Rahl, L.,** 2002b, "The Basics of Hedge Fund Investing: Risk Insights", in: HedgeWorld, *Annual Compendium 2002: The Hedge Fund Industry's Definitive Reference Guide*, Sections 2–5 to 2–10.

**Rahl, L., A. Abdulali  and E. Weinstein,** 2002, "Phantom Prices & Liquidity: the Nuisance of Translucence", in: *A Guide to Fund of Hedge Funds Management and Investment*, Capital Market Risk Advisors (ed) and AIMA Research, October, pp. 48–54.

**Rahl, L., and S. Rahl,** 2002, "Institutionalization of Hedge Funds: How can Hedge Funds be Tamed Without Breaking Their Spirit or Negatively Impairing Their Performance?", in: *Hedge Fund Strategies, A Global Outlook*, B. R. Bruce, pp.69–73

**Rahl, L., and L. Rodriguez,** 2002, "Hedge Fund Diversification", in: *A Guide to Fund of Hedge Funds Management and Investment*, Capital Market Risk Advisors (ed) and AIMA Research, October, pp. 22–33.

**Rao, R., and J. J. Szilagyi,** 1998, "The Coming Evolution of the Hedge Fund Industry: A Case for Growth and Restructuring", RR Capital Management Corp./KPMG Peat Marwick LLP monograph.

**Rees, S.,** 2000, "VAR for Fund Managers", in: *Risk Budgeting: A New Approach to Investing*, L. Rahl (ed), (London: Risk Books) pp. 331–40.

**Reynolds Parker, V.,** 1996, "International Investing Coupled with Enhanced Currency Overlay: An Opportunity for Perfectly Portable Alpha".

**Reynolds Parker, V.,** 2001, *Managing Hedge Fund Risk* (London: Risk Books).

**Ritzi, A.,** 2000, "The Safe Way to Play Hedge Funds", RMF Capital Markets, August.

**Riskdata,** Risk Management Software Provider, www.riskdata.com.

**Risk Standards Working Group,** 1996, "Risk Standards for Institutional Investors".

**Rosenbaum, R. I.,** 2000, "Fund of Funds: The Right Choice for Your Client's Allocation to Hedge Funds", Tremont Advisers, Inc., September/October.

**Rostron, K.,** 1999, "Fund of Funds; Not Just for the Beginner", *AIMA Newsletter*, June/July.

**Samuelson, P. A.,** 1965, *Proof That Properly Anticipated Prices Fluctuate Randomly*, Industrial Management Review, 6, pp. 41–9.

**Schaer, C.,** 2001, "Curve Fitting: A Pernicious Illusion", *AIMA Newsletter*, June.

**Schneeweis, T.,** 1998a, "Dealing with Myths of Managed Futures", *The Journal of Alternative Investments*, Summer, pp. 9–17.

**Schneeweis, T.,** 1998b, "Dealing with Myths of Hedge Funds", *The Journal of Alternative Investments*, Winter, pp.11–15

**Schneeweis, T.,** 1999, "Alpha, Alpha, Who's Got The Alpha?", *The Journal of Alternative Investments*, 2(3), pp. 83–97.

**Schneeweis, T., and S. Chung,** 2000, "Overview of Commodity Investment", Working Paper, March, (http://www.aima.org).

**Schneeweis, T., H. Kazemi and G. Martin,** 2001, "Understanding Hedge Fund Performance: Research Results and Rules of Thumb for the Institutional Investor", Lehman Brothers, November.

**Schneeweis, T., and G. Martin,** 2001, "The Benefits of Hedge Funds: Asset Allocation for the Institutional Investor", *The Journal of Alternative Investments,* 4(3), pp. 27–37.

**Schneeweis, T., and J. F. Pescatore,** 1999, *The Handbook of Alternative Investment Strategies* (Institutional Investor).

**Schneeweis, T., and R. Spurgin,** 1996, "Comparisons of Commodity and Managed Futures Benchmark Indices", CISDM Working Paper Series, August.

**Schneeweis, T., and R. Spurgin,** 1999, "Quantitative Analysis of Hedge Fund and Managed Futures Return and Risk Characteristics", in: *Evaluating and Implementing Hedge Fund Strategies*, P. Lake (ed) Second Edition.

**Schneeweis, T., and R. Spurgin,** 2000a, "Dealing with Myths of Traditional Stock and Bond Performance", *AIMA Newsletter*, February.

**Schneeweis, T., and R. Spurgin,** 2000b, "Hedge Funds: Portfolio Risk Diversifiers, Return Enhancers or Both?", July (http://caiaonline.org/resources/articles/HedgeFundClassification.pdf).

**Schneeweis, T., and R. Spurgin,** 2000c, "The Benefits of Index Option-based Strategies for Institutional Portfolios", *AIMA Newsletter*, June.

**Schneeweis, T., and R. Spurgin,** 2001, "Alternative Investments: What Drives the Returns?", *AIMA Newsletter*, June.

**Schneeweis, T., R. Spurgin and V. N. Karavas,** 2000, "Alternative Investments in the Institutional Portfolio", *AIMA Research*.

**Scholes, M.,** 2000, "Crisis and Risk Management", in: *Risk Budgeting: A New Approach to Investing*, L. Rahl (ed), (London: Risk Books) pp. 27–35.

**Schwager, J. D.,** 1984, *A Complete Guide to the Futures Markets: Fundamental Analysis, Technical Analysis, Trading, Spreads, and Options* (New York: John Wiley & Sons).

**Schwager, J. D.,** 1989, *The Market Wizards: Interviews with Top Traders* (New York: Harper Business).

**Schwager, J. D.,** 1992, *The New Market Wizards: Conversations with America's Top Traders* (New York: Harper Business).

**Shefrin, H.,** 2000, *Beyond Greed and Fear: Finance and the Psychology of Investing* (Oxford University Press).

**Shiller, R. J.,** 1990, *Market Volatility* (MIT Press).

**Soros, G.,** 1994, *The Alchemy of Finance: Reading the Mind of the Market* (New York: John Wiley & Sons).

**Spurgin, R., G. Martin and T. Schneeweis,** "A Method of Estimating Changes in Correlation Between Assets and its Application to Hedge Fund Investment", (http://www.umass.edu/som/cisdm/files/papers/HedgeFundPaper.pdf).

**Spurgin, R.,** 1999, "A Benchmark for Commodity Trading Advisor Performance", *The Journal of Alternative Investments,* 2(1), pp. 11–21.

**Spurgin, R., T. Schneeweis and G. Georgiev,** "Benchmarking Commodity Trading Advisor Performance with a Passive Futures-Based Index", Working Paper, (http://www.umass.edu/som/cisdm/files/papers/CTA_StyleBenchmarks.pdf).

**Steyn, D. B.,** 1998, "Market Neutral: Engineering Return and Risk", Alternative Investing (AIMR).

**Strachman, D. A.,** 2000, *Getting Started in Hedge Funds* (New York: John Wiley & Sons).

**Sutcliffe, C.,** 1997, *Stock Index Futures: Theories and International Evidences* (Massachusetts: Chapman & Hall).

**Swensen, D. F.,** 2000, *Pioneering Portfolio Management – An Unconventional Approach to Institutional Investment* (New York, The Free Press).

**Taleb, N.,** 1997, *Dynamic Hedging, Managing Vanilla and Exotic Options* (New York: John Wiley & Sons).

**Tamarout, Z. B.,** 2001a, "Credit in Convertible Bonds: A Critical View (Part I)", *AIMA Newsletter,* February.

**Tamarout, Z. B.,** 2001b, "Credit in Convertible bonds: A Critical View (Part II)", *AIMA Newsletter,* December.

**Tannenbaum, M. G.,** "U.S. Regulation of Offers of Investment Advisory Services and Hedge Fund Marketing Over the Internet", Tannenbaum, Helpern, Syracuse & Hirschtritt LLP.

**Taylor, S. J.,** 1986, *Modeling Financial Time Series* (New York: John Wiley & Sons).

**Temperton, P.,** 1997, *The Euro* (New York: John Wiley & Sons).

**Temple, P.,** 2001, *Hedge Funds: The Courtesans of Capitalism* (New York: John Wiley & Sons).

**Thomas, L. R. III,** 1990, *The Currency Hedging Debate* (London: IFR Publishing).

**Thomas, L. R. III,** 2000, "Active Management", *The Journal of Portfolio Management,* 26(2), pp. 25–32.

**Tremont Partners Inc.,** 1999, "Mortgage-Backed Securities in the Hedge Fund Marketplace" Tremont White Paper, November.

**Tremont Partners Inc. and TASS Investment Research,** 1999a, "Market Neutral Study", June.

**Tremont Partners Inc. and TASS Investment Research,** 1999b, "The Case For Hedge Funds Report", June.

**Tremont Partners Inc., and Brown, W. A.,** 2000, "Convertible Arbitrage: Opportunity & Risk", Tremont White Paper, September.

**Tremont Partners Inc., and Matos, E.,** 2000, "Distressed Securities Investing", Tremont White Paper, November.

**UBS Warburg Equity Derivatives,** 1999, "20th Century Volatility, A Review of the Stock and Derivatives Markets in the 20th Century", December.

**Wace, I.,** 2000, "Hedge Funds in Europe", Speech at the 2000 Hedge Fund Symposium (EIM/EuroHedge/SFI), "Can Institutions Afford to Ignore Hedge Funds?", 27 April 2000, London.

**Watsham, T.,** 1990, *International Portfolio Management: A Modern Approach* (New York, Longman).

**Weber, T.,** 1999, *Das Einmaleins der Hedge Funds* (Frankfurt: Campus Verlag).

**Weinstein, M. H.,** 1931, *Arbitrage in Securities* (New York: Harper & Brothers).

**Weisman, A. B., and J. Abernathy,** 2000, "The Dangers of Historical Hedge Fund Data", in: *Risk Budgeting: A New Approach to Investing,* L. Rahl (ed), (London: Risk Books) pp. 65–81.

**Weisman, A. B., and T. Birney,** 2002, "The New Diversification Testament", in: *A Guide to Fund of Hedge Funds Management and Investment,* Capital Market Risk Advisors (ed) and AIMA Research, October, pp. 16–21.

**Wermers, R.,** 2000, "Mutual Fund Performance: An Empirical Decomposition into Stock-Picking Talent, Style, Transaction Costs, and Expenses", *Journal of Finance,* 55(4), pp. 1655–95.

**Winkelmann, K.,** 2000, "Risk Budgeting: Managing Active Risk at the Total Fund Level", in *Risk Budgeting: A New Approach to Investing,* L. Rahl (ed), (London: Risk Books) pp. 39–64.

**Zask, E.,** 1999, *Global Investment Risk Management* (New York: McGraw-Hill Trade).

# Index